Communications
in Computer and Information Science 292

K.R. Venugopal   L.M. Patnaik (Eds.)

Wireless Networks and Computational Intelligence

6th International Conference
on Information Processing, ICIP 2012
Bangalore, India, August 10-12, 2012
Proceedings

 Springer

Volume Editors

K.R. Venugopal
University Visvesvaraya College of Engineering
K.R. Circle, Bangalore 56001, India
E-mail: venugopalkr@gmail.com

L.M. Patnaik
Indian Institute of Science
Bangalore, India
E-mail: lalitblr@gmail.com

ISSN 1865-0929   e-ISSN 1865-0937
ISBN 978-3-642-31685-2   e-ISBN 978-3-642-31686-9
DOI 10.1007/978-3-642-31686-9
Springer Heidelberg Dordrecht London New York

Library of Congress Control Number: Applied for

CR Subject Classification (1998): C.2, I.4, H.3, I.5, K.6.5, I.2.7, I.2.10, I.2, H.4, E.3

© Springer-Verlag Berlin Heidelberg 2012
This work is subject to copyright. All rights are reserved, whether the whole or part of the material is
concerned, specifically the rights of translation, reprinting, re-use of illustrations, recitation, broadcasting,
reproduction on microfilms or in any other way, and storage in data banks. Duplication of this publication
or parts thereof is permitted only under the provisions of the German Copyright Law of September 9, 1965,
in its current version, and permission for use must always be obtained from Springer. Violations are liable
to prosecution under the German Copyright Law.
The use of general descriptive names, registered names, trademarks, etc. in this publication does not imply,
even in the absence of a specific statement, that such names are exempt from the relevant protective laws
and regulations and therefore free for general use.

Typesetting: Camera-ready by author, data conversion by Scientific Publishing Services, Chennai, India

Printed on acid-free paper

Springer is part of Springer Science+Business Media (www.springer.com)

Preface

This volume of *Communications in Computer and Information Science* contains the proceedings of the 6th International Conference on Information Processing (ICIP 2012) being held in Bangalore, India, during August 10-12, 2012. Some of the best researchers in the field delivered keynote addresses on the theme areas of the conference. This gave an opportunity to the delegates to interact with these experts and to address some of the challenging interdisciplinary problems in the areas of wireless networks and computational intelligence.

ICIP 2012 attracted over 380 submissions. Through rigorous peer reviews, 75 high-quality papers were recommended by the International Program Committee to be presented at the conference and included in this volume of CCIS. The ICIP Conference series is one of the first series of international conferences on information processing that aptly focuses on the tools and techniques for the development of information systems in general.

Following the success of the past 5 years of ICIP events, ICIP 2012 was devoted to novel methods in the fields of pattern recognition, artificial intelligence, image processing, soft computing, distributed systems, software engineering, wireless networks, network security, signal processing, optimization techniques and data mining. The conference features several keynote addresses in the area of advanced information processing. These areas have been recognized to be the key technologies poised to shape modern society in the next decade.

On behalf of the Organizing Committee, we would like to acknowledge the support from sponsors who helped in one way or the other to achieve our goals for the conference. We wish to express our appreciation to Springer for publishing the proceedings of ICIP 2012. We also wish to acknowledge the dedication and commitment of the CCIS Editorial Staff. We would like to thank the authors for submitting their work, as well as the Technical Program Committee members and reviewers for their enthusiasm, time and valuable suggestions. The invaluable help of the members from the Organizing Committee and volunteers in setting up and maintaining the online submission systems, assigning papers to the reviewers, and preparing the camera-ready version of the proceedings is highly appreciated. We would like to profusely thank them for making ICIP 2012 a success.

August 2012

Venugopal K.R.
Patnaik L.M.

Organization

The 6th International Conference on Information Processing (ICIP-2012) was held in Bangalore, India, and was organized by The Society of Information Processing, Bangalore, India.

Conference Organization

General Chair
L.M. Patnaik   Indian Institute of Science
Bangalore, India

Program Chair
K.R. Venugopal   University Visvesvaraya College of Engineering,
Bangalore University, Bangalore, India

General Co-chairs
S.S. Iyengar   Florida International University, USA
M. Palaniswami   University of Melbourne, Australia
Erol Gelenbee   Imperial College, UK

Advisory Committee
R.L. Kashyap   Purdue University, USA
Dharma P. Aggarwal   University of Cincinnati, USA
M. Vidya Sagar   University of Texas, Dallas, USA

Program Committee
David Kahaner   Association of Independent Information
Professionals, Japan
P. Sreenivasa Kumar   Indian Institute of Technology Madras,
Chennai, India
Sajal K. Das   University of Texas, Arlington, USA
Sharad Purohit   Center for Development of Advanced
Computing, India
K. Sivarajan   Tejas Networks, India
Kentaro Toyama,   Microsoft, India
Vittal S. Rao   National Science Foundation, USA
Rajkumar Buyya   University of Melbourne, Australia
Ram Mohan Rao Kotagiri   University of Melbourne, Australia
Rajeev Shorey   NIIT University, India

Asoke K. Talukdar   International Institute of Information
Technology, Bangalore, India

Dinesh K. Anvekar   Honeywell, Bangalore, India

Bhanu Prasad   Florida Agricultural and Mechanical
University, USA

M. Srinivas   Mentor Graphics, India

Rajib Mall   Indian Institute of Technology, Kharagpur,
India

Bharat Jayaraman   University of Buffalo, USA

J. Mohan Kumar   University of Texas, Arlington, USA

Tomio Hirata   Nagoya University, Japan

Takao Nishizeki   Tohoku University, Japan

G. Shivakumar   Indian Institute of Technology, Mumbai, India

P. Raveendran   University of Malaysia, Malaysia

K. Chandrasekaran   National Institute of Technology, Karnataka,
India

Sneha Kasera   University of Utah, USA

Bhabani P. Sinha   Indian Statistical Institute, Kolkata, India

Francis Lau   University of Hong Kong, Hong Kong

P. Ramaswamy   University of Essex, UK

Nalini Venkatasubramanian   University of Illinois, USA

Suresh M.   University of York, UK

Teo Yong M.   National University of Singapore, Singapore

Organizing Committee

P. Deepa Shenoy   University Visvesvaraya College of Engineering

K.B. Raja   University Visvesvaraya College of Engineering

K. Suresh Babu   University Visvesvaraya College of Engineering

Vibha L.   B.N.M. Institute of Technology

S.H. Manjula   University Visvesvaraya College of Engineering

Sujatha D.N.   B.M. Sreenivasaiah College of Engineering

Thriveni J.   University Visvesvaraya College of Engineering

K.G. Srinivasa   M.S. Ramaiah Institute of Technology

Shaila K.   Vivekananda Institute of Technology

Prashanth C.R.   Vemana Institute of Technology

Ramachandra A.C.   Alpha College of Engineering

Srikantaiah K.C.   S.J.B. Institute of Technology

Sivasankari H.   A.M.C. College of Engineering and Mgmt

ShivaPrakash T.   Vijaya Vittala Institute of Technology

Kumaraswamy M.   S.J.P. Government Polytechnic

Thippeswamy B.M.   Sambhraham Institute of Technology

Viswanath Hullipad   Sambhraham Institute of Technology

Vidya A.   Vivekananda Institute of Technology

Arunalatha J.   University Visvesvaraya College of Engineering

Lata B.T.   University Visvesvaraya College of Engineering

Tanuja R	University Visvesvaraya College of Engineering
Venkatesh	University Visvesvaraya College of Engineering
Pushpa C.N.	University Visvesvaraya College of Engineering
Kiran K.	University Visvesvaraya College of Engineering
Girish K.	B.M. Sreenivasaiah College of Engineering
Nalini L.	University Visvesvaraya College of Engineering

Sponsoring Institutions

Technically Sponsored by:
University Visvesvaraya College of Engineering, Bangalore University,
    Bangalore, India
IEEE-UVCE, India
Alpha College of Engineering, Bangalore, India
Vijaya Vittala Institute of Technology, Bangalore, India

Table of Contents

Section I: Wireless Networks

Section II: Image Processing

Section III: Pattern Recognition and Classification

Section IV: Computer Architecture and Distributed Computing

Section V: Software Engineering, Information Technology and Optimization Techniques

Section VI: Data Mining Techniques

Section VII: Computer Networks and Network Security

Near Field Communication – Applications and Performance Studies

Akshay Uttama Nambi S.N.[1], Prabhakar T.V.[1], Jamadagni H.S.[1],
Kishan Ganapathi[2], Pramod B.K.[2], Rakesh C.M.[2], and Sanjay Naik R.[2]

[1] Department of Electronic Systems Engineering (DESE),
Indian Institute of Science, Bangalore, India
{akshay,tvprabs,hsjam}@cedt.iisc.ernet.in
[2] Department of Electronics and Communication Engineering,
National Institute of Technology Karnataka, Surathkal, India

Abstract. Near Field Communication (NFC), is an integration of Radio Frequency Identification (RFID) technology with mobile devices. NFC offers a quick and convenient method of interaction between humans and NFC enabled devices. Current research concerning NFC appears to mainly focus on development of NFC enabled applications and services. In this paper, we study the performance of NFC devices by considering metrics such as achieved data rates and received power for several distances. Knowledge of these metrics may be useful for application developers to build applications efficiently. We have developed various applications on NFC enabled devices for public transport systems. We also describe the design of 13.56 MHz antenna which was used for measurements of the received power.

Keywords: Near Field Communication (NFC), NFC Antenna, NFC Applications, NFC Performance, RFID.

1 Introduction

Near Field Communication (NFC) is a short range wireless communication using RFID technology. It allows communication between NFC enabled devices. This bidirectional method of communication has a range of around 5-10 cm, with data rates of 106, 212 and 424 kbps. NFC technology has a large potential for mobile services and some of the potential applications include using the mobile phones to (a) Emulate smart cards like credit cards, library cards, etc.; allowing users to exchange their contact information or electronic money with each other; (b) Read information from NFC tags contained in smart posters or items such as DVDs or CDs; (c) Use mobile ticketing services, which enable the mobile phones to be used in public transportation travel cards that are common in large parts of the world. NFC devices can be operated in peer-to-peer mode, card emulation mode and read/write mode.

1. Peer-to-Peer mode: This mode works on the ISO/IEC 18092 standard where data exchange happens between two NFC devices. The data exchanged may be a simple text, image, URL, etc.

K.R. Venugopal and L.M. Patnaik (Eds.): ICIP 2012, CCIS 292, pp. 1–10, 2012.
© Springer-Verlag Berlin Heidelberg 2012

2. Card Emulation mode: In this mode the NFC device acts as an NFC tag for an external reader (similar to contact-less smart card), which enables e-ticketing and contact-less payment.
3. Read/Write mode: In this mode NFC communication is achieved by two devices, one of which is an NFC reader/writer and the other is a passive NFC tag.

Several applications based on NFC technology have been developed over the last few years. However, most of these deal with e-ticketing and smart posters. E-ticketing deals with enabling quick ticketing at bus and train stations and also payment of toll on highways. A similar concept may also be used for carrying out transactions at merchant establishments. A secure payment gateway is required in this class of applications. Smart posters help provide information about objects. This information may be in the form of text, images, URL, etc. Some of the typical advantages of NFC enabled devices include: (i) The NFC technology is compatible with existing RFID structures, existing RFID tags and contact-less smart cards. (ii) NFC technology is easy to use and familiar to people because users have no requirement to possess any prior knowledge about the technology. The user can automatically start a communication by bringing two devices closer. (iii) The transmission range of NFC devices is quite short, so when the user separates the two devices, the communication is aborted. This brings an inherent security in these devices where, if there are no devices close to each other then there is no communication.

Performance of NFC enabled devices is a very important aspect which has to be taken into consideration when developing an application. In this paper we evaluate the performance of these NFC enabled devices by considering the practically achieved data rates and received power via the NFC devices for several distances. These performance metrics are useful for application developers and manufactures which they may have to consider during design and development of a 'viable' application which does not degrade the Quality of Experience for the user. This paper answers the following questions: (a) What is the achieved data rate for transferring a reasonable size file? (b) What is the received power between two devices for several distances? (c) What is the realistic time duration the user has to wait to obtain a particular information from the NFC tag.

2   Related Work

In the last 5 years many NFC applications have been developed and implemented, some even on a large scale. NFC is expected to gain popularity in various fields over the next few years. The current state of applications and their future directions is discussed in [1]. The fundamentals of developing an NFC application and approaches to develop one are dealt in [2] and [3]. A mobile payment system based on RFID-SIM card is discussed in [4]. A discussion of critical aspects involved with the deployment of NFC for e-ticketing applications is presented in [5]. A system that enhances instant messaging tools with real-time location information through the use of NFC enabled mobile devices, called LocaTag, is presented in [6]. However, in all the above mentioned works, the authors do not consider the performance of the NFC devices. The implementation of the game 'Whack-a-Mole' using NFC [7] gives an idea about how NFC may be used for entertainment purposes. The use of NFC to develop and implement educational games and their integration with an educational evaluation system is discussed in [8]. In [9], the authors discuss the use of NFC in the field of healthcare and education through its use for training nurses. Its implementation yielded satisfactory results. Applications of NFC in in the area of Ambient Assisted Living (AAL) is discussed in [10]. The system developed helps the patients to get prescriptions from the comfort of their home, rather than visiting the healthcare centre. A multimodal social application 'Hot in the City', which was developed for social media purposes is discussed in [11]. The paper also discusses how using different modes for the implementation changes the user interface and system design. Different NFC-based use cases in an automotive context are explored in [12]. Nearly all described use cases were implemented in a BMW and the work shows the potential of NFC in an automotive environment to enable additional functionality and ease interactions with the car. The concept of a smart postal system that uses NFC is presented in [13]. Thus, the current literature on NFC mainly focuses on development of applications and use case scenarios without taking performance of these devices into account.

In this rich literature about NFC and its applications, we propose several performance metrics which are useful for application developers. As of our knowledge, this is the first attempt to evaluate performance of NFC devices based on metrics like achieved data rates and received power via the NFC devices for several distances. To conduct performance studies, an antenna for 13.56 MHz was designed and developed. Concepts behind designing the 13.56 MHz antenna are discussed in [14].

3 NFC System Design

In this section, we describe the details of the system architecture of NFC. The NFC architecture includes a application layer, service platform, logical link control protocol and RF layer.

NFC Architecture

The NFC Architecture includes the Application layer, Service platform, Logical Link Control Protocol (LLCP) and the RF layer. The NFC service platform acts as an abstraction layer between the NFC devices and the applications, offering a transparent access to NFC devices of different manufacturers with different hardware interfaces. The service platform offers an abstract, user friendly interface and a convenient notification service, for example, when devices are added or removed. Currently the following tag types are supported: Mifare Ultralight, Mifare 1K, ISO14443-A tags (Smart Cards, DESFire). The NFC LLCP supports peer-to-peer communication between two NFC enabled devices, which is essential for NFC applications that involve bi-directional communications. The specification defines three link service classes: connectionless service, connection-oriented service, and both connectionless and connection-oriented service. The RF layer has the ISO 18092: NFCIP-1 NFC Interface and Protocol. NFCIP-1 supports both active communication mode and passive communication mode. Fig. 1 illustrates the architecture of the NFC platform.

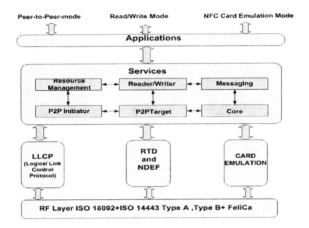

Fig. 1. Near Field Communication Architecture

NFC Interface and Protocol includes the Reader/Writer, Messaging and Core modules. The servicing module includes the Resource management component, the P2P initiator and the P2P target. The messaging component is a language-independent, open-source message broker. The NFC core is an internal library implementing the basic functionality of all NFC devices such as reading from and writing to tags or peer-to-peer (P2P) functionalities. The notification mechanism of the NFC service platform is provided by the NFC messaging component. With this component applications can be notified when devices are detected or removed, when tags appear or disappear in the field or when a message from a P2P device has been received.

4   NFC Applications

In this section, we describe various applications for NFC enabled devices. Firstly, we introduce NFCSK- NFC Smart Kiosk application which is used to broadcast information about bus routes in a bus terminal. Also, we describe an NFC Smart Web Poster application and discuss various cases for using such applications.

4.1   NFC Smart Kiosk – Information Broadcaster

We have designed an NFC Smart Kiosk (NFCSK) system to implement a route information provider at several bus terminals. In centralized and crowded bus terminals, it is often difficult for a traveller to locate the timings and other details regarding his/her bus. This is due to high passenger traffic and also because the existing information counters are insufficient to cater to such traffic in the bus terminal.

We have devised an application that can be used by commuters in such scenarios. The working of the NFCSK is as follows: An array of NFC reader-based information display system is placed in each of the bus terminals with the bus numbers and their routes mentioned on each as shown in Fig. 2. When the user's NFC phone is in the reader's range, it transmits the information about the bus routes. Furthermore, the next bus stipulated to arrive at the specified stop is also part of the information transmitted. Additionally, a logo image of the service provider is also sent for authenticity. Such an application assists in streamlining the information needs of the travellers at a bus station and also facilitates orderly movement of people. The use of this application need not be restricted to only bus terminals; it can also be used in other public transport systems.

Each of the NFC readers is programmed using the TAMA language structure. The application on the NFC reader is implemented using Java on Eclipse Integrated Development Environment (IDE). The application on the phone side communicates using peer-to-peer communication (NFCIP-1) implemented using JSR-257 contact-less communication API. In this application, the NFC reader is used in peer-to-peer mode to dispatch information to any NFC device that comes within its broadcasting range. The information dispatched may be in the form of text, images or both.

Fig. 2. Bus Stop with an Information Broadcasting Poster

4.2 NFC Smart Kiosk – Query Based Information Provider

Often there are situations where the commuter might need specific information from the NFCSK application. This information might be custom queries such as the availability of a bus from 'Place A' to 'Place B'. Additionally, a list of bus routes towards 'Place A' and cost incurred for commuting between two points might also be required. The NFCSK - Query-Based Information Provider application is developed to target such scenarios. This modification to NFCSK - Information Broadcaster assists commuters to place customized queries. The

NFC Tag

NFC enabled phone

Fig. 3. Query-Based Information Service

NFC readers in the bus terminal are programmed to accept such queries and respond with a reply. In our specific application, the user was required to send a route number to the NFC reader. This was done by typing a number and holding it against the reader. The reader gets the number and replies with information requested by the user, as shown in Fig. 3.

4.3   NFC Smart Web Poster

A Smart Poster application was developed using the Reader-Writer mode of the NFC phones. This application is able to write a string (URL) on an emulated card with the phone being in writer mode. The card is of ISO/IEC 14443 Contactless Identification Card standard. The tag has data memory ranging from 256 bytes to 4KB. The string is stored as an NDEF Record of type 'Smart Poster' (ISO/IEC 18092 specifications). The URL is read using the phone in reader mode by holding it near the Mifare card (ISO/IEC 14443) (Fig. 4). The user is redirected to the received URL through the phone's web browser and fetches data from that particular address. This can be implemented by tagging these cards onto any item or article about which the user might need more information. The item tagged may be an artifact in a museum, a product in a shopping mall, or any other poster where the area to display the information is scarce.

There are many merits of using a URL instead of storing the information on the card: (a) The rates of NFC are not sufficient to transfer large data, hence it would be wiser to store data on a remote server and access the data using the internet; (b) The information database can be extremely large. It is sufficient to store the URL once and the information to be displayed maintained in the database.

5   Performance Evaluation on NFC Enabled Devices

In this section, we discuss the evaluation of the performance of NFC readers and NFC enabled mobile phones. The performance metrics described in this section

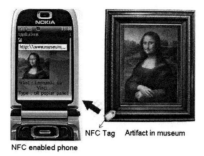

Fig. 4. NFC Smart Web Poster

are achieved data rates and received power of NFC devices for several distances between the NFC transmitter and receiver. In order to model the received power, it was necessary to design and implement a 13.56 MHz antenna.

5.1   Data Rate Measurements for NFC Enabled Devices

To study the data rates achieved by the NFC application we used our NFCSK, Smart web poster applications on the Nokia 6131 mobile phone. The data rates achieved between 2 NFC phones were measured while varying the file size and distance between the phones. Table 1 shows the average data rate achieved for different file sizes with 20 mm distance between the phones.

Table 1. Data Rates for Phone-to-Phone Transmission with Inter-Phone Distance = 20 mm

File Size [KB]	Time [s]	Data rate [kbps]
2.18	0.545	31.99
3.01	0.744	32.08
4.03	1.016	31.73
7.17	1.728	33.08
18.30	4.776	30.61
50.09	11.873	33.75

We also conducted an experiment to find out the average achieved data rate from a NFC enabled mobile phone to NFC reader. We used a *customized image transfer* application, and the transmission time and data rates for files of different sizes between the NFC reader and phone are as shown in Table 2.

From Tables 1 and 2, we observe that the achieved data rates of the NFC enabled devices are significantly lower than the theoretical data rates. For instance, for a file of size 2KB, the achieved data rates is the same as for a file 10 times larger than 2KB. For every command packet sent by the host, a pair of ACK and response packets are sent by the peer device. This clearly indicates the overhead

Table 2. Data Rates for Reader to Phone Data Transmission with Inter-Device Distance = 20 mm

File Size [KB]	Time [s]	Data rate [kbps]
2.18	1.611	11.085
3.01	2.105	11.714
4.02	2.808	11.728
7.17	5.292	11.099
21.80	16.002	11.160
50.95	35.366	11.525

involved in transferring the file using NFC. In our measurements we used "Normal Information frame" for both the commands and their responses. The size of the ACK packet is 6 bytes. Thus, the achieved data rates of NFC enabled devices are low due to (1) the delay in the application layer for peer-to-peer initialization; (2) the transmission of ACK and response messages adding to the overhead. Thus, one has to consider the peer-to-peer initialization time and achieved data rate metrics during application development for NFC enabled devices.

5.2 NFC Antenna Design and Received Power for NFC Devices

To model the received power for NFC devices, we designed and developed a 13.56 MHz antenna. The dimensions of the antenna posed a challenging problem. Since NFC devices operate in the 13.56 MHz frequency, the wavelength is 22.12m; which is a large value as far as the size of NFC tags and receivers are concerned. An antenna operating at this frequency is significantly large in size and requires a size reduction for practical purposes. We have implemented an antenna which is considerably smaller in size. To design such an antenna we used an antenna

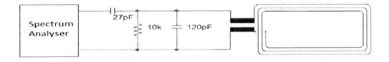

Fig. 5. Loop Antenna and its Matching Circuit

design and simulation tool called Advanced Design System (ADS) from Agilent Technologies. We considered an antenna with a loop structure etched on a PCB. We used FR4 material for the fabrication of the PCB with 1.55 mm thickness, relative magnetic permeability of 1 and a relative electric permittivity of 4.55. The antenna has three rectangular loops with the outer loop measuring 60x30 mm, the thickness of the copper line is 0.2 mm and the spacing between the loops is 2 mm. NFC has a bandwidth of 14 KHz (7 KHz on either side of the centre frequency). The designed antenna was simulated for various frequency ranges and the simulation results indicate that the loop behaves as a pure inductor with inductance 939 nH. The gain of the antenna is 2.45 dBi and directivity is 1.861.

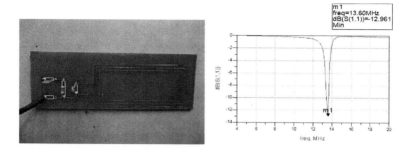

Fig. 6. (a) The Loop Antenna Implemented on a PCB. (b) Simulation Result Showing System Resonating at 13.56 MHz.

A matching circuit for the 13.56 MHz antenna was designed for 50 ohms impedance. This includes a series capacitor, parallel capacitor and a parallel resistance as shown in Fig. 5. The capacitors are used to match the inductive load and resonate at 13.56 MHz and resistance is used to decrease the Q factor for better design. A photograph of the loop antenna on PCB with the matching circuit is also shown in Fig. 6 (a). The simulation result of the 13.56 MHz antenna design is shown in Fig. 6 (b).

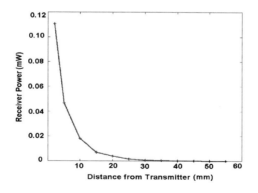

Fig. 7. Received Power Plotted vs. Distance between the Devices

The prototype antenna was used to measure the received power at different distances from the transmitter NFC tag. We connected the prototype antenna to a spectrum analyzer and measured the received power by varying the distance between the transmitter and receiver. Fig. 7 shows a plot of the received power and reveals that the received power varies inversely as the square of the distance. Thus, one has to consider the distances supported between NFC devices while designing NFC enabled applications.

6 Summary and Conclusions

We have shown that NFC technologies integrated into mobile phones provide a niche set of applications. Smart kiosks can be designed for either broadcast mode or unicast mode. Smart Web posters and phone-to-phone data transfers have to be designed such that the degradation of Quality of Experience is insignificant. Therefore, the efficient design of applications requires us to consider performance metrics such as achieved data rates and received power.

References

1. Kerem, O.K., Coskun, V., Aydin, M.N., Ozdenizci, B.: Current Benefits and Future Directions of NFC Services. In: International Conference on Education and Management Technology (2010)
2. Benyó, B., Vilmos, A., Kovacs, K., Kutor, L.: The Design of NFC Based Applications. In: 11th International Conference on Intelligent Engineering Systems (2007)
3. Benyó, B., Sódor, B., Fördős, G., Kovács, L., Vilmos, A.: A generalized approach for NFC Application Development. In: Second International Workshop on NFC (2010)
4. Zou, J., Zhang, C., Dong, C., Fan, C., Wen, Z.: Mobile payment based on RFID-SIM card. In: 10th IEEE Conference on Computer and Information Technology (2010)
5. Juntunen, A., Luukkainen, S., Tuunainen, V.K.: Deploying NFC Technology for Mobile Ticketing Services - Identification of Critical Business Model Issues. In: Ninth International Conference on Mobile Business (2010)
6. Köbler, F., Koene, P., Krcmar, H., Altmann, M., Leimeister, J.M.: LocaTag - An NFC-based System Enhancing Instant Messaging Tools with Real-Time User Location. In: Second International Workshop on NFC (2010)
7. Broll, G., Graebsch, R., Scherr, M., Boring, S., Holleis, P., Wagner, M.: Touch to Play - Exploring Touch-Based Mobile Interaction with Public Displays. In: Third International Workshop on NFC (2011)
8. Garrido, P.C., Miraz, G.M., Ruiz, I.L., Gómez-Nieto, M.A.: Use of NFC-based Pervasive Games for Encouraging Learning and Student Motivation. In: Third International Workshop on NFC (2011)
9. Fontecha, J., Hervás, R., Bravo, J., Villarreal, V.: An NFC Approach for Nursing Care Training. In: Third International Workshop on NFC (2011)
10. Vergara, M., Hellín, P.D., Fontecha, J., Hervás, R., Sánchez-Barba, C., Fuentes, C., Bravo, J.: Mobile Prescription: an NFC-based proposal for AAL. In: Second International Workshop on NFC (2010)
11. Siira, E., Törmänen, V.: The impact of NFC on Multimodal Social Media Application. In: Second International Workshop on NFC (2010)
12. Steffen, R., Preißinger, J., Schöllermann, T., Müller, A., Schnabel, I.: Near Field Communication (NFC) in an Automotive Environment. In: Second International Workshop on NFC (2010)
13. Lou, Z.: NFC Enabled Smart Postal System. In: Second International Workshop on NFC (2010)
14. Gebhart, M., Szoncso, R.: Optimizing Design of Smaller Antennas for Proximity Transponders. In: Second International Workshop on NFC (2010)

Inter-Carrier Interference Power Analysis of OFDM Systems under Slowly Fading Channels

Porselvi Soundararajan and Vidhyacharan Bhaskar

Department of Electronics and Communication Engineering,
SRM University, Kattankulathur - 603203, Kancheepuram Dt., Tamilnadu, India
porselvimaheshwaran@yahoo.co.in

Abstract. OFDM systems suffer significant performance degradation due to Inter-Carrier Interference (ICI) and Carrier Frequency Offset (CFO). The CFO and ICI must be compensated to improve system performance. In this paper, closed form expressions for (a) the power of the Inter-Carrier Interference (ICI) and (b) the mean and variance of the recovered signal under various fading conditions are derived and plotted. Closed form expressions for power of ICI in slowly fading channels are derived and tabulated. Numerical results are presented for Weibull, Nakagami, and Rayleigh fading conditions.

Keywords: Additive White Gaussian Noise (AWGN), Carrier Frequency Offset (CFO), Discrete Fourier Transform (DFT), Inter-Carrier Interference (ICI), Inter Symbol Interference (ISI), Orthogonal Frequency Division Multiplexing (OFDM).

1 Introduction

Orthogonal Frequency Division Multiplexing (OFDM) is a special case of multicarrier transmission and it can accommodate high data rate requirement of multimedia based wireless systems. A major drawback of OFDM is the sensitivity to Inter-Carrier Interference (ICI) and Carrier Frequency Offset (CFO). Thus accurate estimation and compensation of CFO and ICI are very important. In [1], the performance of a blind Minimum Output Variance (MOV) estimator is analyzed by applying the Maximal-Ratio Combining (MRC) technique.

In [2], a new carrier offset estimation technique for OFDM communications over a frequency-selective fading channel is proposed. It is shown that IC1 can be modeled as an additive Gaussian random process that leads to an error floor, which can be determined analytically as a function of the Doppler frequency in [3]. Antenna diversity and trellis coding are examined as methods to reduce this error floor. A Maximum Likelihood estimator is developed by exploiting redundancy in the Cyclic Prefix (CP) [4]. In [5], a blind algorithm for CFO recovery in an OFDM receiver operation over frequency-selective fading channels is proposed.

In this paper, the OFDM system model is briefly described in Section 2. The Numerical results are presented under no fading, Weibull fading, Nakagami

K.R. Venugopal and L.M. Patnaik (Eds.): ICIP 2012, CCIS 292, pp. 11–17, 2012.
© Springer-Verlag Berlin Heidelberg 2012

fading and Rayleigh fading conditions in Section 3. Conclusions are drawn in Section 4.

2 System Description

2.1 OFDM System Description

OFDM is a multicarrier modulation technique which generates waveforms that are mutually orthogonal, and then distributes data over a large number of carriers that are spaced apart at specific frequencies. The system model is illustrated in Figure 1.

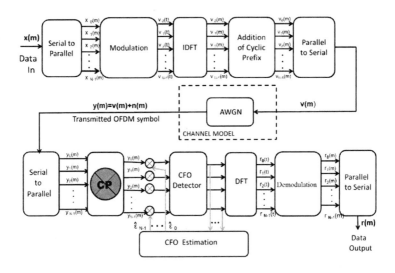

Fig. 1. OFDM System Model

Let us define the N-subcarrier, m^{th} OFDM transmitter data vector as

$$\mathbf{v}(m) = [v_0(m), v_1(m), ..., v_{N-1}(m)]^T. \tag{1}$$

The OFDM signals can be obtained by employing Inverse Discrete Fourier Transform (IDFT) of (1). The mth OFDM transmitted data vector after IDFT is $\mathbf{Fv}(m)$, where $\mathbf{F}$ is the IDFT matrix given by

$$\mathbf{F} = \frac{1}{\sqrt{N}} \begin{bmatrix} 1 & 1 & \cdots & 1 \\ 1 & e^{j\omega} & \cdots & e^{j(N-1)\omega} \\ \cdots & \cdots & \cdots & \cdots \\ 1 & e^{j(N-1)\omega} & \cdots & e^{j(N-1)^2\omega} \end{bmatrix} \tag{2}$$

where $\omega = \frac{2\pi}{N}$. After IDFT modulation and addition of CP, the signal is transmitted over an AWGN channel. The desired signal is recovered by applying DFT.

It is assumed that the received signal contains fading coefficients, denoted as γ. In a slowly fading channel, the received signal in the presence of CFO is denoted as

$$\mathbf{y}(m) = \gamma \mathbf{FHv}(m) + \mathbf{n}(m), \tag{3}$$

where

$$\mathbf{H} = diag\left(\mathbf{H}_0(m), \mathbf{H}_1(m), ..., \mathbf{H}_{N-1}(m)\right) \tag{4}$$

is the frequency response channel matrix, and

$$\Phi = diag\left(1, e^{j\phi_0}, ..., e^{j(N-1)\phi_0}\right) \tag{5}$$

denotes the CFO matrix. The CFO is represented as Δf, $\phi_0 = \frac{2\pi T_s \Delta f}{N}$, γ is the fading coefficient, and T_s is the OFDM block duration.

2.2   Power of Inter-Carrier Interference (P_{ICI})

The received signal after DFT demodulation in the presence of CFO, is given by

$$\mathbf{r}(m) = \mathbf{F}^H \mathbf{y}(m) = \gamma \mathbf{F}^H \Phi \mathbf{FHv}(m) + \mathbf{n}'(m), \tag{6}$$

where $\mathbf{F}^H$ represents the DFT matrix and $\mathbf{n}'(m)$ is the noise term after DFT operation. When $\gamma = 1$, no fading occurs. The recovered signal on the kth subcarrier is given by

$$\mathbf{r}_k = \gamma I_0 \mathbf{v}_k + \sum_{l=0, l\neq k}^{N-1} \gamma I_{l-k} \mathbf{v}_l, \tag{7}$$

where

$$I_n = \frac{\sin\left(\pi \Delta f T_s\right)}{N \sin\left(\left(\frac{\pi}{N}\right)(\Delta f T_s + n)\right)} \exp\left(j\frac{\pi}{N}\left((N-1)\Delta f T_s\right) - n\right).$$

In (7), I_0 is the attenuation and phase rotation of the desired signal, and I_{l-k} is the ICI coefficient from other subcarriers. The power of ICI, P_{ICI}, is denoted as

$$P_{ICI} = E\left|\sum_{l=0, l\neq k}^{N-1} \gamma I_{l-k} \mathbf{v}_l\right|^2. \tag{8}$$

Now, the closed form expressions for power of ICI under (a) No fading case, P_{ICI}^{NF}, [3], (b) Rayleigh fading case, P_{ICI}^{RaF}, (c) Weibull fading case, P_{ICI}^{Wei}, and (d) Nakagami fading case, P_{ICI}^{Nak}, are derived and presented in Table 1.

Here, σ is the standard deviation of Rayleigh fading, λ and k are the scale and shape parameters of Weibull fading and Ω is the Nakagami fading parameter [6]. The ICI term in (8) is assumed as a Gaussian random variable with mean zero [7, 8]. The closed form expressions for the variance of ICI under (a) no fading case, σ_{NF}^2 (b) Rayleigh fading case, σ_{RaF}^2, (c) Weibull fading case, σ_{Wei}^2, (d) Nakagami fading case, σ_{Nak}^2 are calculated and tabulated in Table 2.

The magnitude mean of the dominant signal in the kth subcarrier, $|I_0 \mathbf{v}_k|$ under different fading cases are presented in Table 3. $\epsilon = T_s \Delta f \in (-0.5, 0.5)$ is the CFO normalized to subcarrier spacing.

Table 1. Power of Inter-Carrier Interference (P_{ICI})

S. No.	Power of ICI (P_{ICI})
No Fading	$P_{ICI}^{NF} = 1 - sinc^2(\epsilon)$
Rayleigh Fading	$P_{ICI}^{RaF} = 1 - 2\sigma^2 sinc^2(\epsilon)$
Weibull Fading	$P_{ICI}^{Wei} = \left(1 - sinc^2(\epsilon)\right) \lambda\Gamma\left(1 + \frac{2}{k}\right)$
Nakagami Fading	$P_{ICI}^{Nak} = \Omega\left(1 - sinc^2(\epsilon)\right)$

Table 2. Variance of the ICI (σ^2)

S. No.	Power of ICI (P_{ICI})
No Fading	$\sigma_{NF}^2 = P_{ICI}^{NF} = 1 - sinc^2(\epsilon)$
Rayleigh Fading	$\sigma_{RaF}^2 = P_{ICI}^{RaF} = 1 - 2\sigma^2 sinc^2(\epsilon)$
Weibull Fading	$\sigma_{Wei}^2 = P_{ICI}^{Wei} = \left(1 - sinc^2(\epsilon)\right) \lambda\Gamma\left(1 + \frac{2}{k}\right)$
Nakagami Fading	$\sigma_{Nak}^2 = P_{ICI}^{Nak} = \Omega\left(1 - sinc^2(\epsilon)\right)$

Table 3. Mean of Dominant Signal

S. No.	Mean
No Fading	$m = |I_0 v_k| = sinc(\epsilon)$
Rayleigh Fading	$m = |I_0 v_k| = 1.2533\sigma sinc(\epsilon)$
Weibull Fading	$m = |I_0 v_k| = sinc(\epsilon) \lambda\Gamma\left(1 + \frac{1}{k}\right)$
Nakagami Fading	$m = |I_0 v_k| = sinc(\epsilon) \sqrt{\frac{2\Omega}{\pi}}$

2.3 Expectation and Variance of the Recovered Signal (r_k)

The Probability Density Function (PDF) of the output (r_k) can be approximated as a Gaussian mixture given by

$$p_{|\mathbf{r}_k|}(x) = \left[\frac{1}{\sqrt{2\pi}\sigma}\exp\left(-\frac{(x-m)^2}{2\sigma^2}\right) + \frac{1}{\sqrt{2\pi}\sigma}\exp\left(-\frac{(x+m)^2}{2\sigma^2}\right)\right] u(x), \quad (9)$$

where $u(x)$ is the unit step function. The expectation of (r_k) is given by

$$E\left(|\mathbf{r}_k|\right) = \int_{-\infty}^{\infty} x p_{|\mathbf{r}_k|}(x)dx = \sqrt{\frac{2}{\pi}}\sigma\exp\left(-\frac{m^2}{2\sigma^2}\right) - \frac{m}{\sqrt{\pi}}\Gamma\left(\frac{1}{2}, \frac{m^2}{2\sigma^2}\right), \quad (10)$$

where $\Gamma(\alpha, x) = \int_{x}^{\infty} e^{-t} t^{\alpha-1} dt$ is the Complementary Incomplete Gamma Function (CIGF). The second moment of r_k is given by

$$E\left(|\mathbf{r}_k|^2\right) = \int_{-\infty}^{\infty} x^2 p_{|\mathbf{r}_k|}(x)dx = \frac{2\sigma^2}{\sqrt{\pi}}\Gamma\left(\frac{3}{2}, \frac{m^2}{2\sigma^2}\right) + \frac{m^2\sigma}{\sqrt{\pi}}\Gamma\left(\frac{1}{2}, \frac{m^2}{2\sigma^2}\right). \quad (11)$$

The variance of $\mathbf{r}_k$ is expressed as

$$var\left(|\mathbf{r}_k|\right) = E\left(|\mathbf{r}_k|^2\right) - E^2\left(|\mathbf{r}_k|\right).labeleq:12 \tag{12}$$

From (10), (11), and (12), it is observed that the expectation and variance of $|\mathbf{r}_k|$ are functions of ϵ. The CFO does not change the total signal power in one received symbol [9], but the CFO causes ambiguity in the output.

3   Numerical Results

A comparative analysis of the Power of ICI under different fading conditions is illustrated in Figure 2. It is observed that under Rayleigh, Nakagami and Weibull fading conditions, the power of ICI is significantly greater than that for no fading conditions. The expectation of $\mathbf{r}_k$ versus CFO under no fading and various fading conditions are plotted and illustrated in Figure 3a. It is inferred that the maximum value of expectation is obtained for the no fading case which provides less ambiguity for $\mathbf{r}_k$ under no fading conditions. The variance of the recovered signal, $\sigma^2_{|\mathbf{r}_k|}$, versus CFO for no fading and various fading scenarios are plotted in Figure 3b. It is inferred that CFO is nullified when the variance is zero under no fading conditions.

Figure 4 illustrates the expectation and variance of the recovered signal, $\mathbf{r}_k$ under different fading conditions. Under Rayleigh fading case, it is observed that the expectation of the recovered signal, $|\mathbf{r}_k|$, increases as the standard deviation, σ, of Rayleigh fading increases. Under Weibull fading conditions, the expectation of $\mathbf{r}_k$ increases as the shape parameter, k, increases. An increase in the value of σ, under Nakagami fading, increases the expectation of $|\mathbf{r}_k|$.

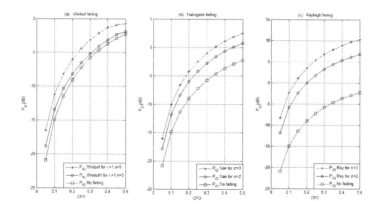

Fig. 2. ICI Power under various Fading cases

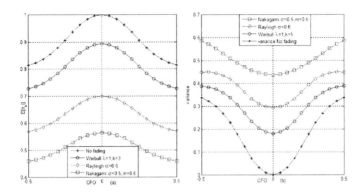

Fig. 3. Comparative Analysis of Variance of $\mathbf{r}_k$

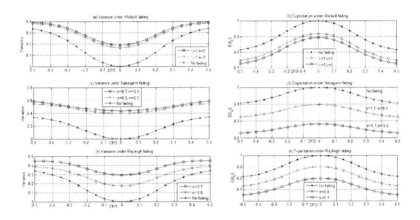

Fig. 4. Expectation and Variance of the Recovered Signal, $\mathbf{r}_k$ under various Fading conditions

4   Conclusions

Closed form expressions for power of ICI in the presence of Nakagami, Weibull, and Rayleigh fading channels are derived and the results are plotted. An increase in PICI is observed in slowly fading channels. Closed form expressions for the Expectation and Variance of the recovered signal, is obtained over slowly fading channels. It is observed that the slowly fading channels introduce uncertainties in the desired signal which is understood by the decrease in the peak value attained by the expectation curve under fading scenarios, thereby affecting the recovery of the desired signal.

References

1. Yang, F., Li, K.H., Teh, K.C.: Performance Analysis of the Blind Minimum Output Variance Estimator for Carrier Frequency Offset in OFDM Systems. EURASIP Journal on Applied Signal Processing, 1–8 (2006)
2. Tureli, U., Liu, H., Zoltowski, D.: OFDM Blind Carrier Offset Estimation ESPRIT. IEEE Transactions on Communications 48, 1459–1461 (2000)
3. Russell, M., Stuber, G.L.: Inter Channel Interference Analysis of OFDM in a Mobile Environment. In: Proceedings of the IEEE Vehicular Technology Conference, Athens, Chicago, USA, vol. 2, pp. 820–824 (1995)
4. Van de Beek, J.J., Sandell, M., Borjesson, P.O.: ML Estimation of Time and Frequency Offset in OFDM Systems. IEEE Transactions on Signal Processing 45, 1800–1805 (1997)
5. Luise, M., Marselli, M., Reggiannini, R.: Low-Complexity Blind Carrier Frequency Recovery for OFDM Signals Over Frequency-Selective Radio Channels. IEEE Transactions on Communications 50, 1182–1188 (2002)
6. Proakis, J.G.: Digital Communications, 4th edn. McGraw Hill Inc., NY (2001)
7. Linnartz, J.P.: Performance Analysis of Synchronous MC-CDMA in Mobile Rayleigh Channel with Both Delay and Doppler Spreads. IEEE Transactions on Vehicular Technology 50, 1375–1387 (2001)
8. Jakes, W.C.: Microware Mobile Communications. John Wiley & Sons, NY (1994)
9. Armstrong, J.: Analysis of New and Existing Methods of Reducing Inter-Carrier Interference due to Carrier Frequency Offset in OFDM. IEEE Transactions on Communications, 365–369 (1999)

RCH-MAC Protocol for Multihop QoS in Wireless Sensor Networks

Kumaraswamy M.[1], Shaila K.[1], Sivasankari H.[1], Tejaswi V.[1],
Venugopal K.R.[1], S.S. Iyengar[2], and L.M. Patnaik[3]

[1] Department of Computer Science and Engineering,
University Visvesvaraya College of Engineering, Bangalore University, Bangalore
kumarasm67@yahoo.co.in
[2] Florida International University, USA
[3] Indian Institute of Science, Bangalore 560 001, India

Abstract. The design of hybrid MAC protocol in Wireless Sensor Networks for delay sensitive data traffic QoS is a challenging work. We present Reservation Control Hybrid MAC (RCH-MAC) protocol, which reduces end-to-end delay, energy efficiency and maximizes the packet delivery ratio by minimizing the contention at the nodes. Here, a node operates the reservation procedure at the contention-based period and reserves a time slot in the adaptive contention-free time. All the neighbor nodes of the sender and receiver receives their own reservation control packets. Once reserved, the sender transmits data and receives ACK packets at the adaptive contention-free time. Since reservation packets occur in nodes along the routing path, the nodes reserve time slots successively in multi-hop. Simulation results demonstrate that the proposed protocol has significantly reduced the end-to-end latency and improved other QoS parameters like energy efficiency and packet delivery ratio.

Keywords: Energy efficiency, Hybrid medium-access control (H-MAC), Latency, Reservation Control, Quality of Service (QoS).

1 Introduction

Wireless Sensor Networks (WSNs) consists of a large number of sensor nodes. A sensor node includes a processor, wireless radio and various sensors. After the initial deployment sensor nodes are responsible for self-organizing an appropriate network infrastructure with multihop connections between sensor nodes. It is used in a wide variety of critical applications such as military, environmental monitoring, industrial process monitoring and health-care units *etc.* Low communication ranges confirm the dense deployment of sensors and only an efficient medium access control (MAC) protocol can handle a number of medium sharing nodes in a better way and form an efficient infrastructure to establish communication links between nodes. In scheduled access, a node can be active only if it is capable of sending or receiving the data. In WSNs, cross-layer design significantly improves energy-efficiency, because WSNs report data wirelessly across multiple hops to a sink node.

K.R. Venugopal and L.M. Patnaik (Eds.): ICIP 2012, CCIS 292, pp. 18–27, 2012.
© Springer-Verlag Berlin Heidelberg 2012

The energy is mainly consumed in MAC protocols when the node is just listening and waiting for a packet to be sent. Traffic in WSNs is very low and is triggered by sensing events which is in the form of bursts[1]. Due to this reason, energy consideration has dominated most of the research at MAC layer level in WSNs[2][3]. A long delay is highly undesirable for time-sensitive applications such as critical situation monitoring and security surveillance. For handling real time traffic of event triggering in monitoring based sensor network requires end-to-end latency within acceptable range and the variation of such delay is acceptable[4].

In this paper, we propose a new hybrid MAC protocol called Reservation Control Hybrid-MAC (RCH-MAC) protocol, which is explicitly designed for WSNs. Almost all hybrid MAC protocols combines two periods, which are contention-based period and contention-free based period. RCH-MAC protocol reserves time slots in contention-based time and nodes transmit data during an assigned slot time using adaptive Time-Division Multiple-Access (TDMA).

Motivation. Most of the existing MAC protocols for Wireless Sensor Networks are classified into three categories: contention-based protocols, schedule-based protocols and hybrid protocols. The Hybrid-MAC uses channel reservation technique to reduce end-to-end delay for delay sensitive applications. It uses short slotted frame format with small size of data packets to achieve high-energy performance, low delivery latency and improved channel utilization. So, the design of adaptive contention-free access time and contention access protocol is required for the variable traffic load.

Contribution. We have designed a novel RCH-MAC protocol for WSNs, which could be efficiently utilised for real-time and energy efficient applications. Our cross-layer RCH-MAC protocol provides quality of service at MAC layer and good performance interms of self-configuration of the nodes easily, high scalability of sensor nodes, minimizes energy consumption by adapting varying traffic conditions inherent to WSNs, low end-to-end latency and increases Packet delivery ratio.

Organization. This paper is divided into seven sections. Literature Survey is discussed in Section II, Background in Section III. Problem Definition and Implementation in Section IV, and Mathematical Model in Section V. Performance Evaluation is discussed in Section VI and Conclusions in Section VII.

2 Literature Survey

Dam et al., [3] propose energy efficiency and throughput of Sensor-MAC by introducing adaptive duty-cycle that dynamically adjusts the length of active periods according to the traffic load variations. T-MAC is proposed to address the S-MAC nodes not participating in the data exchange. Time-out MAC (TMAC) protocol is similar to S-MAC, but adaptively shortens the listen period. The main contribution of the Timeout-MAC protocol is its adaptive duty cycle approach. T-MAC is capable of adapting to traffic fluctuations and outperforms S-MAC.

Ye et al., [5] developed a CSMA/CA based protocol, which uses periodic listening and sleeping to save energy consumption in WSNs. In order to reduce latency due to the low-duty-cycle operation, adaptive listening is employed to improve the sleep delay. Rhee et al., [6] present a hybrid MAC protocol which dynamically switches between CSMA and TDMA depending on the level of contention. Zebra-MAC is hybrid MAC protocol designed for Wireless Sensor Networks and combines different strengths of TDMA and CSMA protocols. Z-MAC uses the DRAND algorithm to assign each node a time slot to guarantee that no two-hop neighbors share the same slot. It operate in either a Low Contention Level (LCL) or High Contention Level (HCL) mode.

3   Background

Wang et al., [7] propose a hybrid MAC protocol that combines energy-efficient scheme of contention-based and TDMA based MAC protocols for WSNs to improve network performance. H-MAC uses channel reservation technique to reduce end-to-end delay for delay sensitive application by allowing packets to go through multihops with a single MAC frame to reduce the queue delay, highest priority is given to channel access and uses a short frame format to speed up packet delivery ratio.

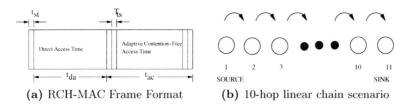

(a) RCH-MAC Frame Format   (b) 10-hop linear chain scenario

Fig. 1. RCH-MAC Protocol Structure

4   Problem Definition

The energy efficiency and end-to-end latency of a WSNs are interdependent on each other. A node operates the reservation procedure at the contention based and reserves a time slot in the adaptive contention-free time. All the neighbor nodes of the sender and receiver receives their own reservation control packets. End-to-end latency is minimized significantly with the presence of the reservation packets in the nodes along the given routing path.

4.1   Assumptions

(i) All the sensor nodes are static and homogeneous.
(ii) Nodes are equipped with omni directional antennas.
(iii) Nodes communicate with each other through packets.

4.2   Objectives

The main objectives of our work is to minimize end-to-end transmission delay, improve packet delivery ratio and minimize the energy-consumption in Wireless Sensor Networks.

4.3   Implementation

We assume that sensor nodes are high-end devices and all nodes are synchronized at the initial stage. The frame format of RCH-MAC protocol is divided into three periods, as shown in Figure 1(a). It consists of sync time t_{st}, direct access time t_{da} followed by adaptive contention-free access time t_{ac}. In this case, a node operates the reservation procedure at the contention-based period and reserves a time slot in the adaptive contention-free time. First reservation control packets are transmitted by all the neighbor nodes of the sender and receiver receives their own reservation control packets. Once reserved, the sender transmits data and receives ACK packets at the adaptive contention-free time. The reservation packets occur in nodes along the routing path and the nodes reserve time slots successively in multi-hop. The traffics are transmitted in the order of RTS/CTS/DATA/ACK sequence at the contention-based time through CSMA/CA technique. Moreover, the traffic is transmitted in the same way as slotted CSMA/CA if there are free slots in adaptive contention-free time.

Once the reservation procedure has been completed, the source node 1 sends data and receives the ACK packet during the reserved slot time in the adaptive contention-free time. The slot information is very important for reserving nodes to avoid collision. In the contention-based time, reservation packets and RTS packets for sending sensor data will contend for channel acquisition. The protocol gives priority to the reservation control packets more than RTS packet.

The H-MAC protocol[7] has long end-to-end delay and QoS cannot be guaranteed, due to unstable wireless channel and collision among the reservation packets, nodes do not maintain neighborhood information. In order to solve this problem, specific nodes broadcast the slot information during reservation packet transmission. The specific nodes that send or receive the reservation control packets during contention-based time should broadcast the slot information according to random back-off scheme. The exact reservation will be maintained among the neighbor nodes.

The adaptive contention-free time consists of number of fixed time slots. The length of a time slot depends on the traffic load. During the free time slots, nodes can transmit data through a slotted CSMA/CA technique. Nodes without sending or receiving data can sleep during the time slots.

5   Mathematical Model

In this paper, we analyse the RCH-MAC performance under multihop linear chain topology for different traffic flows. Figure 1(b). show the topology for

Table 1. Notations

Symbols	Definition
t_{fr}	Frame length time
t_{st}	Synchronization time
t_{da}	Direct access time
t_{ac}	Adaptive Contention-free access time
N	Number of time slots
T_{ts}	Time of adaptive contention-free access slot
T_D	Data transmission time
T_{ACK}	ACK packet time
T_{SIFS}	Time of short interframe space
T_G	Time of guard
L_{pkt}	Data length
T_B	Time of transmission or receive a byte
T_{CW}	Contention window time
N_{hop}	Number of hops
τ	Transmission probability for a node in any time slot

multihop transmission. We find both optimal direct access time and adaptive contention-free access time for minimum end-to-end latency according to traffic load of the sensor network.

Direct access time is a multiple access technique based on CSMA/CA. The time period of this transmission is called the contention window and consists of a pre-determined number of transmission slots. The node, which entered back-off, randomly selects a slot in the contention window. It also continuously senses the medium until it selects the contention slot. If it detects transmission from some other node during that time, it enters the back-off state again. If no transmission is detected, it transmits the access packet and captures the medium. In Figure 1(b), node 1 is a source node that generates data traffic and delivers to sink node 11 through multihop transmission.

We assume processing delay, queuing delay and propagation delay to be negligible at each hop and can be ignored. Efficient scheduling can effectively guarantee quality of service, enable adaptive data rates and minimize end-to-end latency. We study effective scheduling to achieve these goals with respect to RCH-MAC based multihop sensor networks.

Our objective is to minimize the end-to-end latency from source node 1 to sink node 11. We use variables of the optimization problem to determine the number of time slots in adaptive contention-free access time and length of the direct access time. Hence, the optimization problem is

$$min \quad E[EtoE_{latency}] \quad t_{da} \geq 0 \tag{1}$$

The notation for the analysis parameters for the performance evaluation is shown in Table 1. We defined a frame time that consists of three times, synchronization time, direct access time and adaptive contention-free access time. The following equation expresses a total frame time

$$t_{fr} = t_{st} + t_{da} + t_{ac} \tag{2}$$

The adaptive contention-free access time is divided into N time slots. Therefore, adaptive contention-free access time is expressed as the product of N and time slot as,

$$t_{ac} = N * T_{ts} \tag{3}$$

One time slot should have enough time to receive and send data packets. As shown in (4), T_{ts} is the overall time consumed for data transmission time, ACK packet time, receiving time which is three times of short interframe space time and guard time. Overall time consumed is calculated as,

$$T_{ts} = T_D + T_{ACK} + 3 * T_{SIFS} + T_G \tag{4}$$

where, $T_D = L_{pkt}/T_B$

The expected time of a reservation procedure proceeds in the direct access time. In other words, the CSMA/CA technique is used for channel acquisition. The random back-off time for contention follows IFS time. The average value of the random back-off time is half of contention window size. The expected time of a reservation procedure is

$$E[t] = T_{IFS} + T_{CW/2} + 2 * T_{SIFS} \tag{5}$$

The maximum number of completed reservation procedure in a frame time, H_{max}, is expressed in (6). Reservation procedures is performed in direct access time. So, the maximum number of completed reservation procedures is the value of direct access time divided by expected time of a reservation procedure.

$$H_{max} = [t_{da}/E[t]] \tag{6}$$

The probability of one more hop's transmission during a frame time is possible when the sending node reserves a preceeding time slot than a time slot of the relay node in the adaptive contention-free access time. The transmission probability $P[8]$ [9] is expressed in (7) for each node in any time slot is τ. We assume that the number of the unreserved time slots is m. If the sending node selects a time slot, the relay node chooses one of the following time slots than the selected time slot. The probability is independent of the value of m.

$$P = [1 - (1 - \tau)]^{m-1} \tag{7}$$

The probability of one more hop's transmission to find the average hop count of the relayed packets during a frame time. The probability of one more hops transmission is same regardless of the value of m, the average hop count of the relayed packets is expressed as the sum of probability from one hop transmission to maximum hops transmission during a frame time.

$$E[MAX_h] = \sum_{H_{max}=1}^{N_{hop}} H_{max} * P^{H_{max}-1} \tag{8}$$

The average end-to-end latency in the multihop transmission condition is obtained by first finding the average number of a frame time spent for multihop transmission. The value is that the hop number from a source node to a destination node is divided by the average hop count of the relayed packets. The average end-to-end latency is equal to the product of the average number of a frame time and frame period. The following equation shows the average end-to-end latency as,

$$E[EtoE_{latency}] = [N_{hop}/E[MAX_h] * t_{fr} \tag{9}$$

We assume both arrival and service rate are constant and apply D/D/1 queuing model in sensor nodes, where, D/D/1 queuing delay is considered to be negligible. The arrival rate is smaller than the service rate. However, there is waiting delay due to channel contention. The constraint function of direct access time is the product of expected time of a reservation procedure and number of generated data during a frame time:

$$t_{da} \geq E[t] * (d_{rate} * t_{fr}) \tag{10}$$

The following constraint is the minimum number of time slots, i.e., the number of generated data during a frame time. The value N is integer,

$$N \geq [d_{rate} * t_{fr} + 1] \tag{11}$$

The following equation indicates the optimization problem:

$$\begin{aligned} min \quad & E[EtoE_{latency}] \\ such \quad that \quad & t_{da} \geq E[t] * (d_{rate} * t_{fr}) \\ & N \geq [d_{rate} * t_{fr} + 1] \\ & t_{da} \geq 0, and \quad N \geq 0, \end{aligned} \tag{12}$$

The optimal direct access time and number of time slots in each sensor node is calculated according to the data rate from the source node. Hence, the following equation shows the final optimization problem of the end-to-end latency.
minimize

$$E[EtoE_{latency}] = [\frac{N_{hop}}{E[MAX_h]} + 1] * (t_{st} + t_{da} + N * T_{ts})$$
$$for \quad t_{da} \geq 0 \quad and \quad N \geq 0, \tag{13}$$

6 Performance Evaluation

6.1 Simulation Setup

The performance of RCH-MAC has been evaluated using NS2 simulator and compared with S-MAC and H-MAC. The topology that we set up for our simulation model is a ten-hop chain network with source at the first node and sink at the end node as shown in Figure 1(b). In our simulation model, we used two-ray ground reflection model for radio propagation and omnidirectional antenna. Each node is situated at a distance 200 metres from adjacent node and carrier sensing range is 550 meters.

6.2 End-to-End Latency

End-to-End latency plays a very important role in Wireless Sensor Networks. It refers to the total time taken for a single packet to be transmitted across a network from source node 1 to sink node 11. There are many factors affecting the end-to-end latency, among them the routing path and the interference level. Figure 2 shows performance of end-to-end latency with varying number of hops. For the multi-hop chain topology, end-to-end latency in S-MAC, H-MAC and RCH-MAC increases as the number of hop length increases. However, end-to-end latency in S-MAC increases at a much faster rate, because it has a shorter duty cycle. RCH-MAC outperforms both H-MAC and S-MAC. In addition, our proposed RCH-MAC protocol makes shorter end-to-end latency due to low collision rate of the reservation control packets. It stabilize the sensor data traffic transmission through reservation of time slots in adaptive contention-free access time.

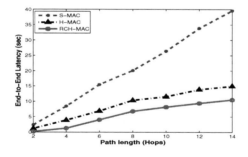

Fig. 2. End-to-End latency in a 10-hop chain scenario

6.3 Packet Delivery Ratio (PDR)

Figure 4 shows the performance of the packet delivery ratio under different packet arrival intervals (sec) in chain topology. RCH-MAC performs better than S-MAC and H-MAC protocols. The packet arrival intervals is varied from 1 packet per second to 1 packet per 40 second to evaluate the network performance for RCH-MAC, H-MAC and S-MAC. Figure 4 shows our simulation results, RCH-MAC outperform than H-MAC and S-MAC.

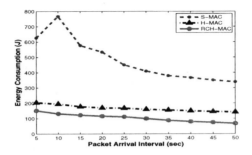

Fig. 3. Energy consumption in a 10-hop chain scenario

6.4   Energy Consumption

We varied our traffic load by varying the packet arrival interval time. If the simulation has multiple packets to send for the chain topology, each CBR flow generate traffic load at the rate of 1 packet every 5 seconds. As the packet arrival interval time increases, H-MAC and S-MAC increase their energy consumption, but RCH-MAC has a smaller rate of increase than other two protocols. In Figure 3, S-MAC node consumes less energy at packet arrival interval time 5 sec than that of arrival time of 10 sec. Because, more packets dropped at nodes due to collision at increased traffic loads and MAC layer does not cache more than one packet. In Figure 3. RCH-MAC is more energy efficient than H-MAC and S-MAC. Therefore, RCH-MAC is efficient contention handling, due to reservation of time slots in adaptive contention-free access time and increases the network lifetime.

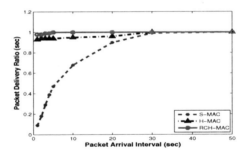

Fig. 4. Packet delivery ratio in a 10-hop chain scenario

7   Conclusions

This paper presents RCH-MAC protocol, a hybrid medium access control protocol specifically designed for Wireless Sensor Networks. It reduces the end-to-end latency in Wireless Sensor Networks for delay sensitive data traffic QoS support for multihop routing in WSNs. In this case, a node operates the reservation procedure during contention-based period and reserves a time slot in the adaptive contention-free time. All the neighbor nodes of the sender and receiver receives their own reservation control packets. The reservation packets occur in nodes along the routing path. As a result, nodes reserve the time slots successively in multi-hop. Simulation results demonstrate that the proposed protocol has significantly reduced end-to-end latency and improved other QoS parameters like energy efficiency and packet delivery ratio.

References

1. Akyildiz, I.F., Su, W., Sankarasubramaniam, Y., Cayirci, E.: A Survey on Sensor Networks. IEEE Communications Magazine, 102–114 (2002)
2. Ye, W., Heidenmann, J., Estrin, D.: An Energy-Efficient MAC Protocol for Wireless Sensor Networks. In: Proceedings IEEE INFOCOM, New York, pp. 1567–1576 (2002)
3. Dam, T.V., Langendoen, K.: An Adaptive Energy-Efficient MAC Protocol for Wireless Sensor Networks. In: Proceedings of the 1st ACM Conference On Embedded Networked SenSys, pp. 171–180 (2003)
4. Younis, M., Akayya, K., Eltowiessy, M., Wadaa, A.: On Handling QoS Traffic in Wireless Sensor Networks. In: Proceedings of the 37th Conference HICSS, Big Island, pp. 902–921 (2004)
5. Ye, W., Heidenmann, J., Estrin, D.: Medium Access Control with Coordinated Adaptive Sleeping for Wireless Sensor Networks. IEEE/ACM Transactions Networking 12(3), 493–506 (2004)
6. Rhee, I., Warrier, A., Aia, M., Min, J.: Z-MAC: A Hybrid MAC for Wireless Sensor Networks. In: Proceedings of the 3rd ACM Conference on Embedded Networked SenSys, pp. 511–524 (2005)
7. Wang, H., Zhang, X., Khokhar, A.: Cross-Layer Optimized MAC to Support Multihop QoS Routing for Wireless Sensor Networks. IEEE Transactions on Vehicular Technology 59(5) (June 2010)
8. Zhai, H., Chen, X., Fang, Y.: How Well can the IEEE 802.11 Wireless LAN Support Quality of Service. IEEE Transactions Wireless Communication, 3084–3094 (2005)
9. Bianchi, G.: Performance Analysis of the IEEE 802.11 Distributed Coordination Function. IEEE Journal Wireless Communication 18(3), 535–547 (2000)

Role Based Dynamic Trust Model for Routing in Mobile Wireless Sensor Networks

Thejaswini S.[1,2], N.R. Sunitha[1,2], and B.B. Amberker[1,3]

[1] Department of Computer Science and Engineering
[2] Siddaganga Institute of Technology, Tumkur, India
[3] National Institute of Technology, Warangal, India
{thejaswinis,nrsunitha}@sit.ac.in, bba@nitw.ac.in

Abstract. In Wireless Sensor Network(WSN), different roles can be associated with sensor nodes. However, depending on the application a node can be dedicated to a particular special role. This paper explores a dynamic role based trust model for route selection mechanism for WSN. In this approach we have identified the different roles of sensor such as packet forwarding and data aggregation. Each node maintains a reputation table which holds reputation values for different roles of all neighboring sensors. Using this table data is routed to destination by evaluating the trustworthiness of the sensors based on different roles. In this paper, an efficient and dynamic symmetric key distribution mechanism is selected for secure communication between nodes in a densely populated mobile WSN. The proposed trust model for routing is reliable, scalable and has simple trust computation for different roles. Using this model secure routing can be provided by detecting malicious and faulty nodes w.r.t different roles.

Keywords: Data Aggregation, Key Distribution, Pairwise, Reputation, Routing, Trust.

1 Introduction

With the rapid technology development of wireless communication and Micro-Electro-Mechanical Systems (MEMS) during these several decades, the WSN technology has found its significant potential use in various fields: environmental monitoring, healthcare, target tracking, and more. Since, sensor nodes are often deployed in open and unattended environments without physical protection, providing security in a stringent resource constraint environment is a hot and challenging issue in WSN. However, an open research problem is how to bootstrap secure communications among sensor nodes, i.e., how to set up secret keys among communicating nodes? Hence, secure communication in WSNs is a rather complex task. To handle large number of keys used for communication in large networks, key management protocols are the core for secure communications. To ensure high level of security in WSNs, there is a need for dynamic key management scheme that can change the administrative keys periodically and on demand or upon detection of node capture. This scheme enhances the network

K.R. Venugopal and L.M. Patnaik (Eds.): ICIP 2012, CCIS 292, pp. 28–34, 2012.
© Springer-Verlag Berlin Heidelberg 2012

survivability. Lewis, Forkia and Govan[1] have proposed trust based dynamic pairwise key distribution and routing mechanism to overcome the drawbacks of static schemes and to provide the high level of security for WSN. Trust and Reputation have been recently suggested as an effective security mechanism for open environments such as the internet. In this paper we consider a Trust/Reputation scheme to provide high level of security for Key Distribution and Routing in WSN. Hence, our contribution in this paper is threefolds :

- To the best of our knowledge, this is the first paper (or one among the only few papers) that employs the concept of role based Reputation to evaluate the trustworthiness of sensor nodes.
- We present the following issues in our proposed scheme :
  - A neighbor based dynamic Key Distribution scheme is selected to provide authentication between the nodes for secure communication in a densely deployed WSN.
  - Role based Dynamic Trust model for route selection to establish secure, reliable path between sensor nodes and base station and also to deal with potential faulty sensors in WSN.
- Simple computation of Trust based on the sensors role and at most to cooperate with other nodes.

2   Proposed Scheme

We consider a large network with densely deployed mobile sensor nodes. In the proposed system we choose an efficient, dynamic neighbor based Key Distribution scheme which provides authenticity between a pair of nodes for secure communication in the WSN. Also we propose a Role Based Dynamic Trust Model for selecting secure and reliable path for successful completion of the task.

2.1   Dynamic Pairwise Key Distribution Scheme

The basic idea of the Key Distribution scheme is to distribute Pairwise key dynamically between the nodes with in the sensor network based on the local computation of the trust. Each sensor node has the ability to distribute a Pairwise key and hence any node in the WSN can be selected by one of its neighbor in order to distribute a Pairwise key for encrypting the communication between two nodes based on trust evaluation[1]. Establishing Trust context will ensure that only trusted nodes within the WSN can share sensed information to provide secure and reliable communication. We assume a set of sensors which are initially deployed in the network as trusted nodes of the Base Station(BS). If a node (source) want to communicate with another node (target), the node can ask (request) one of its trusted neighbor(trusted node of BS) to set up a Pairwise key if the neighbor node has already trusted target node rather than asking (request) the BS to set a Pairwise key between source and target nodes. In case, if none of the trusted neighbors are not available then, key must be set (allocated) by the BS on demand/request. Thus, the neighbor based shared key scheme reduces the number of transmissions required while forwarding key request and key reply messages to and from the BS.

2.2   Role Based Dynamic Trust Model for Route Selection

Recently many trust based secure mechanism in WSNs has been presented[1,2]. In this paper, we propose a Role based Trust framework for Sensor Networks. The sensor node has different Trust rating for different role while cooperating with other nodes. The node considers the Trust rating to decide whether to co-operate with other nodes to finish a certain task. However, if we dont distinguish the different task of a node, we may arrive at wrong evaluation of trust. In fact, a node in WSNs not only send packets but also collect some data to cooperate with its neighbor node. A node can do several tasks to cooperate with other node. Routing refers to delivery of data from source to destination node by selecting a suitable path in the network. In routing process each node has different roles to achieve the task such as sensing, packet forwarding, Data Aggregation, time synchronization, data routing, neighbor found and location report among neighbors and are coupled with each other in the routing approach. If the link fails or do not relay sensor nodes data for a while, the result of routing process may be highly inaccurate, which in turn can have a significant negative impacts on the overall network performance. In our proposed scheme we have identified the sensors roles such as packet forwarding and Data Aggregation depending on their functionality. The roles of the sensor and their Trust evaluation schemes that are identified and proposed in our scheme are as follows:

1. **Packet Forwarding:** Due to selfish/greedy behavior, some nodes want to save its own resources such as power, memory and CPU cycles etc and selectively forwards the packet. Malicious behavior associated node includes the features such as packet dropping, packet modification, packet fabrication, timing attacks and silent route change. Usually such behavior occurs during routing and packet transfer phase of the network deployment. In a mobile WSNs, to detect node acting selfish(malicious) manner, every sensor node monitors and maintain Reputation Table and Trust Table to record the reputations and trust values of all its neighbors based on their roles respectively each time when a source node sends a packet to a neighbor for further forwarding. The Reputation table consists of Trust Metrics that are listed below and these values are periodically updated based on evaluation of their trustworthiness. Using these trust parameters the below specified algorithm is used to compute the Trust value of a node [2] :

Trust Metrics: F: No of Packets Forwarded, D: No of Packets Dropped, M: No of Packets Mis-Routed, I: No of Packets Falsely Injected, R_p: Total no of packets received by B sent from A, S_p: Total no of packets sent by B to A.

Algorithm: To Compute Trust Value:
(a) Collect data for F, D, M, I, R_p and S_p.
(b) Find the threshold values associated to each behavior F_n, D_n, M_n, I_n.

(c) Calculate ratio F_s, D_s, M_s, I_s of each behavior and R_p, S_p total received or sent packet accordingly.

(d) Calculate the deviation F_d, D_d, M_d, I_d from the corresponding threshold:

$$F_s = F/R_p \qquad\qquad F_d = F_n - F_s$$
$$D_s = D/R_p \qquad\qquad D_d = D_n - D_s$$
$$M_s = M/R_p \qquad\qquad M_d = M_n - M_s$$
$$I_s = I/S_p \qquad\qquad I_d = I_n - I_s$$

(e) Calculate the corresponding direct Trust value using the formula:

$$\text{Trust}(T) = (W_1 * F_d) - (W_2 * D_d) + (W_3 * M_d) + (W_4 * I_d)$$

where W_1, W_2, W_3 and w_4 are predefined weights[0,1] for corresponding cooperative and non-cooperative behaviors.

2. **Data Aggregation:** The purpose of Data Aggregation is to eliminate re-dundant data transmission and provide fused information to the BS, to conserve energy and bandwidth of resource constrained sensor nodes and hence reducing the communication cost between sensor nodes in the network (as shown in below fig).

In our proposed scheme, to perform Trust and Reputation mechanism we have identified different roles of sensor nodes in the context of Trust evaluation in Data Aggregation process of sensor networks in order to: i) prolong the network life time ii) have a reliable aggregation iii) reliable data delivery to the destination. Each sensor node must maintain Reputation Table and Trust Table to record the Reputation and Trust values of all its neighbors based on their roles respectively and these values are periodically updated based on their trustworthiness. The following are the different roles of sensors nodes that are considered as the Trust metrics in the Data Aggregation process for WSN :

- **Access Link:** The basic functionality and the idea behind the role of these type of sensor nodes is to judge the accessibility link between its neighboring nodes in WSN. Each sensor node has to send its current sensed data to all of its neighbors periodically. When neighboring nodes receive data, they can deduce whether the link between them and the sender is available or not. If the link is available, then increase the availability parameter value for that link in the Reputation table indicating that these neighboring nodes can be good candidates to relay data from the sender otherwise increase the non availability parameter value.

- **Aggregator:** Data aggregation usually results in alteration in data. If a compromised (captured or faulty) node is selected as data aggregator, it may inject false data or modify aggregated data not only to deceive the BS but also making the mission unreliable. Hence, detecting false data injection during aggregation is a challenging task. In order to detect compromised data aggregators, When aggregator forwards the aggregated data to the BS, BS maintains aggregators nodes reputation based on the behavior of the aggregator nodes. The BS periodically broadcast

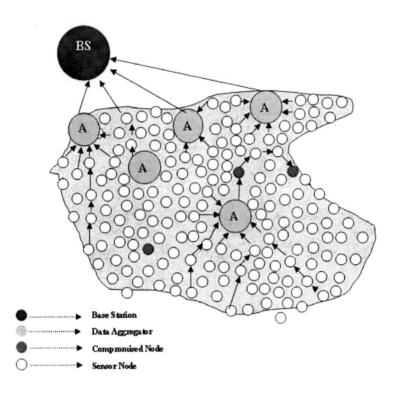

Fig. 1. Data Aggregation Environment in WSN

the Reputation/Trust values of the aggregators node to all the nodes in the network. Based on this, the aggregators neighboring nodes can choose a trustworthy aggregator to relay data to the aggregator node. In case, the broadcast message of BS is not accessible by the nodes in the network due to various reasons such as node facing obstructer or beyond the communication range, then the neighboring nodes of the aggregator can test the trustworthiness of aggregator node before transmission of the data. During the data aggregation session, each neighboring node N_i of the data aggregator A_j sends its own data to A_j and starts listening from its sibling nodes that are within the communication range that sends data to A_j. Once all sensor nodes sends their data to A_j, A_j aggregates data it receives and N_i also aggregates the data sent by its siblings to A_j. When A_j transmits its own aggregated data to its BS, Ni listens the aggregated data of Aj and compares it with its own aggregated data. If the aggregated data of N_i and A_js are correlated then aggregator is treated as trustworthy otherwise untrustworthy (compromised node).

- **Packet Forwarding:** The basic idea of this type of sensor nodes is to find how a neighboring relay node can perform aggregation. Each sensor node has to monitor the local aggregation task of its upstream node. Later on, the sensor node overhears the aggregation result of its relay node and will update the Reputation value and the Trust value for its relay node based on the difference between its aggregated result and result of its relay node.
- **Sensing:** A compromised node may report false sensor reading to deceive BS or to distort the aggregated data. However, due to dense deployment of sensor nodes, neighboring sensor nodes often have overlapping sensing ranges and data sensed by neighboring sensor nodes are highly correlated in the sensor networks. Hence, sensor node that reports false sensor reading is detected by its neighboring nodes that senses the same phenomena by listening to sensing data sent by compromised node.
- **Routing:** To detect the Routing misbehaviors, each sensor node maintains a buffer of the recently sent packets and compare each overheard packet with the packets in the buffer to see if there is a match. Therefore, Reputation values and Trust values are evaluated based on sensor nodes correct behavior and misbehavior i,e., number of false routing and correct routing behavior of a node for a period of time.

To evaluate the trust in the Data Aggregation process, we select Bayesian formulation and to represent Reputation, we utilize BETA distribution, which is based on using beta Proability Density Functions (PDF). Trust can be defined as the probability expectation value of the Reputation function as in [3]. The beta PDF can be described using the gamma function as:

$$f(p|\alpha, \beta) = \frac{\tau(\alpha + \beta)}{\tau(\alpha) + \tau(\beta)} p^{\alpha-1} (1-p)^{\beta-1} \qquad 0 \leq p \leq 1, \alpha \geq 0, \beta \geq 0 \qquad (1)$$

where α and β count the number of satisfaction (cooperative) and unsatisfaction (no-cooperative) of a given criteria respectively. Given a Reputation metric R_{ij}, we define the Trust rate T_{ij} to be expectation of node i about future behavior of node j. T_{ij} is obtained using the statistical expectation of prediction stated as:

$$T_{ij} = E(R_{ij}) = E(Beta(\alpha + 1, \beta + 1)) = \frac{\alpha + 1}{\alpha + \beta + 2} \qquad (2)$$

3   Conclusions and Future Work

The proposed scheme provides more accurate security mechanism as the protocol carefully chooses Trust prediction parameters in different roles of WSNs by identify ing malicious or misbehaved nodes and mitigate different well known active and passive attacks like DOS attacks, Impersonation attacks etc., without depending on a lot of message exchanges and computation. The selected key distribution scheme also provides a better performance on security and storage overhead. We think there is a potential for enhancement to our proposed work in the several issues such as: i) Clock synchronization technique can be integrated with power saving technique to improve the energy efficiency in WSN applications. ii) Trust establishment for Key Distribution mechanisms.

Acknowledgments. We thank AICTE for funding this research work F.No: 8023/BOR/RID/RPS-16/2008-09.

References

1. Nathan, L., Foukia, N., Donovan, G.G.: Using Trust for Key Distribtion and Route Selection in Wireless Sensor Networks. In: Network Operations and Management Symposium, NOMS, pp. 787–790. IEEE (2008)
2. Chatterjee, P., Sengupta, I., Ghosh, S.K.: A Trust Based Clustering Framework for Securing Ad Hoc Networks. In: Prasad, S.K., Routray, S., Khurana, R., Sahni, S. (eds.) ICISTM 2009. CCIS, vol. 31, pp. 313–324. Springer, Heidelberg (2009)
3. Josang, A., Ismail, R.: The Beta Reputation System. In: Proceedings of the 15th Bled Conference, Electronic Commerce, p. 41 (2002)

Distance Based Termite Algorithm
for Mobile Ad-Hoc Networks

Kiran M., Praveenkumar G.H., and G. Ram Mohana Reddy

Department of Information Technology,
National Institute of Technology Karnataka, India
kiranmanjappa@gmail.com

Abstract. Providing Quality of Service (QoS) in Mobile Ad-Hoc Networks (MANET's) is difficult due to dynamic nature of its topology. Today's research trends show that Swarm Intelligence (SI) can be used effectively to provide QoS in MANET and also MANET is not much explored in the area of SI. Motivated by their self organizing behavior and robustness many routing algorithms have been proposed for both wired and wireless networks. SI routing algorithms are driven by mainly two functions, Pheromone update-decay functions and Forwarding functions. In this paper, a new pheromone update and decay function for Termite algorithm is proposed for MANET which reflects the current context of the network that is the distance between the Mobile Nodes at the time of transmitting the packets. Received Signal Strength (Pr) from Physical Layer is used to find the distance and it is made visible at the Network Layer through Cross Layer Model. The proposed model is simulated and the results are compared with the existing methods and the metric used for the comparison are throughout and control packet overhead. The results show that the new distance based pheromone update and decay methods perform better than the other existing methods.

Keywords: MANET, Pheromone Update/Decay Methods, Routing Algorithm, Swarm Intelligence, Termite.

1 Introduction

The dynamic nature of the MANETs topology, lack of centralized coordination or organization structure and real world implementation restrictions have made providing Quality of Service (QoS) more challenging in MANET's than in wired networks thus limiting the usefulness of MANET's. As a result current research trends are focusing more towards providing best QoS in MANET's. A pool of independent wireless Mobile Nodes (MN's) forms a MANET working together to deliver the message from source MN to destination MN. Despite lack of central coordination MN's are able to coordinate together to achieve global task. MANET works on hop by hop basis, thus every MN has to relay on its fellow MN to deliver the message. These fellow MN's receive and forwards the messages towards the destination and are called as intermediate or relay nodes. Thus all

K.R. Venugopal and L.M. Patnaik (Eds.): ICIP 2012, CCIS 292, pp. 35–45, 2012.
© Springer-Verlag Berlin Heidelberg 2012

MN's in MANET play a dual role, a terminal node and router. Due to mobility these MN's are free to move anywhere making the topology of MANET dynamic in nature. This nature of MANET makes route setup and maintenance a difficult job. Due to frequent link breakups source MN has to spend most of its time in route setup and maintenance than sending the messages thus MANET suffers from low throughput and more control packet overhead. Finding the best path in terms of resource richness and stableness between the source MN to destination MN is the main concern. Recent trends in research have incorporated Swarm Intelligence (SI) for finding the best possible path in MANET and have found that it is giving the best results. SI routing algorithms are driven by mainly two functions, Pheromone update functions and Forwarding functions. In this paper, pheromone update and decay function is proposed which reflects the current status of the network in terms of distance between the two MN's. A comparative study has been done on different pheromone update and decay functions in terms of the throughout and control packet overhead.

MANET is not much explored under SI based routing algorithms. The behavior of the ants and bees has attracted more researchers than other social insects. Only a few notable works has been done in an effort to incorporate the intelligence of social insect *termite* in MANET. In [1], Vivekananda Jha et.al. have done a extensive comparative study on different SI inspired routing protocols for MANET. Authors have highlighted the work done in different category of SI in different sections. Also authors have highlighted the advantages and disadvantages of these protocols. In [2], Sharvani G.S et. al. have done a survey on Ant Colony based routing algorithms and also authors have highlighted the principles, characteristics and merits of SI. In [3], Hamideh Shokrani et.al. have explained the operation of ant-based routing algorithms for MANET's along with the survey on SI based routing algorithms mentioning importance of selections of parameter values. Authors have also mentioned that implementation of these algorithms should be done carefully. In [4], Martin Ruth and Stephen Wicker proposed a SI based routing algorithm for MANET called *Termite*. Termite is a per packet, multipath, adaptive routing protocol which works on *stigmergy* to achieve robustness. Termite achieves high data good put while reducing the control packet overhead. But Termite algorithm has still many open questions to be answered. The same authors in [5] have explained the termite algorithm in detail. In [6], Martin Roth has presented a Markov chain model for soft routing algorithm. Author has used Ant Colony Optimization and Termite algorithm for the analysis. The tradeoff between sensitivity, noise, network sample rate and threshold is derived based on the expected cost. The same author extended the work in [7]. In [8], Martin Roth and Stephen Wicker have shown the undesirable behavior of the Termite algorithm that is not taking the full advantage of multipath. Authors have used analytical model to prove the point. Also authors have given a solution for the same. The same authors in [9] have given a analytical justification for three different pheromone update methods for termite namely pheromone filter, Joint Decay IIR Filter (IIR2) and pDijkstra Pheromone update methods. The mean pheromone over a system of single link and two links is studied and parameter relationship is explored. In [10], Praveenkumar G.H et. al. proposed *Opt-Termite*, an extension of basic Termite algorithm. Authors have changed the forwarding function to reflect the new parameter, *traffic load*, while keeping the pheromone update and decay functions as same as basic Termite algorithm. Through simulation authors have shown that Opt-Termite performs better than basic Termite and AODV. In [11], Vineet Srivastava and Mehul Motani have discussed different types of Cross Layer Design along with its definition. Also authors have highlighted the open challenges and new opportunities in CLD. In [12], Kiran M and G Ram Mohana Reddy have proposed a service driven cross layer model for adjusting the Request To Send (RTS) retransmission limit for the prioritized flow dynamically. Authors have compared the performance with AODV and DSR and have shown the proposed method performance better. In [13], the same authors have proposed cross layer model *PrQoS* to improve the throughput of the prioritized flow in Self Aware MANET. *PrQoS* adjusts the RTS retry limit dynamically based on the distance between the transmitting and the receiving node. The rest of the paper is organized as follows. Section 2 explains the Swarm Intelligence also highlights the basic Termite algorithm in brief. In Section 3, the proposed model is explained in detail and Section 4 gives the results and analysis. In Section 5, the paper is concluded with future work.

2   Swarm Intelligence (SI)

SI is defined as An Attempt to design algorithm based on the collective behavior of social insects and other animal societies [14]. The distributed nature of social insects represents a highly structured social organization in accomplishing a complex task by local means. Their characteristics can be easily related to the working of computer networks. The behavior of ants, termites, flocks of birds, bees and school of fishes have attracted the researchers. They have a tremendous problem solving capabilities. Their self organizing behavior, robustness and flexible in nature are the important points to consider while designing a new algorithm. The current research trends have focused on adapting the behavior of the SI such as, its nest building nature, finding the shortest path to the food source, moving together as an organized unit, in designing a new algorithm for computer networks.

2.1   Termite Algorithm Summary

Termites use concept of *stigmergy*, for their coordinated behavior. *Stigmergy* refers to a form of indirect communication. Termites use a chemical substance called *pheromone* to achieve stigmergy. Motivated by their strict self organizing capability a probabilistic biologically inspired routing protocol called Termite is proposed in [4,5]. Termite routing algorithm has been designed for MANET and is inspired by the hill building nature of termite social insect. As termites don't have central coordinator and are independent, they work cooperatively to accomplish the task just like MN's in MANET. Thus the termite's hill building nature can be easily correlated to the behavior of MANET. The packet forwarding technique of MANET is interrelated to the hill building nature of the termite. Termite is an adaptive and per packet probabilistic routing algorithm where for each packet routing decision is taken at every node based on the pheromone deposited on the outgoing links. Through stigmergy it reduces the amount of control traffic thus increasing the data goodput. Rapid route discovery and repair are the additional benefits. Also termite is a multipath routing protocol thus achieving strong routing robustness. The algorithm is explained below. Each MN is treated as a termite hill. The packets are strongly attracted towards the strong pheromone gradient of its destination. But at every hill (MN) the next hop is randomly decided. While moving towards the destination the packets lay pheromone for its source in each hill it visits. Thus it increases the likelihood of packets following the same path to the source while traversing back. Each node maintains a table, called *pheromone table*, analogous to routing tables in traditional routing protocol for tracking the amount of pheromone on each outgoing link. To prevent the stale entries in the pheromone table the concept of pheromone decay over time is introduced. At every MN the pheromone increase is linear and decrease is exponential over time.

Pheromone Update: As soon as packet comes at every MN pheromone is incremented by a constant γ and the nominal value of γ is one. The (1) shows the pheromone update equation when a packet arrives from source node 'S' from previous hop 'p'.

$$P'_{p,s} = P_{p,s} + \gamma \tag{1}$$

Pheromone Decay: Periodically (at every 1 sec) each entry in the pheromone table is multiplied by the decay factor $e^{-\tau}$, where τ is the decay rate. The (2) shows the pheromone decay equation.

$$P'_{n,d} = P_{n,d} \cdot e^{-\tau} \tag{2}$$

Forwarding Function: Based on the amount of destination 'd' pheromone deposited the probability of link usage is calculated for each outgoing link using forwarding function shown in (3) upon arrival of a packet.

$$p_{n,d} = \frac{(P_{n,d} + K)^F}{\sum_{i=1}^{N} (P_{i,d} + K)^F} \tag{3}$$

Here N is the total neighbor nodes and $P_{n,d}$ is the probability of using neighbor node 'n' to reach destination 'd'. The constants 'F' and 'K' are used for tuning the routing behavior of the termite and represents *pheromone sensitivity* and *pheromone threshold*.

3   Proposed Pheromone Update and Decay Functions

Even though the termite algorithm gives promising results with good data good put while maintaining nominal control packet overhead, there are many open questions to be solved, the most important being *decay rate*. A high decay rate quickly decays the amount of pheromone in the pheromone table closing the alternate option to reach destination and a slow decay rate may result in stale entries in the pheromone table. In the proposed method, a new pheromone update function is proposed based on the distance between the two communicating MN's. The pheromone update and decay is proportional to the distance moved by an MN after receiving the previous packet or it is proportional to the mobility of MN. Since mobility effects the performance of the protocol an attempt is made to handle the mobility of MN in an effort to increase the throughput. The distance between the two nodes is found using the Cross Layer Model across Physical Layer and Network Layer where the Received Signal Strength (Pr) being the cross layer parameter.

3.1   Cross Layer Model

Fig. 1 shows the cross layer model for finding the distance between the two MN's. Since Received Signal Strength(Pr) is inversely proportional to the distance between the nodes it is made available at the Network Layer from Physical Layer using the cross layer model since the traditional OSI model does not allow non adjacent layers to communicate or share the variables with each other [13]. As soon as packet comes the Pr is measured from the received packet and the distance of the transmitter is calculated using the free space propagation model shown in (4).

$$d = \sqrt[4]{\frac{Pt.\,Gt.\,Gr.\,ht^2.\,hr^2}{Pr.\,L}}$$

$$(4)$$

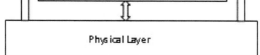

Fig. 1. Cross Layer Model for Finding the Distance

Where,

- Pt : Default transmission power,
- Pr : Received signal power,
- Gt : Antenna gains of the transmitter,
- Gr : Antenna gains of the receiver,
- ht and hr : Heights of the antennas at the transmitter and at the receiver,
- L: System loss (1 by default).

The distance 'd' which is found using (4) along with the time at which it is calculated is maintained in distance table at Network Layer for further processing.

3.2   Distance Based Pheromone Update and Decay Functions

Basic Termite algorithm [4,5] uses constant 'γ', which is one by default, to update the pheromone in the pheromone table and time based exponential decay is used to remove the stale entries in the pheromone table. In the next versions of Termite [7,8], which we call it as Inter Packet Time Based Termite, the pheromone update and decay functions are changed to reflect the inter packet arrival time and are shown in (5). Here the pheromone update and decay are proportional to the inter packet arrival time and if the packet arrives on the current link the pheromone is updated by the amount of pheromone carried by the packet. The amount of pheromone carried by each packet is proportional to the utility of the path.

$$
P_{i,s}^{n'} = \begin{cases} P_{i,s}^n \cdot e^{-(t-\,t_s^n\,)\tau} + \gamma & : i = p \\[2mm] P_{i,s}^n \cdot e^{-(t-\,t_s^n\,)\tau} & : i \neq p \end{cases}
\tag{5}
$$

Where $P_{i,s}^n$ is the amount of pheromone from source node s from neighbor node i at node n. p stands for the previous hop of the packet, γ is the amount of pheromone carried by the packet, τ is the decay rate and t_s^n is the last time a packet from s arrived at node n. While the forwarding functions are borrowed from the basic termite as it is. Unlike basic Termite the pheromone update and decay is based on the packet arrival and not on the time based decay period.

An extension of basic Termite, Opt-Termite [10], differs in forwarding function which finds the less loaded nodes in terms of queue length as the next node to reach the destination. The pheromone update and Decay functions are borrowed from basic termite only that is (1) and (2). Opt-Termite finds the percentage of queue filled in its neighbor MN's and stores in neighbor table which in turn gives the load on these MN's. The forwarding function of opt-Termite uses this load factor to find the next node probability. The forwarding function of Opt-Termite is shown in (6).

$$
p_{n,d} = \frac{\left(P_{n,d}(1-K_n)\right)^F}{\sum_{i \in N}\left(P_{n,d}(1-K_n)\right)^F}
\tag{6}
$$

Where $P_{n,d}$ is pheromone value of destination d at node n. $p_{n,d}$ is the probability of choosing the next node n to reach destination d. A new variable 'K' is introduced which gives the percentage of queue full that is load factor on neighbor node i. The nominal value for the sensitivity parameter 'F' is set to 2. Also the Opt-Termite route discovery and route maintenance is different than the basic Termite algorithm. In this algorithm also the pheromone update and decay is based on the packet arrival and not on the time based decay period.

3.3 Termite with Distance Parameter (BTD)

The basic Termite algorithm is changed to reflect the distance between the MN's. The pheromone update and pheromone decay functions are slightly altered while the forwarding functions are kept as it is.

Pheromone update:

$$P_{k,s}^{n'} = \begin{cases} P_{k,s}^{n} . e^{-(d-d')\tau} + \alpha & : k = l \\ P_{k,s}^{n} . e^{-(d-d')\tau} & : k \neq l \end{cases}$$

(7)

Where $P_{k,s}^{n}$ is the amount of pheromone of source node s from neighbor node k at node n. 'α' is the amount of pheromone carried by the packet and l is the previous hop of the packet. d represents the current distance of neighbor MN while d' is the distance of the same neighbor MN when last packet was received. τ holds the same meaning as the basic termite algorithm that is decay rate.

3.4 Opt-Termite with Distance Parameter(OPTD)

Since Opt-Termite differs only in forwarding function and pheromone update and decay functions are same as the basic termite, distance based pheromone update and decay functions shown in (7) are applied to Opt-Termite to reflect the distance parameter. The forwarding functions are kept same as the original algorithm. Now the algorithm targets on two objectives load balancing as well as finding the stable nodes for the path to the destination. The route discovery and route maintenance is same as the Opt-Termite algorithm.

4   Results and Discussion

The proposed methods are simulated in ns-2 [15]. Different simulation runs for different scenarios with varying mobility of MN's are taken and the average value is used to plot the graph. A comparative study is made among all the methods along with the traditional AODV protocol. The methods are compared against the metrics *throughput* and *control packet overhead*. In the graph OPT stands for Opt-Termite and BT stands for Basic Termite and rest of abbreviations are same as mentioned in the above sections.

Table 1. Simulation Parameters

Parameters	Values
Simulation area	2500 x 200
Number of nodes	100
Initial pheromone	10
Pheromone ceiling	10000
Pheromone floor(PHFLOOR)	0.1
RREQ timeout	2 [seconds]
(decay rate)	0.105
Data TTL	32 [hops]
RREQ TTL	32 [hops]
RREP TTL	32 [hops]
RREQs per Route Request	2

4.1   Experimental Setup

The experimental setup is shown in the Table 1. The simulation is run for 600 seconds. The mobility model considered is random waypoint mobility model. At the MAC layer IEEE 802.11 DCF is used. Transmission range of each node is fixed to 250m and the interference range is set to 550m. FTP is used as the traffic type with the payload of 1500 bytes. The pause time is set to 0 or no pause time is given to any MN's.

4.2   Results and Analysis

The Fig. 2 shows the throughput comparison of different pheromone update and decay methods proposed in the earlier section. The throughput is compared with the Basic Termite and also with traditional protocol AODV as it is considered to be the best protocol for the ad-hoc networks. The graph clearly shows that as mobility increases AODV fails to handle it and throughput decreases. Even though BT performance better than AODV but when compared to other methods it gives low throughput. Among the other three methods OPTD, OPT and BTD, even though results are almost same OPTD gives the good results for all the mobility scenarios. The reason being it balances the load as well as it finds stable nodes for the path. The graph clearly shows that as mobility increases it is handled properly in OPTD, OPT and BTD thus giving good results.

Fig. 3 shows the control packet overhead of all the methods along with AODV. As the advantage of Termite algorithm is low control packet overhead. The graph all Termite extended algorithms are giving good results compared to AODV. Among Termite extended algorithms as like throughput all methods are giving almost same results but OPTD is slightly better than the other methods. The reason is these methods finds the stable nodes for the paths and chances of link breakages are less because of mobility. Where as in AODV as mobility is not handled properly the control packet overhead is more and also it increases as mobility increases.

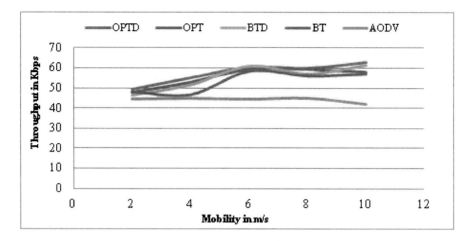

Fig. 2. Throughput Comparison of Different Pheromone Updates Methods with AODV

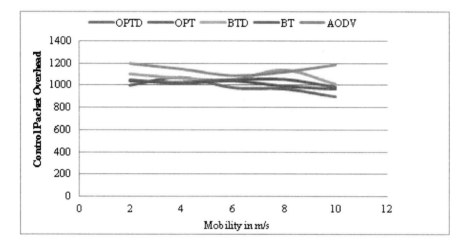

Fig. 3. Control Packet Overhead of Different Pheromone Updates Methods with AODV

5   Conclusion and Future Work

In this paper distance based pheromone update and decay function is proposed as an extension of basic Termite algorithm. Pheromone update and decay is proportional to the distance between the two Mobile Nodes while sending the packets. Also the pheromone update and decay is subjected to packet arrival and not on the time based. Received Signal Strength (Pr) from the Physical Layer is used to find the distance between the two nodes as it is inversely proportional to the distance between the two nodes. Through Cross Layer Model this distance information is made available at the Network Layer. This distance parameter is applied to Basic Termite and Opt-Termite algorithms. The proposed methods are simulated in ns-2 and results are compared using the metrics throughout and control packet overhead. The results show that the Opt-Termite with distance parameter *performs* better than the other methods since the stable nodes are preferred for the path. In the future work authors are concentrating on an analytical model to prove the results.

References

1. Vivekanand, J., Kritika, K., Meghana, S.: A Survey of Nature Inspired Routnig Algorithm for MANET's. In: 3rd IEEE International Conference on Electronics Computer Technology (ICET 2011), April 8-10, pp. 16–24 (2011)
2. Sharvani, G.S., Cauvery, N.K., Rangaswamy, T.M.: Different Types of Swarm Intelligence Algorithm for Routing. In: International Conference on Advances in Recent Technologies in Communication and Computing. IEEE Computer Society (2009)
3. Hamideh, S., Sam, J.: A Survey of AntBased Routing Algorithm for Mobile Ad-Hoc Networks. In: 2009 International Conference on Signal Processing systems, pp. 323–329. IEEE Computer Society (2009)
4. Martin, R., Stephen, W.: Termite: Ad-Hoc Networking with Stigmergy. In: IEEE Global Communication Conference, vol. 5, pp. 2937–2941 (December 2003)
5. Martin, R., Stephen, W.: Termite: Emergent Ad-Hoc Networking. In: 2nd Mediterranean Workshop on Ad-Hoc Networking (MedHoc 2003) (June 2003)
6. Martin, R.: The Markovian Termite: A Soft Routing Framework. In: Swarm Intelligence Symposium (SIS 2007), April 1-5, pp. 213–220. IEEE (2007)
7. Roth, M.: A Framework and Model for Soft Routing: The Markovian Termite and Other Curious Creatures. In: Dorigo, M., Gambardella, L.M., Birattari, M., Martinoli, A., Poli, R., Stützle, T. (eds.) ANTS 2006. LNCS, vol. 4150, pp. 13–24. Springer, Heidelberg (2006)
8. Martin, R., Stephen, W.: Network Routing with Filters: Link Utility Estimation in Swarm Intelligent MANETs. This Research is Sponsored by the Defence Advance Research Project Agency(DARPA) and administrated by the Army Research Office under Emergent Surveilliance Plexus MURI Award No. DAAD 19-01-1-0504
9. Martin, R., Stephen, W.: Asymptotic Pheromone Behavior in Swarm Intelligent MANETS An Analytical Analysis of Routing Behavior. In: Sixth IFIP IEEE International Conference on Mobile and Wireless Communication Networks, MWCN 2004 (2004)
10. Praveenkumar, G.H., Kiran, M., Ram Mohana Reddy, G.: Optimized-Termite: A Bio-inspired Routing Algorithm for MANET's. In: Internationl Conference on Signal Processing and Communications, July 22-25. IEEE, Indian Institute of Science, Bangalore
11. Vineet, S., Mehul, M.: Cross-Layer Design: A Survey and the Road Ahead. IEEE Communication Magazine (December 2005)

12. Kiran, M., Ram Mohana Reddy, G.: Cross Layer Service Driven Adaptive Retry Limit for IEEE 802.11 Mobile Ad-Hoc Networks. In: IEEE Wireless Days 2011 (WD 2011), Niagara Falls, ON, Canada (October 2011)
13. Kiran, M., Ram Mohana Reddy, G.: Throughput Enhancement of the Prioritized Flow in Self Aware MANET based on Neighborhood Node Distances. In: IEEE International Conference on Computer Applications and Industrial Electronics (ICCAIE), Penang, Malaysia (December 2011)
14. Bonabeau, E., Dorigo, M., Theraulaz, G.: Swarm Intelligence: From Natural to Artificial Systems. Oxford University Press, New York (1999)
15. The Network Simulator NS-2, http://www.isi.edu/nsnam/ns/

Outage Probability of Impairments Due to Combining Errors in Rayleigh Fading Channels Incorporating Diversity

J. Subhashini and Vidhyacharan Bhaskar

Department of Electronics and Communication Engineering
SRM University, Tamilnadu, India
subhasivagayaj@gmail.com

Abstract. The principles of diversity combining have been known to the wireless communication fraternity for decades. Diversity requires that a number of transmission paths be available, all carrying the same message but having independent fading statistics. The mean signal strengths of the paths should also be approximately the same. Proper combination of the signals from these transmission paths yields a resultant with greatly reduced severity of fading, and correspondingly improved reliability of transmission. Space diversity is a historical technique that has found many applications over the years and is in wide use in a variety of present-day microwave systems. It is relatively simpler to implement, and does not require additional frequency spectrum. Each of the M antennas in the diversity array provides an independent signal to an M-branch diversity combiner, which then operates on the assembly of signals to produce the most favorable result. A variety of techniques are available to perform the combining process in a fading channel like Rayleigh channel. Maximal Ratio Combining (MRC) is considered as the most efficient among all techniques as it improves the average Signal-to-Noise Ratio (SNR) over that of a single branch in proportion to the number of diversity branches combined, and also provides lowest probability of deep fades.

Keywords: Diversity Combining, Combining Errors, Maximal Ratio Combining, Outage Probability.

1   Introduction

In theory, there are many diversity methods to improve the performance of the transceiver system and to reduce the Bit Error Rate (BER) at the receiver. Diversity methods also reduce the effects of fading as it involves multiple paths carrying the same message, but with independent fading statistics [1]. Proper combination of the signals from multiple transmission paths yields a resultant with greatly reduced severity of fading and correspondingly improved reliability of transmission. Over the years, a number of methods have evolved to capitalize on the uncorrelated fading exhibited by separate antennas in a space-diversity array. In general, the analysis of the mean Signal-to-Noise Ratio (SNR) of the

K.R. Venugopal and L.M. Patnaik (Eds.): ICIP 2012, CCIS 292, pp. 46–55, 2012.
© Springer-Verlag Berlin Heidelberg 2012

combined signal is based on the assumption that the fading signals in the various branches are uncorrelated. In some cases, the antennas in the diversity array could be improperly positioned or the frequency of separation between the diversity signals could be too small [1]. It is thus important to analyze the performance degradation of a diversity system when the diversity branch signals are correlated to a certain extent. It is observed that a moderate amount of correlation between diversity branches is not too damaging. Most of the diversity combining schemes, assume that combining mechanisms operate perfectly. Since information needed to operate a combiner is extracted in some way from the signals themselves, there is a possibility of making an error, thus not completely achieving the expected performance. This effect is studied in detail in [2]. In [3], the Multiple Input Multiple Output (MIMO) channel capacity using exponential correlation matrix model was investigated.

For the system under consideration, increase in correlation is equivalent to a decrease in the Signal-to-Noise Ratio (SNR) using some realistic channel conditions. This might be owing to the fact that information needed to operate a combiner is extracted in some way from the signals themselves and so there is a possibility of making an error which leads to performance degradation. From [4], the behavior of the eigen-modes of a MIMO Rayleigh channel, and the power levels allocated to them by water-filling algorithm with SNR and with channel correlation are analyzed. Capacity of the channel eigen modes and the total capacity of the channel was studied, and is inferred that the strongest eigenmode of the MIMO Rayleigh channel matrix increases with correlation, and the other eigenmodes of the channel decreases.

In [5], the capacity of MIMO Rayleigh fading channels in the presence of spatial fading correlation at both the transmitter and the receiver, assuming the channel is unknown at the transmitter, and perfectly known at the receiver, was analyzed. The analytical framework presented in this paper is valid for arbitrary number of antennas and generalized the previously known results for independent identically distributed or one sided correlated MIMO channels to the case when fading correlation exists on both sides. The capacity of MIMO channels is limited by both spatial fading correlation and rank deficiency of the channel. When spatial correlation reduces the diversity gains, rank deficiency due to double scattering or keyhole effects decreases the spatial multiplexing gains of multiple antenna channels.

In [6], the ergodic (or mean) MIMO capacity for an arbitrary finite number of transmit and receive antennas was analyzed, taking into account realistic propagation environments in the presence of spatial fading correlation, double scattering, and keyhole effects. Mareef and Aissa investigated [7] the impact of spatial fading correlation and keyhole condition on the capacity of MIMO channels when instantaneous Channel State Information (CSI) is available at the transmitter and receiver sides. A separable correlation model was considered, whereby spatial fading correlation was accounted at both sides of the co-located MIMO wireless channel. Two extreme scenarios of a double scattering environment were analyzed: (a) an extremely rich scattering environment corresponding to a conventional semi-correlated Rayleigh fading channel and (b) a doubly-correlated rank deficient keyhole channel with a single degree of freedom.

MIMO systems have the potential to achieve very high capacities, depending on the propagation environment. The measurement of MIMO systems under strong and weak line of sight conditions was presented in [8]. The system capacity decreased as the distance from the transmitter increased. In [9], the capacity of dual antenna array systems under correlated fading via theoretical analysis and ray tracing simulations is explored. It was shown that the empirical capacities converged to the limit capacity predicted from asymptotic theory, and the results were presented for the cases when the transmitter does and does not know the channel realization. In [10], capacity analysis of MIMO Rayleigh channel with spatial correlation at the receiver of multipath taken into account was presented. The incremental improvement of correlated Rayleigh channel was reduced by increasing spatial fading correlation.

Krone and Fettvies studied [11] the capacity of OFDM systems that are impaired by transceiver I/Q imbalance of low cost mobile terminals. Closed forn expressions were derived for the ergodic system capacity and the outage probability considering different types of Rayleigh fading channels. In [12], the channel capacity of a dual-branch MRC diversity system over correlated waveform intensity, which was characterized as correlated Nakagami-m fading was evaluated. The formulae of channel capacity performance were provided with Probability Density Function (PDF) based approach.

In this paper, the effects of correlation between diversity branches, and how it causes deterioration of the performance of diversity system is studied. The purpose of this paper is to compute the outage probability of the Maximal Ratio Combining (MRC) system when the correlation between branches increases using PDF of the instantaneous SNR in [2].

2   System Model and Description

Mobile radio links are subject to severe multipath fading due to the combination of randomly delayed, reflected, scattered, and diffracted signal components. Fading leads to serious degradation in system performance, resulting in either a higher BER or a higher required transmit power for a given multilevel modulation technique. Thus, fading compensation is typically required to improve link performance. One compensation technique uses Pilot Symbol Assisted Modulation (PSAM). This technique inserts a training sequence into a stream of MQAM data symbols to extract channel-induced attenuation and phase shift, which are then used for symbol detection.

Adaptation of certain parameters of the transmitted signal with fading leads to better utilization of channel capacity. The concept of adaptive transmission, which requires accurate channel estimation at the receiver and a reliable feedback path between that estimator and the transmitter, is shown in Fig. 1. These techniques have hardware constraints, requiring good channel estimation techniques and buffering/delay of the input data since the transmission rate varies

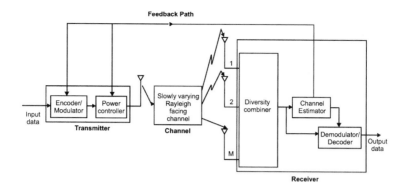

Fig. 1. Block diagram of MRC Transceiver-Rayleigh fading

with channel conditions. The fact that these issues are less constraining in current land mobile radio systems, coupled with the need for spectrally efficient communication, has revived interest in adaptive modulation methods. The idea behind these adaptive modulation schemes is practiced to do real-time balancing of link budget through adaptive variation of the transmitted power level, symbol rate, constellation size, coding rate/scheme, or any combination of these parameters. Thus, without sacrificing BER, these schemes provide a much higher average spectral efficiency by taking advantage of the time-varying nature of the wireless channel, transmitting at high speeds under favorable channel conditions and responding to channel degradation through a smooth reduction of their data throughput.

The performance of these schemes is further improved by combining them with space diversity. The use of diversity systems provides significant improvement in communication when transmitting through a fading propagation medium. Of all diversity linear-combining schemes, maximal ratio combining is considered optimum in that it provides the highest average output SNR and the lowest probability of deep fades.

2.1   MRC Diversity Combining Scheme

In MRC, the signals are co-phased and then summed with the amplitude of each branch signal being weighted by its own SNR. In a fading channel, maximal ratio diversity combining improves the average SNR over that of a single branch in proportion to the number of diversity branches combined as shown in Fig. 1. However, its main advantage is the reduction of the probability of deep fades. The effect of Gaussian errors in the combiner weighting factors on the probability distribution of the output SNR is computed. The limits on allowable error for a specified probability of fades below any given level are indicated. The results are applied to a mobile radio example in which the weighting factor is determined from a pilot transmitted along with the signal.

A particular embodiment of this method involves use of a CW "pilot" signal transmitted adjacent to the message band. To keep the pilot from overlapping the signal, they are separated either in frequency or in time. The phase and amplitude of the pilot signal are sensed, and used to adjust the complex weighting factors of the individual branches so that true MRC results. In this case, Gaussian error is due to decorrelation of the pilot from the signal either because their frequency separation or their time separation is too large.

The fading on the pilot signal is not completely correlated with that of the message, possibly because pilot frequency is too far removed from the message. In this case, complex weighting factors would be somewhat in error, and will degrade its performance. The effects can be completely described in terms of a quantity, ρ, defined as the magnitude of the complex cross-correlation between the transmission coefficients of the medium associated with pilot and message frequencies [1]. In [2], Gans showed that the PDF of the received instantaneous SNR, γ, at the output of a M-branch MRC output (pilot and message signals are not perfectly correlated), i.e., $0<\rho<1$ is expressed as [1]

$$f_M^{(CE)}(\gamma) = \frac{\left(\frac{\rho^2}{1-\rho^2}\right)^n exp(-\frac{\gamma}{\Gamma})}{\Gamma} \sum_{n=0}^{M-1} \binom{M-1}{n} \left(\frac{\gamma\delta}{\Gamma}\right)^n \frac{1}{n!} \quad (1)$$

where

M is the number of diversity branches,

ρ is the correlation between the envelopes of two single sinusoids over the transmission path at the pilot and message,

Γ is the SNR on each individual branch, and

CE stands for Combining Errors.

The Cumulative Distribution Function (CDF) of the received SNR, γ, at the output of a M-branch MRC output when the pilot and message signals are not perfectly correlated is given by

$$F_M^{(CE)}(\gamma) = 1 - exp(-\frac{\gamma}{\Gamma}) \sum_{n=0}^{M-1} \binom{M-1}{n} \rho^{2n}(1-\rho^2)^{M-1-n} \sum_{k=0}^{n} \frac{1}{k!} \left(\frac{\gamma}{\Gamma}\right)^k \quad (2)$$

3   Analysis of Outage Probability

The average SNR of the M-branch MRC output is given by $\langle\gamma\rangle = \Gamma(1 + (M - 1)\rho^2)$ [1]. Note that if $\rho=0$, the pilot and message signals are uncorrelated (worst case), and if $\rho=1$, the pilot and the message signals are perfectly correlated. Given an average transmit power constraint, the channel capacity of a fading channel with received SNR distribution and optimal power and rate adaptation (bps) is given as

$$\langle C_O PRA \rangle = B \int_{\gamma_0}^{\infty} \log_2 \frac{\gamma}{\gamma_0} P_\gamma(\gamma) d\gamma \quad (3)$$

where B [Hz] is the channel bandwidth and γ is the optimal cut off SNR level below which data transmission is suspended. Since no data is sent when $\gamma < \gamma_0$, the optimal policy suffers a probability of outage equal to the probability of no transmission, given by

$$P_{out} = P(\gamma \leq \gamma_0) = \int_0^{\gamma_0} P_\gamma(\gamma)d\gamma = 1 - \int_{\gamma_0}^\infty P_\gamma(\gamma)d\gamma \qquad (4)$$

Given the spectrum efficiency of a fading channel with received SNR distribution, and optimal power and rate adaptation policy under consideration, the optimal cut off SNR, γ_0 , below which data transmission is suspended, must satisfy [12]

$$\int_{\gamma_0}^\infty \left(\frac{1}{\gamma_0} - \frac{1}{\gamma}\right) f_M^{(CE)}(\gamma)d\gamma = 1, \qquad (5)$$

where $f_M^{(CE)}(\gamma)$ is the PDF of the received instantaneous SNR. After substituting PDF of the received instantaneous SNR, γ, in eqn. 5 the optimal cut off SNR (γ_0) is found to satisfy

$$\frac{\Gamma}{(1-\rho^2)^{M-1}} = \sum_{n=0}^{M-1} \binom{M-1}{n} \left(\frac{\gamma\delta}{\Gamma}\right)^n \frac{1}{n!}\left[\frac{\Gamma}{\gamma_0}\Lambda^{(c)}\left(n+1,\frac{\gamma_0}{\Gamma}\right) - \Lambda^{(c)}\left(n,\frac{\gamma_0}{\Gamma}\right)\right]$$
$$\qquad (6)$$

where $\Lambda^{(c)}(x,\alpha) = \int_\alpha^\infty exp(-t)t^{x-1}dt$ is the complementary incomplete gamma function [12]. Let $x = \frac{\gamma_0}{\Gamma}$ and define

$$f(x) = \sum_{n=0}^{M-1} \binom{M-1}{n} \frac{1}{n!} \left(\frac{\rho^2}{1-\rho^2}\right)^n \left[\frac{1}{x}\Lambda^c(n+1,x) - \Lambda^c(n,x)\right] - \frac{\Gamma}{(1-\rho^2)^{M-1}}$$
$$\qquad (7)$$

Note that

$$\frac{\partial f(x)}{\partial x} = -\frac{1}{x^2} \sum_{n=0}^{M-1} \binom{M-1}{n} \frac{1}{n!} \left(\frac{\rho^2}{1-\rho^2}\right)^n \left[\frac{1}{x}\Lambda^c(n+1,x)\right] < 0 \ \forall \ x \geq 0 \quad (8)$$

Moreover from eqn. 5, $\lim_{x\to 0^+} f(x) = +\infty$ and $\lim_{x\to\infty} f(x) = -\frac{\Gamma}{(1-\rho^2)^{M-1}} < 0$. So, we conclude that there is a unique γ_0 for which $f(\gamma_0) = 0$ which satisfies eqn. 6. Numerical results in MATLAB show that $\gamma_0 \in [0,1]$ as $\Gamma \to \infty$. The channel fade level must be tracked at both the receiver and the transmitter, and the transmitter has to adapt its power and rate accordingly, allocating higher power levels and rates for good channel conditions (γ large), lower power levels and rates for unfavourable channel conditions (γ small). Since no data is sent when $\gamma < \gamma_0$, the optimal policy suffers an outage probability, P_{out}, equal to the probability of no transmission, given by

$$P_{out}^{(CE)} = P(\gamma < \gamma_0) = \int_0^{\gamma_0} f_M^{(CE)}(\gamma)d\gamma = 1 - \int_0^\infty f_M^{(CE)}(\gamma)d\gamma \qquad (9)$$

We obtain the outage probability expression, $P_{out}^{(CE)}$, of this optimal adaptation Substituting eqn. 1 into eqn. 7, and simplifying, we have

$$P_{out}^{(CE)} = 1 - (1-\rho^2)^{M-1} \sum_{n=0}^{M-1} \binom{M-1}{n} \frac{\delta^n}{n!}\Lambda^{(c)}\left(n+1,\frac{\gamma_0}{\Gamma}\right) \qquad (10)$$

where $\Lambda^{(c)}(x,\alpha) = \int_x^\infty e^{-t}t^{\alpha-1}dt$ is the Complementary Incomplete Gamma Function (CIGF) [13]. Section IV discusses the effect of ρ, Γ and γ_0 on outage probability.

4   Simulation Results

Fig. 2 shows outage probability of combining errors for various values of ρ. The graph shows that outage probability decreases as ρ increases, and reaches a value close to zero as ρ reaches 0.9. Thus, it is can be concluded that higher the correlation between message and the pilot, lower is the probability of error and outage probability. It is also inferred from Fig. 1 that P_{out} decreases as diversity order M increases. This is due to the fact that as M increases the number of branches carrying the same information increases. So, there is more chance for the receiver to receive at least one copy of the information or data without or with very low BER.

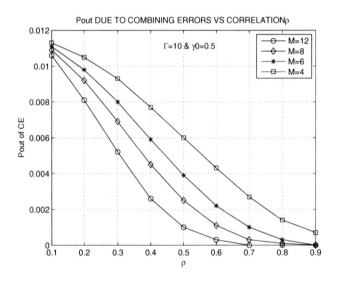

Fig. 2. Outrage Probability vs. Correlation(ρ)

Fig. 3 shows the outage probability of combining errors for various values of Individual branch SNR. It is clearly observed that P_{out} decreases as SNR increases for a particular ρ and γ_0. This is due the fact that channel quality is good at high SNRs and so the CSI at the receiver which is used to adjust weights in the MRC combiner becomes accurate to judge channel performance. So, the message signal is sent with very low BER. Thus, outage capacity which results due to uncorrelated fading of the pilot and message is reduced, as the correlation between the pilot and message signal increases, which is proved mathematically

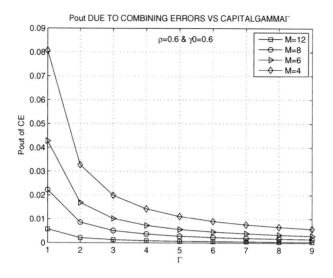

Fig. 3. Outrage Probability vs. Individual Branch SNR

and graphically through numerical analysis of eqn. 2. Also, if the channel is good, even a lesser correlation gives better performance than when the channel is bad.

From Fig. 3, it is also clear that as M increases for the same SNR, performance improves compared to lesser number of branches. So, diversity further enhances performance and leads to true MRC combining.

Fig. 4 shows P_{out} vs. the optimal cutoff SNR, γ_0. Here, outage probability decreases as optimal cutoff SNR increases for a particular value of ρ and Γ. It is known that optimal cut off SNR is the level below which data transmission is suspended. To achieve high capacity, channel fade level must be tracked at both the receiver and the transmitter, and the transmitter has to adapt its power and rate accordingly. It has to allocate higher powers and rates for good channel conditions (γ large) and lower power levels and rates for unfavorable channel conditions (γ small). Since no data is sent when $\gamma_0 < \gamma$, lower the optimal cutoff SNR, higher the channel quality detected at the receiver. So, the channel with higher SNRs alone dominate in combining, and so the channel experiences lower BER which in turn leads to lower outage capacity as shown in Fig. 4 through the numerical results.

Fig. 5 shows P_{out} vs. B=the ratio of optimal cutoff SNR/Individual SNR ($\frac{\gamma_0}{\Gamma}$). Here, the outage probability increases even if the SNR depends on the optimal cutoff SNR. Though the channel is good if the ratio of optimal cutoff to individual branch SNR is more, according to eqn. 3, the outage probability increases, i.e., as B increases, outage probability also increases. This increase in P_{out} is attributed to the optimal cutoff SNR below which no message is transmitted. Hence, if optimal cutoff is maintained at a higher value, even channels with moderate SNRs are not given higher weights in the process of combining, which in turn leads to performance degradation as shown by the simulation results.

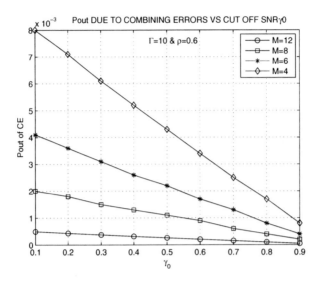

Fig. 4. Outrage Probability vs, Optimal Cutoff SNR(γ_0)

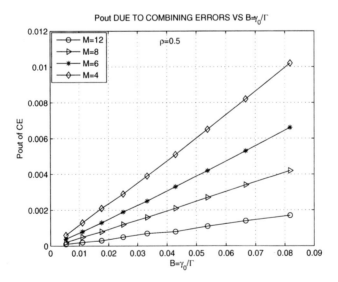

Fig. 5. Outrage Probability vs, B=Optimal Cutoff SNR/Individual SNR(B= $\frac{\gamma_0}{\Gamma}$)

5 Conclusions

The channel outage probability of MRC for Space Combining errors is studied. Furthermore the closed form expression for outage probability of MRC for combining errors was derived and discussed. Our numerical results shows that the outage probability decreases with increase in the diversity order M and/or increase in Individual branch SNR, Γ. Also if the cutoff SNR, γ_0 increases, the outage probability increases.

References

1. Jakes, W.: Microwave Mobile Communications. IEEE Press, Piscataway (1994)
2. Gans, M.: The Effect of Gaussian Error in Maximal Ratio Combiner. IEEE Transactions on Communication Technology 19(4), 492–500 (1971)
3. Lokya, S.: Channel Capacity of MIMO Architecture Using the Exponential Correlation Matrix. IEEE Communication Letters 5(9), 369–371 (2001)
4. Saad, A., Ismail, M., Misran, N.: Rayleigh Multiple Input Multiple Output (MIMO) Channels: Eigenmodes and Capacity Evaluation. In: Proceedings of the International Multiconference of Engineers and Computer Scientists (IMECS), Hong Kong, vol. 2 (March 2009)
5. Shin, H., Win, M., Lee, J., Chiani, M.: On the Capacity of Doubly Correlated MIMO Channels. IEEE Trans. on Wireless Comm. 5(8), 2253–2265 (2006)
6. Shin, H., Lee, J.H.: Capacity of Multiple Antenna Fading Channels: Spatial Fading Correlation, Double Scattering and Keyhole. IEEE Transactions on Information Theory 49(10), 3218–3229 (2003)
7. Mareef, A., Aissa, S.: Impact of Spatial Fading Correlation and Keyhole on the Capacity of MIMO Systems with Transmitter and Receiver CSI. IEEE Transactions on Wireless Communications 7(8), 3218–3229 (2008)
8. Kyritsi, P., Cox, D., Valenzula, R., Wolniansky, P.: Correlation Analysis Based on MIMO Channel Measurements in an Indoor Environment. IEEE Journal on Selected Areas in Communications 31(5), 713–720 (2003)
9. Chuah, C., Tse, D., Kahn, J., Valenzuela, R.: Capacity Scaling in MIMO Wireless Systems Under Correlated Fading. IEEE Transactions on Information Theory 48(3), 637–650 (2002)
10. Trung, H., Benjapolakul, W., Araki, K.: Capacity Analysis of MIMO Rayleigh Channel with Spatial Fading Correlation. IEICE Transactions on Fundamaentals of Electronics, Communications and Computer Sciences E91-A(10), 2818–2826 (2008)
11. Krone, S., Fettveis, G.: Capacity Analysis for OFDM Aystems with Transceievr I/Q Imbalance. In: Proceedings of GLOBECOM, New Orleans, LA, pp. 4572–4577 (2008)
12. Alouini, M., Goldsmith, A.: Capacity of Nakagami Multipath Fading Channels. In: Proc. IEEE Vehicular Tech. Conf. VTC 1997, Phoenix, AZ, pp. 358–362 (May 1997)
13. Gradshteyn, I., Ryzhik, I.: Table of Integrals, Series, and Products. Academic Press, San Diego (1994)

Energy Efficient Transmission Control Protocol in Wireless Sensor Networks

Prabhudutta Mohanty, Manas Ranjan Kabat, and Manoj Kumar Patel

Department of Computer Science & Engineering,
VSS University of Technology, Burla,
Odisha, India
prabhu99.mohanty@gmail.com

Abstract. One of the most important challenges in the design of Wireless Senor Networks (WSN) is to maximize their lifetime. Sensor nodes are energy constrained in nature. Therefore, energy efficient communication techniques are necessary to increase the lifetime of sensor nodes. Maximum energy is consumed during transmission in comparison to sensing and processing of data. Redundant data increases the energy consumption during data transmission. In this paper, we present an Energy Efficient Transmission Control Protocol (EETCP) for the data gathering and data transmission within the network. Our objective is to maximize the network lifetime by controlling the transmission rate. We tried to minimize the redundant data transmission with the co-ordination of Base-station, to increases the lifetime of network.

Keywords: EETCP, Energy Efficient Transmission, Redundancy, WSN.

1 Introduction

A sensor network consists of hundreds or thousands of inexpensive, tiny recourse constraints sensor nodes which has some computational power and sensing capabilities. It is a self configured dynamic Network. WSN can be deployed in various domains and applications like agriculture or environmental sensing, object tracking, wild life monitoring, health care, military surveillance, industrial control, home automation, security etc. [1,2,3]. Some of its application areas deal with redundant data and some deal with non- redundant data [4]. There are many reasons of redundant data in WSN such as multiple sensor sensing same phenomena, slow change in phenomena,presence of malicious nodes in WSN, flooding techniques or multipath data transmission techniques etc. The lifetime of the sensor nodes mostly depend on the power supply unit. Power is stored either in Batteries or Capacitors in a sensor node. A sensor network consumes energy while sensing a phenomenon, transmitting and processing data. Energy required for data communication is more than that for sensing and data processing. Redundant data transmission affects the WSN severely. It drains the energy of the node. Redundant data increases congestion, communication and computational overhead. Malicious nodes may take the advantage of redundant

K.R. Venugopal and L.M. Patnaik (Eds.): ICIP 2012, CCIS 292, pp. 56–65, 2012.
© Springer-Verlag Berlin Heidelberg 2012

data and cause energy drain by injecting redundant data in the network (i.e., replay attack)[5]. That may lead to routing holes[5].

A sensor network transmits all its collected data using different modes of communication [5,6]. The power consumption of the network depends on the communication mode and type of traffic. Traffic in sensor networks can be classified into one of three categories one-to-many, many-to-one and local communication. In many-to-one mode of communication multiple sensor nodes send sensor readings to a base station or aggregation point in the network. In one-to-many mode of communication a single node (typically a base station or a cluster head) multicast or flood a query or control information to several sensor nodes. In Local communication, neighbouring nodes send localized messages to discover and coordinate with each other. In WSNs, sensor nodes sense and transmit the data to the sink nodes in two techniques [7] such as direct communication and multi hop communication.In direct communication mode, each sensor sends its data directly to the base station (Fig. 1a)[6]. In multi hop communication mode, each node sends its data to the base station through intermediate nodes (Fig. 1b). Multi-hopping both leads to less power consumption and lower cost than direct communication. Clustering is the technique which can further reduce energy consumption in a network as well as providing the scalability. In a cluster technique the whole network is partitioned into disjoint set/group consisting of sensor nodes is called cluster. Each cluster has a designated leader, called cluster head. If the cluster head directly transmits [8] to the base station is called direct mode of communication with clustering (Fig. 1c). If the cluster head transmit data to next level cluster head [9,10] and then the next level cluster head send data to base station is called multi hop mode of communication with clustering (Fig. 1d). A sensor network has three data delivery models [11,12]. These are event driven, query driven and continuous. In event driven model, data transmission is triggered by an event. In query driven model base station generate queries to enquire about an event and that query is sent to the sensor node. The sensor node replays with data. In continuous model, sensor nodes send data to the sink node at a pre-specified transmission rate. In network redundancy of data is checked by packet sequence number. This technique helps the receiver to identify the duplicate data and discard it. A packet sequence number cannot help a sender to control redundant data transmission.The other way to eliminate redundant data is data aggregation. In data aggregation [4,6], multiple sources send their data to aggregation point. The data aggregation point (typically a sensor node) generates a data without redundancy by using various methods [13].

In this paper, our objective is to maximize the network lifetime by controlling the duplicate data transmission with the co-ordination of Base-station. Sensor senses the redundant data in many applications and transmits it to the base station. We propose a method to identify the redundant data at the sender side instead of receiver side and minimize the transmission overheads by reducing the redundant data transmission. Base station is an intended data receiver in WSN, which is energy empowered device. We propose an algorithm for base

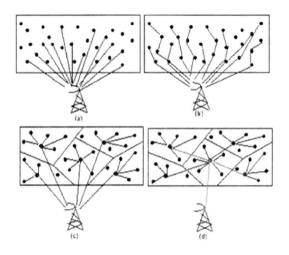

Fig. 1. Sensor Information Forwarding with and without Clustering and Aggregation. (a) Direct Communication. (b) Multi Hops without Clustering. (c) Single Hop with Clustering. (d) Multi Hops with Clustering.

station that computes and processes redundant data without being received. Our aim is to design a suitable model, that can compatible with different modes of communication. Our model fits well in a continuous data delivery model. It also works for both event driven and query driven model.

The paper is organized as follows. In Section II, the proposed energy efficient transmission control protocol is presented. The simulation results and analysis is presented in section III. In section IV, we conclude the paper.

2   Proposed EETCP

We tried to minimize the number of communication between sensor nodes and base station by eliminating redundant data transmission. This is a combined effort of both source node and base station. Our protocol works in four phases. It starts with sensing phase followed by validation and transmission phase, finally ends with data updation phase. Based on these phases we presented our proposed model and the algorithms required to be implemented in the source node and base station.

2.1   EETCP Layering Model

The proposed model (Fig. 2) is divided into two parts, source side and destination side processes. Source side includes three phases i.e. data sensing, data validation and data transmission. In data sensing phase, each sensor node senses the phenomena and gathers information. These gathered data are passed to the validation phase. In validation phase,the data currently sensed compared with

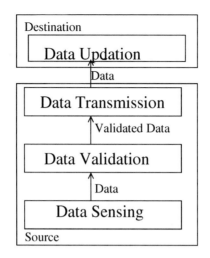

Fig. 2. EETCP Layering Model

Table 1. Data Table for Base station/sink

Node id	Node status	Node co-ordinate points	Last data received time	Time counter	Previous data	Current data

the data sensed previously for redundancy check. Then the validity of the data is checked. A data is valid for transmission if it is non redundant or its no of redundancy is greater than the predefined threshold value. The valid data for transmission triggers the transmission phase and invalid data is ignored. In transmission phase, the transmitter is activated first and then distance to the destination is adjusted. For a direct mode of transmission, the transmitter is adjusted according to the distance of the base station. If any multi-hop transmission is followed, then the transmitter is adjusted to the neighbour node. The transmission phase forwards the data to the base station. After data is received from the source or the period for receiving the data for a node lapse, then the updation phase starts. Base station maintains a Table (Table 1) for data updation. The entire updation process is based on the co-ordination between a sensor node and the base station.

When the base station receives data from a node it updates the table and sets the time counter to zero. If no data is received from a node in an expected duration then it checks the node status If status is alive then previous received data is processed as current data and time counter is increased. When the time counter exceeds a predefined threshold value, base station initiates to know the status of the node by sending control packet. The status checking process allots the base station about the network status.

2.2 Proposed Algorithms

The efficiency of the proposed model lies on the data validation and data updation. Based on the model discussed above two algorithms are proposed. One needs to run in source side (i.e., sensor node) for validation of data and another in the destination side (i.e., base station) to update the database maintaining sensor readings. The algorithms that run in the source side and receiver side are shown in Fig. 3 and Fig. 4 respectively.

Algorithm Data_Gathering(Battery_Power)
begin:
    initialize $tpower=$ minimum power required to sense the data
    + power required to transmit to the destination;
    initialize $prevdata = \Phi, read\_data = \Phi$;
    initialize $node\_th\_count = 0, th = 5$;
    while($Battery\_Power \geq tpower$) **do**
        $read_data = $ sense_data();
        if($prevdata = \Phi$)or($readdata \neq prevdata$) **then**
          $prevdata = readdata$;
          $transmit\_data(read\_data)$;
          $node\_th\_count = 0$;
        else
          if($node\_th\_count \neq th$) **then**
            $node\_th\_count + +$;
          else
            $transmit\_data(read\_data)$;
            $node\_th\_count = 0$;
          endif
        endif
    end while
end

Fig. 3. Algorithm for Sensor Nodes in EETCP

Data sensing is initiated by a node when its battery power is greater than or equal to the threshold power i.e. $tpower = $ minimum power required to sense the data + power required to transmit to the destination. Once data is sensed ($read\_data$) it is compared with the previously sensed data ($prev\_data$) for redundancy check. If a node is sensing the data for first time then the data sensed previously by the same node is made NULL and it proceeds to data transmission phase. If the data is redundant then the node compares the number of times it senses redundant data ($node\_th\_count$) with the maximum number of times the redundant data transmission can be avoided (th). This parameter can be decided and set by the base station depending on the application requirement. This parameter is either set at the time of node deployment or during network setup phase. If the $node\_th\_count$ is less than or equal to th, then the data is invalid for transmission. If the $node\_th\_count$ is greater than th, then the data is valid for transmission even if it is redundant. This gives a robustness to identify nodes status (alive or dead). For non redundant data it simply enters into transmission phase because it is a valid data. Base station initiates data updation phase.

Algorithm Data_Compute(Received_data)
begin:
    initialize $rdata = received\_data$;
    if$(rdata \neq currentdata)$ **then**
        $currentdata = rdata$;
        $previous\_data = currentdata$;
        $timecounter = 0$;
        $Lastdatareceivedtime = current\_time()$;
    else
        if$(rdata = currentdata)$ and $(timecounter > th)$ **then**
        $timecounter = 0$;
        $Lastdatareceivedtime = current\_time()$;
        else
         if$((nodatareceived)$and$(timecounter \leq th))$ **then**
           $currentdata = previousdata$;
           $timecounter = timecounter + 1$;
           $Lastdatareceivedtime = current\_time()$;
         else
          if$((nodatareceived)$ and $(timecounter > th)$
           $checks\ status\ of\ the\ node\ if\ no\ replay$
           $nodestatus = dead$;
         endif
        endif
        endif
    endif

Fig. 4. Algorithm for BS/sink to Compute Value

When the base station receives data from a node it updates the Table(Table 1) and sets the time counter to zero. Base station maintains the data received time for every sensor node. The data received time helps the base station to compute and identify the nodes that has exceeds the expected data received time. If no data is received from a node then it checks the node status if status is alive then previous received data is processed as current data and time counter is increased. When the time counter exceeds the th value base station initiates to know the status of the node by sending control packet.

Table 2. Radio Characteristics

Operation	Energy Dissipated
Transmitter Electronics(ETx-elec)	50 nJ/bit
Receiver Electronics(ERx-elec)	50 nJ/bit
Transmit Amplifier(amp)	100 pJ/bit/m2
Data Aggregation in Receiver	5 nJ/bit/message for k = 2000 bit messages
Signal-to-Noise Ratio (SNR)	typically 10db

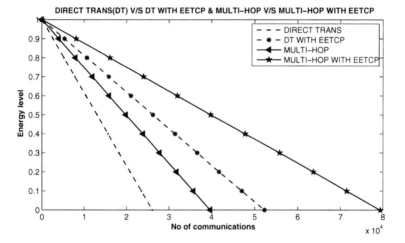

Fig. 5. Direct Transmission Vs Direct transmission with EETCP and Multi-Hop Vs Multi-Hop with EETCP

3   Simulation Results

The proposed EETCP is implemented Intel(R) core(TM) i3 @ 2.10 GHz system with C. We use first order radio model [6,10] for message transmission and reception. The radio characteristics have two modes, transmit and receive, in power dissipation. We randomly distribute 100 nodes in a sensor field of area 50 $50m^2$ with sink located at location (25,50). We also assume the initial energy levels as 1.0J for each node. Data packet length is assumed to be of 2000 bits. The radio channel is assumed to be symmetric. Table 2 summarizes the radio model characteristics. In order to construct the best possible result we iterated each analysis hundred times and considered the average result.

In Fig. 5 we analyzed the performance of direct transmission and direct transmission with EETCP. We consider energy level as 1.0 Joule for a node and placed that node randomly away from the base station in the sensing field. In the analysis we considered an average data redundancy (i.e., 50%-60%). In the same Figure we analyzed the performance of multi-hop transmission and multi-hop transmission with EETCP. Fig. 6 compares direct and multi-hop cluster communication

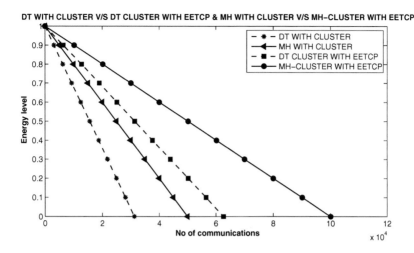

Fig. 6. Comparision between Cluster Based Direct Transmission and Multi-hop Transmission with Cluster Based Direct Transmission and Multi-hop Communication with EETCP

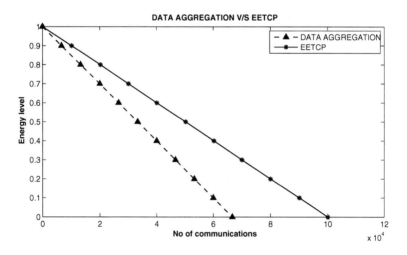

Fig. 7. Comparision between Data Aggregation with EETCP

with cluster communication adapted EETCP. According to B. Krishnamachari, D. Estrin ,S. Wicker [4] by aggregating data in multi hop transmission 50% to 80% of energy can be conserved. In Fig. 7 we analyzed the energy consumption of data transmission using data aggregation with EETCP. In data aggregation sensor nodes send data to an aggregate point. The aggregate point (i.e. a sensor node) aggregates data and forwards data to base station. We considered each node as an aggregation point for its neighbours. Data aggregation consumes 5nJ/bit/message amount of energy for aggregation. In our simulation scenario

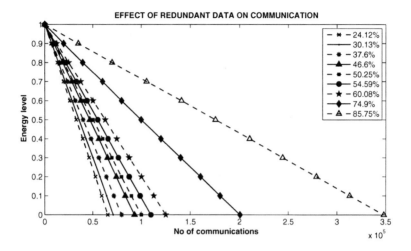

Fig. 8. Effect of Different level of Redundancy on Transmission Performance Analysis

we considered data aggregation in a multi-hop cluster based communication as multi-hop cluster communication [9,10] saves more energy than direct, multi-hop and direct communication with cluster. In Fig. 8, we analyzed the effect of different level of redundancy on data communication. The figure shows that average number of communications increases With the increase of redundancy.

4   Conclusion

In this paper, we make a comprehensive study about the effect of redundant data on transmission. We minimize the redundant data transmission with the co-ordination of base station. Our proposed model processes the redundant data at base station without being transmitted by the sensor node. Our proposed transmission control protocol is compatible with different modes of communication. We simulated our proposed protocol with all modes of communication and it is observed that our proposed protocol increases the life time of network significantly.

References

1. Ruizhong, L., Zhi, W., Youxian, S.: Wireless Sensor Networks Solutions for Real Time Monitoring of Nuclear Power Plant. In: The Proceedings of the 5th World Congress on Intelligent Control and Automation, Hangzhou, P.R. China, pp. 3663–3667 (2004)
2. Romer, K.: The Design Space of Wireless Sensor Networks. IEEE Wireless Communications, 54–61 (2004)
3. Yoneki, E., Bacon, J.: A Survey of Wireless Sensor Network Technologies Research Trends and Middlewares Role. Technical Report (2005)

4. Krishnamachari, B., Estrin, D., Wicker, S.: Modelling Data-Centric Routing in Wireless Sensor Networks. In: IEEE INFOCOM, pp. 1–11 (2002)
5. Karlof, C., Wagner, D.: Secure Routing in Wireless Sensor Networks Attacks and Countermeasures. University of California, Berkeley (2003)
6. Wang, J., Niu, Y., Cho, J., Lee, S.: Analysis of Energy Consumption in Direct Transmission and Multi-hop Transmission for Wireless Sensor Networks. In: Third International IEEE Conference on Signal-Image Technologies and Internet-Based System, SITIS, pp. 270–280 (2007)
7. Younis, O., Fahmy, Y.S.: HEED: A Hybrid, Energy-Efficient, Distributed Clustering Approach for Ad Hoc Sensor Networks. IEEE Transactions on Mobile Computing 3, 366–379 (2004)
8. Heinzelman, W.B., Chandrakasan, A.P., Balakrishnan, H.: Energy-Efficient Communication Protocol for Wireless Microsensor Networks. In: Proceedings of the 33rd Hawaii International Conference on System Sciences, HICSS, Hawaii, vol. 8 (2000)
9. Manjeshwar, A., Agarwal, D.P.: TEEN: A Routing Protocol for Enhanced Efficiency in Wireless Sensor Networks. In: 1st International Workshop on Parallel and Distributed Computing Issues in Wireless Networks and Mobile Computing (2001)
10. Mohanty, P., Panigrahi, S., Sarma, N., Satapathy, S.S.: HCEPSN: A Hierarchical Cluster based Energy Efficient Data Gathering Protocol for Sensor Network. In: ICIT, Bhubneswar, pp. 207–212 (2009)
11. Bhuyan, B., Sarma, H.K.D., Sharma, N., Kar, A., Mall, R.: Quality of Service(QoS) Provisions in Wireless Sensor Networks and Related Challenges. Scientific Research Journal for Wireless Sensor Networks, 861–868 (2010)
12. Talak, S., Abu-Ghazaleh, N., Heinzelman, W.: A Taxonomy of Wireless Micro Sensor Network Communication Models. ACM Mobile Computing and Communications 7, 16–27 (2000)
13. El Faouzi, N.E., Leung, H., Kurian, A.: Data Fusion in Intelligent Transportation Systems Progress and Challenges Survey, pp. 4–10. Elsevier (2010)

AODV-MBR: A New Routing Protocol with Modified Backup Approach

Vijayendra Chaudhary, Utkarsh Patel, Shivaji, and Rakesh Kumar

Department of Computer Science and Engineering
Madan Mohan Malaviya Engineering College, Gorakhpur-273010, India
vijayendra.mmmec@gmail.com

Abstract. Nodes in mobile ad hoc networks communicate with one another via packet radios on wireless multi-hop links. Because of node mobility and power limitations, the network topology changes frequently. Routing protocols therefore play an important role in mobile multi-hop network communications. A prominent trend in ad hoc network routing is the reactive on-demand (AODV) philosophy where routes are established only when required. Given that AODV requires a new route discovery procedure whenever a link breaks, such frequent route discoveries incur a high routing overhead and increase end-to-end delay. Most of the protocols in this category, however, use single route and do not utilize multiple alternate paths. In this paper, we propose a scheme to improve existing on-demand routing protocols by creating a mesh and providing multiple alternate routes with the assurance of no link failure. Our algorithm establishes the link failure prediction embedded within the existing protocol. We improve the Ad hoc On-Demand Distance Vector Backup Routing (AODV-BR) protocol and compare our proposed approach with existing ones through simulation on various performance metrics by varying Traffic Load.

Keywords: Alternate Node, Alternate Route, Mess Structure.

1 Introduction

A mobile ad hoc network [1] is a self-configuring infrastructure less network of mobile nodes, moving independently, communicate with each other through direct wireless links or multi-hop wireless links. The Ad hoc On-Demand Distance Vector (AODV [2]) protocol, one of the on-demand routing algorithms that are receiving the most attention, however, does not utilize multiple paths. An improved version of AODV, AODV-LFP [3] consists of a mechanism of link failure forecast in process of data transmission. The strength of the packet signal, which the node receives may be defined as:

$$p_r = \frac{p_t G_r G_t H_r^2 H_t^2}{d^4} \qquad (1)$$

p_r, p_t are the Strength of received and transmitted signal, G_r, G_t are the antenna gain of receiver and transmitter , H_r, H_t are the antenna altitude of receiver and transmitter respectively, d is the distance between sending and receiving node

K.R. Venugopal and L.M. Patnaik (Eds.): ICIP 2012, CCIS 292, pp. 66–73, 2012.
© Springer-Verlag Berlin Heidelberg 2012

$$d = \sqrt[4]{\frac{p_t G_r G_t H_r^2 H_t^2}{p_r}} \qquad (2)$$

We propose a scheme utilizing a mesh structure to provide multiple alternate routes with link failure prediction by signal strength detection technique with few additional control messages. Therefore our scheme gives better performance as compared to AODV-BR [4], [5], routing protocol in terms of packet delivery ratio, end-to-end delay.

2 Related Work

There are a couple of multicast protocols that rely on the mesh topology for communications between multicast members: the On-Demand Multicast Routing Protocol [2] (ODMRP), and the Core Assisted Mesh Protocol [6] (CAMP).The scheme called 'Duct Routing', proposed in 1980s suffers from some limitations: excessive redundancy and congestion.The scheme by Nasipuri and Das, Temporary Ordered Routing Algorithm (TORA) [7]and Routing On-Demand Acyclic Multipath [2] using multiple routes , but these algorithms require additional control messages.Marina and Das developed an extension for AODV, called Ad hoc On-Demand Multipath Distance Vector (AOMDV) [2] routing. It provides loop-free and disjointed alternate path.

3 Proposed Protocol

In this section, we present the operational details of our proposed scheme,aiming at performance improvement existing protocols(AODV-BR).

3.1 Route Discovery Phase

Our scheme operates similar like AODV in Route discovery phase. when a source wants to initiate a data session to a destination but it does not have any route information, it initiates route discovery process.we slightly modify the route reply phase of AODV protocol to establish mesh structure and alternate paths. Taking advantage of the broadcast nature of wireless communications, a node promiscuously "over-hears" packets that are transmitted by their neighboring nodes. From these packets, a node obtains alternate path information and becomes part of the mesh as follows. When a node that is not part of the route overhears a RREP packet not directed to it-self transmitted by a neighbor (on the primary route), it records that neighbor as the next hop to the destination in its alternate route table.

A node may receive numerous RREPs for the same route if the node is within the radio propagation range of more than one intermediate node of the primary route. When a node that is not part of the route overhears a RREP packet not directed to itself transmitted by a neighbor (on the primary route), it records that neighbor as the next hop to the destination in its alternate route table.

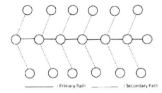

Fig. 1. Multiple Routes forming fish bone like structure

Example of Route Construction

Fig. 2. Is an example showing how the mesh and alternate routes are constructed and used in data delivery. When the RREQ reaches the destination node D, a primary route (S-A-B-C-D) is selected. The destination D sends a RREP to nodes that are within the propagation range of it i.e, Nodes C, Y and Z, who overhear the packet and insert an entry into their alternate route tables. This process is pictorially described in Fig. 2(a). After receiving this REPLY, only node C relays the packet to node B since it is part of the route Again, one hop neighboring nodes can overhear the packet Nodes W and X record node C as the next hop to the destination D in their alternate route table. On the other hand Node Y and Z do not update their table since they already have consisted a path to D. Likewise, node D does not react to the RREP transmission by node C since it is the destination (and part of the route). Fig. 2(c) reflects the state when the RREP reaches the source node S and builds the primary and multiple alternate routes. The final state when primary route and alternate paths are established is shown in Fig. 2(d). Each Alternate Node Routing table entry is as follow{ Next_Hope, Destination_Node, Hop_count }

3.2   Route Maintenance Phase

Data packets are delivered through the primary route unless there is a route disconnection.

Link Failure Detection Mechanism: In Ad Hoc networks, the communication among nodes is done through wireless channel. The strength of the packet signal which the node receives can be calculated through the formula (1). Suppose each node has the same transmit power, and the loss of transmission energy entirely depends on the distance between the sending and receiving nodes. Through formula (1), we know that the changing strength of the received packet node signal reflects the fluctuation of the distance among nodes. Therefore, we establish a signal intensity threshold Pr_THRESHOLD, when the received signal intensity is lower than the established threshold, then it prompts the link to be at the unstable state and be likely to have link interrupt. In this situation, the receiving node sends a message to the sending node to restart local route repairs process.

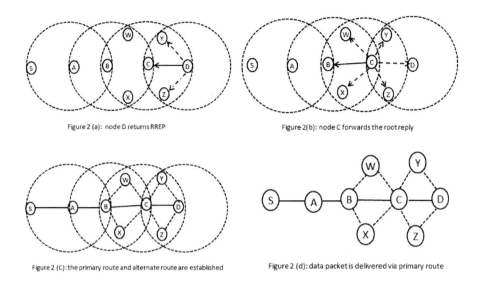

Figure 2 (a): node D returns RREP   Figure 2(b): node C forwards the root reply

Figure 2 (C): the primary route and alternate route are established   Figure 2 (d): data packet is delivered via primary route

Fig. 2. Route Discovery Phase [4]

Action Taken by Receiving Node (Upstream Node) Before Link Failure

In our proposed algorithm we predict the link which is going to break by signal strength detection technique. If the strength of link weakens gradually, the receiving node sends an interrupt to the transmitting node (predecessor node). After receiving this interrupt predecessor node broadcasts the control message to all nodes that are in the radio range of transmitting node. If any alternate node has an entry in its alternate routing table to destination via next hop entry, sends acknowledgment to the transmitting node. Transmitting node forwards a acknowledgment status(P_ACK or N_ACK) to the receiving node which has made interrupt to transmitting node. In case of link failure,the transmitting node will check the availability of alternate route, if available then data transmission will be done through that alternate route otherwise a RERR message is sent to the source node to inform that there is failure in the communication path.

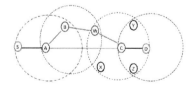

Fig. 3. Data Packet will be forwarded through alternate route in case of link failure(S-A-B-W-C-D)

Our proposed scheme has the considerable advantage over AODV-BR routing protocol approach, as we are only broadcasting the control message instead of broadcasting a data packet that reduces collision and congestion in the ad hoc network and the alternate route will be used for some time in data transmission.In the above fig[3] there is a link breakage (A-B-C) due to movement of node B. Now communication starts through an alternate route (A-B-W-C) because of availability of alternate route according to our scheme.

4   Proposed Algorithm

Proposed Protocol Pseudo Code for Route Maintenance

Algorithm 1. proposed protocol

1: Computation of received Signal Strength by each(mobile or stationary) node
2: **if** Computed Signal Strength lies in range of threshold value **then**
3:        "Receiving node will send a message to predecessor node"
4: **else**
5:        go to line number 25
6: **end if**
7: Predecessor node Broadcasts Control Message to it's neighbors
8: **if** Predecessor node receives reply message i.e. Acknowledgment from its neighbors **then**
9:        **if** reply message includes P-ACK **then**
10:               Alt-Route := P-ACK //P-ACK shows availability of alternate route
11:        **else**
12:               Alt-Route := N-ACK // N-ACK shows unavailability of alternate route
13:        **end if**
14: **else**
15:        Alt-Route := NULL
16: **end if**
17: Predecessor Node forwards Alt-Route status to receiving node
18: **if** Link failure occurs **then**
19:        **if** Alt-Route = = P-ACK **then**
20:               go to line number 7
21:        **end if**
22: **else**
23:        RERR message sent to source
24: **end if**
25: Continue data transmission with available path

Working of the proposed algorithm is explained in fig[4] Whenever receiving node detects weak signal strength then it will send a control message to transmitting node. That node will start local route discovery process by broadcasting the control message with one hop count. After then availability of alternate route is acknowledged by alternate nodes, lying in radio range of transmitting node. message contains information (Either P-ACK or N-ACK) and this route status is forwarded to the receiving node.

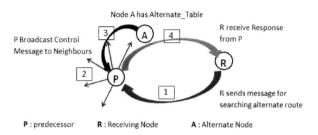

Fig. 4. Working of Proposed Algorithm

5   Performance Evaluation

We can see that our scheme improves throughput as AODV and AODV-BR. As the mobility increases(i.e.,pause time gets shorter),the performance gain by alternate routes will becomes more significant. AODV simply drops data packets when routes are disconnected. AODV-BR also has some packet losses. Alternate

Table 1. Simulation Parameter

Parameter	Value
number of node	20
Terrain size	1500 x 300 meter
Max speed	0,10,20 meter/sec
Pause Time	0 - 300 sec
Simulation Time	350 sec
Packet Type	CBR
Channel Capacity	2 MB/sec

paths may be broken as well as the primary route because of mobility, or be unavailable and not discovered during the route reply phase. Moreover, packets can be lost because of collisions and contention problems.For Performance evaluation of our proposed protocol with existing ones i.e, AODV and AODV-BR Protocols we used NS 2.35 under Fedora 14.The common Simulation Parameters are given in table 1 [3].

5.1   Effect of Traffic Load

The above mentioned factor (traffic load) affects the performance of our proposed scheme considerably, that can be summarized under following metrics:

Packet Delivery Ratio
Packet delivery ratio in our proposed scheme is more than AODV-BR because in AODV-BR packets may be dropped during the route rediscovery process when

data packets are forwarded using
alternate path and RERR message
is send to the source node.In our
scheme alternate path can be used
for some duration but in AODV-
BR this is used for sending the
packet that is dropped during the
link failure only. Therefore substantial link failure may increase
the throughput in our scheme.

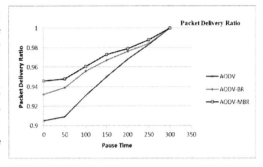

Fig. 5. Packet Delivery Ratio

Number of RERR Message

In our scheme, even the link failure can't cause RERR message due to availability of alternate route. Therefore there is decrement in RERR messages. On
the other hand, AODV as well as AODV-BR generate RERR message in case of
each link failure.

End-to-End Delay

In our scheme end-to-end delay will be slightly higher than AODV-BR, because it utilizes alternate route as a mean of data transmission for short period
of time while in contrast, AODV-BR uses it only once when there is a break

in primary route. Alternate routes
makes data transmission through
more number of links, that contributes to the increment of end
-to -end delay. Among these three
AODV has least end-to-end delay
because of transmission of packets
occur through primary route only.
Even in case of link failure, a new
primary route has to be set up for
data transmission.

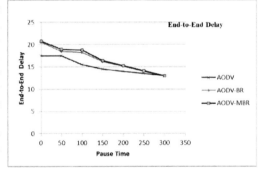

Fig. 6. End-to-End Delay

6 Conclusion

We have presented a scheme that utilizes a mesh structure and alternate paths.
Our scheme can be incorporated into any ad hoc on-demand unicast routing
protocol to improve reliable packet delivery in case of node movements and
route breaks. The mesh configuration provides multiple alternate routes and is
constructed without yielding any extra overhead. Alternate routes are utilized
only when data packets cannot be delivered through the primary route. As a
case study, we applied our algorithm to AODV-BR and obtained performance
improvements.our scheme does not perform well under heavy traffic networks
and frequently breaks in primary as well as alternate routes due to high mobility
of nodes. We are currently investigating ways to make our scheme consisting of
control message-performance trade off, robustness to traffic load.

References

1. Corson, M.S., Macker, J.P., Cirincione, G.H.: Internet-Based Mobile Ad Hoc Networking (Preprint), DTIC Document (1999)
2. Arain, W.M., Ghani, S.: An Instantiation of Way Point Routing for Mobile Ad-Hoc Networks. In: Proceedings of IEEE International Conference on Information and Communication Technologies, ICICT 2009, pp. 52–56 (2009)
3. Li, Q., Liu, C., Jiang, H.H.: The Routing Protocol of AODV Based on Link Failure Prediction. In: Proceedings of IEEE 9th International Conference on Signal Processing, ICSP, pp. 1993–1996 (2008)
4. Lee, S.J., Gerla, M.: AODV-BR: Backup Routing in Ad-Hoc Networks. In: Proceedings of IEEE Wireless Communications and Networking Conference, WCNC, vol. 3, pp. 1311–1316 (2000)
5. Huang, T.C., Huang, S.Y., Tang, L.: AODV-Based Backup Routing Scheme in Mobile Ad-Hoc Networks. In: Proceedings of IEEE International Conference on Communications and Mobile Computing (CMC), vol. 3, pp. 254–258 (2010)
6. Garcia-Luna-Aceves, J.J., Madruga, E.L.: The Core-Assisted Mesh Protocol. IEEE Journal on Selected Areas in Communications 17(8), 1380–1394 (1999)
7. Kuppusamy, P.: A Study and Comparison of OLSR, AODV and TORA Routing Protocols in Ad-Hoc Networks. In: Proceedings of IEEE 3rd International Conference on Electronics Computer Technology (ICECT), vol. 5, pp. 143–147 (2011)

EGC Diversity Incorporated BER Performance Analysis of M-DCSK Schemes in MIMO Nakagami Channels

Sangeetha Manoharan and Vidhyacharan Bhaskar

Department of Electronics and Communication Engineering,
SRM University, Tamilnadu, India
sangeetha.m@ktr.srmuniv.ac.in

Abstract. In this paper, we consider chaotic digital communications in Multiple-Input-Multiple-Output (MIMO) wireless multipath fading channels. In particular, we focus on a system that employs M-ary Differential Chaos Shift Keying (M-DCSK). We consider a transceiver scheme that requires no channel state information at either the transmitter or the receiver. It employs a distinct chaotic sequence at each transmit antenna to spread the same data symbols and transmit omnidirectionally. At each receive antenna, the corresponding differential detection statistics is formed and these statistics are then combined with equal gain combining for symbol detection. The Quality of Service (QoS) parameter is the Bit Error Rate (BER) which is calculated for various space diversity levels and average SNRs. Also the performance of the system is evaluated for various chaotic sequence lengths.

Keywords: Chaotic Communications, Equal Gain Combining, Multiple Input Multiple Output Systems, M-ary Differential Chaos Shift Keying.

1 Introduction

Since 1970s, there has been a great deal of research effort spent on studying chaotic systems and the properties of the chaotic signals generated. Chaos-based communications has attracted a lot of research interest ever since synchronization was demonstrated possible between two chaotic systems. Characterized by their wideband, impulse-like autocorrelation and low cross-correlation properties, chaotic signals were considered to be useful spread spectrum signals to carry digital information [1].

Chaotic signals are nonperiodic, random-like and bounded signals that are generated in a deterministic manner. Chaotic systems, *i.e*, systems that produce chaotic signals, form a special category in deterministic dynamical systems. In addition, the chaotic systems exhibit sensitive dependence on initial conditions, which means that the chaotic signals produced are very different even with very small difference in the initial conditions. Chaotic signals appear noise like hence they can be used to provide security at the physical level [2]. A number of chaotic modulations have been proposed [3]-[4], among which Differential Chaos Shift

K.R. Venugopal and L.M. Patnaik (Eds.): ICIP 2012, CCIS 292, pp. 74–83, 2012.
© Springer-Verlag Berlin Heidelberg 2012

Keying (DCSK) is the most suitable one in wireless communications due to its good noise performance over multipath fading channels with a simple receiver structure.

Multiple-Input-Multiple-Output (MIMO) techniques can effectively enhance the capacity of wireless communications and recent works address MIMO chaotic communications. In particular, chaotic shift keying, combined with Space-Time Coding (STC) was presented in [5], and a DCSK-STC scheme based on the Alamouti code was proposed in [6]. Both schemes require Channel State Information (CSI) to perform maximum-likelihood space-time decoding.

Channel estimation in a MIMO multipath environment is difficult, especially for chaotic communications, due to the difficulty in obtaining synchronization. In this brief, we propose MIMO chaotic communication schemes that do not require CSI and yet can effectively exploit the inherent spatial diversity of the system. In particular, we focus on a system that employs M-ary DCSK. We consider a transceiver scheme, which requires no CSI at either the transmitter or the receiver. It employs a distinct chaotic sequence at each transmit antenna to spread the same data symbols and transmit omnidirectionally. At each receive antenna, the corresponding differential detection statistics is formed, and these statistics are then combined with equal gain combining for symbol detection.

The remainder of this brief is organized as follows: Section 2 describes the system model. The proposed transceiver scheme for MIMO chaotic communication is presented in Section 3. Simulation results are shown in Section 4. Finally, Section 5 presents the conclusions.

2   System Description

2.1   M-DCSK Modulation

In M-DCSK modulation each transmitted symbol is divided into two identical time slots. The first one is used to transmit a chaotic reference signal, while the second time slot sends an information-bearing signal. During the second time slot, if a symbol "+1" is transmitted, the chaotic reference signal is repeated; if the symbol "−1" is to be transmitted, an inverted copy of the reference signal will be sent. Hence, the discrete time transmitted signal corresponding to one information symbol $b \in \{\pm 1\}$ is given by [7].

$$s(n) = \begin{cases} c(n), & 0 < n \leq L_c \\ bc(n - L_c), & L_c + 1 < n \leq 2L_c \end{cases}. \tag{1}$$

The reference signal is a segment $\mathbf{c} = [c(1),\ c(2),\ ...,\ c(L_c)]$ of L_c successive samples which forms a chaotic waveform in discrete time generated by a Chebyshev map of degree $\mu = 3$ which is defined as $\tau(c) = \cos\left(\mu \cos^{-1}(c)\right),\ -1 \leq x \leq 1$ from [8]. The distinct chaotic sequences are generated by $c_i(k + 1) = \tau\left(c_i(k)\right)$ with different initial values of $c_i(0)$ with a spreading factor $L_c = 64$. It can be observed that the signal never repeats itself, looks random-like and is bounded in the interval $[-1, 1]$. We normalize the length L_c chaotic vector $\mathbf{c}$ to have a unit norm for each symbol. The initial conditions for the generation of chaotic sequence should be between $+1$ and -1. The mean value of the chaotic sequence is necessarily zero; i.e., $E\left[c_k(i)\right] = 0$ in order to avoid transmission of any D.C. component which is a waste of power. The chaotic sequences are generated independently of one another. In other words, the covariance of two different chaotic sequence is zero, i.e., $cov\left[c_k(i)^2,\ x_m(i)^2\right] = 0\ \forall\ k \neq m$.

2.2   Multicode Transmission with EGC

We consider differential chaos-shift keying communication systems for MIMO systems with N_t transmit antennas and N_r receive antennas as shown in Fig. 1. A discrete-time approach will be adopted for the analysis.

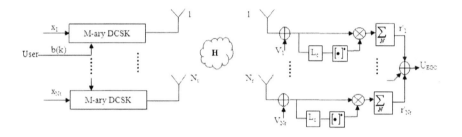

Fig. 1. MC-EGC Transceiver structure

Let $b(k)$ denote the kth binary symbol transmitted by the user, which is "$+1$" or "-1", each with a probability of $\frac{1}{2}$. Also, the symbols sent by each transmitting antenna are independent of one another. Essentially, there are N_t chaos generators corresponding to N_t different transmit antennas. The overall transmitted signal of the system is denoted by $\mathbf{X}$. As the signal goes through a wireless communication channel, multipath effects and noise are being added. Hence, the input-output relationship can be described as

$$\mathbf{Y} = \mathbf{HX} + \mathbf{N}. \tag{2}$$

Let $\mathbf{X} = \begin{bmatrix} x_1 & x_2 & ...x_{N_t}\end{bmatrix}^T$ be the $N_t \times 1$ vector of transmitted symbols, $\mathbf{Y}$ and $\mathbf{N}$ are the $N_r \times 1$ vector of received symbols and additive white Gaussian noise with zero mean and variance $\frac{N_o}{2}$, respectively. Let $\mathbf{H}$ be the $N_r \times N_t$ matrix of channel coefficients. A time-varying multipath Nakagami fading channel is considered. At each receive antenna, the corresponding differential detection statistics is formed, and these statistics are then combined with equal gain combining for symbol detection. The decision parameter is the combiner output U and the recovered symbol, denoted by $\hat{b}(k)$, is given by

$$\hat{b}(k) = sgn(U), \tag{3}$$

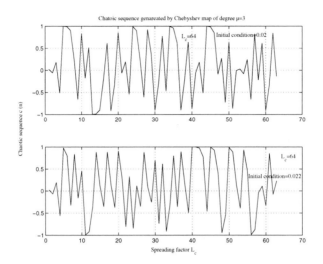

Fig. 2. Generation of Chaotic Sequence by Chebyshev map of degree $\mu = 3$

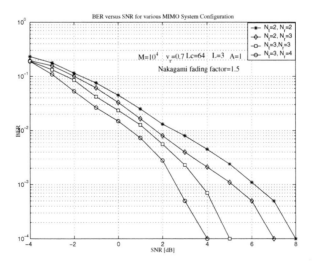

Fig. 3. BER vs. SNR (dB) for various MIMO configurations

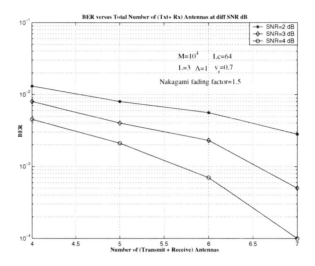

Fig. 4. BER vs. Number of (Transmit + Receive) Antennas

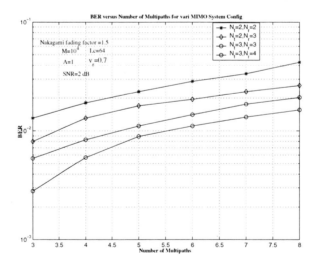

Fig. 5. BER vs. Number of Multipaths for various MIMO Configurations

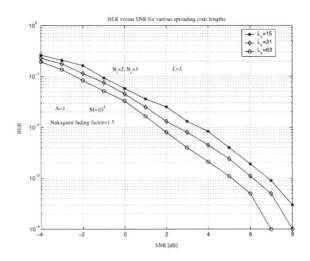

Fig. 6. BER vs. SNR (dB) for various spreading code lengths

where $sgn(.)$ is the signum function. The above decoding rule says that for each user, the recovered symbol is "+1" if $U > 0$, and is "−1" otherwise. We refer to this scheme as Multicode transmission with Equal Gain Combining (MC-EGC).

3 Data Formulation

Let the chaotic sequence used at the ith transmit antenna be
$\mathbf{c}_i = [c_i(1),\ c_i(2),\ ...,\ c_i(L_c)]$, which is generated by distinct chaotic maps or one map with different initial conditions given by (1). The discrete-time transmitted signal from the ith antenna corresponding to information symbols, $b(k)$, be a sequence of length $2L_c$. In the first time slot, a reference chaotic signal which serves as the signature waveform for the ith transmit antenna is sent. Let

$$\mathbf{X}_i(n) = \sqrt{\frac{\rho}{N_t}}\mathbf{c}_i(n);\ \ \forall\ 0 < n \le L_c,\ \ i = 1, 2, ..., N_t. \tag{4}$$

In the second time slot, the modulated chip sequence of the user is sent, which is given as

$$\mathbf{X}_i(n) = \sqrt{\frac{\rho}{N_t}}b(k)\mathbf{c}_i(n - L_c);\ \ \forall\ L_c + 1 < n \le 2L_c,\ \ k = 1, 2, ..., M, \tag{5}$$

where ρ denotes the total transmit Signal to Noise Ratio (SNR). We assume $L_c >> L$, and that the chaotic sequence has good autocorrelation, and cross correlation properties, i.e., each sequence is approximately orthogonal to its delayed version with some delay and two different sequences c_i and c_i' are approximately orthogonal with any relative delay.

3.1   MIMO Multipath Fading Channel

We consider a MIMO system with N_t transmit antennas and N_r receive antennas over time-varying multipath Nakagami fading channels. The channel between the ith transmit antenna and the jth receive antenna is modeled as [1]

$$h_{j,i}(t) = \sum_{l=0}^{L-1} h_{j,i}^{(l)}(t)\delta\left(t - lT_c\right), \tag{6}$$

where $\delta(.)$ is the Dirac delta function, T_c is the duration of chaotic chips, and L is the channel order. Note that the information symbol duration is $T_s = 2L_cT_c$. We assume that the channel coefficient $h_{j,i}^{(l)}(t)$ is constant over symbol duration T_s, but varies from symbol to symbol.

3.2   Detection Strategies

The received signal at the jth receive antenna is given by

$$r_j(n) = \sum_{l=1}^{N_t} \sum_{l=0}^{L-1} h_{j,i}^{(l)} x_i(n - l) + v_j(n), \ \forall \ 0 < n \le L_c, \tag{7}$$

$$r_j(n) = \sum_{l=1}^{N_t} \sum_{k=1}^{M} b(k) \sum_{l=0}^{L-1} h_{j,i}^{l)} x_i(n - l) + v_j(n) \tag{8}$$

$\forall \ L_c + 1 < n \le 2L_c$, where $v_j(n)$ is the additive white Gaussian noise. The corresponding correlator output is given by

$$r'_j = \sum_{n=L_c+1}^{2L_c} r_j(n)r_j(n - L_c)^*, i.e., \tag{9}$$

$$r'_j = \left(\frac{\rho}{N_t}\right) \sum_{n=L_c+1}^{2L_c} \sum_{i=1}^{N_t} \sum_{l=0}^{L-1} |h_{j,i}^{(l)}|^2 x_i(n - l)x_i\left(n - l - L_c\right)^* + noise$$

$$\forall \ 0 < n \le L_c, i.e., \tag{10}$$

$$r'_j = \left(\frac{\rho}{N_t}\right) \sum_{k=1}^{M} d(k) \sum_{n=L_c+1}^{2L_c} \sum_{i=1}^{N_t} \sum_{l=0}^{L-1} |h_{j,i}^{(l)}|^2 x_i(n - l)x_i(n - l - L_c)^* + noise$$

$$\forall \ L_c + 1 < n \le 2L_c, \tag{11}$$

where $*$ denotes the complex conjugate and the noise is considered to be complex gaussian noise with zero mean and variance σ^2. These correlator outputs are then combined with equal gain to yield the decision statistic for the data symbols, $b(k)$, i.e.,

$$U_{EGC} = \sum_{j=1}^{N_r} r'_j. \tag{12}$$

Note that the aforementioned MIMO transmission strategy does not require CSI at the transmitter or the receiver. Nevertheless, by employing orthogonal chaotic spreading sequences, it can be effectively exploited for full multipath diversity and spatial diversity inherent in MIMO multipath channels.

4   Simulation Results

Figure 2 plots chaotic signals, generated by a one dimensional chaotic map, against spreading factor L_c. The chaotic sequences are generated with initial conditions, $c_1(0) = 0.02$ and $c_2(0) = 0.022$ with a spreading factor, $L_c = 64$. It can be observed that the signal never repeats itself, looks random-like and is bounded in the interval $[-1, +1]$. The two chaotic signals have a difference of 0.002 in their initial conditions. Even though a small difference is introduced between the initial values, the two chaotic signals differ rapidly from each other within a short time period. The covariance between the two different chaotic sequences is found to be 0.004. It shows that the two sequences have good cross correlation properties.

Figure 3 shows the performance of MC-EGC scheme for various MIMO configurations. Here, the number of information symbols is $M = 10^4$, the chaotic sequences are independent and Nakagami distributed with parameter, $m = 1.5$. The multipath channel consists of $L = 3$ resolvable paths with delay of $0, T_c, 2T_c$. It is observed that BER decreases as SNR increases. Moreover, we observe that BER for a 3×4 MIMO configuration at $SNR = 5$dB is very negligible when compared to other MIMO configuration (2×2, 2×3, 3×3) where the BER is around 0.0024. This shows that the performance improves with spatial diversity provided by the MIMO system.

The system performance is analyzed with respect to the total number of transmit and receive antennas used in various MIMO system configurations at a particular SNR (dB). In this simulation, $M = 10^4$ information symbols are used to analyze system performance while SNR is set as 4 dB.

From Figure 4, we observe that the BER for a system with 7 total transmit and receive antenna is 10^{-4} , which is very low compared to MIMO systems with total transmit and receive antennas as four, where the BER is 45×10^{-4} with the same system specifications. Thus we observe that higher the numbers of antennas, better will be the spatial diversity.

Figure 5 shows the performance of the MIMO system with varying multipath lengths. As the number of multipath increases, the BER becomes worse. The BER improves for larger values of transmit and receive antennas. From Figure 6, we observe that the BERs improve (decrease) when the spreading factor increases. Furthermore, the BERs agree very well with the simulation results for large spreading factors (31 and 63). This is because the validity of the assumption of normal distribution of the correlator output holds better for higher spreading factors.

Table 1 shows a comparison of BER for different number of multipaths. The BER increases for 3×3 MIMO antenna configurations at $SNR = 2$ dB as the

Table 1. BER versus Number of multipaths (L) for System specifications: $M = 10^4$, $L_c = 63$, Nakagami factor, $m = 1.5$, SNR = 2 dB

Space diversity	QoS	$L = 3$	$L = 4$	$L = 5$	$L = 6$	$L = 7$	$L = 8$
$N_t = N_r = 3$	BER	0.0056	0.0083	0.0111	0.0141	0.0176	0.0203

Table 2. BER versus Spreading code lengths (L_c) for System and Channel specifications: $M = 10^4$, $L = 3$, Nakagami factor, $m = 1.5$, SNR = 5 dB

Space diversity	QoS	$L_c = 15$	$L_c = 31$	$L_c = 63$
$N_t = 2, N_r = 3$	BER	0.004	0.0024	0.0011

number of multipaths increases. There is a 2% increase in the BER between L = 8 and L = 3. Table 2 shows the comparison of BER for various spreading factor lengths. Higher the spreading factor, better is the BER of the system for 2×3 MIMO antenna configurations at SNR = 5 dB.

5   Conclusions

We have considered chaotic digital communication systems in MIMO multipath fading channels employing M-DCSK without the need of CSI at the transmitter or at the receiver. The MC-EGC scheme employs a distinct chaotic sequence at each transmit antenna for symbol spreading and transmit omnidirectionally; the receiver performs EGC on the decision statistics from the receive antennas. The following observations are realized from the simulation results:

- Chaotic sequence generated by Chebyshev map of degree $\mu = 3$ has good cross correlation properties,
- The BERs improve (decrease) with increase in spatial diversity provided by the MIMO system,
- As the number of multipath increases, the BER becomes worse,
- The BERs improve (decrease) when the spreading factor increases.

Furthermore, the performance can be improved by extending the proposed M-DCSK scheme for MIMO systems by incorporating hybrid combining techniques at the receiver side. Moreover, like other forms of spread-spectrum communication systems, chaos-based systems allow multiple access in order to make efficient use of the available bandwidth. Future scope of the paper is to implement the proposed scheme for multiuser MIMO with hybrid combining techniques.

References

1. Carroll, T.L., Pe Pecora, L.M.: Synchronizing Chaotic Circuits. IEEE Transactions on Circuits and Systems 38, 453–456 (1991)
2. Kolumban, G., Kennedy, M.P., Chua, L.O.: The Role of Synchronization in Digital Communications using Chaos - Part II: Chaotic Modulation and Chaotic Synchronization. IEEE Transactions on Circuits and Systems 45, 1129–1140 (1998)

3. Kolumban, G., Kennedy, M.P., Jako, Z., Kis, G.: Chaotic Communications with Correlator Receivers: Theory and Performance Limits. Proceedings of the IEEE 90, 711–731 (2002)
4. Wang, L., Zhang, X., Chen, G.R.: Performance of an SIMO FM-DCSK communication System. IEEE Transactions on Circuits and Systems II 55, 457–461 (2008)
5. Lau, Y.S., Lin, K.H., Hussain, Z.M.: Space-Time Encoded Secure Chaos Communications with Transmit Beamforming. In: Proceedings of the TENCON IEEE Region 10 Conference, Melbourne, Australia, pp. 1–5 (2005)
6. Thapaliya, K., Yang, Q., Kwak, K.S.: Chaotic Communications in MIMO Systems. In: Lee, Y.-H., Kim, H.-N., Kim, J., Park, Y.W., Yang, L.T., Kim, S.W. (eds.) ICESS 2007. LNCS, vol. 4523, pp. 708–717. Springer, Heidelberg (2007)
7. Wang, S., Wang, X.: M-DCSK-based Chaotic Communications in MIMO Multipath Channels with no Channel State Information. IEEE Transactions on Circuits and Systems II 57, 1001–1005 (2010)
8. Schimming, T., Schwarz, W.: Signal Modeling using Piece-Wise Linear Chaotic Generators. In: Proceedings of the European Signal Processing Conference, Las Vegas, USA, pp. 1377–1380 (1998)

Cognitive Network Layer
in MANETs Mobility Aware Routing Protocol

Zakeerhusen A.G., Kiran M., and G. Rama Mohana Reddy

Department of Information Technology,
National Institute of Technology Karnataka,
Mangalore, India
{zakeer56,kiranmanjappa,profgrmreddy}@gmail.com

Abstract. It is intended to add cognition to make cognitive network layer in order to design and develop Quality of Service (QoS) aware adaptive routing protocol in Mobile Adhoc Networks (MANETs). QoS-aware routing is challenging as nodes in the network are free to move, the topology will be changing dynamically. Performance of AODV will be less when nodes in the network are highly mobile. In this paper, Mobility Aware Routing Protocol (MARP) model is proposed to extract a core part in MANET that is stable in terms of mobility of the nodes. This core part is a subset of MANET mobile nodes through which transmission will be done. Here selection of paths through this extracted core can ensure more QoS in time. The MARP model not only provides a better way to discover a QoS but it considers an efficient route maintenance scheme by selecting the route which has more stability as source is having knowledge about other available paths. Since MARP is multipath routing protocol, route maintenance is easy and it robust. By simulation MARP show better performance over existing AODV-on demand routing protocol.

Keywords: AODV, Load, MANETs, Mobility, QoS.

1 Introduction

Mobile Adhoc Networks (MANETs) has been recognized as an area of research in its own rights, but their practical implementation in real world has been limited so far. Due to dynamic topology, and lack of central coordination in MANETs, the provision of Quality of Service (QoS) is much more challenging than in wired networks. The difficulties in the provision of such guarantees have limited the usefulness of MANETs. As a result research focus has been shifted from best effort services to the provision of higher and better defined QoS in MANETs. QoS Routing protocols play an important role in a QoS mechanism, since their task to find which nodes, if any, can serve an applications requirements. The link among nodes through which transmission will take place may live for longer period, as nodes in range move out. Control packet overhead is more here since it allows single path, once it breaks route discovery process will be started again. The QoS routing algorithm for wired networks cant be applied directly to adhoc networks.

K.R. Venugopal and L.M. Patnaik (Eds.): ICIP 2012, CCIS 292, pp. 84–92, 2012.
© Springer-Verlag Berlin Heidelberg 2012

The performance of most of the wireless routing algorithm relies on the availability of the precise state information [1]. However, the dynamic nature of adhoc network makes the available state information inherently imprecise. Second, nodes may join, leave and rejoin an adhoc network at any time, any location. Existing links may disappear and, new links may be found as the nodes move. With the increase in demand for QoS in evolving applications, it is necessary to support this QoS in MANETs. The characteristics of these networks make QoS support a very complex process.

Due to the fact that Mobile Nodes (MNs) change their physical location by moving around, the network topology may unpredictably change [2]. This causes changes in link status between each MN and its neighbors. Thus, MNs which join and/or leave the communication range of a given MN in the network will certainly change its relationship with its neighbors by detecting new link breakages and/or link additions. This can produce a large number of updates in the routing table of each MN in MANET. Furthermore, this topology change makes an overhead traffic in the process of path maintenance assured by the implemented routing protocol in MANET. Hence, the performance of a MANET is closely related to the capability of the routing protocol to adapt itself to topology changes. It is more judicious that the QoS-aware routing takes in to consideration the mobility of MNs in the network. Our approach to evaluate and quantify this mobility of MNs is based on the link changes of each MN with its neighboring MNs. Consequently, MNs with low mobility composing path of required QoS are more reliable amongst each other. Otherwise, the QoS provided by QoS-aware routing can be assured and guaranteed in time.

1.1   Issues for QoS-Aware Routing in MANETs

Providing QoS-aware routing in MANETs is really challenging task and it is an active research area. MANETs have certain unique characteristics that pose several issues and difficulties in provisioning QoS-aware routing. These issues include features of the MANET environment like predictable link properties, node mobility and route maintenance. These issues are summarized as follows [2].

a. Link properties: Wireless media is very unpredictable. Packet collision is intrinsic to wireless network. Signal propagation faces difficulties such as signal fading, interference, and multi-path cancellation. All these properties make measures such as bandwidth and delay of a wireless link unpredictable.

b. Mobility: Mobility of the MNs creates a dynamic network topology. Links will be dynamically formed when two MNs come into the transmission range of each other and are torn down when they move out of range.

c. Route maintenance: The dynamic nature of the network topology and the changing behavior of the communication medium make precise maintenance of network state information very difficult. Thus, the QoS-aware routing in MANETs have to operate with inherently imprecise information. Furthermore, in MANET environments, MNs can join or leave at any time. The established routing paths may be broken even during the process of data transfer. Thus, the need arises for maintenance and reconstruction of routing paths with minimal overhead and delay.

In AODV [3] QoS support in MANETs includes issues at the application layer, transport layer, network layer, medium access control (MAC) layer, and physical layer of the network infrastructure. In particular, the primary goal of the QoS-aware routing protocols is to determine a path from a source to the destination that satisfies the needs of the desired QoS. The QoS-aware path is determined within the constraints of bandwidth, minimal search, distance, and traffic conditions. Since path selection is based on the desired QoS, the routing protocol can be termed QoS-aware. Here the QoS is provided in terms of mobility hence the protocol is mobility aware.

In this work, MARP model is proposed to extract a stable core in MANET in terms of mobility with the goal to serve QoS-aware routing. Such an extraction can define a subset of MNs in the network where this mobility is low the links between them are reliable in time. In this model, source broadcast the RREQ message to destination through among available paths. Unlike in AODV the destination is allowed to accept multiple requests and replies back. Furthermore, source will be having the information about the mobility of each path. Over the time, MNs are move out of the range or new MNs are come into range. When the link failure is occurred, then source immediately switch the transmission to other path as it has knowledge of other paths instead of starting with route discovery mechanism again. Therefore, the selected path through this core is more stable in terms of mobility and consequently the required QoS are more guaranteed.

2 Related Work

Due to the dynamic nature of network topology in MANETs many research work has been done in routing protocols by modifying route discovery mechanism in order to improve the performance. These improvements are made on the basis of different MANET parameters like mobility, node status, link status, congestion, packet overhead, power consumption, and others.

In [4], Yaser Taj and Karim Faez have proposed a SSBR model which describes novel routing metric for MANETs, by measuring signal strength changes of neighbour nodes, nodes that have a lot of mobility are identified which can cause link failure. Thus, these nodes will not be the part of route to be selected. Selection of the reliable nodes can create a stable route that it has long lifetime. Emphasizing on the contention delay, in [5] S.T. Sheu and J. Chen proposed a Novel Delay-Oriented Shortest Path Routing Protocol that analyzed the medium access delay of a mobile node in IEEE 802.11 wireless network. In consideration of the real time traffic in [6], S. Jain, et al. proposed a protocol which includes load field value in the RREQ message during route discovery process that helps in the selection of route with low congestion and end to end delay for real time traffic will be less. In [7], L. Ting, et al. proposed status adoptive routing protocol includes the shortest route selection criteria of AODV routing protocol with real network status including the remaining power capacity, link quality and traffic load. The status of traffic load is defined as a ratio of maximum length of queue and number of packets that are buffered. In [8], S. Baboo and B. Narasimhan proposed a congestion aware routing protocol for heterogeneous MANET which employ combined weight value as routing metric based on link status, data rate, queuing delay and MAC overhead. In [9], H. Jutao, et al. used the traffic load calculation with load status, node processing power and link state between nodes a forward mechanism is developed for broadcast of message. This methodology is not suitable for large-scale transmissions but results in higher packet delivery ratio and decreases routing overhead. Y. Khamayseh, et al. proposed protocol in [10], which extends the ideas of both AODV and VON schemes. The proposed model depends on the traffic load of the nodes and the velocity to decide which nodes will rebroadcast in order to build a stable route. The nodes with the high velocity do not participate in the route discovery phase, since they result into unstable routes. In [11], Y. Kim and S. Cho proposed a model that rediscovers route after a fixed interval of time by considering the node mobility and route is resettled after rediscovery phase. If a node in the selected route is part of multi-path route then load on that node increases and degrades the performance. In [12], D. A. Tran and H. Raghavendra proposed a protocol which is congestion adaptive routing protocol (CBR) for MANET. In this scheme, a by-pass is implemented as a sub route that connecting the node with next non congested node. If congestion is expected on the next node then by-pass path is adopted. This model tried to prevent congestion in first attempt, but it will not deal reactively over the time. Because traffic is divided over two different paths, load balancing is there for some extent which improves performance.

The study of literature gives a clear view of different routing protocols that have been proposed for MANET to achieve optimal performance in the given network scenarios. And it is quite clear that because of the varying nature of MANET, not any single routing protocol work well with all network scenarios. It motivated our work on routing protocol by considering the QoS constraint. This not only gives the optimum performance but also suitable for longer period transmission as the links between the MNs are reliable over the time.

3 Proposed MARP Model

Here we consider mobility scheme, in which each MN in a MANET can be found in three states with its neighbors:

a. MN moves and its neighbors are static
b. MN is static and its neighbors move
c. Both node and its neighbors move

As a result, these three possible states lead to change of the links status of the MN with its neighbors, hence as the nodes move in the wireless network, the link status changes over the time.

3.1   Packet Design

There are three types of packets used by MARP. These are data, route request (RREQ), and route reply (RREP). Here RREQ and RREP are control messages. Each packet type contains at least six fields, including source address, destination address, previous hop address, next hop address, message identification, and Time-To-Live (TTL). Data packets may contain additional fields such as data length and bulk data. In this MARP model, structure of both RREQ message and RREP message is modified by adding one more field named mobility field to handle the mobility. This model proposes a modification in the basic AODV route discovery mechanism.

a. RREQ packets: RREQ packets are broadcasted when a source needs to find a path to an unknown destination. If a RREQ cannot be forwarded, it is dropped. Any number of RREQ packets may be sent for each route request. When a neighbor receives RREQ message it will calculate the mobility in terms of the change in distance over time from its previous hop and adds the value in the mobility field of the RREQ message. This process is done at each node in the route to the destination.

b. RREP packets: Unlike in AODV, destination is allowed to accept as many as RREQ messages which are broadcasted by source in MARP. The RREP message is created such that the source of the packet appears to be the requested destination and the destination of the packet is the requestor. The mobility field in RREP has total mobility value of all MNs occurred in that route. This value is sent back to source in RREP message. At the source the average mobility is calculated. The source decides on the basis of average value that to which route it has to send the data packets.

3.2   Cross Layer Framework

Since our objective is to get the distance value in Network Layer (NL) Cross layer framework is designed so that distance information is accepted from Physical Layer (PL). Here some parameters of PL should be made visible to upper NL. It is hard to achieve this goal in the legacy protocol stack since it will not allow non adjacent layers to communication with each other. With this requirement, a

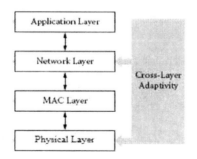

Fig. 1. Cross Layer Model

cross layer framework is designed for MARP across the protocol stack as shown in the Fig. 1. Through the shared registry, PL shares distance information to upper layers for further processing.

3.3   The Mobility Quantification

Cross layer architecture has been used where the distance factor from Physical Layer (PL) is used in Network Layer (NL) [13]. Distance will be calculated by using Eq. 1. The distance d is maintained in a neighbor table at every node and it is done only for the neighbor node which participates in the active route and not for all the neighbors.

$$d = \sqrt[4]{\frac{P_t G_t G_r \lambda^2}{(4\pi)^2 P_r L}} \tag{1}$$

Where,
P_t: is the default transmission power,
P_r: the received signal strength,
G_t and G_r: are the antenna gains of the transmitter and receiver,
λ: is the wavelength, and
L: is the system loss experienced.

Once distance between the nodes is calculated, it is then possible to determine whether the nodes are moving apart or moving closer by calculating the difference between the distances. This information along with the time at which d is calculated are kept in the neighbor table for further processing. Based on this distance information, using Eq. 2, mobility will be calculated for each node.

After each packet is transmitted, we represent this relative mobility quantification by the change of the neighbors of each node. The node mobility measure at a given time t for node i in the wireless network is defined as the change in its neighbors compared to the previous (state) for example at time t2-t1. Eq. 2 is used for the computation of mobility of each node with respect to its neighbor. Thus, nodes that join and/or leave the neighbors of node i will surely have an impact on the evaluation of its mobility measure.

We define two mobility measures representing node mobility and mobility of the path. These mobility measures are mainly used for extracting the core part where the MNs are more stable and dont depend upon simulation characteristics such as mobility parameters or movement patterns.

$$Mobility of the Node(X) = \frac{|d_n - d_{n-1}|}{t_n - t_{n-1}} \tag{2}$$

Where d_n and d_{n-1} are distances at time t_n and t_{n-1}.

$$Mobility of the Path = \frac{1}{n} \sum_{i=0}^{n-1} X(i) \tag{3}$$

Mobility of the path can be calculated by using Eq. 3 which is nothing but the average mobility of the nodes of that path, where n total number of the nodes present in that path and i ranges from 0 to n-1 nodes. At source node average mobility is computed in order to select the path for data transmission. This route will be more stable which can define a subset of MNs in the network where the mobility is low and the links between them are reliable in time.

4   Implementation and Results

The proposed model MARP was simulated in the network simulator ns2.34, with the simulation parameters as mentioned in the Table 1. We analyzed the results against throughput and end to end delay to compare the performance. For different simulation time, throughput and end to end delay is calculated for both basic AODV and MARP model and compared as shown in Fig.2 and Fig.3 respectively. Since MARP uses multi path routing, route maintenance is easy which yields high throughput, reducing control traffic in the network.

Table 1. Simulation Parameters

Channel type	WirelessChannel
Propagation model	TwoRayGround
Mac protocol type	Mac/802.11
Queue type	DropTail
Max Packet in queue	50
Number of mobile nodes	25
Routing protocol	AODV
Link layer type	LL
Data rate	2 Mbps
Simulation time	600 seconds

Here we run the network scenario in two cases, one is using traditional basic AODV protocol and other one is MARP, where latter case considers the mobility factor of the nodes in the network. And following results will show the performance of routing protocols. We compared our enhanced MARP model with basic AODV and evaluate the performance according to following metric.

a. Average throughput: It is the total number of packets received successfully in the given time.
b. End-to-end delay: Refers to the time taken for a packet to be transmitted across a network from source to destination.

In this way a node which normally must be selected as in case of basic AODV is avoided so stable path will be selected and transmission will be for longer period. The above performance metrics are plotted on the graphs for both traditional AODV and MARP. In Fig. 2, throughput is shown for our proposed MARP

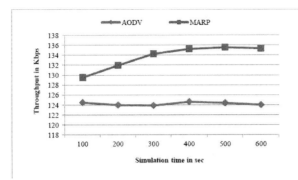

Fig. 2. Throughput versus Simulation Time

model. It shows performance of this model is constantly up as compared to basic AODV, why because the source will be having knowledge about alternative paths, if link has been broken then it immediately switches transmission to the other path. Hence the number of packets transmitted is more. Route maintenance is quick enough so the end to end delay is less as shown in Fig. 3. Hence in this model time taken for packets transmission is less to that of basic AODV.

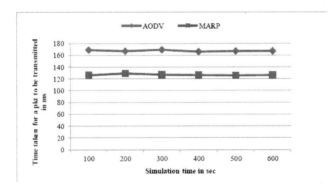

Fig. 3. End to End Delay versus Simulation time

5   Conclusions

In this work, MARP model has been proposed, for finding the stable routes in terms of mobility in MANETs. MARP finds a route from a source to destination with end to end QoS constraints like less mobility of MNs. The selected path through which data packets are transmitted is having the links between MNs which are reliable in time. Since MARP uses multipath routing, route maintenance is easy which yields high throughput, reducing control traffic in the network hence it is robust. Future work concentrates on extending MARP to consider other parameters like traffic load and bandwidth.

References

1. Jacquet, P., Muhlethaler, P., Clausen, T., Laouiti, A., Qayyum, A., Viennot, L.: OLSR: Optimized Link State Routing Protocol. In: IEEE INMIC 2001, pp. 62–68 (December 2001)
2. Enneya, N., Elmeziane, R., Elkoutbi, M.: A Game Theory Approach for Enhancing QoS Aware Routing in Mobile Ad-hoc Networks. In: First International Conference on Networked Digital Technologies, NDT (2009)
3. Perkins, C.E.: Ad hoc On Demand Distance Vector (AODV) Routing, Internet Draft, Draft-ietfmanet-aodv-01.txt (1998)
4. Taj, Y., Faez, K.: Signal Strength Based Reliability: A Novel Routing Metric in MANETs. In: Second International Conference on Networks Security, Wireless Communications and Trusted Computing (2010)
5. Sheu, S.T., Chen, J.: A Novel Delay-Oriented Shortest Path Routing Protocol for Mobile Ad Hoc Networks. In: Proceedings IEEE ICC 2001, Helsinki, Finland (June 2001)
6. Jain, S., Pitti, V., Verma, B.: Real Time On-demand Distance Vector in Mobile Ad hoc Networks. Asian Journal of Information Technology 5(4), 454–459 (2005)
7. Ting, L., Rui-bu, T., Hong, J.: Status Adaptive Routing with Delayed Rebroadcast Scheme in AODV-based MANETs Science Direct (September 2008)
8. Baboo, S., Narasimhan, B.: A Hop-by-Hop Congestion-Aware Routing Protocol for Heterogeneous Mobile Ad-hoc Networks. International Journal of Computer Science and Information Security 3(1) (2009)
9. Jutao, H., Jingjing, Z., Minglu, L.: Energy Level and Link State Aware AODV Route Request Forwarding Mechanism Research. WSEAS Transactions on Communications 8(2) (February 2009)
10. Khamayseh, Y., Obeidat, G., Alhassan, A.: Enhanced VON-AODV Based on Delayed Rebroadcast Scheme. ACM (October 26, 2009)
11. Kim, Y., Moon, I.I., Cho, S.: Enhanced AODV Routing Protocol through Fixed Expire-time in MANET. In: International Conference on Network Application, Protocol and Services 2008, pp. 21–22 (November 2008)
12. Tran, D.A., Raghvendra, H.: Congestion Adaptive Routing in Mobile Ad Hoc Networks. IEEE Transactions on Parallel and Distributed Systems 17(11) (November 2006)
13. Soo, W.K., Phang, K.K., Ling, T.C., Ang, T.F.: Intelligent IEEE 802.11B Wireless Networks Mac Layer Diagnostic Controller in Mobile Ad Hoc Network. Malaysian Journal of Computer Science 20(2) (2007)

Spectrum Efficiency of Lognormal Fading Channels under Different Adaptation Policies with MRC Diversity

Vivek G. Rajendran and Vidhyacharan Bhaskar

Department of Electronics and Communication Engineering,
SRM University, Kattankulathur - 603203, Kancheepuram Dt., Tamilnadu, India
vivek89@yahoo.co.in

Abstract. We consider a Single Input Multiple Output (SIMO) system in the presence of Lognormal Multipath Fading (LMF) channel. We study Shannon capacity of different adaptive transmission policies in conjunction with diversity combining techniques and provide an upper bound on spectral efficiency using these techniques. We obtain closed-form expressions for spectrum efficiency in a Lognormal fading channel under these adaptation policies: (i) Optimal Power and Rate Adaptation (OPRA), and (ii) Truncated channel Inversion with Fixed Rate (TIFR). Numerical results show that there is an increase in spectrum efficiency when these adaptation policies are used in conjunction with diversity combining techniques.

Keywords: Spectrum Efficiency, Lognormal Fading, Optimal Power and Rate Adaptation (OPRA), Truncated Channel Inversion with Fixed Rate (TIFR), Maximal Ratio Combining (MRC) Diversity.

1 Introduction

Radio spectrum available for wireless communications is extremely scarce, while the need for these services is increasing rapidly. Hence, spectrum efficiency has to be studied for the design of future wireless communication systems. Due to multipath propagation of the transmitted signal, fading occurs. For indoor channels, the fading model follows a Lognormal distribution. Multipath effects can be mitigated by employing receive antenna diversity.

Over the last few decades, researchers have looked at efficient ways of including multilevel modulation schemes, diversity combining techniques, adaptive transmission techniques to improve spectrum efficiency. These adaptive transmission techniques along with diversity combining techniques provide a much higher average spectral efficiency without sacrificing Bit Error Rate (BER).

Numerous researchers have worked in the area of channel capacity measurements over fading channels. Goldsmith and Varaiya derived for Shannon capacity adaptive transmission techniques in a fading channel with side information at the transmitter and the receiver, and at the receiver alone in [1]. In [2], Shannon capacity of adaptive transmission techniques with diversity combining is studied.

K.R. Venugopal and L.M. Patnaik (Eds.): ICIP 2012, CCIS 292, pp. 93–99, 2012.
© Springer-Verlag Berlin Heidelberg 2012

In [3] and [4], closed-form expressions for capacities per unit bandwidth are derived for various adaptation policies for Generalized Rayleigh and Generalized Rician fading channels, respectively. Laourine, et al. investigated the capacity of Lognormal fading channels with receiver channel state information in [5].

This paper is organized as follows: In Section 2, we outline the channel and communication system model. We derive capacity of a Lognormal fading channel (with and without diversity) for OPRA and TIFR policies in Sections 3 and 4, respectively. In Section 5, we present numerical results of spectrum efficiency in bps/Hz plotted against SNR in dB. We review our results in Section 6.

2   System Model and Description

A block diagram of the transmission system is shown in Figure 1. We assume a slowly varying channel. We consider a Lognormal fading channel, whose Probability Density Function (PDF) of the instantaneous SNR (γ) is given by [6]

$$p_\gamma(\gamma) = \frac{\exp\left(-l\left(k\ln\gamma - 1\right)^2\right)}{\gamma\sigma\sqrt{2\pi}} \ \forall \ \gamma > 0. \tag{1}$$

Here, let $k = \frac{1}{\mu}$ and $l^2 = \frac{\mu^2}{2\sigma^2}$ for convenience. Let μ and σ^2 be the mean and variance of a Gaussian random variable making up the Lognormal distribution.

MRC combining is the optimal diversity scheme, and it provides maximum capacity improvement relative to the other diversity combining techniques [7]. Let the instantaneous received SNR at the output of an M-branch MRC combiner [5] be $\gamma_{mrc} = \sum_{m=1}^{M} \gamma_m$. The PDF of received instantaneous SNR at the output of a perfect M-branch MRC can be expressed as

$$p_\gamma(\gamma) = \frac{\exp\left(-l_{mrc}\left(k_{mrc}\ln\gamma - 1\right)\right)^2}{\gamma\sigma_{mrc}\sqrt{2\pi}} \ \forall \ \gamma > 0. \tag{2}$$

Let $k_{mrc} = \frac{1}{\mu_{mrc}}$, $l_{mrc} = \frac{\mu_{mrc}^2}{2\sigma_{mrc}^2}$, where $\sigma_{mrc}^2 = \ln\left(\frac{(M-1)\exp\left(\rho\sigma^2\right)+\exp\left(\sigma^2\right)}{M}\right)$, and $\mu_{mrc} = \ln M\Gamma - \frac{\sigma_{mrc}^2}{2}$ be the variance and mean of the MRC random variable, γ_{mrc} [5]. We assume that the variation in the combiner output SNR, γ, is tracked perfectly by the receiver. We also assume that the variation in instantaneous SNR, γ, is sent back to the transmitter through the noise-free feedback path. The time delay in this feedback path is assumed to be negligible when compared to the rate of the channel variation.

3   OPRA Policy

Given an average transmit power constraint, the spectrum efficiency of a fading channel with received instantaneous SNR distribution, $p_\gamma(\gamma)$, and OPRA is given as [1]

$$\frac{\langle C \rangle_{opra}}{B} = \int\limits_{\gamma_0}^{\infty} \log_2 \left(\frac{\gamma}{\gamma_0} \right) p_\gamma(\gamma) d\gamma, \tag{3}$$

where B is the channel bandwidth in Hz, and γ_0 is the optimal cutoff SNR below which data transmission is suspended. The optimal cutoff SNR in (3) must satisfy the equation [1]

$$\int\limits_{\gamma_0}^{\infty} \left(\frac{1}{\gamma_0} - \frac{1}{\gamma} \right) p_\gamma(\gamma) d\gamma = 1. \tag{4}$$

To achieve capacity in (3), the channel fade level must be known both at the transmitter and receiver, and the transmitter has to adapt its power and rate accordingly, allocating high power levels and rates for good channel conditions (γ large), and lower power levels and rates for unfavorable channel conditions (γ small). Since no data is sent during $\gamma < \gamma_0$, this policy suffers a probability of outage, P_{out} is equal to the probability of no transmission [1],

$$P_{out} = P(\gamma \leq \gamma_0) = 1 - \int\limits_{\gamma_0}^{\infty} p_\gamma(\gamma) d\gamma. \tag{5}$$

3.1   No Diversity Case

Substituting (1) into (4) and simplifying, we find that γ_0 must satisfy

$$\frac{1}{\sigma\sqrt{2\pi}} \left(\frac{1}{\gamma_0} \int\limits_{\gamma_0}^{\infty} \frac{\exp\left(-l\left(k\ln\gamma - 1\right)^2\right)}{\gamma} d\gamma - \int\limits_{\gamma_0}^{\infty} \frac{\exp\left(-l\left(k\ln\gamma - 1\right)^2\right)}{\gamma^2} d\gamma \right) = 1.$$

Simplifying, we have

$$\frac{1}{2k\sigma\gamma_0\sqrt{2l\pi}} \Gamma_c \left(\frac{1}{2}, l\left(k\ln\gamma_0 - 1\right)^2 \right)$$
$$- \frac{\exp\left(-\frac{1}{k} + \frac{1}{4k^2l}\right)}{2k\sigma\sqrt{2l}} \left(1 - \Phi\left(\sqrt{l}\left(k\ln\gamma_0 - 1\right) + \frac{1}{2k\sqrt{l}} \right) \right) = 1, \tag{6}$$

where $\Gamma_c(\alpha, x) = \int\limits_{x}^{\infty} t^{\alpha-1} e^{-t} dt, \quad \alpha > 0$ is the Complementary Incomplete Gamma

Function (CIGF) defined in Equation (5) of [2] and $\Phi(x) = \frac{2}{\sqrt{\pi}} \int\limits_{0}^{x} e^{-t^2} dt$ is the error function (erf) (from [8], section 7.1.1, page no. 86). The optimal cutoff SNR, γ_0, can be computed by substituting $x = \gamma_0$ in (6),

$$g(x) = \frac{1}{2kx\sigma\sqrt{2\pi l}} \Gamma_c \left(\frac{1}{2}, l\left(k\ln x - 1\right)^2 \right)$$
$$- \frac{\exp\left(-\frac{1}{k} + \frac{1}{4k^2l}\right)}{2k\sigma\sqrt{2l}} \left(1 - \Phi\left(\sqrt{l}\left(k\ln x - 1\right) + \frac{1}{2k\sqrt{l}} \right) \right) - 1. \tag{7}$$

Then,

$$\frac{\partial g(x)}{\partial x} = -\frac{1}{2kx^2\sigma\sqrt{2\pi l}}\Gamma_c\left(\frac{1}{2}, l\left(k\ln x - 1\right)^2\right). \tag{8}$$

Note that $\frac{\partial g(x)}{\partial x} < 0 \quad \forall\ x > 0$. Moreover, from (7), $\lim_{x\to 0^+} g(x) \to \infty$ and $\lim_{x\to\infty} g(x) < 0$. Thus, it can be concluded that there is a unique positive x_0 for which $g(x_0) = 0$, or equivalently, there is a unique γ_0 which satisfies (6). Substituting (1) into (3), the spectrum efficiency of a Lognormal fading channel with no diversity for OPRA policy is given as

$$\frac{\langle C\rangle_{opra}^{(ND)}}{B} = \frac{\log_2 e}{2k^2 l\sigma\sqrt{2\pi}}\left(\sqrt{l}\left(1 - k\ln\gamma_0\right)\Gamma_c\left(\frac{1}{2}, l\left(k\ln\gamma_0 - 1\right)^2\right)\right.$$
$$\left. + \exp\left(-l\left(k\ln\gamma_0 - 1\right)^2\right)\right). \tag{9}$$

Substituting (1) into (5), the probability of outage is given as

$$P_{out}^{(ND)} = 1 - \frac{1}{2k\sigma\sqrt{2l}}\left(1 - \Phi\left(\sqrt{l}\left(k\ln\gamma_0 - 1\right)\right)\right). \tag{10}$$

3.2   MRC Diversity Case

Given the average received SNR, the spectrum efficiency at the output of a M-branch MRC is obtained by substituting (2) into (3), and is given as

$$\frac{\langle C\rangle_{opra}^{(MRC)}}{B} = a\left(\sqrt{l_{mrc}}\left(1 - k_{mrc}\ln\gamma_0\right)\Gamma_c\left(\frac{1}{2}, l_{mrc}\left(k_{mrc}\ln\gamma_0 - 1\right)^2\right)\right)$$
$$+ a\exp\left(-l_{mrc}\left(k_{mrc}\ln\gamma_0 - 1\right)^2\right), \tag{11}$$

where $a = \frac{\log_2 e}{2k_{mrc}^2 l_{mrc}\sigma_{mrc}\sqrt{2\pi}}$. The corresponding outage probability, $P_{out}^{(MRC)}$, is obtained by substituting (2) into (5), and can be expressed as

$$P_{out}^{(MRC)} = 1 - \frac{1}{2k_{mrc}\sigma\sqrt{2l_{mrc}}}\left(1 - \Phi\left(\sqrt{l_{mrc}}\left(k_{mrc}\ln\gamma_0 - 1\right)\right)\right). \tag{12}$$

4   TIFR Policy

TIFR policy is the another approach which uses a modified inversion policy which inverts channel fading only above a fixed cutoff fade depth γ_0. The spectrum efficiency with truncated channel inversion and fixed rate policy, is given as

$$\frac{\langle C\rangle_{tifr}}{B} = \log_2\left(1 + \frac{1}{\int_{\gamma_0}^{\infty}\frac{p_\gamma(\gamma)}{\gamma}d\gamma}\right)\left(1 - P_{out}\right). \tag{13}$$

4.1   No Diversity Case

Substituting (1) into (13) and simplifying, the spectrum efficiency of a Lognormal fading channel with no diversity for TIFR policy is given as

$$\frac{\langle C \rangle_{tifr}^{(ND)}}{B} = \log_2 \left(1 - \frac{2k\sigma\sqrt{2l}\left(\exp\left(\frac{1}{k} - \frac{1}{4k^2l}\right)\right)}{\left(1 - \Phi\left(\sqrt{l}\left(k\ln\gamma_0 - 1\right) + \frac{1}{2k\sqrt{l}}\right)\right)} \right) \left(1 - P_{out}^{(ND)}\right). \quad (14)$$

Substituting (10) into (14), we have

$$\frac{\langle C \rangle_{tifr}^{(ND)}}{B} = \log_2 \left(1 - \frac{2k\sigma\sqrt{2l}\exp\left(\frac{1}{k} - \frac{1}{4k^2l}\right)}{1 - \Phi\left(\sqrt{l}\left(k\ln\gamma_0 - 1\right) + \frac{1}{2k\sqrt{l}}\right)} \right) \left(\frac{1 - \Phi\left(\sqrt{l}\left(k\ln\gamma_0 - 1\right)\right)}{2k\sigma\sqrt{2l}}\right)$$

$$(15)$$

This is the closed-form expression for spectrum efficiency for LMF channel for TIFR policy without diversity combining schemes.

4.2   MRC Diversity Case

Substituting (2) into (13) and simplifying, the spectrum efficiency of a Lognormal fading channel with MRC diversity for TIFR policy is given as

$$\frac{\langle C \rangle_{tifr}^{(MRC)}}{B} = q\log_2 \left(1 - \frac{2k_{mrc}\sigma_{mrc}\sqrt{2l_{mrc}}\exp\left(\frac{1}{k_{mrc}} - \frac{1}{4k_{mrc}^2 l_{mrc}}\right)}{1 - \Phi\left(\sqrt{l_{mrc}}\left(k_{mrc}\ln\gamma_0 - 1\right) + \frac{1}{2k_{mrc}\sqrt{l_{mrc}}}\right)} \right), \quad (16)$$

where $q = 1 - P_{out}^{(MRC)}$. Substituting (12) into (16), and simplifying, we have

$$\frac{\langle C \rangle_{tifr}^{(MRC)}}{B} = \log_2 \left(1 - \frac{2\exp\left(\mu_{mrc} - \frac{\sigma_{mrc}^2}{2}\right)}{1 - \Phi\left(z + \frac{\sigma_{mrc}}{\sqrt{2}}\right)} \right) \left(\frac{1 - \Phi(z)}{2}\right), \quad (17)$$

where $z = \sqrt{l_{mrc}}\left(k_{mrc}\ln\gamma_0 - 1\right)$. This is the closed-form expression for spectrum efficiency for LMF channels under MRC diversity case for TIFR policy.

5   Numerical Results

Figure 2a shows the spectrum efficiency of Lognormal fading channel without diversity combining techniques for various instantaneous SNR values. At 10 dB, the spectrum efficiencies of TIFR policy is higher than that of OPRA policy. But, at the higher SNR OPRA provides higher spectrum efficiency than TIFR policy. This shows that OPRA holds good at higher SNR values and TIFR holds good at lower SNR values with no diversity case. Figure 2b shows the probability of outage for a Lognormal fading channel under OPRA policy for various instantaneous SNR values. The variation in the probability of outage between the receivers with MRC diversity and without diversity combining is shown in Figure 2b. Here M = 6 represents the number of branches that have been combined by the MRC i.e. diversity order. Figure 2c shows the spectrum efficiency of Lognormal fading channel under MRC diversity case for various instantaneous SNR values. The difference in spectral efficiencies increases as the instantaneous SNR increases. At 10 dB, the difference between the spectrum efficiencies of OPRA and TIFR policy is 1.05 bps/Hz approximately. In MRC diversity case, the diversity order (M) and correlation factor (ρ) are considered.

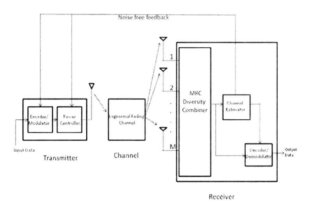

Fig. 1. SIMO System Model for a Lognormal Fading Channel [2]

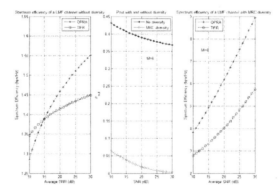

Fig. 2. (a) Spectrum Efficiency of a Lognormal Fading Channel without Diversity Combining for OPRA and TIFR Adaptation Policies,(b)Outage Probability of a Lognormal Fading Channel for OPRA Policy, (c) Spectrum Efficiency of a Lognormal Fading Channel with MRC Diversity Combining for OPRA and TIFR Adaptation Policies

6   Conclusions

We have obtained closed-form expressions for spectral efficiency of a Lognormal fading channel under different adaptation policies with MRC diversity combining techniques in this paper. The dependence of optimal cut-off SNR on the average received SNR is also studied. From our analyses, OPRA policy performs better in improving the spectral efficiency for a Lognormal fading channels, when it is used in combination with diversity combining techniques. For lower values of average received SNR, outage probability for the MRC diversity case is much lower than the no diversity case, which is expected. Also, MRC diversity case improves the spectral efficiency much more than that for the no diversity case.

References

1. Goldsmith, A., Varaiya, P.: Capacity of Fading Channels with Channel Side Information. IEEE Transactions on Information Theory 43, 1986–1992 (1997)
2. Alouini, M., Goldsmith, A.: Capacity of Rayleigh Fading Channels under Different Adaptive Transmission and Diversity Combining Techniques. IEEE Transactions on Vehicular Technology 48, 1165–1181 (1999)
3. Bhaskar, V.: Spectrum Efficiency Evaluation for MRC Diversity Schemes under Different Adaptation Policies over Generalized Rayleigh Fading Channels. International Journal of Wireless Information Networks 14, 191–203 (2007)
4. Bhaskar, V.: Spectrum Efficiency Evaluation for MRC Diversity Schemes under Different Adaptation Policies over Generalized Rician Fading Channels. International Journal of Wireless Information Networks 14, 209–223 (2007)
5. Laourine, A., Stephenne, A., Affes, S.: Capacity of Lognormal Fading Channels. In: Proceedings of the 2007 International Conference on Wireless Communications and Mobile Computing, Honolulu, Hawai, USA, pp. 13–17 (2007)
6. Proakis, J.G.: Digital Communications, 4th edn. McGraw Hill Inc., NY (2001)
7. Alouini, M., Goldsmith, A.: Capacity of Nakagami Multipath Fading Channels. In: Proceedings of the IEEE Vehicular Technology Conference, VTC 1997, Phoenix, AZ, USA, pp. 358–362 (1997)
8. Abramowitz, M., Stegun, I.A.: Handbook of Mathematical Funstions with Formulas, Graphs, and Mathematical Tables, U.S. Government Printing Office, 10th edn., Washington (1972)

FTSMR: A Failure Tolerant and Scalable Multipath Routing Protocol in MANET

V. Jayalakhsmi

Department of Computer Applications,
Sudharsan Engineering College,
Anna University, Tamilnadu, India
jayasekar1996@yahoo.co.in

Abstract. Multipath routing in Mobile Ad-hoc Networks (MANET) allow the establishment of multiple paths for routing between a source-destination pair. Multipath routing protocols address the problem of scalability, security, life time of networks, instability of wireless transmissions, and their adaptation to applications. This paper proposes a multipath protocol called Failure Tolerant and Scalable Multipath Routing FTSMR. This proposed FTSMR protocol uses multipath Dijkstra Algorithm to obtain multiple paths. The algorithm gains great flexibility and extensibility by employing different link metrics and cost functions. Route recovery and loop detection are also implemented in FTSMR in order to improve quality of service. Simulation based on NS2 simulator is performed in different scenarios. The simulation results reveal that the proposed FTSMR is suitable for mobile, large and dense networks with large traffic, and could satisfy critical multimedia applications with high on time constraints.

Keywords: Dijkstra Algorithm, End-to-end delay, Mobile Ad Hoc Networks, Multipath Routing, Link Metrics.

1 Introduction

MANET is the network completely self-organizing and self-configuring, requiring no existing network infrastructure or administration. Some routing policies[1][3][6] have been proposed in order to establish and maintain the routes in MANET. There are many common routing algorithms used in Adhoc networks but AODV[2][3] and DSR[1], which both are on-demand algorithms. In some multi-path algorithms once different paths are discovered, they are all stored but only one of them is used for transferring the data. The other stored paths will become useful once the current one is broken. There are also other multi-path algorithms that transfer data over all discovered paths concurrently which reduces end to end delay and increases end to end bandwidth.

Unlike its wired counterpart, the ad hoc network is more prone to both link and node failures due to expired node power or node mobility. As a result, the route used for routing might break down for different reasons. To increase the routing resilience against link or and node failures, one solution is to route a

K.R. Venugopal and L.M. Patnaik (Eds.): ICIP 2012, CCIS 292, pp. 100–108, 2012.
© Springer-Verlag Berlin Heidelberg 2012

message via multiple disjoint paths simultaneously. Thus, the destination node is still able to receive the message even if there is only one surviving routing path. This approach attempts to mainly address the problems of the scalability, mobility and link instability of the network. The multipath approach takes advantage from the large and dense networks. Several multipath routing protocols[10] were proposed for ad hoc networks. The main objectives of multipath routing protocols are to provide reliable communication and to ensure load balancing as well as to improve quality.

At the protocol level, The design of multipath routing[13] needs to consider failure models, characteristics of redundant routes, Coordinating nodes to construct routes, Mechanisms for locating mobile destination And intermediate forwarding nodes, and failure recovery.

The multiple paths obtained can be grouped into three categories:

1. Disjoint: This group can be classified into node-disjoint and link-disjoint. In the node-disjoint multipath type, there are no shared nodes between the calculated paths that links source and destination. The link-disjoint multipath type may share some nodes, but all the links are different.
2. Inter-twisted: The inter-twisted multipath type may share one or more route links.
3. Hybrid paths: The combination of previous two kinds.

Of all the multipath types, the node-disjoint type is the most disjointed; as all the nodes/links of two routes are different i.e. the network resource is exclusive for the respective routes. Nevertheless, the pure disjoint approach is not always the optimal solution, especially for sparse networks and multi-criteria computing. In the proposed protocol, a modification of Dijkstra algorithm allows for multiple paths both for sparse and dense topology. Two cost functions are used to generate node-disjoint or link-disjoint paths. To support the frequent topology changes of the network, auxiliary functions, i.e. route recovery and loop check, are implemented. The remainder of the paper is organized as follows. In Section 2, related works on multipath routing protocols are summarized. In Section 3, FTSMR protocol and its functionalities are implemented. Simulation and performance evaluation are presented in Section 4. Finally, conclusion of this paper is given in section 5.

2   Related Works

Most of the proposed multipath protocols are based on the single-path version of an existing routing protocol: AODV and AOMDV[4], DSR[1] and SMR[5].Most of these protocols are based on a reactive routing protocol (AODV[2]or DSR[1]. In fact, reactive multipath routing protocols[9] improve network performances (load balancing, delay and energy efficiency), but they also have some disadvantages: Route request storm: Multipath reactive routing protocols can generate a large number of route request messages. When the intermediate nodes have to process duplicate request messages, redundant overhead packets can be introduced in the networks[6]. Inefficient route discovery: To find node-disjoint or link disjoint paths, some multipath routing protocols prevent an intermediate node from sending a reply from its route cache[7]. Thus, a source node has to wait until a destination replies. Hence, the route discovery Process of a multipath routing protocol takes longer compared to that of DSR or AODV protocols.

Compared to reactive routing, the proactive routing protocols need to send periodic control messages. Hence, several researchers consider proactive routing protocols as not suitable for ad hoc networks[3]. For a network with low mobility and network load, the reactive routing protocols generate fewer control messages. However, given a network with high mobility and large traffic, the cost of destination.DSR does not require any periodic update messages, thus avoiding route discovery and route maintenance will raise significantly.

On the other hand, the proactive protocols try to keep a routing table for all possible destinations and therefore provide a transmission delay shorter than reactive routing protocols[8]. Furthermore, because the proactive protocols try to maintain the information of the whole network by periodical control messages, they can discover multiple routes more efficiently without much extra cost.

In our work, we propose a new Multipath Dijkstra Algorithm, which provides node-disjoint or link-disjoint paths when necessary by adjusting distinct cost functions. Additional functionalities are used to adapt to the topology changes.

3   Proposed FTSMR Protocol

The FTSMR can be regarded as a kind of hybrid multipath routing protocol which combines the proactive and reactive features. It sends out HELLO and TC messages periodically to detect the network topology just like AOMDV[4]. AOMDV mainly computes the multiple paths during route discovery process and it consists of two main components: a rule for route updates to find multiple paths at each node, and a distributed protocol to calculate the link-disjoint paths. However, FTSMR does not always keep a routing table. It only computes the multiple routes when data packets need to be sent out.

The core functionality of FTSMR has two parts: topology sensing and route computation. The topology sensing is to make the nodes aware of the information of the network. The route computation uses the Multipath Dijkstra Algorithm[8] to calculate the multipath based on the information obtained from the topology sensing. The source route (all the hops from the source to the destination) is saved in the header of the data packets. The topology sensing and route computation make it possible to find multiple paths from source to destination. In the specification of the algorithm, the paths will be available and loop-free. However, in practice, the situation will be much more complicated due to the change of the topology and the instability of the wireless medium.

3.1   Topology Sensing

To get the topology information of the network, the nodes use topology sensing which includes link sensing, neighbor detection and topology discovery. Link sensing populates the local link information base (link set). Neighbor detection populates the neighborhood information base (neighbor set and 2-hop neighbor set)[11][5] and concerns itself with nodes and node main addresses. Both link sensing and neighbor detection is based on the periodic exchange of HELLO messages. Topology Discovery generates the information base which concerns the nodes that are more than two hops away (topology set). It is based on the flooding of the TC messages through topology sensing, each node in the network can get sufficient information of the topology to enable routing.

3.2   Route Computation

For FTSMR, an on-demand scheme is used to avoid the heavy computation of multiple routes for every possible destination. For a source node sin the network FTSMR will keep an updated flag for every possible node in the network to identify the validity of the routes to the corresponding node.

- Initially, for every node i, the updatedFlagi is set to false, which means the route to the corresponding destination does not exist or needs to be renewed. When there is a route request to a certain node i, the source node will first check the updatedFlagi. If the updatedFlagi equals false, the multiple paths to node i , save it into the multipath routing table, and renew the corresponding updatedFlagi to true.
- If the udpdatedFlagi equals true, the node will find a valid route to node i in the multipath routing table route request to a certain node i, the source node will first check the updatedFlagi.
- If the udpdatedFlagi equals true, the node will find a valid route to node i in the multipath routing table.

Every time the node receives a new TC or HELLO message and results in the changes in the topology information base, all the updatedFlags will be set to false.In Figure 1, node S is trying to get multiple paths to node D. For MultiPath Dijkstra Algorithm, we use the number of hops as link cost metric. For the first step, the shortest path S-A-B-G-D will be found.. Then for the next step, the second shortest path S-C-E-F-G-D will be found. If we use the algorithm proposed in[4], and we delete the intermediate nodes A, B and G after the first step, it is impossible to obtain the second path. As illustrated above, another benefit of using cost functions is that we can get a different multiple path set (node-disjoint or link-disjoint) by choosing different cost functions according to our preference and the network requirements. The network topology in Figure 2 is presented as an example.

3.3   Route Recovery

In the proposed protocol , route recovery is used to overcome the disadvantage of the source routing. The principle is very simple: before an intermediate node tries to forward a packet to the next hop according to the source route, the node

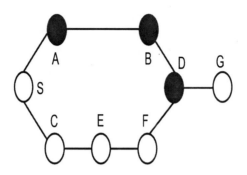

Fig. 1. Multiple Dijkstra Algorithm in Sparse Case. The Node-disjoint Path is Non-desirable after Nodes A,B and G are Removed.

first checks whether the next hop in the source route is one of its neighbors (by checking the neighbor set). If so, the packet is forwarded normally. If not, then it is possible that the next hop is not available anymore. Then the node will re compute the route and forward the packet by using the new route.

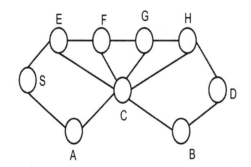

Fig. 2. Obtaining Different Path Sets by using Different Cost Functions. Path S-A-C-B-D will First be Chosen but the Second one might be Link-disjoint or Node disjoint (the bold lines) Depending on the Choice of Cost Functions.

4   Performance Evaluation Results

4.1   Simulation Environment

The simulation environment is ns2[12] and it consists of N mobile nodes in a rectangular region of size 1000 meters by 1000 meters. Each node has a radio propagation range of 250 m and channel capacity was 2Mbps. The IEEE 802.11 Distribution Coordination Function (DCF) is used as Medium Access Control (MAC). The random waypoint model was adopted as the mobility model. In the random waypoint model, a node randomly selects a destination from the physical terrain. It moves in the direction of the destination in a speed uniformly chosen between a minimum and maximum speed specified. After it reaches its destination, the node stays there for a time period specified as the pause time. In our simulation, minimum speed was set constant to zero. The simulated traffic is Constant Bit Rate (CBR) and all data packets are 512 Bytes. Each simulation is run for 300 seconds.

To compare the performances of the protocols, the following metrics are used.

- Packet delivery ratio: The ratio of the data packets successfully delivered at destination.
- Average end-to-end delay: Averaged over all surviving data packets from the sources to the destinations. This includes queuing delay and propagation delay.
- Average time in FIFO queue: Average time spent by packets in the queue.
- Distribution of delay of received packets: This measurement can give an idea of the jitter effect.

4.2   Simulation Results

In Figure 3, the data delivery ratio of the two protocols is given. AOMDV has a slightly better delivery ratio (about 3%) than FTSMRonly at the speed of 1 m/s (3.6 km/h). This is because with more paths transmitting packets at the same time, there is a higher possibility of collision at the MAC layer. This inter-path interference can be eliminated by using multichannel techniques, which guarantee a different frequency band for each path. In our case, there is only one channel used, so FTSMR has more packets dropped due to the collision at the MAC layer. However, as the speed of the nodes increases, the links become

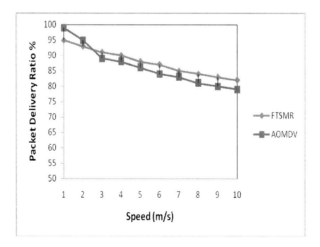

Fig. 3. Delivery Ratio of FTSMR and AOMDV

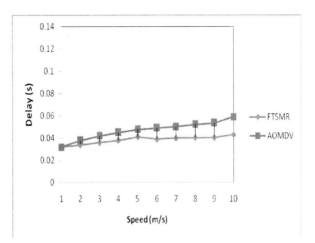

Fig. 4. Average End-to-End Delay of FTSMR and AOMDV

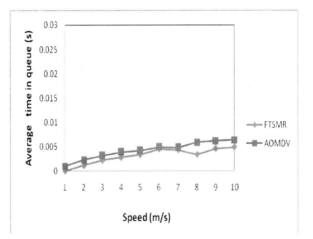

Fig. 5. Average Time in Queue of MP-OLSR and OLSR in a scenario of 81 nodes and 4 sources

more unstable, and there are also more loops in the network. The delivery ratio of AOMDV then decreases quickly and FTSMR outperforms AOMDV.

Compared to the slight gain in the delivery ratio (about 3% at high speed), the multipath protocol performs much better on average end-to-end delay than the single path, as shown in Figure 4. The end-to-end delay includes the propagation delay from the source to the destination and the queue delay in every relay nodes. The multipath protocol might have a longer propagation delay because some of the packets are forwarded through longer paths. However, what matters most is that it can effectively reduce the queue delay by distributing the packets to different paths rather than to a single one. In addition, the proposed loop detection mechanism can also reduce the unnecessary transmissions by avoiding the loops. As shown in Figure 5, the FTSMR has much shorter average time in the queue compared to AOMDV.

5   Conclusions

Any form of multipath technique always performs substantially better than single path routing. Providing multiple paths is useful in ad hoc networks because when one of the routes is disconnected, the source can simply use other available routes without performing the route recovery process. In this paper, Failure Tolerant and Scalable Multipath Routing Protocol (FTSMR) protocol is proposed. This proposed algorithm includes a major modification of the Dijkstra algorithm which uses two cost functions are now used to produce multiple disjoint or non-disjoint paths, auxiliary functions, i.e. route recovery and loop detection to guarantee quality of service.. The FTSMR can effectively improve the performance of the network (especially in the scenarios with high mobility and heavy network load). Simulations results show that the proposed protocol outperforms the AOMDV protocol in terms of packet delivery ratio and average end to end delay. The best benefit of FTSMR for QoS occurs in end-to end delay and jitter that is precisely required for critical multimedia services. Routing decision based on different types of scalable streams (especially video streams) can be further exploited, combined with the study on the metrics of link quality to fulfil the QoS. This constitutes the subject of future work.

References

1. Johnson, D., Maltz, D.: Dynamic Source Routing in Ad Hoc Wireless Networks. In: Imielinski, T., Korth, H. (eds.) Mobile Computing, ch. 5. Kluwer Academic, Hingham (1996)
2. Perkins, C.E., Royer, E.M.: Ad Hoc On-Demand Distance Vector Routing. In: Proceedings of IEEE Workshop On Mobile Computing Systems and Applications, WMCSA (1999)
3. Perkins, C.E., Bhagwat, P.: Highly Dynamic Destination-Sequenced Distance-Vector Routing (DSDV) for Mobile Computers. In: Proceedings of ACM SIGCOMM (1994)
4. Marina, M.K., Das, S.R.: On-Demand Multipath Distance Vector Routing for Ad Hoc Networks. In: Proceedings of 9th IEEE International Conference on Network Protocols, pp. 14–23 (2001)
5. Yao, Z., Jiang, J.J., Fan, P., Cao, Z., Li, V.: A Neighbor Table Based Multipath Routing in Ad Hoc Networks. In: 57th IEEE Semi Annual Vehicular Technology Conference, pp. 1739–1743 (2003)
6. Ye, Z., Krishnamurthy, S.V., Tripathi, S.K.: A Framework for Reliable Routing in Mobile Ad Hoc Networks. In: IEEE INFOCOM, San Francisco, CA, USA, pp. 270–280 (2003)

7. Cizeron, E., Hamma, S.: A Multiple Description Coding Strategy for Multi-path in Mobile Ad Hoc Networks. In: International Conference on the Latest Advances in Networks (ICLAN), Paris, France (2007)

8. Poussard, A.M., Hamidouche, W., Vauzelle, R., Pousset, Y., Parrein, B.: Realistic SISO and MIMO Physical Layer Implemented In Two Routing Protocols for Vehicular Ad Hoc Network. In: IEEE ITST, Lille, France (2009)

9. Jayalakshmi, V., Rameshkumar, R.: Multipath Fault Tolerant Routing Protocols in MANET. International Journal on AdHoc Networking Systems 2(1) (January 2012)

10. Zhou, X., Lu, Y., Xi, B.: A Novel Routing Protocol for Ad Hoc Sensor Networks using Multiple Disjoint Paths. In: 2nd International Conference on Broadband Networks, Boston, MA, USA (2005)

11. Clausen, T., Dearlove, C., Dean, J.: IETF Internet Draft, MANET Neighborhood Discovery Protocol (NHDP), draft-ietf-manet-nhdp-10 (July 2009)

12. Network Simulator-2, `http://www.isi.edu/nsnam/ns`

13. Tarique, M., Tepe, K.E., Adibi, S., Erfani, S.: Survey of Multipath Routing Protocols for Mobile Ad Hoc Networks. Journal of Network and Computer Applications, 1125–1143 (2009)

Secure Reputation Update for Target Localization in Wireless Sensor Networks

Tanuja R.[1], Anoosha V.[1], Manjula S.H.[1],
Venugopal K.R.[1], Iyengar S.S.[2], and L.M. Patnaik[3]

[1] Department of Computer Science and Engineering,
University Visvesvaraya College of Engineering, Bangalore University, Bangalore
r_tanuja@yahoo.com
[2] Florida International University, USA
[3] Indian Institute of Science, Bangalore

Abstract. Wireless Sensor Networks (WSNs) are by its nature more prone to security attacks and data losses. Security and data privacy have become need of the day. The most challenging area in WSNs which needs security is target localization. In addition to this complexity we are here concentrating on acoustic sensor nodes which uses Particle Swarm Optimization (PSO) algorithm for Location Estimation. We propose Secure Reputation Update Target Localization (SRUTL) algorithm which addresses target localization and security issues viz., bad-mouth attack, Sybil attack, on-off attack and malicious node attack at different levels of target localization. Simulation results shows positive response in attack detection hence contribute in building a secure wireless sensor network.

Keywords: Insider Attacks, Security, Reputation System, Target Localization, Wireless Sensor Networks (WSNs).

1 Introduction

Wireless Sensor Networks are known for their environment sensitive data collection and analysis which helps to solve most of the real world problems. Besides its resource constraint characteristics like, limited battery power, bandwidth, limited memory and network characteristics like, unreliable communication, higher latency, etc., it has emerged as a platform for signal processing and communication. Geographical information is one of the most important parameter in WSNs. The data stream is relevant only if location information of monitoring event is known. This issue is usually known as acoustic target localization (ATL) problem. Along with sensing, computing and communicating, the WSNs should also provide security to the sensor network.

Military base, which requires fast and accurate location information of its groups and secure channel to guard against enemy intervening our military signals can explain why ATL problem is so important in WSNs. In this scenario, the communication network should be fast and accurate with less overhead and

K.R. Venugopal and L.M. Patnaik (Eds.): ICIP 2012, CCIS 292, pp. 109–118, 2012.
© Springer-Verlag Berlin Heidelberg 2012

at the same time defend itself against various attacks like node compromise, replay attack, malicious nodes, etc., from the other side. Another example to show importance of ATL problem is vehicle monitoring scenario. As sound emitted by vehicles are not Omni-directional, target location estimation become complex. The complexity increase with addition of environmental noise, multi targets presence and thus the robust reputation system come to the rescue.

The target location estimation in WSNs can be performed using either centralized or de-centralized localization techniques. Reputation system provides a method of de-centralized localization, wherein every node is qualified based in its reputation score to perform target estimation. This helps in achieving node level security issues viz., false node (may be faulty node), node malfunction, node outage and physical attacks in WSNs. The resources and information communicated in WSNs should be protected and as well as defend security attacks. Most important security measures that should be addressed are : Data Confidentiality, Data Integrity, Availability, Data freshness, Self-Organization, Secure Localization, Time Synchronization and Authentication.

Secure Localization, determines accuracy and automatic location estimation in WSNs. Defending attacks on target localization networks which can be using either range-based or range free techniques, is a potential problem. Our proposed scheme addresses this issue. Reputation is vital to achieve security in a non-cryptographic scenario. This helps in analyzing untrustworthy sensors which hamper the network performance. By data synthesis (fusion) process on each nodes reputation score helps in reducing impact of faulty or malicious nodes in WSNs. Reputation computation is a challenging task as it should be strong enough to sustain internal attacks in WSNs. Previously, a watch-dog module was used to monitor nodes behavior, but this is a high energy consumption technique. Thus to ensure lower energy usage and better network functioning, a reputation system here is built based on powerful *Dirichlet distribution.*

Motivation: Researches have derived several algorithms and techniques which provide location estimation, high performance factor, low communication cost, defense against various attacks like wormhole attack, Sybil attack, node malfunction etc., but with their own drawbacks. None of them combine the efficiency and security for target localization in WSNs, which is our area of interest. With the help of better security framework which can overcome some of the most dangerous attacks in WSNs along with a highly efficient target localization scheme to address the current challenge in WSNs.

Contributions: We propose a new algorithm known as Secure Reputation Update for Target Localization (SRUTL). This scheme adds security measures to the existing reputation system in acoustic WSNs. The main focus is on secure update of reputation value at each individual node during transmission control phase. A node is allowed to increase its reputation if and only if its sensed data has contributed in location estimation. If there is a sudden increase or decrease in reputation value, then that node is ignored from the network. When a faulty node enters back to network, it will be given initial reputation score as assigned during deployment phase, thus protecting the whole network from malicious nodes and safeguarding network performance.

Organization: The rest of the paper is organized as follows: Section 2 deals with study of previous techniques in support to the proposed system. Section 3 gives background work and base algorithms used in our system. The acoustic sensing model and proposed SRUTL algorithm are explained in Section 4. Section 5 gives implementation and performance evaluation. Section 6 gives conclusions and future enhancement.

2   Related Works

Many applications find WSNs advantageous than compared to other networks. A data without its origin is insignificant. Thus a sensed data signal in any WSNs is only valid until its source location is known, which is commonly addressed as Acoustic Target Localization (ATL) problem in WSNs. A simple scenario to explain ATL problem is shown in the form of localization in [1] using two step Acoustic mapping for multiple speakers based localization. It shows a comparative study of Global Coherence Field (GCF) and Oriented Global Coherence Field (OGCF) techniques which are widely used.

Zaher et al.,[2] have proposed a EB-MAC protocol for event-based system that characterizes acoustic target location system using Time Difference on Arrival (TDOA). Fuzzy Art data fusion center is designed to detect errors and fuses estimates to a decision based on spatial correlation and consensus vote. On MICAZ motes with Tiny-OS this protocol provides reliable fault tolerant communication platform that maximizes throughput, lowers channel contention and latency with huge enhancement over other fusion algorithm. It has a drawback of single point failure and performance poorly in dense sensor networks and outdoor deployments.

Alexander et al.,[3] have demonstrated an automatic self-localization scheme using non parametric belief propagation (NBP) for location estimation and resending uncertain location information. As its implemented in distributed environment it helps various statistical models and multi-model uncertainty. It has low cost in-terms of messages per sensors and low bit rate approximation for messages which results in no impact on network performance. This method is extensible to non-Gaussian noise models so as to increase robustness of the network. Other message-passing inference algorithm viz., max-product might help to improve performance which is not considered here. Also alternative graphical models can provide more accuracy than that of the proposed NBP technique. NBP can serve as a useful tool for estimating unknown sensors location in large ad-hoc networks.

Pramod et al.,[4] have described a new approach for target localization which uses quantized sensor data and channel statistics of WSNs. This novel approach uses Cramer-Rao Lower Bounds (CRLBs) for location estimation. Three different types of target location estimators are developed for various link layer designs viz., Hard decoding Binary-Channel (BC), Soft decoding in Rayleigh

Fading Channel with Coherent Reception and Soft decoding in Rayleigh Fading Channel with Non-coherent Reception. A channel-aware estimator is derived from CRLBs even with a relatively small number of sensors. Results show coherent reception scheme performance better that non-coherent reception scheme for both soft and hard decoding links. Improve localization performance by designing an optimal local sensor threshold needs to be addressed. This scheme can be incorporated in larger dimensions of performance optimization by adding physical layer parameters and other functional characteristics such as various modulation and coding schemes. This can be generalized to extend for multiple target estimation scenarios.

Most of research works on ATL problem either design localization algorithms [5] or target estimation schemes [6] for a better solution in WSNs. These localization algorithms are required to report the origin of event, assist group querying of sensors, routing and answering questions on the network coverage. Whereas target estimation schemes concentrate on specific parameters like, using mobile agents for collaboration and classification, mobile anchor nodes [7], channel aware data quantization to find location information.

One of the most efficient algorithm for target localization is known as Particle Swarm Optimization (PSO) which is described in Raghavendra et al., [7], Xu et al., [8], Panigrahi et al., [9], along with Xue et al., [10] which is base of this paper. All the above works have explored PSO in different direction like network-centric, mobile anchor assisted, maximum likelihood function etc., to arrive to one simple solution for ATL problem. Most of their experiments were carried out using MICAz motes. The acoustic network model is derived from [10], which help in providing a realistic network view.

3   Background

Reputation system designed for accurate target sensing in WSNs, provides security at each individual node[10]. Based on weighted measurement of each node in data fusion a reputation is calculated and thus effect of untrustworthy nodes is eliminated from the network.(i) All the initial network parameters assigned while building sensor network model and acoustic sensing model. (ii) Each nodes rating value is expressed by its probability distribution of measurement error (PDME) of possible outcomes along with positive real parameters which is efficiently expressed using Dirichlet distribution for variable vector and parameter vector. (iii) Reconstruction of the sensing model is carried out with pre-defined threshold for along with its rating bounds, to detect a targets existence. By solving an objective function of least-square estimation as in [2] helps to determine sensing parameters along with deviation factor from true measurement.

The earlier works concentrates only on target location estimation with high accuracy, reliable data delivery and node failure due to physical tampering and high inter-device or environmental noise. Our concern is to make a realistic secure model for ATL which can protect itself from most common WSN attacks like bad-mouth attack, Sybil attack, on-off attack and malicious nodes.

Table 1. Notations used in the Algorithm

$Symbols$	$Definition$
S_{ssth}	sensed signal strength threshold
s_i	sensed data at node i
g	sensor gain
c	sensor measurement bias
NS_R	neighbor set reputation value
NS_{status}	neighbor set node status
r_i	reliability of node i
r_{ij}	link reliability between node i and j
γ	stability value
R_{th}	threshold value of reputation
R_i	reputation value of node i

4   Problem Definition and Algorithm

4.1   Problem Definition

Given a set of Wireless Sensor Nodes $S_i \in V$ where $i = 1, 2, \ldots, n$ as an acoustic sensor network established by either throwing sensor nodes through an air bound vehicle to the fields where the data has to be read from stationary objects and target object is expected to pass by through the designated region. These sensor nodes have to sense data and provide location estimation. There may be a faulty node or malicious node estimation which should be identified and discarded.

The objectives of the algorithm are :

(i) Calulate reputation trust values and estimate target location.
(ii) To make a realistic secure model which can protect itself from most common WSN attacks like bad-mouth attack, Sybil attack, on-off attack and malicious nodes.

4.2   Algorithm

The proposed scheme provides a security framework for WSNs used for target location estimation. We introduce new algorithm, Secure Reputation Update for Target Localization (SRUTL) to securely modify reputation value at each node.

There are three phases of the algorithm applied at three different levels.

Phase1. After construction sensing model for the uniform distributed WSNs using Dirichlet distribution and least square estimation, stability factor every node is verified. This can be same as trust value (or inter-device noise) of that node. This prevents malicious attack and on-off attack at node level. Later these nodes are considered as Cluster Members (CMs).

Table 2. Secure Reputation Update for Target Localization (SRUTL)

Phase 1: Create cluster members
begin
Initially γ is set to 0.5 and all nodes are considered normal.
for every node i
if event sensed AND $s_i \leq S_{ssth}$ then
broadcast ID Packets consisting of position and bias.
update γ by 0.1 and nodes status as Cluster Member(CM). **else**
wait for an event.
endif
endfor
end
Phase 2: Create cluster decoders
begin
for every node i $\in$ set of CMs
if $w_i \leq 500$ then
apply local voting algorithm to neighbor set NS of node i
for every node j, $R_j \leq R_{th}/2$	j $\in$NS$_R$AND NS$status$
update γ by 0.15 and nodes status as Cluster Decoder(CD).
calculate r_j and r_{ij}
endfor
else
apply local voting algorithm to neighbor set NS of node i
along with prior value.
for every node j, $\gamma_j \geq 0.7$ AND $R_j \leq R_{th}$
update γ by 0.15 and nodes status as Cluster Decoder(CD).
update r_j and r_{ij}
endfor
endif
endfor
end

Phase2. After applying local voting scheme [10] for data filtering, the nodes identity is verified. This helps in detecting malicious nodes and defends against Sybil and on-off attacks, in turn efficiently identify Cluster Decoders (CDs.)

Phase3. During the process of execution of PSO algorithm at Cluster Heads (CHs), if a CH disconnects with the network then second highest reputed and stable CD is promoted as CH and carries its task. The probability of second elected CH suffering on-off attack is very less and thus can guarantee smooth network performance.

Table 2 shows the first two phases of the algorithm. During the first phase the nodes may be experience malicious attack and onoff attack. The nodes with faulty data (stale data) could be identified based on carefully selected signal strength threshold. So to next phase the nodes which are verified to be normal are added to cluster member set. The stability value assigned to each node plays a major role in selecting nodes which can resist it from the security attacks that

Table 3. Secure Reputation Update for Target Localization (SRUTL)

Phase 3: Create cluster Heads
begin
while $(num_{ch} \leq 2)$
for every node $i \in$ set of CDs
exchange new trust value with other CDs
if $\gamma_i \leq 0.7$ OR 0.8 AND $R_j \leq R_j \mid j \in$ set of CDs-node i **then**
elect that node as Cluster Head(CH) ; $num_{ch}++$
endif
endfor
endwhile
// Applying PSO algorithm
for every node $i \in$ set of CHs
apply PSO algorithm.
calculate approx. $S_j \mid j \in$ set of CDs and inform all other CDs.
verify the newly calculated S_j with precalculated approx. S_j
if no match **then**
broadcast node j is malicious node and update its status as faulty.
decrement R_j and γ_j
else
update its status normal and increment R_j and γ_j
endif
endfor
end

are interested. It also accounts the accumulated evidence matrix to determine nodes behavior. The difference in position information exchanged in ID packet to the one known at deployment phase should not exceed error_threshold [10].

In phase two, initially when communication has not crossed window size w=500, the local voting algorithm is applied on neighboring set of CMs. Then the nodes with higher rating level and valid status information, updates stability value and consider it as CDs. Meanwhile, nodes reliability and link reliability is also calculated. If the prior communication history is available then it contributes in estimating nodes behavior and thus reduces number of faulty nodes.

Table 3 shows the phase 3 of the algorithm. The following steps take place during phase 3 at CHs : (i) If the node is a cluster head then, estimate target location and then send update packet which contains, new target location and that nodes contribution factor using nodes sensed data reading, s_i. Else, wait for the cluster heads response for the nodes measurement epochs. (ii) Once update packet is received (which is unique), the nodes compute reputation based on its contribution for the target estimation by computing its new $s_{i,new}$ and increase its score accordingly using : $s_i = g_i a_i + n_i$, where a_i is the signal strength at every sensor node which is a polynomial distance function, n_i is combination of sensor network parameters like environmental and inter device noise which can determine nodes status. The cluster heads will increase its score once it sends out update packet to its members. (iii) During next ID packet communication it includes its position, sensed data along with its new reputation score R_i, which will be verified by its cluster head of previous iteration. (iv) If a mismatch is found, that node is ignored for any further computation in the network. If it retunes back as normal node then its given initial reputation score and allowed to participate in location estimation, but will be taken into account only after crossing pre-determined threshold reputation score $R_t h$, which is monitored consistently.

Every node in the network stores the reputation value of its neighboring node set along with its status (active/ inactive) information. By applying the above algorithm a reputation score is checked to identify any abnormal nodes behavior. Reputation score updation is applied and monitored by current CHs. While selecting a node as Effective Node the participating Featuring Nodes should verify that it is not an abnormal/ malicious node. The communication from the estimated target information of Effective Node to sink should be decided based on nodes and links reliability factor (50% of each). Once a node is identified as malicious by a rapid increase in its reputation score, should be ignored by the network.

5   Implementation and Performance Evaluation

5.1   Simulation Setup

We evaluate the performance of our scheme by simulation conducted in MATLAB with a 100x100 units region under observation. The nodes are uniformly distributed and targets are assumed to be randomly placed. All the network parameters are initialized at deployment phase and all nodes are assumed to be normal. This algorithm is distributed in nature and stability is achieved in a short span. The signal threshold for target detection is 2.6. The window size w=500 and error_threshold=0.1.

5.2   Results and Analysis

Table 4 shows the SRUTL algorithm addressing various security attacks at different levels. The network performance is evaluated in terms of success probability at all 3 groups of nodes i.e., cluster members, cluster decoders and cluster heads.

Table 4. SRUTL Algorithm and its Defense to Various Attacks at Different Levels

Security Attacks	Bad Mouth Attack	Sybil Attack	On-off Attack	Malicious Node Attack
Phase 1			CMs	CMs
Phase 2	CDs	CDs		CDs
Phase 3			CHs	CHs

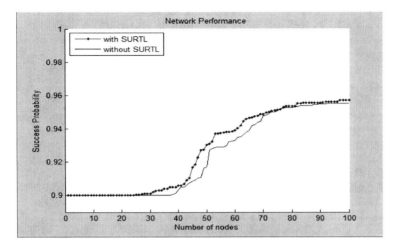

Fig. 1. Network Performance with SRUTL algorithm

The Figure 1 show the number of nodes contributing in solving ATL problem is defended by the use of SRUTL algorithm. This is due to filtering of faulty nodes in 3 phases and different levels of target location estimation process. The use of stability factor along with reputation value has shown positive results in identifying malicious nodes and other attacks.

6 Conclusions and Future Work

The proposed SRUTL algorithm presents a simple and effective security framework for WSNs. The results show a high overall performance when compared with the network without this algorithm. The energy efficiency and high accuracy adds to its advantage. With reputation update better target localization is performed. The various node attacks considered viz., bad-mouth attack, Sybil attack, on-off attack and malicious nodes are detected at earlier stages, so that network remains stable and unaffected. The special cases of nodes failing at cluster head level are not addressed and hence would be continued in our future works. Simulation results show that SRUTL can successfully overcome various attacks at different levels of the algorithm for target localization using reputation.

References

1. Zaher, M.M., Mohamed, A.E., Magdy, A.B.: A Lightweight Collaborative Fault Tolerant Target Localization System for Wireless Sensor Networks. IEEE Transactions on Mobile Computing 8(12), 1690–1704 (2009)
2. Zhong, Z., Zheng, P., Jun-Hong, C., Zhijie, S., Amvrossios, C.B.: Scalable Localization with Mobility Prediction for Underwater Sensor Networks. IEEE Transactions on Mobile Computing 10(3), 335–348 (2011)

3. Alexander, T.I., John, W.F., Randolph, L.M., Alan, S.W.: Nonparameteric Belief Propagation for Self-Localization of Sensor Networks. IEEE Journal on Selected Areas in Communications 23(4), 809–819 (2005)
4. Ozdemir, O., Niu, R., Pramod, K.V.: Channel Aware Target Localization with Quantized Data in Wireless Sensor Networks. IEEE Transactions on Signal Processing 57(3), 1190–1202 (2009)
5. Amitangshu, P.: Localization Algorithms in Wireless Sensor Networks: Current Approaches and Future Challenges. Network Protocols and Algorithms 2(1), 45–74 (2010) ISSN 1943-3581
6. Xue, W., Dao-wei, B., Liang, D., Sheng, W.: Agent Collaborative Target Localization and Classification in Wireless Sensor Networks. Sensors, 1359–1386 (2007), ISSN 1424-8220, http://www.mdpi.org/sensors
7. Raghavendra, V.K., Venayagamoorthy, G.K., Ann, M., Cihan, H.D.: Networkcentric Localization in MANETs based on Particle Swarm Optimization. In: IEEE Swarm Intelligence Symposium, St. Louis, MO, USA (2008)
8. Xu, L., Zhang, H., Shi, W.: Mobile Anchor Assisted Node Localization in Sensor Networks based on Particle Swarm Optimization. In: IEEE Conferences (2010)
9. Panigrahi, T., Panda, G., Mulgrew, B., Majhi, B.: Maximum Likelihood Source Localization in Wireless Sensor Networks Using Particle Swarm Optimization. In: IEEE ICES, pp. 111–115 (2011)
10. Xue, W., Liang, D., Daowei, B.: Reputation-Enabled Self-Modification for Target Sensing in Wireless Sensor Networks. IEEE Transactions on Instrumentation and Measurement 59(1) (2010)

Local Histogram Based Descriptor
for Tracking in Wide Area Imagery

Alex Mathew and Vijayan K. Asari

Department of Electrical and Computer Engineering,
University of Dayton, Dayton, Ohio, USA
vijayan.asari@notes.udayton.edu

Abstract. In this paper we propose a novel feature extraction technique and show its application in tracking in low resolution videos. The aspects that make tracking particularly challenging are global camera motion, large target movement, poor gradient and texture information and absence of color information. Global camera motion is reduced or eliminated by registering the images from frame to frame employing SURF (Speeded Up Robust Feature). The proposed method is based on intensity histogram, but with a variant that encodes both spatial and intensity information. The method is evaluated on CLIF (Columbus Large Image Format) data. The robustness of the feature eliminates the need for background subtraction in videos. A performance comparison of our approach with other object descriptors such as HOG (Histogram of Gradients), SURF and SIFT (Scale Invariant Feature Transform) shows the effectiveness of the proposed descriptor.

Keywords: Aerial Images, CLIF Data, Low Resolution Object Detection, Tracking, Wide Area Surveillance.

1   Introduction

Finding reliable features for visual tracking in low resolution imagery is a hard problem. The proposed method focuses finding robust features for detection and tracking in wide area motion imagery. This problem is of immense interest in the area of Wide Area Surveillance. Although there are several feature extraction techniques available for high resolution images, these methods fail in low resolution scenarios. The method described in this paper is evaluated on Columbus Large Image Format(CLIF) data [1]. The data is captured using cameras mounted on flying platforms at a height of approximately 7000 ft. The camera captures images of size 2672 x 4008 at a rate of 2 frames per second. Targets of interest span only a few pixels.

In object recognition, any available cue is of interest. They include-

Physical Characteristics: Color, texture, physical structure, location, orientation, depth map etc. These features are not available in long range.

Behavioral Patterns: This includes the behavioral patterns such as the gait of a person, the trajectory, acceleration and speed of a vehicle etc. Low video frame

K.R. Venugopal and L.M. Patnaik (Eds.): ICIP 2012, CCIS 292, pp. 119–128, 2012.
© Springer-Verlag Berlin Heidelberg 2012

rate in this data results in large variations between consecutive frames making trajectory prediction hard.

Environment Context: This includes the physical environment features. For example, a car is likely to be on a road or a parking spot rather than on the top of a building. Such contexts are very useful for effective search and recognition of objects. However in this data, areas such as road cannot be reliably extracted since there is very little texture information.

There are two sub areas in object recognition - model-based recognition and feature based recognition. In model based recognition, the algorithm tries to find areas in the image and compare them with parts of an object of interest. In low resolution images, parts of objects of interest are not well defined. Feature based methods find local interest points. Small target sizes combined with poor gradient and textural information render traditional feature extraction techniques impractical. There is also significant change in viewpoint between frames. Hence two problems need to be tackled for object tracking - image registration and finding robust features. In this paper, we propose an intensity distribution based descriptor that offers good target localization and accuracy. The paper is organized as follows. In Section 2 we present the proposed method that includes image registration and feature extraction. Section 3 details the process of tracking. In Section 4 we give a comparison of our descriptor with other available descriptors. A comparison of our method with mean-shift tracking is also presented. Finally in Section 5, we present our conclusions.

2   Proposed Method

The first step involved is the image registration step which is performed using the SURF(Speeded Up Robust Features) descriptor [2]. This is described in Section 2.1. To track a target, the target is first selected in the frame. The target features are used in subsequent frames to track it. The feature extraction process is described in Section 2.2.

2.1   Image Registration

Registration is the process of transforming data into a particular coordinate system. Global camera motion is eliminated or reduced by the process of image registration. For registration, descriptors such as SURF or SIFT (Scale Invariant Feature Transform) can be used [3]. SIFT feature extraction technique consists of four steps detecting scale-space extrema, keypoint localization, orientation assignment and keypoint descriptor computation. To compute scale-space extrema, the image is convolved with Gaussian kernel at different scales. This gives a scale-space representation of the image. The difference of Gaussian images are then computed as the difference of successive scale-space representations. Candidate keypoints are those at which maxima or minima (extrema) of the difference of Gaussian images. Unstable keypoints, for example, those along edges and with low contrast, are eliminated. Keypoints are localized in scale and position by

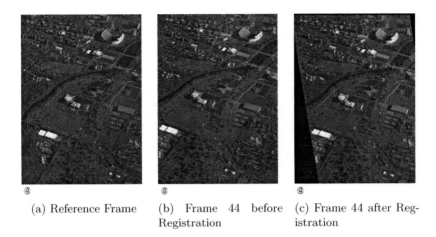

(a) Reference Frame   (b) Frame 44 before Registration   (c) Frame 44 after Registration

Fig. 1. Image Registration with SURF keypoints and Image wraping

interpolating between nearby data. Orientations are assigned a keypoints based on image gradient information around it. The spatial - orientation histogram at a keypoint gives the SIFT feature vector. The computation of the SIFT descriptor is relatively expensive. SURF, on the other hand, is several times faster than SIFT. The increase in speed is achieved by using integral images to compute approximations of Laplacian of Gaussians using a box filters. Since SIFT is slower than SURF the proposed method uses SURF for registration [4]. In our implementation we have used the Matlab code available at [5]. Speed is further increased by downsizing the image and fitting the frame to frame registration homography on the larger images. Fig. 1. shows two frames registered with respect to one another.[1]

2.2   Feature Extraction

Local feature based methods do not consider the object as a whole, instead such algorithms look for distinguishable local features such as gradients or texture. Standard methods used for object recognition in close range are not suitable in long range scenario, as details are progressively lost with distance. In long range images, appearance based models do not work since object geometries and their structural integrity are not well defined. Stable keypoints are also few and unavailable. As objects in long range span only a few pixels, corners and edges are not well defined. Absence of these cues and texture information make point descriptors like SIFT and SURF poor choices for detection, recognition or tracking. The objects in such images have very little gradient information. For this reason, gradient based descriptors such as HOG (Histogram of Gradients) are also not very useful [6]. Tracking methods that rely on color information such as the one described in [7] cannot be used since there is no color information in CLIF data.

---

[1] @ CLIF data, ID: HAAA08E09D, URL: https://www.sdms.afrl.af.mil

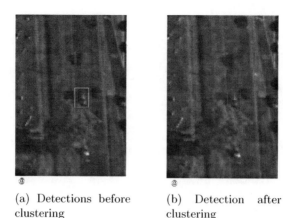

(a) Detections before
clustering

(b) Detection after
clustering

Fig. 2. Detection with the Proposed Method. The Region Bounded by the Green Rectangle is the Actual Target. Multiple Detections are Fused and False Detections are Eliminated with Clustering as shown in (b).

Using grey level histogram for classification is not capable of providing good localization. As other features are not available, we propose a novel descriptor based on local histograms. The work is motivated by the fact that local intensity distribution within an object do not change drastically from frame to frame. In this method, we divide the object into regions and compute the normalized intensity histogram in each region. Normalizing the histogram makes the descriptor partially scale invariant. These histograms are concatenated to form a larger feature vector. The vector retains both spatial and intensity information. In our experiments, we divided the target into four regions. The region sizes roughly correspond to the size of vehicle parts such as windshields and roof. This method is conceptually similar to the method used in face recognition with Local Binary Patterns [8]. However, LBP descriptors are texture descriptors and are not powerful in low resolution domain. The proposed descriptor offers good localization and is useful for detection and tracking in long range. The features are compared using the histogram comparison techniques. Histogram comparisons are widely used in texture analysis and in content based image retrieval. Experiments were carried out using the different techniques available for Histogram comparison. Common histogram dissimilarity measures are Histogram intersection, Log-likelihood statistics and Chi square statistic as given in equation 1, 2 and 3 respectively.

$$D(S, M) = \sum_i min(S_i, M_i) \tag{1}$$

$$L(S, M) = -\sum_i S_i log M_i \tag{2}$$

Fig. 3. Detections with HOG. Red Rectangles are the Detections given by HOG. Green Rectangle Represents the Actual Target.

Fig. 4. SIFT keypoints. The Actual Target is shown in the Green Rectangle. There are no Matches between the Images.

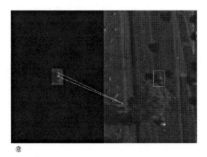

Fig. 5. Incorrect Matches with SURF Keypoints. The Actual Target is shown in the Green Rectangle.

$$\chi^2(S, M) = \sum_i \frac{(S_i - M_i)^2}{(S_i + M_i)} \qquad (3)$$

$S = \{S_i\}$ and $M = \{M_i\}$ are the two histograms that are compared. We have experimentally found out that chi-square statistic gives the best results with the proposed descriptor.

3   Tracking

Object tracking is the problem of estimating the position of targets of interest. The main difficulties in the reliable tracking in long range aerial images are the absence of cues such as corners and occlusion. For tracking in such a complex scenario we use a combination of a Kalman filter and the proposed feature extraction technique. The filter predicts the position of the target when there are occlusions. Kalman filter model can be written as

$$x_k = Ax_{k-1} + w_k \tag{4}$$

$$z_k = Hx_k + v_k \tag{5}$$

w_k and v_k are assumed to be zero mean Gaussian noise. The state model $x_k = [x, y, v_x, v_y]$ consists of position and velocity information. A and H are the state transition matrix and the measurement matrix. The measurement vector z_k is the position [x y]. The registration process is computationally expensive. This requires that the computational cost associated with the trackers be kept to a minimum. Using a prediction mechanism such as Kalman filter reduces the search area to a small window, in addition to handling conclusions.

The feature descriptor of the target selected is compared in subsequent frames using chi-square statistic. To increase the probability of correct detection, we take the closest 10 neighbors. Since the feature is robust, the algorithm gives multiple detections for an object. The multiple detections are fused together using a robust mode seeking algorithm such as mean shift algorithm [9]. An alternative is to use density based clustering algorithms such as DBSCAN [10].

4   Results and Discussion

Fig. 2(a). shows the target detections with the proposed method. The target vehicle is shown in a green rectangle. The detections are shown in red rectangles. Fig. 2(b). shows the detection obtained after eliminating false detections and fusing multiple correct detections. Detections given by HOG descriptor are shown in Fig. 3. SIFT keypoints are shown in Fig. 4. However, there are no matches between the target image and the frame. As shown in Fig. 5., SURF keypoints are incorrectly matched between the target image and the frame. Experiments on several video sequences with the proposed descriptor gave promising results. Fig. 6. shows the result of feature tracking with the proposed descriptor in a particular video sequence. The three objects selected are accurately tracked using the proposed method. Mean shift tracking is another histogram based tracking method [11]. It computes the most probable location of the target based on mean-shift iterations. For target modeling, it uses a metric based on Bhattacharya coefficient. For two normalized m-bin histograms, $p = \{p_i\}_{i=1,2...m}$ and $q = \{q_i\}_{i=1,2...m}$ ($\sum_{i=1}^{m} p_i = 1$, $\sum_{i=1}^{m} q_i = 1$), the sample estimate of the Bhattacharya coefficient is

$$\rho(p, q) = \sum_{i=1}^{m} \sqrt{p_i q_i} \tag{6}$$

(a) Multi-Object Tracking with the Proposed Method - Frame 1.

(b) Multi-Object Tracking with the Proposed Method - Frame 3.

(c) Multi-Object Tracking with the Proposed Method - Frame 5.

(d) Multi-Object Tracking with the Proposed Method - Frame 7.

(e) Multi-Object Tracking with the Proposed Method - Frame 9.

(f) Multi-Object Tracking with the Proposed Method - Frame 13.

Fig. 6. Tracking Results for Frame 1, Frame 3, Frame 5, Frame 7, Frame 9 and Frame 13 using the Proposed Method

(a) Multi-Object Tracking with the Mean Shift Tracking - Frame 1.

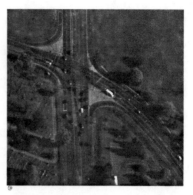

(b) Multi-Object Tracking with the Mean Shift Tracking - Frame 3.

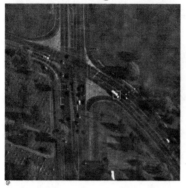

(c) Multi-Object Tracking with the Mean Shift Tracking - Frame 5.

(d) Multi-Object Tracking with the Mean Shift Tracking - Frame 7.

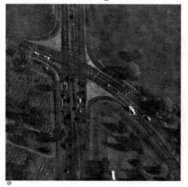

(e) Multi-Object Tracking with the Mean Shift Tracking - Frame 9.

(f) Multi-Object Tracking with the Mean Shift Tracking - Frame 13.

Fig. 7. Tracking Results for Frame 1, Frame 3, Frame 5, Frame 7, Frame 9 and Frame 13 using Mean Shift Tracking

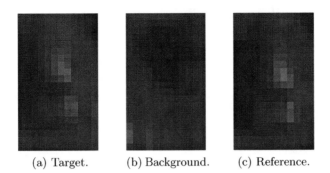

(a) Target.   (b) Background.   (c) Reference.

Fig. 8. Target, Background and Reference Images

Using equation 4 , the distance between the two distributions is defined as

$$d(y) = \sqrt{1 - \rho(p, q)} \qquad (7)$$

Fig. 7. shows tracking three targets using mean-shift. As can be seen only one target is tracked correctly. This is because mean-shift tracking cannot cope with large target movements. For the computation of the mean-shift vector, successive target locations need to be overlapping. Fig. 8. shows a target image, part of the background region and the reference image. For the target to be matched correctly with the reference, the distance between the reference and the target has to be less than that between the reference and the background. Table 1 shows

Table 1. Performance Comparison of Histogram Similarity Metrics

	Our method	Undivided Image Histogram	Metric in mean shift tracking
dist(reference,target)	3.1654	0.2968	0.3252
dist(reference,background)	4.2863	0.2902	0.3120

a comparison of the metric used in our method, using chi-square metric without dividing the image into regions and the metric used in mean-shift tracking (equation 7). Dividing the image into grids is the key to correct matching and localization. As noted in Table 1, the target cannot be correctly matched when the histograms are compared with chi-square metric without dividing the image or when the metric used in mean-shift tracking is employed.

5   Conclusions

We have presented a novel feature extraction technique that addresses the problem of detection and tracking in low resolution domain. A comparison with other techniques such as HOG, SURF, SIFT and mean-shift tracking shows that our descriptor is far superior to such techniques when there is very little textural and structural information. In addition, since the approach is based on histogram, it is less computationally intensive than most other methods. We have shown the effectiveness of our approach in tracking in wide area CLIF data. A scheme that uses cross bin similarity metrics instead of bin-bin similarity metrics like chi-square is currently being developed.

References

1. AFRL CLIF Dataset (2007),
   https://www.sdms.afrl.af.mil/index.php?collection=clif2007
2. Bay, H., Ess, A., Tuytelaars, T., Gool, L.: SURF: Speeded Up Robust Features. Computer Vision and Image Understanding (CVIU) 110(3), 346–359 (2008)
3. Lowe, D.G.: Distinctive Image Features from Scale-invariant Keypoints. International Journal Computer Vision 60(2), 91–110 (2004)
4. Juan, L., Gwun, O.: A Comparison of SIFT, PCA-SIFT and SURF. International Journal of Image Processing (IJIP) 3(4), 143–152 (2009)
5. http://www.mathworks.com/matlabcentral/fileexchange/
   28300-opensurf-including-image-warp
6. Dalal, N., Triggs, B.: Histograms of Oriented Gradients for Human Detection. In: International Conference on Computer Vision and Pattern Recognition, vol. 2, pp. 886–893 (2005)
7. Pérez, P., Hue, C., Vermaak, J., Gangnet, M.: Color-Based Probabilistic Tracking. In: Heyden, A., Sparr, G., Nielsen, M., Johansen, P. (eds.) ECCV 2002, Part I. LNCS, vol. 2350, pp. 661–675. Springer, Heidelberg (2002)
8. Ahonen, T., Hadid, A., Pietikäinen, M.: Face Recognition with Local Binary Patterns. In: Pajdla, T., Matas, J(G.) (eds.) ECCV 2004, Part I. LNCS, vol. 3021, pp. 469–481. Springer, Heidelberg (2004)
9. Comaniciu, D., Meer, P.: Mean Shift: A Robust Approach Toward Feature Space Analysis. IEEE Trans. Pattern Analysis and Machine Intelligence 24(5), 603–619 (2002)
10. Ester, M., Kriegel, H., Sander, J., Xu, X.: A Density Based Algorithm for Discovering Clusters in Large Spatial Databases with Noise. In: 2nd International Conference on Knowledge Discovery and Data Mining, Portland, pp. 226–231 (1996)
11. Comaniciu, D., Ramesh, V., Meer, P.: Real-time Tracking of Non-rigid Objects Using Mean Shift. In: IEEE Conference on Computer Vision and Pattern Recognition, vol. 2, pp. 142–149 (2000)

Shot-Based Genre Identification in Musicals

Sher Muhammad Doudpota, Sumanta Guha, and Junaid Baber

Computer Science and Information Management,
Asian Institute of Technology, Bangkok, Thailand
sher.muhammad.doudpota@ait.ac.th

Abstract. The phenomenal growth of World Wide Web has caused an easier and faster access to multimedia contents. The volume of available multimedia contents like Hindi movies' music databases online has been exponentially increased. It results in dire need of automatic music retrieval from such databases. In recent years content-based music retrieval has been viewed as a potential solution to it. The ability of content based music retrieval is to automatically identify different characteristics of music data such as its genre. Unfortunately, the existing genre identifiers that are mostly tested on western music databases, has very low accuracy on Hindi movies' music databases. Moreover, all the existing approaches of genre identification are based on music audio. In this paper, we propose a framework to automatically identify genre of a Hindi movie song using its video features. We used video shot duration and actor movement to classify the songs in pop, romantic, and tragic classes. We performed our experiments on 105 popular Hindi movies' songs falling evenly in three proposed genres. An accuracy of 89.5% has been achieved that proves the effect of music video on its genre.

Keywords: Actor Movement, Content-Based Video Retrieval, Genre Identification, Shot Duration, Song Genre Identification.

1   Introduction

Bollywood has become an important part of South Asian culture. The most common Bollywood genre, the song-and-dance movie, colloquially called the masala movie, typically with a simple melodramatic plot along the lines of poor good guy wins the rich beautiful gal, resonates strongly across the subcontinent. Often derided as escapist fare, Bollywood movies, nevertheless, are hugely popular amongst all strata of South Asian society, from daily wage workers to millionaire industrialists, from the uneducated to the college-going. Families gathering around the TV at home to watch a Bollywood movie is a favorite leisure pastime in South Asia. South Asians abroad, in fact, are often even more fanatical in collecting and viewing Bollywood movies, an activity which transports them, at least vicariously, back to their homeland. Popular film songs often form the musical backdrop for various festive occasions in South Asia, from weddings to political rallies.

K.R. Venugopal and L.M. Patnaik (Eds.): ICIP 2012, CCIS 292, pp. 129–138, 2012.
© Springer-Verlag Berlin Heidelberg 2012

Not surprisingly, songs are a crucial determinant and integral part of a Bollywood movie's success. In fact, a main purpose of the plot line is to provide a sequence of pegs on which to hang song sequences. Typically, there are usually three to ten songs in a Bollywood movie of two to three hours, with every song having length of three to ten minutes. Songs in Bollywood movies are mixed depending on their genre. Generally, a movie song falls in one of three categories: romantic, tragic, and pop music song. Like film making, there are few conventions followed for song making as well. For example, a tragic song can have low or no actor movement with long short duration in order to capture sad expression of on-screen actor, whereas for a pop song, there should be high actor movement with short shot duration in order to increase excitement in the pop song. The features of romantic songs are generally closer to tragic songs however with increased actor movement.

The popularity of Bollywood songs causes a separate industry to exist for production their cassettes and CD's containing songs from many Bollywood movies. These CD's and cassettes have a huge sale in India as well as other countries where Indian movies are screened. There are also many online databases hosting these songs. A Bollywood songs CD/cassette generally contains songs from many movies and these songs are mainly included based upon their genre. For examples, there are many CDs comprising of multiple tragic songs from different movies. It would be a difficult task for a CD/cassette producer to extract all the songs of a particular genre from a music databases. An automatic song genre identifier may help in production of such CDs and cassettes.

The search and indexing of online music databases like YouTube can also be made efficient with automatic genre identifier. An online user may easily query a music database for his/her desired genres. Currently, the genre of a song is identified by the text caption added with a song. However, if that caption is not reflecting genre of a song, in current databases, the genre of a song become impossible to identify. In video sharing websites where songs are uploaded by users, it is not feasible to expect them to add genre information every time they upload, thus currently songs genre is not helping in indexing and search. In this paper, we propose an approach to identify genre of Bollywood movie songs using visual features of the song video. W use shot duration and actor movement to classify songs in three genres: pop, tragic, and romantic. The proposed approach shows that there is a strong relationship between song genre and video of a song.

The rest of the paper is organized as follows. The related work on genre identification is given in Section 2. The details of the proposed framework are given in Section 3. An entropy based video shot duration calculation is discussed in Section 4. The mechanism of actor movement estimation in a video is presented in Section 5. Section 6 shows the experimental results, and finally Section 7 concludes the paper.

2   Related Work

The content-based music genre classification in music information retrieval (MIR) has gained a substantial attention in recent times. It mainly uses content-based acoustic features of a music peace to classify in a genre. These features are classified into timber texture features, rhythmic content features, and pitch content features as explained by Shen et al. in [1]. The timber features are borrowed from the research done in speech recognition field. It conveys the timber information of song's vocal component. Rabiner et al. in [2] calculated these features by performing short time Fourier transform on audio frames of a music peace. Shen et al. in [1] in their work, proposed Linear Perdition Cepstral Coefficient (LPCC) to estimate timber texture features. The other features which convey timber information are zero crossing, spectral roll off, spectral flux, and Mel-frequency Cepstral Coefficient (MFCC).

The rhythmic content features contains information about regularity of rhythm, beat and tempo information [3]. The rhythm, tempo and beat are found clear parameters to differentiate between different genres of songs. Finally, pitch content describes the harmonic information of a song. Tolonen et al. in [4] proposed an algorithm for features extraction that are used for modeling of music pitch features.

Tao et al. [3] proposed a new feature extraction method for music genre classification using Daubechies Wavelet Coefficient Histogram (DWCH). They claim that local and global information of a music signal can be computed by DWCHs that helps in genre identification of a song. They used Support Vector Machine (SVM) on DWCHs to classify a music audio song in ten genres including blues, classical, country, disco, jazz, metal, pop, hiphop, reggae, and rock. Their proposed accuracies in different genres are ranging from 91% to 98%. The same features are also used by Shen et al. [1] to classify songs in different genre that help them in singer identification.

Shahram et al. [5] used beat related features to classify traditional Malay music in different genres. They have tested their results with selected features on a range of classifiers and found out the best results that is 88.6% with Multi-layer Perceptron (MLP) classifier. Tzanetakis et al. [6] selected three feature sets for representing timber texture, rhythmic content and pitch content. They described a real time frame-based classification technique to classify song in ten music genres. They achieved classification accuracy of 61% on their selected dataset. These and various other attempts at music genre identification has mainly focused on audio features because most of the western songs are either recorded in a studio or in a concert thus their video has no relation with genre of song. However, because Bollywood songs are part of a movie thus every song has a video that conveys a lot of meaning about the genre of song. Moreover, the genre like jazz, country, blue, and rock are rarely observed in these movie songs, thus there is a need to re-define genres for Bollywood movie songs.

With the analysis of many Bollywood movies, it has been observed that a movie song falls in one of three categories: romantic, tragic, and pop. A romantic song is mixed with a romantic scene of movie. On the other hand, a sad scene like funeral or break-up scene of hero and heroine may be accompanied by a tragic song. A pop music song can be added in dancing scenes to add fun and excitement in movie.

3   Video Assisted Song Genre Identifier System

Hindi movie songs can be broadly classified in two major genres: pop and classic. The songs belonging to pop genre are high paced songs with a lot of actor movement and camera motion in it and targeted toward young audience. In order to keep the pace of a song high, the shot duration is kept very low in pop songs. The classic genre songs are mostly slow paced with low actor movement and camera motion. The slow pace of classic songs is accomplished by high shot duration. These are mostly targeted towards mature audience and having strong lyrics.

The classic genre is further classified in two sub-genres: romantic and tragic. A romantic genre song is mostly mixed in a movie with a love scene between actor and actress. On the other hand, a tragic song in a movie can be found in sad scenes like during the break-up of hero-heroine. Table 1 shows different video features observed in songs belonging to these three genres. It can be observed

Table 1. Video Features of Song Genres

Song Genre	Shot Duration	Actor Movement	Camera Motion
pop	low	high	high
romantic	high	meduim	low
tragic	high	low	low

from Table 1 that pop songs can be separated from other two genres on the basis of shot duration. In classic songs it is usual to see shots of longer duration greater than 10 seconds. However in pop songs, the shot duration is mostly observed in a range of 2 to 5 seconds. Although it is practice of keeping shot duration high in classic songs, however all the shots do not have high duration. There are many shots in classic songs with duration less than a second. These unusual shots of low duration show that a simple mean calculation might not prove a good indicator to separate classic songs from pop. Thus we used standard deviation to separate two genres.

Given a song S, the shot duration average $Av_{sd}(S)$ and shot duration deviation $Std_{sd}(S)$ are defined as,

$$Av_{shotDuration}(S) = \frac{\sum_{k=1}^{n}(D_k)}{n}. \tag{1}$$

$$Std_{shotDuration}(S) = \sqrt{\frac{\sum_{k=1}^{n}(D_k - Av_{shotDuration}(S))^2}{n}}. \tag{2}$$

Where n represents number of the shots in a song, and D_k represents the shot duration of kth shot. Thus given a song S, its genre is defined as,

$$Genre(S) = \begin{cases} classic \text{ if } Std_{shotDuration}(S) \geq t_1; \\ \\ pop \quad \text{ if } Std_{shotDuration}(S) < t_1. \end{cases}$$

Where t_1 is threshold for shot duration. Its value is set through experiments performed on 105 songs belonging different genres.

The next step is to break classic genre songs in two sub-genres: tragic and romantic. As discussed earlier, the actor movement is a good separator between tragic and romantic genre songs. In tragic songs, all the efforts are done to capture the emotional expressions of actor, thus an actor rarely moves in a shot. On the other hand, during romantic songs, hero and heroine may move around in a field to perform some light dance steps that cause their movement in shots.

Given a classic song S, its sub-genre is defined as,

$$Genre(S) = \begin{cases} romantic \text{ if } Av_{actorMovement}(S) \geq t_2; \\ \\ tragic \quad \text{ if } Av_{actorMovement}(S) < t_2. \end{cases}$$

Figure 1 summarizes the whole process of genre identification in a flow chart. Sections 4 and 5 describe the processes of computing shot duration and actor movement in a song.

4   Shot Duration Calculation

For shot duration calculation, we need to determine shot boundaries. There are many attempts in literature to detect shot boundary in a video. We use the approach proposed in [7,8,9]. However, rather using simple RGB color values, we use image entropy to detect shot boundary as proposed by Baber et al. in [10]. The entropy for an image i, quantized to M levels is defined as,

$$E_i = \sum_{k=0}^{M} P_k log_2 \frac{1}{P_k}$$

$$= -\sum_{k=0}^{M} P_k log_2 P_k. \tag{3}$$

where p_k is the probability of ith quantize level being used and obtained from histogram of the pel intensities.

The process of shot detection is depicted in Figure 2. A frame is considered shot boundary if,

- its image entropy value is considerably different (greater than threshold t_1) from previous frame or,
- its image entropy values is considerably different (greater than threshold t_2) from previous shot boundary.

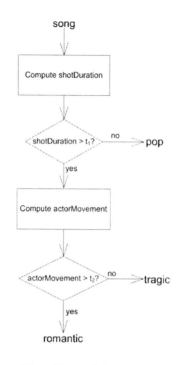

Fig. 1. Flow Chart of Genre Identification

The values for t_1 and t_2 are set through experiments performed on 105 popular Bollywood songs.

After detecting shot boundaries, the next step is to calculate shot duration. The duration of a shot is difference between its start time and end time. The calculated shot durations are used in equation 1 and 2 to compute overall shot duration average and standard deviation that is then used to classify a song in either pop or classic genre.

5   Actor Movement Estimation

The actor movement in classic songs is used to differentiate between tragic and romantic songs. As discussed earlier, its values are higher in the romantic songs than the tragic songs due to possible dance sequence in these songs. In order to compute actor movement we capture three images per second from all the shots of a song and perform simple threshold based image comparison.

We break every image taken from shots in 48 regions. These sub-images (region) from two subsequent images are compared to find out their difference. Given two images, $image_i$ and $image_j$, their difference is defined as,

$$D = \sum_{r=1}^{48} ABS(image_i(r) - image_j(r)). \tag{4}$$

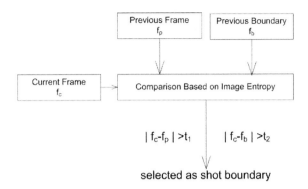

Fig. 2. Shot Boundary Detection

where r represents a region in an image. The actor movement M in a shot with n images is average difference between all images in a shot and is defined as,

$$M = \frac{\sum_{i=1}^{n} D_i}{n}. \tag{5}$$

Figure 3 shows the actor movement in romantic and tragic songs. Figure 5, and Figure 5 show two consecutive images of a romantic song. In this song, due to the existence of dance sequence, there is a lot of actress movement that causes change in many regions of the image grid. On the other hand, Figure 5, and Figure 5, show two consecutive images of a tragic song. The movements of actors is nearly zero. It causes very low changes in any region of the whole image grid. We use this change to differentiate between romantic and tragic songs.

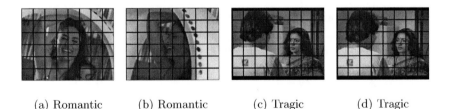

(a) Romantic   (b) Romantic   (c) Tragic   (d) Tragic

Fig. 3. Actor Movement: Romantic vs Tragic Songs

6   Experimental Results

Given the current inconsistent state of genre information with Bollywood movie songs, we had a trouble of deciding manually the actual genre of the songs selected for the experimental purpose. In order to solve this problem, we selected a total of 200 Bollywood movie songs and conducted an online survey from 50

Table 2. Video Assisted Genre Identification Results

Genre	No. of Songs	Correctly Identified	Accuracy (%)
Pop	35	33	94.29
Romantic	35	31	88.57
Tragic	35	30	85.71
Total	**105**	**94**	**89.52**

respondents. The respondents were Bollywood music lovers. We requested them to listen a few seconds of every song and decide the genre of a song: romantic, tragic, or pop. We then selected 105 undisputed songs for the automatic genre identification purpose. The undisputed songs were those, for which all the respondents agreed on one genre.

There were 35 songs from each genre in the dataset of 105 songs. First of all, we tested our dataset using different audio features proposed in music genre identification literature. The selected audio features were zero crossing rate, spectral flux, spectral centroid, MFCC, and spectral roll off point. We selected 20% songs of each genre for training the classifier. We tested the remaining 80% of the dataset using different classifiers and best results were observed using SVM. We used LibSVM implementation for SVM classifier proposed by Chang et al. in [11]. We also tested same dataset on genre identification approach based on Daubechies Wavelet Coefficient Histograms (DWCH) proposed by Tao et al. in [3]. The experimental results are shown Table 2, 3, and 4 for different configurations. The best results (89.52%) were achieved using video assisted genre identification. The lower accuracies on traditional genre identification approaches might be because of the difference between composition of western and Hindi music. There is difference in musical instruments used in different genres in western music and Hindi music. For example, the use of drum is mostly in pop music songs in western music, whereas in Hindi music, it is found in all three genres. This is reason why, audio features are not true indicators of song genres in Hindi music.

Table 3. Genre Identification Results Using DWCH with SVM Classifier

Genre	No. of Songs	Correctly Identified	Accuracy (%)
Pop	27	22	81.48
Romantic	27	20	74.07
Tragic	27	19	70.37
Total	**81**	**61**	**75.31**

Table 4. Genre Identification Results Using ZCR+Spectral Flux+Spectral Rolloff+MFCC+Spectral Centroid on SVM Classifier

Genre	No. of Songs	Correctly Identified	Accuracy (%)
Pop	27	22	81.48
Romantic	27	18	66.67
Tragic	27	19	70.37
Total	**81**	**59**	**72.84**

7 Conclusions

Song genre information, in its current implementation, is a textual caption associated with each song. This information is usually inserted manually, initially by the song creator. This information may not be available with those songs which are uploaded to online music databases by ordinary users. Thus, in order to index online music databases, there is a dire need of an automatic mechanism of identifying genre information for a music peace.

A Bollywood movie song is associated with a part of movie video that has strong relationship with genre of the song. For example, if a song is mixed in a movie during a sad scene, it must be a tragic song. In similar way, a pop or romantic song might be mixed in a movie during love or celebration scenes.

There are certain video making rules for the movie songs that are followed every time a new songs is recorded. For example, a tragic song video might have long shot duration and low actor movement. On the other hand, for a pop song the shot duration may be kept low with high actor movement that is caused by dance sequences availability in these songs. In romantic songs, mostly the shot duration is found high with medium actor movement although it is not as high as in pop songs.

In this paper, we presented a video based song genre identification system that uses these song making rules in Bollywood movies. We tested the proposed approach on a dataset of 105 movie songs and achieved correct genre identification on 89.52% songs that is much better than the approaches based on audio features when tested on the same dataset.

References

1. Shen, J., Shepherd, J., Cui, B., Tan, K.L.: A Novel Framework for Efficient Automated Singer Identification in Large Music Databases. ACM Transactions on Information Systems 27(3), 1–31 (2009)
2. Rabiner, L., Juang, B.: Fundamentals of Speech Recognition. Prentice-Hall, N.J. (1993)
3. Tao, L., Ogihara, M., Li, Q.: A Comparative Study on Content-Based Music Genre Classification. In: 26th Annual International ACM SIGIR Conference on Research and Development in Informaion Retrieval. ACM, New York (2003)

4. Tolonen, T., Karjalainen, M.: A Computationally Efficient Multi Pitch Analysis Model. IEEE Trans. Speech Aud. Process 8(4), 708–716 (2000)

5. Shahram, G., Shyamala, D., Noris, M.N., Sulaiman, M.N., Udzir, N.I.: A Comprehensive Study in Benchmarking Feature Selection and Classification Approaches for Traditional Malay Music Genre Classification. In: DMIN, pp. 71–77 (2008)

6. Tzanetakis, G., Cook, P.: Musical Genre Classification of Audio Signals. IEEE Transactions on Speech and Audio Processing 10(5) (July 2002)

7. Zhang, H.J., Kankanhalli, A., Smoliar, S.W.: Automatic Partitioning of Full-Motion Video. Multimedia System 1, 10–28 (1993)

8. Zhang, H.J., Low, C.Y., Smoliar, S.W.: Video Parsing and Browsing using Compressed Data. Multimedia Tools and Appl. 1, 89–111 (1995)

9. Anil, J., Aditya, V., Wei, X.: Query by Video Clip. In: International Conference on Pattern Recognition (ICPR 1998), pp. 90–99 (1998)

10. Baber, J., Afzulpurkar, N., Dailey, M.N., Bakhtyar, M.: Shot Boundary Detection from Videos Using Entropy and Local Descriptor. In: Proceedings of 17th International Conference Digital Signal Processing, pp. 6–8 (July 2011)

11. Chang, C.C., Lin, C.J.: LIBSVM: A Library for Support Vector Machines (2001), http://www.csie.ntu.edu.tw/~cjlin/libsvm

Color Image Quantization Quality Assessment

Mohammed Hassan and Chakravarthy Bhagvati

Department of Computer and Information Sciences, University of Hyderabad,
Hyderabad 500 046, India
mohdnow@yahoo.com

Abstract. In this paper we present a novel objective image quality measure that fully uses image's color information for the quality assessment of color quantized images. The proposed measure models any color quantization distortion as a combination of three similarities: color similarity, edge similarity, and structural similarity. We validate the performance of the proposed measure with an extensive subjective study involving 875 color quantized images and show that the new measure outperforms recent state-of-the-art image quality measures in the quality assessment of color quantization distortion.

Keywords: Color Quantization, Objective Image Quality Assessment, Subjective Image Quality Assessment.

1 Introduction

Image quality assessment is an important tool in image processing systems. Image quality assessment methods can be classified into two categories: subjective and objective. The subjective image quality assessment methods are accurate in estimating the visual quality of an image because they are carried out by human subjects but are costly process which requires a large number of observers and takes a significant time. On the other hand the objective image quality assessment methods are computer based methods that can automatically predict the perceived image quality. Hence the objective image quality assessment methods gained more popularity.

Originally, color quantization has been used to satisfy the display hardware constraints that allow a limited number of colors to be displayed simultaneously. Today the original motivation of color quantization has changed due to availability of inexpensive full color displays. However, color quantization is still an important problem in the fields of image processing and computer graphics, it can be used in mobile and hand-held devices where memory is usually small [1], for low-cost color display and printing devices where only a small number of colors can be displayed or printed simultaneously [2], it also can be used in lossy compression techniques [3]. Another aspect of importance of color quantization is that the human visual system can't perceive more than 20,000 different colors at any given time [4] while a full color image may contain up to 16 million different colors, this large number of colors makes it difficult to handle a variety of color-based tasks such as computing histograms or other useful statistics.

K.R. Venugopal and L.M. Patnaik (Eds.): ICIP 2012, CCIS 292, pp. 139–148, 2012.
© Springer-Verlag Berlin Heidelberg 2012

Many researchers have contributed significant research in the design of objective image quality methods starting from the widely used mean square error (MSE) metric and its correlated peak signal to noise ratio (PSNR). The weighted signal to noise ratio (WSNR) [5] simulates the human visual system properties by filtering both the reference and distorted images with contrast sensitivity function and then compute the SNR. Miyahara [6] proposed a picture quality scale (PQS) based on three distortion factors; namely the amount, location and structure of error. Wang and Bovik [7] proposed a new universal image quality index (UQI) and its improved form the single-scale structural similarity index (SSIM) [8] by modeling the image distortion as the combination of loss of luminance, contrast, and correlation. In [9] the single-scale structural similarity index was extended in to a multi-scale structural similarity index (MSSIM) that works in multi scales of an image and achieved a better result than SSIM. Information fidelity criterion (IFC) [10] and visual information fidelity (VIF) [11] both are based on information-theory in which the distorted image is modeled as a sequence of passing the reference images through distortion channels, and quantify the visual quality as a mutual information between the test image and the reference image. Shnayderman [12] explored the feasibility of singular value decomposition (SVD) for quality measurement. In [13] a two a two staged wavelet based visual signal to noise ratio (VSNR) was proposed based on the low-level and the mid-level properties of human vision.

In this paper we present a new image quality measure for the quality assessment of color quantized images which is based on color, edge, and structural similarities. Section 2 describes the proposed color quantization quality measure. In section 3, the experimental data is presented including the subjective tests. The results are discussed in Section 4. We conclude the paper in Section 5.

2   The Proposed Color Quantization Quality Measure

In color quantization, three main factors define the quality of color quantized images namely: how close the set of representative colors to the original set of colors is, the presence of spurious edges, and the overall image structure. Based on these main factors our new index is proposed by modeling any color image quantization distortion as a combination of three similarities: color similarity, edge similarity, and structure similarity. For two image signals x and y, the proposed quality metric is defined as

$$CQM(x,y) = C^{\alpha}(x,y) \cdot E^{\beta}(x,y) \cdot S^{\gamma}(x,y). \tag{1}$$

Where C is the color similarity, E is the edge similarity, and S is the structure similarity. α, β and γ are parameters to define the relative importance of the three similarities. The optimal values of the parameters are $\alpha = 0.05$, $\beta = 0.7$ and $\gamma = 0.7$. The three statistical features are measured locally by moving a 3×3 window through all the image pixels starting from the top left pixel to the bottom right one.

2.1 Color Similarity

The CIELAB color space is designed to improve the organization of colors that are not uniform in a linear color space so that Euclidean distances between different colors in the CIELAB correspond approximately to perceived color differences. A useful rule of thumb in CIELAB color space is that any two colors can be distinguished if the Euclidean distance between these two colors is greater than threshold 3 [14]. This threshold is known as the Just Noticeable Color Difference (JNCD) threshold. Therefore all the colors within a sphere of radius equal to the JNCD threshold are perceptually indistinguishable from each other. The Color similarity can be obtained by the following steps:

1. The reference and the test images are preprocessed by spatial filtering to simulate the spatial blurring by the human visual system in a way that the filtering operation to the color image affects only the fine-patterned colors [15].
2. Then, the reference and the test images are transformed to the CIELAB color space.
3. After that the color distortion profile is created by locally averaging the number of colors in the reference image that are undistinguishable from their corresponding colors in the test image based on the JNCD threshold 3.

2.2 Edge Similarity

Difference vector (DV) edge detection operator[16] is a 3×3 well-known color based edge detector in image processing. Each pixel represents a vector in the RGB color space and the maximum gradient is calculated across the central pixel in each of the four possible directions (0, 45, 90, and 135 deg). The gradients are defined as:

$$|\nabla f|_{d\,\deg} = \|U_{d\,\deg} - V_{d\,\deg}\|. \tag{2}$$

Where $d=$ 0, 45, 90, 135 and $\|\cdot\|$ denotes the L_2 norm, U and V are RGB color vectors in the neighborhood of the central pixel. Then the difference vector is given by

$$DV = \max(|\nabla f|_{0\,\deg}, |\nabla f|_{45\,\deg}, |\nabla f|_{90\,\deg}, |\nabla f|_{135\,\deg}). \tag{3}$$

A threshold can be applied to the maximum gradient vector to locate edges. Then the edge similarity of two image signals x and y is given as:

$$E = \frac{2E_x E_y + C_1}{E_x^2 + E_y^2 + C_1}. \tag{4}$$

Where E_x and E_y are the edge responses of applying the DV edge detector over the image signals x and y respectively. C_1 is a stabilizing constant to a void division by zero.

2.3   Structural Similarity

Structure of an image signal is defined by removing the luminance (mean) and contrast (variance) normalization. Thus the structure similarity is defined as [8]

$$S(x,y) = \frac{\sigma_{xy} + C_2}{\sigma_x \sigma_x + C_2}. \tag{5}$$

Where σ_x and σ_y are the sample standard deviations of x and y, respectively, σ_{xy} is the sample correlation coefficient between x and y, and C_2 is a stabilizing constant.

Fig. 1. Some of the Reference Images used in the Study

3   Subjective Experiments Setup

Our human subjective evaluation data [17] contains 25 reference images collected from the Internet based on the number of segments and number of distinct colors. Those images reflect a variety of image contents includes important objects, uniform regions, slowly varying color gradients, edges, and high level of details. Fig. 1 shows some of the reference images used in the study. All images in our database are of size 512x512 pixels for the purpose of carrying out subjective experiments. Each of the resized images has been quantized into seven levels (4, 8, 16, 32, 64, 128, and 256 colors) using five different color image quantization algorithms that are popular in literature. The quantization algorithms are as follows: Kmeans algorithm [18], Median Cut algorithm [19], Wu's Algorithm [20], Octree [21], and Dekker's SOM [22].

To evaluate the quality of the quantized images a subjective quality test is used in which a number of human subjects are asked to judge the quality of the sequence images. In our tests we followed the recommendations given by ITU [23] that define how to carry out subjective quality tests. A group of twenty two undergraduate students participated in our psychometric experiment. The majority of the subjects were males and they were non-experts with image quality assessment. The reliability of the assessors was qualitatively evaluated by checking their behavior when reference/reference pairs where reliable subjects are expected to give evaluations very close to the maximum point in the quality scale.

Before carrying out the experiments the observers were briefly explained what they are going to see, what they have to evaluate and how they express their opinion, the grading scale, the sequence, and timing. The subjects also have been shown some examples in how to evaluate the quality of quantized images; those examples approximate the range of quality of the images for different quantization levels. Images in the training phase were different from those used in the actual experiment.

Since fidelity of the quantized images to the reference images has to be evaluated, simultaneous double stimulus for continuous evaluation (SDSCE) method [23] was used in conducting the psychometric experiment where a set of subjects is watching simultaneously the two images (the reference and the quantized images). The observers are asked to assess the overall quantized image quality with respect to the reference image of each presentation by simply dragging a slider on a quality scale. The quality scale which is of range [0,100] was labeled and divided into five equal categories: "Bad," "Poor," "Fair," "Good," and "Excellent." The position of the slider reflects the rate given by the observer for that image and its position was reset after each presentation.

There are 875 test images and each session should not last more than 30 minutes [23], therefore overall subjective tests were divided into six sessions (175 test images for each session). Five dummy images were added at the beginning of the first session and not considered in the calculation; their purpose is to stabilize the subjects to the rating process. Subjects were shown images in a random order and this order is unique for each subject.

Before starting the analysis of the data, a screening of the subjective raw values was conducted [23] to eliminate observers with unstable values. The generalized ESD many-outlier procedure [24] was run twice to detect outliers within the subjective raw data. About 2.66 % of subjective raw data was considered as outlier and one of the observers was rejected.

To calculate Mean Opinion Score (MOS), the subjective raw data is first converted to Z-score (after outliers removal) to minimize the variation between individual subjective values due to not using the full range of quality scale by the different subjects during the image quality rating process[25], then the final MOS for each test image is obtained by averaging all Z-scores given to that image by all subjects.

4   Results and Discussions

In this section, the performance of the proposed image quality measure in terms of the ability of predicting the subjective ratings is analyzed. The proposed quality measure was applied to the set of images used in the psychometric experiment and the results were compared to the subjective mean opinion scores. For comparison, the same set of images were presented to eight well-known objective image quality measures that are commonly used and their implementations are publicly available on the Internet namely: Peak Signal to Noise Ratio (PSNR), Weighted Signal to Noise Ratio (WSNR) [5], Universal Image Quality Index(UQI) [7], Structural Similarity Index (SSIM) [8], Multiscale Structural Similarity Index (MSSIM) [9], Information Fidelity Criterion (IFC) [10], Visual Information Fidelity(VIF) [11], and Visual Signal-to-Noise Ratio (VSNR) [13].

The scores given by an objective image quality measure (IQM) are transferred into a predicted MOS to map the IQM's scores into the range of the subjective MOS and to remove any nonlinearity between them using non-linear regression [23]. The function chosen for regression is a four parameters logistic function [26]:

$$MOS_p(Q) = \frac{p_1 - p_2}{1 + \exp\left(\frac{Q - p_3}{p_4}\right)} + p_2. \tag{6}$$

Where MOS_p is the predicted MOS, Q is the quality rating given by the measure, and p_1, p_2, p_3, and p_4 are parameters.

Table 1. Pearson's Correlation Coefficient between Subjective MOS and MOS_p

	PSNR	WPSNR	UQI	SSIM	MSSIM	IFC	VIF	VSNR	CQM
SOM	0.956	0.942	0.732	0.929	0.935	0.806	0.950	0.949	**0.967**
Median	0.965	0.935	0.772	0.940	0.934	0.783	0.938	0.929	**0.969**
Kmeans	0.960	0.940	0.662	0.911	0.910	0.791	0.951	0.943	**0.971**
Octree	0.970	0.957	0.804	0.935	0.944	0.869	0.967	0.955	**0.981**
Wu	0.957	0.945	0.720	0.930	0.940	0.812	0.957	0.953	**0.964**
All Data	0.945	0.920	0.728	0.913	0.917	0.805	0.942	0.926	**0.966**

Table 2. Spearman's Rank Order Correlation Coefficient between MOS and MOS_p

	PSNR	WPSNR	UQI	SSIM	MSSIM	IFC	VIF	VSNR	CQM
SOM	0.950	0.934	0.742	0.921	0.934	0.812	0.945	0.944	**0.962**
Median	0.961	0.932	0.774	0.938	0.931	0.790	0.936	0.925	**0.962**
Kmeans	0.952	0.933	0.679	0.909	0.912	0.798	0.946	0.938	**0.961**
Octree	0.965	0.952	0.802	0.934	0.950	0.873	0.962	0.954	**0.980**
Wu	0.953	0.941	0.728	0.929	0.939	0.816	0.955	0.952	**0.960**
All Data	0.939	0.916	0.735	0.911	0.918	0.810	0.938	0.923	**0.960**

Table 3. Root Mean Square Error

	PSNR	WPSNR	UQI	SSIM	MSSIM	IFC	VIF	VSNR	CQM
SOM	8.540	9.801	19.871	10.831	10.334	17.283	9.127	9.168	**7.385**
Median	8.004	10.908	19.511	10.490	10.970	19.099	10.609	11.372	**7.592**
Kmeans	8.678	10.603	23.205	12.787	12.862	18.938	9.586	10.304	**7.423**
Octree	7.008	8.383	17.243	10.302	9.532	14.332	7.409	8.629	**5.579**
Wu	8.815	9.974	21.147	11.176	10.390	17.774	8.815	9.187	**8.087**
All Data	9.774	11.722	20.574	12.209	11.933	17.811	10.100	11.289	**7.716**

Tables 1-3 show Pearson's correlation coefficient, Spearman's rank order correlation coefficient, and root mean square error between the subjective MOS and the ratings given by each objective IQM after nonlinear mapping. It is clear from those tables that CQM outperforms all image quality measures included in this study on all datasets.

To evaluate the statistical significance of the performance of CQM over the other IQMs, the F-test was performed on the set of residuals (prediction errors) from each IQM. This test was deemed to be a more informative measure of the prediction accuracy of an image quality measure [23]. For variances σ_A^2 and σ_B^2 of two metrics A and B respectively; the F statistic is defined as $F = \frac{\sigma_A^2}{\sigma_B^2}$. If $F > F_{critical}$ $(F < 1/F_{critical})$ then it signifies that at a given confidence level, metric A has significantly larger (smaller) residuals than metric B. The $F_{critical}$

Table 4. Normality Test for Residuals (Skewness/Kurtosis)

	SOM	Median	Kmeans	Octree	Wu	All Data
PSNR	-0.08/4.14	0.25/4.0	-0.13/4.16	0.02/3.6	0.48/4.3	0.13/3.6
WSNR	-0.22/4.22	0.29/3.5	0.06/4.2	-0.19/3.86	0.05/4.8	0.13/3.7
UQI	-0.21/2.71	-0.16/3.05	0.10/2.7	0.39/3.4	-0.13/3.02	-0.01/3.01
SSIM	-0.30/3.81	-0.47/4.80	-0.50/4.12	-0.15/3.67	-0.06/4.81	-0.11/4.01
MSSIM	-0.66/4.50	-0.64/4.49	-0.39/5.80	0.14/4.1	-0.96/6.05	-0.35/4.94
IFC	0.01/3.3	0.40/3.5	0.05/3.6	0.63/4.3	0.01/3.7	0.12/3.6
VIF	-0.37/4.02	0.16/4.3	-0.43/4.55	0.94/5.7	-0.22/4.73	-0.04/4.47
VSNR	-0.17/3.50	0.41/3.9	0.14/4.7	-0.20/4.50	0.17/4.9	0.28/3.9
CQM	-0.09/2.52	0.09/2.7	-0.10/2.70	0.06/2.8	-0.02/2.59	-0.07/2.97

Table 5. The F-test Statistics for each IQM against CQM

	SOM	Median	Kmeans	Octree	Wu	All Data
$\boldsymbol{F_{critical}}$	1.284	1.284	1.284	1.284	1.284	1.118
$\boldsymbol{1/F_{critical}}$	0.779	0.779	0.779	0.779	0.779	0.895
PSNR	**1.337**	1.112	**1.367**	**1.578**	1.188	**1.604**
WSNR	**1.761**	**2.064**	**2.040**	**2.258**	**1.521**	**2.308**
UQI	**7.240**	**6.605**	**9.772**	**9.552**	**6.837**	**7.109**
SSIM	**2.151**	**1.909**	**2.967**	**3.410**	**1.910**	**2.503**
MSSIM	**1.958**	**2.088**	**3.002**	**2.919**	**1.650**	**2.392**
IFC	**5.478**	**6.329**	**6.509**	**6.599**	**4.830**	**5.328**
VIF	**1.528**	**1.953**	**1.668**	**1.763**	1.188	**1.713**
VSNR	**1.541**	**2.244**	**1.927**	**2.392**	**1.290**	**2.140**
CQM	1.000	1.000	1.000	1.000	1.000	1.000

is computed based on the number of residuals and the confidence level [13]. In our study, we used 95% confidence level. The F-test assumes that the residuals are normally distributed; the results of the normality test are given in Table 4 based on the rule of thumb that a set of values is reasonably normally distributed if its kurtosis and skewness values between 2 to 4, and -1 to 1 respectively [26] (the Normal distribution has a kurtosis of 3 and a skewness of zero).

Table 5 lists the F statistics of the F-test carried out on the set of residuals of each IQM against the set of residuals of CQM. Values with $F > F_{critical}$ which are shown in boldface signify that an IQM from the row has significantly larger residuals (greater prediction errors) than CQM for the dataset from the column. Thus in terms of statistical significance, CQM has smaller prediction errors than all other image quality measures for all datasets except that it is indistinguishable for Wu's quantizer dataset from PSNR and VIF, and for Median cut dataset from PSNR.

5   Conclusion and Future Work

In this paper, we presented a novel image quality measure for the quality assessment of color quantized images based on the main factors that define the quality of any color quantized image. Our proposed measure models any image distortion as combination of three similarities: color similarity, edge similarity, and structural similarity. The performance of the proposed measure was validated with an extensive subjective study involving 875 color quantized images and the results show that the new measure outperforms recent state-of-the-art image quality assessment measures. Future work includes using this new application-specific image quality measure to guide the process of color quantization in a color quantization algorithm in order to improve the perceptual quality of the delivered color quantized images.

References

1. Rui, X., Chang, C., Srikanthan, T.: On the Initialization and Training Methods for Kohonen Self-Organizing Feature Maps in Color Image Quantization. In: First IEEE International Workshop on Electronic Design, Test and Applications, pp. 321-325 (2002)
2. Scheunders, P.: A Genetic C-means Clustering Algorithm Applied to Color Image Quantization. Pattern Recognition, 30, 859-866 (1997)
3. Velho, L., Gomes, J., Sobreiro, M.: Color Image Quantization by Pairwise Clustering. In: 10th Brazilian Symposium on Computer Graphics and Image Processing, IEEE Computer Society, pp. 203-207 (1997)
4. Sharma, G.: Digital Color Imaging. CRC Press (1996)
5. Mitsa, T., and Varkur, K.: Evaluation of Contrast Sensitivity Functions for the Formulation of Quality Measures Incorporated in Halftoning Algorithms. In: IEEE International Conference on Acoustic, Speech and Signal processing, 5, pp. 301-304 (1993)
6. Miyahara, M., Kotani, K., Algazi, V.R.: Objective Picture Quality Scale (PQS) for Image Coding. IEEE Transactions on Communications, 46, 1215-1226 (1998)
7. Wang, Z., Bovik, A. C.: A Universal Image Quality Index. IEEE Signal Processing Letters, 9, 81–84 (2002)
8. Wang, Z., Bovik, A.C., Sheikh, H.R., Simoncelli, E.P.: Image Quality Assessment: From error Measurement to Structural Similarity. IEEE Transaction on Image Processing, 13, 600-612 (2004)
9. Wang, Z., Simoncelli, E.P., Bovik, A.C.: Multiscale Structural Similarity for Image Quality Assessment. In: 37th IEEE Asilomar Conference on Signals, Systems and Computers, 2, pp. 1398-1402 (2003)
10. Sheikh, H. R., Bovik, A.C., de Veciana, G.: An Information Fidelity Criterion for Image Quality Assessment using Natural Scene Statistics. IEEE Transactions on Image Processing, 14, 2117-2128 (2005)
11. Sheikh, H. R., Bovik, A. C.: Image Information and Visual Quality. IEEE Transactions on Image Processing, 15, 430-444 (2006)
12. Shnayderman, A., Gusev, A., Eskicioglu, A.M.: An SVD-Based Gray-Scale Image Quality Measure for Local and Global Assessment. IEEE Transaction on Image Processing, 15, 422-429 (2006)
13. Chandler, D.M., Hemami, S. S.: VSNR: A Wavelet Base Visual Signal-to-Noise Ratio for Natural Images. IEEE Transaction on Image Processing, 16, 2284-2298 (2007)
14. Mahy, M., Van Eycken, L., Oosterlinck, A.: Evaluation of Uniform Color Spaces Developed after the Adoption of CIELAB and CIELUV. Journal of Color Research and Application, 19, 105-121 (1994)
15. Zhang, X., Wandell, B. A.: A spatial Extension of CIELAB for Digital Color Image Reproduction. In: The SID Symposium Technical Digest, 27, pp. 731-734 (1996)
16. Yang, Y.,: Colour Edge Detection and Segmentation using Vector Analysis, Master's Thesis, Electrical and Computer Engineering, University of Toronto, Toronto, Canada (1995)
17. Color Quantization Database Available, http://dcis.uohyd.ernet.in/~hassan/Color_Quantization_Database.rar
18. Lloyd, S. P.: Least Squares Quantization in PCM. IEEE Transactions on Information Theory, 28,129-137(1982)

19. Heckbert, P.: Color Image Quantization for Frame Buffer Display. ACM Trans. Computer Graphics (SIGGRAPH), 16, 297-307 (1982)
20. Wu, X.: Efficient Statistical Computations for Optimal Color Quantization. Graphics Gems, 11, J. Arvo, Ed. New York: Academic, 126-133 (1991)
21. Gervautz, M., and Purgathofer, W.: A Simple Method for Color Quantization: Octree Quantization. In: New Trends in Computer Graphics, Springer Verlag, Berlin, pp. 219-231 (1988)
22. Dekker, A. H.: Kohonen Neural Networks for Optimal Colour Quantization. Network: Computation in Neural Systems, 5, 351-367 (1994)
23. ITU-R: Methodology for the Subjective Assessment of the Quality for Television Pictures, Recommendation ITU-R BT.500-11. Geneva (2002)
24. Rosner, B.: Percentage Points for a Generalized ESD Many-Outlier Procedure. Technometrics, American Statistical Association, 25, 165-172 (1983)
25. Van Dijk, A. M, Martens, J-B, Watson, A.: Quality Assessment of Coded Images using Numerical Category Scaling. In: Proc. SPIE, 2451, pp. 90-101 (1995)
26. Sheikh, H. R., Sabir, M. F., Bovik, A. C.: A Statistical Evaluation of Recent Full Reference Image Quality Assessment Algorithms. IEEE Transactions on Image Processing, 15, 3441-3452 (2006)

Enhanced Approach
for 3d Model Reconstruction from Silhouettes

Ashwin Sekhar T.K. and V.K. Govindan

National Institute of Technology Calicut,
Calicut, Kerala, India
{ashwin_mcs10,vkg}@nitc.ac.in

Abstract. Silhouette based 3d reconstruction is the method to reconstruct the model of an object using calibrated images of the object taken in a controlled environment. Photos of the object are taken from different viewpoints and silhouettes are extracted from these photographs. Then these silhouettes are projected into a discretized 3d space made up of voxels to reconstruct the object model. Voxels projecting outside the silhouettes are carved out and others are retained. Extensive study has been done on this area and various methods are well documented in literature. This paper does not go into the subtleties of camera calibration and silhouette extraction. Rather it focuses on the actual reconstruction algorithm i.e., the projection of the silhouettes into the 3d space and the carving of the voxels. The main contribution of this paper comes in the form of a simple region testing approach. Also a simple visibility check is used to color the model assuming Lambertian surfaces. The algorithm provides improved time performance when compared to existing works of comparable reconstruction performance.

Keywords: 3d Reconstruction, Region Testing, Silhouette, Visibility, Voxel.

1 Introduction

3d model reconstruction from multiple images is an important and challenging problem in the field of computer vision. Silhouette based reconstruction is one of the methods to reconstruct the model from multiple views. Without prior information about the imaging environment and camera, this becomes a difficult task. Normally it is done in a controlled environment where images are taken from prior known camera coordinates [1]. After camera calibration, the silhouettes are extracted out from the calibrated images. Here, we do not go into the subtleties of camera calibration and silhouette extraction as they are research fields on their own. We use a dataset [2] which already contains calibrated images with the silhouettes extracted out and more concentration is laid on improving the actual reconstruction process.

The actual reconstruction process makes use of a silhouette based volume intersection algorithm to reconstruct the model. First, a bounding cube is calculated which is guaranteed to contain the whole object [1]. Then, this bounding

K.R. Venugopal and L.M. Patnaik (Eds.): ICIP 2012, CCIS 292, pp. 149–158, 2012.
© Springer-Verlag Berlin Heidelberg 2012

cube is discretized into voxels. Voxel size can be varied according to the resolution required. Smaller the voxel size, higher will be the resolution. Then each of these voxels is projected into the silhouettes, to determine whether they are inside the model or outside. If a voxel projects inside in all of the silhouettes then it is inside the model. If it projects outside in at least one of the silhouettes then it is outside and is carved out. To check whether a voxel is projecting inside or outside a silhouette, region testing is used. In normal region testing approaches, all the corners of the voxel will be projected back into the silhouettes. Here a simple region testing approach is used which varies according to the size of the voxels and will project only the center of the voxel into the silhouettes.

After carving out all unwanted voxels, we will be left with visual hull. The next step is to color the voxels. In order to color the voxels, we need to first determine the visibility of the voxels from the cameras. We need to take color from an image only if it is visible from the corresponding camera. In order to determine visibility, a simple visibility check is used. Coloring of the voxels is further simplified under the assumption of Lambertian surfaces.

This paper is organized as follows. Section 2 gives a brief literature survey of the existing methods. Section 3 describes the reconstruction algorithm in detail. The new region testing and coloring approaches are given in Sections 4 and 5 respectively. The implementation of the algorithm and the results are presented in Section 6. Section 7 concludes the paper.

2   Literature Survey

Automatic construction of 3D object models from multiple views is an important problem in computer vision. It involves taking photos of objects from different viewpoints and trying to infer the 3D surface structure of the object from these photographs. Fast and accurate reconstruction of 3D models is required in applications like interactive visualization of remote environments, virtual modification of a real scene, virtual reality applications, robot vision, product presentations, computer games etc. Considerable research has been done in this field. Several methods ranging from stereo imaging to space carving have developed over the course of last 20 years [3–9].

Stereo matching [3, 6] is one of the earliest methods that tries to establish correspondences between pixels in images in closely separated views and calculate depth maps of the pixels. But this method has the disadvantage that it cannot properly handle occlusions in the scene. It requires views very close to each other so that corresponding point matching can be done easily and effectively. The correspondences must be maintained over many views spanning large changes in viewpoint. Also, many partial models must often be computed with respect to a set of base viewpoints, and these surface patches must then be fused into a single, consistent model.

Volumetric scene reconstruction [4, 5] is based on computations in three-dimensional scene space in order to construct the volumes or surfaces in the world that are consistent with the input images. Volumetric scene modelling explicitly represents a world coordinate frame and the volume of space in which the scene occurs and makes occupancy decisions about whether a volumetric primitive contains objects in the scene. The volumetric primitive is normally a voxel. These methods allow widely separated views but generally depend on calibrated cameras to determine the absolute relationship between points in space and visual rays. Also volumetric approach can handle occlusions in scene better and there is no need of fusing partial models since the volume being reconstructed is always consistent with all views.

Camera Calibration is an important step in volumetric approach [10, 11]. Earlier methods used a controlled setup, normally in labs, so that determination of camera parameters can be done accurately. This controlled environment normally consists of a turn table and fixed camera. The turn table can be rotated to take the images of the object from different angles [1]. Zhang [10] proposed an easy method to calibrate camera which only requires the camera to observe a planar pattern shown at a few different orientations. Either the camera or the planar pattern can be freely moved. Compared with classical techniques, the proposed method is inexpensive as it does not require any special equipment.

Under the volumetric approaches, two important classifications are shape from silhouettes [1] and shape from photo-consistency [7–9]. Shape from silhouettes involves finding the silhouette of the objects from the views by separating out the foreground object from the background. Silhouettes are binary images where foreground is colored white and background is colored black. These silhouettes are projected into the 3D space and are intersected in order to get the visual hull. Visual hull is guaranteed to contain the object. This method has the disadvantage that it cannot detect concavities on the object surface as it does make use of the color information in the images. A complete silhouette based reconstruction system is described in [1].

Different methods are employed for silhouette extraction. First easy method is to set the background of the imaging environment to a known color. This color will be different from the color of the object so that it can be easily extracted out. Second method is to take two photographs of the object from the same viewpoint with varying backgrounds. The background in this case can be extracted out by image subtraction. Methods to extract out silhouettes from unknown backgrounds also exist. These methods generally employ segmentation techniques to segment out background and foreground separately.

Voxel coloring [7, 8] and space carving [9] are the volumetric approaches falling under the second category which makes use of color information in the images. These methods are based on the concept of photo-consistency. Photo consistency is the property where the color of a voxel in the 3D scene should be consistent with all the photographs. These methods can detect concavities on the surface. But determining the photo-consistency between images requires additional knowledge about camera models and scene model, i.e., camera positions, scene geometry, surface reflectance, and illumination.

The work described in this paper is a silhouette based 3d reconstruction algorithm. It has several points common to [1]. It differs mainly in the region testing and coloring of voxels. Here a simpler region testing criteria is used which depends upon the size of the voxels. Also a simpler coloring scheme is used under the assumption of Lambertian surfaces.

3 Reconstruction Algorithm

The first step in the reconstruction algorithm is to determine a bounding cube which is guaranteed to contain the object. After determining the bounding cube, the whole cube is discretized into voxels. Then all the voxels on the surface of the cube are initialized into a Surface Voxel List (SVL).

In this reconstruction algorithm, each silhouette is processed one by one. This avoids the need to store all the silhouettes in the memory at the same time hence saving memory space.

A single silhouette is taken at a time and all the voxels in the SVL are projected into this silhouette. If a voxel is projecting to the inside of the silhouette, it is retained in the SVL. If a voxel is not getting projected to inside, then it can be removed from the SVL as that voxel is guaranteed to be located outside the object model. And further the neighboring voxels of the removed voxel are added to the SVL if they are not already in the SVL. A marked flag is used to identify whether a voxel has already been added to the SVL or not. Once all the voxels in the SVL are projected into the silhouette, the next silhouette is taken and the projection is continued. After all the silhouettes are processed, all the remaining surface voxels will be consistent with all the silhouettes. These surface voxels will give the visual hull of the model. The pseudo code for this is given in Table 1.

4 Enhanced Approach to Region Testing

Region Testing is used to determine whether a voxel is projecting to the inside or outside of a silhouette. In normal region testing approaches, the eight corners of the voxel are first projected into the silhouette. Then a bounding rectangle of these corner projections is found out. Then the pixels in this bounding rectangle are evaluated. If majority of the pixels is falling within the silhouette then the voxel is considered to be projecting to inside else it is considered to be projecting to outside.

Projecting a 3d point onto the silhouettes normally requires 2 matrix multiplications [10]. Let X be the 3d point in the world coordinates. The relation between this point and its image projection x is given by the following formula.

$$x = X \ [R \ t] \ A. \tag{1}$$

$[R \ t]$ is called the extrinsic parameters. It is the rotation and translation matrices that relate the world coordinate system to the camera coordinate system. A is called the camera intrinsic matrix.

Table 1. Algorithm: 3d Reconstruction from Silhouettes

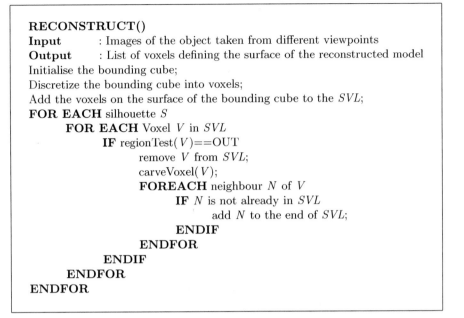

$$A = \begin{bmatrix} f_x & \alpha & u_0 \\ 0 & f_y & v_0 \\ 0 & 0 & 1 \end{bmatrix} \qquad (2)$$

u_0 and v_0 are the coordinates of the principal point, f_x and f_y are the focal lengths, and γ is the parameter describing the skew of the two image axes.

Hence, in normal region testing approaches a total of 16 matrix multiplications would be required, as all 8 corners of the voxel are projected. Also the determination of the bounding rectangle of these 8 corner projections is also necessary.

Here, we employ a simpler method. Only the voxel center is projected into the silhouette taking up only 2 matrix multiplications. Then the bounding square is found out in the following way. The bounding square will be centered at the voxel center projection. The side length s of the bounding square is determined as follows. The distance between the voxel center and camera origin, d, is first calculated. Let VC be the voxel center in the world coordinates. Let $CC = [0\ 0\ 0]$ be the camera center in the camera coordinates. This camera center is converted to the world coordinates by multiplying it with the inverse of the camera extrinsic parameters.

$$CC' = CC\ [R^T \quad -t]. \qquad (3)$$

The world coordinates of the camera center can be stored with the corresponding silhouette itself to avoid calculation each and every time. Then distance between the VC and CC' is found out and stored in d. The side, s of the bounding square is estimated as a function of voxel size S and distance of the voxel center from the camera center d.

$$s \; \alpha \; \frac{S}{d} \tag{4}$$

The larger the voxel size S, the longer will be the bounding square side length s since larger voxels will project to a larger area in the image. The bounding square side length will decrease with increasing d, as the projection area will decrease with increasing distances from the camera center. After determining the bounding square, the pixels in this square will be evaluated to determine whether the majority of them are inside or outside the silhouette.

Here only 2 matrix multiplications and a distance calculation are required as opposed to the 16 matrix multiplications in normal approaches. When the voxel size becomes very less, we need not even calculate the bounding square hence avoiding the distance calculation. We can just check whether the projection of the voxel center is inside the silhouette or not.

5   Coloring the Voxels

To color the voxels, the visibility of the voxels from the cameras needs to be estimated. We take the color from an image only if the voxel is visible from the corresponding camera. In order to determine the visibility of a voxel from a camera, a ray was traversed from the voxel center to the camera center in the world coordinates [12]. If the ray is not blocked by any other voxel, then the voxel is visible otherwise not visible. If visible, the voxel center is projected into the image from the camera and color of the projected pixel is taken as the color of the voxel. The basic idea in this method is shown in Figure 1.

A further simplification was done under the assumption of Lambertian surfaces. If a voxel is found to be visible from one camera, then no more visibility checks are performed. This is because the colors from all images will be the same if surface is Lambertian. Hence, we can stop with the color obtained from a single image.

A heuristic approach was used to color the voxels that were not visible from any of the cameras. To color such a voxel, the distance of the voxel center to each of the camera centers were calculated. Then the closest camera center to the voxel was found out and the color was taken from the corresponding image. The pseudo code is given in Table 2.

6   Implementation and Results

The reconstruction was implemented in C++ using the OpenCV library. For rendering the 3D structure of the model OpenGL library was used. The dataset

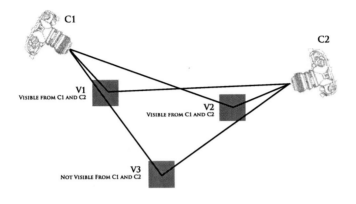

Fig. 1. Visibility of the Voxels from the Cameras

Table 2. Algorithm: Coloring the Voxels

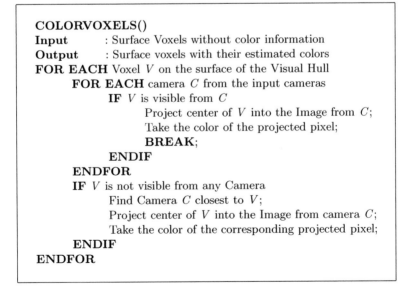

COLORVOXELS()
Input   : Surface Voxels without color information
Output   : Surface voxels with their estimated colors
FOR EACH Voxel V on the surface of the Visual Hull
    FOR EACH camera C from the input cameras
        IF V is visible from C
            Project center of V into the Image from C;
            Take the color of the projected pixel;
            BREAK;
        ENDIF
    ENDFOR
    IF V is not visible from any Camera
        Find Camera C closest to V;
        Project center of V into the Image from camera C;
        Take the color of the corresponding projected pixel;
    ENDIF
ENDFOR

images and corresponding camera parameters were taken from the Voxel Coloring Blog of Rob Hess. The dataset consists of 20 images of a bird doll. Figure 2 shows four of the dataset images.

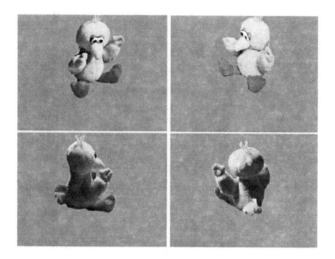

Fig. 2. Four of the Input Dataset Images

The dataset images were converted into silhouette data structures which had all the information required for reconstruction including the intrinsic and extrinsic parameters, world coordinates of the camera center, and a mask indicating which pixels of the image were within the silhouette and which were not.

The voxels were implemented in the form of a grid. Each voxel had pointers to 6 of its neighbors. Also a global hash table was used which hashed the center coordinates of a voxel to the corresponding voxel pointer. The use of the hash table enables easy searching of voxel space to check whether a voxel is present or not.

After constructing the grid and the hash table, the Surface Voxel List was initialized consisting of only the surface voxels. The voxels in the surface list were projected onto the silhouettes using the new region testing approach to create the visual hull. Figure 3 shows the visual hull that is created after reconstruction.

After the construction of the visual hull coloring was done using the new approach. The ray traversal to check the visibility can be done using the method defined in [12]. But here we used simple increments to traverse the ray. A small increment was made and the nearest voxel center to the current point on the ray was found out. If this voxel center is equal to the previous center encountered, it means that we are in the same voxel. Hence further increments were made repeatedly until the ray steps into a new voxel. Then this voxel was evaluated to see whether it is transparent or not. If not then the ray is blocked and hence the corresponding voxel is considered to be not visible. If the voxel is transparent, the ray is stepped further. The voxel was considered to be visible if the ray reaches the camera center without any blocks. Figure 3 shows the final reconstructed model after coloring. The details of the reconstruction under different resolutions are shown in Table 3.

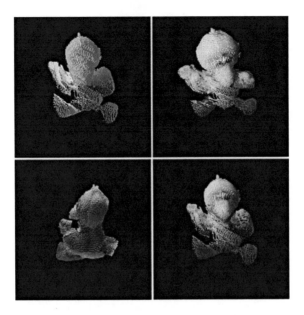

Fig. 3. Visual Hull (Top Left) and the Final Reconstructed Models

Table 3. Reconstruction Details

Voxel Size	Number of Surface Voxels	Size of Bounding Box	Running Time in seconds
2	24687	126x126x126	2111
3	10542	85x85x85	238
4	5888	64x64x64	55
5	3647	51x51x51	21

7   Conclusion and Future Work

An enhanced silhouette based 3d model reconstruction method has been proposed. The implementation was focused mainly on the reconstruction process and not on silhouette extraction or camera calibration. A simple novel region testing approach was used in the reconstruction algorithm which varies according to the size of the voxels. This region testing approach requires only the projection of the voxel centers to determine whether a voxel is inside or outside the silhouette. Also a simple visibility check was used to color the model.

The reconstruction can be further improved in several ways. First of all, better bounding cube estimation will help in avoiding unnecessary calculations. The number of voxels that need to be evaluated will be drastically reduced.

Secondly, silhouette-based reconstruction has the disadvantage that it cannot model concavities as these will never appear in any of the silhouettes. In order to model concavities, we need to consider the color information in images while carving out the voxels. This work can be extended to a space carving like approach. The current visibility check itself can be used to check the photo-consistency of the voxels. Also, the final reconstructed model will be in the form of voxels. This can be transformed into triangular patches using the marching cubes algorithm for better visualization.

References

1. Mulayim, A.Y., Ulas, Y., Volkan, A.: Silhouette-based 3D Model Reconstruction from Multiple Images. IEEE Transactions on Systems, Man and Cybernetics (2003)
2. Hess, R.: Adventures in Voxel Coloring. Oregon State University (2005)
3. Barnard, S.T., Fischler, M.A.: Computational Stereo. ACM Computing Surveys 14(4) (1982)
4. Dyer, C.R.: Volumetric Scene Reconstruction from Multiple Views, ch. 16, pp. 469–489. Kluwer, Boston (2001)
5. Eisert, P.: Reconstruction of Volumetric 3D Models, ch. 8. John Wiley & Sons Ltd., Chichester (2006)
6. Szeliski, R.: Stereo Algorithms and Representations for Image-Based Rendering. In: British Machine Vision Conference, pp. 314–328 (1999)
7. Seitz, S.M., Dyer, C.R.: Photorealistic Scene Reconstruction by Voxel Coloring. International Journal of Computer Vision 35, 1067–1073 (1997)
8. Culbertson, W.B., Malzbender, T., Slabaugh, G.: Generalized Voxel Coloring. In: ICCV 1999: Proceedings of the International Workshop on Vision Algorithms: Theory and Practice, pp. 100–115 (2000)
9. Kutulakos, K.N., Seitz, S.M.: A Theory of Shape by Space Carving. International Journal of Computer Vision 38(3), 199–218 (2000)
10. Zhang, Z.: A Flexible New Technique for Camera Calibration. IEEE Transactions on Pattern Analysis And Machine Intelligence 22(11) (2000)
11. Brown, D.C.: Close-Range Camera Calibration. Photogrammetric Engineering 37(8), 855–866 (1971)
12. Amanatides, J., Woo, A.: A Fast Voxel Traversal Algorithm for Ray Tracing. In: Eurographics 1987, pp. 3–10. Elsevier Science Publishers, Amsterdam (1987)

Computationally Efficient Implementation of Convolution-Based Locally Adaptive Binarization Techniques

Ayatullah Faruk Mollah[1], Subhadip Basu[2], and Mita Nasipuri[2]

[1] School of Mobile Computing and Communication,
Jadavpur University, India
[2] Department of Computer Science & Engineering,
Jadavpur University, India
afmollah@gmail.com

Abstract. One of the most important steps of document image processing is binarization. The computational requirements of locally adaptive binarization techniques make them unsuitable for devices with limited computing facilities. In this paper, we have presented a computationally efficient implementation of convolution based locally adaptive binarization techniques keeping the performance comparable to the original implementation. The computational complexity has been reduced from $O(W^2N^2)$ to $O(WN^2)$ where $W \times W$ is the window size and $N \times N$ is the image size. Experiments over benchmark datasets show that the computation time has been reduced by 5 to 15 times depending on the window size while memory consumption remains the same with respect to the state-of-the-art algorithmic implementation.

Keywords: Binarization, Computational Complexity, Mobile Device.

1 Introduction

Document image binarization is an extensively studied topic over the past decades. It is one of the most important steps of any document processing systems. It can be defined as a process of converting a multi-chromatic digital image into a bi-chromatic one. A multi-chromatic image also called as color image consists of color pixels each of which is represented by a combination of three basic color components viz. red (r), green (g) and blue (b). The range of values for all these color components is 0-255. So, the corresponding gray scale value $f(x, y)$ for a pixel located at (x, y) may be obtained by using Eq. 1.

$$f(x, y) = w_r \times r(x, y) + w_g \times g(x, y) + w_b \times b(x, y) \tag{1}$$

where $w_r = 0.299$, $w_g = 0.587$ and $w_b = 0.114$. As $\sum w_i = 1$, the range of $f(x, y)$ is also 0-255. So, a gray scale image can be represented as a matrix of gray level intensities $F_{M \times N} = [f(x, y)]_{M \times N}$ where M and N denote the number of rows i.e. the height of the image and the number of the columns i.e. the width of the

K.R. Venugopal and L.M. Patnaik (Eds.): ICIP 2012, CCIS 292, pp. 159–168, 2012.
© Springer-Verlag Berlin Heidelberg 2012

image respectively. Similarly, a binarized image $G_{M \times N}$ can be represented as $[g(x,y)]_{M \times N}$ such that $g(x,y) \in \{0, 255\}$.

Techniques developed so far for document image binarization are categorized into two types - global binarization techniques and locally adaptive binarization techniques. In the first case, pixels constituting the image are binarized with a single threshold T as shown in Eq. 2. A number of such techniques [1]-[4] have been developed, of which Otsu's technique [4] has been found to be the best in a study conducted by Trier et al. [5]-[6].

$$g(x,y) = \begin{cases} 0 & \text{if } f(x,y) < T \\ 255 & \text{Otherwise} \end{cases} \tag{2}$$

Global binarization techniques in general produce good results for noise free and homogeneous document images of good quality. But, it fails to properly binarize the images with uneven illumination and noise. Locally adaptive binarization techniques evolved to overcome this problem by binarizing pixels with pixel specific threshold $t(x,y)$ as shown in Eq. 3.

$$g(x,y) = \begin{cases} 0 & \text{if } f(x,y) < t(x,y) \\ 255 & \text{Otherwise} \end{cases} \tag{3}$$

Quite a good number of such adaptive techniques have been found in the literature [7]-[14]. Among these techniques, the best one has been found to be Niblack's one [11] in the same study by Trier et al. Later, more advanced techniques have been designed and some of them have been reported in [15]-[19]. Sauvola's [15] Text Binarization Method (TBM) is one of them. This method calculates $t(x,y)$ from mean $m(x,y)$ and standard deviation $s(x,y)$ of the gray levels of the pixels within a window around the subject pixel (x,y) as described in Eq. 4.

$$t(x,y) = m(x,y)[1 + k(\frac{s(x,y)}{R} - 1)] \tag{4}$$

where k is a positive constant and R is the dynamic range of standard deviation. A good number of the locally adaptive binarization techniques including Sauvola [15] are convolution based. As a result, the computational complexity and computation time of such techniques are very high. So far, binarization techniques are evaluated on the basis of binarization accuracy only [20]-[21]. But, study on computational requirements of algorithms is also required especially for real time systems and low-resourceful computing devices such as cell-phones, Personal Digital Assistants (PDA), iPhones, iPod-Touch, etc.

The present work is an attempt to reduce the computational complexity of convolution based binarization techniques while retaining comparable accuracies. The computational complexity of the global binarization technique is usually $O(N^2)$ where $N \times N$ is the image size. In case of convolution based binarization techniques, selection of threshold for each pixel requires computation of mean and standard deviation of the gray level intensities of the surrounding pixels within the window. So, computation of individual threshold value for each pixel has a complexity of $O(W^2)$ where $W \times W$ is the window size and overall complexity is $O(W^2 N^2)$ for an image of $N \times N$ pixels.

As the study [22] shows, handheld/mobile devices may not be capable of running algorithms of $O(W^2 N^2)$ within affordable time. Even, the time taken for such algorithms on desktop computers may lead to dissatisfaction to many. In [23], Shafait et al. have suggested an implementation for such algorithm with computational complexity of $O(N^2)$. They proposed a faster calculation of $m(x, y)$ and $s(x, y)$ using integral images, but at the cost of 5 to 6 times more memory. In the present work, we have proposed a novel implementation of the convolution based binarization algorithms, which has a computational complexity of $O(WN^2)$ and does not require any additional memory. Experimental results on publicly available standard datasets and our own dataset have also been presented.

2   Present Work

The computation of mean $m(x,y)$ and standard deviation $s(x,y)$ for each pixel (x,y) is the most time consuming operation in convolution based locally adaptive binarization techniques. If a window of size $W \times W$ pixels is taken around a pixel (x,y), then the set of window pixels, S, will have $W \times W$ number of elements. The performance of such methods is heavily dependent on the size of the window. Window size is decided on the basis of pattern stroke and pattern size. It cannot be made arbitrarily small.

A possible way to reduce the execution time of such binarization methods is to reduce the number of pixels in S by considering only the pixels which effectively contribute in computation of mean and variance within the window. In our present work, we have tried to reduce this number by sampling pixels from S following some geometrical order to form a reduced set $S' \subset S$.

Different geometric structures can be defined to select the contributive pixels. A few of such geometric structures have been shown in Fig. 1. S' contains pixels corresponding to black boxes marked in the geometric structures of Fig. 1. It may be observed that in S', the number of foreground pixels is much lesser than that of the background pixels for the windows of same size around both foreground and background pixels. The mean and standard deviation computed from S' are denoted as $m'(x, y)$ and $s'(x, y)$ respectively.

It is evident that S' is a very small subset of S for all possible geometric structures of Fig. 1. Also, in this context, the formulation of Sauvola's method is as given in Eq. 5.

$$t'(x, y) = m'(x, y)[1 + k(\frac{s'(x, y)}{R'} - 1)] \tag{5}$$

where $t'(x, y)$ denotes the threshold calculated from the reduced set S' for the pixel (x, y), R' is the dynamic range of $s'(x, y)$ and k is a positive constant.

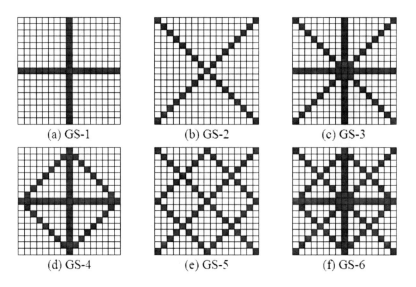

Fig. 1. Various Geometric Structures for Selection of Representative Pixels in a Window

3   Experimental Results

The proposed implementation has been tested on the printed as well as hand-written images used for benchmarking the performance of various binarization techniques in the recent Document Image Binarization Contest (DIBCO) 2009 [24] and Handwritten Document Image Binarization Contest (H-DIBCO) 2010 [25]. It has also been tested on our own dataset (CMATERdb-6) as well. This dataset contains 5 representative images. The first one is of a handwritten Bengali document in which the texts on the rear side are visible from the front side and the image is unevenly illuminated. The second image is of an old historical printed Bengali document. The third one is an image of printed English text and has been captured from a notice board by a cell-phone camera. The fourth image is of an old printed document having texts of multiple fonts and font-sizes. The last one is a cell-phone camera captured business card image.

Ground truth data for the DIBCO and H-DIBCO datasets are publicly available. We have prepared the ground truth data for the images of CMATERdb-6 dataset. The original and ground truth images of this dataset are publicly available for research purposes at [26]. These three datasets together have 25 representative images containing various kinds of degradations and deformations. The results obtained with the proposed implementation have been compared with the original/algorithmic implementation of Sauvola's binarization method, since it is one of the best convolution-based binarization methods. Results obtained with Niblack as well as Otsu's binarization technique have also been given.

3.1   Performance Analysis

Current implementation incepts from a conjecture that the threshold value $t'(x,y)$ obtained from $m'(x,y)$ and $s'(x,y)$ are not considerably different from $t(x,y)$ computed from $m(x,y)$ and $s(x,y)$. As a result, the performance remains comparable. The binarized result obtained with the new threshold $t'(x,y)$ may not be exactly same with that obtained with $t(x,y)$, but experiments show that the results obtained with the presented technique serves the purpose of binarization very well.

Comparing the output images obtained using various geometric structure of Fig.1(a-f) with their ground truth images, we find the number of true positives (TP), number of true negatives (TN), number of false positives (FP) and the number of false negatives (FN). The definition for F-Measure (FM) in terms of Recall rate (R) and precision rate (P) has been given in Eq. 6.

$$FM = \frac{2 \times R \times P}{R + P} \tag{6}$$

where $R = \frac{TP}{TP+FN}$ and $P = \frac{TP}{TP+FP}$. In an ideal situation i.e. when the output image is identical with the ground truth image, R, P and FM should be all 100%. While calculating the F-Measure, the best combination of window size (W) and k has been considered in all cases.

Table 1 shows F-Measures achieved with Otsu, Niblack, Sauvola and proposed implementations of Sauvola's method for DIBCO image dataset. It contains 5 (1-5) printed and 5 (6-10) handwritten images. Bold cells represent the highest F-Measure achieved for the corresponding image. It may be noted that the highest mean F-Measure (91.13%) has been achieved with GS-3. Moreover, mean F-Measures achieved with GS-4, GS-5 and GS-6 are greater than that of Sauvola's method. F-Measure with GS-2 is equal to that of Sauvola.

Table 1. F-Measures Achieved with Different Techniques/Implementations for DIBCO Images (**Bold** cells Represent the Highest F-Measure for the Corresponding Image)

Image	F-Measures (%)								
	Otsu	Niblack	Sauvola	GS-1	GS-2	GS-3	GS-4	GS-5	GS-6
1	91.06	88.12	91.64	91.18	91.83	91.88	91.61	**91.91**	91.71
2	**96.56**	94.76	96.39	95.58	96.27	96.16	96.14	96.40	96.25
3	**96.71**	88.65	95.82	94.90	95.83	95.58	95.68	95.96	95.77
4	82.59	90.29	92.93	91.70	93.02	92.88	92.56	**92.93**	92.86
5	89.58	85.59	89.81	88.49	89.85	89.36	89.33	**89.87**	89.62
6	90.85	**92.70**	92.34	91.64	91.96	92.15	91.77	91.78	91.98
7	86.15	75.02	86.65	**89.64**	88.99	89.41	89.21	89.06	89.23
8	84.11	88.19	87.99	88.08	88.02	**89.08**	88.74	88.46	88.92
9	40.56	86.20	88.62	88.09	88.65	**89.24**	88.52	88.79	88.99
10	28.04	85.62	85.38	**86.36**	83.13	85.59	85.13	85.05	84.81
Mean	78.62	87.51	90.76	90.57	90.76	**91.13**	90.89	91.02	91.01

Similar to Table 1, Table 2 shows F-Measures achieved with H-DIBCO Images. It contains 10 representative Handwritten Document Images. Proposed implementations have achieved highest F-Measures for 6 images out of 10. The implementation referred to as GS-3 alone has yielded 3 highest F-Measures. Although, The Mean F-Measure is highest in case of Sauvola, F-Measures of the proposed implementations are close to that.

Table 2. F-Measures Achieved with Different Techniques/Implementations for H-DIBCO Images (**Bold** cells Represent the Highest F-Measure for the Corresponding Image)

Image	F-Measures (%)								
	Otsu	Niblack	Sauvola	GS-1	GS-2	GS-3	GS-4	GS-5	GS-6
1	**91.47**	90.98	91.23	89.39	90.82	89.71	90.28	91.37	90.57
2	88.18	88.46	89.03	**89.86**	88.32	89.47	89.53	88.64	89.26
3	84.36	81.78	**85.64**	84.16	85.01	84.36	84.45	85.15	84.63
4	85.62	89.80	89.67	89.29	89.82	**89.84**	89.45	89.60	89.69
5	88.28	84.57	92.26	92.91	93.20	**93.51**	93.19	93.23	93.38
6	80.38	84.38	84.09	84.04	83.77	84.11	**84.42**	84.33	84.33
7	90.12	89.57	90.87	90.76	90.69	**91.13**	90.84	90.79	91.09
8	85.68	88.32	88.23	87.27	88.01	88.29	88.30	88.12	**88.32**
9	81.28	**88.43**	88.42	88.40	87.88	87.88	87.85	87.92	87.92
10	79.25	87.67	87.60	**87.90**	86.00	85.91	85.54	85.67	85.66
Mean	85.46	87.40	**88.70**	88.40	88.35	88.42	88.39	88.48	88.49

Table 3. F-Measures Achieved with Different Techniques/Implementations for CMA-TERdb6 Images (**Bold** cells Represent the Highest F-Measure for the Corresponding Image)

Image	F-Measures (%)								
	Otsu	Niblack	Sauvola	GS-1	GS-2	GS-3	GS-4	GS-5	GS-6
1	88.00	89.71	89.98	90.10	90.09	**90.16**	90.05	89.96	90.14
2	88.88	88.68	89.04	88.97	**89.07**	89.05	89.06	89.07	89.07
3	91.93	92.89	93.41	93.00	93.37	**93.46**	93.29	93.38	93.46
4	**99.04**	95.64	98.02	97.01	97.42	97.90	97.80	97.82	97.94
5	91.06	90.94	91.65	91.40	91.63	91.70	**91.81**	91.77	91.80
Mean	91.78	91.57	92.42	92.10	92.32	92.45	92.40	92.40	**92.48**

Table 3 shows The F-Measures Achieved with CMATERdb-6 Images. It is noteworthy that Highest Mean F-Measure i.e. 92.48% has been achieved for GS-6 whereas The mean F-Measure for Sauvola's Method is 92.42%. It may also be noted that Otsu's Global Binarization Method has given the Highest F-Measure for the fourth Image.

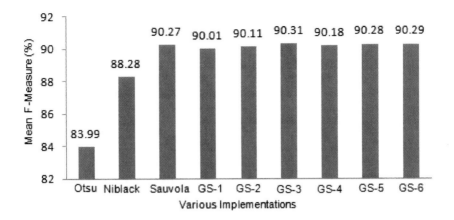

Fig. 2. Mean F-Measures Computed for All Images of the 3 Benchmarking Datasets with Various Techniques and Implementations

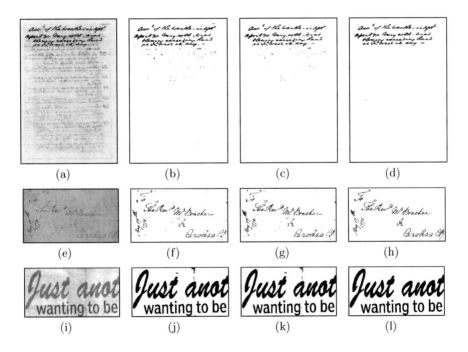

Fig. 3. Sample Images and Binarized Results with Various Techniques. (a,e,i) Image #7 of [24], #2 of [25] and #4 of [26] respectively, (b,f,j) Binarized Images with Sauvola's method, (c,g,k) Binarized images with GS-3, GS-1 and GS-3 respectively, (d) Ground Truth Images.

A comparison of the mean F-Measures achieved for all 25 images of the 3 datasets with various techniques has been shown in Fig. 2. The highest F-Measure i.e. 90.31% is achieved with GS-3. F-Measures achieved with all present implementations are greater than that of Niblack. Three implementations viz. GS–1, GS–2 and GS–4 have yielded F-Measures slightly less than that of Sauvola and the remaining implementations viz. GS–3, GS–5 and GS–6 have yielded slightly improved F-Measures than that of Sauvola. This shows that the results with the proposed implementations are comparable with the result of Sauvola. Fig. 3 show some sample images of the above datasets and their binarized images for some techniques.

3.2   Computational Complexity and Computation Time

The proposed technique calculates the threshold for each pixel with computation time of $O(W)$ time. So, computational complexity of the proposed technique is $O(WN^2)$. Plot of mean computation times of Niblack, Sauvola and proposed techniques has been shown in Fig. 4 with respect to a moderately powerful notebook (DualCore T2370, 1.73 GHz, 1GB RAM, 1MB L2 Cache). It may be observed from Fig. 4 that the computation time of the proposed technique is much lesser than Niblack's and Sauvola's implementations.

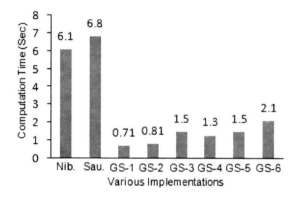

Fig. 4. Plot of Mean Computation times of Niblack, Sauvola and Proposed Techniques (for the Images of Resolution 1024x768 with 20x20 Window size)

3.3   Memory Consumption

As storing a pixel of a gray scale image requires 1 byte of memory, an $N \times N$ image requires $S_z = N \times N$ bytes of memory. The algorithmic implementation of Niblack's and Sauvola's technique makes a copy of the image before binarizing its pixels by convolving the window. So, the amount of memory consumption of this algorithm is $2 \times S_z + c_1$ bytes where c_1 is a constant.

The implementation proposed by Shafait et al. [23] is faster, but it requires additional memory. It prepares two types of integral images from the given image - one for intensity values and the other for square of the intensity values. To store these integral images with 32 bit and 64 bit integers respectively, we need $4 \times S_z$ and $8 \times S_z$ bytes of memory. So, the amount of memory consumption in this case is $12 \times S_z + c_2$ where c_2 is another constant. It may be noted that the memory consumption is 6 times higher than that of the algorithmic implementation.

Memory consumption of our implementation can be given as $2 \times S_z + c_3$ where c_3 is another constant. It may be noted that this implementation requires no additional memory compared to the original/algorithmic implementation.

4   Conclusions

In this paper, we have presented a novel implementation of convolution based locally adaptive binarization techniques. Both the computational complexity and computation time are significantly reduced while keeping the performance close to the ordinary implementation. The computational complexity has been reduced from $O(W^2 N^2)$ to $O(W N^2)$ and the time computation has been reduced by 5 to 15 times depending on the window size. At the same time, memory consumption is the same with the original implementation. This type of implementation is especially useful in image analysis and document processing systems for real-time systems and on handheld mobile devices having limited computational facilities. As the trend in designing camera based applications on mobile devices has recently increased considerably, the presented technique will be highly useful.

Acknowledgments. We are thankful to the *Center for Microprocessor Application for Training Education and Research (CMATER)*, Jadavpur University for providing infrastructure support for the research work. The first author is also thankful to the *School of Mobile Computing and Communication (SMCC)* for providing fellowship to him.

References

1. Abutaleb, A.S.: Automatic Thresholding of Gray-Level Pictures using Two-Dimensional Entropy. Computer Vision, Graphics and Image Processing 47, 22–32 (1989)
2. Kapur, J.N., Sahoo, P.K., Wong, A.K.C.: A New Method Thresholding using the Entropy of the Histogram. Computer Vision, Graphics and Image Processing 29, 273–285 (1985)
3. Kittler, J., Illingworth, J.: Minimum Error Thresholding. Pattern Recognition 19(1), 41–47 (1986)
4. Otsu, N.: A Threshold Selection Method from Gray-Level Histograms. IEEE Transactions on Systems, Man and Cybernetics 9(1), 62–66 (1979)
5. Trier, D., Taxt, T.: Evaluation of Binarization Methods for Document Images. IEEE Transactions on Pattern Analysis and Machine Intelligence 17(3), 312–315 (1995)

6. Trier, D., Jain, A.K.: Goal-Directed Evaluation of Binarization Methods. IEEE Transactions on Pattern Analysis and Machine Intelligence 17(12), 1191–1201 (1995)
7. Bernsen, J.: Dynamic Thresholding of Gray-Level Images. In: Proceedings of Eighth International Conference on Pattern Recognition, Paris, pp. 1251–1255 (1986)
8. Nakagawa, Y., Rosenfeld, A.: Some Experiments on Variable Thresholding. Pattern Recognition 11(3), 191–204 (1979)
9. Eikvil, L., Taxt, T., Moen, K.: A Fast Adaptive Method for Binarization of Document Images. In: Proceedings of First International Conference on Document Analysis and Recognition, Saint-Malo, France, pp. 435–443 (1991)
10. Mardia, K.V., Hainsworth, T.J.: A Spatial Thresholding Method for Image Segmentation. IEEE Transactions on Pattern Analysis and Machine Intelligence 10(6), 919–927 (1988)
11. Niblack, W.: An Introduction to Digital Image Processing, pp. 115–116. Prentice-Hall, Englewood Cliffs (1986)
12. White, J.M., Rohrer, G.D.: Image Thresholding for Optical Character Recognition and other Applications Requiring Character Image Extraction. IBM J. Research and Development 27(4), 400–411 (1983)
13. Parker, J.R.: Gray Level Thresholding in Badly Illuminated Images. IEEE Transactions on Pattern Analysis and Machine Intelligence 13(8), 813–819 (1991)
14. Trier, D., Taxt, T.: Improvement of Integrated Function Algorithm for Binarization of Document Images. Pattern Recognition Letters 16(3), 277–283 (1995)
15. Sauvola, J., Pietikainen, M.: Adaptive Document Image Binarization. Pattern Recognition 33, 225–236 (2000)
16. Seeger, M., Dance, C.: Binarizing Camera Images for OCR. In: 6th International Conference on Document Analysis and Recognition, pp. 54–58 (2001)
17. Wolf, C., Jolion, J.M., Chassaing, F.: Text Localization, Enhancement and Binarization in Multimedia Documents. In: Proceedings of International Conference on Pattern Recognition, pp. 1037–1040 (2002)
18. Gatos, B., Pratikakis, I., Perantonis, S.J.: Adaptive Degraded Document Image Binarization. Pattern Recognition 39(3), 317–327 (2006)
19. Shin, K.T., Jang, I.H., Kim, N.C.: Block Adaptive Binarization of ill-conditioned Business Card Images Acquired in a PDA using a Modified Quadratic Filter. IET Image Processing 1(1), 56–66 (2007)
20. Gatos, B., Ntirogiannis, K., Pratikakis, I.: ICDAR 2009 Document Image Binarization Contest (DIBCO 2009). In: Proceedings of 10th International Conference on Document Analysis and Recognition, Spain, pp. 1375–1382 (2009)
21. Pratikakis, I., Gatos, B., Ntirogiannis, K.: H-DIBCO 2010 – Handwritten Document Image Binarization Competition. In: Proceedings of 12th International Conference on Frontiers in Handwriting Recognition, India, pp. 727–732 (2010)
22. Dunlop, M.D., Brewster, S.A.: The Challenge of Mobile Devices for Human Computer Interaction. Personal and Ubiquitous Computing 6(4), 235–236 (2002)
23. Shafait, F., Keysers, D., Breuel, T.M.: Efficient Implementation of Local Adaptive Thresholding Techniques using Integral Images. In: Proceedings of Document Recognition and Retrieval XV, San Jose, USA (2008)
24. DIBCO 2009 Benchmarking Dataset,
    http://users.iit.demokritos.gr/~bgat/DIBCO2009/benchmark
25. H-DIBCO 2010 Benchmarking Dataset,
    http://users.iit.demokritos.gr/~bgat/H-DIBCO2010/benchmark
26. CMATER Database Repository, http://code.google.com/p/cmaterdb

Study of Sampled Data Control Approach towards Prosthetic Eye Model for Initiating the Non Deterministic Aspect

Arghadeep Mazumder[1], Soumya Ghosal[2],
Susmita Das[3], and Biswarup Neogi[3]

[1] EE Dept., Hooghly Engineering & Technology College, Hooghly, India
[2] IEEE, IT Dept., RCCIIT, Kolkata, India
[3] ECE Dept., JIS College of Engineering, Kolkata India
amazumder21@gmail.com

Abstract. Our paper is based on the glimpse of prosthetic or robotic eye modelling by incorporating advanced discrete domain control approaches as well as sample data control representation. A short review and preface about prosthetic or robotic eye is given in the introductory part. The linear control representation is given in the next portion. The discrete domain analysis with step responses has been furnished in the next portion. Effective stability analysis has been carried out in discrete domain. Sample data control representation for prosthetic eye control modelling has been shown in the next part of our paper. Moreover, an effective and advanced control strategy has been shown in our paper for achieving an efficient hardware based prosthetic or robotic vision system which can be an effective and pre- innovative research in the field of prosthesis and human machine interaction.

Keywords: Data Control Approach, Prosthetic Eye Model.

1 Introduction

Vision is one of the recent and developing research fields. Robotic or prosthesis has emerged and developing the robotic or prosthetic eye has been a challenge from the past to produce artificial vision, tracking and object recognitions like human. An object when viewed, eyeball automatically gets directed to capture the intelligent message as governed by the brain. This message is subsequently processed by the brain and brain in turn initiates the functionality of the concerned neuron-motor for the associated movement of various parts and sub parts to have the completeness towards the study and analysis of any object getting viewed. Still, ergonomics in the construction and modeling of prosthetic or robotic eye has yet to come. A short review on researches about prosthetic eye is given here. A comparative training and learning procedure for gathering useful information for drawing the virtual reality of robotic vision is shown in this

K.R. Venugopal and L.M. Patnaik (Eds.): ICIP 2012, CCIS 292, pp. 169–177, 2012.
© Springer-Verlag Berlin Heidelberg 2012

work [2]. The construction of two prototype robotic prosthetic eyes- one using an external infrared sensor array mounted on a frame of a pair of eyeglasses to detect natural eye movement and to feed the control system to drive the artificial eye to move with the natural eye and another using human brain EOG (ElectroOculoGraphy) signals picked up by electrodes placed on both sides of a person's head to carry out the same eye movement detection and control tasks is also a novel research work and is published in [3]. Designing of the control system of an assistive device that will help patients with eye-implant to have natural eye movement is a also another important research on proswhetic eye moielling [4]. The introduction of stereo vision is a growing field for artificial vision and intetligence research. A work on robot feedback control based on stereo vision with calibration-free hand-eye coordination is shown in [5]. Our paper aims to produce an effective and advanced control system for designing artificial or prosthetic eye. The initiation of the transfer function for robotic eye, which was attained in our previous research[1] to the discrete domain, its step response analysis, stability analysis and sample data control representation is shown chronologicecly in this paper.

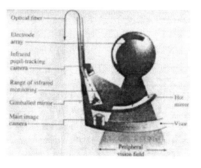

Fig. 1. Construction of the Prosthetic Eye [6]

2   Short Review on Our Past Research Work on Control Model of Prosthetic Eye

Our previous research work is based on the control model preparation of human prosthetic eye and a paper was publiseed on this work [1]. The concept of object image fetching to the camera when some of its part are routed to the brain made the basis of the feedback control modelllng. As hhe brain causes the eye to rotate, a mirror rotates via gimbals, deflecting on infrared (IR) beam towards the eyes lens, with resulting impact on the electronic retinal detector. As the mirror gimbals in the correct direction, the detector accepts more input until IR level equaling that of the reference IR beam is reacted. The mirror links to the camera so that the camera follows the eyes angle, creating artificial vision. The electrode array movement bounded by an oval shape and object osition is located in brain to view it. The micro-motor actn to move the electrode as per the brain signal. The picture of pyosthetic eye construction is given in fig [1].

To design the compensator Gc(s) and gimballed mirror Gp(s), the properties of normal human vision is considered. To obtain a smooth response in image tracking and having lower steady state errors, Gc(s) and Gp(s) are chosen as they both have a pole at s=0. The values for K, a and b needed to be selected from the closed loop transfer function. Now, choosing the time constant to 0.6 and the poles perfectly, the coefficient a, b and k values were found. Putting the values in equation the transfer function is found and is given below.

$$T(s) = \frac{252.5(0+).045)}{s^3 + 55.04545s^2 + 252.5s + 11.3625} \tag{1}$$

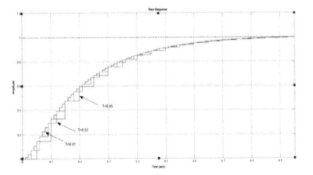

Fig. 2. Step Response Curves of T(s) for Sampling Time 0.01, 0.03, 0.05 sec

3 Background

3.1 Discrete Domain Analysis for Different Sampling Time

The transfer function is transformed from s-domain to z- domain for different sampling time. Among the different test signals step response is taken because transient response and steady state value is obtained more quickly than that of other responses. Moreover by using the step response the error can be minimized more precisely.

The different transfer function obtained for different sampling time is given in the following table.

Table 1. Transfer functions for different Sampling Time

Sampling Time	Transfer Function
0.0008	$T(z) = \dfrac{0.007006z^2 - 0.0009524z - 0.006048}{z^3 - 2.631z^2 + 2.275z - 0.6438}$
0.010	$T(z) = \dfrac{0.01058z^2 - 0.001764z - 0.008802}{z^3 - 2.557z^2 + 2.134z - 0.5767}$
0.025	$T(z) = \dfrac{0.05179z^2 - 0.01885z - 0.03284}{z^3 - 2.168z^2 + 1.421z - 0.2526}$
0.030	$T(z) = \dfrac{0.06913z^2 - 0.02888z - 0.0401}{z^3 - 2.082z^2 + 1.274z - 0.1918}$
0.050	$T(z) = \dfrac{0.1452z^2 - 0.08505z - 0.05971}{z^3 - 1.859z^2 + 0.9229z - 0.06378}$

4 Stability Analysis in Discrete Domain for Prosthetic Eye Transfer Function

Among the different values, the transfer function of sampling time t = 0.0008 sec is taken because the system is properly optimized in this sampling time. The transfer function is given by

$$T(z) = \frac{0.007006z^2 - 0.0009524z - 0.006048}{z^3 - 2.613z^2 + 2.275z - 0.6438} \tag{2}$$

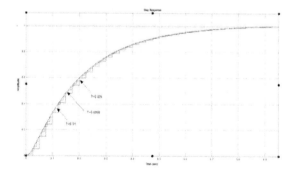

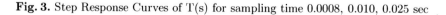

Fig. 3. Step Response Curves of T(s) for sampling time 0.0008, 0.010, 0.025 sec

Table 2. Transfer functions for different Sampling Time

Sampling Time	Transfer Function
0.0008	$T(z) = \dfrac{0.007006z^2 - 0.0009524z - 0.006048}{z^3 - 2.631z^2 + 2.275z - 0.6438}$
0.010	$T(z) = \dfrac{0.01058z^2 - 0.001764z - 0.008802}{z^3 - 2.557z^2 + 2.134z - 0.5767}$
0.025	$T(z) = \dfrac{0.05179z^2 - 0.01885z - 0.03284}{z^3 - 2.168z^2 + 1.421z - 0.2526}$
0.030	$T(z) = \dfrac{0.06913z^2 - 0.02888z - 0.0401}{z^3 - 2.082z^2 + 1.274z - 0.1918}$
0.050	$T(z) = \dfrac{0.1452z^2 - 0.08505z - 0.05971}{z^3 - 1.859z^2 + 0.9229z - 0.06378}$

The stability of the system is tested by using Region of convergence (ROC) is applied for checking the stability of the system in the z-domain. The ROC of the transfer function is the set of all values of z for which the system attains a finite value. To be a system stable, the roots of the characteristic equation should lie within the unit circle.

$$T(z) = \frac{0.007006z^2 - 0.0009524z - 0.006048}{z^3 - 2.613z^2 + 2.275z - 0.6438} \tag{3}$$

$$T(z) = \frac{(z - 0.9995)(z + 0.86)}{(z - 0.668)(z - 0.98)(z - 0.98)} \tag{4}$$

Now, comparing the equation with,

$$T(z) = \frac{(z - x_1)(z - x_2)}{(z - p_1)(z - p_2)(z - p_3)} \tag{5}$$

$x_1 = 0.9995$, $x_2 = -0.86$, $p_1 = 0.668$, $p_2 = 0.98$, $p_3 = 0.98$. From the above expression, it is found that the zeros and poles are lying inside the unit circle.

Again, the stability of the system is tested by using Jurys Stability Test. The Jury stability criterion is a method of determining the stability of a linear

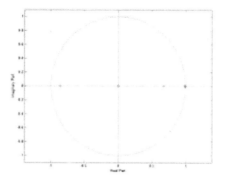

Fig. 4. Region of Convergence (ROC) for Prosthetic eye transfer function T(z)

discrete system by analysis of the coefficients of its characteristics polynomial. The theory of Jury Stability Test was first introduced by E. I. Jury to provide simple analytic test for closed loop system[7,8,9].

The conditions for the system to be stable are:

$F(-1)>0$ where $F(z)$= the characteristics equation of the transfer function.

$$(-1)^n F(-1)>0$$

Here, the characteristics equation is given by

$$F(z) = a_3 z^3 + a_2 z^2 + a_1 z^1 + a_0 z^0 \qquad (6)$$

Comparing with equation(5),

$$F(z) = z^3 - 2.631 z^2 + 2.275 z - 0.6438 \qquad (7)$$

$$So, F(1) = 1 - 2.631 + 2.275 - 0.6438 = 0.0002 \qquad (8)$$

$$F(1)>0$$

$$(-1)^n F(-1) = (-1)^3 [(-1)^3 - 2.631(-1)^2 + 2.275(-1) - 0.6438] = 6.4598 \qquad (9)$$

$$(-1)^n F(-1)>0$$

So, by using ROC and Jurys stability test it is found that the system is stable.

Table 3. Sample Data Analysis of Equation (9)

p	$C(p) - 2.631C(p-1) + 2.275C(p-2) - 0.6438C(p-3) =$ $0.007006R(p-1) + 0.0009524R(p-2) - 0.006048R(p-3)$	$C(p)$
0	$C(0) - 2.631C(-1) + 2.275C(-2) - 0.6438C(-3) =$ $0.007006R(-1) + 0.0009524R(-2) - 0.006048R(-3)$	$C(0) = 0$
1	$C(1) - 2.631C(0) + 2.275C(-1) - 0.6438C(-2) =$ $0.007006R(0) + 0.0009524R(-1) - 0.006048R(-2)$	$C(1) = 0.007006$
2	$C(2) - 2.631C(1) + 2.275C(0) =$ $0.007006R(1) + 0.0009524R(0) - 0.006048R(-1)$	$C(2) = 0.02448$
3	$C(3) - 2.631C(2) + 2.275C(1) - 0.6438C(0) =$ $0.007006R(2) + 0.0009524R(1) - 0.006048R(0)$	$C(3) = 0.05037$
4	$C(4) - 2.631C(3) + 2.275C(2) - 0.6438C(1) =$ $0.007006R(3) + 0.0009524R(2) - 0.006048R(1)$	$C(4) = 0.08325$
5	$C(5) - 2.631C(4) + 2.275C(3) - 0.6438C(2) =$ $0.007006R(4) + 0.0009524R(3) - 0.006048R(2)$	$C(5) = 0.12210$
6	$C(6) - 2.631C(5) + 2.275C(4) - 0.6438C(3) =$ $0.007006R(5) + 0.0009524R(4) - 0.006048R(3)$	$C(6) = 0.1680$
7	$C(7) - 2.631C(6) + 2.275C(5) - 0.6438C(4) =$ $0.007006R(6) + 0.0009524R(5) - 0.006048R(4)$	$C(7) = 0.2197$

5 Sample Data Control Domain Aspect towards the Prosthetic Eye Model

The sampled data systems have received significant attention to describe nonlinear system characteristics. The approach of modern control systems are implemented digitally as shown below. Apart from deterministic test response (step, ramp, impulse etc.) the study of non-deterministic test response for a system retains the special aspects of modern control system.

Table 4. Structure of Jury Array

Row	z^0	z^1	z^2	z^3
1	$a_0 = -0.6438$	$a_1 = 2.275$	$a_2 = -2.631$	$a_3 = 1$
2	$a_3 = 1$	$a_2 = -2.631$	$a_1 = 2.275$	$a_0 = -0.6438$
3	$b_0 = -1.4144$	$b_1 = 1.166$	$b_2 = 0.5812$	-
4	$b_2 = 0.5812$	$b_1 = 1.166$	$b_0 = -1.4144$	-

$$T(z) = \frac{C(z)}{R(z)} = \frac{0.007006z^2 - 0.0009524z - 0.006048}{z^3 - 2.631z^2 + 2.275z - 0.6438} \tag{10}$$

or, $C(z)[z^3$-2.631z^2+2.275z-0.6438]
= $R(z)[0.007006z^2$-0.0009524z-0.006048]

or, $C(z)$-2.631$z^{-1}C(z)$+2.275$z^{-2}C(z)$-0.6438$z^{-3}C(z)]$
= 0.007006$z^{-1}R(z)$+0.0009524$z^{-2}R(z)$-0.006048$z^{-3}R(z)$

or, $C(z$-0)-2.631$C(z$-1)+2.275$C(z$-2)-0.6438$C(z$-3)]$
= 0.007006$R(z$-1)+0.0009524$R(z$-2)-0.006048$R(z$-3)

S0, $C(p)$-2.631$C(p$-1)+2.275$C(p$-2)-0.6438$C(p$-3)]$
= 0.007006$R(p$-1)+0.0009524$R(p$-2)-0.006048$R(p$-3)

6   Conclusions

Eye is one of the important sense organs of human body. Prosthesis or Artificial organ research is divided into three major types Internal, Sense and External organs. It is well known that the second domain or the sense organ based research domain is the most challenging field of Prosthesis. In our paper, an effective and advanced control system based approach for designing prosthetic eye is shown. Initiation of discrete domain analysis, stability performances, step responses and sample data control representation have been carried out for setting a robust control system for prosthetic eye. In future, application on computational intelligence will be carried out on prosthetic eye control and modelling.

References

1. Neogi, B., Darbar, R., Ghosal, S., Das, A., Tibarewala, D.N.: Simulation Approach Towards Eye Prosthesis with Clinical Comparisons of Original Human Vision Capture Procedure. In: Proceeding 3rd IEEE Conference on Recent Trends in Information Systems (ReTIS), Kolkata, India, pp. 185–190 (2011)
2. Chen, S.C., Hallum, L.E., Lovell, N.H., Suaning, G.J.: Learning Prosthetic Vision: A Virtual-Reality Study. IEEE Transaction on Neural System and Rehabilitation Engineering 13(3), 249–255 (2005)
3. Gu, J.J., Meng, M., Cook, A., Faulkner, M.G., Liu, P.X.: Sensing and Control of a Robotic Prosthetic Eye for Ocular Implant. In: IEEE International Conference on Intelligent Robots and Systems, USA, pp. 2166–2171 (2001)
4. Gu, J., Meng, M., Faulkner, M.G., Cook, A.: Movement Control System Design for an Artificial Eye Implant. In: IEEE International Conference on SMC, USA, pp. 3735–3740 (1998)
5. Raymond, T.S., Savant Jr., C.J., Shahian, B., Hostetter, G.H.: Design of Feedback Control System, pp. 236–240. Saunders College Publishing (1994); Research 22(10-11), 941–954 (2003)

6. Hager, G.D., Chang, W.-C., Morse, A.S.: Robot Feedback Control Based on Stereo Vision: Towards Calibration-free Hand-Eye Coordination. In: IEEE International Conference on Robotics and Automation, USA, pp. 2850–2856 (1994)
7. Raible, R.H.: A Simplification of Jurys Tabular Form. IEEE Transaction on Automatic Control 250, 248–250 (1974)
8. Jury, E.I.: Inners and Stability of Dynamic System (1982)
9. Neogi, B., Roy, A., Mukherjee, S., Ghosal, S., Ghosh, S., Chatterjee, A., Datta, S., Das, A., Tibrewla, D.N.: Simulator Generation of Jurys Stability Test In Z Domain. International J. of Engg. Research and Indu. Appls. (IJERIA) 3(4), 411–421 (2010)
10. Khalil, H.K.: Performance Recovery Under Output Feedback Sampled Data Stabilization of a Class of Nonlinear Systems. IEEE Transaction Automat., 2173–2184 (2004)
11. Barbot, J.P., Monaco, S., Normand-Cyrot, D.: Discrete-Time Approximated Linearization of SISO Systems under Output Feedback. IEEE Trans. Automat. 44, 1729–1733 (1999)
12. Kawabe, T., Motoyama, T.: Receding Horizon Control of Sampled Data Systems Based on Dividing Genetic Computation. In: Proceeding Artificial Intelligence and Soft Computing (2006)

Localization of Optic Disc
in Color Fundus Images

Shilpa Joshi and P.T. Karule

Lokmanya Tilak College of Engineering, Navi Mumbai
Yashwantrao Chavan College of Engineering, Nagpur
joshishilpa10@rediffmail.com

Abstract. The objective of Medical image analysis field is to develop computational tools which will assist quantification and visualization of interesting pathology and anatomical structures. Diabetic retinopathy is a medical condition where the ratina is damaged because fluid leaks from blood vessels into the retina. The detection of the optic disk and the quantitative analysis of the evolution of its shape and its size can bring clinical information of big importance. This paper describes a novel method for localization of the optic disk boundary of retinal images. The proposed method consists of two steps: in the first step, a circular region of interest is found by first isolating the brightest area in the image by means of contrast enhancement and in the second step, the Hough transform is used to detect the main normal circular feature, the optical disk within the positive horizontal gradient image within this region of interest. The technique is tested on publicly available DRIVE, diaretdb0, diaretdb1 databases and Live images form hospital. Results obtained by applying these are presented on GUI (Graphic User Interface). Initial results on a database of fundus images show that the proposed method is effective and favorable in relation to comparable techniques. The intention of using GUI as an automated detection program is to allow simple and easy access for doctors or nurses to perform quick analysis and observation without the need of programming skills. The proposed method achieves an average accuracy of 94.7 percentage for localization of optic disk.

Keywords: Fundus Images, Hough Transform, Optic disc, Retinal Images.

1 Introduction

The fast progression of diabetes is one of the main challenges of current health care. The number of people afflicted with the disease continues to grow at an alarming rate. The World Health Organization expects the number of people with diabetics to increase over the next years. The situation is made worse by the fact that only one half of the patients are aware of the disease. Retinal photography is an essential mean to document and diagnose this various eye diseases in clinics. Color retinal images are widely used to mass screen systemic diseases such as diabetic retinopathy. Early detection and treatment of these diseases

K.R. Venugopal and L.M. Patnaik (Eds.): ICIP 2012, CCIS 292, pp. 178–186, 2012.
© Springer-Verlag Berlin Heidelberg 2012

are crucial to avoid preventable vision loss. In the traditional way of diagnosis, the ophthalmologists will examine retinal images, search the possible anomalies and give the diagnostic results. The automatic processing and analysis of retinal images could save workloads and may give objective detection to the ophthalmologists. Feature extraction, which is the fundamental step in an automated analyzing system, is investigated in this paper. Accurate optic disk localization and detection of its boundary is main and basic step for automated diagnosis systems [1–4]. The optic disk is the region on the retina at which optic nerve axons enter and leave the eye. Optic disc is a bright yellowish disk in human retina from where the blood vessels and optic nerves emerge [5–7]. The shape, color and size of optic disk help in localization and detection. However, these properties show a large variance. Localizing the centre and rim of the optic disk is necessary to differentiate the optic disk from other features of the retina and as an important landmark. Localization of the retinal optic disk has been attempted by several researchers recently. The optic disc is usually the brightest component on the fundus, and therefore a cluster of high intensity pixels will identify the optic disc location. In [8], an approximate location of the optic disk is estimated where the location of the optic disk is intensity, diversity of gradient directions, and hypothesized by searching for regions of high convergence of blood vessels. Principal component analysis has been used by Chutatape and Li to differentiate the optic disc from other sources [9].They produced a training set using the brightest pixels that were firstly clustered as candidate optic disc regions. Principal component analysis was then applied to project a new image to the 'disc space'. Then, the location of the optic disc centre was found by calculating the minimum distance between the original retinal image and its projection. Sinthanayothin [10, 11] located the position of the optic disk by finding the region with the highest local variation in the intensity. Hoover [12, 13] utilized the geometric relationship between the optic disk and main blood vessels to identify the disk location. He described a method based on a fuzzy voting mechanism to find the optic disc location. Mendels et al.[14] and Osareh et al. [15] introduced a method for the disk boundary identification using free-form deformable model technique. Li and Chutatape [4, 16] used a PCA method to locate the optic disk and a modified Active Shape Model (ASM) to refine the optic disk boundary based on Point Distribution Model (PDM) from the training sets. A method based on pyramidal decomposition and Hausdorff distance based template matching was proposed by Lalonde et al. [17, 18]. In this paper, we propose a Hough Transformation based technique for OD localization and detection. In our proposed method, firstly, optic disk localization is done by detecting the maximum gray values from an image histogram. Secondly, ROI is extracted and optic disk detection is done by taking Circular Hough Transform of an image. We test the validity of our method on publicly available databases i.e. DRIVE [19], diaretdb0, diaretdb1 and Live images form hospital. This method could form the basis of a quick and accurate test for feature extraction of diabetic retinopathy which would have hug benefits it terms of improved access to screening people for risk or presence of diabetes.

2   Methods

2.1   Systematic Overview

A systematic overview of the proposed technique is shown in Figure 1. In summary, given a color retinal image, the first step is pre-processing the input retinal images, the second step localizes the optic disk center and in the third step on the extracted ROI optic disk detection takes place.

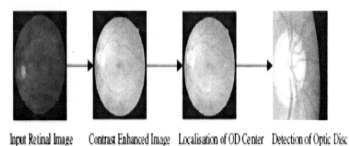

Input Retinal Image   Contrast Enhanced Image   Localisation of OD Center   Detection of Optic Disc

Fig. 1. Systematic Overview of Proposed Technique

2.2   Optic Disc Localization and Detection

The optic disk appears in color fundus images as a bright yellowish or white region. Its shape is more or less circular, interrupted by outgoing vessels. Although sometimes due to the nature of the photographic projection it has the form of an ellipse. First the original image is converted from the RGB color model to gray scale image. The resulting image is processed by local contrast enhancement in order to remove the background artifacts which can cause false localization of optic disc center. Local contrast enhancement is a signal to noise enhancement process to create images which are improved for the subsequent retinal optic disc detection. It emphasizes the local contrast of the intensity values of an image so that the optic discs are more clearly distinguished from the background and other features. Then localization of optic disc center is done by detecting the maximum gray values from an image histogram. After localizing the optic disc we have to define the Region Of Interest (ROI) for increasing the performance of optic disc detection. After smoothing the size of ROI, we have to detect the optic disc boundary using Hough Transform [20, 21]. The Hough Transform is used to identify the locations and orientations of retinal image features. This transform consists of parameterized description of a feature at any given location in the original image space. It can be used for representing objects that can be parameterized mathematically as in our case, a circle, can be parameterized by equation 1.

$$(x - a)^2 + (y - b)^2 = c^2 \tag{1}$$

Where (a, b) is the coordinate of center of the circle that passes through (x, y) and c is its radius [22, 23]. The procedure to detect circles involves the following steps:

1)Obtain a binary edge map of the image.

2)Set values for a and b.

3)Solve for the value of c that satisfies Eq. (1).

4)Increment the accumulator that corresponds to (a, b, c).

5)Update value for a and b within range of interest and go back to step 3.

Each local maximum in each plane of the Hough space corresponds to a possible circle with the corresponding radius and center in the original image. By analyzing the various local maxima in the Hough space, we can find the best-fitting circular approximation of the optic disc with the corresponding center and radius. The Hough accumulator is a 3D array, each cell of which is incremented for each nonzero pixel of the edge map that meets the stated condition. The value for the cell (a, b, c) in the Hough accumulator is equal to the number of edge map pixels of a potential circle in the image. In the case of the images in the DRIVE dataset, the size of each image is 584 X 565 pixels; the spatial resolution of the images is about 20m/pixel. The physical diameter of the optic disc is about 1.8 mm, on average. Hence, the size of the Hough accumulator was set to be 584 X 565 X 20. The potential circles indicated by the Hough accumulator. Results obtained by applying these along with the centriode are presented on GUI. GUI is a graphical interface to allow simple and user friendly access to the program. There is a set of tools provided for in Matlab to simplify designing and building of GUIs. Programming codes can be added to the function events of GUIDE to carry out the intended functions.

2.3   Experimental Results

We have extensively tested our optic disk localization and detection technique on standard diabetic retinopathy databases. We have used publicly available datasets DRIVE, diaretdb1, diaretdb0 and Live images form hospital. Planes of the Hough space for the Diaretdb1 and Diaretdb0 images are shown in Figure 2 and Figure 3. Planes of the Hough space for the Training, Testing image in the DRIVE dataset are shown in Figure 4 and 5, respectively. Optic Disc detection for the image from Live images form hospital are shown in Fig.6 and in Fig. 7 results for Live fundus on gray images are shown. In Fig 8. Some of the results from above mentioned database for the gray scale images are shown. The DRIVE [19] database consists of 40 RGB color images of the retina. Diaretdb0 [22] database contains 130 retinal images while diaretdb1 database contains 89 retinal images. These databases contain retinal images with a resolution of 1500 x 1152 pixels and 20 Live images form hospital a resolution of 1936 x 1296 pixels of different qualities in terms of noise and illumination. The decision for successful localization or failed localization is based on human eye observation. The experimental results demonstrated that our method performs well in locating and detecting optic disk. The proposed method achieves an average accuracy of 94.7 percent summarizes the results of optic disk localization for all databases. Although a number of methods have been published for optic disc localization, many are unreliable when confronted with images of diseased retina including strong distractors, and the reliable methods tend to be quite computationally complex. We have presented a simple but effective algorithm for localization.

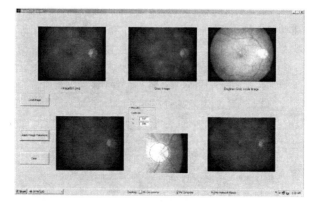

Fig. 2. Results for Diaretdb1 Fundus Images

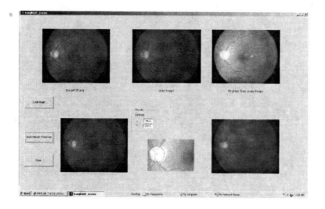

Fig. 3. Results for Diaretdb0 Fundus Images

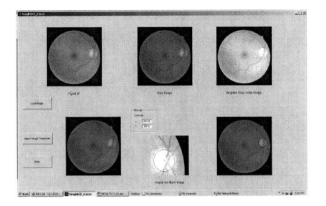

Fig. 4. Results for Drive Training Fundus Images

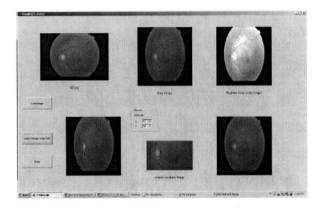

Fig. 5. Results for Drive Test Fundus Images

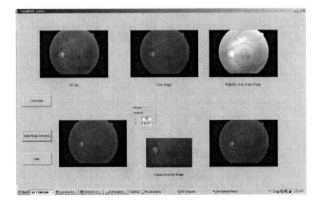

Fig. 6. Results for Live Fundus Images

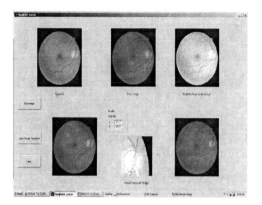

Fig. 7. Results for Live1 Fundus Images

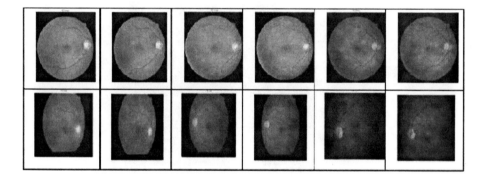

Fig. 8. Results for Live Fundus on Gray Scale Images

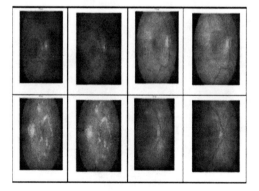

Fig. 9. More Results from Database

2.4   Conclusion

Our proposed approach for automated optic disk localization and detection is effective in handling retinal images under various conditions with reasonable accuracy and reliability for medical diagnosis. The problem with retinal images is that the visibility and detection of optic disk are usually not easy especially in presence of some lesions. In this paper, retinal images are pre-processed and ROI is extracted prior to optic disk detection. Optic disk is localized using contrast enhancement, thresholding and it is detected using Hough transform. We have tested our technique on publicly available DRIVE, diaretdb0, diaretdb1 and live images form hospital. The experimental results demonstrated that our method performs well in locating and detecting optic disk.

References

1. Osareh, A., Mirmehdi, M., Thomas, B., Markham, R.: Automated Identification of Diabetic Retinal Exudates in Digital Colour Images. British Journal of Ophthalmology 87(10), 1220–1223 (2003)
2. Shankar, S.R., Jain, A., Mittal, A.: Automated Feature Extraction for Early Detection of Diabetic Retinopathy in Fundus Images. IEEE Transaction on Medicine (2009) 978-1-4244-3991
3. Ayres, F.J., Rangayyan, R.M.: Design and Performance Analysis of Oriented Feature Detectors. Journal of Electronics Imaging 16(2), 023007 (2007)
4. Vijayamadheswaran, R., Arthanari, M., Sivakumar, M.: Detection of Diabetic Retinopathy using Radial Basis Function. International Journal of Innovative Technology and Creative Enggineering (2011)
5. Park, M., Jin, J.S., Luo, S.: Locating the Optic Disc in Retinal Images. In: Proceedings of the International Conference on Computer Graphics, Imaging and Visualisation. IEEE, Sydney (2006)
6. Reza, A.W., Eswaran, C., Dimyati, K.: Diagnosis Diabetic Retinopathy: Automatic Extraction of Optic Disc and Exudates from Retinal Images using Marker-controlled Watershed Transformation. Journal of Medical System (2010)
7. Park, J., Kien, N.T., Lee, G.: Optic Disc Detection in Retinal Images using Tensor Voting and Adaptive Mean-Shift. In: IEEE 3rd International Conference on Intelligent Computer Communication and Processing, ICCP, Romania, pp. 237–241 (2007)
8. Narasimha-Iyer, H., Can, A., Roysam, B., Stewart, C.V., Tanenbaum, H.L., Majerovics, A., Singh, H.: Robust Detection and Classification of Longitudinal Changes in Color Retinal Fundus Images for Monitoring Diabetic Retinopathy. IEEE Transactions on Biomedical Engineering 53(6), 1084–1098 (2006)
9. Li, H., Chutatape, O.: Automated Feature Extraction in Color Retinal Images by a Model based Approach. IEEE Transactions on Biomedical Engineering 51, 246–254 (2004)
10. Sinthanayothin, C., Boyce, J.A., Cook, H.L., Williamson, T.H.: Automated Localization of the Optic Disc, Fovea, and Retinal Blood Vessels from Digital Fundus Color Images. British Journal of Ophthalmology 83, 902–910 (1999)
11. Kim, S.K., Kong, H.J., Seo, J.M., Cho, B.J., Park, K.H., Hwang, J.M., Kim, D.M., Chung, H., Kim, H.C.: Segmentation of Optic Nerve Head using Warping and RANSAC. In: Proceedings of the 29th Annual International Conference of the IEEE Engineering in Medicine and Biology Society, pp. 900–903. IEEE, Lyon (2007)

12. Hoover, A., Goldbaum, M.: Locating the Optic Nerve in a Retinal Image using the Fuzzy Convergence of the Blood Vessels. IEEE Transactions on Medical Imaging 22(8), 951–958 (2003)
13. Carmona, E.J., Rincon, M., García-Feijoó, J., Martínez de-la Casa, J.M.: Identification of the Optic Nerve Head with Genetic Algorithms. Artificial Intelligence Journal of Med. 43(3), 243–259 (2008)
14. Mendels, F., Heneghan, C., Thiran, J.P.: Identification of the Optic Disc Boundary in Retinal Images using Active Contours. In: Proceedigs IMVIP Conference, pp. 103–115 (1999)
15. Osareh, A., Mirmehd, M., Thomas, B., Markham, R.: Comparison of Color Spaces for Optic Disc Localization in Retinal Images. In: 16th International Conference on Pattern Recognition, vol. 1, pp. 743–746 (2002)
16. Li, H., Chutatape, O.: Boundary Detection of Optic Disk by a Modified ASM Method. Pattern Recognition 36(9), 2093–2104 (2003)
17. Lalonde, M., Beaulieu, M., Gagnon, L.: Fast and Robust Optic Disc Detection using Pyramidal Decomposition and Hausdorff-based Template Matching. IEEE Transaction on Medical Imaging 20(11), 1193–1200 (2001)
18. Usman Akram, M., Khan, A., Iqbal, K., Butt, W.H.: Retinal Images: Optic Disk Localization and Detection. In: Campilho, A., Kamel, M. (eds.) ICIAR 2010, Part II. LNCS, vol. 6112, pp. 40–49. Springer, Heidelberg (2010)
19. Niemeijer, van Ginneken, B.: (2002),
    http://www.isi.uu.nl/Reseach/Databases/DRIVE/results.php
20. Sekhar, S., Al-Nuaimy, W., Nandi, A.K.: Automated localization of retinal optic disk using Hough transform. In: 5th IEEE International Symposium on Biomedical Imaging, pp. 1577–1580 (2008)
21. Hajer, J., Kamel, H., Noureddine, E.: Localization of Optic Disc in Retinal Image using the "watersnake". In: Proceedings of the International Conference on Computer and Communication Engineering, Kuala Lumpur, Malaysia, May 13-15 (2008)
22. Gonzalez, R.C., Woods, R.E.: Digital Image Processing, 2nd edn. Prentice Hall, Upper Saddle River (2002)
23. Ayres, F.J., Rangayyan, R.M.: Design and Performance Analysis of Oriented Feature Detectors. Journal of Electronics Imaging 16(2), 023007 (2007)

Robust Color Image Watermarking Scheme Using JFIF -YCbCr Color Space in Wavelet Domain

A.K. Verma[1], C. Patvardhan[1], and C. Vasantha Lakshmi[2]

[1] Electrical Engineering Department
Faculty of Engineering, Dayalbagh Educational Institute
Dayalbagh, Agra, UP, India
[2] Department of Physics and Computer Science
Faculty of Science, Dayalbagh Educational Institute
Dayalbagh, Agra, UP, India
ajaykrverma@yahoo.com

Abstract. In this paper, a wavelet based color image watermarking scheme is proposed which utilizes a specific version of gamma corrected YCbCr color space used in JPEG File Interchange Format (JFIF) to achieve maximum compatibility in cross platform JPEG file interchange and robustness against JPEG compression. To achieve both robustness and imperceptibility to the maximum possible extent, the watermark payload is divided into two parts. A smaller part with less embedding strength is embedded in Y (Luma) channel for good imperceptibility and robustness against compression attacks. The other larger part with higher embedding strength is embedded in Cr (Chroma) channel to achieve robustness against other types of attacks such as geometrical attacks and good imperceptibility. The proposed watermarking scheme utilizes spread spectrum technique. The performance results show that proposed scheme is more robust against a variety of attacks than other schemes available in literature.

Keywords: Bior6.8, Correlation, Embedding Strength, Human Visual System, JFIF-YCbCr, RGB, Robustness, Wavelets.

1 Introduction

Digital watermarking of multimedia content has evolved as a solution to unauthorized manipulation of images and videos and has become an active field of research. In the last few years, a sizable amount of work in the area of watermarking has been reported for grayscale images in the literature [1, 2, 3]. Typically it is suggested that the same scheme can also be applied for color images. Direct conversion from grayscale watermarking to color image watermarking needs taking care of some key points such as proper selection of color space representation; inter relations of color planes etc. Some work on color image watermarking has also been reported in literature. A block probability based spatial domain approach is suggested in [4]. This method does not show enough robustness against

K.R. Venugopal and L.M. Patnaik (Eds.): ICIP 2012, CCIS 292, pp. 187–192, 2012.
© Springer-Verlag Berlin Heidelberg 2012

JPEG compression. A collusion attack resistant scheme, based on averaging of middle frequency coefficients of block of Discrete Cosine Transform (DCT) coefficients of an image is presented in [5]. This scheme utilizes the blue channel for watermark insertion. Substantial work based on wavelet based watermarking of color images is also reported in literature. A DWT based color image watermarking scheme resistant to JPEG and JPEG 2000 is proposed in [6]. In this scheme, RGB color model is used and watermark with different embedding strengths considering relative perception of R, G and B channel. A comparative analysis to find suitability of various color-spaces in DWT based watermarking is presented in [7]. A good survey of various techniques for color image watermarking is presented in [8]. In this paper, a robust scheme is proposed which utilizes JFIF-YCbCr color-space showing better performance against compression and proposes watermark embedding in both Y channel and Cr channel with different embedding strength for better robustness and better imperceptibility. The rest of the paper is organized as follows. Section 2 describes about chosen color space, Section 3 describes the proposed watermark embedding and watermark extraction algorithms. Section 4 presents the experimental results and some conclusions are given in Section 5.

2 Selection of Color Space Representation and Watermark Embedding Channel

Several color space representations viz., RGB, YIQ, YCbCr, YUV, HSI, HSV etc. have been used for watermarking. Most of the early work used RGB representation and watermark embedding in Blue channel but blue channel embedding suffers against JPEG compression. Selection of appropriate color space and choice of suitable channel for watermark embedding is investigated in [7]. It is shown that the Y-channel in YCbCr system is the ideal space for data hiding whenever tolerance against JPEG compression and noise addition are the most important concerns. Cr-channel in the same color space is the best choice when the proposed algorithm should resist scaling and rotation attacks while Cb-channel is a better option for resistance against cropping. To achieve maximum compatibility with JPEG standard, a specific version of gamma corrected YCbCr color space of JPEG File Interchange Format (JFIF) as defined in CCIR 601 (256 levels) standard is chosen for proposed scheme [9]. The conversion rule for RGB to JFIF-YCbCr is given below,

$$\begin{bmatrix} Y \\ Cb \\ Cr \end{bmatrix} = \begin{bmatrix} 0.299 & 0.587 & 0.114 \\ -0.168736 & -0.331264 & 0.5 \\ 0.5 & -0.418688 & -0.081312 \end{bmatrix} \begin{bmatrix} R \\ G \\ B \end{bmatrix} + \begin{bmatrix} 0 \\ 128 \\ 128 \end{bmatrix}$$

The reverse conversion from YCbCr to RGB is simply obtained by above matrix equation.

3 Watermark Embedding and Extraction Algorithms

In this paper, the spread spectrum watermarking scheme [10] is utilized. In the proposed scheme, the watermark is divided into two parts (WM1 and WM2). The smaller part (WM1) is embedded in Y channel with lesser embedding strength. The motivation behind this is that eyes are very sensitive to luminance (Y channel). Therefore, minimum possible modifications should be done in Y channel. The watermark is embedded in Y channel for robustness against compression attacks. The other part of bigger size (WM2) is embedded in Cr channel with higher embedding strength to survive attacks other than compression. As Cr channel is not very sensitive to eyes, more payload and more embedding strength do not spoil the visual quality of watermarked image but provide good robustness. Enhanced security is also achieved by using two different pseudo random sequences generated by two different keys.

3.1 Watermark Embedding Algorithm

Input: RGB Color image (I) of type uint8 and of size $M \times M$ and two binary watermarks $(WM1$ and $WM2)$.
Output: Watermarked Image (I_w).

1. Convert input RGB color image (I) in to JFIF-YCbCr color space and select Y channel and Cr channel for watermarking.
2. Perform the two-level wavelet decomposition of Y channel obtaining four coefficients matrices cA, cH, cV and cD. The high frequency band cD is selected for watermark embedding.
3. Select a seed to generate a pseudo random sequence $(PRS1)$ of size equal to the size of frequency band cD. Modify $PRS1$ to get another sequence, which contains only +1, -1 and 0 according to the equation $PRS = R1 \times (PRS1 - R2)$. Where, $R1 = 2$ and $R2 = 0.5$.
4. If watermark bit is 0 (Black) then modify the cD wavelet coefficients as, $cD' = cD + k.PRS$, Where k is embedding strength. If watermark bit is 1 (white) then wavelet coefficients are left unchanged.
5. Repeat the steps 3 and 4 for all '0' watermark bits with every time newly generated pseudo random sequence.
6. Take modified cD' to its original position and take inverse DWT to get back the watermarked Y channel.
7. The similar procedure (from step 2 to step 6) is also followed for Cr channel with different watermark and get watermarked Cr channel.
8. With watermarked Y, watermarked Cr channel and unmodified Cb channel, convert modified YCbCr image back into RGB image. Which is watermarked color image (I_w) and Compute the PSNR for I and I_w.

3.2 Watermark Extraction Algorithm

Input: Watermarked RGB Color Image (I_w).
Output: Extracted Watermarks $(WM_R1$ and $WM_R2)$.

1. Convert watermarked RGB color image (I_w) in to JFIF-YCbCr color space and select Y channel (Yr) and Cr channel (Cr) for watermark extraction.
2. Perform the two-level wavelet decomposition of Y channel obtaining four coefficients matrices cAr, cHr, cVr and cDr.
3. Generate the same pseudo random sequence (PRS) with same seed value that was used in embedding and compute the correlation coefficients between (PRS) and modified coefficient metrics cDr as $r = corr2\,(PRS,\ cDr)$. Repeat step 3 for all watermark bits and compute all correlation values r.
4. Compute the Threshold value as ($T = mean\,(r)$) and initialize a row matrix ($WM'1$) having all values '1' equivalent to the size of watermark. For every watermark bit, compare r with T and modify the $WM'1$ as follows,

$$WM'1 = \begin{cases} 0, & r > T \\ 1, & otherwise \end{cases}$$

5. Reshape the row matrix $WM'1$ into a matrix equivalent to the size of original watermark matrix to get recovered watermark (WM_R1) and compute the correlation between original watermark ($WM1$) and recovered watermark (WM_R1).
6. Repeat the same process to recover the second watermark (WM_R2) from Cr channel and compute the correlation between original watermark ($WM2$) and recovered watermark (WM_R2).

4   Experimental Work and Result Analysis

This section presents the experimental results. As host images four RGB color images (Pepper, Lena, F16 and Splash) of size 512×512 are tested. These images are shown in figure 1. The watermark image taken is a binary image of size 21×12 as shown in figure 2. The binary watermark as shown in figure 2 is divided into two parts '**DE**' and '**I**' as per the scheme of embedding two watermarks suggested in section 3. The embedding strength for Y channel ($k1$) and Cr channel ($k2$) is found empirically to be 2 and 4 according to the desired balance of imperceptibility and robustness. In the scheme proposed, higher order Bi-Orthogonal wavelet 'Bior6.8' is used due to its several advantages such as perfect reconstruction and smoothness.

Fig. 1. Test Images (RGB, 512×512)

Fig. 2. Binary Watermark Image

After watermark embedding, PSNR between original image (I) and watermarked image (I_w) is calculated using, $PSNR = \frac{1}{3}[PSNR_{red} + PSNR_{green} + PSNR_{blue}]$, Where, $PSNR_{red}$, $PSNR_{green}$ and $PSNR_{blue}$ are calculated for each R, G and B channel. For the test images of figure 1, PSNR values after watermarking are shown in the table 1.

Table 1. Comparison of PSNR

Images	Pepper	Lena	F16	Splash
PSNR (dB)	38.1405	38.0634	38.0093	38.3131

As observed from table 1, the obtained value of PSNR is good. The performance of proposed watermarking scheme is tested under several attack cases such as compression, noise addition, filtering and geometric distortions. The quality of extracted watermark is judged by finding Normalized Correlation Coefficient (NC) between original watermark (WM) and recovered watermark (WM_R). The results are shown for variousn attacks in table 2.

Table 2. Values of NC under various types of attacks

Attack Type	Parameters	Water marks	Test Image		
			Pepper	Lena	F16	Splash
JPEG Compression	Quality Factor=20	WM1	0.8003	0.7460	0.6958	0.6958
		WM2	0.2580	0.1662	0.1345	0.1498
JPEG2000 Compression	Compression Ratio=80	WM1	0.6502	0.6959	0.6958	0.4438
		WM2	0.8324	1.0000	1.0000	1.0000
Blurring	Averaging by [3 × 3] mask	WM1	1.0000	1.0000	1.0000	1.0000
		WM2	1.0000	1.0000	1.0000	1.0000
Median Filtering	[3 × 3] mask	WM1	1.0000	1.0000	1.0000	1.0000
		WM2	1.0000	1.0000	1.0000	1.0000
Gaussion Noise	$\mu = 0$, $\sigma^2 = 0.03$	WM1	0.9350	1.0000	0.9350	0.9348
		WM2	1.0000	1.0000	1.0000	1.0000
Sharpening	[3 × 3] mask	WM1	1.0000	1.0000	1.0000	1.0000
		WM2	1.0000	1.0000	1.0000	1.0000
Cropping	Upper half is cut	WM1	1.0000	1.0000	1.0000	1.0000
		WM2	1.0000	1.0000	1.0000	1.0000

Besides the attacks as mentioned in table 2, proposed scheme is also tested against several other attackes such as Auto Level, Auto Contrast, Diffuse Glow,

Unsharp Mask, High Pass, Invert, Equalize and Fish Eye. In all these attacks, both the embedded watermarks recovered fully with NC value of 1.

5   Conclusions

In this paper, a robust spread spectrum method of digital image watermarking for color images in wavelet domain is presented. The proposed scheme represents the RGB image in JFIF-YCbCr color space and utilizes Y channel and Cr channel for watermarking. The embedding in Y channel provides robustness against compression attacks such as JPEG compression while embedding in Cr channel provides robustness against various other attacks. As Y channel (Luminance) is more sensitive to human eyes, a smaller watermark with less embedding strength is used. The Cr channel has very less contribution in luminance and therefore, it is watermarked with larger watermark with more embedding strength to achieve better robustness. The results of Section 5 validate these.

References

1. Serdean, C.V., Tomlinson, M., Wade, J.G., Ambroze, M.A.: Protecting Intellectual Rights: Digital WM in the Wavelet Domain. In: Proceedings of the IEEE International Workshop on Trends and Recent Achievements in Information Technology, Cluj-Napoca, Romania, May 16-18 (2002) ISBN: 973-8335-49-3
2. Patvardhan, C., Verma, A.K., Vasantha, L.C.: A Comparative Analysis of Spread Spectrum Watermarking Technique in Wavelet Domain. Journal of Computer Science and Engineering (JCSE) 9(2) (October 2011)
3. Patvardhan, C., Verma, A.K., Vasantha, L.C.: A Robust Wavelet Packet based Blind Digital Image Watermarking using HVS Characteristics. International Journal of Computer Applications (IJCA) (0975 – 8887) 36(9) (December 2011)
4. Nasir, I., Weng, Y., Jiang, J.: A New Robust Watermarking Scheme for Color Image in Spatial Domain. In: Third International IEEE Conference on Signal-Image Technologies and Internet-Based System (SITIS), Shanghai, December 16-18, pp. 942–947 (2007)
5. Saxena, V., Gupta, J.P.: Collusion Attack Resistant Watermarking Scheme for Colored Images using DCT, IAENG. International Journal of Computer Science (IJCS) 34(2), IJCS_34_2_02 (November 2007)
6. Caramma, M., Lancini, R., Mapelli, F., Tubaro, S.: A Blind and Readable Watermarking Technique for Color Images. In: International Conference on Image Processing, Vancouver, Canada, vol. 1, pp. 442–445 (2000)
7. Vahedi, E., Zoroofi, R.A., Shiva, M.: On Optimal Color Coordinate Selection for Wavelet based Color Image Watermarking. In: International Conference on Intelligent and Advanced Systems, Kuala Lumpur, pp. 635–640 (2007)
8. Zhang, Y., Wu, Q., Wang, J., Chu, M.: Progresses of Color Image Watermark Methods. In: 2nd International Conference on Intelligent Control and Information Processing, Harbin, vol. 1, pp. 238–242 (2011)
9. JPEG File Interchange Format (JFIF) Version 1.02 from http://www.jpeg.org/public/jfif.pdf (accessed February 10, 2012)
10. Cox, I.J., Joe, K., Thomson, L.F., Talal, S.: Secure Spread Spectrum Watermarking for Multimedia. IEEE Transactions on Image Processing 6(12) (December 1997)

Novel Shannon's Entropy Based Segmentation Technique for SAR Images

Debabrata Samanta and Goutam Sanyal

Department of CSE,
National Institute of Technology, West Bengal, India - 713209
debabrata.samanta369@gmail.com

Abstract. Segmentation of SAR image plays an imperative function in analysis of huge amount of satellite data. The good recital of recognition algorithms based on the quality of segmented image. In case of SAR image, it is one of the most complicated and challenging tasks in image processing, and determines the quality of the final results of the analysis. The capability of SAR image is to penetrate cloud cover to predict the weather condition at any particular instant of time. Image data can also be used to classify the land, forest, hills, oceans etc.

In this paper a novel methodology has been carried out to segment a SAR images based on Shannon's definition of information entropy. Since entropy is a statistical measure of randomness that can be used to characterize the texture of the input image. The basic concept is that the background remains informatively poor, whereas the objects carry relevant information. This method preserves the details, highlights edges, and decreases random noise; all of this is done in one calculation.

Keywords: Fuzzy c-Means Clustering Algorithm, Shannon's Entropy, Probability, Shannon's Filter.

1 Introduction

Segmentation of SAR images has established a fabulous amount of research attention since it is unaffected by seasonal variations and weather conditions. It has its own specific characteristics that are quite different from optical and infrared remote sensing.

In case of SAR image, segmentation is based on global features. Basically gray level is taken as the primary features and the average of the gray level returns entropy. The motivation of this work is to develop a novel shannon's entropy based segmentation algorithm, which can be used to segment the SAR images and improve the overall accuracy. The term of Entropy is not a new concept in the field based on information theory.

A. Nakib, H. Oulhadj and P. Siarry[1] used a microscopic image segmentation method with two-dimensional (2D) exponential entropy based on hybrid micro canonical. Wang Lei, Shen Ting-zhi [2] proposed two-dimensional entropy followed by both the gray value and the local average gray value of a pixel.Wen-Bing Tao,Jin-Wen Tian, Jian Liu[3] has used fuzzy entropy probability analysis

K.R. Venugopal and L.M. Patnaik (Eds.): ICIP 2012, CCIS 292, pp. 193–199, 2012.
© Springer-Verlag Berlin Heidelberg 2012

based on three parts, namely, dark, gray and white part of an image. Wenbing Tao,Hai Jin,Liman Liu[4] investigate the performance of the fuzzy entropy approach when it is applied to the segmentation of infrared objects of images. Yanhui Guo,H.D. Cheng, Wei Zhao1, Yingtao Zhang [5] proposed neutrosophic set approach in image segmentation, based on fuzzy c-means cluster analysis . Theodor Richardson [6] has usedalgorithms to aid the accuracy of the entropy image registration algorithm, which is based on the maximization of mutual information. Roberto Rodrguez and Ana G. Suarez [7] proposed as stopping criterion in the segmentation process by using recursively the mean shift filtering . H. B. Kekre, Saylee Gharge, Tanuja K. Sarode[8] used segmentation using vector uantization technique on entropy image based on Kekres FastCodebook Generation (KFCG) algorithm.

In this work, a new SAR image segmentation strategy is proposed by using the shannon's entropy and to collects the information of small change in properties of SAR images to measure statistical value of randomness that can be used to characterize the texture of the input SAR image.

2   Proposed Methodology

2.1   Shannon's Entropy

Let us start with a reminder of the form of Shannon's entropy from information theory with respect to the image analysis terminology. Any given normalized discrete probability distribution $p=p_1,p_2,p_3,......p_n$ fulfills the conditions:

$$P_v \geqslant 0 \tag{1}$$

$$\sum_{v=1}^{n} P_v = 1 \tag{2}$$

Hear an intensity image, there exists an approximation of the probability distribution given by the histogram function $H(v)$. H is an intensity function that shows the count of the pixels $f(i;j)$ with an intensity equal to v, independent of the image position $(i;j)$. The histogram is then normalized by the number of pixels that fulfill condition (1). More conditions are assumed when measuring the information. Information must be additive for two independent events w, z:

$$I(wz) = I(w) + I(z) \tag{3}$$

If different amounts of information occur with different probabilities, the total amount of information is the average of the individual information, weighted by the probabilities of their individual occurrences. Therefore, the total amount of information is:

$$P_v \geqslant 0 \tag{4}$$

$$\sum_{v} P_v I_v \tag{5}$$

which leads us to the definition of Shannon's entropy (S_h) as a measure of information:

$$S_h = -\sum_v P_v log_2 P_v \tag{6}$$

2.2 Shannon's Filter

Shannon's entropy gives all the information content of the entire SAR image to be measured. However, when we change the number of pixels in the histogram estimation, we obtain partial information content that is strictly dependent on the area entering the computation. Shannon's entropy filtering is based on the replacement of pixel values in the image by values of entropy. Entropy is computed in a specified area, usually from the pixel's n-by-n symmetric neighborhood in the input image. The shape of the neighborhood should be also defined by the users. The computed entropy is:

$$S_{h1} = -\sum_v S_h log_2 S_h \tag{7}$$

It is clear that the output image is strongly dependent on the area selected $i.e,$ segmented reason.

2.3 Adaptive Shannon's Thresholding

In this paper probability image has been taken as an input image to find Adaptive Shannon's thresholding. Here it becomes necessary to select analyzing window size to find Adaptive Shannon's thresholding for neighborhood of each pixel in the input image. After that 3x3 and 5x5 window sizes were used to find local entropy. By moving analyzing window on complete image, calculating entropy for each window, new Adaptive Shannon's thresholding image was formed by replacing the central pixel of the particular window by entropy and displayed as entropy image.

2.4 Region Merging

In grayscale SAR images, the region merging based on Fuzzy c-means clustering algorithm, is relatively simple: neighboring regions that do not differ by more than a specified contrast value can be merged into each other. The Fuzzy c-means clustering algorithm is an iterative clustering method that produces an optimal c partition by minimizing the weighted within group sum of squared error objective function S_{fc}

$$S_{fc} = \sum_{j=1}^{n}\sum_{i=1}^{m}(W_{ij})^v f^2(U_j, V_i) \tag{8}$$

Where $U = u_1, u_2, u_3, \ldots \ldots u_n \subseteq Q^v$ is the data set in the p-dimensional vector space, is the number of data items. A solution of the object function S_{fc} can be follows:

1. Set values for the SAR image are $c, q,$,
2. Initialize the fuzzy partition matrix of segmented region.
3. Set a loop counter $j=0$.
4. Calculate c cluster for $V_i^{(b)}$ with $U(b)$.

$$V_i^{(b)} = (\sum_{j=1}^{n} (U_{ij}^{(b)})^q u_j)/(\sum_{j=1}^{n} (U_{ij}^{(b)})^q) \qquad (9)$$

In this case we can write for a SAR image:

$$2 \sum_{j=1}^{n} (U_{ij})^q (U_j - V_i) = 0 \qquad (10)$$

3   Proposed Algorithm

Input: SAR Images of variable size.
Output: Segmented region of SAR image.

1. Start.
2. Taken a SAR images.
3. Consider a 3X3 window.
4. Calculate the Shannon's entropy of that SAR Images.
5. Store the color feature in the Shannon's Filter.
6. Segmentation is obtained using Adaptive Shannon's thresholding and Fuzzy c-means clustering algorithm.
7. Stop.

4   Proposed Work Flow Diagram

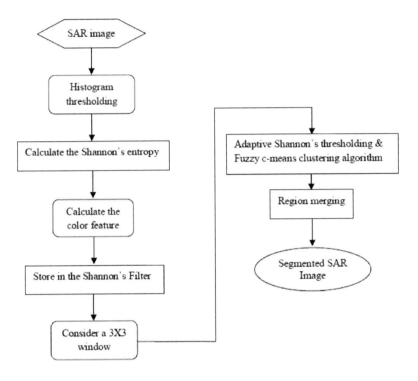

5   Experimental Results

In this work SAR image is used to test proposed algorithm. First entropy was calculated from probability for original image. Images were tested for analyzing window size of 3x3 and 5x5 to find entropy. Finally Fuzzy c-means clustering algorithm was used on entropy image for segmentation. The Figures (Fig 1 to Fig 2) shows the original SAR images and segmented SAR images.

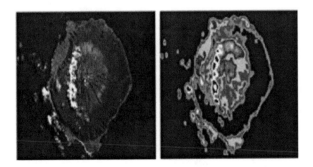

Fig. 1. Input 1st SAR Image and Segmented 1st SAR Image

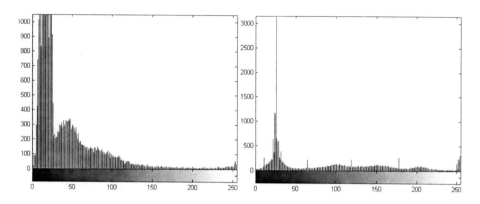

Fig. 2. Histogram of Input 1st SAR Image and Segmented 1st SAR Image

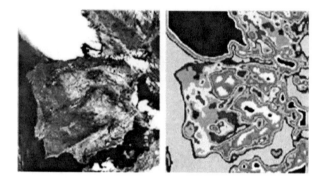

Fig. 3. Input 2nd SAR Image and Segmented 2nd SAR Image

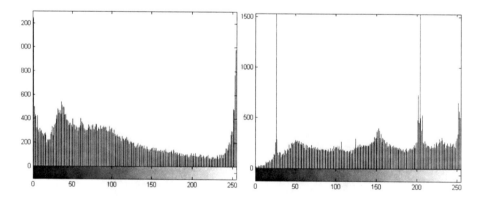

Fig. 4. Histogram of Input 2nd SAR Image and Segmented 2nd SAR Image

6   Conclusions

In this paper a new Shannon's Entropy based image segmentation technique for SAR image is proposed. This technique based on considering a 3X3 window and calculates the local Entropy based on Shannon's Filter of that SAR Images then store the color feature by calculating Shannon's Filter. Next, Segmentation is obtained using Adaptive Shannon's thresholding and Fuzzy c-means clustering algorithm. It was evidenced that this segmentation procedure is a straightforward extension of the filtering algorithm based on Shannon's Entropy. For this reason, our algorithm did not make mistakes; that is, a segmented image very different to get the originality of the SAR images. This may be extended to the color image segmentation. The results from this preliminary study indicated that the proposed strategy was effective.

References

1. Nakib, A., Oulhadj, H., Siarry, P.: Microscopic Image Segmentation with Two-Dimensional Exponential Entropy based on Hybrid Microcanonical Annealing. In: MVA 2007 IAPR Conference on Machine Vision Applications, Tokyo, Japan, May 16-18 (2007)
2. Wang, L., Shen, T.-Z.: Two-Dimensional Entropy Method Based on Genetic Algorithm. Intelligent Control and Automation, 6783–6788 (June 2008)
3. Tao, W.-B., Tian, J.-W., Liu, J.: Image Segmentation by Three-level Thresholding based on Maximum Fuzzy Entropy and Genetic Algorithm. Pattern Recognition Letters 24, 3069–3078 (2003)
4. Tao, W., Jin, H., Liu, L.: Object Segmentation using Ant Colony Optimization Algorithm and Fuzzy Entropy. Pattern Recognition Letters 28, 788–796 (2007)
5. Guo, Y., Cheng, H.D., Zhao, W., Zhang, Y.: A Novel Image Segmentation Algorithm Based on Fuzzy C-means Algorithm and Neutrosophic Set. Journal New Mathematics and Natural Computation 07, 155–171 (2011)
6. Richardson, T.: Improving the Entropy Algorithm with Image Segmentation (2003) (online document),
http://www.cse.sc.edu/songwang/CourseProj/proj2003/Richardson/richardson.pdf
7. Rodrguez, R., Suarez, A.G.: A New Algorithm for Image Segmentation by using Iteratively the Mean Shift Filtering. Scientific Research and Essay 1(2), 043–048 (2006)
8. Kekre, H.B., Gharge, S., Sarode, T.K.: SAR Image Segmentation using Vector Quantization Technique on Entropy Images. (IJCSIS) International Journal of Computer Science and Information Security 7(3) (March 2010)

Hybrid Approach for Image Encryption Using Hill Cipher Technique

Sharath Kumar H.S., Panduranga H.T., and Naveen Kumar S.K.

Department of Electronics, University of Mysore,
PG-Center, Hemagangothri, Hassan, Karnataka
sharath.kr83@gmail.com

Abstract. In this paper, we describe a method for image encryption which has three stages. In first stage pixel position manipulation technique is applied, where position of each row and column of input image is permuted into *Bit-Reversed-Order*. In second stage, each pixel of image is converted to its equivalent eight bit binary number and in that eight bit number, number of bits equal to the length of password are rotated and then reversed. In third stage, hill cipher technique is applied by using self-invertible matrix generated by same password given in second stage to make encryption more secured. This proposed hybrid approach is implemented for different images using MATLAB. Decryption involves the reverse process of encryption.

Keywords: Bits Reverse, Bits Rotation, Hill Cipher, Image Encryption.

1   Introduction

With the fast development in communication and information technology, huge data is transmitted over a communication channel which needs security. There are many applications like information storage, information management, patient information security, satellite image security, confidential video conferencing, telemedicine, military information security and many other applications which require information security.

Komal D Patel and Sonal Belani [1] have presented a survey on existing work which is used different techniques for image encryption and also given a general introduction about cryptography. There are several methods for image encryption with some advantages and disadvantages. Ismet Ozturk and Ibrahim Sogukpinaar [2] have discussed the analysis and comparison of image encryption algorithms. And they classify the image encryption methods in to three major types: position permutation, value transformation and visual transformation. Mitra et al [3] have presented a new approach for image encryption using combination of different permutation techniques. The intelligible information present in an image is due to the correlations among the bits, pixels and blocks in a given arrangement. This perceivable information can be reduced by decreasing the correlation among the bits, pixels and blocks using certain permutation techniques. Panduranga H T and Naveen Kumar S K [4] have proposed an approach

K.R. Venugopal and L.M. Patnaik (Eds.): ICIP 2012, CCIS 292, pp. 200–205, 2012.
© Springer-Verlag Berlin Heidelberg 2012

using bit reversal method. Bibhudendra Acharya et al [5] have proposed several methods of generating self invertible matrix which can be used in Hill Cipher algorithm. Saroj Kumar Panigrahy et al [6] have implemented image encryption using Self-Invertible key matrix of Hill Cipher algorithm.

The organization of the paper is as follows. Following the introduction, the concept of pixel position manipulation is explained in Section 2. Section 3 explains the image encryption technique by using *bits rotation and reversal* method based on password. In section 4, proposed image encryption method is explained. Finally, results and discussions are explained in Section 5. This paper is concluded by providing the summary of the present work in section 6.

2   Proposed Position Manipulation Technique for Image Encryption

This method includes two stages: *Row Shuffling* and *Column Shuffling* of input image which results positional manipulated encrypted image. In Row Shuffling, index value of each row of input image is converted into x-bit binary number, where x is number of bits present in binary equivalent of index value of last row of input image. The resultant x-bit binary number is rearranged in reverse order. This reversed-x-bit binary number is converted into its equivalent decimal number. Therefore weight of index value of each row changes and hence position of all rows of input image changes. i.e., Positions of all the rows of input image are rearranged in *Bit-Reversed-Order*. Similarly, positions of all columns of input image are also rearranged in *Bit-Reversed-Order*. Positional change of rows and columns of input image gives encrypted image by means of *Pixel Position Manipulation*. Figure 1(a) shows the input image. Figure 1(b) and Figure 1(c) show output images.

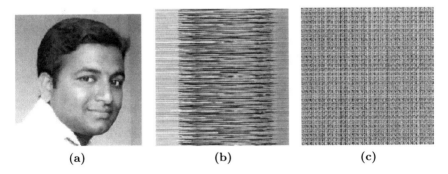

(a)   (b)   (c)

Fig. 1. (a) Input image. (b) Encrypted Image after Row Shuffling. (c) Encrypted Image after Column Shuffling.

3 Bits Rotation and Reversal Technique for Image Encryption

In this method, a password is given along with input image. Value of each pixel of input image is converted into equivalent eight bit binary number. Now length of password is considered for bit rotation and reversal. i.e., number of bits to be rotated to left and reversed will be decided by the length of password. Let L be the length of the password and L_R be the number of bits to be rotated to left and reversed (i.e. L_R is the effective length of password). The relation between L and L_R is represented by equation 1.

$$L_R = L \bmod 7 \tag{1}$$

where '7' is the number of iterations required to reverse entire input byte.

For example, $P_{in}(i,j)$ is the value of a pixel of an input image. $[B_1B_2B_3B_4B_5B_6B_7B_8]$ is equivalent eight bit binary representation of $P_{in}(i,j)$.

$$i.e.\ P_{in}(i,j) \xrightarrow{\text{decimal to 8 bit binary}} [B_1B_2B_3B_4B_5B_6B_7B_8]$$

If $L_R = 5$, five bits of input byte are rotated left to generate resultant byte as $[B_6B_7B_8B_1B_2B_3B_4B_5]$. After rotation, rotated five bits i.e., $B_1B_2B_3B_4B_5$, get reversed as $B_5B_4B_3B_2B_1$ and hence we get the resultant byte as $[B_6B_7B_8B_5B_4B_3B_2B_1]$. This resultant byte is converted to equivalent decimal number $P_{out}(i,j)$.

$$[B_6B_7B_8B_5B_4B_3B_2B_1] \xrightarrow{\text{8 bit binary to decimal}} P_{out}(i,j)$$

where $P_{out}(i,j)$ is the value of output pixel of resultant image.

Since the weight of each pixel is responsible for its colour, the change occurred in the weight of each pixel of input image due to *Bits Rotation and Reversal* generates the encrypted image. Figure 2(a) and Figure 2(b) show input and encrypted images respectively. For this encryption process given password is "sharu" whose effective length $(L_R) = 5$.

(a)   (b)

Fig. 2. (a) Input Image (b) Encrypted Image for Password "sharu"

Note:- If $L = 7$, then $L_R = 0$. In this condition, the whole byte of pixel gets reversed.

4   Proposed Technique

This image encryption method consist of three stages, among which one stage belongs to *Position Manipulation* and other two stages belong to *Pixel Manipulation*.

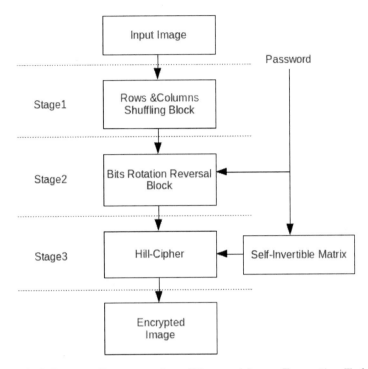

Fig. 3. Block Diagram Representation of Proposed Image Encryption Technique

In first stage, positions of all the pixels of input image are manipulated by permuting positions of rows & columns of pixels of input image into *Bit-Reversed-Order* as explained in Section 2. In second stage, output image of first stage is taken as input image along with an *alphanumeric password*. The encryption process is carried out as explained in Section 3. But the encrypted image generated in second stage can be decrypted by other passwords of same length as original password. To avoid this inconvenience third stage of encryption has designed. In third stage, a *Self-Invertible-Matrix* is generated by using the *alphanumeric password* given in second stage. By using password generated self-invertible-matrix, *Hill-Cipher* technique is applied on encrypted image generated from second stage to obtain more secured final encrypted image. To generate a self invertible matrix, minimum length of alphanumeric password should be four. Figure.3 shows block diagram representation of Proposed Image Encryption Technique.

5   Results and Discussions

Here, the above mentioned technique is implemented for different images and also histograms are plotted for all stages. From the histogram it can be observed that histogram of encrypted image by pixel position manipulation technique remains same as the histogram of original image. But histogram of encrypted image due to *Bits Rotation and Reversal* technique is altered as compared to histogram of original image, and also the histogram of encrypted image due to *Hill-Cipher* technique is altered as compared to histograms of encrypted images of previous stages. Results of the encryption process for different images along with their histogram are tabulated in Table 1 & Table 2.

Table 1.

Password	Input Image	Encryption Stage 1 (using pixel position manipulation technique)	Encryption Stage 2 (using bits rotation & reversal technique)	Encryption Stage 3(using Hill-Cipher technique)
Sharu				

Table 2.

Password	Input Image	Encryption Stage 1 (using pixel position manipulation technique)	Encryption Stage 2 (using bits rotation & reversal technique)	Encryption Stage 3(using Hill-Cipher technique)
Sharath				

6   Conclusions

In this paper we presented a hybrid technique which has three stages for image encryption. For first stage, password is not needed. But for second and third stages, only one alphanumeric password is needed. From the experimental result we can conclude that we can predict the original image by observing its histogram if we use only position manipulation technique, but it is difficult if we use pixel-value manipulation technique. We can also guess the original image if there is a uniform background in an image in case of pixel-value manipulation technique. If we use the hybrid technique of pixel position manipulation and bits rotation & reversal technique along with the Hill-Cipher technique, it is very difficult to decode the image. We conclude that the encrypted images using hybrid approach is more scrambled as compared to individual technique.

Acknowledgment. The work described in this paper is supported by a grant from the *University Grants Commission,* New Delhi, India.

References

1. Patel, K.D., Belani, S.: Image Encryption using Different Techniques: A Review. International Journal of Emerging Technology and Advanced Engineering 1(1) (November 2011) ISSN 2250-2459
2. Ozturk, I., Sogukpinaar, I.: Analysis and Comparison of Image Encryption Algorithms. Transaction on Engineering, Computer and Technology 3, 38–42 (2004)
3. Mitra, et al.: A New Image Encryption Approach using Combinational Permutation Techniques. IJCS 1(2), 127–131 (2006)
4. Panduranga, H.T., Naveenkumar, S.K.: An Image Encryption Approach using Bit-Reversal Method. In: NCIMP, pp. 181–183 (2010)
5. Acharya, B., Rath, G.S., Patra, S.K., Panigrahy, S.K.: Novel Methods of Generating Self-Invertible Matrix for Hill Cipher Algorithm. International Journal of Security 1(1), 14–21 (2007)
6. Panigrahy, S.K., Acharya, B., Jena, D.: Image Encryption using Self-Invertible Key Matrix of Hill Cipher Algorithm. In: First International Conference on Advances in Computing, Chikhli, India, February 21-22 (2008)

A Fast Brain Image Registration
Using Axial Transformation

Sithara Kanakaraj, Govindan V.K., and Pournami P.N.

National Institute of Technology,
Calicut, Kerala, India
sithara_mcs10@nitc.ac.in

Abstract. The registration process in the medical field has evolved rapidly making the physicians to rely on computer algorithms for processing and diagnosing the diseases. Registration has been used for studying disease growth and treatment responses of the diseases. Brain image registration enables physicians to diagnose diseases like Alzheimer's based on the changes in the internal structure of the brain. One of the main challenges in this topic is the huge computational requirements of the registration processes. In this paper we propose a method for the fast and accurate registration of MR brain images using the shape property of the axial slice of the brain. The algorithm exhibits reduced computational time when compared to a standard existing approach, which makes it useful for real time applications.

Keywords: Axial Transformation, Image Registration, Magnetic Resonance Imaging, Medical Image Registration, Multi-resolution.

1 Introduction

Image Registration is the process of geometrically aligning two images onto a common coordinate system [1]. It calculates the transformation required by one image, to overlay on the other image with maximum similarity. The two images may be taken at different times or using different devices or from different angles. The results of registration help to detect subtle changes between the two images. Registration is the primary step in many medical applications that use 2D or 3D images. It is widely used for monitoring tumour growth, measuring volume of tissues, treatment verification, etc.

The different components in the registration process are as follows [2]:

1. Feature Space: Information used for matching is extracted from the images.
2. Search Space: The transformation capable of aligning the images is defined.
3. Similarity Metric: Defines a method to measure the similarity between the features extracted in the feature space.
4. Search Strategy: Defines how the search for optimal transformation has to be done.

K.R. Venugopal and L.M. Patnaik (Eds.): ICIP 2012, CCIS 292, pp. 206–212, 2012.
© Springer-Verlag Berlin Heidelberg 2012

Classification of the registration process is done based on several criteria; for example, based on the similarity criteria-intensity or feature based; based on the modality used-single or multi; based on mode of operation-automatic or interactive, etc. There have been numerable image registration techniques that have been developed in the past several years. The results of the techniques are different in each case of registration, however, the basic steps such as finding the feature space, search space, determining the search strategy and similarity metric are the same for every registration process. The choice of the algorithm used in each of the steps determines the registration process and its results. Hence, a single method that can be used for all applications does not exist.

In many of the experiments conducted in the area of disease growth and treatment response of the disease, registration techniques have been used to monitor them. Diseases such as Alzheimer's, Epilepsy etc., wherein the progress of the disease and treatment responses cannot be detected by the patients external conditions, registration methods have proved to be helpful.

The brain imaging approaches convey a lot of information depending on its modality. The two modalities in brain imaging are functional and structural. The functional imaging techniques like Positron Emission Tomography (PET) and Single-Photon Emission Computed Tomography (SPECT) gives information about the activity of the cell in the region. Whereas, structural imaging techniques like Magnetic Resonance Imaging (MRI) and Computed Tomography (CT) gives information on the structural aspects, the bones and tissues. In this paper, an approach specific to the registration of axial MRI slices has been proposed. It aims at the reduction of time taken for the registration process. The Paper is organized as follows. Section 2 deals with the review of some of the existing approaches in brain image registration. Section 3 presents the basic theory of our approach. The comparative performance study of the proposed method with the mutual information based registration method is given in Section 4. Finally, the work is concluded in Section 5.

2 Related Works

Some of the important related works in this area are reviewed briefly in the following:

A brief description of some of the general methods used for medical image registration, the issues to be addressed and a few examples of the registration technique used have been illustrated in [3]. The authors also comment on the difficulty of the problem of image registration and the variability/ diversity of possible solutions.

Teverovskiy et al., [4] presents the performance evaluation of the intensity versus feature based method for brain image registration. A mutual information method was used for the evaluation process. The algorithms in ITK package and HAMMER [5] are evaluated based on their performances at both local and global levels. The authors concluded that each of the algorithms differed in their performance aspect over the other at different regions of the brain, i.e. the algorithm performance was specific to the brain regions.

In contrast with using purely feature-based or intensity-based methods, a hybrid method that integrates the merits of both approaches has been proposed in [6] by Xiaolei et al., In this method an entropy based detector is used to select the salient region features initially and then the likelihood of the regions is determined. For a test data of 50 moving images the runtime was calculated in 4 cases based on different artificial transformation parameters. An average from all the 4 cases showcased a computation time of 150 seconds for each 50 images.

A recent work on improving the accuracy and speed of the registration process was done by Kim et al., [7] using a Support Vector Regression (SVR) model. In this work, the SVR first learns the brain image appearances and their corresponding shape deformations with respect to a template, for a set of training samples. The learnt SVR models are then applied to rapidly predict a good initial deformation for a given new subject. To test 50 images of size 256x256x198, HAMMER [5] took 5400 seconds and Diffeomorphic demons [8] took 219 seconds without using the framework. A reduced computation time of 960 seconds for HAMMER and 71 seconds for Diffeomorphic demons was obtained by using the framework.

Jean Francois Mangin, et al., [9] proposed a non-supervised 3D registration of images from different modalities. Initially the discrete representations of the region of interest are extracted from the PET and MR images. The required transformation is found from the shape-independent matching algorithm. The registration process required five minutes on a conventional work station.

A new method using Fast Walsh Hadamard Transform for image registration has been put forth in [10]. Applying Fast Walsh Hadamard transform on images results in detecting the local structures of the image; these are used as the features in this approach. The algorithm was tested on 21 sets of CT-MR image pairs, for bases 1 to 5. The results show a reduced runtime that averages to 3.7 seconds in base 1 and 7 seconds in base 5. Another method [11], using wavelet as the edge detector and mutual information as the similarity metric, aligns the MR and CT images with an increased accuracy and reduced processing time.

In the work by Lepore et al., [12], the fluid image registration method incorporated with multi-resolution is suggested to be used when large anatomical differences are expected. This method was tested on a 2D phantom image which was highly deformed. The commonly used elastic registration completely failed for this test set. The computational time required to calculate the numerical solution of viscous fluid has been significantly reduced.

Raj Shekhar, et al., [13] proposed a high speed registration method for 3D and 4D images using mutual information (MI) as the voxel similarity measure. The long execution time is a major drawback of the MI method. To overcome this, a low-cost hardware was developed to accelerate the process of registration. Results show an acceleration ratio of 16.5 for registering images of size 256^3. The execution time to register MRI to a PET image takes 18-22 minutes for the software, whereas the hardware needs only 80-100 seconds.

The works reviewed above reveals that in general most of the algorithms take huge computational time, thus making the real-time registration process a difficult task. The present work proposes a fast approach for brain image registration.

3 Proposed Method

Our approach is dependent on MR images, particularly images of the axial view. We know that, the axial view of the brain and the skull together resembles the shape of an egg or rather it is oval in shape although not perfect. Using this property, it can be said that the length from the frontal lobe to the occipital lobe will be the longest distance of the line that can be plotted in the axial view as shown in Figure 1. This algorithm aims to align the line joining the farthest points to be parallel to the y-axis.

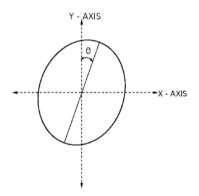

Fig. 1. Axial Slice of the Brain Depicting the Angle of Inclination, θ, Towards the y-axis

Initially an edge detection algorithm is applied to the slice to extract the outermost circumference of the skull. Then using the distance formula, the points on the circumference (x_1, y_1) and (x_2, y_2) that are the farthest from each other are found and a line is plotted between them. The slope of this line towards the y-axis is calculated using the formula (1), for the line joining the points (x_1, y_1) and (x_2, y_2).

$$\theta = tan^{-1} \left[\frac{x_2 - x_1}{y_2 - y_1} \right] . \tag{1}$$

θ gives the angle of rotation required. It has to be noted that, for an MRI image the point of rotation is at the occipital lobe or rather the base of the MRI slice, so therefore a rotation to align the base of the image would be the actual value of the rotation parameter. A bounding box is constructed around the image, which will therefore include only the brain and the skull. Hence the need for translation is completely eliminated. To align two images the corners of the bounding box have to be aligned. A scaling factor is also calculated between the two images and then images are rescaled. A GUI based on wavelet is used for fusing the images.

4 Performance Evaluation and Discussion

A global registration technique that uses mutual information as the similarity metric has been used for comparison in this paper. The method includes a multi-resolution technique to reduce the search space of the algorithm. The two images for registration, the reference image, R, and the float image, F, are given as the input. Different transformations in the search space are applied to the image F and its mutual information is calculated along with the image R. A maximum value of MI results in the correct transformation required for F in order to align itself with R.

Table 1 depicts the performance of both, the existing and the new methods on 1 set of images. It includes the resulting transformation parameters after registration, the MI value of the registered images, the runtime of the algorithm, the fused image and the difference image. Notations used in Table 1 are given in Table 2.

Table 1. Result of Registration Performed on 1 Set of Images

METHOD	EXISTING		PROPOSED
Transformation Parameters	$t_x = 23$ mm	$r_x = 8^o$	$R_R = 12.4552^o$
	$t_y = 21$ mm	$r_y = 0^o$	$R_F = 14.9314^o$
	$t_z = 0$ mm	$r_z = 0^o$	
Mutual Information	0.2437		0.3323
Time (in seconds)	483.06		2.687
Registered Image			
Difference Image			

R   F

Evaluation of the proposed method is performed on DICOM images of size 256x256 retrieved from the ADNI database [14]. The images are taken from the same subject at different times. 15 set of MR images were tested with the

Table 2. Notations

t_x - translation w.r.t x-axis	r_x - rotation w.r.t x-axis
t_y - translation w.r.t y-axis	r_y - rotation w.r.t y-axis
t_z - translation w.r.t z-axis	r_z - rotation w.r.t z-axis
R_R - angle of inclination of the reference image w.r.t y-axis	R_F - angle of inclination of the float image w.r.t y-axis

proposed and the existing techniques. The results are tabulated in Table 3. The drastic reduction of computational time with the proposed method makes it suitable for real time applications. The image dependent nature of the method is a major limitation of this method.

Table 3. Comparison of the Proposed Method and the Existing Method

IMAGE SET	MUTUAL INFORMATION VALUE		TIME in seconds	
	EXISTING	PROPOSED	EXISTING	PROPOSED
1	0.2585	0.3097	404.96	1.227
2	0.2665	0.3079	410.14	1.090
3	0.2869	0.3225	401.69	1.100
4	0.2754	0.3247	405.46	1.105
5	0.2777	0.3175	403.59	1.119
6	0.2743	0.3156	411.807	1.152
7	0.2719	0.3165	416.283	1.129
8	0.2721	0.3212	412.802	1.103
9	0.2654	0.3166	403.326	1.139
10	0.2680	0.3022	403.786	1.119
11	0.2794	0.3173	399.566	1.128
12	0.2670	0.2955	399.557	1.108
13	0.2563	0.2856	397.289	1.121
14	0.2505	0.2864	396.941	1.159
15	0.2424	0.2888	399.044	1.154

5   Conclusions

A new algorithm for brain image registration has been proposed in this paper. This method reduces the computational time required for registration of brain images. A reduced runtime makes the registration technique to be used in real time applications. The method proposed here is specific for the axial slice MR brain images.

References

1. Wyawahare, M.V., Patil, P.M., Abhyankar, H.K.: Image Registration Techniques: An Overview. International Journal of Signal Processing, Image Processing and Pattern Recognition 2(3), 1–5 (2009)
2. Brown, L.G.: A Survey of Image Registration Techniques. ACM Computing Surveys 24(4) (1992)
3. Kostelec, P.J., Periaswamy, S.: Image Registration for MRI. Modern Signal Processing 46, 161–184 (2003)
4. Teverovskiy, L., Carmichael, O.T., Aizenstein, H.J., Lazar, N., Liu, Y.: Feature-Based vs. Intensity-based Brain Image Registration: Voxel Level and Structure Level Performance Evaluation. CMU-ML, p. 2 (2006)
5. Shen, D., Davatzikos, C.: HAMMER: Hierarchical Attribute Matching Mechanism for Elastic Registration. IEEE Transactions on Medical Imaging 21, 1421–1439 (2002)
6. Huang, X., Sun, Y., Metaxas, D., Sauer, F., Xu, C.: Hybrid Image Registration Based on Configural Matching of Scale-invariant Salient Region Features. In: Computer Vision and Pattern Recognition Workshop, p. 167 (2004)
7. Kim, M., Wu, G., Yap, P.-T., Shen, D.: A Generalized Learning Based Framework for Fast Brain Image Registration. In: Jiang, T., Navab, N., Pluim, J.P.W., Viergever, M.A. (eds.) MICCAI 2010, Part II. LNCS, vol. 6362, pp. 306–314. Springer, Heidelberg (2010)
8. Vercauteren, T., Pennec, X., Perchant, A., Ayache, N.: Diffeomorphic Demons Efficient Non-parametric Image Registration. NeuroImage 72, S61–S72 (2009)
9. Mangin, J.F., Frouin, V., Bloch, I., Bendriem, B., Lopez-Krahe, J.: Fast Nonsupervised 3-D Registration of PET and MR Images of the Brain. J. Cerebr. Blood Flow Metab. 14(5), 749–762 (1994)
10. Sasikala, D., Neelaveni, R.: Registration of Brain Images Using Fast Walsh HadamardTransform. International Journal of Computer Science and Information Security Publication 8(2), 96–105 (2010)
11. Yamamura, Y., Kim, H., Tan, J., Ishikawa, S., Yamamoto, A.: A Method for Reducing of Computational Time on Image Registration Employing Wavelet Transformation. Control, Automation and Systems, 1286–1291 (2007)
12. Lepore, N., Chou, Y.Y., Lopez, O.L., Aizenstein, H.J., Becker, J.T., Toga, A.W., Thompson, P.M.: Fast 3D Fluid Registration of Brain Magnetic Resonance Images. In: SPIE, vol. 6916, pp. 69160Z–69160Z-8 (2008)
13. Shekhar, R., Zagrodsky, V., Castro-Pareja, C.R., Walimbe, V., Jagadeesh, J.M.: High-speed Registration of Three- and Four-dimensional Medical Images by Using Voxel Similarity. Radiographics 23, 1673–1681 (2003)
14. Alzheimers Disease Neuroimaging Initiative, http://adni.loni.ucla.edu

A Fuzzy Based Automatic Bridge Detection Technique for Satellite Images

Lizy Abraham[1] and M. Sasikumar[2]

[1] Department of Electronics and Communication Engineering,
LBS Institute of Technology for Women, Kerala University, Trivandrum, India
lizytvm@yahoo.com
[2] Head of the Department, Marian Engineering College, Kerala, India

Abstract. Automatic detection of artificial objects from satellite images are important source of information in many applications such as terrain mapping by remote sensing and GIS (Geographic Information System) applications. In this paper, a fuzzy based integrated algorithm for automatic detection of bridges over water is proposed. In the first step, the multispectral satellite image is given to a fuzzy based thresholding method to segment water regions from the background. Then candidate bridge pixels are extracted according to area analysis and bridge extraction algorithm developed. The algorithm is formulated in such a way that, the method can be applied to any complexity levels and any spatial resolutions. The approach in this paper has been implemented and tested with different types of satellite images to validate the superior performance of the algorithm.

Keywords: Area analysis, Bridge extraction, Fuzzy segmentation, Hough transform, Otsu's thresholding.

1 Introduction

Automatic detection of geographical objects such as roads, buildings and bridges from remote sensing imagery is a very meaningful but difficult work. Bridges over water is a typical geographical object and its automatic detection is of great significance whether for military or civilian application.

A number of methods have been developed for bridge extraction from high resolution satellite imagery [1, 2] but they are based on detecting linear features after segmentation and can be applied only for very high resolution SAR images. Trias-Sanz et al. [3] suggest techniques to automatically detect bridges on small high-resolution panchromatic satellite images that rely on radiometric features and geometric models. Although the approach is effective,computation of texture parameters for a large image takes a significant amount of time. Most existing methods are based on knowledge base, which is not derived automatically [4, 5]. But since these rules are developed by an observer, the methods are not well suited for all types of images. In [6] segmentation is greatly influenced by gray level value which changes with elevation angle of sun and turbidity of water.

K.R. Venugopal and L.M. Patnaik (Eds.): ICIP 2012, CCIS 292, pp. 213–219, 2012.
© Springer-Verlag Berlin Heidelberg 2012

A fuzzy based thresholding method can be used for accurately segmenting water regions from background [7]. But the knowledge model proposed in the approach can not be applied for any complexity levels and spatial resolutions.

In this paper after fuzzy based segmentation, exact location of bridges are obtained by knowledge models and spatial resolution of the image. These knowledge models are applied in the algorithm in such a way that the thresholds are automatically fixed depending on the quality of the image. Then candidate bridge pixels are extracted according to area analysis and bridge extraction algorithm developed. Panchromatic and multispectral images can be processed using this method. Results are presented and it can be observed that the road extraction is done with high accuracy for different types of images of varying complexity and resolution levels.

2 Methodology

The approach of bridge recognition strategy has been applied to various satellite images to test the validity of the method. All the images are three-band pan-sharpened multispectral (PS-MS) images with different resolutions. The multispectral data contain four individual bands: red (R), green (G), blue (B) and near infrared (NIR). Here we discard NIR band as our algorithm of bridge detection does not require that band. The overall flow of the system is shown in Fig. 1.

2.1 Fuzzy Based Thresholding

The algorithm based on histogram works well for most of the satellite images as the water areas have significant difference in gray level compared to other regions. But some shadow regions and urban areas can also be misclassified as water regions. Depending on sun elevation and azimuth angles and the sensor azimuth angle gray level intensities may vary widely and this method is not possible. In this paper, fuzzy threshold segmentation [7] is used for pre-processing the image. If $\mu_x(x_{ij})$ represent membership value of gray value x at location i, j then the original image X of size (m, n) is defined as [1]:

$$X = \{(x_{ij}, \mu_x(x_{ij}))\} \tag{1}$$

where $0 \leq \mu_x(x_{ij}) \leq 1, i = 0, 1, ...m - 1, j = 0, 1, ...n - 1$. Choose an arbitrary threshold t and find $\mu_x(x_{ij})$ of each pixel values as [2]:

$$\mu_x(x_{mct}) = \begin{cases} \dfrac{1}{1+|x_{mr} - \mu_0|/C}, & x_{mr} \leq t \\ \dfrac{1}{1+|x_{mr} - \mu_1|/C}, & x_{mn} > t \end{cases} \tag{2}$$

$$C = min\{|t - \mu_0|, |t - \mu_1|\} \tag{3}$$

where μ_0 is the average gray value of background ($x_{ij} \leq t$) and μ_1 is average gray value of foreground ($x_{ij} > t$). Then find the expectation value for all threshold

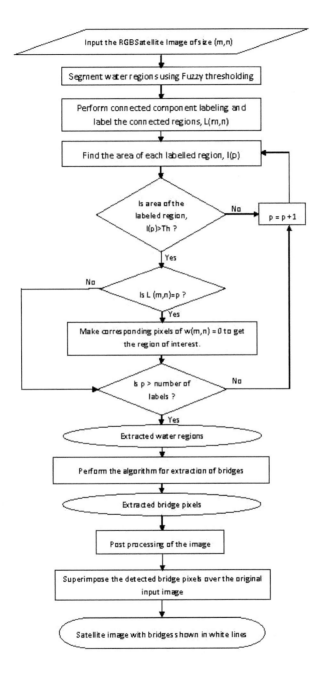

Fig. 1. Schematic Diagram of the Method

values. The t corresponding to the minimum of all expectation values is selected as the optimum threshold for that particular image.

2.2   Fine Segmentation to Remove Noise

By a sequence of morphological erosion and dilation steps undesired small objects are removed and the bridge gaps are closed. Binary morphological operators such as erosion and dilation combine a local neighborhood of pixels with a pixel mask to achieve the desired result. The expectation area can be further scaled down by a logical exclusive OR operation with the initial threshold result and subsequent noise reduction. The Fig. 3(a) shows the result of fine segmented image. An IKONOS satellite image of 1-m resolution (Fig. 2(a)) and corresponding fuzzy segmented image (Fig. 2(b)) is shown below.

2.3   Area Analysis

After morphological operations, there are still a lot of regions which are similar to water areas. The size of these areas are very small compared to other regions and can be eliminated by connected component labelling. To verify the hypothesized connected components as water regions, area analysis is performed. A suitable threshold for area is determined by using Otsu's method [8] and this is applied for the fine segmented image. The aim is to find the threshold value where the sum of foreground and background spreads is at its minimum. After otsu's thresholding regions having area size greater than the threshold is considered as the region of interest which is shown in Fig. 2(c).

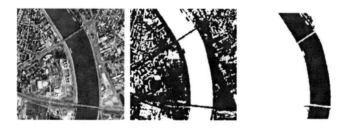

Fig. 2. (a)IKONOS Satellite Image (b)Fine Segmented Image after Fuzzy Thresholding (c)Image after Area Analysis

2.4   Extraction of Bridges

Bridges are extracted from the image using the logic that at bridge edges there is a transition between black and white pixels. If the number of pixels between the transitions is less than at least 10% percentage of width of the image for an 1-m resolution image, they are considered as bridge pixels. But if the resolution of the satellite image varies this threshold is modified accordingly. The algorithm is formulated as follows (Table. 1):

Table 1. Algorithm - Bridge Extraction

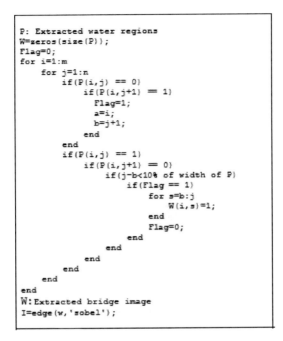

```
P: Extracted water regions
W=zeros(size(P));
Flag=0;
for i=1:m
    for j=1:n
        if(P(i,j) == 0)
            if(P(i,j+1) = 1)
                Flag=1;
                a=i;
                b=j+1;
            end
        end
        if(P(i,j) == 1)
            if(P(i,j+1) = 0)
                if(j-b<10% of width of P)
                    if(Flag == 1)
                        for s=b:j
                            W(i,s)=1;
                        end
                        Flag=0;
                    end
                end
            end
        end
    end
end
W: Extracted bridge image
I=edge(w,'sobel');
```

Using the algorithm any type of bridges are extracted irrespective of their inclination angle,shape and size. As the algorithm is carefully formulated without considering the geometrical features, further processing is not much required in the test process. The below figures show the extracted bridge regions (Fig. 3(a)) and the detected edge lines of the bridge (Fig. 3(b)).

2.5   Post Processing of the Extracted Image

The output image includes error specified by the scattered white points which may be detected as bridges. This can be eliminated using hough transform Fig. 3(c).

Finally superimpose the detected bridge pixels over the original input image. Satellite RGB image with bridges shown in white pixels is the resultant image Fig. 3(d).

3   Results and Discussions

The proposed algorithm has been tested on various images obtained from different satellite sensors and the outputs are shown in the following figures (Fig. 4(a) - Fig. 4(d)).

The algorithm proposed here uses fuzzy based segmentation and Otsu's thresholding for area analysis, which increase the applicability of this work over a wide range of images since the threshold is not fixed. This algorithm is designed to perform on images of varying resolutions. Using the algorithm any type of bridges are extracted irrespective of their inclination and shape. Also segmentation is not affected by gray level value which changes with elevation angle of sun and turbidity of water. Panchromatic and multispectral images can be processed using this method. PAN images can be directly processed whereas for multispectral, we have to subject the image to preprocessing to extract only its luminance component (Y) before processing the image using the proposed algorithm.

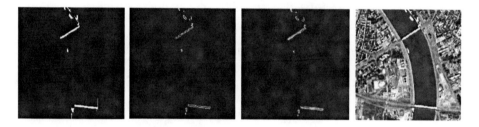

Fig. 3. (a)Extracted Bridge Regions (b)Detected Edge Lines of the Bridge (c)Image after Post Processing (d)Resultant Image

(a)IKONOS image (1-m) (b)Quickbird image (60-cm) (c)SPOT5 image (2.5-m) (d)SPOT5 image (4-m)

Fig. 4. Bridge Detected Results

4   Conclusions

In this paper, a fuzzy based automatic bridge detection technique is designed for any type of satellite images including low resolution images, images taken at different sum azimuth and elevation angles and images having bridges of different angle of inclinations. Considering the results, acceptable accuracy for the resultant images is obtained and so the efficiency of the bridge detection process is improved by using our algorithm. If we use multispectral images and prior processing, the background regions are masked depending on spectral properties further improvements are possible.

References

1. Robalo, J., Lichtenegger, J.: ERS-SAR Images a Bridge. ESA, Earth Oberservation Quarterly, 7–10 (December 1999), http://esapub.esrin.esa.it/eoq/eoq64/bridge.pdf

2. May, P., Ehrlich, H.-C., Steinke, T.: ZIB Structure Prediction Pipeline: Composing a Complex Biological Workflow Through Web Services. In: Nagel, W.E., Walter, W.V., Lehner, W. (eds.) Euro-Par 2006. LNCS, vol. 4128, pp. 1148–1158. Springer, Heidelberg (2006)

3. Trias-Sanz, R., Lomenie, N., Barbeau, J.: Using Textural and Geometric Information for an Automatic Bridge Detection System. In: Proc. ACIVS, Brussels, Belgium, August 31-September 3, pp. 325–332 (2004)

4. Du, Z.G., et al.: Recognition of Bridge Over Water in Air-Plane Image. Journal of Wuhan University of Technology 29, 230–233 (2005)

5. Chaudhuri, D., Samal, A.: An Automatic Bridge Detection Technique for Multispectral Images. IEEE Transaction on Geoscience and Remote Sensing 46(9), 2720–2727 (2008)

6. Han, Y., Zheng, H., Cao, Q., Wang, Y.: An Effective Method for Bridge Detection from Satellite Imagery. In: 2nd IEEE Conference on Industrial Electronics and Applications, Harbin, China, pp. 2753–2757 (2007)

7. Yili, F., Kun, X., YongJie, H., Yongfei, X.: Recognition of Bridge Over Water in High-Resolution Remote Sensing Images. In: World Congress on Computer Science and Information Engineering, Los Angeles/Anaheim, USA, March 31-April 2 (2009)

8. Otsu, N.: A Threshold Selection Method from Graylevel Histograms. IEEE Transactions on Systems, Man, and Cybernetics 9(1), 62–66 (1979)

Capsule Endoscopic Colour Image Denoising Using Complex Wavelet Transform

Varun P. Gopi, P. Palanisamy, and S. Issac Niwas

Department of Electronics and Communication Engineering
National Institute of Technology (NIT), Tiruchirappalli, Tamilnadu-620015
vpg@ieee.org

Abstract. In this paper, wavelet transform based capsule endoscopic colour image denoising method is proposed. Recent research in image denoising methods mainly focused on wavelet transform as its superior performance over other transforms. In this proposed method double density dual tree complex wavelet transform (DDDT-CWT) is used due to its ability to implement as complex and multi-directional wavelet transform. Denoising is done in YCbCr colour space, which provides good results in terms of peak signal to noise ratio (PSNR) and structural similarity (SSIM) than RGB colour space.

Keywords: Wireless Capsule Endoscopy, Image Denoising, PSNR, Structural Similarity.

1 Introduction

In medical diagnostics, Wireless Capsule Endoscopy (WCE) is used to acquire the images of human intestine [1-4]. The capsule consist of imaging and wireless circuitry embedded in it. The patient ingests this electronic capsule, it captures images during a slow squirm process and transmits them wirelessly to an outside workstation. Due to the complicated environment of the intestine and intrinsic restrictions of the equipment used for image acquisition and transmission results in noisy images. The wavelet transform is a simple and elegant tool that can be used for many digital signal and image processing applications. Many techniques for image analysis based on wavelet have been proposed. In Image Denoising using wavelets, signal and noise are seperated in the wavelet domain through discrete wavelet transform (DWT) and noise is removed by thresholding the wavelet coefficients [5].

Thresholding of wavelet coefficients is a popular denoising technique due to its good edge preserving properties [6-10]. Small coefficients correspond to smooth regions of the image, while large coefficients occur in the edge regions. The main idea of wavelet denoising is to modify the coefficients according to this classification. Grayscale Image Denoising can be straightforwardly extended to color images by applying it to each color component independently. However, it is important to properly choose the color space for the best possible performance. For example, our study suggests that denoising in YCbCr (luma and chroma) space

K.R. Venugopal and L.M. Patnaik (Eds.): ICIP 2012, CCIS 292, pp. 220–229, 2012.
© Springer-Verlag Berlin Heidelberg 2012

[11] is better than RGB. Wavelet transform is a powerful tool for Image Denoising. Inspite of its sparse representation and efficient computation, the wavelet transform suffers from four fundamental shortcomings like oscillation of wavelet coefficients into positive and negative around singularities, shift variance, aliasing due to iterated discrete-time downsampling operations, lack of directionality as given in [12]. Due to these shortcomings, double density dual tree complex wavelet transform (DDDT-CWT) is used in this work. To produce better colour estimates, first convert the image into YCbCr space, then apply the gray scale denoising method based on DDDT-CWT seperately on each component. The noise is added in RGB (Red, Blue, Green) space, but denoising is performed in both RGB and YCbCr spaces.

2   Framework of DDDT-CWT

DDDT-CWT is a combination of both double-density and the dual-tree DWT, so the resultant transform have taken the advantages of both, which ensures that:

- Two wavelets of the first pair are offset from one other by one half.
- The other pair of wavelets form an approximate Hilbert transform pair.

By doing this, the DDDT-CWT can be used to implement complex and directional wavelet transforms. The following comparisons clarifies the differences between the double-density DWT and the dual-tree DWT.

1. In double-density DWT, the two wavelets are offset by one half, whereas in dual-tree DWT, the two wavelets form an approximate Hilbert transform pair.
2. For the dual-tree DWT, there are fewer degrees of freedom for design whereas for the double-density DWT, there are more degrees of freedom for design
3. Different filterbank structures are used to implement the dual-tree and double-density DWTs.
4. The dual-tree DWT can be used to implement 2-D transforms with directional Gabor-like wavelets, which is highly desirable for image processing (the double-density DWT cannot be, although it can be used in conjunction with specialized post-filters to implement a complex wavelet transform with low-redundancy, as developed in [13])

This transform forms a new family of dyadic wavelet frames based on two scaling functions and four distinct wavelets $\psi_{h,i}(t)$ and $\psi_{g,i}(t)$, $i = 1, 2$.

where

$$\psi_{g,1}(t) = H\{\psi_{h,1}(t)\}, \psi_{g,2}(t) = H\{\psi_{h,2}(t)\} \tag{1}$$

and

$$\psi_{h,1}(t) = \psi_{h,2}(t - 0.5), \psi_{g,1}(t) = \psi_{g,2}(t - 0.5), \tag{2}$$

Eq. 1 indicates that $\psi_{h,1}(t)$ and $\psi_{h,2}(t)$ are offset from one another by one half and similarly for $\psi_{g,i}(t)$. The second equation shows that the two wavelets $\psi_{h,1}(t)$ and $\psi_{g,1}(t)$ form an approximate Hilbert transform pair and $\psi_{g,2}(t)$, $\psi_{h,2}(t)$ likewise. Threfore they are suitable for directional and complex wavelet transforms. The design procedure for the DDDT-CWT introduced in this paper draws on the design procedures for the double-density DWT and the dual-tree DWT described in [14-17].

The DDDT-CWT is obtained by concatenating two oversampled DWTs. Like dual-tree DWT, the filterbank structure for the DDDT-CWT consists of two oversampled iterated filterbanks operating in parallel. Fig. 1 shows the structure of oversampled filter bank. Filters in the first filter (analysis filter) bank is denoted by $h_i(n)$ and the second filter bank (synthesis filter) is denoted by $g_i(n)$, for $i = 0, 1, 2$. The synthesis filters should be the time reversed version of analysis filters. Main aim is to design a FIR filter which satisfies the following properties:

1. Perfect reconstruction (PR)
2. The wavelets form two approximate Hilbert transform pairs
3. Wavelets have specified vanishing moments
4. The filters are of short support

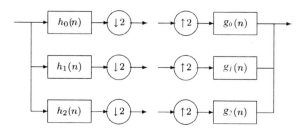

Fig. 1. Oversampled Analysis and Synthesis Filter Bank Structure

From basic multirate identities, the PR conditions for $h_i(n)$ and $g_i(n)$ are the following

$$H_0(z)H_0(1/z) + H_1(z)H_1(1/z) + H_2(z)H_2(1/z) = 2 \tag{3}$$

$$H_0(z)H_0(-1/z) + H_1(z)H_1(-1/z) + H_2(z)H_2(-1/z) = 0 \tag{4}$$

and

$$G_0(z)G_0(1/z) + G_1(z)G_1(1/z) + G_2(z)G_2(1/z) = 2 \tag{5}$$

$$G_0(z)G_0(-1/z) + G_1(z)G_1(-1/z) + G_2(z)G_2(-1/z) = 0 \tag{6}$$

The scaling and wavelet functions are defined by the dilation and wavelet equations,

$$\phi_h(t) = \sqrt{2} \sum_n h_0(n)\phi_h(2t - n) \tag{7}$$

$$\psi_{h,1}(t) = \sqrt{2} \sum_n h_1(n)\phi_h(2t - n), \psi_{h,2}(t) = \sqrt{2} \sum_n h_2(n)\phi_h(2t - n) \tag{8}$$

and

$$\phi_g(t) = \sqrt{2} \sum_n g_0(n)\phi_g(2t - n) \tag{9}$$

$$\psi_{g,1}(t) = \sqrt{2} \sum_n g_1(n)\phi_g(2t - n), \psi_{g,2}(t) = \sqrt{2} \sum_n g_2(n)\phi_g'(2t - n) \tag{10}$$

The iterated oversampled filter bank pair, corresponding to the simultaneous implementation of the DDDT-CWT is illustrated in Fig. 2. There are two separate filter banks denoted by $h_i(n)$ and $g_i(n)$ where i=0, 1, 2. The filter banks $h_i(n)$ and $g_i(n)$ are unique and designed in a specific way so the subband signals of the upper DWT can be interpreted as the real part of a complex wavelet transform, and the subband signals of the lower DWT can be interpreted as the imaginary part. Equivalently, for specially designed sets of filters, the wavelets associated with the upper DWT can be approximate Hilbert transforms of the wavelets associated with the lower DWT. The wavelet coefficients w are stored in a cell array data structure $w\{j\}\{i\}\{k\}\{d\}$, for j=1 to J, i=1 to 2, k=1 to 2, d=1 to 8. Where j represents the scale, i=1 real part (tree 1), i=2 imaginary part (tree 2), (k, d) represents the orientation and J represents number of stages.

3   Proposed Algorithm

The proposed algorithm includes the following steps for colour Image Denoising

1. Image selection: Select an endoscopic image of size 512 x 512.
2. Preprocessing: First convert the selected image in to double data type and then add Gaussian noise to the image.
3. Colour conversion : Convert the preprocessed image in to YCbCr space.
4. Transform: Take the forward wavelet transform over 4 scales using DDDT-CWT.
5. Thresholding: Threshold the wavelet coefficients through all the subbands using soft thresholding based on MAP estimator
6. Inverse transform: After thresholding, take the inverse wavelet transform using DDDT-CWT.

4   Soft Thresholding Based on MAP Estimator

Let y be noisy wavelet coefficient of the form $y = w + n$, in transform domain, where w is the noise-free coefficient and n is noise, which is zero-mean Gaussian. The main goal is to estimate w from noisy observation y. The estimate depends on the observed (noisy) value y, so it can be denoted as $\hat{w}(y)$.

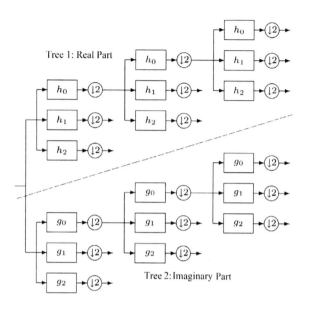

Fig. 2. Schematic of Iterated Oversampled Filterbank for the DDDT-CWT

As expalined in [18], the MAP estimate of w can be written as

$$\hat{w}(y) = sign(y).(|y| - T)_+ \qquad (11)$$

where $(a)_+$ and threshold T are defined as

$$(a)_+ = \begin{cases} 0 \ if \ a < 0 \\ a \ if \ a \geq 0 \end{cases} \qquad (12)$$

and

$$T = \frac{\sqrt{2}\sigma_n^2}{\sigma} \qquad (13)$$

Finally MAP estimator can be written as

$$\hat{w}(y) = soft(y, T) \qquad (14)$$

5   Image Quality Assesment

In this denoising, the performance of the denoised image is quantitatively analyzed by means of two measures such as PSNR and Structural Similarity Index (SSIM).

5.1   PSNR

PSNR of colour image is computed as

$$PSNR = 10\log_{10}(\frac{255^2}{MSE_c})\qquad(15)$$

$$MSE_c = \frac{1}{3}MSE_{c\in R,G,B}\qquad(16)$$

Mean Square Error (MSE) which is the cumulative squared error between original and denoised image and is defined as

$$MSE_{c\in R,G,B} = \frac{1}{MN}\sum_{i=1}^{M}\sum_{j=1}^{N}(I_c(i,j) - \widehat{I}_c(i,j))^2\qquad(17)$$

where $I_c(i,j)$ and $\widehat{I}_c(i,j)$ are the original and denoised image rspectively.

5.2   SSIM

The PSNR measurement gives a numerical value on the damage, but it does not describe its type. Moreover, as is noted in [19-20], it does not quite represent the quality perceived by human observers. For medical imaging applications, where images are degraded must eventually be examined by experts, traditional evaluation remains insufficient. For this reason, objective approaches are needed to assess the medical imaging quality. We then evaluate a new paradigm to estimate the quality of medical images, specifically the ones compressed by wavelet transform, based on the assumption that the human visual system (HVS) is highly adapted to extract structural information. The similarity index compares the brightness $I(x, y)$, contrast $c(x, y)$ and structure $s(x, y)$ between each pair of vectors, where the SSIM index between two signals x and y is given by the following expression [21-22].

$$SSIM(x, y) = I(x, y)c(x, y)s(x, y)\qquad(18)$$

However, the comparison of brightness is determined by the following expression

$$I(x, y) = \frac{2\mu_x\mu_y + C_1}{\mu_x + \mu_y + C_1}\qquad(19)$$

where the average intensity of signal x is given by

$$\mu_x = \frac{1}{N}\sum_{i=1}^{N}x_i, C_1 = (K_1 L)^2\qquad(20)$$

the constant $K_1 \ll 1$, and L is the dynamic row of the pixel values (255 for an image coded on 8 bits). The function of contrast comparison takes the following form

$$c(x,y) = \frac{2\sigma_x \sigma_y}{\sigma_x^2 + \sigma_y^2 + C_2} \tag{21}$$

where $\sigma_x = \sqrt{\mu_x(x^2) - \mu_x^2(x)}$ is the standard deviation of the original signal x, $C_2 = (K_2 L)^2$ and the constant $K_2 \ll 1$.

The function of structure comparison is defined as follows

$$s(x,y) = \frac{\sigma_{xy} + C_3}{\sigma_x \sigma_y + C_3} = \frac{cov(x,y) + C_3}{\sigma_x \sigma_y + C_3} \tag{22}$$

where $cov(x,y) = \mu_{xy} - \mu_x \mu_y$ and $C_3 = C_2/2$

Then the expression of the Structural Similarity index becomes

$$SSIM(x,y) = \frac{(2\mu_x \mu_y + C_1)(2\sigma_{xy} + C_2)}{(\mu_x^2 + \mu_y^2 + C_1)(\sigma_x^2 + \sigma_y^2 + C_2)} \tag{23}$$

6   Results and Discussion

The proposed Image Denoising method is implemented as an algorithm tested by MATLAB simulation with the aid of endoscopic images. To prove the effectiveness of the proposed method, it is compared to some other denoising techniques like Bayesian methods for subband-adaptive, spatially-adaptive, and multivalued Image Denoising (ProbShrink-MB) [23], Sparse 3-D Transform-Domain Collaborative Filtering (C-BM3D) [24] and locally adaptive, variance based filtering

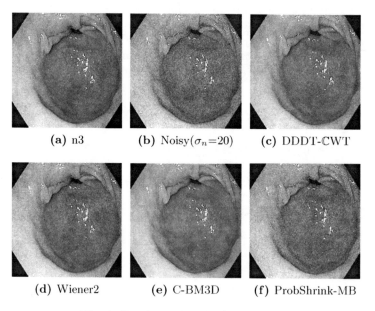

(a) n3   (b) Noisy(σ_n=20)   (c) DDDT-CWT

(d) Wiener2   (e) C-BM3D   (f) ProbShrink-MB

Fig. 3. Simulation Results (RGB Space)

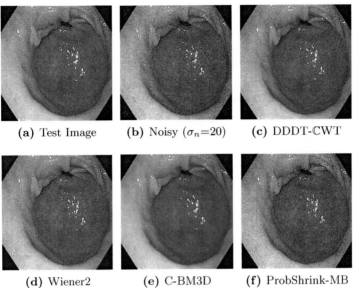

(a) Test Image   (b) Noisy (σ_n=20)   (c) DDDT-CWT

(d) Wiener2   (e) C-BM3D   (f) ProbShrink-MB

Fig. 4. Simulation Results (YCbCr Space)

Table 1. Performance Comparison

	Method	PSNR (dB)		SSIM	
		RGB	**YCbCr**	**RGB**	**YCbCr**
σ_n=10	DDDT-ℂ WT	35.20	41.94	0.7927	0.9413
	Wiener2	36.26	41.76	0.7754	0.9317
	C-BMD3	36.08	38.03	0.7434	0.9127
	ProbShrink-MB	33.57	39.08	0.7320	0.8110
σ_n=20	DDDT-ℂ WT	31.74	38.38	0.5791	0.8859
	Wiener2	33.13	37.60	0.6724	0.8366
	C-BMD3	33.02	35.88	0.6521	0.8113
	ProbShrink-MB	30.75	34.21	0.5464	0.6435
σ_n=30	DDDT-ℂ WT	30.34	36.28	0.4248	0.8269
	Wiener2	31.22	34.62	0.5357	0.7121
	C-BMD3	31.69	34.50	0.4272	0.7081
	ProbShrink-MB	29.89	32.60	0.3928	0.4719
σ_n=40	DDDT-ℂ WT	29.56	34.84	0.3195	0.7716
	Wiener2	30.20	32.83	0.4214	0.6297
	C-BMD3	30.36	33.54	0.4142	0.5787
	ProbShrink-MB	29.47	31.60	0.2723	0.3685

method (Wiener2)[25]. Image denoised in RBG space and YCbCr space is shown in Fig. 3 and 4 respectively for a noise level (σ_n) of 20. Table 1 represents the PSNR and SSIM values of denoised images at different noise levels.

7   Conclusion and Future Work

In this paper, study of removal of noise from corrupted image by using complex wavelet transform is performed. In this method, Image Denoising in YCbCr space based on DDDT-CWT is proposed. Performance of the proposed algorithm is compared with other colour Image Denoising techniques. The results of the proposed work has shown better performance than the other denoising methods. Future work will be Image Denoising based on other complex wavelets and other thresholding thechniques to enhance the results.

References

1. Moglia, A., Menciassi, A., Dario, P.: Recent Patents on Wireless Capsule Endoscopy. Recent Patents on Biomedical Engineering 1(1), 24–33 (2008)
2. Faigel, D.O., Cave, D.R.: Capsule Endoscopy. Saunders Elsevier, Amsterdam (2008)
3. Swain, P.: The Future of Wireless Capsule Endoscopy. World Journal of Gastroenterology 14(26), 4142–4145 (2008)
4. McCaffrey, C., Chevalerias, O., OMathuna, C., Twomey, K.: Swallowable-Capsule Technology. IEEE Pervasive Computing 7(1), 23–29 (2008)
5. Mallat, S.: A Wavelet Tour of Signal Processing. Academic, MA (1998)
6. Donoho, D.L., Johnstone, I.M.: Adapting to Unknown Smoothness via Wavelet Strinkage. J. American Statistical Association 90, 1200–1224 (1995)
7. Crouse, M.S., Nowak, R.D., Baraniuk, R.G.: Wavelet-based Statistical Signal Processing Using Hidden Markov Models. IEEE Transaction. Signal Process. 46(4), 886–902 (1998)
8. Malfait, M., Roose, D.: Wavelet-based Image Denoising Using a Markov Random Field a Prior Model. IEEE Transaction Image Processing 6(4), 549–565 (1997)
9. Romberg, J., Choi, H., Baraniuk, R.G.: Bayesian Tree-Structured Image Modeling Using Wavelet-Domain Hidden Markov Models. IEEE Transaction Image Processing 10(7), 1056–1068 (2001)
10. Bao, P., Zhang, L.: Noise Reduction for Magnetic Resonance Images *via* Adaptive Multiscale Products Thresholding. IEEE Transaction Medical Imaging 22(9), 1089–1099 (2003)
11. Bhaskaran, V., Konstantinides, K.: Image and Video Compression Standards. Kluwer, Norwell (1995)
12. Dragotti, P.L., Vetterli, M.: Wavelet footprints.: Theory, Algorithms, and Applications. IEEE Transaction Signal Processing 51(5), 1306–1323 (2003)
13. Fernandes, F., van Spaendonck, R., Burrus, C.S.: A New Directional, Low-Redundancy Complex-Wavelet Transform. In: Proceedings IEEE International Conference Acoust., Speech, Signal Processing (2001)
14. Chui, C., He, W.: Compactly Supported Tight Frames Associated with Refinable Functions. Appl. Comput. Harmon. Anal. 8(3), 293–319 (2000)
15. Selesnick, I.W.: The Design of Hilbert Transform Pairs of Wavelet Bases *via* the Flat Delay Filter. In: Proceedings IEEE International Conference Acoust., Speech, Signal Process. (2001)
16. The Double Density DWT. In: Petrosian, A., Meyer, F.G. (eds.) Wavelets in Signal and Image Analysis: From Theory to Practice. Kluwer, Boston (2001)

17. Selesnick, I.W.: The Design of Approximate Hilbert Transform Pairs of Wavelet Bases. IEEE Transaction Signal Processing 50, 1144–1152 (2002)
18. Selesnick, I.W.: A Derivation of the Soft-Thresholding Function. Polytechnic Institute of New York University (2009/2010)
19. Geisler, W.S., Banks, M.S.: Visual Performance. Handbook of Optics, vol. 1. McGraw-Hill, NY (1995)
20. Watson, A.B., Kreslake, L.B.: Measurement of Visual Impairment Scales for Digital Video. In: Human Vision and Electronic Imaging Conference, San Jose, CA, USA. SPIE, vol. 4299, pp. 79–89 (2001)
21. Wang, Z., Bovik, A.C., Sheikh, H.R., Simoncelli, E.P.: Image Quality Assessment: From Error Visibility to Structural Similarity. IEEE Transactions on Image Processing 13, 600–612 (2004)
22. Wang, Z., Bovik, A.C.: A Universal Image Quality Index. IEEE Signal Processing Letters 9, 81–84 (2002)
23. Pizurica, A., Philips, W.: Estimating the Probability of the Presence of a Signal of Interest in Multiresolution Single and Multiband Image Denoising. IEEE Transaction Image Processing 15(3), 645–665 (2006)
24. Dabov, Foi, A., Katkovnik, V., Egiazarian, K.: Image Denoising by Sparse 3D Transform-Domain Collaborative Filtering. IEEE Transaction Image Processing 16(8), 2080–2095 (2007)
25. Lee, J.S.: Digital Image Enhancement and Noise Filtering by use of Local Statistics. IEEE Transaction Pattern Analysis and Machine Intelligence, PAMI 2(2), 165–168 (1980)

An Improved Adaptive Border Marching Algorithm for Inclusion of Juxtapleural Nodule in Lung Segmentation of CT-Images

P.R. Varshini[1], S. Baskar[2], and S. Alagappan[3]

[1] Depatrment of Electrical and Electronics Engineering
prvarshini@tce.edu
[2] Department of Electrical and Electronics Engineering Department
Thiagarajar College of Engineering, Madurai, Tamil Nadu
[3] Chief Consultant Radiologist, Devaki MRI & CT scans, Madurai, Tamil Nadu

Abstract. Lung segmentation is an important preprocessing step in the diagnosis of lung cancer using chest Computed Tomography (CT) images. Presence of Juxtapleural nodules makes lung segmentation more complex. In this paper, an Improved Adaptive Border Marching (IABM) algorithm is proposed for lung segmentation. This algorithm reliably includes Juxtapleural nodules while avoiding under-segmentation of convex regions. The proposed algorithm is a simple, reliable and efficient approach for segmenting lungs from a two dimensional CT-image.

Keywords: Computed Tomography, Improved Adaptive Border Marching, Juxtapleural Nodule, Lung Cancer, Lung Segmentation.

1 Introduction

A report of the Early Lung Cancer Action Project (ELCAP) indicated that low dose CT can detect four times more malignant lung nodules than a chest X-ray. Automatic lung segmentation from CT-images is an important part of the Computer Aided Diagnosis (CAD) systems for the lung. Number of techniques has been developed for computer assisted segmentation of lung region from CT-images. In many semi-automatic approaches, some manual interaction is required to select threshold values or edit the resulting segmentation [1]-[4]. Recently, many automatic lung segmentation methods have been developed [5]-[13]. Thresholding and morphological methods [5], [6], region growing methods [7], [13] feature extraction [8] and classification methods, rolling ball algorithm [9], [10] image registration methods [11], [12] have been proposed for lung segmentation.

Pu et al., [1] have proposed an Adaptive Border Marching (ABM) algorithm to segment the lung by smoothing the lung border in a geometric way and to include Juxtapleural nodules. This also minimizes over-segmentation of adjacent regions such as the abdomen and mediastinum. Shiying et al., [5] have proposed a fully automatic method for identifying the lungs in three-dimensional

K.R. Venugopal and L.M. Patnaik (Eds.): ICIP 2012, CCIS 292, pp. 230–235, 2012.
© Springer-Verlag Berlin Heidelberg 2012

(3-D) pulmonary X-ray CT images. The lung region is extracted by gray-level thresholding. Then, the left and right lungs are separated by identifying the anterior and posterior junctions by dynamic programming. Finally, a sequence of morphological operations is used to smooth the irregular boundary along the mediastinum. Armato et al., [10] have introduced the use of Ball-Algorithm for the segmentation of lungs. At first stage, each CT-image is gray level thresholded and a rolling ball algorithm is applied to the lung segmentation contours to avoid the loss of Juxtapleural nodules. It is difficult to find a properly-sized rolling ball a priori that works well for all juxtapleural nodules. Sluimer et al., [11] have proposed segmentation-by-registration approach to segment the lung fields from thin-slice CT scans. A scan of a normal subject is elastically registered to each of the abnormal scans. Applying the found deformations to a lung mask created for the normal subject, a segmentation of the abnormal lungs is found.

In this paper, an Improved Adaptive Border Marching algorithm that segments the lung regions from CT scans with successful inclusion of Juxtapleural nodules avoiding under-segmentation of convex region is proposed. This method uses two threshold values namely a smaller value of threshold to include Juxtapleural nodule and a higher value of threshold to avoid under-segmentation of convex region instead of single threshold used in ABM algorithm [1].

Section 2 describes the lung segmentation and Section 3 describes the steps involved in creating the lung mask. Section 4 illustrates the two lung border smoothing algorithms: ABM, IABM and explains the how IABM overcomes the drawbacks of ABM and finally Section 5 discusses the conclusions.

2   Lung Segmentation

The lungs are complex organs. Imprecision in the segmentation process of the lung field can cause distortion to the noticeable subjects in the lung area that are chosen to investigate. Therefore, it is important to preserve the features of the lung field as completely as possible during the segmentation procedure to avoid artifacts. Several image processing techniques have been proposed for segmentation in medical imaging, such as thresholding, region growing, and morphological operations [2]. 2D CT-scan images of thorax were captured by SOMATOM Emotion Duo CT Scanner with 10mm slice thickness. The segmentation of lung is done in three steps: lung mask creation, lung border smoothing and lung field segmentation.

3   Lung Mask Creation

Lung mask is created using conventional gray scale thresholding and morphological operations. In CT images, the blood vessels and other regions of interest are brighter than the lung region[2]. The threshold value is chosen from the input CT scan image and gray scale thresholding is done. A morphological closing operation is used to fill the indentation caused by the exclusion of the pixels

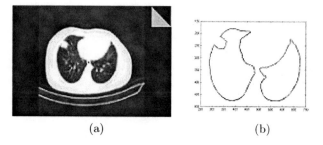

(a)   (b)

Fig. 1. Basic steps of Pulmonary Nodule Detection Scheme: (a)CT-Image (b) Boundary of Lung Mask

representing the pulmonary vessels. After the closing operation, some small islands within the lung region remain. To allocate a complete contour of the lung region margin automatically, a labeling technique is used to find the island slots within the lung regions and fill them up. This creates a lung mask and the lung boundaries obtained is given in Fig.1 (b).

4 Lung Border Smoothing

Inner border tracing algorithm is used to compute the lung border by tracing the lung region. The border of the lung region in each slice is traced in a sequence of pixels, thus forming a collection of directed closed contours [1]:

$$Lungborder = \{L_i \,|(p_1, p_2, ..., p_{ni}), i \in [1, m]\}. \tag{1}$$

where m is the number of directed loops forming the lung border, L_i is the ith direction loop of the lung border, p_x is the pixel of the lung border.

4.1 Adaptive Border Marching Algorithm (ABM)

To bridge the local concavities formed by improperly excluded Juxtapleural nodules, the Adaptive Border Marching algorithm marches along the border with a marching step length and finds all of the convex tracks. The convex track is defined as the line segment connecting the starting point and the rightmost or leftmost point within the marching step. When the marching direction is clockwise, the leftmost line within the marching step is defined as the convex track; when the marching direction is counter-clockwise, the rightmost line within the marching step is defined as the convex track.The marching step length n is chosen adaptively according to the threshold condition [1]:

$$\lambda = \frac{H_{max}}{W} = \frac{R - \sqrt{R^2 - \frac{1}{4}W^2}}{W}. \tag{2}$$

where W is the Euclidean distance between two consecutive points after the marching operation, and Hmax is the maximum height perpendicular to this connecting line segment. Given a local region, if λ is smaller than a threshold λ_0, then the marching step for this region is decreased by a scaling factor δ ε [0,1], and the smoothing operation is executed again until λ within the new marching step is smaller than λ_0. The threshold λ_0 can be optimized to the specific appearance of Juxtapleural nodules. Adaptive border marching is applied to images and the resultant lung segments are shown in Fig.2. The boundaries of the lungs are border marched with a threshold of 0.33.

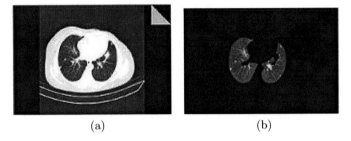

(a)   (b)

Fig. 2. Results of Adaptive Border Marching algorithm: Sample Images and their corresponding segmented lungs after border marching using ABM (a) Sample Image1 (b) lung segment of sample image1

In CT lung images, one lung lobe may have a larger Juxtapleural nodule and the other lung lobe may not have any but its boundary may be convex. If the ABM is applied to this type of CT-image, then for a fixed threshold, exclusion of either Juxtapleural nodule or convex region of the lobe may occur. The ABM algorithm works with a fixed threshold value λ_0. This threshold λ_0 must be a small value λ_{min} in the order of 0.00005, if the Juxtapleural nodule to be included is large in size. This small value of λ_0 does not include the convex regions of the lung lobes as given in Fig.3 (a). In order to include the convex regions within the lung boundary after border marching operations, a value of threshold λ_{max} in the order of 0.33 is to be used which fails in including Juxtapleural nodule as given in Fig.3 (b).

4.2   Improved Adaptive Border Marching Algorithm (IABM)

The problem with the ABM algorithm is that, if this CT image is used for lung segmentation, then border marching with fixed threshold may fail. The lung lobe containing Juxtapleural nodule needs a smaller threshold λ_{min} while the lung lobe without Juxtapleural nodule and containing convex region requires higher threshold λ_{max}. In the proposed algorithm (IABM), the lung boundaries are initially border marched with the smaller value of threshold λ_{min} to include the Juxtapleural nodule. Then the boundaries are border marched with higher value of threshold λ_{max}. The two images are then merged together by image stitching.

A sample image containing a Juxtapleural nodule on the right lung lobe and no pleural nodules on the left lobe is chosen for demonstration as given in Fig. 4(a).

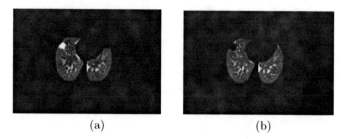

(a)   (b)

Fig. 3. Segments of Lung Obtained after Adaptive Border Marching applied to the Lung Boundaries with Fixed Threshold Values (a) λ_0=0.00005, Under-Segmentation of Convex Regions in Left Lobe, (b) λ_0=0.33, Juxtapleural Nodule are not included

To these images, Improved Adaptive Border Marching algorithm is applied. The lung mask is created by grayscale thresholding and morphological operations. The boundary of the lung mask is obtained by conventional inner border tracing algorithm. To these boundaries, the proposed border marching algorithm is applied with two different threshold values $\lambda_{min} = 0.00005$ and λ_{max} =0.33. The segmented lung lobes after border marching is obtained and these lung segments are then merged together as shown in Fig.4 (b). The total processing time is 25 secs.

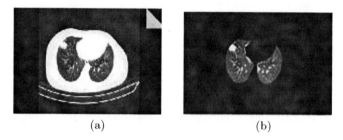

(a)   (b)

Fig. 4. Results of Improved Adaptive Border Marching algorithm. (a) Sample Image (b) Corresponding Lung Segment Obtained after Improved Adaptive Border Marching.

5   Conclusions

An Improved Adaptive Border Marching (IABM) algorithm for smoothing of lung border to segment lung from a CT-image which is an important preprocessing step in diagnosis of lung cancer is proposed. This border marching algorithm uses lung mask created by grayscale thresholding and morphological operations. ABM uses a fixed threshold value which cannot be applied for lung regions with larger Juxtapleural nodule and more convex lung lobe. This Improved Adaptive Border Marching algorithm uses two values of threshold for border marching:

One smaller threshold value to incorporate the Juxtapleural nodule and another higher threshold value to avoid under-segmentation of convex region of lung lobe. The IABM overcomes the failure in ABM algorithm for CT-images with larger pleural nodules and more convex lobes. The proposed algorithm is easy to implement and gives robust and efficient segmentation of lungs with less computational time.

References

1. Pu, J., Justus, R., Chin, A.Y., Sandy, N., Geoffrey, D.R., David, S.P.: Adaptive Border Marching Algorithm: Automatic Lung Segmentation on Chest CT Images. J. Comput. Medical Imaging Graphics 32(6), 452–462 (2008)
2. Daw-Tung, L., Chung-Ren, Y., Wen-Tai, C.: Autonomous Detection of Pulmonary Nodules on CT Images with a Neural Network-Based Fuzzy System. J. Comp. Medical Imaging and Graphics 29, 447–558 (2005)
3. Kalender, W.A., Fichte, H., Bautz, W., Skalej, M.: Semiautomatic Evaluation In: Procedures for Quantitative CT of the Lung. J. Comput. Assist. Tomogr. 15(2), 248–255 (1991)
4. Keller, J.M., Edwards, F.M., Rundle, R.: Automatic Outlining of Regions on CT Scans. J. Comput. Assist. Tomogr. 5(2), 240–245 (1981)
5. Shiying, H., Eric, A.H., Joseph, M.R.: Automatic Lung Segmentation for Accurate Quantitation of Volumetric X-Ray CT Images. IEEE Transactions on Medical Imaging 20(6), 490–498 (2001)
6. Ozkan, H., Osman, O., Sahin, S., Atasoy, M.M., Barutca, H., Boz, A.F., Olsun, A.: Lung Segmentation Algorithm for CAD System in CTA Images. World Academy of Science, Engineering and Technology 77, 306–309 (2011)
7. Regina, P., Klaus, D.T.: Otto-von-Guericke: Segmentation of Medical Images Using Adaptive Region Growing. In: Proceedings SPIE, vol. 4322, p. 1337 (2001)
8. Avishkar, M., Mamatha, R., Arcot, S.: Automatic Lung Segmentation. A Comparison of Anatomical and Machine Learning Approaches. In: Proceedings of the 2004 Intelligent Sensors Sensor Networks and Information Processing Conference, pp. 451–456. IEEE (2004)
9. Bae, K.T., Kim, J.S., Na, Y.H., Kim, K.G., Kim, J.H.: Pulmonary Nodules: Automated Detection on CT Images with Morphologic Matching Algorithm–Preliminary Results. Radiology 236, 286–294 (2005)
10. Armato III, S.G., Giger, M.I., Moran, C.J., Blackburn, J.T., Doi, K., MacMahon, H.: Computerized Detection of Pulmonary Nodules on CT Scans. Radiographics 19, 1303–1311 (1999)
11. Sluimer, I.C., Meindert, N., Bram, V.G.: Lung Field Segmentation from Thin-Slice CT Scans in Presence of Severe Pathology. In: Proceedings of the SPIE Medical Imaging, vol. 5370, pp. 1447–1455 (2004)
12. Muenzing, E.A., Murphy, K., Van, G.B., Pluim, J.P.W.: Automatic Detection of Registration Errors for Quality Assessment in Medical Image Registration. In: Proceedings of the SPIE Medical Imaging, vol. 7259, pp. 72590K1–72590K9 (2009)
13. Iqbal, S., Iqbal, K.: Lungs Segmentation for Computer Aided Diagnosis. Inter. J. Academic Research 3(5), 161–166 (2004)

Document Classification after Dimension Reduction through a Modified Gram-Schmidt Process

Sumanta Guha and Ananta Raj Lamichhane

Asian Institute of Technology (A.I.T.),
Pathumthani 12120, Thailand
guha@ait.ac.th

Abstract. This paper proposes a modified Gram-Schmidt algorithm for dimension reduction of a document vector space in order to do classification. We also evaluate the performance of the proposed algorithm by comparing with commonly known algorithms such as the centroid-based algorithm and latent semantic indexing. Further, to measure efficiency, a modified Gram-Schmidt training set is applied in the centroid-based algorithm and latent semantic indexing as well. Performance measurement was based on two different parameters, viz., classification accuracy and closeness of similarity with the corresponding training set. The results shows that modified Gram-Schmidt algorithm is indeed an effective method for dimension reduction prior classification. Moreover, it is easy to code and computationally inexpensive.

Keywords: Centroid, Document Classification, Dimension Reduction, Gram-Schmidt, LSI, Vector Space Model.

1 Introduction

A problem which faces researchers nowadays is the huge volume of papers and reports available digitally. A researcher may have to sift through hundreds of documents in order to find just a few relevant ones. A first step in the search, typically, is to classify into broad categories the documents returned by the initial query.

Automatic document classification is the task of assigning text documents to pre-specified categories [1]. Generally, it is defined as content-based assignment to one or more of such categories. Automatic classifiers have been developed using statistical pattern recognition, neural network and machine learning approaches [2].

Automatic classification helps researchers, scientists and students to find required documents. It is vital as well in organizing information in giant digital banks, e.g., on-line libraries. retrieving, categorizing, routing and filtering of the documents are all based on text classification.

In document categorization, typically, we already have human indexed training data at hand. A classifier is used to automatically determine to which class

K.R. Venugopal and L.M. Patnaik (Eds.): ICIP 2012, CCIS 292, pp. 236–243, 2012.
© Springer-Verlag Berlin Heidelberg 2012

a new document should be added [3]. The efficiency and quality of document classification clearly depends on the representation of documents [4]. Generally, classification involves phases such as document indexing, dimensionality reduction, classifier learning, classification and evaluation [5].

Automatic document classication can be a key component of storage and retrieval operations, which are central in databases and data mining [3]. Moreover, in handling massive amounts of data, computational efficiency is crucial. At present various algorithms has been proposed for document classification. The vector space model [6] which represents documents as vectors has been used most widely. Centroid [7] classification techniques use the vector space model to classify the documents. Classification by dimension reduction in the vector space model is an important concept. Some algorithms that perform dimension reduction are Latent semantic analysis (LSI) [8], probabilistic latent semantic analysis (PLSI) [9], principle component analysis (PCA) [10], IDR/QR [3] etc.

In this paper we propose a new and practical algorithm based on the vector space model, which performs classification by representing data in a space of reduced dimension..

2   Gram-Schmidt Process Definitions and Algebraic Framework

2.1   Gram-Schmidt Orthonormalization

Let $u \cdot v$ denote the inner product of vectors u and v. Define the projection of v on a non-null u by

$$\text{proj}_u(v) = \frac{u \cdot v}{u \cdot u} u. \tag{1}$$

Of course, $u \cdot u = |u|^2$, where $|u|$ is the magnitude of u. See Figure 1 for the geometric view.

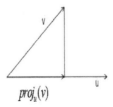

Fig. 1. The projection of v on u is bold

An orthogonal set $S = \{u_1, \ldots, u_n\}$ of vectors is one where $u_i \cdot u_j = 0$, for any $1 \leq i < j \leq n$, i.e., members of S are mutually perpendicular. If, additionally, each member of S is of unit magnitude, then S is said to be orthonormal.

The projection of v on a subspace spanned by an orthogonal set $S = \{u_1, \ldots, u_n\}$ can be shown to be

$$\text{proj}_S(v) = \sum_{i=1}^{n} \text{proj}_{u_i}(v). \tag{2}$$

Denote the subspace spanned by a set of vectors $\{u_1, \ldots, u_n\}$ by $\text{span}(u_1, \ldots, u_k)$. The Gram-Schmidt orthonormalization process takes as input a linearly independent set of vectors $\{v_1, \ldots, v_n\}$ and outputs an orthonormal set $\{u_1, \ldots, u_n\}$ such that $\text{span}(u_1, \ldots, u_k)$ is the same as $\text{span}(v_1, \ldots, v_k)$, for $1 \leq k \leq n$. [11] Pseudo-code for Gram-Schmidt is below:

<u>Gram-Schmidt</u>
```
u₁ = v₁/|v₁|;
S = {u₁};
for i = 2 to n do
{
    uᵢ = vᵢ − projₛ(vᵢ);
    uᵢ = uᵢ/|uᵢ|;
    S = S ∪ {uᵢ};
}
output S;
```

Note that if the input set is not assured *a priori* to be linearly independent then checks are easily added into the code above.

2.2   Modified Gram-Schmidt

We consider the setting where the input set $I = \{v_1, \ldots, v_n\}$ is of document vectors of unit magnitude each, and the "closeness" of two documents is measured by the angle between them. In particular, denote the angle between two vector u and v by $\text{angle}(u, v)$. Evidently, generally,

$$\text{angle}(u, v) = \cos^{-1} \frac{u \cdot v}{|u||v|}. \tag{3}$$

which simplifies to $\text{angle}(u, v) = \cos^{-1}(u \cdot v)$, if u and v are unit vectors. Note that $\text{angle}(u, v)$ is a metric on the space of unit vectors in a fixed dimension; in particular, it is equivalent to the metric of geodesic distances measured on the unit sphere.

For computational efficiency, one would like to reduce substantially the dimension of the subspace to be computed in from that of the subspace spanned by the initial input set I (whose dimension may be in the thousands). Our process of doing so is based upon modifying the Gram-Schmidt orthonormalization process: in particular, at each step, if the next input vector makes a sufficiently small angle with the subspace spanned by the current configuration of the output set S, then we do not use this vector.

The modification is simple to implement. Let $0 < \alpha < \pi/2$ be a given threshold angle. Here then is the modified code:

Modified Gram-Schmidt
```
u₁ = v₁/|v₁|;
Sα = {u₁};
for i = 2 to n do
if angle(vᵢ, projS_α(vᵢ)) > α then
  {
      uᵢ = vᵢ − projS_α(vᵢ);
      uᵢ = uᵢ/|uᵢ|;
      Sα = Sα ∪ {uᵢ};
  }
output Sα;
```

The output $S_\alpha = \{u_1, \ldots, u_n\}$ of the modified Gram-Schmidt process may no longer span the same subspace as the input set I, as in the original algorithm. In fact, clearly, span(S_α) is a (possibly, proper) subspace of span(I).

2.3 Query Answering

Say, the input set $I = \{v_1, \ldots, v_n\}$ is of document vectors of unit magnitude each. Select a threshold angle α in $0 < \alpha < \pi/2$ and apply the modified Gram-Schmidt process described above to obtain the output set S_α. Project each v_i, $1 \leq i \leq n$, onto S_α, denoting the projection by v_i'. Project the query vector, say q, onto S_α as well, the projection being q'.

Now, if θ is a user-determined requirement of closeness, then the answer to the query q is the set of all document vectors $v_i \in I$, such that angle(q', v_i') $\leq \theta$. Clearly, once the input set I is preprocessed by applying modified Gram-Schmidt to output S_α, followed by projection onto S_α, then each query can be answered by operations in span(S_α), whose dimension may be orders of magnitude smaller than that of span(I). Computational saving, therefore, is potentially enormous.

2.4 Classification

Let's say, d is the input document vector. If there are k classes in the training set, this gives k subspace $\{S_\alpha^1, \cdots, S_\alpha^k\}$ where S_α^i is the subspace for the ith class from modified Gram-Schmidt. Project d onto all k subspace, denoting the projection by d_i' for the ith subspace. Next, compute similarity of d to all d_k' using Equation 2. Finally, based on these similarities d is assigned to the class corresponding to the most similar subspace. That is the class of d is given by

$$max_{1\ldots k}(Cos(d, d'_k)) \tag{4}$$

3   Experimental Results

The performance of the modified Gram-Schmidt classifier has been evaluated by comparing with Centroid, Latent Semantic Indexing classification (LSI), centroid using modified Gram-Schmidt training set and LSI using modified Gram Schmidt training set. The results of all classification algorithms have been obtained by implementation. The implementation was done by using standard Java library packages, e.g., common-math2.0. jar, lucene-analyzers-2.3.0.jar, lucene-core 2.4.0.jar. Common-math2.0.jar was used for matrix manipulation, whereas Lucene for indexing and stemming the terms in documents.

3.1   Documents Collection

All the documents for testing have been collected from buzzle.com. 200 documents have been extracted, 50 documents for the four categories sport, food, health and religion. Each document collected was tagged with its category name followed by index number. For example, the 50 documents in the sports document set are tagged $\{sports1.txt, sport2.txt, \cdots, sports50.txt\}$.

Susequently, 25 documents from each category was randomly selected and placed in the training set for all three classifier. Alpha was taken to be 60° as a threshold angle to obtain the training set for modified Gram-Schmidt (MGS). After processing the training set by MGS classifier, 20 documents for sport, 22 documents for health, 21 documents for food and 23 documents for religion were obtained for each category as shown in Table 1.

3.2   Classification Performance

Classification Accuracy. True classification experiment was done by comparing the percentage of accuracy in classification provided by the classifiers. To perform this experiment, 20 document from each category were selected. All the selected documents were processed with the classification algorithms. For example, if for a sports input document the classification result is indeed "sports" then the result is said to be the correct, else classification is incorrect. The summary of the test is presented in Table 2. The results shows that MGS shows good classification performance. Centroid classifier and centroid treated with MGS training set shows equivalent performance. This means with reduced set using MGS, same classfication performance can be achieved. Thus MGS reduced the computational complexity in classification for centroid classifier. Similary in LSI we can see the increase in performance after treating with MGS training set.

Similarity Measure. Similarity measure tries to find out the classifier that provides best similarity values to input document's predefined class. Now to test the performance of classiers, 10 documents from each category was selected. Each of the 10 documents was passed to the different classfiers. Cosine similarity score given by each document treated with their corresponding training set on different classifiers was recorded and compared with all the other classifiers. The results are presented in the Figure 2. The results shows that almost in all the documents MGS show more similarity value to the document's category than other classifier. Hence MGS outputs similar document more precisely.

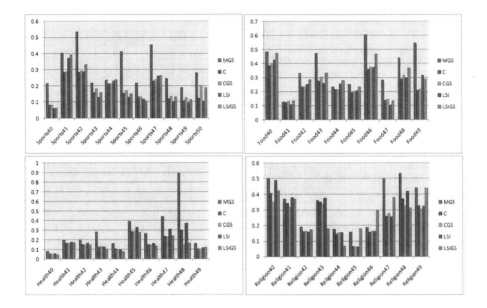

Fig. 2. Cosine similarity score given by each document treated with their corresponding training set on different classifiers

Table 1. Number of documents before and after MGS

Training set	Before Dimension Reduction	After Dimension Reduction
Sport	25	20
Food	25	21
Health	25	22
religion	25	23

4   Classification Model

Modifed Gram-Schmidt classification model is simple and straight forward. The good performance of MGS suggests that it employs a sound underlying classification model. The algorithm makes an effort to find out the low-dimensional

Table 2. The Percentage Classification Accuracy Achieved by the Different Classification Algorithms

	Modified GS	Centroid	Centroid using MGS	LSI	LSI using MGS
Sport	80	85	85	85	85
Food	90	90	90	90	90
Health	60	70	70	80	80
religion	90	90	90	90	95
Sum	320	335	335	345	350

subspace of the original span of the training set-obtained through a modified Gram-Schmidt process. Data in Table 1 shows that the dimension has been substantially reduced. All vector of the original vector space make angle less than alpha with this reduced dimension space. Reduced parameters in the algorithm are obtained by writing the projected vectors in the new reduced subspace in terms of a basis of that reduced subspace. Thus data are represented in the reduced dimensional space and hence computational efficiency has been achieved.

5   Conclusions and Future Work

This research paper focuses on data representation in a reduced space created using modified a Gram-Schmidt process. The experimental evaluation shows that a modified Gram-Schmidt process based classification algorithm performs well on multiple ranges of data sets. It also shows that the strength of this classifier is its consideration of a threshold angle between document vectors and its projection on the original space to form a reduced space. The centroid algorithm doesn't perform dimension reduction. The LSI algorithm does, but has lot of computational overhead during dimension reduction [8]. However MGS is efficient and less computationally intensive. As the test range for our experiments is limited, it is not possible to conclusively compare the performance of MGS versus LSI. However it can be claimed that our work shows a new and plausible approach to dimension reduction.

To further prove this new technique as competitive with established methods, more work is needed. Sound experiments of the proposed technique with other established methods should be a goal for future work. Also as all the document vectors of the original vector space make angle less than α – which is some arbitrary user-decided value – with reduced dimension space, a theoretical question is to be able to determine some optimality condition on α.

References

1. Torkkola, K.: Linear Discriminant Analysis in Document Classigfication. In: Proceedings, IEEE ICDM Workshop Text Mining (2001)
2. Goller, C., Loning, J., Will, T., Wolf, W.: Automatic Document Classifcation thorough Evaluation of Various Methods. Machine Learning 1, 1–11 (2000)
3. Ye, J., Li, Q., Xiong, H., Park, H., Janardan, R., Kumar, V.: An Incremental Dimension Reduction Algorithm *via* Decomposition. IEEE Transactions on Knowledge and Data Engineering 17(9), 1208–1222 (2005)
4. Biro, I.: Document Classification with Latent Dirichlet Allocation. Unpublished Doctoral Dissertation, Eotvos Lorand University (2009)
5. Li, J., Sun, M.: Scalable Term Selection for Text Categorization. Computational Linguistics, 774–782 (June 2007)
6. Salton, G., Wong, A., Yang, C.S.: A Vector Space Model for Automatic Indexing. Communications of the ACM 18(11), 613–620 (1975)
7. Han, E.-H., Karypis, G.: Centroid-based Document Classification Analysis and Experimental Results (2000)
8. Deerwester, S., Dumais, S.T., Furnas, G.W., Landaurer, T.K., Harshman, R.: Indexing by Latent Semantic Analysis. Journal of the American Society for Information Science 41(1), 391–407 (1990)
9. Hofmann, T.: Unsupervised Learning by Probabilistic Latent Semantic Analysis. Machine Learning, 177–196 (2001)
10. Jollife, I.T.: Principal Component Analysis. Springer, New York (1986)
11. Rorres, C., Anton, H.: Elementary Linear Algebra, 9th edn., Application Version

Automatic Facial Expression Recognition Using Extended AR-LBP

Naika Shrinivasa C.L., Jha Shashi Shekhar,
Das Pradip K., and Nair Shivashankar B.

Indian Institute of Technology Guwahati, India
{shrinivasa,j.shashi,pkdas,sbnair}@iitg.ernet.in

Abstract. The Local Binary Pattern (LBP) based operators are sensitive to localization errors. To mitigate these errors input images are manually aligned, face is localized using eyes co-ordinates in the image before feature extraction and multi-scale or multi operators are used, which restricts the use of LBP based operators for automatic facial expression recognition. This paper proposes an Extended Asymmetric Region Local Binary Pattern (EAR-LBP) operator and automatic face localization heuristics to mitigate the localization errors for automatic facial expression recognition. The proposed operator along with face localization heuristics was evaluated for person-independent facial expression recognition on JAFFE and CK+ databases using a multi-class SVM with Linear and Radial Basis Function (RBF) as kernels. It is observed that face localization and the EAR-LBP method are able to mitigate the localization errors to produce reasonably better performance. Maximum 10-fold cross validation average performance of 58.74% and 60.35% were obtained on JAFFE and in case of CK+ database, maximum performance of 83.09% and 82.21% were obtained using Linear and RBF kernels for SVM multi-class classifier respectively.

Keywords: AR-LBP, Facial Expression Recognition, Feature Extraction, Face Representation, Convolution, Extended AR-LB.

1 Introduction

Humans being social animal, use different modalities to communicate with others. Among different modalities such as speech, visual and touch, facial expressions form major modalities in human communication [1]. Automatic analysis of percepted facial expression is challenging and difficult due to variation in pose, scale and lighting conditions, but it has applications in Human Computer Interaction (HCI) such as online searching, information retrieval, Human-Robot Interaction (HRI) and animation. To realize an ideal system for automatic facial expression analysis, it should posses characteristics as listed in [2]. This paper addresses some of the characteristics such as, automatic face detection using Viola and Jones method [3], automatic facial expression feature extraction using Extended Asymmetric region local binary pattern (EAR-LBP) method based on

K.R. Venugopal and L.M. Patnaik (Eds.): ICIP 2012, CCIS 292, pp. 244–252, 2012.
© Springer-Verlag Berlin Heidelberg 2012

Local Binary Pattern (LBP) and Support Vector Machine (SVM) with Linear and Radial Basis Function (RBF) as kernels.

LBP is non-parametric descriptor used in different applications [4]. Due to less computational cost and robustness to monotonic illumination, LBP based operators are extensively used for facial representation in facial expression analysis [4], but it has several pitfalls such as, lack of generalization across databases, performance of LBP based facial expression representations varies due to localization errors, size of the image and the grid size used to divide the input image to get concatenated spatial histogram [5]. To mitigate the localization errors and to increase the recognition performance, most of the facial expression analysis work done using LBP based operators, one or more of listed techniques are used: (i) the face is manually cropped and geometric transforms are used to align the images with respect to the position of the eyes to reduce the registration errors [6], [7] but it restricts the use of LBP operators for automatic facial expression analysis. (ii) Overlapping grids [6] are used to derive the facial expression representation which in-turn increases the feature histogram length. (iii) Multi-scale [7] and multi-level operators are used to represent features of facial expression which increases the feature histogram length as well. Moore *et.al* [7] investigated automatic face localization using frontal and profile Viola and Jones face detectors available in OpenCV [8] on the multi-pie database [9]. The false positive detections by the face detector are removed manually from the database. The authors have not considered face localization as the part of automatic feature extraction but as a preprocessing operation. A performance of 76.7% was reported for frontal facial expression recognition using multi-scale LBP^{ms} operator with feature histogram length of 30208 extracted on 100 x 100 sized facial expression images. To the best of our knowledge most of the existing work on facial expression analysis using LBP based operators are not able to achieve the ideal characteristics of automatic facial expression representation and recognition system due to manual face localization, facial expression image alignments and pitfalls of LBP based operators. In order to attain automatic facial representation there is a need to derive good face localization methods or derive new LBP based operators which are intrinsically robust to misalignment errors and achieve good generalization capability for different databases.

This paper proposes an LBP based operator called Extended Asymmetric Region-Local Binary Pattern (EAR-LBP) which is an extended version of the previous work described in [10] and an automatic face localization method using Viola and Jones method available in OpenCV 2.3 [8]. Further, the proposed operator efficiency was investigated for person-independent automatic facial expression recognition without using above listed techniques to reduce misalignment errors. The proposed operator inherits the properties of AR-LBP and reduce the averaging effect of texture by considering only the border pixels for calculating the average of the region contrary to AR-LBP operator. As EAR-LBP is robust to monotonic illumination, input facial expression images were not preprocessed to remove illumination or misalignments.

2   EAR-LBP Operator

The discriminative capabilities of AR-LBP [10] operator is reduced for larger neighborhood size or with larger scales. This is due to averaging effect (smoothing) for a larger area. To increase the discriminative ability of the operator, the effect of averaging has to be reduced. The effect of the averaging can be reduced by considering boundary pixels of each sub-regions. With this idea the EAR-LBP is proposed which has the properties of AR-LBP and enhances the discriminative ability by considering the outer boundary pixels of the sub-regions. EAR-LBP is computationally efficient since the average of outer boundary grey-pixels value of a region is computed using integral image or summed-area tables as in [10].

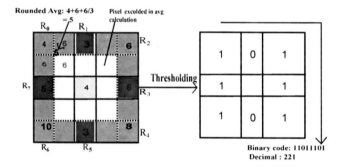

Fig. 1. Example of 5 x 5 sized EAR-LBP

Fig. 1 shows EAR-LBP operator consisting of nine regions, R_i (i= 0...7) and central region (not labeled). These regions has the properties of AR-LBP [10] except that the boundary pixels of each region is considered in order to calculate average of each region. Fig. 1 also shows how a pixel of an image is coded using EAR-LBP of size 5 x 5, as decimal 221. Each region's rounded average is shown in the region with bold numerals except for central region for illustration. The non boundary pixels are in white color (example pixel value 6 in region R_0). Formally, given a center pixel (x_c, y_c) of the face image, the resultant EAR-LBP code can be expressed in decimal form as follows:

$$EAR - LBP(x_c, y_c) = \sum_{i=0}^{7} s(a_i - a_c)2^i \tag{1}$$

Where, a_i and a_c are rounded (to higher value) average grey values of the outer boundary pixels of surrounding region i, (i=0...7) and central region respectively, the function $s(x)$ is defined as:

$$s(x) = \begin{cases} 1, & \text{if } x \geq 0 \\ 0, & \text{if } x < 0 \end{cases} \tag{2}$$

2.1 Automatic Face Localization

In the input image the face needs to be localized prior to the facial expression recognition task. This paper addresses face localization using Viola and Jones face and eye detectors available in OpenCV library. The eye detectors (left and right eyes) are used to reduce the false positives of the face detector. It is observed that the eye detectors also produce false positives by detecting eye brows as eyes. The combination of face and eye detector can reduce false positives efficiently but they can introduce inconsistency in localization of facial features. Facial expression is outcome of contraction of several facial muscles. For example predominately lower part of the face muscles will involve in producing *Happy* facial expression. Since facial expressions are spatial dependent, inconsistency in localization of the face is critical which needs to be addressed.

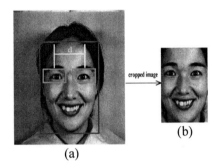

(b)

(a)

Fig. 2. (a) Facial Features Localization using Viola and Jones method for a JAFFE [11] Input Face Image. (b) The Cropped Image using Proposed Face Localization method.

$$d = [x_{\mathrm{RE}} + (width_{\mathrm{RE}}/2)] - [x_{\mathrm{LE}} + (width_{\mathrm{LE}}/2)] \tag{3}$$

$$x_{\mathrm{Face'}} = \begin{cases} x_{\mathrm{LE}}, & \text{if } y_{\mathrm{RE}} \geqslant y_{\mathrm{LE}} \\ x_{\mathrm{RE}} - d, & \text{otherwise} \end{cases} \tag{4}$$

$$y_{\mathrm{Face'}} = \begin{cases} y_{\mathrm{LE}} - d/2, & \text{if } y_{\mathrm{RE}} \geqslant y_{\mathrm{LE}} \\ y_{\mathrm{RE}} - d/2, & \text{otherwise} \end{cases} \tag{5}$$

$$width_{\mathrm{Face'}} = width_{\mathrm{LE}}/2 + width_{\mathrm{RE}}/2 \tag{6}$$

$$height_{\mathrm{Face'}} = \begin{cases} y_{\mathrm{RE}} - y_{\mathrm{Face'}} + (2*d) - k, & \text{if } y_{\mathrm{RE}} \geqslant y_{\mathrm{LE}} \\ y_{\mathrm{LE}} - y_{\mathrm{Face'}} + (2*d) - k, & \text{otherwise} \end{cases} \tag{7}$$

To minimize the inconsistency in localization of face, this paper proposes a heuristic localization method using Viola and Jones face and eye detectors rectangles. Given the three rectangles as shown in Figure 2 (a) and face rectangle parameter as $(x_{Face}, y_{Face}, width_{Face}, height_{Face})$, $(x_{LE}, y_{LE}, width_{LE}, height_{LE})$ for left eye (LE) rectangle, and $(x_{RE}, y_{RE}, width_{RE}, height_{RE})$ for right eye (RE) rectangle, we can derive rectangle $Face'$ whose parameters can be obtained using equations 3, 4, 5, 6 and 7. The x and y are co-ordinates measured from top left corner of the input image and d is approximate distance between two eyes. *Left* and *Right* directions are with respective to the observer point of view. The Fig. 2 (b) shows the localized face image using obtained $Face'$ rectangle.

2.2   Automatic Facial Expression Recognition

In this paper EAR-LBP features automatically extracted from the input face images and facial expression is classified without manual intervention. The SVM multi-class classifier [13] is used extensively for LBP based facial expression recognition. The SVM classifier is considered since it can be trained faster and it generalizes well for small arbitrary number of examples of particular class. SVM training and testing methods provided in OpenCV 2.3 with Radial Basis Function (RBF) and Linear function as kernels are used. For each size of the EAR-LBP operator, images from CK+ [12] and JAFFE [11] dataset is convoluted and feature histograms were obtained as in [10]. A multi-class SVM classifier with seven facial expressions (*Neutral, Happy, Sad, Surprise, Fear, Disgust* and *Angry*) is derived from training dataset and 10 fold person independent cross validation is carried on test dataset and average performance were recorded for each size of the EAR-LBP operator. To set parameters of kernels for each size of the operator, a grid search approach available in OpenCV 2.3 was used.

2.3   Experiments and Results

The proposed EAR-LBP operator is used to derive facial expression representation to images from CK+ and JAFFE databases. The CK+ database consists of 123 adults aged in the range of 18-50 years of which 69% are females, 81% Euro-American, 13% African-American and 6% other groups. The subjects were instructed to display the prototypic facial expression from neutral to the target expression. These image sequences are digitized to 640 x 490 pixels with 8-bit representation. The database consists of 593 sequences with peak frame FACS (Facial Action Coding System) coded and 327 sequences out of 593 peak frames are emotion coded (*Neutral, Happy, Sad, Surprise, Fear, Disgust, Angry* and *Contempt*) using Active Appearance Model and Support Vector Machine. This database can be used for AU (Action Unit) recognition or for Facial Expression Recognition and consists of posed and non-posed facial expression. The JAFFE database consists of 213 TIFF images sized 256 x 256 posed by 10 Japanese models. Each subject has posed seven facial expression (six basic expressions and one neutral) photographed with constant illumination and uniform background. For our experiments, we selected 309 emotion coded sequences from CK+ database leaving *Contempt* labeled sequences. We selected total of 1236 images (309 neutral, 210 happy, 84 sad, 249 surprise, 138 angry, 75 fear and 171 disgust) from each 309 sequences maximum of three peak frames and minimum of one peak frame such that each frame can be categorized into one of seven prototypical expression. From JAFFE data base we considered all 213 images (30 neutral, 31 happy, 31 sad, 30 surprise, 30 angry, 32 fear and 29 disgust).

The face in images were localized using the proposed method. Then the cropped face image was resized to 64 x 64. As EAR-LBP operator is robust to monotonic illumination, we did not remove illumination changes and no further pre-processing steps were applied to face images. The cropped 64 x 64-pixel face image was divided into 16 sub-regions of size 16 x 16 pixels. From each divided sub-region, a 256 bin-length histogram was derived and a concatenated histogram of length 16 * 256 was obtained as the facial expression image representation similar to [10]. For all the sizes of EAR-LBP operator, the length of feature histogram was kept constant at 4096. For each size of the EAR-LBP operator the CK+ database was divided into 10 random parts without overlap of persons facial expression between parts making the training and testing set as person-independent. A multi-class SVM is trained using 9 parts and remaining one part was used as test set. The training and testing experiment was repeated 10 times giving 10-fold cross validation recognition rate. For different sizes of the EAR-LBP operator, average facial recognition rate from 10 fold cross validation are tabulated in respective tables. The parameters[1] of SVM for RBF and Linear kernels was set using OpenCV 2.3 grid search method for all the size of the EAR-LBP operator for both databases.

Table 1. Average Facial Expression Recognition Rate (%) for SVM 7-class Facial Expressions on JAFFE Database with Linear Kernel

		Height						
		3	**5**	**7**	**9**	**11**	**13**	**15**
	3	56.68	52.55	56.43	48.83	47.65	50.28	49.80
	5	57.70	55.77	55.95	49.85	52.15	56.78	56.70
Width	**7**	56.31	51.53	55.27	55.93	49.85	51.53	56.27
	9	55.81	52.60	51.96	51.57	51.75	52.05	54.26
	11	54.02	51.98	49.75	51.19	51.27	49.89	50.42
	13	56.84	54.37	47.60	55.38	52.59	50.70	53.87
	15	**58.74**	53.96	47.60	54.38	53.61	57.13	53.88

---

[1] For JAFFE database SVM with Linear kernel C=12.5 for all size of the EAR-LBP, for RBF kernel C=312.5 and γ=0.033750 to 3x9, 5x5, 5x13, 7x15, 9x9, 11x13 and 11x15 size of the EAR-LBP. For Remaining size of the operator C=12.5 and γ=0.506250 was set. In the case of CK+ database SVM with Linear kernel C=2.5 for 7x9, 7x11, 11x11, 11x13 and for other sizes C=12.5 was set. For SVM with RBF kernel for the size of opeartor 3x7, 5x3, 5x5, 5x11, 7x3, 11x3, 11x13, 13x3,13x7, 13x11, 15x11, 15x15 C=312.5 γ=0.033750 for 5x13, 7x9, 9x5, 9x7, 9x13, 9x15, 13x13, 13x15 C=62.5, γ=0.033750, for 9x9 C=2.5 γ=0.506250 and for other size of the operator C=12.5 γ=0.506250 was set.

Table 2. Average Facial Expression Recognition Rate (%) for SVM 7-class Facial Expressions on JAFFE Database with RBF Kernel

		Height						
		3	**5**	**7**	**9**	**11**	**13**	**15**
Width	**3**	55.38	51.13	53.66	48.18	47.23	48.46	48.91
	5	**60.35**	55.06	54.89	49.89	49.97	54.74	51.95
	7	55.32	52.28	56.67	55.54	50.80	49.36	54.95
	9	52.77	54.28	51.30	50.52	49.23	50.69	51.19
	11	52.75	55.07	52.06	52.29	52.24	49.51	50.62
	13	55.99	54.88	49.94	54.51	53.67	52.60	49.24
	15	58.02	53.13	54.34	53.58	51.77	52.93	48.21

Table 1 and Table 2 shows person independent SVM facial expression average recognition rate for each size of the EAR-LBP operator with linear and RBF kernels on JAFFE database. For example using 3 x 3 (*width* x *height*) size, average recognition rate was 56.68% and 55.38% respectively. We can observe that recognition rate is considerably higher for size when *width* is larger than the *height* of the operator. A maximum of 58.74% and 60.35% recognition rate was obtained with Linear and RBF kernel respectively.

In Table 3 and Table 4 similar observations on CK+ database can be made as in the case of JAFFE and maximum performance of 83.09% and 82.21% recognition rate was obtained with Linear and RBF kernel respectively. Further, when *width* and *height* of the operator is greater than 9, the recognition rate was less compared to the lesser sizes of the operator (observe 4th to 7th columns of all tables). On the contrary, better performance was obtained when the *width* and *height* of the operator was less than 9 (observe 1st to 3rd columns of all tables) for both databases.

Table 3. Average Facial Expression Recognition Rate (%) for SVM 7-class Facial Expressions on JAFFE Database with RBF Kernel

		Height						
		3	**5**	**7**	**9**	**11**	**13**	**15**
Width	**3**	80.07	79.03	79.23	78.79	78.52	77.34	77.20
	5	81.30	82.17	80.91	80.60	77.55	78.49	79.00
	7	81.89	82.49	80.61	79.16	79.29	78.74	79.81
	9	81.17	81.42	80.52	79.37	79.49	78.70	80.70
	11	80.18	82.24	79.32	79.61	82.23	80.49	81.30
	13	82.30	**83.09**	79.65	79.30	80.52	81.01	81.12
	15	80.61	82.20	79.19	79.30	79.38	79.98	80.17

Table 4. Average Facial Expression Recognition rate (%) for SVM 7-class Facial Expressions on JAFFE Database with RBF Kernel

		Height						
		3	**5**	**7**	**9**	**11**	**13**	**15**
	3	78.24	79.31	78.13	75.32	76.35	75.56	74.75
	5	81.68	81.02	77.93	77.05	78.31	78.46	75.50
Width	**7**	80.02	79.83	78.97	79.41	77.27	76.72	76.37
	9	78.24	**82.21**	80.44	78.35	77.78	78.45	79.81
	11	80.42	79.92	78.87	78.26	78.25	80.60	77.04
	13	80.85	79.36	79.93	77.88	79.73	80.35	81.40
	15	76.43	79.44	77.94	77.56	79.49	78.25	79.80

2.4 Conclusions

This paper proposes automatic facial expression recognition using Extended AR-LBP operator and a face localization method to mitigate the misalignment errors. The facial expression representation was obtained without any manual intervention so as to satisfy the ideal characteristics of automatic facial expression recognition system. The proposed operator is robust to misalignment errors as its facial representation gave better results comparable to existing work in the literature with manual intervention for facial expression recognition. When the *width* and the *height* of the operator is greater than 9 it is observed that the performance is reduced and the performance was comparatively increased otherwise. This may be due to the averaging of orthogonal pixels which are not correlated for larger neighborhoods but correlated for small neighborhoods of the diagonal regions (R_0, R_2, R_4 and R_6) of the operator. It is observed that the performance is higher when *width* is larger than the *height* of the operator, which suggests that the operator is able to represent the horizontal features like edges, bulges and furrows of the face rather than vertical ones.

Acknowledgments. We would like to thank Prof. P. Lucey for the use of CK+ database and Dr. Michael J. Lyons for the use of the JAFFE database.

References

1. Mehrabian, A.: Communication without Words. Psychology Today 2(4), 53–56 (1968)
2. Pantic, M., Rothkrantz, L.: Automatic Analysis of Facial Expressions: The State of the Art. IEEE Transactions on Pattern Analysis and Machine Intelligence 22(12), 1424–1445 (2000)
3. Viola, P., Jones, M.: Rapid Object Detection using a Boosted Cascade of Simple Features. In: Proceedings of the 2001 IEEE Computer Society Conference on Computer Vision and Pattern Recognition (CVPR), vol. 1, pp. 511–518 (2001)

4. Huang, D., Shan, C., Ardabilian, M., Wang, Y., Chen, L.: Local Binary Patterns and its Application to Facial Image Analysis: A Survey. IEEE Transactions on Systems, Man and Cybernetics, Part C: Applications and Reviews (99), 1–17 (2011)
5. Ahonen, T., Hadid, A., Pietikäinen, M.: Face Recognition with Local Binary Patterns. In: Pajdla, T., Matas, J(G.) (eds.) ECCV 2004, Part I. LNCS, vol. 3021, pp. 469–481. Springer, Heidelberg (2004)
6. Shan, C., Gong, S., McOwan, P.W.: Facial Expression Recognition Based on Local Binary Patterns: A Comprehensive Study. Image and Vision Computing 27(6), 803–816 (2009)
7. Moore, S., Bowden, R.: Local binary patterns for Multi-view Facial Expression Recognition. Computer Vision and Image Understanding 115(4), 541–558 (2011)
8. Opencv (October 2011), http://opencv.willowgarage.com/wiki/Welcome
9. Gross, R., Matthews, I., Cohn, J., Kanade, T., Baker, S.: Multi-pie Image and Vision Computing 28(5), 807–813 (2010)
10. Naika C.L., Shrinivasa, Das, Pradip K., Nair, Shivashankar B.: Asymmetric Region Local Binary Pattern Operator for Person-Dependent Facial Expression Recognition. In: Proceedings of International Conference on Computing Communication and Applications (ICCCA), pp. 1–5 (2012)
11. Lyons, M., Akamatsu, S., Kamachi, M., Gyoba, J.: Coding Facial Expressions with Gabor Wavelets. In: Proceedings 3rd IEEE International Conference on Automatic Face and Gesture Recognition, pp. 200–205 (1998)
12. Lucey, P., Cohn, J.F., Kanade, T., Saragih, J., Ambadar, Z., Matthews, I.: The Extended Cohn-Kanade Dataset (CK+): A Complete Dataset for Action Unit and Emotion-Specified Expression. In: Proceedings of IEEE Workshop on CVPR for Human Communicative Behavior Analysis, San Francisco, USA (2010)
13. Cortes, C., Vapnik, V.: Support Vector Networks. Machaine Learning 20, 273–297 (1995)

Formation of a Compact Reduct Set Based on Discernibility Relation and Attribute Dependency of Rough Set Theory

Asit Kumar Das[1], Saikat Chakrabarty[1], and Shampa Sengupta[2]

[1] Department of Computer Science and Technology,
Bengal Engineering and Science University, Shibpur,
Howrah - 711 103, West Bengal, India
akdas@cs.becs.ac.in, saikatchakrabarty187@gmail.com
[2] Department of Information Technology,
MCKV Institute of Engineering, Liluah,
Howrah - 711 204, West Bengal, India
shampa2512@yahoo.co.in

Abstract. Large amount of data have been collected routinely in the course of day-to-day work in different fields. Typically, the datasets constantly grow accumulating a large number of features, which are not equally important in decision-making. Moreover, the information often lacks completeness and has relatively low information density. Dimensionality reduction is a fundamental area of research in data mining domain. Rough Set Theory (RST), based on a mathematical concept, has become very popular in dimensionality reduction of large datasets. The method is used to determine a subset of attributes called reduct which can predict the decision concepts. In the paper, the concepts of discernibility relation and attribute dependency are integrated for the formation of a compact reduct set which not only reduces the complexity but also helps to achieve higher accuracy of the system. Performance of the proposed method has been evaluated by comparing classification accuracy with some existing dimension reduction algorithms, demonstrating superior result.

Keywords: Attribute Dependency, Core, Decision System, Discernibility, Reduct.

1 Introduction

Rough set theory (RST) is an efficient mathematical concept used for dimensionality reduction [1, 2] as well as classification of data [3, 4]. A series of reduction algorithms [5, 6] were constructed for all kinds of applications based on rough set models. However, determining minimal set of attributes, called reduct, is NP-complete [7] problem. There is usually more than one reduct for real world datasets. It is not very clear which subset of reducts should be selected for learning. Exhaustive search for finding reduct is infeasible and therefore, heuristic methods based on distinct meas-ures of significance of attributes, such as discernibility matrix [8] based algorithm, dependency based [9] algorithm, mutual

K.R. Venugopal and L.M. Patnaik (Eds.): ICIP 2012, CCIS 292, pp. 253–261, 2012.
© Springer-Verlag Berlin Heidelberg 2012

information [10] based algorithm, genetic algorithm [11] and dynamic reduction algorithm [12] are applied. In reality, there are multiple reducts in a given information system used for developing classifiers, amongst which the best performer is chosen as the final solution to the problem. But this is not always true and according to the Occams razor and minimal description length principle [13-15], the minimal reduct is preferred. However, Roman [16] has found that the minimal reduct is good for ideal situations where a given dataset fully represents a domain of interest. But for real life situations and limited size datasets, those other than the minimal reducts might be better for prediction. Selecting a reduct with good performance is time expensive, as there might be many reducts of a given dataset. Therefore, obtaining a best performer classifier is not practical rather ensemble of different classifiers may lead to better classification accuracy. However, combining [17-19] large number of classifiers increases complexity of the system. So, there must be a tradeoff between these two approaches.

In the proposed method, a novel heuristic approach is used that tries to find out only a compact reduct set based on the concepts like discernibility relation and attribute dependency of the rough set theory. The method tries to tradeoff between the two approaches popularly used by different researchers by forming only a few reducts without spending much time to compute all possible reducts. Firstly, a discernibility matrix is constructed from the decision system based on which the core and noncore attributes are identified. Then, rank of all noncore attributes are calculated from their frequency in the discernibility matrix. Obviously, higher rank attribute is more important than the others. Finally, highest ranked noncore attribute is added to the core in each iteration provided attribute dependency of the resultant set increases and subsequently a reduct (final resultant set) is formed after certain iteration when dependency of the decision attribute on the resultant set is equal to that of the decision attribute on the whole condition attribute set. The same process is repeated with the core and remaining noncore attributes for generating other reducts. Thus, a compact set of reducts is generated.

The paper is organized as follows: the proposed dimension reduction method have been discussed in section 2. Experimental results are demonstrated and comparative studies are made in Section 3. Finally, conclusion and future work are given in section 4.

2   Dimension Reduction Using Rough Set Theory

As all attributes are not equally important, selecting only the significant attributes is the most important task in dimension reduction techniques. The reduced dimension not only reduces the complexity of the overall system but also takes an important role to increase the accuracy of the system. The final dimension (reduct) is determined integrating the concepts like discernibility relation and attribute dependency of rough set theory. So, before going to the details of the reduct generation method, some related concepts of rough set theory are discussed here.

2.1 Basic Concepts of Rough Sets

The rough set theory is based on indiscernibility relations and approximations. Indiscernibility relation is usually assumed to be equivalence relation, interpreted so that two objects are equivalent if they are not distinguishable by their properties. Given a decision system $DS = (U, A, C, D)$, where U is the universe of discourse and A is the total number of attributes, the system consists of two types of attributes namely conditional attributes (C) and decision attributes (D) so that $A = C \cup D$. Let the universe $U = \{x_1, x_2, .., x_n\}$, then with any $P \subseteq A$, there is an associated P-indiscernibility relation $IND(P)$ defined by Eq. (1).

$$IND(P) = \{(x, y) \in U^2 | \forall a \in P, \ a(x) = a(y)\} . \tag{1}$$

If $(x, y) \in IND(P)$, then x and y are indiscernible with respect to attribute set P. These indistinguishable sets of objects, therefore define an indiscernibilty relation referred to as the P-indiscernibility relation and the class of objects are denoted by $[x]_P$. The lower approximation of a target set X with respect to P is the set of all objects which certainly belongs to X, as defined by Eq. (2).

$$\underline{P}X = \{x | [x]_P \subseteq X\} . \tag{2}$$

The upper approximation of the target set X with respect to P is the set of all objects which can possibly belong to X, as defined by Eq. (3).

$$\overline{P}X = \{x | [x]_P \cap X \neq \phi\} . \tag{3}$$

As rough set theory models dissimilarities of objects based on the notions of discernibility, a discernibility matrix is constructed to represent the family of discernibility relations. Each cell in a discernibility matrix consists of all the attributes on which the two objects have the different values. Two objects are discernible with respect to a set of attributes if the set is a subset of the corresponding cell of the discernibility matrix.

Discernibility Matrix and Core. Given a decision system $DS = (U, A, C, D)$, where U is the universe of discourse and A is the total number of attributes. The system consists of two types of attributes namely conditional attributes (C) and decision attributes (D) so that $A = C \cup D$. Let the universe $U = \{x_1, x_2, .., x_n\}$, then discernibility matrix $M = (m_{ij})$ is a $|U| \times |U|$ matrix, in which the element m_{ij} for an object pair (x_i, x_j) is defined by Eq. (4).

$$m_{ij} = \{a \in C | (a(x_i) \neq a(x_j)) \wedge (d \in D, d(x_i) \neq d(x_j))\} . \tag{4}$$

where, $i, j = 1, 2, 3, .., n$.

Thus, each entry (i, j) in the matrix S contains the attributes which distinguish the objects i and j. So, if an entry contains a single attribute say, A_s, it implies that the attribute is self-sufficient to distinguish two objects and thus it is considered as the most important attribute, or core attribute. But in reality, several entries may contain single attribute, union of which is known as core CR of the dataset, as defined in Eq. (5).

$$CR = \cup \{m_{ij} | (m_{ij} \neq \phi) \wedge (|m_{ij}| = 1), \forall i, j = 1, 2, .., n\} . \tag{5}$$

Attribute Dependency and Reduct. One of the most important aspects of database analysis or data acquisition is the discovery of attribute dependencies; that establishes a relationship by finding which variables are strongly related to which other variables. In rough set theory, the notion of dependency is defined very simply. Assume two (disjoint) sets of attributes, P and Q, and inquire what degree of dependency is present between them. Each attribute set induces an (indiscernibility) equivalence class structure. Say, the equivalence classes induced by P is $[x]_P$, and the equivalence classes induced by Q is $[x]_Q$. Then, the dependency of attribute set Q on attribute set P is denoted by $\gamma_P(Q)$ and is given by Eq. (6).

$$\gamma_P(Q) = \frac{\sum_{i=1}^{N} |\underline{P} X_i|}{|U|} .$$

(6)

where, X_i is a class of objects in $[x]_Q$, $\forall$ i = 1, 2, .., N.

A reduct can be thought of as a sufficient set of attributes to represent the category structure and the decision system. Projected on just these attributes, the decision system, possesses the same equivalence class structure as that expressed by the full attribute set. Taking the partition induced by decision attribute D as the target class and R as the minimal attribute set, R is called the reduct if it satisfies Eq. (7). In other words, R is a reduct if the dependency of decision attribute D on R is exactly equal to that of D on whole conditional attribute set C.

$$\gamma_R(D) = \gamma_C(D) .$$

(7)

The reduct of an information system is not unique. There may be many subsets of attributes which preserve the equivalence-class structure (i.e., the knowledge) expressed in the decision system.

2.2   Formation of Reducts

The various concepts of rough set theory like discernibility matrix, core and attribute dependency are applied together to compute quick reducts of a decision system. The term quick reduct is used in the sense that the method computes a compact set of reducts very quickly without unnecessarily increasing the complexity since they are sufficient to represent the system. Based on the discernibility matrix M, the attributes are divided into the core set CR and noncore set NC. The proposed method uses (i) a forward attribute selection method and (ii) a backward attribute removal method for the computation of final reduct set RED.

Forward Attribute Selection. Rank of all noncore attributes in NC is calculated from their frequency in the discernibility matrix M. Obviously, attribute having higher frequency has higher rank and is more important than the other attributes. Next, highest ranked element of NC is added to the core CR in each iteration; provided the dependency of the decision attribute D on the resultant set increases; otherwise it is ignored and next iteration with the remaining elements in NC is performed. The process terminates when the resultant set satisfies Eq. (7) and is considered as a reduct. After getting one reduct, the same process is repeated with core CR and remaining noncore attributes in NC and finally, a compact set of reducts is obtained.

Backward Attribute Removal. The demerit of forward attribute selection is that it always selects the higher ranked attribute before the lower one. In some cases, one higher ranked attribute (say, in i^{th} iteration) together with another comparatively lower ranked attribute (say, in $(i+2)^{th}$ iteration) may have higher attribute dependency compared to that in the case which arises in forward selection method by three consecutive, namely, i^{th}, $(i+1)^{th}$ and $(i+2)^{th}$ iterations. In such situations, the non-core attribute added in $(i+1)^{th}$ iteration may be removed from the generated reduct. So for each noncore attribute x in generated reduct R, it is checked whether Eq. (7) is satisfied using $R - \{ x \}$, instead of R. If it is satisfied, then x is redundant and must be removed. Thus, all redundant attributes are obtained and stored in set RM. Now, if Eq. (7) is satisfied using $R - RM$ instead of R, then $R - RM$ is a final reduct; otherwise, repeatedly compute all subsets of RM taking |RM| - 1 elements together and check Eq. (7) for all those subsets. For any subset S satisfying Eq. (7), removing S from R gives us a reduct and further processing with the subsets of S is not required. This acts as the terminating condition for the process. Thus, for a single reduct obtained by the forward selection method, a set of reducts may be formed. Repeating the process for all reducts obtained in forward selection method gives a compact set of reducts.

The algorithm of a compact set of reducts formation for a decision system $DS = (U, A, C, D)$ is given below in Table 1, where, forward selection method is described in the 'Reduct_Formation' algorithm and for each generated reduct, backward removal algorithm 'Back_Removal', as given in Table 2, is invoked to obtain the possible set of reducts.

3   Experimental Results

The proposed method is illustrated by a sample decision system with 4 conditional attributes and a decision attribute, listed in Table 3. The discernibility matrix of Table 3 is given by Table 4. Table 4 shows that core $CR = \{d'\}$ and noncore attributes are $NC = \{a', b', c'\}$. Since, the frequency of $a' = 15$, $b' = 17$ and $c' = 14$, so according to the rank of decreasing order, the attribute set is $NC = \{b', a', c'\}$. The forward selection method gives us two reducts $RED = \{\{b', d'\}, \{a', c', d'\}\}$. Here, both the reducts contains no redundant attributes, so backward removal method cannot eliminate any attribute from the reducts in RED. So, $RED = \{\{b', d'\}, \{a', c', d'\}\}$ is the final reduct of the decision system.

The method is also applied on some benchmark datasets obtained from UCI repository 'http://www.ics.uci.edu/mlearn/MLRepository'. The wine dataset

Table 1. Forward Selection Algorithm

```
Algorithm: Reduct_Formation(DS, CR, NC)
Input: DS, the decision system with C conditional attributes and D decisions,
CR, the core and NC, the non-core attributes
Output: RED, a compact set of reducts
Begin
     Repeat
         R = CR   /* core is considered as initial reduct*/
         NC_OLD = NC /* take a copy of initial elements of NC*/
         /*Repeat-until below forward selection to give one reduct*/
         Repeat
             x = highest ranked element of NC
             If (x = φ) break   /*if no element found in NC*/
             If (γ_{R∪{x}}(D) > γ_R(D))
                 {
                     R = R ∪ {x}
                     NC = NC - {x}
                 }
         Until (γ_R(D) = γ_C(D))
         If (γ_R(D) = γ_C(D))   //R is a reduct, apply backward removal
            { /*one reduct obtained by forward selection is used in backward
removal to get actual reducts*/
                RD = Call Back_Removal(DS, CR, R) //RD is a set of reducts
from R
                RED = RED ∪ RD
            }
         If (NC_OLD = NC)
             NC = φ
    Until (NC is empty)
End.
```

Table 2. Backward Removal Algorithm

```
Algorithm: Back_Removal(DS, CR, R)
Input: DS, the decision system, CR, the core and R, the reduct obtained by
forward selection
Output: RD, a set reducts
Begin
     RD = RM = φ //RM contains all redundant attributes
     For each x in (R - CR)
             If (γ_{R-{x}}(D) = γ_C(D))
                 RM = RM ∪ {x}
     Insert (RM) into Queue Q
     While (Q is not empty) {
             RM = Remove (Q)
             If (γ_{R-RM}(D) = γ_C(D))
                 RD = RD ∪ {R - RM}
             Else
                 Compute all subsets of length |RM| - 1 of RM
                 Insert all subsets into Q
         } //end while

         Return (RD)
End.
```

Table 3. A Sample Decision System

a′	b′	c′	d′	D
M	L	3	M	1
M	L	1	H	1
L	L	1	M	1
L	R	3	M	2
M	R	2	M	2
L	R	3	L	3
H	R	3	L	3
H	N	3	L	3

Table 4. Discernibility Matrix of the Decision System

			a′b′	b′c′	a′b′d′	a′b′d′	a′b′d′
			b′c′d′	b′c′d′	a′b′c′d′	a′b′c′ d′	a′b′c′ d′
			b′c′	a′b′c′	b′c′d′	a′b′c′ d′	a′b′c′ d′
				d′	a′d′	a′b′d′	
				a′c′d′	a′c′d′	a′b′c′ d′	

Table 5. Reducts of Wine Dataset with Accuracies given by Various Classifiers

Classifiers	Reducts					Average accuracy for all reducts
	{BFGJKM}	{BGHJKM}	{ADEGJL}	{ABEGJKL}	{ADEFGJL}	
Naïve Bayes	97.18	98.87	99.44	99.44	98.31	98.65
SVM	95.48	96.61	97.18	97.74	96.61	96.72
SMO	95.48	94.92	96.05	96.61	96.06	95.82
KSTAR	96.05	98.31	94.92	94.92	94.92	95.82
Bagging	94.35	94.92	96.05	94.92	95.48	95.14
MultiClass	98.87	99.44	98.87	98.31	97.18	98.53
J48	97.74	97.74	95.48	96.61	95.48	96.61
PART	97.18	97.18	96.05	96.05	96.05	96.50
Average accuracy against all classifiers	96.55	97.24	96.75	96.83	96.26	96.72

contains 178 instances and 13 conditional attributes. The attributes are abbreviated by letters A, B and so on, starting from their column position in the dataset. Here, core is the only attribute J appearing in 10th position. Now, the forward selection method generates two reducts RED = { { ABFGHJKLM }, { ABDEFGHIJKL } }, each of which is further modified by backward removal method, yielding five reducts in total, listed in Table 5 with their accuracies for various classifiers, based on 10-fold cross-validation using 'Weka' tool.

The same process is applied for other benchmark datasets and accuracies are computed and compared with existing attribute reduction techniques like 'Correlation-based Feature Selection' (CFS) and 'Consistency-based Subset Evaluation' (CSE), as shown in Table 6. The proposed method, on average, contains lesser number of attributes compared to CFS and CSE and at the same time achieves higher accuracy, which shows the effectiveness of the method.

Table 6. Classification Accuracy of Reducts obtained by Proposed and Existing Methods

Dataset (Instance / attribute)	Reduction Method (attribute)	Classifiers					Average accuracy (%)
		Naïve Bayes	SVM	Multi Class Classifier	J48	PART	
Wine (178/13)	PROP(6.4)	98.65	96.72	98.53	96.61	96.50	97.40
	CFS(8)	98.47	96.58	97.08	96.58	97.08	97.16
	CSE(8)	98.31	96.84	97.71	96.23	97.08	97.23
Heart (270/13)	PROP(9)	84.79	84.53	84.27	83.90	82.49	84
	CFS(8)	84.19	84.19	84.01	82.33	81.14	83.17
	CSE (11)	85.12	83.17	83.64	82.06	79.35	82.67
Machine (209/7)	PROP(5)	34.35	50.23	34.79	50.89	51.85	44.42
	CFS(2)	30.47	45.87	21.79	48.18	46.55	38.57
	CSE (4)	33.15	50.00	32.72	49.59	52.32	43.56
Liver Disorder (345 /6)	PROP(5)	68.73	70.80	69.77	69.19	69.77	69.65
	CFS(5)	68.31	68.89	68.60	68.31	69.48	68.72
	CSE (4)	68.60	68.31	70.64	69.48	68.60	69.13

4   Conclusion

The proposed method used only the concepts of rough set theory which does not require any additional information except the decision system itself. Since, reduct generation is a NP-complete problem, so different researchers use different heuristics to compute multiple reducts used for developing classifiers. However, using large number of reducts increases complexity of the system. Also, selecting single reduct is not always good in ideal situation for better prediction. The method tries to tradeoff between the two approaches and produces a compact set of reducts. The experimental results show that, the accuracies given by various classifiers are also comparable with that of the popular existing methods.

The method fails to compute the core of a decision system only if no entry of the associated discernibility matrix contains a single attribute. In this situation, the approximate core may be obtained by combining all attributes from the entries of the discernibility matrix with minimum number of attributes. The proposed method may be extended by computing the core from the approximate core, which is the future work of this study.

References

1. Raymer, M.L., et al.: Dimensionality Reduction using Genetic Algorithms. IEEE Transactions on Evolutionary Computation 4(2), 164–171 (2000)
2. Carreira-Perpinan, M.A.: A Review of Dimension Reduction Techniques. Technical Report CS-96-09, Department of Computer Science, University of Sheffield (1997)
3. Gordon, A.D.: Classification, 2nd edn. Monographs on Statistics and Applied Probability. Chapman and Hall/CRC, London (1999) ISBN: 9781584880134
4. Pal, S.K., Mitra, S.: Multi-Layer Perceptron, fuzzy Sets and Classification. IEEE Trans. Neural Networks 3, 683–697 (1992)
5. Komorowski, J., Pawalk, Z., Polkowski, S.A.: Rough Sets: A Tutorial. In: Pal, S.K., Skowron, A. (eds.) Rough Fuzzy Hybridization: A New Trend in Decision-Making, pp. 3–98. Springer, Berlin (1999)
6. Pawlak, Z.: Rough Set Theory and Its Applications to Data Analysis. Cybernetics and Systems 29, 661–688 (1998)
7. Garey, M., Johnson, D.: Computers and Intractability- A Guide to the Theory of NP-Completeness. Freeman, New York (1979)
8. Swiniarski, R.W.: Rough Sets Methods in Feature Reduction and Classification. International Journal of Applied Mathematics and Computer Science 11(3), 565–582 (2001)
9. Qu, G., Hariri, S., Yousif, M.: A New Dependency and Correlation Analysis for Features. IEEE Transactions on Knowledge and Data Engineering 17(9), 1199–1207 (2005)
10. Novovičová, J., Somol, P., Haindl, M., Pudil, P.: Conditional Mutual Information Based Feature Selection for Classification Task. In: Rueda, L., Mery, D., Kittler, J. (eds.) CIARP 2007. LNCS, vol. 4756, pp. 417–426. Springer, Heidelberg (2007)
11. Freitas, A.: A Genetic Programming Framework for Two Data Mining Tasks- Classification and Generalized Rule Induction. In: Conf. on Genetic Programming, USA, pp. 96–101 (1997)
12. Deng, D., Huang, H.: Dynamic Reduction Based on Rough Sets in Incomplete Decision Systems. In: Yao, J., Lingras, P., Wu, W.-Z., Szczuka, M.S., Cercone, N.J., Ślęzak, D. (eds.) RSKT 2007. LNCS (LNAI), vol. 4481, pp. 76–83. Springer, Heidelberg (2007)
13. Quinlan, J., Rivest, R.: Inferring Decision Trees using the Minimum Description Length Principle. Inf. Comput. 80, 227–248 (1989)
14. Hansen, M., Yu, B.: Model Selection and the Principle of Minimum Description Length. J. Am. Stat. Assoc. 96, 746–774 (2001)
15. Quinlan, J.R.: The Minimum Description Length and Categorical Theories. In: Proceedings 11th International Conference on Machine Learning, New Brunswick, pp. 233–241. Morgan Kaufmann, San Francisco (1994)
16. Roman, W.S., Larry, H.: Rough sets as a Frontend as Neural-Networks Texture Classifiers. Neuro-Computing 36, 85–102 (2001)
17. Kuncheva, L.I.: Combining Pattern Classifiers, Methods and Algorithms. Wiley Interscience, New York (2005)
18. Fumera, G., Roli, F.: Analysis of Error-Reject Trade off in Linearly Combined Multiple Classifiers. Pattern Recognition 37, 1245–1265 (2004)
19. Kittler, J., Hatef M.: On Combining Classifiers. IEEE Transactions on Pattern Analysis and Machine Intelligence 20(3), 226–239 (1998)

Isolated Word Recognition for Kannada Language Using Support Vector Machine

Sarika Hegde[1], Achary K.K.[2], and Surendra Shetty[1]

[1] Department of Computer Applications, NMAMIT, Nitte,
Udupi District, Karnataka, India-574110
sarika.hegde@yahoo.in, hsshetty@yahoo.com
[2] Department of Statistics Mangalore University, Mangalagangothri, Mangalore
Karnataka, India-574199
kka@mangaloreuniversity.ac.in

Abstract. An ideal Automatic Speech Recognition system has to accurately and efficiently convert a speech signal into a text message transcription of the spoken words, independent of the device used to record the speech (i.e., the transducer or microphone), the speaker, or the environment. There are three approaches to speech recognition, Acoustic-phonetic approach, Pattern recognition approach and Artificial intelligence approach, where in the pattern recognition approach statistical methods are used. We have developed an Isolated Word Recognition (IWR) system for identification of spoken words for the database created by recording the words in Kannada Language. The developed system is tested and evaluated with a performance of 79% accuracy.

Keywords: Isolated Word Recognition, Kannada Language, Speech Recognition, Support Vector Machine.

1 Introduction

The Automatic Speech Recognition problems have been solved using pattern recognition technique in most of the cases. In pattern recognition approach for speech recognition, speech patterns are used directly without explicit feature determination (like in acoustic) and segmentation. The method has mainly two steps, training of speech pattern and recognition of speech pattern via pattern comparison. The concept is that the enough versions of a pattern to be recognized are included in the training pattern. Machine learns the acoustic properties of speech class that are reliable and repeatable across all training tokens of the pattern. The process of classification of a given speech signal into a particular class has four steps, feature measurement, pattern training, and pattern classification and decision logic [1].

2 Previous Works

The ASR problem can be researched in many ways like, how the speech data can be enhanced for improving the quality of speech, reducing the level of noise in

K.R. Venugopal and L.M. Patnaik (Eds.): ICIP 2012, CCIS 292, pp. 262–269, 2012.
© Springer-Verlag Berlin Heidelberg 2012

the speech signals, detecting the presence/absence of voice(VAD) or how signal can be segmented into different units; (the unit may be phone, syllable or word etc). Some of the major works relating to noise and speech-end point detection can be seen in [2][3][4][5]. Many authors have considered phone/triphone model as the basic unit of speech and segmentation of speech and recognition is done based on it [6]. IWR is an area of ASR where the input speech is an isolated word unit in contrary to a speech signal where continuous speech sentence is uttered. There are also significant research done on segmenting speech into syllabic like models and we can find more detail on such works in the following papers [7][8][9]. The research has also been focused as to what parametric representation would best suit to categories the speech into different units. Mel Frequency Cepstral Coefficients (MFCC) and Linear Predictive Coefficients (LPC) features have been the most successful feature representation for the speech signal[10].The enhancements in pattern recognition techniques like SVM, Bayes classifier, HMM or hybrid models etc as suitable for ASR is another important aspect [11][12][13].

Since the final goal of an ASR would be to generate a system that recognizes speech removing all the constraints of type of speaker, environment of recording, the mood , accent, region , language etc, there is also a great need that every important language in the world would be considered and experimented in the context of ASR problem. The English language has been very commonly used; many researches are mainly focused on the database that is created for English language and also the database is easily available. Apart from English there are many other European, Asian languages have been considered. But research on Indian languages started very recently; there are 14 languages in India which has been constitutionally approved and is very commonly spoken in different parts of the nation. Though we can find some works on languages Hindi, Bangali, Panjabi, Marathi, Tamil, Malayalam significant works have been done in Tamil language [8][9].

In this paper, we are considering Kannada language which has not been used by many for the research in the context of Speech Recognition. We have developed a system where we created the database of some words in Kannada language, trained and tested a classifier model to identify these words successfully using the well known technique, Support Vector Machines (SVM). The content of the paper is organized as follows; section 1 gives brief information regarding the ASR problem and in section 2 we discuss the problem in the light of the various research works being done. The section 3 explains the overall system design with the brief detail on the techniques that are used at different stages. In the section 4 we describe the method that is used to conduct the experiment, the detail about the database used and the results. The last section we present conclusions and also highlight the direction towards the future work.

3   System Design and Implementation

The ASR problem solution would have mainly two parts or module. The first module, known as front end, converts the signal into representative features. The second module also called as the back end deals with the machine learning technique have been used. We have designed a system where the front end extracts the MFCC feature and SVM is used as a back-end. We explain the system in detail in the following section.

3.1   Feature Calculation (Front-end) Method

The first step is to process each of the wave-file (speech signal) from the database and convert it into sequence of feature vectors(FV) where each FV_i corresponds to the feature vector of the ith frame given as $FV_i=\{fv_{i1}, fv_{i2},\ldots, fv_{i12}\}$. The twelve attributes represents the 12 MFCC coefficients. The Mel-scaled Cepstral Coefficients (MFCC) filter bank is a feature extracted by applying more than one Fourier Transform to the original signal in sequence. The term Cepstrum (an anagram of spectrum) derives from this repeated use of the Fast Fourier Transform (FFT) [9]. The collection of feature vectors FV is generated for each input speech signal (wave-file) and stored in a separate file. The algorithm given in Figure 1 below list the steps followed for implementing the first step.

At the end of this module we get a database with collection of files, where each file stores the feature vectors of the corresponding speech wave file of the main database. But before extracting the feature, we reduce the level of noise by applying spectral subtraction method. Then we apply the speech end point detection for identifying the exact marking of the beginning and end of the speech uttered in the signal. To do this, the input speech signal is divided into number of frames with frame size of 10ms. Then the log of short time energy is calculated for each of these frames. The frames with lower energy than the threshold value are rejected. The signal is reconstructed with the remaining frames. The threshold value is decided dynamically by clustering the log-energy values into two parts with K-means clustering technique. The cluster which has larger means log-energy value compared to other is considered for further processing. The target labels are assigned as $1\ldots n$, sequentially for 'n' number of classes/words. For the feature vector FV_i, which represent the 12 MFCC coefficients, we also add one more attribute (fv_{i13}), a target label that identify class/word to which the speech signal belongs. This information is used while training and also for evaluating the results.

3.2   Machine Learning Algorithm (Back-end)

We have used Support vector Machine as it is one of the well known, successful pattern recognition technique. Support Vector Machines (SVMs) represent a new approach to pattern classification which has attracted much interest. This is due to their great ability to generalize, often resulting in better performance than traditional techniques, such as artificial neural networks. SVMs have been successfully used in many applications, e.g., handwritten digit recognition.

The support vector machine is a supervised classification system that searches for the hyperplane with the largest margin called as Maximal Margin Classifier.

```
Algorithm Feature-Extraction()
    (INPUT: database of *.wav files
    OUTPUT: database of *.mat(FV) files)

For all the wave-files in the database
    Fname=next wave-file in database
    Signal_sample=wavread('fname.wav')
    j=target_label('fname.wav')
    New_sample=spectral_subtraction(Signal_sample)
    Frames=enframe(New_sample,10ms)
    Log_energy=compute_logEnergy(Frames)
    Re_signal=reconstruct(New_sample,Log_energy>Threshold)
    Frames=enframe(Re_signal,30ms)
    For each fᵢ in Frames
                        FVᵢ(1:12) = mfcc(fᵢ)
                        FVᵢ(13) = j
    End
    saveFile('fname.mat,' FV')

End
```

Fig. 1. Feature Extraction Procedure

SVMs are linear classifiers (i.e., the classes are separated by hyperplanes) but they can be used for non-linear classification by the so-called kernel trick.

Instead of applying the SVM directly to the input space R^n they are applied to a higher dimensional feature space F , which is nonlinearly related to the input space: : $R^n->F$, The kernel trick can be used since the algorithms of the SVM use the training vectors only in the form of Euclidean dot-products $(x.y)$. It is then only necessary to calculate the dot-product in feature space, which is equal to the so-called kernel function $k(x, y)$.

Important kernel functions which fulfill these conditions are the polynomial kernel

$$k(x, y) = (x.y + 1)^d \tag{1}$$

and the Gaussian radial basis function (RBF) kernel,

$$k(x, y) = exp(-\gamma \|x - y\|^2) \tag{2}$$

Given a training set x_i, y_i of N training vectors $x_i \epsilon Rn$ and corresponding labels, $yi \epsilon \{-1, +1\}$, a kernel function $k(x, y)$ and a parameter C, the SVM finds an optimal separating hyperplane in F. This is done by solving the quadratic programming problem[15]. There are three main modules in the back end. The TRAINING module generates the SVM model based on the training dataset feature vectors. The TESTING modules test each of the file with the SVM model. The final predicted label for a file is computed using the DECISION LOGIC module, since file has many feature vectors. We test each of the feature vectors (corresponding to each frame) and consider the predicted label that appears for the highest number of times.

The database of feature vectors created in the first module is used as input for training the SVM system. We extract the content of each file and create a database which has collection of $'M'$ number of feature vectors (all the files) where each feature vector has the target label of the corresponding class/word. The database is given as, $D=\{FV_i\}^M{}_{i=1}$. We apply Hold-out method for generating the training set from the database. The hold-out method divides the database into two parts where the ratio of dividing is 1:5. Here the first number indicates the percentage of data that should be there in the training data out of the total records in the database. The less number of training data ensures the less time taken for training and also works with better generalization. Let us assume that 't' number of records has to be selected for the training. The training set is chosen by generating the t number of indices randomly out of total 1 to 'M' number indices. While generating the indices randomly, we ensure that equal proportion of records is chosen from each class/word. The following Figure 2 shows the graphical representation of the steps that are used in the training process. The training set given as $TR=\{FV^i\}^t{}_{i=1}$ is used for the training purpose. The training set is divided into two parts $TR=\{FV(1:12)^i,$ $Y^i\}^t{}_{i=1}$, the last attribute $FV(13)_i$ is sperated into vector Y holding the target labels of all the corresponding feature vector $FV(1:12)_i$. The database TR is given for SVM learning algorithm for generating the classifier model. Usually in Hold-out method, the remaining records in the database D which are not used in the training set TR is considered for testing purpose. But we have considered the feature vectors of individuals files from the Feature Vector Files Database separately. This helps us to identify how many files of each class/word have been identified accurately. The following diagram shows the overall method used for training and testing the word files. The testing set may have some of the records used in training set. The diagram Figure 3 shows the method used in the testing procedure.

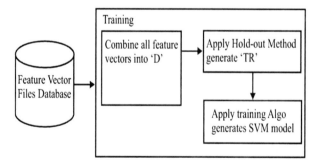

Fig. 2. Feature Extraction Procedure

3.3   Experimental Results

We created a database with ten words of Kannada Language which are the words for numbers one to ten. The words are listed as follows, One(*Ondu*), Two(*Eradu*), Three(*Mooru*), Four(*Naalku*), Five(*Aidu*), Six(*Aaru*), Seven(*Elu*), Eight(*Entu*), Nine(*Ombattu*), Ten(*Hattu*). The word in bracket indicates the actual word that

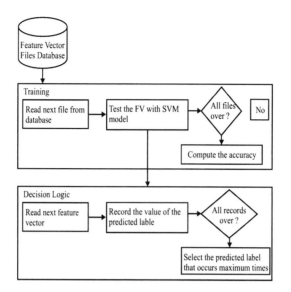

Fig. 3. Feature Extraction Procedure

WORD	Number of Files	Correctly Recognized
One("*Ondu*")	10	8
Two("*Eradu*")	10	7
Three("*Mooru*")	10	9
Four("*Naalku*")	10	10
Five("*Aidu*")	10	9
Six("*Aaru*")	10	8
Seven("*Elu*")	10	7
Eight("*Entu*")	10	9
Nine("*Ombattu*")	10	5
Ten("*Hattu*")	10	8
	100	80
Classification Accuracy --- 80%		

Fig. 4. The Table Showing the Results of Classifying *ten Kannada* Words

is uttered in Kannada for recording. Totally five speakers that is two males and three females have uttered the all the ten words, in a room environment. The recording was done twice so that we have two samples of each of the word with each speaker. The total number of samples for each word is ten, so totally 100 files for ten words. The words are recorded using the Voice recorder facility present in the mobile and then the audio files have been converted from AMR file format to wav file format. The ten words are assigned target labels from 1 to 10. The task of recognition is, given an unknown speech signal assign target label from1 to 10 that corresponds to the ten words. The frame size for computing the log-energy values is 10ms and for computing the MFCC feature is 30ms. Each of the file is converted into sequence of nearly 50 number of feature vectors totally constituting around 5000 number of records. After applying Hold-out method, we extracted nearly 1/6th of the records that is 900 records for training. The following table shows the accuracy result of testing the 100 files with the trained SVM model. The first column gives the word uttered with the meaning given in both English and Kannada. The second column gives the total number of files for each word. We have done ten iterations and the average class recognition accuracy is 78.4%.

4   Conclusions

The speech recognition problem has application in many diverse areas. Due to the complex nature of the signals the ASR problem has not been solved to its full extent. Especially Indian languages need more focus so that it can be easily accommodated into the existing ASR system. The database creation for Indian languages spoken words is challenging job. We have demonstrated that the technique SVM combined with MFCC feature extraction, systematic method of noise reduction and speech end point detection yields generating classifier model that could classify the considered words with a good accuracy rate. We can test the same model with a large database and analyze the results. We can also consider the continuous speech database in the next step, in which case we should for efficient segmentation techniques.

References

1. Rabiner, L., Juang, B.H.: Fundamentals of Speech Recognition. Prentice Hall PTR, NY (1993) ISBN: 0-13-015157-2
2. Sohn, J., Kim, N.S., Sung, W.: A Statistical Model-based Voice Activity Detection. IEEE Signal Processing Letters 6(1), 1–3 (1999)
3. Lori, F.L., Lawrence, R.R., Aaron, E.R., Jay, G.W.: An Improved End Point Detector for Isolated Speech Recognition. IEEE Transactions On Acoustics, Speech, and Signal Processing 29(4), 777–785 (1981)
4. Main, G.R., Juang, B.-H.: Signal Bias Removal by Maximum Likelihood Estimation for Robust Telephone Speech Recognition. IEEE Transactions on Speech and Audio Processing 4 (1996)
5. Ephraim, Y.: Statistical Model Based Speech Enhancement Systems. Proceedings of the IEEE 80(10), 1526–1555 (1992)
6. Hawkins, S.: Contribution of Fine Phonetic Detail to Speech Understanding. In: Proceedings of the 15th International Congress of Phonetic Sciences, pp. 293–296 (2003)

7. James, R.G.: A Probabilistic Framework for Segment Based Speech Recognition. Computer, Speech and Language 17(3), 137–152 (2003)
8. Lakshmi, A., Hema, A.M.: Syllable Based Continuous Speech Recognizer for Tamil. In: Proceedings of International Conference on Spoken Language, INTERSPEECH 2006 ICSLP, Pittsburgh, Pennsylvania, September 17-21, pp. 1878–1881 (2006)
9. Thangarajan, R., Natarajan, A.M.: Syllable Based Continuous Speech Recognition for Tamil. South Asian Language Review XVIII(1), 72–85 (2008)
10. Steven, B.D., Paul, M.: Comparison of Parametric Representation for Monosyllabic Word Recognition In Continuous Speech Recognition. IEEE Transactions on Acoustics, Speech and Signal Processing Assp-28(4), 357–365 (1980)
11. Chien, J.-T., Shinoda, K., Furui, S.: Predictive Minimum Bayes Risk Classification for Robust Speech Recognition. In: INTERSPEECH 2007, Antwerp, Belgium, August 27-31, pp. 1062–1065 (2007)
12. Li, X., Jiang, H.C.-J.: Large Margin HMM for Speech Recognition. IEEE Transaction on Audio, Speech and Language Processing 14(5), 1584–1595 (2006)
13. Scott, A., Maison, B.: Combination of Hmm with Dtw For Speech Recognition. In: Proceedings Internation Conference on Acoustics, Speech and Signal Processing (ICASSP 2004), pp. 173–176 (2004)
14. Jelinek, F.: Continuous Speech Recognition by Statistical Methods. Proceedings of the IEEE 64(4), 532–556 (1976)
15. He, X., Zhou, X.-Z.: Audio Classification by Hybrid Support Vector Machine/ Hidden Markov Model. World Journal of Modeling and Simulation 1(1), 56–59 (2005)

Vein Identification and Localization for Automated Intravenous Drug Delivery System

Deepa Prabhu, Mohanavelu K., Sundersheshu B.S., and Padaki V.C.

Defence Bioengineering and Electromedical Laboratory (DEBEL),
Defence Research and Development Organization,
P.B. No: 9326, ADE Campus, Bangalore-560093
missdeepaprabhu@gmail.com

Abstract. Intravenous (IV) drug administration of fluids or medication and blood drawing procedures require the medical practitioner to access the veins in patients. This procedure is of prime importance in saving an injured soldiers life on the battlefield by intravenously administering haemostatic agents to prevent blood loss due to haemorrhage. This paper presents an image acquisition system that captures images of subcutaneous veinpatterns and processes these to conclude the location for intravenous needle-insertion. The system consists of a camera, receptive to near-infrared light, which captures an image of the subcutaneous veins illuminated by a suitable source of light. The contrast-enhanced image of the veins thus obtained is processed using an algorithm to conclude an ideal site for needle-insertion. Subcutaneous vein-images were captured using a modified web-camera that works well under the illumination of near-infrared light and a DSLR (Digital Single Lens Reflex) camera with an external filter to block visible light. An algorithm was developed to extract vein-segments from these images. The system will be used for automated delivery of haemostatic agent.

Keywords: DSLR, Intravenous, Near-Infrared-Light, Veins, Web-Camera.

1   Introduction

A drug-delivery system can be defined as a system that enables the introduction of a therapeutic agent in the form of a drug or necessary fluids in to the body. The system would act as an interface between the drug and the human body. The popular anatomical route used to administer the drugs is *via* veins. This is called Intravenous Therapy or IV Therapy. IV Therapy can quickly deliverelectrolytes, nutrients and water to the body. Many drugs and procedures like blood transfusion can be administered only intravenously [1].

According to a recent study, it has been estimated that there are nearly 500 million IV insertions done every year. Other studies have shown that 95.2 - 97.3 percent of them are successful in the first attempt which indicates that it

K.R. Venugopal and L.M. Patnaik (Eds.): ICIP 2012, CCIS 292, pp. 270–281, 2012.
© Springer-Verlag Berlin Heidelberg 2012

is difficult to find veins in around 14 million cases on the first attempt. Also, 15,000 patients per day are subjected to four or more attempts to draw blood or other fluids from the vein causing them to experience a lot of discomfort and pain [2]. The main reason for faulty IV insertions is the failure to gain correct vascular access for insertion of the needle. The conventional method used by medical professionals for the IV needle insertion is based on visual cues which can be described as feeling and stabbing. Practitioners often have great difficulty seeing or feeling small veins found in women and children, or veins that lie beneath a layer of fat, as found in obese patients. Also, if the patient has a recent venipuncture history, the veins tend to be damaged and are not easy to locate. Anxiety causes the patients blood pressure to rise, thereby, narrowing the veins.

The success of this method depends largely on the practitioners experience and judgment. As many of these cases are not performed in an emergency setting, establishing vein access in a short time is not crucial, but the patients comfort becomes a priority. False insertion leads to stabbing and bruising of the vein and surrounding tissues [1]. But this step becomes more crucial in an emergency situation like the one faced on the battlefield. In such a situation, quick and precise vein localization and needle-insertion for drug administration will constitute the most important step which eventually helps in saving the soldiers life.

On the battlefield, many soldiers are wounded in combat. Serious injuries are caused to the head, torso and limbs which lead to heavy bleeding. According to statistics, released by the American Army Medical Department, in the years 1939 to 1945 during World War II, of the 904,755 American soldiers who were seriously injured, 20,810 died from their wounds. So 2.3% of the soldiers lives could have been saved with timely administration of coagulants to control bleeding. Many years later, during the wars in Iraq and Afghanistan, of the 17,501 soldiers who were injured, 383 soldiers died from their wounds. So 2.1% of the soldiers lives could have been saved with timely administration of coagulants to stop bleeding. This shows that after so many years, the percentage of soldiers whose lives could have been saved, with timely medical aid still remains approximately the same [3].

On the battlefield, when the soldier is seriously wounded and major arteries are severed, the resulting loss of blood occurs at a very fast rate. Additionally, the soldier may be incapacitated due to his injury and unable to administer any kind of self-aid. The time taken for medical aid to arrive may vary from few minutes to hours or sometimes days. In such crucial situations, there is a need to develop technologies to stabilize a wounded soldier [4]. In medical emergencies, like the ones faced on the battlefield, an automated system for the intravenous drug-administration would dramatically shorten the time it takes to help soldiers wounded in combat - a factor that could save many lives when a soldiers life may hang in balance [4]. Such a system would capture a contrast-enhanced image of the veins and also localize the region where the needle needs to be inserted. This is very useful in the poor lighting conditions on the battlefield and when proper medical help is immediately unavailable.

2   Vein Imaging

Vein-imaging forms an integral part of the automated intravenous system. It consists of a camera that captures images of the patients subcutaneous veins under the illumination of near-infrared light at a specific wavelength. This camera is receptive in near-infrared light.

2.1   Near-Infrared Light

Human eyes can only detect visible light that occupies a narrow band (approximately 400 nm 700 nm) of the entire electromagnetic spectrum. However, there is much more information contained in other bands of the electromagnetic spectrum. For subcutaneous veins, their visibility under normal visible light conditions is fairly low [5]. However, the near-infrared region (NIR) is of special advantage since the skin tissue becomes relatively transparent and the venous blood absorbs near-infrared light well [6].

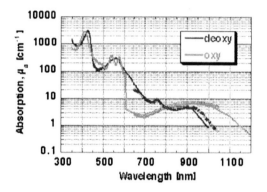

Fig. 1. Absorption Properties of Oxygenated Haemoglobin and Deoxygenated Haemoglobin

Near-infrared (NIR) wavelength lies between 700 nm to 1400 nm. The blood that is present in the veins is dominated by deoxygenated haemoglobin with the oxygenated haemoglobin content concentration around 47% while that in the arteries contains more oxygenated haemoglobin at around 90%-95% [2]. Oxygenated and deoxygenated haemoglobin posses different light absorption properties as illustrated in Fig. 1 [7].

Both oxygenated haemoglobin and deoxygenated haemoglobin, posses the same absorption properties up to wavelength of 600 nm. It can be understood that the absorption of light by deoxygenated haemoglobin present in veins is higher than that of oxygenated haemoglobin present in arteries in the wavelength of 700 nm to 900 nm [2]. Biologically, this is the medical spectral window which extends approximately from about 700 to 900 nm. Light in this spectral window penetrates deeply into tissues, thus allowing non-invasive investigation of subcutaneous veins [7]. The reduced haemoglobin in venous blood absorbs more of the incident near-infrared radiation at 850 nm more than the surrounding tissue [8]. Therefore, in the resulting image, the vein-segments appear darker than the surrounding parts and are easily discernible.

3   Choice of Vein

The preferred veins for IV therapy are the peripheral veins. A peripheral vein is any vein that is not present in the chest or abdomen area [9]. Arm, hand, leg and foot veins are the common peripheral veins chosen for IV therapy. For intravenous administration, the veins preferred generally are the superficial veins of the palma dorsa (outer side of the palm). This consists of the basiclic vein and the cephalic vein. The palma dorsum is preferred as the incidences of arterial abnorrmalities are minimal. These veins are illustrated in Fig. 2.

Further the veins in the palm are preferred for IV because:

1) It is usually an uncovered part of the body.
2) It has sufficient mobility.
3) It has reduced amount of hair.
4) The veins of palm are closer to the surface than in any of the other body parts, therefore easier to locate.
5) These veins are less susceptible to damage [10].

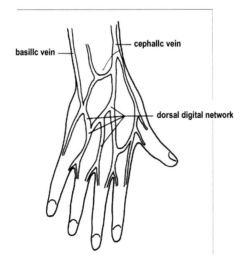

Fig. 2. Common Vascular Pattern of the Dorsal Digital Network Preferred Site for Intravenous Therapy

4   Previous Work

A lot of research has been done concerning an ideal way to image subcutaneous veins. A lot of information is available about the camera most suitable to image the subcutaneous veins. It was experimented with a Hitachi CCD camera that was made sensitive to IR light by use of infrared filters like the commercially available Hoya R72 among others [11]. In more recent experiments, researchers have successfully captured good quality images with an off- the shelf web-cam after converting it to be IR sensitive [12]. Some researchers used a Philips ToU USB camera to acquire vein images. It was a low cost, easy to use web-cam having a CCD sensor array [10]. Some scientist in USA used a Videre stoc stereo camera with the IR filter removed which was able to provide monochrome images [13]. Once the vein-segments were captured in an image using the camera they were processed to achieve the results. Scientists have applied a threshold to the image and then performed edge detection followed by thinning to get the desired region of interest where the needle can be inserted for IV therapy. Further, some researchers believe that it is best to insert the needle where the vein bifurcates because this has lesser connective tissues rather than in the midsection of the vein [13]. They use an approach of tracking the vein-pattern from a known point and then detecting a bifurcation and concluding that point to be an ideal spot for needle insertion.

A commercially available prototype for automatic intravenous needle insertion developed at the Health Science Centre of The University of Tennessee processes the image to retain the veins and then projects it back onto the patients skin. This helps in viewing the veins and makes needle insertion very convenient and easy [14].

Some scientists first eliminated the palm as the region of interest and reduced noise using a smoothing filter. This was further processed to retain the veins in the palm by applying a threshold. Here the value for threshold is chosen based on average around each pixel in the image [6]. It was found that a gradient based method used along with a threshold on the vein-segments images also works well and gives good results. Good results were also achieved by applying morphological thinning on images after the threshold was used [10][15][16].

5   Method

This paper aims at the design of an automated system for the purpose of intravenous drug administration. This system can be used on the battlefield to help soldiers wounded in combat. Soldiers suffer a lot of bleeding due to wounds caused to the head, torso and limbs. Proper medical aid is often not available close-by and may take hours and sometimes even days to arrive. In such a situation, the soldier needs to be administered with coagulants like Recombinant activated factor VII (rfVIIa) that will heal the wounds and reduce blood loss which could save the soldiers life. Recombinant activated factor VII (rfVIIa) is used for treating uncontrolled massive haemorrhage, and it plays a role as an

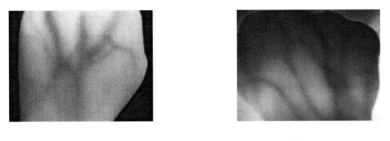

Fig. 3.   **Fig. 4.**

adjunct to surgical haemostasis in patients with severe post operative bleeding following general surgery. Therefore, administration of this drug to the soldier will speed up the coagulation process and helps prevent further blood loss. Recombinant activated factor VII (rfVIIa) is administered to the blood stream intravenously. In the absence of immediate medical aid to administer an IV injection, there is a need for an automated system to do the same. The system developed consists of a camera for capturing images of subcutaneous veins and an algorithm to process these images.

5.1   Source of Light

A medical spectral window extends from approximately 700 to 900 nm, where light penetrates deeply into veins and helps with imaging. Thus, Light Emitting Diodes (LEDs) with their peak velocity at 850 nm were used as a light source. The LEDs were connected to form an array. This LED array was focused on the target area which is the palma dorsa. For the sake of experimentation, LED arrays were designed in two different configurations: concentric and rectangular. With the concentric LED array a circular diffusing filter was used. The diffuser helped the light to spread out evenly. With the use of the filter the light was more focused.

Apart from the LED arrays other light sources, like torchlight, sunlight and normal lighting conditions in the laboratory were experimented with. This is because even these light sources have some near-infrared light present in them and will be detected by the camera.

5.2   Camera

Venous blood contains deoxygenated haemoglobin which absorbs light at 850 nm. Whereas the oxygenated haemoglobin present in the blood surrounding the veins remains transparent to light at this wavelength. Keeping this in mind, a camera that works in the near-infrared region was used. A webcamera modified to work in the near-infrared region and a DSLR with an external filter were used.

A commercially available web-camera was used after converting it so as to work in the NIR region. All web-cameras are sensitive to both IR as well as visible light. But IR light is blocked out completely due to the presence of an inbuilt IR filter.

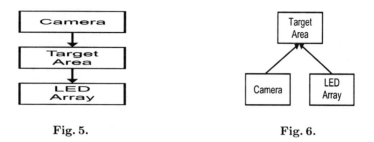

Fig. 5.   **Fig. 6.**

The removal of the IR filter made the web-camera sensitive to IR light. Special care was taken while removing the filter, as any minor damage to the close-by image sensing chip could render the web-camera useless. Also, the web-camera was made exclusively sensitive only to the IR region and not the visible region. To do so, once the IR filter was removed, it was replaced with a filter to block the visible light. This blocked out the visible light completely and made the web-camera sensitive to only IR region of light. Fig. 3 illustrates an image of the subcutaneous veins captured by the modified webcamera.

The second type of camera that was used was a DSLR with an external filter to block visible light. A DSLR is digital single-lens reflex camera. The sensors fitted in all DSLRs have the ability to capture a large portion of the electromagnetic spectrum, from the ultra-violet light (400 nm) right up to near-infrared light (900 nm). However, because infrared radiation contaminates images taken under normal visible light conditions all modern day DSLRs are fitted with an infrared blocking filter, called a hot mirror or a cut filter. This filter blocks out light from the infrared spectrum, above 700nm.

Therefore, in order to capture IR images, an external filter that blocks all visible light below 700 nm was used. This made the DSLR receptive in the 700 nm to 900 nm wavelength range- near-infrared range. The HOYA R72 was used and it blocked all light below 720 nm. The DSLR that was used along with the HOYA R72 is the Canon Rebel T2i. Fig. 4 illustrates an image captured by the DSLR along with HOYA R72.

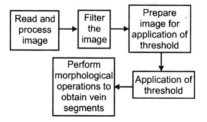

Fig. 7. Flowchart of the Algorithm

5.3   System Set-Up

The camera and the light source were set up in two different configurations. In the transmission method, the LED array and camera were placed on either sides of the target area (palma dorsa). The light was shone through the target area to be captured by the camera.

Fig 5 illustrates the arrangement of the LED array and camera for the transmission method.

In the reflection method, the LED array and camera were placed on the same side of the target area. The light was shone on the target area (palma dorsa) to be captured by the camera on the same side.

Fig 6 illustrates the arrangement of the LED array and camera for the transmission method. The distance between the camera and the target area was experimented with. The best results were obtained when the distance was set at 14 cms.

5.4   Vein Identification and Localisation

nce the images were captured they were analyzed and processed to determine the region where the vein-segments are present. The software that was used for this is MATLAB 7 Image Processing Toolbox (IPT). Fig. 7 illustrates the steps involved in this algorithm.

Firstly, the image is read from the folder and is processed. It was converted to grayscale and the contrast was enhanced. The RGB infrared (IR) image was converted to gray scale image by eliminating the hue and saturation information and retaining the luminance.

Contrast enhancement was done by setting all gray pixel values below a specified lower limit to zero, and all gray pixel values above a specified upper limit to the maximum intensity value, which was 255. All gray pixel values between the upper and lower limit were set to a linear ramp of values between 0 and 255. Because the upper limit must be greater than the lower limit, the lower limit must be between 0 and 254, and the upper limit must be between 1 and 255.

Contrast enhancement improved the visual appearance of the grayscale image. After this the veins were more prominent as compared to the surrounding areas.

Contrast enhancement made the overall image noisy. Filtering this image to smooth it out gave a better image. A two dimensional median filter was used to filter the image. Each pixel was replaced neighborhood. This preserved the useful the by the median of intensity values in its neighbourhood. This reduced the noise in the image. A median filter of 50 x 50 size was used. Each of the pixel values was replaced by median value of pixels in a 50 x 50 neighbourhood.

The median filtered image had a discernable vein region. This image can further be processed before the application of the threshold. On comparison of the median filtered image with the contrast enhanced image, the area occupied by the surrounding region remains almost the same. Keeping this in mind, the two images were subtracted. In the resulting image, the vein-segments are a lighter colour as compared to the surrounding area which is very dark. A differentiation

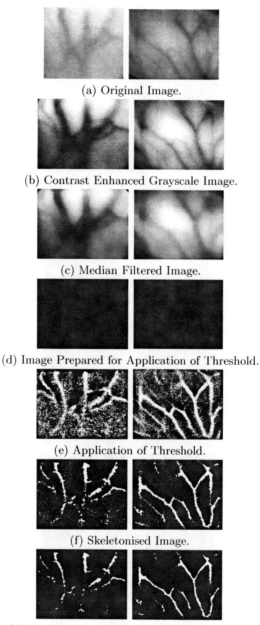

(a) Original Image.

(b) Contrast Enhanced Grayscale Image.

(c) Median Filtered Image.

(d) Image Prepared for Application of Threshold.

(e) Application of Threshold.

(f) Skeletonised Image.

(g) Final Image with Detected Vein-Segments.

Fig. 8. (a-g) Processing of Images using Algorithm. Each Image Represents the Steps in Processing for an Image Captured with the Modified Webcamera on the Left and an Image Captured with DSLR on the Right.

between the two can be made by means of applying a threshold value that will segment the image to make a clear distinction between vein regions and surrounding regions. The image contains 256 gray levels meaning the value of each of the pixels ranges from 0 to 255. The smallest value that any pixel can have would be 0 which represents a black pixel and the largest value would be 255 which represents white. All the other pixels have values ranging between 0 and 255. After the application of the threshold for this image, each gray level that is less than or equal to some prescribed value T called the threshold value is set to 0, and each gray level greater than T is changed to 255.

A threshold of 2 was applied on the subtracted image. This resulted in a binary image containing only white and black pixels was obtained. The vein-segments are retained as white pixels. There are some other unwanted white pixels too, which were eliminated by morphological operations.

Binary morphology uses only set membership and does not consider other factors like the value, such as gray level or colour, of a pixel. To eliminate the unwanted white pixels surrounding the vein-segments, only those white pixels were retained, which had at least five white pixels in their 3 x 3 neighbourhood. After this, the image was skeletonised. This reduced the remaining surrounding unwanted pixels and also made the vein segments thinner. After this, erosion operation was performed on the image using a suitable structural element. This eroded the unwanted pixels further, which resulted in the vein-segments from the original image. The final image obtained had the vein-segments represented by white pixels.

The processing of captured vein images was done using MATLAB 7 Image Processing Tool Box.

6   Results and Conclusions

The images captured by the webcamera and the DSLR were processed using the algorithm. Fig. 8 illustrates the processing of images. The final image obtained after erosion represents the vein segments of the palma dorsa. The co-ordinates of these vein segments will act as a guide for needle-insertion.

A database of images was collected using the modified webcamera and the DSLR. The transmission method provided better results as compared to the reflection method with both types of camera. The configuration of LEDs made no difference to the quality of images captured. The camera was placed at a distance of 14 cms from the palma dorsa.

Further, the images were processed using the aforementioned algorithm. Accurate results were achieved with most of the images in the database. It was observed that better results were achieved for the images captured with the DSLR. Poor results for images with the webcamera can be attributed to the low contrast quality of these images.

7 Future Work

The vein segments have been obtained using the algorithm. A robotic intravenous needle guide can be developed for the automated intravenous system. Once the vein segments have been determined, it can be used as a guide for the needle for insertion. The needle can be guided to enter the vein-segments by a microcontroller. This system would then involve minimal human assistance.

With an accurate guide to the correct veins, the system can be used in civilian applications that involve IV therapy. It can be used to locate and localize veins in patients who have darker skin making them less translucent for the practitioner to determine the location of a vein. Additionally, it can assist IV therapy in heavier patients whose veins are more deep seated under a thick layer of fat. It also alleviates a lot of physical discomfort during the IV procedure in infants, toddlers and geriatric patients. Thus, it can be used in a wide range of civilian applications like hospitals, emergency care wards, paediatric centres, blood banks and geriatric centres among others.

References

1. Sharon, M.: Plumers Principle and Practice of Intravenous Therapy, 8th edn. Lippincott Williams and Wilkins, ISBN 0781759447
2. Soujanya, G.: Depth and Size Limits for the Visibility of Veins using Veinveiwer Imaging System. Master of Science Thesis, The University of Tennessee, Memphis, USA, pp. 2–7 (2007)
3. Ronald, B., John, H., Howard, R., Lynn, S., Charles, W.: Understanding Combat Casualty Care Statics. The Journal of Trauma, Injury, Infection and Critical Care 60, 399 (2006)
4. Pete, M.: Vein Viewing Technology Provides Life Saving Imagery for Battlefield Wounded, Materials and Manufacturing Directorate, Air Force Research Laboratory, Press Release
5. Wang, L., Graham, L.: Near and Far-Infrared Imaging for Vein-segments Biometrics. In: Proceedings of the IEEE International Conference on Video and Signal Based Surveillance (AVSS 2006), pp. 2–3 (2006)
6. Ahmed, B.: Hand Vein Biometric Verification Prototype: A Testing Performance and Patterns Similarity. In: Proceedings of the 2006 International Conference on Image Processing, Computer Vision and Pattern Recognition (IPCV 2006), Las Vegas, USA, pp. 1–3 (2006)
7. Cross, J., Smith, C.: Thermographic Imaging of Subcutaneous Vascular network of the Back of the Hand for Biometric Identification. In: Proceedings of IEEE 29th International Carnahan Conference on Security Technology, Sanderstead, Surrey, England, pp. 20–35 (October 1995)
8. Wang, L., Graham, L.: Near and Far-Infrared Imaging for Vein-segments Biometrics. In: Proceedings of the IEEE International Conference on Video and Signal Based Surveillance (AVSS 2006), p. 2 (2006)
9. Zeman, H.D., Lovhoiden, G., Vrancken, C., Danish, R.K.: Prototype Vein Contrast Enhancer. Optical Engineering 44(8), 8 (2005)
10. Brewer, R.D., Salisbury, K.J.: Visual Vein Finding for Robotic IV Insertion. In: IEEE International Conference on Robotics and Automation, Convention District, Anchorage, Alaska, USA, May 3-8, pp. 4600–4602 (2010)

11. Shrotri, A., Rethrekar, S.C., Patil, M.H., Kore, S.N.: IR-Webcam Imaging and Vascular Pattern Analysis towards Hand Vein Authentication. In: Computer and Automation Engineering (ICCAE), Singapore, vol. 5, pp. 877–879 (2010)
12. Septimiu, C., IonGavril, T., Eduard, C.T.: A Low Cost Vein Detection System Using Near-infrared Radiation. In: SAS 2007 - IEEE Sensors Application Symposium, San Diego, California USA, pp. 1–8 (February 2007)
13. Allen, G.D., Everett Gaither, B.: Intravenous Therapy-A Review of Site Selection and Technique. Anaesthesia Progress, 283
14. Henry, G.: Anatomy of the Human Body, 40th edn., p. 608. Lea & Febiger, Philadelphia (2009) ISBN: 9780443066849
15. Wang, Y., Wand, H.: Gradient Based Image Segmentation for Vein-segments. In: Fourth International Conference on Computer Sciences and Convergence Information Technology, pp. 1615–1616 (2009)
16. Fantini, S., Franceschini, M.A.: Handbook of Optical Biomedical Diagnostics, vol. TM107. SPIE Press (2002) ISBN: 9780819442383

A New Manifold Learning Technique for Face Recognition

Mohammad Moinul Islam[1], Mohammed Nazrul Islam[2],
Vijayan K. Asari[3], and Mohammad A. Karim[1]

[1] Old Dominion University
[2] Farmingdale State University of New York
[3] University of Dayton
vijayan.asari@notes.udayton.edu

Abstract. One of the fundamental problems in pattern recognition is the curse of dimensionality in data representation. Many algorithms have been proposed to find a compact representation of data as well as to facilitate the recognition task. In this paper, we propose a novel Dimensionality Reduction technique called Marginality Preserving Embedding (MPE). Unlike Principal Component Analysis (PCA) and Linear Discriminant Analysis (LDA) which projects data in a global sense, MPE seeks for local structure in the manifold. This is similar to other subspace learning techniques but the difference with them is that MPE preserves marginality in local reconstruction. Experimental results show that the proposed method provides better representation in low dimensional space and achieves lower error rates in face recognition.

Keywords: Dimensionality Reduction, Manifold Learning, Marginality preserving embedding (MPE).

1   Introduction

In many applications of computer vision and machine learning we often need to deal with very high dimensional data but the intrinsic structure of the data may lie in a low dimensional space. Learning such high dimensional data is computationally expensive and not suitable for all practical applications. Moreover, it is also desirable to reduce the dimension for visualization. But this low dimensional data must preserve the underlying structure of high dimensional data in order to be of use. This leads researchers to develop methods of Dimensionality Reduction that can extract manifold structure of data on which data may reside. Recently various research works[1]-[4] on face images have shown that the data may reside on a nonlinear submanifold. As a result manifold learning becomes popular for face recognition. Some popular nonlinear techniques include Laplacian Eigenmap[5], Locally Linear Embedding (LLE)[2] and Isomap[6]. All these methods showed impressive results on artificial datasets and in some real applications. But they are defined only on training data points and it is unclear how the map can be evaluated for a new data point. Some linear manifold learning techniques have also been proposed such as Locality Preserving Projection

K.R. Venugopal and L.M. Patnaik (Eds.): ICIP 2012, CCIS 292, pp. 282–286, 2012.
© Springer-Verlag Berlin Heidelberg 2012

(LPP)[4] and Augmented Relation Embedding (ARE)[7]. LPP uncovers manifold structure by preserving local structure of data while ARE learns manifold by using user's feedback. Yan et al [8] proposed Marginal Fisher Analysis (MFA) for Dimensionality Reduction. It redefines LDA in a graph embedding framework by constructing two graphs- one for intra-class compactness and the other for inter-class separability. Another graph embedding network called Maximum Margin Projection (MPP)[9] which maximizes the margin between within-class graph and between-class graph. In this paper, we propose a new Dimensionality Reduction technique called Marginality Preserving Embedding (MPE). The proposed method considers manifold structure which is modeled by two adjacency graphs: one from same class level and the other from local neighborhood. Thus it has more discriminant power and it is defined everywhere.

2   Marginality Preserving Embedding

The basic idea of Marginality Preserving Embedding (MPE) is to find both geometrical and discriminant features in data manifold. It focuses on Locally Linear Embedding (LLE) in the sense of reconstruction from local neighborhood. But LLE is defined only on the training data and it is not clear how to evaluate a new data point. If the number of training sample is small, reconstruction based on minimizing the error may not be the optimum one since the classes with the more frequent examples tend to dominate the prediction of the new vector, as they tend to come up in the k nearest neighbors. This limitation of LLE may be overcome by developing new criteria that minimize the contribution from inter-class samples in reconstruction. Toward this end, we propose MPE based on a graph embedding framework that uses both label information and the advantage of LLE to enhance the recognition rate. First, we construct a graph that uses class information and preserves marginality in reconstruction. Then we construct another graph that uses both class information and neighborhood information.

Given a set of points $x_1, x_2, ..., x_m$ in R^n our goal is to find a transformation matrix,$\mathbf{A}$ that maps all these points to a set of points $y_1, y_2, ..., y_m$ in R^d such that $d << n$. Let $W_{i,j}^s$ be a $m \times m$ coefficient matrix of reconstruction from all the members of the same class. The objective function that minimizes the reconstruction error can be defined as

$$\phi(W^s) = \sum_i \|x_i - \sum_j W_{i,j}^s x_j\|^2 \tag{1}$$

which adds up the squared distances between all the data points and their reconstruction. The weights $W_{i,j}^s$ summarize the contribution of the j th data point to i th reconstruction. The minimization is subjected to two constraints:

$$W_{i,j}^s = 0 \qquad \text{if } x_j \notin C(x_i)$$

where $C(x_i)$ is the class of the pattern x_i

and
$$\sum_{x_i \in C(x_i)} W_{i,j}^s = 1 \tag{2}$$

Consider the problem of mapping original data point to a line so that each data point on the line can be represented as a linear combination of its class members with coefficients $W_{i,j}^s$. Let $(y_1, y_2, ..., y_m)^T$ be such a map. A reasonable criterion for choosing a "good" map is to minimize the following cost function

$$\phi(y) = \sum_i (y_i - \sum_j W_{i,j}^s y_j)^2 \tag{3}$$

under appropriate constraints. Here the weights $W_{i,j}^s$ is fixed while the coordinates y_i is optimized. Now we define another cost function which adds up reconstruction error from neighbors that belong to different class. So, the objective here is to maximize the following cost function:

$$\phi(y) = \sum_i (y_i - \sum_j W_{i,j}^d y_j)^2 \tag{4}$$

with the following constraints

$$W_{i,j}^d = 0 \text{ if } x_j \notin N_k(x_i) \text{ and } C(x_i) \neq C(x_j)$$

and
$$\sum_{x_j \in N_k(x_i), x_j \notin C(x_i)} W_{i,j}^d = 1 \tag{5}$$

where $N_k(x_i)$ is the k nearest neighbors of x_i and $C(x_k)$ is the class of k th pattern. It can be shown that equation (3) is reduced to

$$\phi(y) = a^T X M^s X^T a \tag{6}$$

where
$$M^s = (I - W^s)^T (I - W^s) \tag{7}$$

By combining equation (3) and equation (4), the objective function finally reduces to solve the following optimization problem

$$argmax_a \quad \frac{a^T X M^d X^T a}{a^T X M^s X^T a} \tag{8}$$

The optimal a's are the eigenvectors corresponding to the following maximum eigenvalue solution:

$$X M^d X^T a = \lambda X M^s X^T a \tag{9}$$

It is easy to show that the matrices $X M^d X^T$ and $X M^s X^T$ are symmetric and positive semidefinite.

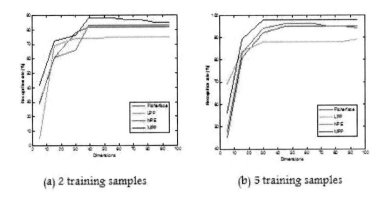

(a) 2 training samples   (b) 5 training samples

Fig. 1. (a-c) An Example Image with Three Different Illuminations and their Corresponding (d) LBP image and (e) MLBP image

3   Experiments and Analysis

We use ORL (Olivetti Research Laboratory) face database in our experiments. The database consists of 10 different images each of 40 different subjects. The images were taken at different times with varying lighting conditions and facial expressions (open/closed eyes, smiling/not smiling, open/closed mouth) and facial details (glasses/no glasses). All images were taken against a dark homogeneous background with the subjects in an upright, frontal position (with tolerance for some tilting and rotation of face up to 20 degrees). Original images were cropped to locate only the face regions and resized to 32×32 pixels with gray levels/pixel. Thus each face image can be represented by a -dimensional vector. For each subject we use $n = 2$ and 5. images of each individual for training and the rest for testing the algorithm. For each n we use random selection for training images and estimate the mean of the results. For comparison, we run the test against some popular techniques in face recognition such as Eigenface[10], Fisherface[11], LPP[4] and NPE[3]. Figure 1 shows the error rate of different methods against dimensionality. It shows that the recognition rate is affected with number of dimensions in face subspace. From the figure, we see that the proposed MPE attains maximum value at 39 dimensions (for 2 samples) and 30 (for 5 samples). To illustrate the advantage of our method over other methods we compare the classification accuracy for different number of training samples and listed in Table 1. It can be seen that Fisherface, LPP and NPE have outperformed the baseline and Eigenfaces for both small and large training sizes. But our proposed MPE outperforms all the other state of the art methods.

Table 1. Face Recognition Results (%) on ORL database

Method	2 Samples	5 Samples
Baseline	71	89
Eigenfaces	53	75.14
Fisherfaces	74.6	91.52
LPP	69.22	87.28
NPE	76.04	92.38
MPE	79.51	94.64

4   Conclusions

In this paper, we propose a new Dimensionality Reduction technique called Marginality Preserving Embedding (MPE). Several papers also addressed subspace learning technique for Dimensionality Reduction both supervised and unsupervised way. Two related algorithms called LLE[2] and NPE[3] also shares locality preserving projections. In addition to that our method also considers similarity and dissimilarity measures by formulating an optimization problem that involves both intra-class and inter-class data in the local neighborhood. It is simple and defined everywhere on test data. Performance of this method is demonstrated through several experiments and it shows lower error rate in face recognition.

References

1. He, X., Yan, S., Hu, Y., Niyogi, P., Zhang, H.: Face Recognition using Laplacianface. IEEE Trans. Pattern Analysis and Machine Intelligence 27(3), 328–340 (2005)
2. Roweis, S., Saul, L.: Nonlinear Dimensionality Reduction by Locally Linear Embedding. Science 290, 2323–2326 (2000)
3. He, X., Cai, D., Yan, S., Zhang, H.: Neighborhood Preserving Embedding. In: Proceedings 11th International Conference, Computer Vision, ICCV 2005 (2005)
4. He, X., Niyogi, P.: Locality Preserving Projections. In: Advances in Neural Information Processing Systems, vol. 16. MIT Press (2003)
5. Belkin, M., Niyogi, P.: Laplacian Eigenmaps and Spectral Techniques for Embedding and Clustering. In: Proceedings Conference Advances in Neural Information Processing System, vol. 15 (2001)
6. Tanenbaum, J., Silva, V., Langford, J.: A Global Geometric Framework for Nonlinear Dimensionality Reduction. Science 290(22), 2319–2323 (2000)
7. Lin, Y., Liu, T., Chen, H.: Semantic Manifold Learning for Image Retrieval. In: Proceedings 13th Ann. ACM International Conference, Multimedia (2005)
8. Yan, S., Xu, D., Zhang, B., Zhang, H., Yang, Q., Lin, S.: Graph Embedding and Extensions: A General Framework for Dimensionality Reduction. IEEE Transactions Pattern Analysis and Machine Intelligence 29(1), 40–51 (2007)
9. He, X., Cai, D., Han, J.: Learning a Maximum Margin Subspace for Image Retrieval. IEEE Transaction Knowledge and Data Engineering 20(2), 189–201 (2008)
10. Joliffe, I.: Principal Component Analysis. Springer (1986)
11. Belhumeur, P., Hespanha, J., Kriegman, D.: Eigenfaces vs. Fisherfaces: Recognition using class specific linear projection. IEEE Transactions Pattern Analysis and Machine Intelligence 19(7), 711–720 (1997)

An Innovative ANN Based Assamese Character Recognition System Configured with Radon Transform

Purnima Kumari Sharma, Mondira Deori,
Balbindar Kaur, Chandralekha Dey, and Karen Das

Department of Electronics and Communication Engineering,
Don Bosco College of Engineering and Technology, Guwahati, India
purnimasoni4018@rediffmail.com

Abstract. Character Recognition is a process of understanding a human readable text document by machines and today many researchers in the academia and industry are interested in this direction. This paper describes a novel method of Character Recognition. The main objective of this is to use the ANN and Radon Transform to obtain a set of invariant features, on basis of which a character will be recognized.

Keywords: Recognition, ANN, MLP, Radon Transform, PCA.

1 Introduction

Storing the old books and written scripts safely is a sacred mission as it represents the culture and convey the historical information of a particular area or a particular class of people. An efficient character recognition system can give a higher order dimension to this thought since as much copy of a digital book can be easily stored than a hard copy of that one. This paper describes a novel method of Assamese Character Recognition System (ACRS) based on Radon Transform (RT) and Artificial Neural Network(ANN).

Our work starts with training of an ANN and the trained network is implemented to classify the tested characters. In phase1, a network is a trained, and the trained network is used to recognize the character input to the system in phase2. In the block diagram given in Fig.1, it is seen that an image is taken as input by scanning and then various image enhancement techniques are applied followed binarization. Then, RT of the preprocessed sample is done to get the required feature vector for creating the trained network in Phase 1. The testing sample is first preprocessed and then feature extracted using RT is input to the trained network to get a decision.

1.1 Different Techniques Used for Character Recognition

Many methods have been proposed till date for printed and handwritten character recognition. But still it remains a highly challenging task to implement a

K.R. Venugopal and L.M. Patnaik (Eds.): ICIP 2012, CCIS 292, pp. 287–292, 2012.
© Springer-Verlag Berlin Heidelberg 2012

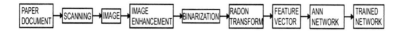

Fig. 1. Block Diagram for Training Phase

Fig. 2. Block Diagram for Testing Phase

character recognition system that works under all possible conditions and gives highly accurate results. So on considering these effects character recognition system is made using various techniques like Quad tree-based Fractal encoding, Hidden Markov Models, SVM Classifier, Principal Component Analysis etc.

In using Quad tree-based Fractal Encoding Scheme for Arabic numerals[1], a better result was obtained using Fractal Nearest Neighbor classifier in the training phase i.e. 100% but by using Fractal Transformation classifier the performance was 96.2%. Hidden Markov Models focus mainly on offline handwritten character recognition. It improves classification accuracy from 62.7% to 71.0%. Using SVM classifier [2], recognition rates between 95.51% to 98.78% have been obtained.

2   Theoritical Background

2.1   Radon Transform

The Radon Transform finds projection of a two dimensional function. The Radon function computes the line integrals $f(x,y)$ from multiple sources along parallel paths, or beams, in a certain direction at different angles by rotating the source around the center of the image. The figure 3 shows a single projection at a specified rotation angle. The radial coordinates are the values along the x'-axis, which is oriented at θ degrees counter clockwise from the x-axis. Let $(x) = (x,y)$ be a continuous function vanishing outside some large disc in the Euclidean plane R^2. The Radon Transform is a function defined on the space of straight lines L in R^2 by the line integral along each such line:

$$Rf(L) = \int_L f(x)dx \tag{1}$$

It follows that the quantities (α,s) can be considered as coordinates on the space of all lines in R^2, and the Radon transform can be expressed in these coordinates by:

$$Rf(\alpha, s) = \int_{-x}^{x} f(x(t).y(t))dt = \int_{-x}^{x} f((tsin\alpha + scos\alpha), (-tcos\alpha + sin\alpha))dt \tag{2}$$

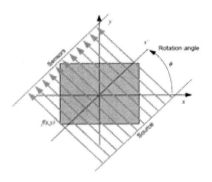

Fig. 3. Single projection at a specified rotation angle

Thus the Identification by Radon transformation is rotated and mirrored invariable so, any character in any angle can be recognized and helps in giving better performance.

2.2 Artificial Neural Network

In ANN based OCR system segmentation is done by using Multi Layered Perceptron (MLP) . By exploiting the input/output behavior of ANNs it is possible to train an ANN with known classification data to predict the classification of unclassified data. ANN has two phases of working- first training during which it learns the patterns and testing which ascertains the extent of learning.

3 Experimental Work

The work consists of application of ANN for Assamese character recognition in two different aspects. First is application of ANN directly on the character images and the second one is the application of ANN on the features of the characters extracted using Radon Transform. With this two methods the system performance is checked and efficiency of both the systems are being recorded.

Before using either ANN or Radon Transform Based ANN, the Assamese characters are preprocessed. The characters are filtered using median filter. Then, the filtered images are enhanced using histogram equalization technique. The image is also cropped perfectly so that the extra regions are cut out which may affect to give better results. After enhancement and sharpening the gray level image is converted into binary form so as to ease the computational load of the subsequent stages. At last,the image is thinned because while taking samples different writers use different pen which results in few thin and few thick characters.

3.1 ANN Based Recognition

The training input used for ANN training is the pre-processed image of the assamese characters. The complete training set includes variations of 100 different persons. For training purpose a three layered MLP is considered with one hidden layer. It has the following configuration: Length of input layer = row size of the input ; Length of hidden layer = .75 times of the input; Length of output layer = row size of target. Say, for a 25x25 image, length of input layer = 625 and length of hidden layer = 469.

Several methods of Back Propagation have been used for training the ANN. These are : Gradient Descent with Adaptive Learning rate Back Propagation (GDALBP); Gradient Descent with Momentum and Adaptive Learning Rate Back Propagation (GDMALRBP) and Resilient Back Propagation (RBP).

The number of epochs required to obtain Mean Square Error (MSE) of 10^{-4} for different training methods are tabulated in Table 1. The best performance is given by RBP. Table 2 shows epochs and time required for different image sizes. It is seen that number of epochs required and time is lowest for the smallest image size i.e. 15x15. This is due to its smallest size.

Table 1. Epochs and Time required for Training of Assamese Characters to reach 10^{-4} MSE using Different Training Algorithms for 15x15 image with Learning Rate 0.1

Algorithm	Time	Regression rate	Epochs
GDMALRBP	50 sec	99.945 %	520
GDALBP	1 min 20 sec	99.945 %	1418
RBP	7 sec	99.945%	211

Table 2. Epoch and Time required to get 10^{-4} MSE using RBP for Different Sizes

Image size	Time	Regression Rate	Epoch
20x20	52 sec	99.991 %	523
18x18	11 sec	99.995 %	296
15x15	7 sec	99.946 %	211

Table 3. Table for RT Curve for the Assamese Character 'oi', at Different Angles

Degree of Rotation	Test Character	Radon Transform Curve
10		
35		
70		

Table 4. Epochs and Time Required for Training to reach 10^{-4} MSE using Different Training Algorithms considering 64x64 image size with Learning Rate 0.1

Algorithm	Time	Regression Rate	Epoch
GDMALRBP	18 sec	99.945%	375
GDALBP	58 sec	99.931%	934
RBP	9 sec	99.946%	293

Table 5. Epochs and Time required for training to reach 10^{-6} MSE using RBP. Different image sizes are used with Learning Rate 0.1

Image size	Feature vector size	Time	Regression Rate	Epoch
96x96	139	1 min 1 sec	99.99%	3551
64x64	95	1 min 4 sec	99.99%	4487
32x32	49	2 min 19 sec	99.99%	8198

3.2 ANN Configured with Radon Transform

In this the ANN training is applied on the character samples after doing Radon Transform. This reduces dimensionality and also increases speed. On application of Radon Transform on different Assamese characters, we have obtained the corresponding radon transform curves for the same at different angles. For example we have taken a character 'oi', and applied radon transform on it in matlab at various angles such as $10^0, 35^0, 70^0$ etc. and obtained the corresponding Radon Transform curve for the corresponding figure as shown in Table 3. From Table 4 we can see that though it is comparable to Table 1 used for only ANN but it was done for 15x15 image size. This method gives better performance even with 64x64 image. Table 5 shows the fast and accurate behavior of this method. Time required is much lesser than the one with only ANN for attaining MSE of 10^{-6} whereas using ANN alone gives MSE of 10^{-4} only for different variant sizes.

4 Conclusions and Future Work

A comparative analysis was done considering both the above methods and it was found out that the latter method gives better efficiency and is also faster than ANN alone as shown in Table 7. The testing set includes handwritten scripts of another 100 different persons. Table 6 shows the testing results of 'ka' and 'ri' for different training algorithms. By observing the training and testing results RBP algorithm was found to be the most efficient followed by GDMALRBP. In future we will try to use more samples and incorporate PCA to improve the efficiency much more. We will also consider Assamese numerals. Segmentation will also be done for separating alphanumeric characters and vowel signs from written document.

Table 6. Testing Efficiency Rates of Different Test Samples and Training Algorithms

Algorithm	Test sample	Efficiency rate (%) (ANN+Radon Transform)	Efficiency rate (%) (only ANN)
GDMALRBP	ক	95.1	89.7
GDMALRBP	খ	94.8	87.9
GDALBP	ক	90.3	86.9
GDALBP	খ	91.9	85.8
RBP	ক	98.1	90.4
RBP	খ	96.9	90.7

Table 7. Comparison between ANN and ANN based on Radon Transform

Character	ANN average efficiency rate (%)	ANN based on RT average efficiency rate (%)
GDMALRBP	86.6	95.8
GDALBP	83.9	93.9
RBP	90.3	97.43

References

1. Mozaffari, S., Faez, K., Ziaratban, M.: Character Representation and Recognition Using Quadtree-based Fractal Encoding Scheme. In: Proceedings of the 2005 Eight International Conference on Document Analysis and Recognition (ICDAR 2005), 1520-5263/05. IEEE (2005)
2. Philip, B., Samuel, R.D.S.: Preffered Computational Approaches for the Recognition of different classes of printed Malayalam Characters using Hierarchical SVM classifiers. IJCA (0975-8887) 1(16) (2010)
3. Sarma, K.K.: Bi-lingual Handwritten Character and Numeral Recognition using Multi-Dimensional Recurrent Neural Networks (MDRNN). International Journal of Electrical and Electronics Engineering 3(7) (2009)
4. Bhattacharyya, K., Sarma, K.K.: ANN-based Innovative Segmentation Method for Handwritten text in Assamese. International Journal of Computer Science Issues, IJCSI 5 (2009) (in press)

Implementation Scheme for Clinical Diagnosis System Using Multi-Agent System(MAS)

Shibakali Gupta, Arindam Sarkar, and Sripati Mukherjee

University Institute of Technology, Burdwan University, Golapbag
(north), Burdwan (W.B)-713104
skgupta.81@gmail.com

Abstract. In present days, it is a true fact that computerized intelligent health care system can provide better healthcare than the traditional medical system. In the framework of this paper it is interesting to consider the possibility of deploying agents that provide Health Care-related services. In this paper we report the design and construction of a Multi-Agent System (MAS) that is composed of agents that provide medical services. The MAS contains agents that allow the user to have a solution for his/her symptoms. In our previous research paper, we proposed Clinical Diagnosis System (CDS), an advanced scheme of agent-based healthcare and medical diagnosis system. Using the knowledge base and collaborative as well as co-operative intelligent agents and residing on a multi-agent platform, that CDS provides a communicative task-sharing environment. In this paper we have tried to implement the above mentioned intelligent medical diagnosis system through JADE(Java Agent Development Enviroment).

Keywords: Health Care System, Intelligent Agent, JADE, Knowledge Base, Multi-Agent System.

1 Introduction

Modernization of conventional healthcare system is an emerging research direction today. Health care problem seems to be a major problem in the third world developing countries like India. In our country a large number of people are very poor. Conventional medical and healthcare system of our country can't give them proper chance to get proper service. Growing population and poor economy [1] is a very big problem in this issue. Beside these issues a major portion of the total population of our country resides in the remote areas [2], where proper health care and community medical services are almost beyond the reach of the native people. The problem is due to acute scarcity of medical practitioners as well as proper infrastructure. Keeping the medical diagnosis system in mind, we notice that the whole system depends on some basic factors like proper medical healthcare infrastructure, healthy economic condition, global awareness and user friendly environment or setup. In our research paper we have tried to give focus on that technical infrastructure problem. Generally technical

K.R. Venugopal and L.M. Patnaik (Eds.): ICIP 2012, CCIS 292, pp. 293–298, 2012.
© Springer-Verlag Berlin Heidelberg 2012

infrastructure means the practitioners, tools, medicines and modern technology based platform. And it's a fact that the factors are quite indispensable, mainly for those community health centers situated at remote villages as well as at other places. Lack of proper user friendly environment also stands against the proper treatment and diagnosis. Not only those limitations, there persists many other problems that affects the overall situation of our social environment and health situation. Due to the lack of proper medical system, many people go to some local unqualified practitioners. This is really a threat for our health care system. To overcome those unwanted problem in this arena, in our previous work [3] we have proposed a new agent oriented, much better to say, multi agent system (MAS) oriented intelligent diagnosis scheme called Clinical Diagnosis System or CDS. That very system can take care of the initial checkup of the patient, do the treatment and generate the solution or report for the patient very easily. In this paper we have mentioned the working concept of CDS first, and then we have tried to implement the individual transactions of that CDS through JADE.

2   Significance of Using Multi-Agent System

As per Michael Wooldridge [4], an agent is a computer system that is capable of independent action on behalf of its user or owner. And a multi agent system [5] is one that consists of a number of agents, which interact with one another, typically by exchanging messages through some computer network infrastructure. In MAS the agents are able to cooperate, coordinate, and negotiate with each other. Using the interdepedencies [6] of the agents MAS can decompose any problem. If we analyze the Clinical diagnosis and Health care system, we shall find that the knowledge required for solving a problem is spatially distributed in different locations. For example, diagnosis of general diseases differs from eye, or cardiology section. Each specialist doctor uses their own knowledge to solve the problem. Tests are carried on to some different location with the help of some different set of knowledge. Giving solution to a particular case involves better coordination between different individuals with their different skills and functionalities. It is obvious that medical diagnosis system is a complex system and there is no straightway software engineering standardization. A multi agent based system may be a better approach at that place.

2.1   Architecture of the CDS

In Clinical Diagnosis System [3], an agent called User Agent (UA) is responsible for taking the user inputs i.e. symptoms from the patients with the help of a user interface(which can be a website here). The user interface helps the practitioner or any person engaged in taking the symptom to feed the input as measured form and observation. Duty of this UA is to take patient symptoms in the form of raw data. The UA takes the raw input, and to apply some analysis method upon those data with the help of Master Agent (MA) to convert it to knowledge. This analysis is done with the help of the user interface i.e, the patient symptom

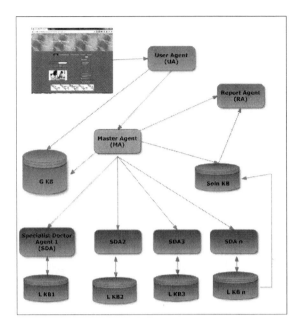

Fig. 1. Architectural Design of the Clinical Diagnosis System

form. That knowledge is stored in the Global Knowledge base (GKB). Role of the Master Agent (MA) is to select a specialist doctor agent (SDA) for handling the particular case and handover the case to that specific specialist doctor agent (SDA). The MA has the responsibility to give the task and to provide the proper knowledge from the Global Knowledge base (GKB) to the specialist doctor agents. For each SDA, there is individual local knowledge bases (LKB) associated with them. After having the solution, SDA will give the solution to the Master Agent (MA) and that solution will be stored in the Solution knowledge base (S KB). A report agent will be responsible for generating the report after getting the final instruction from the master agent. For instance, if a patient will come with symptoms such as high fever with convulsion, headache and weakness etc, the person will take those symptoms with the help of the user interface i.e. the form. User agent will help the person to refine the queries. After getting the queries or symptoms in the measured way, those inputs will be converted to knowledge and will be kept to the Global knowledge base. That knowledge will tell the master agent that the symptoms are likely to be of malaria. Then on the basis of that knowledge, the master agent will select the proper doctor agent. MA will also help SDA to access the global knowledge base. That SDA will then give the proper solution. That solution will also be kept in the Local knowledge bases of each SDA. After getting the particular solution for a particular case, that solution will be stored in form of knowledge at a different knowledge base called Solution knowledge base (SKB). A Report Agent (RA) can access this knowledge base for generating report with the help of MA.

2.2   Experimental Design and Software Architecture

The above architecture of the MAS can be implemented using the JADE(Java Agent Development Environment) [7]-[8] for agent development and different interfaces can be implemented using the J2EE technology, the knowledge base can be created using the KQML [9]language and the database can be created using MYSQL server.The standard model of an agent platform, as defined by FIPA[10], is represented in the following Fig. 2,

Agent Management System: The Agent Management System (AMS) is the agent who exerts supervisory control over access to and use of the Agent Platform. Only one AMS will exist in a single platform.

Agent Communication Channel: The Message Transport System, also called Agent Communication Channel (ACC), is the software component controlling all the exchange of messages within the platform, including messages to from remote platforms. JADE fully complies with this reference architecture and when a JADE platform is launched, the AMS and DF are immediately created and the ACC module is set to allow message communication. The main-container,

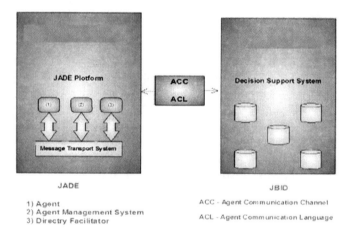

JADE

1) Agent
2) Agent Management System
3) Directry Facilitator

JBID

ACC - Agent Communication Channel

ACL - Agent Communication Language

Fig. 2. Reference Architecture of the FIPA Platform

or front-end, is the agent container where the AMS and DF lives and where the RMI registry, that is used internally by JADE, is created. The other agent containers, instead, connect to the main container and provide a complete runtime environment for the execution of any set of JADE agents. According to the FIPA specifications, DF and AMS agents communicate by using the FIPA-SL content language, the FIPA-agent-management ontology, and the FIPA-request interaction protocol. JADE provides compliant implementations for all these components. The following messages are used by agents to communicate with other agents,

1. Accept Proposal - One Agent accepts the proposal of another agent.
2. Agree - The process of mutual agreement between agents for request and response.
3. Inform - One agent informs to the agent about the process.
4. Failure - The communication failure is send as the response.
5. Propose - One agent submits some task to the other agent.
6. Refuse - The process of denying some task.
7. Request - Request for some action to be performed.

2.3   JADE and Master Agent Communication

Once the user agent is authenticated as shown in Fig. 3, he has been taken into website user part developed using J2EE. The user may give his/her symptoms here. The Coordinator Agent(CA) developed using JADE takes these symptoms through the parser and using its Knowledge Base(KB) it gives some solution to the user which can be generated using the Reporter Agent(RA). Now Suppose if

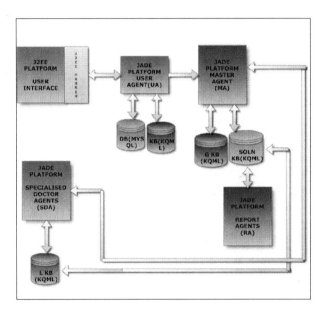

Fig. 3. Software Architectural Design for Clinical Diagnosis System

CA does not have a solution then it refers the case to the Master Agent(MA) and the MA now searches for the Specialised Doctor Agent(SDA) using its Global Knowledge Base(GKB). The SDA then using its Knowledge Base(KB) generates a XML file of the solution and gives it to the Master Agent(MA).The specific requirement of XML file is that, in near future JADE may be moved to some other server. It gives flexibility to transfer the data from one server to another server.

The XML file is parsed using J2EE Parser and data is transferred to JADE. Intern it is forwarded to Master Agent(MA). Master Agent(MA) is connected with Decision Support System. Master Agent(MA) made intelligent analysis and returns the best solution to the user whose report can be generated using the Report Agent(RA).

3   Conclusions and Future Work

The proposed implemented version of Clinical Diagnosis System(CDS) can take care of every stage of patients such as intial checkup,treatment and report for the patients. We believe that the implemented scheme can bring a revolution in our Clinical Diagnosis System mainly for Indian enviroment.In future correspondence the incorporation of KQML(Knowledge Query Manipulation Language) can be done to have more efficient data mining or knowledge mining.

References

1. PricewaterhouseCoopers.: Emerging Market Report: Health in India 2007 (2007)
2. Gill, K.: A Primary Evaluation of Service Delivery under the National Rural Health Mission (NRHM): Findings from a Study in Andhra Pradesh, Uttar Pradesh, Bihar and Rajasthan, Planning Commission of India (May 2009)
3. Gupta, S., Pujari, S.: A Multi Agent System (MAS) based Scheme for Health Care and Medical Diagnosis System. In: IAMA 2009. IEEExplore (2009) ISBN 978-1-4244-4710-7
4. Wooldridge, M.: An Introduction to Multi Agent Systems, Department of Computer Science, University of Liverpool, UK. John Wiley and Sons Ltd.
5. Sycara, K.P.: Multi Agent Systems. AI Magazine 19(2) (1998), Intelligent Agents Summer
6. Moreno, A.: Medical Applications of Multi-Agent Systems, Computer Science and Mathematics Department, Universitat Rovira, Virgili, ETSE. Campus Sescelades. Av. dels Països Catalans, 26, 43007-Tarragona-Spain
7. JADE: Java Framework for Agent Development, http://sharon.cselt.it/projects/jade
8. JADE: Java Framework for Agent Development, http://www.jade.tilab.com
9. Finin, T., Labrou, Y., Mayfield, J.: KQML as an Agent Communication Language. In: Bradshaw, J. (ed.) Software Agents. MIT Press, Cambridge (1997) (to appear)
10. FIPA: Foundation for Intelligent Physical Agents, http://www.fipa.org

Applying Restrained Genetic Algorithm for Attribute Reduction Using Attribute Dependency and Discernibility Matrix

Asit Kumar Das[1], Saikat Chakrabarty[2],
Soumen Kumar Pati[3], and Ajijul Haque Sahaji[4]

[1,2,4] Department of Computer Science and Technology,
Bengal Engineering and Science University, Shibpur,
Howrah - 711 103, West Bengal, India
[3] Department of Computer Science and Information Technology,
St. Thomas' College of Engineering and Technology
akdas@cs.becs.ac.in, saikatchakrabarty187@gmail.com,
soumen_pati@rediffmail.com

Abstract. Microarray gene dataset often contains huge number of attributes many of which are irrelevant and redundant with respect to classification. Presence of such attributes may sometimes reduce the classification accuracy of the dataset. Therefore, the data should be pre-processed to filter out the unimportant attributes before passing them on to the classifier. In the paper, the concepts of Rough Set Theory (RST) and Genetic Algorithm (GA) are used for selecting only the relevant attributes of the dataset. The method constructs relative discernibility matrix to compute the core attributes based on which attributes are encoded to strings used as an initial population for running the genetic algorithm. The method runs each time by adding a single attribute to the initial strings to select only a minimal attribute set known as reduct. The fitness function is defined based on the attribute dependency of the formed rough set. Attribute dependency gives a measure of the degree of influence of the selected attribute subset on the decision. The experimental results show that, the proposed method yields better result than some well-known attribute reduction algorithms for some real-world microarray cancerous datasets.

Keywords: Attribute dependency, Attribute reduction, Discernibility matrix, Genetic algorithm, Gene data analysis, Rough set theory.

1 Introduction

Now-a-days, an increasing number of applications in different fields, especially on the field of natural and social sciences, produce massive volumes of very high dimensional data under a variety of experimental conditions. In scientific databases like gene microarray dataset, it is common to encounter large sets of observations, represented by hundreds or even thousands of coordinates. The performance of data analysis such as clustering and classification degrades in such high dimensional spaces. Gene microarray high dimensional data provides

K.R. Venugopal and L.M. Patnaik (Eds.): ICIP 2012, CCIS 292, pp. 299–308, 2012.
© Springer-Verlag Berlin Heidelberg 2012

the opportunity to measure the expression level of thousands of genes simultaneously and this kind of high-throughput data has a wide application in bioinformatics research. In DNA microarray data analysis generally biologists measure the expression levels of genes in the tissue samples from patients, and find explanations about how the genes of patients relate to the types of cancers they had. Many genes could strongly be correlated to a particular type of cancer, however, biologists prefer to focal point on a small subset of genes that dominates the outcomes before performing in-depth analysis and expensive experiments with a high dimensional dataset. Therefore, automated selection of the minimal set of attributes (i.e., reduct), is highly advantageous. There can be multiple reducts in a dataset, intersection of which, known as core, are indispensable to the decision system of the dataset.

Finding reducts by exhaustive search of all possible combination of attributes is an NP-complete [1] problem. Therefore, different strategies, like Rough Set Theory [2–4], Heuristic Search [5] and so on are used to accomplish this task. Heuristic searches find a good (not the best) solution efficiently by sacrificing completeness of the search. Genetic algorithms [6, 7] can also be applied in search problems. Rough set theory, a mathematical model, is popularly employed by researchers as it does not require any additional information like probability [8], fuzzy [9] or Dempster-Shafer [10] strategies.

Skowron and Rauszer [11] developed a novel idea for reduct generation using discernibility matrix. Baoquing Jiang, Meng Liang and Ling Mei [12] developed a reduct generation technique based on discernibility matrix and itemset lattice. Y.Y. Yao and Y. Zhao worked on discernibility matrix simplification for constructing reducts [13]. Pappa, Freitas and Kaestner used multi-objective GA for attribute reduction [14]. They used error rate and tree size as objective functions. Hong Shi and Jin-Zong Fu used heuristic GA to find reduct [15]. An adaptive GA which adjusts its crossover and mutation probability was formulated by Bing Xiang Liu et al. [16].

The proposed method of reduct generation firstly identifies the core attributes by constructing and inspecting relative discernibility matrix. Based on the core attributes, all attributes are encoded to strings and an initial population is generated for the Genetic Algorithm (GA) used for computing optimal set of reducts. GA does well in performing search of relevant attributes as long as a strong fitness function is designed. The proposed method combines the concepts of RST and GA. Here, GA is run iteratively, starting with the initial population consisting of core attributes and adding one attribute at a time till high dependency of the selected attribute set is achieved. The reducts are obtained from the encoded attribute strings of the final generation. The proposed method yields better result compared to well-known attribute reduction algorithms for some real-world datasets, which shows its effectiveness.

The rest of the paper is organized as follows: Section 2 describes the proposed reduct(s) generation method. Section 3 contains the experimental results and finally, section 4 gives conclusion and the areas of further research.

2   Proposed Work

The proposed work finds multiple reducts of a dataset using the concepts of RST and GA. It first uses (relative) discernibility matrix to find the core attributes and then GA is employed in a controlled manner to find the reducts. Fitness function of the GA maximizes attribute dependency to search for reducts.

2.1   Core Selection

The proposed method, firstly, computes the discernibility matrix (using Eq. (1)) to find the core attributes of the dataset. Each cell of the discernibility matrix holds the conditional attributes that distinguishes the objects in that particular row and column. If any of the cells contains a single conditional attribute, then that attribute is necessary to distinguish two objects associated with the cell and so definitely belongs to the core.

$$m_{ij} = \{a \in C | (f_a(x_i) \neq f_a(x_j)) \wedge (d \in D, f_d(x_i) \neq f_d(x_j))\} \qquad (1)$$

where, $i, j = 1, 2, 3, \ldots, n$ and $f_a(x)$ is the value of attribute a for object x in U.

Therefore, the union of such singleton sets in the relative discernibility matrix gives the core attribute set CR of the dataset, computed using Eq. (2).

$$CR = \bigcup \{m_{ij} | m_{ij} \neq \phi \text{ and } |m_{ij}| = 1, \forall i, j = 1, 2, 3 \ldots, n\} \qquad (2)$$

Now, for some datasets, it may happen that none of the cells contain a single attribute. If more than one attributes are present in a cell, then it cannot be inferred that all of them belong to core. Some of them may not appear in all the reducts because presence of other attributes of that cell is enough to discern the object pair. Hence, they are non-core attributes. In such a case, the proposed method looks for approximate core attributes. It searches for cells with the minimum number of attributes and considers their union as approximate set of core attributes.

In this way, a few attributes are considered as core attributes, even though some of them may be non-core attributes (in case of approximate core set). If any of those non-core attributes are unimportant then the GA will eliminate them from reducts. Thus, the first step is completed giving the set of possible core attributes.

2.2   Multiple Reducts Generation

The next step of the proposed method aims at generating multiple reducts. Core or approximate core attributes have already been identified using the procedure explained above. Now GA is applied to find the reducts. But to ensure that the reducts are of minimal lengths, the number of attributes on which the GA runs is restricted. It is not allowed to run on arbitrary number of attributes. The idea is to find the combinations of attributes of particular lengths, that form reducts. The task of finding these combinations is done using GA. This is why it is being called restrained genetic algorithm. Initially, the reduct generation algorithm runs with the approximate core attributes. If it yields reducts, the process halts. Otherwise, it is repeated with number of attributes incremented by one. This continues till reducts are obtained. Therefore, in each iteration, the search space of GA has solutions with equal number of attributes.

Initial Population. In GA, the initial population of size N needs to be provided representing multiple points in the search space. In the method, the initial population for the first iteration of the reduct generation algorithm contains only the (approximate) core attributes. Then, all associated steps like encoding, reproduction, crossover, mutation, etc. are performed producing further generations of the population. When change in average fitness value of two successive generations is 0.001 or less, no further generations are created and the GA stops. If the last generation contains reducts, then the process terminates. Otherwise, a new initial population is created for the next iteration of the reduct generation algorithm. This new initial population contains strings with one more attribute randomly chosen from the remaining non-core attributes. So, initial strings in i^{th} iteration of the algorithm has one more non-core attribute than that in its $(i-1)^{th}$ iteration.

Encoding. The strings in the initial population of GA have to be encoded to represent chromosomes. Here, the strings have been encoded as binary strings containing 0 and 1, where each bit, i.e. an allele, represents a conditional attribute. All the encoded strings, or chromosomes, are of same length which is the number of conditional attributes in the dataset. Bit '1' in p^{th} position of a chromosome means that the pth conditional attribute of the dataset is in the selected attribute subset and bit '0' means it is not in the attribute subset. In this way, strings are encoded in each iteration.

Fitness Function. Fitness function determines the quality of a chromosome. So, a strong fitness function is imperative for giving good result. Our fitness function judges a chromosome by its dependency value for the attribute subset represented by the chromosome, as explained below.

For calculating dependency of decision attribute D on an attribute subset P, indiscernibility relation (Eq. (3)) is used. Equivalence classes $[x]_P$ are hence generated by the attribute subset P. Equivalence classes $[x]_D$ formed by the decision attribute are considered to be the target sets X, i.e., $X \in U/D$. The lower approximation $\underline{P}X$ of X under P is computed using Eq. (4), for all $X \in U/D$. Similarly, upper approximation $\overline{P}X$ can be computed using Eq. (5). The positive region $POS_P(D)$ is obtained by taking the union of the lower approximations $\underline{P}X$ under P for all $X \in U/D$, using Eq. (6). Then, dependency of D on P (i.e., $\gamma_P(D)$) is obtained using Eq. (7).

$$IND(P) = \{(x,y) \in U \times U | \forall a \in P, f_a(x) = f_a(y)\} \qquad (3)$$

where, $f_a(x)$ denotes the value of attribute a for object x in U.

$$\underline{P}X = \{x|[x]_P \subseteq X\} \tag{4}$$

$$\overline{P}X = \{x|[x]_P \cap X \neq \phi\} \tag{5}$$

$$POS_P(D) = \bigcup_{X \in U/D} \underline{P}X \tag{6}$$

$$\gamma_P(D) = \frac{|POS_P(D)|}{|U|} \tag{7}$$

Our fitness function, given by Eq. (8), maximizes the dependency of decision attribute D on attribute subset P represented by the chromosome ch. Obviously, higher the dependency value $\gamma_P(D)$, higher the fitness value F(ch) and better the quality of the chromosome (or encoded string) ch.

$$F(ch) = \gamma_P(D) \tag{8}$$

Reproduction. Reproduction is a parent selection process by which the best strings in a generation are replicated and placed in a mating pool for further genetic operations. It is an artificial simulation of natural selection by which only the fittest survive. Inferior quality chromosomes are eliminated. In our method, deterministic sampling scheme is used for reproduction. In this scheme, the probability $p(ch_i)$ of selection of chromosome ch_i is given by Eq. (9) and expected number $e(ch_i)$ of replicas i.e., offspring, is given by Eq. (10), where $F(ch_i)$ denotes the fitness value of chromosome ch_i.

$$P(ch_i) = \frac{F(ch_i)}{\sum_1^N F(ch_i)} \tag{9}$$

$$e(ch_i) = \lfloor N.p(ch_i) \rfloor \tag{10}$$

New chromosomes are created by applying crossover operation on these selected chromosomes.

Multipoint Crossover. Reproduction directs the search towards the best existing individuals but is unable to create new individuals. To create new individuals, crossover operation is required. In nature, offspring has two parents and inherits some of their characteristics. Crossover does the same. For a selected pair of parents, two new offspring are generated by applying crossover with probability 0.95. In our method 2-point crossover has been used. Here, two random numbers, indicating positions of bits in chromosome, are generated. Then, the substrings of the parent strings, lying between the two randomly generated positions, are interchanged. Thus, two new individuals are created. The motivation for using 2-point crossover is that, the new individuals generated are more similar to one of their high quality parents, than they are in 1-point crossover. So, convergence is expected to occur earlier. During crossover the number of 1's in the offspring may change.

Elitism. The elitist strategy copies some of the best individuals in the ith generation to the $(i+1)^{th}$ generation. It often improves performance of GA. Let M be the number of new individuals created by crossover. Then, the remaining $N - M$ individuals of the $(i+1)^{th}$ generation are filled up using elitism. The best $N - M$ individuals of the ith generation are copied to the $(i+1)^{th}$ generation.

Mutation. Using crossover, new strings are generated but no new information is introduced at the bit level. As a source of new bits, mutation is applied on the strings with probability 0.001. Mutation inverts a randomly chosen bit in a string. It adds a flavor of uncertainty to the GA. Thus, during mutation too, like crossover, the number of 1's in the strings may change.

Reducts. Based on the core attributes CR, initial population of chromosomes is generated and the above mentioned genetic operations are applied on the population to create new generations until difference in the average fitness values of two successive generations converges (here, less than 0.001). Thus, a final population is obtained. Dependency for each chromosome, of the final population, with number of 1's equal to |CR| is computed and checked to see whether it is equal to $\gamma_C(D)$. If any such chromosome is obtained in the final population, then the set of attributes representing that chromosome is considered as reduct and the process is terminated. Presence of more than one such chromosome gives multiple reducts. If no reduct is found in the final population then a new initial population of chromosomes, for the next iteration of the reduct generation algorithm, is generated with number of 1's one more than that in its previous iteration, always including core attributes in each iteration. The whole process is repeated based on this new initial population until a set of reduct(s) is found. The overall reduct generation algorithm is given in Table 1.

3   Experimental Results

Experimental studies presented here provide an evidence of effectiveness of the proposed dimension reduction technique. Experiments were carried out on large number of different kinds of microarray gene datasets (cancerous data), few of which described below are summarized.

▶ Prostate Cancer dataset : Training dataset contains 52 samples (labeled as "relapse") and 50 patients having remained relapse free (labeled as "non-relapse") prostate samples with around 12600 genes. The raw data available at http://www.genome.wi.mit.edu/mpr/prostate.

▶ Lung Cancer dataset : Training dataset contains 16 samples (labeled as "MPM") and 16 samples (labeled as "ADCA") lung samples with around 12533 genes. The raw data available at http://www.chestsurg.org/microarray.htm.

▶ Leukemia (ALL vs. AML) dataset : Training dataset consists of 38 bone marrow samples (27 ALL and 11 AML), over 7129 human genes. The raw data is available at http://www-genome.wi.mit.edu/cgi-bin/cancer/datasets.cgi.

Table 1. Reduct Generation Algorithm

Algorithm: ***REDUCT_GENERATION(DS, CR, RED)***
/* Generates reducts of the decision system */
input : DS = (U, A, C, D) and CR = set of core attributes
output: RED = set of reduct(s)

begin
    RED = { }
    n = $|CR|$
    Compute $\gamma_C(D)$
  repeat
      Generate N binary strings of length $|C|$ with '0' in each bit
      Set '1' for core and n-$|CR|$ non-core attributes in each string
      avg_old = 0   //average fitness of previous generation
      repeat
        sum = 0
        for *i=1 to N* **do**
          Calculate $F(ch_i)$ for string ch_i //$F(ch_i) = \gamma_P(D)$
          count = number of '1's in ch_i
          if $\gamma_P(D) = \gamma_C(D)$ *and count = n* **then**
            RED = $RED \bigcup P$;
          else
            sum=sum+$F(ch_i)$;
          end
        end
        avg_new = sum / N
        change = avg_new - avg_old
        /* change is the difference of average fitness of two successive
        generations */
        avg_old = avg_new
        Perform reproduction
        Perform crossover
        Perform elitism
        Perform mutation
      until *change*≤ 0.001;
      n = n + 1
    until $RED \neq \phi$;
    return RED
end

First of all, all the numeric attributes are discretized by ChiMerge [17] discretization algorithm. To measure the efficiency of the method, k-fold cross-validations, where k ranges from 1 to 10 have been carried out on the dataset and classified using 'Weka' tool [18]. The proposed method (PRP) and well known dimensionality reduction methods such as, Correlated Feature Subset (CFS) [19] and Consistency Subset Evaluator (CON) [20] methods have been applied on the dataset for dimension reduction and the reduced datasets were classified on various classifiers such as Nave Bayes, SMO, K-STAR, etc. Original number of attributes, number of attributes after applying various reduction methods and the average accuracies (in %) of the datasets were computed and listed in Table 2. Figure 1 shows the graphs plotted on the basis of the results obtained. In case of Prostate dataset, the proposed method selects 20 features with classification accuracy 77.79%, whereas CON gives 74.01% accuracy inspite of selecting 68 features. For the other two datasets, CON selects fewer features but its accuracy decreases significantly. On the other hand, when CFS is applied, it selects fewer attributes compared to the proposed method but gives much lesser accuracy for prostate dataset. For the other two datasets, it does not reduce any attribute but gives only marginal increase (about 0.5%) in accuracy. This proves the superiority of the proposed method.

Table 2. Accuracy Comparison of Proposed, CFS and CON methods

Classifiers Dataset		Naïve Bayes	J48	Random Forest	Ada-Boost	Bagging	PART	K-Star	Average
Prostate (102)	PRP (20)	79.33	80.01	84.48	57.19	84.61	81.29	77.64	77.79
	CFS (15)	66.76	74.04	77.58	56.05	78.71	72.74	73.21	71.30
	CON (68)	71.73	73.85	81.95	57.69	82.09	75.54	75.23	74.01
Lung (32)	PRP (20)	87.65	85.39	90.42	66.69	89.65	87.58	84.01	84.48
	CFS (32)	89.09	85.98	91.28	66.49	90.44	88.40	83.81	85.07
	CON (9)	80.53	82.03	85.16	66.48	86.84	84.19	82.95	81.17
Leukemia (38)	PRP (26)	81.95	81.77	88.52	51.66	87.24	83.42	85.01	79.94
	CFS (38)	82.52	81.94	89.46	51.66	88.31	84.85	85.21	80.56
	CON (10)	80.75	81.12	86.15	51.66	84.83	81.66	82.42	78.37

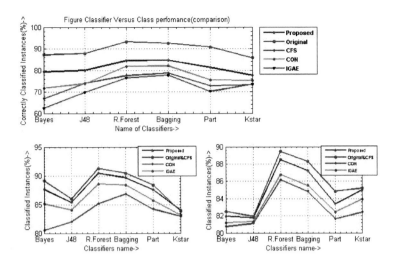

Fig. 1. Classification performance of (a) Prostate cancer (b) Lung cancer and (c) Leukemia datasets

4 Conclusion and Future Enhancements

This paper describes a new method of attribute reduction. In this method multiple reducts are generated using concepts of Rough Set Theory and Genetic Algorithm. Here, GA has been iteratively applied to search reducts in a microarray dataset and also ensure minimal length of the reducts. The GA applied was restrained by controlling the number of attributes on which it works, in each iteration. This could have been done by incorporating the minimum length criterion into the fitness function. But the disadvantage is that, one criterion may dominate the other and hence lead to inaccurate fitness value. Hence, GA was basically used to find reducts of particular length. The length was incremented by one in each iteration, starting from minimum.

Future enhancements to this work may include use of boundary region of RST for designing a better fitness function. A better encoding technique may also be formulated. Also, application of optimization techniques other than GA, like PSO, Ant-colony optimization, etc., is also worth a try. Moreover, the method gives multiple reducts. Some technique may be used to combine these reducts to a single reduct.

References

1. Garey, M., Johnson, D.: Computers and Intractability- A Guide to the Theory of NP-completeness. Freeman, New York (1979)
2. Pawlak, Z.: Rough Sets. International Journal of Information and Computer Sciences 11, 341–356 (1982)

3. Pawlak, Z.: Rough Set Theory and its Applications to Data Analysis. Cybernetics and Systems 29, 661–688 (1998)
4. Komorowski, J., Pawalk, Z., Polkowski, S.A.: Rough sets: A Tutorial. In: Pal, S.K., Skowron, A. (eds.) Rough Fuzzy Hybridization: A New Trend in Decision-Making, pp. 3–98. Springer, Berlin (1999)
5. Zhong, N., Dong, J., Ohsuga, S.: Using Rough Sets with Heuristics for Feature Selection. J. Intelligent Information System, 199–214 (2001)
6. Goldberg, D.E.: Genetic Algorithms in Search, Optimization, and Machine Learning, pp. 432–440. Addison-Wesley (1989)
7. Beasley, D., Bull, D.R., Martin, R.R.: An Overview of Genetic Algorithms: Part 2 Research Topics. University Computing 15, 170–181 (1993)
8. Devroye, L., Gyorfi, L., Lugosi, G.: A Probabilistic Theory of Pattern Recognition. Springer, New York (1996)
9. Pal, S.K., Mitra, S.: Neuro-Fuzzy Pattern Recognition: Methods in Soft Computing. Willey, New York (1999)
10. Gupta, S.C., Kapoor, V.K.: Fundamental of Mathematical Statistics. Sultan Chand & Sons, A.S. Printing Press, India (1994)
11. Skowron, A., Rauszer, C.: The Discernibility Matrices and Functions in Information Systems. In: Slowinski, R. (ed.) Intelligent Decision Support. Handbook of Applications and Advances of the Rough Sets Theory. Kluwer, Dordrecht (1992)
12. Jiang, B., Liang, M., Mei, L.: Attribute Reduction Algorithm based on Discernibility Matrix of Skowron and Itemset Lattice. In: Intl. Conf. AICI (2010)
13. Yao, Y.Y., Zhao, Y.: Discernibility Matrix Simplification for Constructing at Tribute Reducts. Information Sciences 179(5), 867–882 (2009)
14. Pappa, G.L., Freitas, A.A., Kaestner, C.A.A.: Attribute Selection with a Multi-objective Genetic Algorithm. In: Bittencourt, G., Ramalho, G.L. (eds.) SBIA 2002. LNCS (LNAI), vol. 2507, pp. 280–290. Springer, Heidelberg (2002)
15. Shi, H., Fu, J.-Z.: A Heuristic Genetic Algorithm for Attribute Reduction. In: Fifth International Conference on Machine Learning and Cybernetics (2006)
16. Liu, B.X., Liu, F., Cheng, X.: An Adaptive Genetic Algorithm based on Rough Set Attribute Reduction. In: Third International Conference on Biomedical Engineering and Informatics (2010)
17. Kerber, R.: ChiMerge: Discretization of Numeric Attributes. In: Proc. of AAAI 1992, Ninth Intl. Conf. Artificial Intelligence, pp. 123–128. AAAI-Press (1992)
18. WEKA: Machine Learning Software, http://www.cs.waikato.ac.nz/~ml
19. Hall, M.A.: Correlation-Based Feature Selection for Machine Learning. Ph.D thesis, Dept. of Computer Science, University of Waikato, Hamilton, New Zealand (1998)
20. Liu, Setiono, R.: A Probabilistic Approach to Feature Selection: A Filter Solution. In: Proceedings of 13th International Conference on Machine Learning, pp. 319–327 (1996)

Improving Generalization Ability of Classifier with Multiple Imputation Techniques

Dipak V. Patil[1] and R.S. Bichkar[2]

[1] Department of Computer Engineering Sandip Institute of Technology and Research Centre Nasik, M.S., India
dvspatil@yahoo.co.in
[2] Department of Computer Engineering G.H. Raisoni College of Engineering & Management, Pune, M.S., India

Abstract. A main objective of research in machine learning is to learn to identify complex patterns and make intelligent decisions based on that data automatically; but the set of all possible behaviors is too large to be covered by the set of available training data. Hence it is desirable that learner must generalize from the given examples, so that it can provide a useful output in new cases; otherwise the number of training instances available in training data must be sufficient. We can have another case where the data set may contain some instances with multiple missing attributes, these instances need to be deleted; in such case sufficient data samples are required to improve generalization ability of the classifier. The proposed algorithm generates additional training instances and adds it to original training data to improve generalization ability of the decision tree classifiers. The proposed algorithm imputes missing attribute values with domain values and thus generates additional training instances. The proposed method is permutation and combination based multiple imputation method and it is also useful for imputation of missing data. The proposed method demonstrates good generalization ability on decision trees. This paper proposes a new method for imputation of missing data and same method is used to generate additional data instances to generalize the decision tree learning.

Keywords: Decision Trees, Generalization, Multiple Imputations.

1 Introduction

The most important objective in machine learning is to learn and predict accurately on unseen data; that is the learner must generalize from the given examples, so that it can provide a useful output in new cases [1]. Decision trees cannot generalize to variations that are not available in the training set. A decision tree creates a partition of the input space and requires at least one case instance in each of the regions associated with a class leaf in order to make a sensible prediction in that region [2].

Sufficient numbers of data sample are required to improve generalization ability of the classifier. However, the training data may contain insufficient data

K.R. Venugopal and L.M. Patnaik (Eds.): ICIP 2012, CCIS 292, pp. 309–317, 2012.
© Springer-Verlag Berlin Heidelberg 2012

samples by its inception or in another case where the data set may contain some instances with multiple missing attributes and these instances need to be deleted; in such cases we need to add extra training data to original data set to improve generalization ability of the classifier. In this paper we propose multiple imputation method to generate additional training data instances and these additional data instances are added to the original data set to create new training data and decision trees are learned on this data that generalize.

The proposed multiple imputation method is also useful in imputation of missing data. Missing data is the missing form of information about phenomena, which is important, and it is the information in which we are interested. The existence of missing data is one significant problem in data quality. Data quality plays major role in machine learning, data mining and knowledge discovery from databases. Machine learning algorithms handle missing data in a quite naive way. To avoid biasing in induced hypothesis missing data treatment should be carefully handled. Imputation is a process that replaces the missing values in instance by some reasonable values.

1.1   Handling Missing Data

Missing data handling methods are categorized as follows

Ignoring Data: There are two core methods for discarding data with missing values. The methods are complete case analysis and discarding. These methods are executed only if missing data are missing completely at random. Little and Rubin [3] stated that it is the dangers to delete instances. Instance deletion presumes that the deleted instances are a relatively small quantity of the entire dataset and when cases are missing completely at random. The deletion can bring in significant bias into the experimentation. In addition, the reduced sample size can significantly hamper the analysis. The thumb rule for deletion instances is, if data sets have more than 5% missing values, cases are not deleted.

Imputation: In imputation-based procedures missing values are imputed with reasonable, probable values rather than being deleted totally. The objective is to use known associations that can be recognized in the valid range values of the data set to facilitate in estimating the missing values [4].

Multiple Imputations: This method [3] provides multiple simulated values for each incomplete information, and then iteratively validates data instance with each simulated value substituted in every turn. With modest amounts of missing data 5 imputation replicates are often sufficient. Other than these methods there are more estimations i.e. replacement of missing values with the series mean, by the mean or median of nearby points, or linear interpolation between prior and subsequent known points, interpolating between the adjacent valid values above and below the missing one, or substitution of the linear regression trend value for that point i.e. missing values are replaced with their predicted values.

2   Related Work

In this review two types of algorithms are discussed, first type is algorithms for generalization of decision trees and another type is algorithms for imputation of data.

Zhou and Jiang [5] proposed a variation of C4.5 decision tree algorithm named NeC4.5 that utilizes neural network ensemble to preprocess the training data for decision tree construction. The algorithm trains a neural network ensemble and the trained ensemble is used to produce a new training set. It substitutes the preferred class labels of the original training tuples with the output from the trained ensemble. Some extra training tuples produced by the trained ensemble are also added to the new training set. The new training set is used for training C4.5. The processed training data by neural network improves classification accuracy of the decision tree classifier.

Kuligowski and Barros [6] proposed a use of a back propagation neural network for estimation of missing data by using concurrent rainfall data from neighboring gauges. Empirical comparative analysis of deletion and imputation techniques is provided in [7]. Abebe et al. [8] proposed a use of a fuzzy-rule-based model for substitution in missing rainfall data using data from neighboring stations.

Sinharay et al. [9] experimented on the use of multiple imputations for the analysis of missing data. Khalil et al. [10] proposed cyclic federation of data intended for budding ANN models to estimate missing values in monthly surplus datasets. Bhattacharya et al. [11] used ANN models to substitute the missing values of wave data. Fessant & Midenet [12] proposed use of a self-organizing map (SOM) for imputation of data along with the multilayer perceptron (MLP) and hot deck methods.

Musil et al. [13] provided empirical comparative analysis on list wise deletion, mean substitution, simple regression, regression with an error term and the EM algorithm. Junninen et al. [14] experimented on univariate linear, spline and nearest-neighbor interpolation algorithm, multivariate regularized expectation-maximization algorithm, nearest-neighbor, self-organizing map, multilayer perceptron (MLP) as well as hybrid methods. M. Subasi, et al. [15] proposed new imputation method for incomplete binary data. Amman Mohammad Kalteh & Peder Hjorth [16] experimented on imputation of missing values with self organizing map, multilayer perceptron, multivariate nearest neighbor, regularized expectation maximization algorithm and multiple imputation for precipitation runoff process data set.

3   The Decision Tree Construction

Decision tree [17]-[22] is a classifier in the form of tree data structure that contains a decision node and leaves. A leave specifies a classification. A decision node specifies a test to be carried on single attributes value. A solution is present for each probable outcome of the test in the form of child node. A performance measure of a decision tree over a set of cases is called classification accuracy. A hybrid learning methodologies that integrates genetic algorithms (GAs) and decision tree learning in order to evolve optimal decision trees has been proposed by [17], [22].

4   Problem Definition and Proposed Algorithm

The training data may contain insufficient data samples or the training data may have data instances with multiple missing attributes, and in this case these instances need to be deleted. In these cases sufficient data samples are required to improve generalization ability of the classifier. In this paper we propose multiple imputation method to generate additional training data instances and these additional data instances are added to the original data set to create new training data and decision trees are learned on this new data set that generalize. The proposed multiple imputation method is also useful in imputation of missing data. Here missing data is added in training data set manually with random function. The instances and attributes are selected randomly.

Let T_f be a set of all available n training instances. Let the training instance be denoted by t. An instance denotes values for set of attributes and a class. Let the attributes be denoted by $\{A_1, A_2, ..., A_n\}$ and the classes be denoted by the set values $\{C_1, C_2, ..., C_n\}$. Add missing attribute values randomly in some data instances if required (if missing attribute values are not there). Let A_n be the attribute with missing values and let T_e be a set of instances that includes set of instances with missing attribute values along with normal data instances. Find domain values for all attribute A_n with missing values.

In multiple imputations generally 3 to 5 imputations are done. But here in this experimentation, the number of imputed instances depends on domain values and their combinations and thus we have not restricted it 3 to 5 imputed values. The pool of solutions is available for multiple imputations. Details are explained in next sections.

The ratio $\mu = n/m * 100$; where n be a number of instances in training data and m be extra training instances produced and added to training data. In this experimentation we have used $\mu = 30\%$ for small sized data sets i.e. data set size up to100 data samples; and $\mu = 50\%$ for moderate sized data sets i.e. data set size from 100 to 500 data samples by using our own thumb rule and it worked well. Zhi-Hua Zhou and Yuan Jiang [5] used $\mu = 0\%$ and 100% but as per Oates and Jensen [23] increasing data size does not improve classification performance after some limit but it increses the complexity of the decision tree and thus we have tried to optimize the size of the data set and generalization ability of the classifier with classification accuracy as performance criteria. Another limitation on adding or generating new training instances is due following factors: dependence on number of tuples in a data set, number of attributes in tuple and number of domain values for an attribute.

The proposed algorithm works as follows.

1. Find instance I with missing attribute value/values in T_e
2. Find Dom(A)

3. Impute (A, Dom(A))
4. ∀ A in I repeat step 2 to 3
5. ∀ I repeat step 1 to 4
6. Induce(H, T_F)
7. ∀ I on H if X(I) = 1⇒ I ∈T_A
8. Else Del(I)
9. Delete erroneous data from T_e
10. Find Dup(I, T_A ,T_F)
11. Delete duplicate I in T_A
12. $T_i = T_e ∪ T_A$
13. Induce(H_i, T_i)
14. End.

Find attribute with missing value/values. For every attribute with missing values, find set of domain values for those attributes. Substitute missing attribute values with domain values and make all possible combinations with available domain values for various missing attributes in instance. Repeat above steps for all instances with missing values. Thus multiple instances with imputed attributes are available. The original data set T_F is used to train the classifier. The classifier is used for validation of imputed data instances. The imputed data instances are used as test instance on this classifier. The test instance which gets classified is considered as correctly imputed instance else invalidated. The successfully imputed data instances are added to set T_A . Find out data instances with missing attribute value/values in Te (which is inserted by us or which is already there since its inception). Find out duplicate data instances in T_A as compared to original data set T_F. If any duplicate data instance is found delete it. The two sets T_A and T_e are merged to form T_i. The hypothesis is learned on new imputed data setT_i and the hypothesis is expected to perform better in terms of classification performance.

5   Experimentation and Results

Using five dataset [24] from University of California Irvine repository experiments were performed. The missing data was introduced in some data instances. The missing values were substituted as per proposed algorithm. The datasets T_F,T_i and T_e were used to learn the decision trees. Readings of classification accuracy of these trees was obtained using 10 fold cross validation method which gives accurate results. The validity of proposed algorithm was done on J48, Simple CART [25] and GATree [17].

The results for proposed algorithm as per experimental method explained above are summarized in Table 1. Let X_i be classification accuracy of the trees build on data set T_i and similarly X_e on T_e and X_F on T_F. The result table summarizes the enhancement in accuracy $Δ X_F$ and $Δ X_e$. $Δ X_F$ is enhancement in accuracy with respect to original full data set. Where $Δ X_F = X_i$-X_F. Similarly $Δ X_e$ is enhancement in accuracy with respect to erroneous full data set.

Table 1. Enhancement in Accuracy with Proposed Method

Sr. No.	Data set	$|T_F|$	μ	X_e	X_F	X_i	ΔX_F	ΔX_e	Classifier
1.	Breast	286	30%	74.5	74.13	79.89	5.39	5.76	J48
2.	Lymph	148	30%	76.61	76.35	82.84	6.23	6.49	J48
3	Post	90	50%	74.44	74.44	81.59	7.15	7.15	J48
4	Shuttle	15	50%	60.00	60.00	95.00	35.00	35.00	J48
5	Weather	14	50%	50.00	51.14	71.43	21.43	20.29	J48
1	Breast	286	30%	69.23	69.23	79.31	10.08	10.08	CART
2	Lymph	148	30%	76.35	75.00	81.86	5.51	6.86	CART
3	Post	90	50%	72.22	72.22	84.21	11.99	11.99	CART
4	Shuttle	15	50%	60.00	60.00	95.00	35.00	35.00	CART
5	Weather	14	50%	42.85	57.14	66.66	23.81	9.52	CART
1	Breast	286	30%	73.21	71.79	80.57	7.36	8.78	GATree
2	Lymph	148	30%	80.00	72.86	84.21	4.21	11.35	GATree
3	Post	90	50%	73.33	73.33	84.61	11.28	11.28	GATree
4	Shuttle	15	50%	60.00	60.00	85.00	25.00	25.00	GATree
5	Weather	14	50%	60.00	60.00	70.00	10.00	10.00	GATree
	Average	-	-	66.85	67.18	81.48	14.63	14.30	

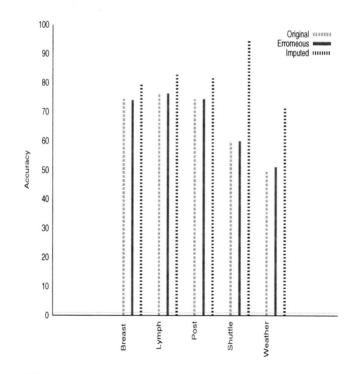

Fig. 1. Comparison Accuracy with Proposed Method on J48

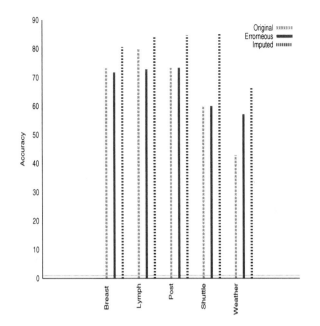

Fig. 2. Comparison Accuracy with Proposed Method on CART

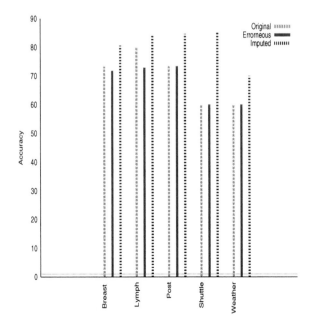

Fig. 3. Comparison Accuracy with Proposed Method on GATree

It has been observed that percentage enhancement in tree classification accuracy on imputed data set is significant as compared to original data set and data set with missing attribute values on all data sets on all classifiers. The method is more effective on small data sets with moderate classification performance. The Average Δ X for all experiments on GATree, J48 and Simple CART jointly is around 14%. Figure 1, 2 and 3 presents graphical visualization of results on J48, CART and GATree algorithms respectively. For moderate sized data sets we propose to use expert vote for validation of imputed data instances. In this experimentation some data sets were small in size and implementing expert vote was not possible.

6 Conclusions

The algorithm generates additional data instances with multiple imputations and adds it to original training data to improve generalization ability of the decision tree classifiers. A new multiple imputation methodology is proposed. The proposed algorithm uses all permutations and combinations of domain values for imputations of intrinsic and extrinsic missing attribute values. The associations among attributes are verified on decision tree classifier built on complete data set. The method is experimented on categorical values only. The proposed method significantly improves generalization ability on decision trees. The method is more effective on small data sets with lower classification performance.

The proposed algorithm is also useful for imputation of missing data. The proposed algorithm when applied on missing data provides us sufficient instances with imputed data values for knowledge acquisition. The data imputation on training data set helps in induction of enhanced and accurate hypothesis.

References

1. Alpaydin, E.: Introduction to Machine Learning. MIT Press (2004)
2. Bengio, Y., Delalleau, O., Simard, C.: Decision Trees do not Generalize to New Variations. Computational Intelligence 26(4), 449–467 (2010)
3. Little, R.J., Rubin, D.B.: Statistical Analysis with Missing Data. John Wiley and Sons, New York (1987)
4. Schafer, J.L., Graham, J.W.: Missing data: Ourview of the State of the Art. Psychology Methods 7(2), 147–177 (2002)
5. Zhou, Z.-H., Jiang, Y.: NeC4.5.: Neural Ensemble based C4.5. IEEE Transactions on Knowledge and Data Engineering 16(6), 770–773 (2004)
6. Kuligowski, R.J., Barros, A.P.: Using Artificial Neural Networks to Estimate Missing Rainfall Data. Journal AWRA 34(6), 14 (1998)
7. Brockmeier, L.L., Kromrey, J.D., Hines, C.V.: Systematically Missing Data and Multiple Regression Analysis: An Empirical Comparison of Deletion and Imputation Techniques. Multiple Linear Regression Viewpoints 25, 20–39 (1998)
8. Abebe, A.J., Solomatine, D.P., Venneker, R.G.W.: Application of Adaptive Fuzzy Rule-Based Models for Reconstruction of Missing Precipitation Events. Hydrological Sciences Journal 45(3), 425–436 (2000)

9. Sinharay, S., Stern, H.S., Russell, D.: The Use of Multiple Imputations for the Analysis of Missing Data. Psychological Methods 4, 317–329 (2001)
10. Khalil, K., Panu, M., Lennox, W.C.: Groups and Neural Networks Based Stream Flow Data Infilling Procedures. Journal of Hydrology 241, 153–176 (2001)
11. Bhattacharya, B., Shrestha, D.L., Solomatine, D.P.: Neural Networks in Reconstructing Missing Wave Data in Sedimentation Modeling. In: Proceedings of 30th IAHR Congress, Thessaloniki, Greece Congress, pp. 24–29 (2003)
12. Fessant, F., Midenet, S.: Self-organizing Map for Data Imputation and Correction in Surveys. Neural Computation Applications 10, 300–310 (2002)
13. Musil, C.M., Warner, C.B., Yobas, P.K., Jones, S.L.: A Comparison of Imputation Techniques for Handling Missing Data. Weston Journal of Nursing Research 24(7), 815–829 (2002)
14. Junninen, H., Niska, H., Tuppurainen, K., Ruuskanen, J., Kolehmainen, M.: Methods for Imputation of Missing Values in Air Quality Data Sets. Atoms, Environment 38, 2895–2907 (2004)
15. Subasi, M., Subasi, E., Hammer, P.L.: New Imputation Method for Incomplete Binary Data. Rutcor Research Report (August 2009)
16. Kalteh, A.M., Hjorth, P.: Imputation of Missing values in Precipitation-Runoff Process Database. Journal of Hydrology Research 40(4), 420–432 (2009)
17. Papagelis, A., Kalles, D.: GAtree: Genetically Evolved Decision Trees. In: Proceedings of the 12th International Conference on Tools with Artificial Intelligence, vol. 13-15, pp. 203–206 (2000)
18. Rajasekaran, G.A., Pai, V.: Neural Networks Fuzzy Logic and Genetic Algorithms Synthesis and Applications. Prentice-Hall of India (2004)
19. Quinlan, J.R.: C4.5.: Programs for Machine Learning. Morgan Kaufman, San Mateo (1993)
20. Ruggieri, S.: Efficient C4.5. IEEE Transaction on Knowledge and Data Engineering 14(2) (March/April 2002)
21. Quinlan, J.R.: Decision Trees and Decision making. IEEE Transaction on Systems, Man, and Cybernetics 20(2) (March/April 1990)
22. Fu, Z., Mae, F.: A Computational Study of Using Genetic Algorithms to Develop Intelligent Decision Trees. In: Proceedings of the IEEE Congress on Evolutionary Computation (2001)
23. Oates, T., Jensen, D.: The Effect of Training Set Size on Decision Tree Complexity. In: Proceedings of the 14th International Conference on Machine Learning, pp. 254–262 (1997)
24. Frank, A., Asuncion, A.: UCI Machine Learning Repository. University of California, School of Information and Computer Science, Irvine (2010), http://archive.ics.uci.edu/ml
25. Hall, M., Frank, E., Holmes, G., Pfahringer, B., Reutemann, P., Witten, I.H.: The WEKA Data Mining Software: An Update. SIGKDD Explorations 11(1) (2009)

Clustering of Ragas Based on Jump Sequence for Automatic Raga Identification

Surendra Shetty[1], K.K. Achary[2], and Sarika Hegde[1]

[1] Department of Computer Applications,
NMAMIT, Nitte, Udupi District, Karnataka, India
hsshetty4u@yahoo.com, sarika.hegde@yahoo.in
[2] Department of Statistics, Mangalore University,
Mangalagangothri, Mangalore Karnataka, India
kka@mangaloreuniversity.ac.in

Abstract. Raga is a soul of Indian Music and the Indian Music has been studied on the basis of Raga. It can also be the main parameter for content based retrieval of audio in Music Information Retrieval(MIR) system. In Western music, melody has not many variations, but in Indian music melody has many variations in the form of ragas. Difficulty in understanding the complex structure of raga makes automatic Raga Identification problem a critical one. Many different attempts have been made to address the raga identification problem but realization of such a system for a large collection of raga is a long way to go. There are many issues in regard to this that need to be solved. We have designed solution to tackle two issues in our work and present the methods and the experimental analysis in this paper. The first issue is to handle the large number of raga classes which is solved through the clustering technique based on jump sequence. The second issue that is addressed here is avoiding the calculation of the scale (tonic) of the song to identify the notes in the song. So approaching a method where raga identification can be done even without knowing tonic (scale) of the song. We present the importance of jump sequence in raga identification in this paper. We also present the experimental results on naturally clustering the ragas along with cluster identification for a given song.

Keywords: Raga Identification, Music Information Retrieval, Hidden Markov Model.

1 Introduction

Music Information Retrieval (MIR) is a process of searching and indexing an audio clip from a large database collection based on the content of the audio clip. One of the approaches to solve MIR is by High-Level Music Content Description where musical concepts such as melody or harmony are used to describe the content of music. The design of MIR for Indian Music collections would require the intelligence of retrieving the piece of audio sample based on the underlying raga used to compose the musical piece. Also, managing the vast audio collections of classical music will require greater human intervention for classifying the

K.R. Venugopal and L.M. Patnaik (Eds.): ICIP 2012, CCIS 292, pp. 318–328, 2012.
© Springer-Verlag Berlin Heidelberg 2012

songs into different categories based on the concept of Raga. Raga is the most fundamental concept of Indian classical music both in Hindustani and Carnatic Musical traditions. We have addressed the two most important issues that are not yet dealt with raga identification problem. The kind of work done in this paper has been initiated in the previous work [1], where clusters have been defined manually which is a tedious job. But in this paper we discuss the methods where clusters are formed automatically by applying the K-means clustering algorithm. The organization of the paper s as follows. We present the previous works that are related to the raga identification problems. In the next section, we present the theoretical concepts of raga along with the techniques that are used for raga identification. We discuss the experimental analysis and results in the next section and conclude at the end with the highlight of the future works.

1.1 Previous Works

In Western music the research has been mainly focused on to the note transcription that is to convert the given musical audio into notational script. But in Indian music, the research works mainly have been done based on the identification of the ragas in the song. In paper [2], Shridhar and Geetha have described an approach for raga identification where they first identify the singer in the audio. With the identification of singer they determine the scale of the song by retrieving the information from the database where scale of each singer is stored. A Krishnaswamy [1], has described a method on how Pitch Tracking is useful for Note Transcription of South Indian Classical Music. He presented the results of applying pitch trackers to samples of South Indian classical (Carnatic) music. He investigated the various musical notes used and their intonation and tried different pitch tracking methods and observed their performance in Carnatic music analysis. G. Pandey, in his paper explained the method of development of raga identification system called Tansen where HMM technique has been used. The HMM created, models the sequence of swaras as a sequence of states. Chordia has used the concept pitch-class distribution profile as the feature vector for distinguishing one raga from another [3]. A similar approach has been used by Kodori et al. [4] for raga identification problem which is accompanied with robust polyphonic pitch detection technique. An arohana/avarohana approach has been used for raga identification as describe in paper [5]. In this paper the swara combination and list of vakra pair has been used as a feature vector. In paper [6] another method for raga identification is used where pitch values are converted into the corresponding notes and then distribution of pair of notes is used as a feature vector for training the ANN classifier.

Most of the works described have been done by using different approaches. But all the works does have limitation; the main one is regarding the scale calculation. The second one is regarding the number of ragas tested. The accuracy of the system can be proven only when many ragas has been tested. In this paper we attempt to address these solutions by designing a feature vector that can be computed even if the scale is unknown and two-level raga identification helps reducing the complexity of discriminating large number of raga classes in a single classifier.

1.2   Raga

Understanding and designing an automatic Raga identification system requires an intense knowledge of a Raga, which is a complex structure. In spite of its complexity, the Raga structure is clearly defined in a systematic way. Raga in simpler term is a combination and permutation of swaras or notes in western term decorated in such a way that when combined with the feel of the song creates pleasant melody for a listener. As the words in any language are formed with combination of letters to give a particular meaning so as Raga is a combination of swaras which creates melody. A swara is a basic unit of Indian music. Hindustani and Carnatic Music are two forms of Indian music, where the basic concepts of these two are same but differ by the set of Ragas defined in those. In Carnatic Music, there are seven swaras, named as S, R, G, M, P, D, N. More detail on the Raga structure required to understand automated technique can be found in [7] [8].

1.3   Problem Definition

Having defined the Raga and Carnatic Music, we define the problem statement of work. The goal of our work is, given a piece of Carnatic Music; identify the Raga of the song. The solution to the problem is difficult due to the following reasons. As we have mentioned above that there are thousands of ragas defined in Carnatic music. So the classification problem has to deal with large number of classes at a time to make a decision about a given piece of music. To know the Raga, we must know what swaras used in the song. It is not simple because after calculating the pitch we cannot relate it directly to a particular swara without knowing the scale of the song.

We cluster the ragas for identifying the natural grouping among the ragas based on the jump sequence which is feature computed without knowing the scale of the song. Then we test the new given song with these cluster to identify the cluster to which it belongs.

2   Proposed Solution

The approach used by us for solving the raga identification is described as below. The audio file in wave-file format is converted into sequence of pitch values. The jump sequence is calculated from the sequence of pitch values and is used as feature vector. First we apply k-means clustering technique on the set of collection of all the jump sequence for identifying the natural clusters of ragas based on the jump sequence. Each of the clusters formed are then analyzed to identify the ragas that are grouped under the clusters. In the next level, we create HMM model for each of the cluster separately. The HMM model is trained using the set of jump sequences of the particular cluster. While in the testing phase the raga identification can be done at two levels. The first level identifies the cluster to which the musical audio clip belongs and in the second level, identifies the raga by matching the song across the ragas of only the selected cluster. In this paper, we mainly present the experimental analysis of the first level of cluster identification in detail.

2.1   Compute Pitch Sequence

For the purpose of raga identification, we have mainly focused on the relationship of the definition of raga with the ascending/descending scale of the raga. Since the structure of the ascending/descending scale is clearly defined theoretically; such an approach makes the analysis of the results easy and the theoretical proofs also lessen the burden of testing the enormous number of ragas. The audio signal with array of sample values are divided into 'n' number of frames with a frame-size of 50ms [6]. In the first step we divide the signal into frames given as F = $(f_1, f_2,...,f_M)$, where 'M' indicates the total number of frames. Now for each of the frame we calculate the pitch values using the auto-correlation algorithm, the result are given as P = $(p_1, p_2,...,p_M)$ for M number of frames. In addition to calculating the pitch value, we also calculate the log energy for each frame with a Frame-Size of 'L' is given as below,

$$E = \frac{\sum_i^L x_i^2}{N} \tag{1}$$

Here x_i, represents the value of the ith sample value within the frame. The variable E in simple term represents the energy of the frame. The log-energy by taking the log of the value given as below,

$$le = 10 * log_{10}(E + \varepsilon) \tag{2}$$

The value of ε represents a very small value considered as $1.e^{-007}$ The list of Log-energy values for **M** number of frames are given as **LE**=$(le_1, le_2,...,le_M)$. The list of pitch values which corresponds to the frame with the higher log-energy value is considered for the further evaluation. The Fig. 1 shows the result of pitch tracking for an instrumental audio clip.

In the figure, first graph shows the plotting of raw audio signal with the sample values along time axis. The second graph shows the value of log-energy for each frame. The third pot shows that the frames are separated with high and low log-energy values. The last plot shows the values of pitch computed for each frame.

2.2   Jump Sequence

The jump sequence reflects the variation in pitch value in terms of the position of the swaras on the scale of the 12 notes. In paper [7] more detail on jump sequence is given with example. The ratio of the adjacent notes in Western music is fixed and given as,

$$\frac{f_{i+1}}{f_i} = 1.059 \tag{3}$$

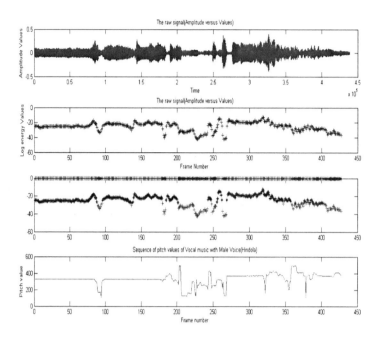

Fig. 1. Sequence of Pitch Values for a Monophonic Instrumental Song

But in Indian music the ratio between adjacent notes are given as related to the fundamental frequency of the first swara Sa as given in Table 1. Using this table we derive the ratios between the adjacent swaras in Carnatic music given in the table below,

Table 1. Ratios of Fundamental Frequencies of Adjacent Swaras

Swara	Ratio with Swara 'Sa'	Ratio with next Swara	Swara	Ratio with Swara 'Sa'	Ratio with next Swara
Sa	1	1	Ma_2	729/512	1.06787
Re_1	256/243	1.05349	Pa	3/2	1.0535
Re_2	9/8	1.06789	Da_1	128/81	1.05349
Ga_1	32/27	1.05349	Da_2	27/16	1.067902
Ga_2	81/64	1.06803	Ni_1	16/9	1.05381
Ma_1	4/3	1.054	Ni_2	243/128	1.0678

So given two adjacent values p_i and p_{i+1} from the list P, we need to identify the difference of position between the corresponding swara numbers n_i and n_{i+1}. This is solved by calculating the value x that indicates how many times the pitch value p_i should be multiplied by the value 1.067 to get the approximated value of p_{i+1}. So we need to solve the following equation,

$$p_{i+1} \cong (1.067^x) * p_i \qquad (4)$$

Solved as,

$$(1.067^x) \cong \frac{p_{i+1}}{p_i} x = \frac{log_{10} \frac{p_{i+1}}{p_i}}{log_{10} 1.067} \tag{5}$$

The following algorithm gives the steps required to calculate the jump sequence for a given audio file.

Table 2. Algorithm for Computing the Jump Sequence

Algorithm: Generating the Jump Sequence
Input: Sampled value array x
Output: Jump sequence J
Set the Frame-Size (L)=50ms
Frame-Inc (INC)=25ms
Divide the signal x into M number of frames F=$(f_1, f_2,...,f_M)$ each with size L
For each frame f_i i=1:M
Calculate log-energy value le_i
End
(Clust1, Clust2) = k-means(LE=$(le_1, le_2,...,le_M)$, k = 2)
if mean(Clust1) >mean(Clust2)
INDX=$I_1, I_2,...,I_{c1}$ of Clust1
else
INDX=$I_1, I_2,...,I_{c2}$ of Clust2
end
for each i=1:length(INDX)
pos=INDX(i)
p_i=pitch_calculate(f_{pos})
end
$unique_{pitch}$=unique(p)
for i=1:length($unique_{pitch}$)-1
$pair_1$=$unique_{pitch}$(i)
$pair_2$=$unique_{pitch}$(i+1)
J(i)=round($\frac{log_{10} \frac{p_{i+1}}{p_i}}{log_{10} 1.067}$)
End

2.3   Clustering of Ragas

Raga identification problem is solved as a two level classification problem. We have used Hidden Markov model (HMM) classifier for identifying the cluster for a new song. The following diagram shows the overall method used to design the solution for the problem of raga identification. The Fig. 2 shows the sequence of steps used for clustering the jump sequence. The jump sequence given as, J=$(j_1,j_2,...,j_n)$ In paper [7] same concept is implemented but the clusters are defined manually using the theoretical concepts. Since defining the clusters manually requires too much human intervention and becomes tedious for large number of raga classes, we go for natural clustering. The collection of such jump sequences form a database D=J^i, i=1:n, where 'n' indicates the total number of feature vectors. Such a database D is given to a K-means clustering algorithm for dividing the jump sequences into 'k' number of clusters. By analyzing that, to which cluster maximum number of jump sequence of a particular raga assigned; the set of ragas under a cluster is decided. Next, we explain the method used to

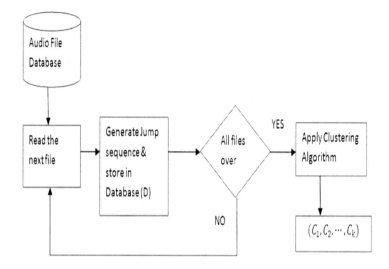

Fig. 2. Clustering of the Jump Sequence Database

describe each of the clusters in terms of the list of raga labels within it. Assuming that we have a vector R=(r^i) for i=1 to n, where the value r^i indicates the value for the raga label ID for ith data record in D. The k-means clustering algorithm returns a list 'C' which gives the mapping between the data record number and the cluster number. Using the list 'C' and the value R, we define each of the clusters by listing the ragas that are clustered together. Since the clusters are not very exclusive, a raga can belong to two clusters. After computing each cluster in terms of ragas, the set of jump sequence of all the ragas under the clusters are collected. In other words, the dataset D is divided into 'k' subsets each one listing the set of jump sequences for a particular cluster. Using these 'k' subsets of jump sequences, 'k' number of Hidden Markov Models (HMM) are trained and stored in the database for further testing as shown in Fig. 3.

2.4   Experimental Results for Clustering Ragas

We collected monophonic songs belonging to 21 ragas, the choice of which, is made based on the availability of the songs. The list of 21 ragas are *Ananda-bhairavi, Thodi, Reethigaula, Shree-raga, Kharaharapriya, Kambhoji, Harikam-bhoji, Khamaj, Shahana, Arabhi, Bilahari, Begade, Shankarabharana, Kalyani,*

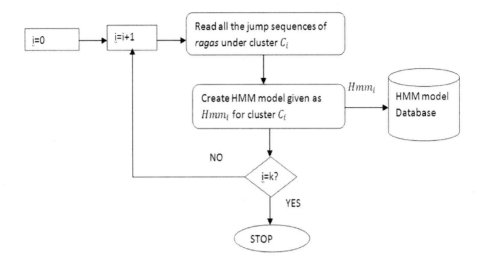

Fig. 3. Training of a HMM Model with the Jump Sequences of a Particular Cluster

Table 3. Cluster-Raga Assignment for the Dataset with 119 Numbers of Records

Cluster No.	List of Ragas	Cluster No.	List of Ragas
1	1. Begade	5	1. Madhayma
	2. Darbar		2. Saveri
	3. Harikambhoji	6	1. Arabhi
	4. Kalyani		2. Mohana
	5. Reethigaula		3. Reethigaula
	6. Shankara		4. Anandabhairavi
	7. Thodi		5. Hansadhwani
	8. Kambhoji		6. Shriranjani
	9. Kharaharapriya		
2	1. Arabhi	7	1. Bilahari
	2. Bilahari		2. Darbar
	3. Hindola		3. Dhanyasi
	4. Madhyama		4. Kalyani
	5. Mohana		5. Shankarabarana
	6. Shreeraga		6. Shreeraga
	7. Hansadhwani		7. Thodi
3	1. Harikakambhoji		8. Anandabhairavi
	2. Kamas		9. Khamboji
4	1. Begade		10. Shriranjini
	2. Dhanyasi		11. Kharaharapriya
	3. Hindola		
	4. Kamas		
	5. Saveri		

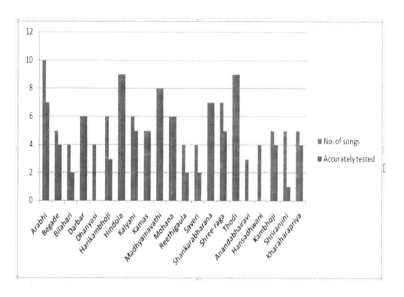

Fig. 4. Cluster Identification Accuracy Result

*D*hanyasi, *S*aaveri, *H*indola, *M*ohana, *M*adhyamavathi, *S*hreeranjini and *H*amsadhwani. We considered totally 100 number of songs with each song of a duration up to 1 minute. The jump sequence calculation method generated 119 number of jump sequences for the collection of the 100 audio songs. In the database D=$(J^i Y^i)$, the value Y^i indicates the raga class label to which the jump sequence J^i belongs to. K-means clustering algorithm is applied by choosing the value of k=7. For choosing the cluster centers, we chose the random 10% sub-sample of the dataset and apply the clustering algorithm which generates the 'k' cluster centers considered as the initial centers for the next step. If any of the clusters happens to be empty then a new cluster (with no records assigned) is initiated again with a single data record with the maximum value of point-to-centroid distance. Since the result of clustering is highly random, we have iterated the k-means algorithm for 20 times in one run and computed the value for $SUMD_i = sumd^j$ for j=1 to k, where the value of sumdj indicates the value for within-cluster sums of point-to-centroid (cluster) for jth cluster in ith repetition. Then we chose the result of the repetition with minimum value of *a*verage(SUMD). The result of clustering is very random; here it also strongly depends on the accuracy with which the pitch values are computed. The Table 3 below shows the ragas assigned for each cluster based on the jump sequences.

2.5 Experimental Results for Training and Testing Cluster HMM Models

Now we test the data records in the database with the cluster model for assigning each of the test record to one of the clusters formed. We have used Hidden

Markov Model (HMM) technique for modeling the sequence of jump values. Such techniques have been used by some of the authors [9][10][11][12][13] in the context of music. The HMM model is designed by defining eight number of states given as S=(s_1, s_2,...,s_8). The sequence of observation symbols given as V={1, 2,...,6}, assuming that maximum value jump value can be 6. The prior, transition and emission table are computed for each HMM model. Each of the record from the test database is matched against all the HMM model to compute the probability. The HMM cluster model with the highest probability is chosen as the cluster to which the data record belongs to. The results are shown in Graph, with average cluster recognition rate is 70.69%. The result is low compared to the results described in [7] since in that paper, cluster properties are defined manually using the theoretical concepts.

3 Conclusions

Automatic raga identification system would be one of the very useful and important tasks, especially for musician and MIR systems. Even though many authors are researching in this field for realizing such a system; the task is proved to be very challenging. We have demonstrated a new way of problem solution in our paper which would help design a raga identification system for a vast number of ragas. But the success of such system highly depend accurate pitch calculation for the audio file. Since accurate pitch values corresponds to the sequence of swaras in the audio. To avoid the complexity of pitch calculation we have conducted the experiments on monophonic audio. In future we have planned to implement the robust polyphonic pitch detection described in the literature and combine it with the clustering approach.

References

1. Krishnaswamy, A.: Application of Pitch Tracking to South Indian Classical Music. In: IEEE Workshop on Applications of Signal Processing to Audio and Acoustics, pp. 19–22 (October 2003)
2. Rajeswari, S., Geetha, T.V.: Raga Identification of Carnatic Music for Music Information Retrieval. International Journal of Recent Trends in Engineering 1(1), 571–574 (2009)
3. Chordia, P., Rae, A.: Raag Recognition using Pitch-Class and Pitch-Class Dyad Distributions. In: Proceedings of the ISMIR, pp. 431–436 (2007)
4. Gopala, K.K., Preeti, R., Sankalp, G.: A Survey of Raaga Recognition Techniques and Improvements to the State-of-the-Art. In: Sound and Music Computing, Padova, Italy, Europe (2011)
5. Shetty, S., Achary, K.: Raga Mining of Indian Music by Extracting Arohana-Avarohana Pattern. International Journal of Recent Trends in Engineering 1(1), 362–366 (2009)
6. Shetty, S., Achary, K.: Audio Data Mining for Indian Classical Music by Extracting Raga Patterns. In: 4th Indian International Conference on Artificial Intelligence (IICAI 2009), Tumkur (December 2009)

7. Shetty, S., Achary, K., Sarika, H.: Raga identification in Cranatic Music using Hidden Markov Model Technique. In: Proceedings of 4th International Conference on Computing, Communication and Information Technologies, Vellor (December 2012)

8. Padmanabha, S.K.A.: PanchamaVeda. Published by S.K. Padmanabha Acharya, Kasargod, India (2008)

9. Wei, C., Barry, V.: Folk Music Classification using Hidden Markov Models. In: Proceedings of International Conference on Artificial Intelligence (June 2001)

10. Aggelos, P., Sergios, T., Demirits, K.: Classification Musical Patterns Using Variable Duration Hidden Markov Models. In: Proceedings EUSIPCO, pp. 1281–1291 (2004)

11. Krishna, A.S., Rajkumar, P.V., Saishankar, K.P., John, M.: Identificaton of Carnatic Ragas using Hidden Markov Models. In: Proceedings of the 9th IEEE International Symposium on Applied Machine Intelligence and Informatics, Smoleniu, Slovakia (January 2011)

12. Pandey, G., Mishra, C., Tansen, P.I.: A System for Automatic Raga Identification. In: Proceedings of the Indian International Conference on Artificial Intelligence, pp. 1350–1363 (2003)

13. Sinith, M., Rajeev, K.: Hidden Markov Model based Recognition of Musical Pattern in South Indian Classical Music. In: IEEE International Conference on Signal and Image Processing, Hubli, India (2006)

14. Rabiner, L.R.: Fundamentals of Speech Recognition. Prentice Hall, PTR USA, ISBN-10: 0130151572

15. Geekie, G.: Carnatic Ragas as Music Information Retrieval Entities. In: Proceedings of ISMIR, pp. 257–258 (2002)

16. Belle, S., Joshi, R., Rao, P.: Raga Identification by using Swara Intonation. Journal of ITC Sangeet Research Academy 23 (2009)

17. Rao, V., Rao, P.: Vocal Melody Extraction in the Presence of Pitched Accompaniment in Polyphonic Music. IEEE Transactions on Audio, Speech, and Language Processing 18(8), 2145–2154 (2010)

Syntactic and Semantic Feature Extraction and Preprocessing to Reduce Noise in Bug Classification

Ruchi Agrawal and G. Ram Mohan Reddy

National Institute of Technology, Karnataka, India
{agrawalruchi01,profgrmreddy}@gmail.com

Abstract. In software industry a lot of effort is spent in analyzing the bug report to classify the bugs. This Classification helps in assigning the bugs to the specific team for Bug Fixing according to the nature of the bug. In this paper, we have proposed a data mining technique applying syntactic and semantic Feature Extraction to assist developers in bug Classification. Extracted features are organized into different feature groups then a specific preprocessing technique is applied to each feature group. The applied methods have reduced the noise in the bug data compared to traditional approach of word frequency for text categorization. We have analyzed our approach on a collection of bug reports collected from a networking based organization (CISCO).The experiments are performed using Naive Bayes Multinomial Model and Support Vector Machine on features obtained after preprocessing.

Keywords: Bug Fixing, Classification, Feature Extraction, Naive Bayes, Support Vector Machine.

1 Introduction

Large organizations like CISCO require a bug classifier system. Since these organization are having many products and different maintenance team to handle different types of bugs. Assigning a bug to a particular team, so that it can be resolved quickly is a challenging task. This system helps to classify the bugs according to different maintenance teams of the organization. Thus, it aims to reduce the overall time to fix the bug.

Like most of the big organizations, CISCO is also having its own bug tracking system which contains bug information in form of various attachments. Attachments refer to the links for accessing the data regarding bug such as description, crash log info, and stack trace decode and other information. It also has provision to add comments and information after static analysis of the bug report as a separate attachment. This system of posting comments is also similar to most open source bug tracking system like bugzilla [1].

The attachments added manually such as description and static analysis are in natural language format (semantic information) whereas the crash log file collected from the crashed system contain information in programming language

K.R. Venugopal and L.M. Patnaik (Eds.): ICIP 2012, CCIS 292, pp. 329–339, 2012.
© Springer-Verlag Berlin Heidelberg 2012

format (syntactic information). Instead of using traditional approach of word frequency for text categorization, information from the attachments can be mined to find out some specific pattern for Feature Extraction and classification. This paper aims at reducing the noise in the data so that bugs can be classified correctly and quickly.

In this paper, we analyze the network bugs and depending on the static analysis of the bug report, the Feature Extraction is performed .The features are grouped into different feature groups and different preprocessing technique is applied to the extracted features to reduce the level of noise in the data. Any classification approach can be applied on the extracted features; we had analyzed our approach using Bayesian probability approach and Support Vector Machine.

2   Related Work

Davor Cubranic et.al. [9] have proposed an approach for automatic bug triage using text categorization. They proposed a prototype for bug assignment to developer using supervised Bayesian learning. Their prototype used the word frequency as input to the classifier. In our approach instead of considering word frequency we had taken bug semantics into consideration. Our approach helps to reduce noise in the extracted features.

Nicholas et.al. [8] have proposed a system that automatically classifies duplicate bug reports as they arrive to save developer time. Their system used surface features, textual semantics, and graph clustering to predict duplicate status. They had considered only textual features that are title and description. In our approach ,syntactic features along with the textual features are used to increase the accuracy of classification.

Deqing Wang et.al [7] have implemented a tool Rebug-Detector, to detect related bugs using bug information and code features. The extracted features related to bugs and used relationship between different methods that is overloaded or overridden methods. In our approach we had used the sequence of the function call present in the stack at the time crash happened. Since the stack image is present for all the bugs irrespective of the product or organization, our approach can be applied on any bug database.

Karl-Michael Schneider in the paper [5] used Naive Bayes Method for Spam Classification. Kian Ming Adam Chai, Hwee Tou Ng and Hai Leong Chieus in their paper [6], explores the use of Bayesian probability approach for text classification. They showed through experiments that Bayesian is good approach for text classification. The words can be considered as unigram features obtained irrespective of the type of bugs.

3   Feature Extraction and Preprocessing

3.1   Overview of the Bug Site

In bug site, bug reports are organized in the form of different attachments and attachments are grouped into General, Commit, Build, Test, Fix Entries category.

According to us, attachments of General category are relevant for classification purpose. General category attachments contain information which is available before the bug is analyzed, tested and fixed by the developer. General category attachments are further divided into Description, Crash info, Decode file, Event log, Email, Static analysis etc attachments. Then bug information is extracted by analyzing the attachments and irrelevant attachments are discarded. For example, Email information is discarded from General category. The information is retrieved from the bug site in html format; html tags are then removed to get individual paragraphs. Information is then statically analyzed to find some pattern for automatic Feature Extraction.

3.2   Feature Extraction

The features are extracted automatically (applying pattern matching) from the bug information in the bug site after html tag removal. The information retrieved from the bugs are of two type one is textual semantics obtained from title and description and other is syntactic features which includes stack trace decode, commands and syslog events. The textual information is in natural language format hence normal natural language processing technique can be applied. For example, title and description are in natural language, so word frequency information is retrieved.

Syntactic features include stack trace decode, commands and syslog events. For syntactic features first static analysis of the bug information is done to find out the patterns for their retrieval. The stack trace decode is the sequence of function call retrieved from the stack. Here not only the function name but the order in which they are called is also important. This chunk of function call obtained from the stack is very important for classification task. The trace decode occurs in two patterns in bug report (1) starts with %[0x]: and ends with + symbol and (2)starts with %[0x]--→ and ends with + symbol. For example, the trace decode chunk retrieved from the bug CSCek63114 is as shown in Fig. 1.

create_cce_target_class_group   ccm_add_class_in_class_group
qm_create_hw_policy
ccm_return_new_param
iccshim_merge_resp

Fig. 1. Stack Trace Decode Function Call Sequence

Commands have two types of pattern (1) start with CMD: like CMD:<feature> (2) Data present between "Current Configuration" and "end" having commands in each line. For example the command of the bug CSCek61132 is "CMD: 'no aaa new-model' 19:30:05 EST Sat Nov 11 2006, CMD: 'ip subnet-zero' 19:30:05 EST Sat Nov 11 2006". The events that happened in response to the crash actually represent the cause of the crash. These events are called syslog events or log events. The log events will start with % sign and end with colon (:) like

%<feature>:. For bug CSCtn56006, the event log contains messages as shown in Fig. 2 . We had considered all these features as for different type of bugs different commands will be executed and events happened in response to the function calls are also different for bugs related to different component.

```
*Nov 12 00:30:02.699: %LINEPROTO-5-UPDOWN: Line rotocol on Interface
GigabitEthernet0/1, changed state to up
*Nov 12 00:30:02.699: %LINEPROTO-5-UPDOWN: Line protocol on Interface VoIP-Null0,
changed state to up
*Nov 12 00:30:03.479: %LINK-3-UPDOWN: Interface Serial0/0/0, changed state to down
*Nov 12 00:30:03.479: %LINEPROTO-5-UPDOWN: Line protocol on Interface IPv6-mpls,
changed state to up
```

Fig. 2. Syslog Events Collected from Crash Log of a Bug

3.3   Feature Preprocessing to Reduce Noise

The features extracted by pattern matching process contain lots of noise as the pattern which we followed for extracting the required features may match to some other data which is in the specified pattern but is not relevant with respect to our classification task. The features extracted themselves cannot be used directly for classification as they are not structured .The unwanted data retrieved after pattern matching which is not relevant for classification is called noise. This noise tends to reduce the accuracy of the classification algorithm hence there is a need for noise reduction in extracted features.

Removing Configuration Changes. Sometimes the two bugs reported in two different versions of the same product are similar but due to configuration changes of the different versions when normal text matching is applied, there is a chance that they will be reported as two different bugs by the matching process. In order to overcome this effect, the two different configurations should be recognized as single. This approach should be applied after the confirmation that the bug has not occurred due to configuration change. For example consider the two bugs shown in Table 1. The two bugs have occurred because of the same reason that is bad memory access but are recognized as two different bugs due to configuration changes. For command checking purpose, a repository containing the standard commands used by the product or organization is required. In our case, CISCO is already having a repository called CISCO COMMAD LOOKUP TOOL. The commands are checked with the repository for example, if Interface Ethernet 2/0 is checked it will not be recognized as standard command whereas the Interface will be recognized as standard command. The commands extracted after preprocessing steps are used as features for classification.

Preprocessing of Stack Trace Decode Using Frequent Pattern Tree. The sequence of functions which are called at the moment when the crash happened gets saved in the stack. The functions taken from stack in order is called

Table 1. Configuration Details of Two Bugs taken from Crash Log File

Bug1 Configuration Detail	Bug2 Configuration Detail
Version 12.4	Version 12.5
Interface Ethernet 2/0	Interface Ethernet 4/0
Interface Ethernet 2/1	Interface Ethernet 4/1
Interface FastEthernet2/0	Interface Ethernet 4/2
Interface FastEthernet2/1	Interface Ethernet 4/3
Controller T1 2/1contoroller	Controller T2 2/1contoroller
T1 2/2 Processor xyz	T2 2/2 Processor abc

stack trace decode. The concept of stack trace decode can be applied to any type of bug irrespective of the product and organization as stack trace will be available for all the bugs. In trace decode preprocessing order is very important and it is very difficult to find the complete match for the traces but a part of trace can match with the part of other trace. To find the matching pattern in traces, a separate frequent pattern tree is constructed for each and every class under consideration. Consider the traces shown in Table 2 functions are represented using symbol F1, F2, F3 and soon.

Table 2. Trace Decode Sequence of Bugs Belonging to One Class

Traceid	TraceDecode Sequence
1	F1→F2→F3
2	F3→F4→F5
3	F1→F4
4	F3→F4→F6

Construction of FP Tree. An FP-tree is constructed by reading traces one by one and mapping each trace sequence onto a path on the FP-tree [2]. As different traces may have same function, their path may overlap. The sequence of the function obtained from the stack when trace 1, 2, 3, 4 occurred is shown in Table 2. The tree start with an empty node called NULL node. A node in the tree contains the function name and the count (frequency of the function).When the first trace is added, a new branch will be constructed in the FP tree and the count of all nodes will become one .When trace2 comes than a new branch is created, for trace3 the node corresponding to function F4 will be added to branch starting with F1 and count of F1 will be increased to 2.Continuing in the similar manner the FP tree can be completed as shown in Figure 3(a). A separate FP tree will be constructed for each class. So for N input class, N number of FP tree will be constructed in the manner as explained.

Ranking Based on FP Tree. When a new bug arrives, its trace is retrieved and checked through against FP tree for each class and all the pattern which are

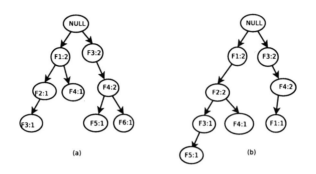

Fig. 3. FP Tree for Trace Sequence of two Different Class

matched are retrieved along with count. Count of the matched sequence is the count of the last function matched. Consider the two FP tree shown in Figure 3 (a) and (b) as FP tree for two different classes A and B respectively. If a new trace t comes, it will be matched with FP tree of all the classes and ranking will be done according to following rules

- If the length of the matched trace is equal to length of a complete branch in any of the tree than probability of the new trace t_new belonging to that class is highest. So corresponding to that class high rank will be assigned. For example consider the trace F1→F2→F3, it is having match in both the tree but in tree (a) it matches a complete branch whereas in (b) it matches only with a sub branch. Hence corresponding to class A rank should be high compared to class B.
- If the length of the trace is not equal to any complete branch in any of the tree then the length of the maximum match is considered. For example consider trace F1→F2, it is not matching to any complete branch in any tree then:
  • If there are two matches with the same length then the match having high count will be assigned high rank. Trace F1→F2 is matching with both the tree but in tree (b) the count is more hence t will be assigned high rank corresponding to class B.
  • If there is a single match than that match is given highest rank. For example trace F3→F4 is matching with only one tree hence high rank is assigned corresponding to class A.

For traces instead of considering frequency vector, rank vector calculated according to FP tree will be considered for further classification process.

Removing the Noise Caused Due to Two Process Trying to Write into Crash Log at Same Time. While writing the events in crash log, it may happen that some other process may try to write at the same time. In case when process1 is writing, process2 comes and takes control will create noise. Process2 will be suspended and process1 will continue writing. For example, Consider the syslog events in Figure 4 all six syslog events are same but will be recognized as six different events by the classification algorithm. Hence it is necessary to reduce this internal noise in the data. In order to overcome, buckets will be created one bucket for one syslog event. Starting with a single bucket the incoming syslog will be added to the bucket and after that every syslog message will be checked against the bucket. A threshold value will be set and if the number of characters matched in sequence is greater than the threshold than the syslog will be added to that bucket. In case it will not match with any of the bucket a new bucket will be created for that syslog message. At the end, the number of bucket becomes equal to the number of original syslog events. To find the original syslog event from the bucket length of the syslog events in that bucket will be considered. The event with least length will be the original syslog as the length will always increase in case two process tries to write it will never decrease.

DUAFLa-5-NBRCHANGE
DUAL-5-CNBRCHANGE
DUAL-5-NBRCHANGEa
DUAL-5-NiBgRCHANGE
DUALa-5-CNBRCHANGE
DUAL-5-NBRCHANGE

Fig. 4. Variants of Syslog Event DUAL-5-NBRCHANGE

4   Classification Technique

The classification of the bugs is done based on the component in which the problem has occurred for example OS (i.e. Operating System related bugs), SNMP (Simple Network Management Protocol), BGP (Border Gateway Protocol). After Feature Extraction and preprocessing, any classification algorithm can be applied. We had evaluated our results using Nave Bayes Multinomial Approach and Support Vector Machine.

4.1   Probabilistic Framework for Nave Bayes Classification

A Naive Bayes Classifier can be defined as an independent feature model that deals with a simple probabilistic classifier based on Bayes' theorem with strong independence assumptions [4]. There are several models which assume different fitting for Nave Bayes. The traditional Multinomial Model for classification consider word frequency as input but in our case we have applied Multinomial on the multigram features obtained after pattern matching and preprocessing. The Multinomial model is applied on all the feature group one by one and the final result is obtained. Consider the bug classification into n different classes $C = \{C_1, C_2., C_n\}$. The unseen bug(B_i) will be classified using 1 to class with higher posterior probability.

$$P(C_k, B_i) = P(B_i|C_k)(P(C_k)/P(B_i)) \tag{1}$$

$P(C_k)$ is the prior probability of class C_k calculated using 2, N is the number of bugs in the training data and N_k is used to denote total number of bugs from training data which belong to class.

$$C_k.P(C_k) = N_k/N \tag{2}$$

nstead of taking word information as input we are using feature information for bug specific features and for features of natural language type we are considering word information. Words are unigram features but extracted features from bug information may be Bi-gram, Trigram or Multigram. Bug specific features may be a combination of number of words as in Trace Decode and Commands.

Multinomial Event Model. The multinomial model captures feature frequency information in bugs. Consider, for example, M_i is the multinomial model feature vector for the ith bug data B_i. M_{it}, is the number of times feature F_t occurs in bug data B_i; $n_i = \sum t$. M_{it} the total number of features in B_i. In the multinomial model, a bug is an ordered sequence of feature events, drawn from the same vocabulary V. We assume that the lengths of bugs are independent of class. We make a Naive Bayes assumption: that the probability of each feature event in a bug is independent of the feature's context and position in the document. $P(F_t|C_k)$ is estimated using word frequency information from the multinomial model feature vectors. Generation of bugs is modeled by repeatedly drawing features from a multinomial distribution.

4.2 Support Vector Machine

Support Vector Machines are based on the concept of decision planes that define decision boundaries. A decision plane is one that separates between a set of objects having different class memberships. Support Vector Machine (SVM) is primarily a classier method that performs classification tasks by constructing hyperplanes in a multidimensional space that separates cases of different class labels. In our approach, we have applied SVM on the extracted features of all the feature groups considering linear kernel Function.

5   Experimental Results

5.1   Dataset Information and Implementation

The data from six different categories os, bgp, ip, ipv6, aaa, snmp are collected from the site of one of the networking based organization. The training data contains 1000-1500 bugs from each category. Five different types of features are extracted by static analysis and pattern matching. The Syslog Event contain around 8,000 Syslog messages, for Commands the vocabulary size is around 600 commands, for Title and Description word frequency data is taken and their respective vocabulary sizes are around 9000 and 30000. For Trace decode, there are 400 chunks available for the classification purpose. The Feature Extraction and preprocessing is performed using python and for Support Vector Machine LIBSVM [3] library is used.

5.2   Results and Discussion

The experiments are performed on the data collected from six different categories (i.e. OS, BGP, SNMP, AAA, IP, IPV6). The binary classification is performed using Multinomial Nave Bayes Model, the binary classifier using traditional approach of word frequency gives an accuracy of 67%. But when the classifier is extended for multiclass classification its accuracy is very low (below 10%). The word frequency data contains huge amount of noise as it is not the usual natural language data but it is combination of natural language and programming language data. So, to overcome noise our approach of syntactic and semantic Feature Extraction is applied. The extracted features are given as input to the Nave Bayes Multinomial model and Support Vector Machine. The results using extracted features before preprocessing is shown in Table 3 and Table 4.

Table 3. Average Performance (Accuracy) of the Multinomial Naive Bayes Classifier

Classification Model	Title	Description	Syslogs	Commands	Stack Trace
Multinomial Naive Bayes (before preprocessing)	0.3249	0.3424	0.2403	0.1484	0.0719
Multinomial Naive Bayes (after preprocessing)	0.3443	0.3942	0.3249	0.2951	0.1581

The extracted features found to contain noise which is removed using the preprocessing techniques discussed in Section 3.The features after preprocessing are given as input to the classification algorithms. The performance of the classification techniques has found to improve after preprocessing. The Nave Bayes Multinomial Model gives less accuracy compared to Support Vector Machine. The Support Vector Machine when applied on the features one by one and the final overall accuracy is found to be 52.36%.The Major improvement is in accuracy w.r.t Commands and Stack Trace Features .The Stack trace is found to be very useful in the classification task even though the accuracy is less but its reliability is more. If the Stack Trace of the two bugs matches exactly it can be concluded that the two bugs are similar. The exact matching is very rare hence the rank is calculated according to the portion matched. The rank vector used for the classification has found to be efficient in classification task. It is clear from the Figure 5 and Figure 6 that applied Feature Extraction and preprocessing had reduced the noise in the bug data and helps to increase the classification accuracy.

Table 4. Average Performance (Accuracy) of the Support Vector Machine

Classification Model	Title	Description	Syslogs	Commands	Stack Trace
Support Vector Machine (before preprocessing)	0.42	0.4102	0.2819	0.2195	0.1216
Support Vector Machine (after preprocessing)	0.4453	0.4943	0.3782	0.3249	0.2981

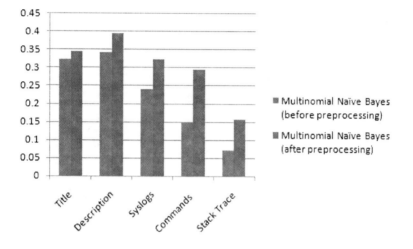

Fig. 5. Performance of Multinomial Naive Bayes Model using Extracted Features

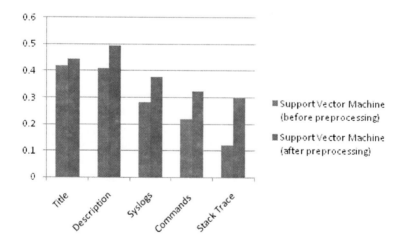

Fig. 6. Performance of Support Vector Machine using Extracted Features

6   Conclusions

The experimental results shows that the features extracted and the preprocessing technique applied helps to reduce noise in the bug data. The stack trace, commands and the syslog events has found be very useful in classification. The syntactic features when used along with the semantic feature will tend to increase the overall accuracy of the classification algorithm. The features obtained after preprocessing are very useful for CISCO in Bug Fixing task. The work can further be used by the CISCO to make automated bug tracking system. The Stack trace FP tree method, Configuration changes removal and the removal of noise caused due to process synchronization can be applied to any type of bugs irrespective of the organization. The accuracy can further be increased depending on the classification algorithm that is applied.

References

1. BugZilla official website, http://www.bugzilla.org/
2. FP Tree, www.cis.hut.fi/Opinnot/T-61.6020/2008/fptree.pdf
3. Chang, C.C., Lin, C.J.: LIBSVM: A Library for Support Vector Machines. ACM Transactions on Intelligent Systems and Technology 2, 27:1–27:27 (2011)
4. Qiang, G.: An Effective Algorithm for Improving the Performance of Naive Bayes for Text Classification. In: Second International Conference on Computer Research and Development, pp. 699–701 (2010)
5. Schneider, K.M.: A Comparison of Event Models for Naive Bayes Anti-Spam E-Mail Filtering. In: Proceedings of the Tenth Conference on European Chapter of the Association for Computational Linguistics, EACL 2003, pp. 307–314 (2003)
6. Chai, M.A., Ng, H.T., Chieu, H.L.: Bayesian Online Classifiers for Text Classification and Filtering. In: 25th Annual International ACM SIGIR Conference on Research and Development in Information Retrieval, SIGIR (2002)
7. Wang, D., Lin, M., Zhang, H., Hu, H.: Detect Related Bugs from Source Code Using Bug Information, Information. In: IEEE 34th Annual Computer Software and Applications Conference, pp. 228–237 (2010)
8. Jalbert, N., Weimer, W.: Automated Duplicate Detection for Bug Tracking Systems. In: IEEE International Conference on Dependable Systems and Networks with FTCS and DCC DSN (2008)
9. Cubranic, D., Gail, C.M.: Automatic Bug Triage Using Text Classification. In: Proceedings of the Sixteenth International Conference on Software Engineering and Knowledge Engineering, pp. 92–97 (June 2004)

Analysis of Blind Source Separation Techniques for Eye Artifact Removal

Theus H. Aspiras and Vijayan K. Asari

Department of Electrical and Computer Engineering
University of Dayton, Dayton, USA
aspirast1@udayton.edu

Abstract. Evaluation of several different eye artifact removal techniques for electroencephalographic data is presented in this paper. Data is taken from an emotion recognition experiment, in which subjects undergo five different emotions (joy, sadness, disgust, fear, and neutral). Preprocessing for the EEG Data includes filtering with a Butterworth band-pass filter and a 60Hz notch filter. Three different types of eye artifact removal techniques are explored using the preprocessed data: EOG based linear regression, Principal Component Analysis, and Independent Component Analysis. All techniques used electrooculographic (EOG) data to determine the criteria for feature extraction and removal. Evaluations from our experiments show that all techniques significantly reduce the effects of eye blinks and eye movements in the EEG. The developed metric used in experimentation shows that Independent Component Analysis reduced eye artifacts the best while keeping EEG portions unchanged (Average SSE of 0.1126 for clean EEG portions).

Keywords: Electroencephalography, Electrooculography, Eye Artifact Removal, Independent Component Analysis, Strength of Eye Blink.

1 Introduction

Noise/artifact removal is an important area of study for Electroencephalography (EEG). While EEG electrodes detect diminutive activations in the brain, they are succeptible to a wide array of noises. A comparison between the recorded EEG and the electrocardiogram (ECG) by Dirlich et al., [1], who showed that cardiac field artifacts are high amplitude potentials which affect EEG performance. Dewan et al., [2] were able to remove these ECG-type artifacts by developing a noise model based on energy functions to subtract the noise from the recorded EEG. Muscle activations, such as jaw clenching and facial movements, are also potential sources of artifacts in the EEG. Narasimhan and Dutt [3] found that muscle artifacts hidden in EEG potentials can be removed by least mean squared adaptive predictive filtering. De Clercq et al., [4] found that using a blind source separation technique called Canonical Correlation Analysis proved to be better for muscular artifact removal than low pass filters and Independent Component Analysis. Ferdjallah and Barr [5] developed different types of adaptive FIR and IIR notch filters to remove power line noise in EEG signals.

K.R. Venugopal and L.M. Patnaik (Eds.): ICIP 2012, CCIS 292, pp. 340–349, 2012.
© Springer-Verlag Berlin Heidelberg 2012

The noise/artifact removal research is most prevalent in the removal of eye blink/movement artifacts. One method by Jervis et al., [6] finds the cross-correlation between the Electroculography (EOG) recordings and the EEG and subtracts a fraction of the EOG signals from the recorded EEG to yield a cleaned EEG. Ramanan et al., [7] used Haar wavelets to distinguish between eye artifacts and clean EEG, offering an algorithm that can detect and remove artifacts in epileptic EEG. Neural networks have been used by Erfanian and Mahmoudi [8] to suppress eye artifacts in the EEG as with many others [9, 10]. The techniques that are most widely used are the Blind Source Separation (BSS) techniques. Gomez-Herrero et al., [11] used BSS to develop an automated artifact removal system without the use of an EOG signal. Liu and Yao [12] used Principal Component Analysis to correctly identify EOG sources and correct the EEG from them. From the different types of blind source separation techniques used, Independent Component Analysis has been used extensively to remove ocular artifacts in EEG. Zhou et al., [13] used ICA to remove both eye artifacts and power line noise. Several others [14–17] also used Independent Component Analysis to isolate eye artifacts in the EEG and remove them to create a clean EEG. We will extensively analyze the Blind Source Separation techniques along with the EOG subtraction method for its effectiveness in obtaining eye artifacts and removing them in the EEG.

2   Data Acquisition and Preprocessing

We used the Geodesic EEG System from EGI, Inc. to capture our EEG data. The system has a high density 256-channel network for high resolution imaging and a stimulus presentation software to give stimuli to subjects. The data was taken from an emotion study [18, 19], in which five different emotions were classified (joy, sadness, disgust, fear, and neutral). Images were displayed to elicit these emotions and were recorded through our system. We used a sampling rate of 250Hz for our data acquisition. Once our EEG data has been recorded, we used two preprocessing steps to remove frequency-based noise. We first used a Butterworth band-pass filter from 0.1Hz to 100Hz to remove EEG biases. We then used a 60Hz notch filter to remove potential noise from electrical equipment.

3   Artifact Removal Techniques

With the 256-channel EEG system, there are several electrodes used for capturing eye blinks and eye movement artifacts, specifically the EOG channels. Table 1 shows the pairs of electrodes used for capturing these artifacts. We used these electrodes as a source of information when developing these artifact removal techniques.

3.1   EOG Based Eye Artifact Removal

For this type of artifact removal, an EOG signal is taken along with the set of EEG signals to allow removal of eye blink and eye movement signals. This

Table 1. Electrodes used for EOG Channels

Electrode Pair	Electrode Numbers
Left Eye Blink Pair 1	37 and 241
Left Eye Blink Pair 2	32 and 241
Right Eye Blink Pair 1	18 and 238
Right Eye Blink Pair 2	25 and 238
Eye Movement Pair	226 and 252

assumes that the recorded signals are a linear combination of clean EEG signals and noisy EEG signals from the EOG channel. The following equation shows this.

$$Y = X + \alpha N \tag{1}$$

where Y is the recorded EEG signal, X is the clean EEG signal, N is the noise due to the EOG signal, and α is the coefficient for the noise channel. Since we have recorded the EOG channels, we can solve for the clean EEG signal which results in the following equation.

$$X = Y - \alpha N \tag{2}$$

Some assumptions must be made when using this artifact removal technique. Since the EOG contains mostly eye blink and eye movement data, we can use the recorded EOG signal for correction of the EEG, but the recorded signal may contain some brain EEG signals, which may be subtracted out when using the technique. Filtering may be used to remove most of the brain signal from the recorded EEG signal, but for this experiment, has not been used.

3.2 Blind Source Separation

For these techniques, we want to separate the signals without any information on the signals themselves and how they were combined. We also assume that the signals are not correlated. Therefore, we must separate the signals with each technique, find what signals are eye artifact signals and remove them, and then recombine the separated signals into a clean EEG signal.

When doing these blind source separation techniques, we generally assume a linear mixing of sources as shown in the equation below.

$$Y = XA \tag{3}$$

where Y is the recorded EEG signal, X is the source matrix, and A is the linear mixing matrix. We also assume that the number of sources is less than the number of variables and that the mixing of sources is instantaneous.

Principal Component Analysis: Principal component analysis (PCA) is an orthogonal transformation that decomposes a set of signals into principal components, which are uncorrelated and ordered based on the highest variance of the data. To compute this transformation, we use the covariance matrix of Y given by the following equation.

$$\begin{aligned} cov(Y) &= E[YY^T] \\ &= E[(P^T X)(P^T X)^T] \\ &= P^T E[XX^T]P \\ &= P^T cov(X)P \end{aligned} \tag{4}$$

We can then create the orthonormal transformation by realigning the equation as shown below.

$$\begin{aligned} Pcov(Y) &= PP^T cov(X)P \\ &= cov(X)P \end{aligned} \tag{5}$$

We solve for the transformation P since the resulting equation is based on a simple eigenvalue problem. This type of transformation would be useful in eye artifact removal because large variances in the data are due to eye blinks in the data. We can therefore assume that the first set of principal components can be classified as eye blink and eye movement components and can be removed when recombining the components to recreate the EEG signal.

Independent Component Analysis: Independent Component Analysis is also an orthogonal transformation that decomposes a set of signals into independent components, which are signals that are statistically independent. This means that the ICA algorithm tries to maximize the independence between components. Independence can be defined as the maximum amount of information of a component while minimizing the amount of mutual information of other components. This can be shown through the following equation.

$$H(x, y) = H(x) + H(y) - H(xy) \tag{6}$$

We can also say that a mixture of Gaussian random variables, specifically Gaussian sources, cannot be separated into different sources and that they have the largest entropy. Therefore, we can develop methods that maximize the non-Gaussianity of the independent components, like negentropy which minimizes the entropy. Several preprocessing steps are used when using Independent Component Analysis. Centering the data allows biases to be removed when finding components. Whitening decorrelates the variables by uncorrelating the data and shaping the data to have a variance of one. There are several different types of algorithms for ICA like maximum likelihood estimation, Infomax [20], and FastICA [21], but we use FastICA for our experiments.

Strength of Eye Blink: When using blind source separation techniques, we can develop different criteria to remove specific components that are noise components and recombine the other components to form clean signals. For ocular artifact removal, we assume that the components that will contain most of the noise are from the eyes. Therefore, based on the weights that were created from the blind source separation techniques, we can see which electrodes have the highest weightage and remove those components that contain high weights for the EOG electrodes. The criteria we specified for our experiment is the Strength of Eye Blink (SEB), which is based on the mean square weights, as shown by the equation below.

$$SEB = \frac{\frac{1}{M}\sum_{i=1}^{M} v_i^2}{\frac{1}{N}\sum_{j=1}^{N} w_j^2} \times 100 > \epsilon \qquad (7)$$

where v_i are the eye electrodes, M is the number of eye electrodes, w_j are all of the electrodes, and N is the number of total electrodes. We can define ϵ as a threshold which is a specific percentage of EOG signal as compared to the normal EEG signal found in each component, meaning that to remove a specific component, the power of the eye blinks should be greater than ϵ.

Figure 1 shows the amount of components removed versus various values of ϵ. We can see that as ϵ is increased, the amount of components decrease. With ICA, eye components seem to have a higher amount of weightage as compared to the other signals in the EEG. PCA seems to have less components containing strictly eye blinks/movements, so it is expected that ICA will perform better due to isolation of eye components.

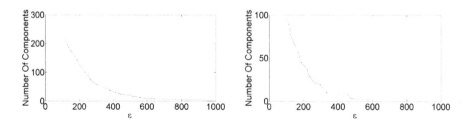

Fig. 1. Number of Components vs ϵ for ICA (left) and PCA (right)

4   Results

To illustrate the effectiveness of each of the algorithms, we considered the results of three different electrodes. We also used specific criteria optimized for each method. For the EOG-based subtraction model, we decided to use $\alpha = 1$. For

PCA, we used $\epsilon = 450\%$. For ICA, we used $\epsilon = 700\%$. Figure 2 shows EEG Channel 26 depicting the front of the head, where most of the noise for the EEG occurs. We can see that all the methods are able to remove the eye artifacts in the EEG, specifically the eye blinks. One thing we can note is that the overall shape of the corrected EEG using ICA maintains the overall shape of the clean portions of the EEG while the other methods seem to remove more components than necessary. Figure 3 shows EEG Channel 126 depicting the back of the head, where noise from the eyes does not affect the EEG as much. Also with these results, we can see that all the algorithms remove the eye blink data, but only ICA seems to remove only the eye blink data. The other methods seem to remove actual EEG components along with the EOG components. Figure 4 shows EOG Channel 18 to illustrate how there is some EEG information in the EOG Channel which can be used for analysis. We can see that even in the EOG, there are actual portions of EEG data, so subtracting out the EOG signal using the EOG-based subtraction model from all other electrodes would remove some EEG components. Also since the EOG signals are subtracted out, those signals would be discarded. With PCA, it seems to delete even more parts of the EEG than the EOG-based subtraction, even though it will still use the EOG electrodes as viable sources of EEG information.

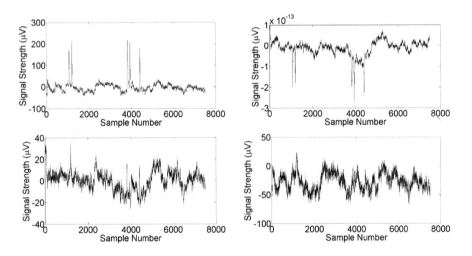

Fig. 2. Experiment 1: EEG Channel 26 - Front of Head for Original(top left), EOG-Based (top right), PCA (bottom left), and ICA (bottom right)

4.1   Clean EEG Metric

To establish how well the different types of eye artifact removal algorithms work, we need to develop a metric to quantify this. Since the data used for the eye artifact removal is not artificial, instead of developing a metric to quantify how well the noise is removed, we can quantify how much the EEG changes in portions

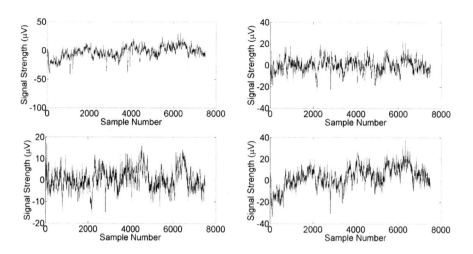

Fig. 3. Experiment 2: EEG Channel 126 - Back of Head for Original(top left), EOG-Based (top right), PCA (bottom left), and ICA (bottom right)

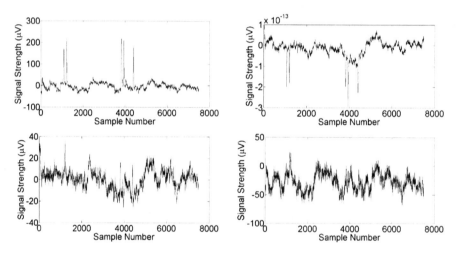

Fig. 4. Experiment 3: EOG Channel 18 - Eye Blink Channel for Original(top left), EOG-Based (top right), PCA (bottom left), and ICA (bottom right)

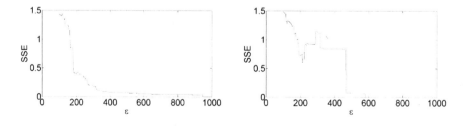

Fig. 5. Changes in Sum Squared Error vs ϵ for ICA (left) and PCA (right)

of the EEG that have no visible eye artifacts. To calculate the metric, first subtract the mean for both the original signal and the processed signal, as shown in Equation 8.

$$x_{mean,i} = x_i - \frac{1}{N}\sum_{j=1}^{N} x_j \tag{8}$$

where x_i is the signal, N is the number of samples in the signal, and $x_{mean,i}$ is the zero-mean signal. Once you subtract the mean from the signals, you can then normalize the signals by dividing by the norm, as shown in Equation 9.

$$x_{norm} = \frac{x_{mean}}{\|x_{mean}\|} \tag{9}$$

where x_{norm} is the zero-mean normalized signal. We then calculate the metric by finding the sum squared error between the original signal and the processed signal, as shown in Equation 10.

$$E = \sum_{i=1}^{N}(x_{norm,i} - y_{norm,i})^2 \tag{10}$$

where $x_{norm,i}$ is the original signal and $y_{norm,i}$ is the processed signal. This metric shows that as the processed signal is changed more, the E value will increase, thus quantifying the changes which are invariant to the mean and norm of the signals. We use this measure to show the changes before and after processing in noiseless portions of the EEG. Figure 5 shows these changes for both ICA and PCA when using EEG Channel 126. We can see that PCA changes the EEG almost immediately when taking out the highest weighted eye component. It was found that the eye components were the first couple of principal components. ICA seems to change the EEG the least with the same amount of components

Table 2. Sum Squared Error for each Eye Artifact Removal Technique on different EEG Channels

Type	Linear	PCA	ICA
Chan 26	1.4446	1.8032	0.5175
Chan 126	0.5984	0.8326	0.0427
Chan 18	0.6726	0.7363	0.1541
Chan 15 (Fz)	1.2159	0.3673	0.1850
Chan 101 (Pz)	0.0159	0.0070	0.0060
Chan 137 (Oz)	0.8937	0.9815	0.0446
Chan 95 (T5)	1.5447	0.3671	0.0476
Chan 178 (T6)	1.2779	1.3803	0.0419
Chan 59 (C3)	0.7380	0.6239	0.0372
Chan 183 (C4)	1.2401	1.8705	0.0491
Average	0.9642	0.8970	0.1126

removed. This is due to the high amount of weightage placed on the eyes in the component creation. Table 2 shows this metric for all methods across the EEG. PCA and the EOG-based subtraction technique gave the highest SSE values across the different EEG channels while the ICA technique gave the lowest SSE value, which is due to the isolation of eye components.

5   Conclusions

In this paper, we observed that using Independent Component Analysis gave the best eye artifact removal by removing the artifacts from the EEG while maintaining the integrity of the EEG signal (Average SSE of 0.1126). This artifact removal technique is able to localize specific components that are generated by the eyes, in which our automated component selection criteria defines a threshold by which these components are removed. Principal Component Analysis does remove eye artifacts using the automated component selection criteria but tends to remove other EEG components as well due to the components maximizing variance. The EOG based linear model also offers great artifact removal, but due to the EOG channels having some EEG components, the linear model affects the clean EEG portions. For future work, we will experiment with other types of artifact removal algorithms and develop new algorithms to improve the speed and accuracy of these techniques.

References

1. Dirlich, G., Vogl, L., Plaschke, M., Strian, F.: Cardiac Field Effects on the EEG. Electroencephalography and Clinical Neurophysiology 102, 307–315 (1997)
2. Dewan, M., Hossain, M., Hoque, M., Chae, O.: Contaminated ECG Artifact Detection and Elimination from EEG using Energy Function Based Transformation. In: Information and Communication Technology, ICICT, pp. 52–56 (2007)
3. Narasimhan, S., Dutt, D.: Application of LMS Adaptive Predictive Filtering for Muscle Artifact (noise) Cancellation from EEG Signals. Computers and Electrical Engineering 22, 13–30 (1996)
4. De Clercq, W., Vergult, A., Vanrumste, B., Van Hees, J., Palmini, A., Van Paesschen, W., Van Huffel, S.: A New Muscle Artifact Removal Technique to Improve the Interpretation of the Ictal Scalp Electroencephalogram. In: Engineering in Medicine and Biology Society, IEEE-EMBS, pp. 944–947 (2005)
5. Ferdjallah, M., Barr, R.: Adaptive Digital Notch Filter Design on the Unit Circle for the Removal of Powerline Noise from Biomedical Signals. IEEE Transactions Biomedical Engineering 41, 529–536 (1994)
6. Jervis, B., Nichols, M., Allen, E., Hudson, N., Johnson, T.: The Assessment of Two Methods for Removing Eye Movement Artefact from the EEG. Electroencephalography and Clinical Neurophysiology 61, 444–452 (1985)
7. Ramanan, S., Kalpakam, N., Sahambi, J.: A Novel Wavelet Based Technique for Detection and De-noising of Ocular Artifact in Normal and Epileptic Electroencephalogram. In: Communications, Circuits and Systems, ICCCAS, pp. 1027–1031 (2004)

8. Erfanian, A., Mahmoudi, B.: Real-Time Eye-Blink Suppression using Neural Adaptive Filters for EEG-based Brain Computer Interface. In: 24th Annual Conference and the Annual Fall Meeting of the Biomedical Engineering Society EMBS/BMES Conference, Engineering in Medicine and Biology, vol. 1, pp. 44–45 (2002)

9. Sovierzoski, M., Schwarz, L., Azevedo, F.: Binary Neural Classifier of Raw EEG Data to Separate Spike and Sharp Wave of the Eye Blink Artifact. Natural Computation, ICNC 2, 126–130 (2009)

10. Selvan, S., Srinivasan, R.: Removal of Ocular Artifacts from EEG using an Efficient Neural Network based Adaptive Filtering Technique. IEEE Signal Processing Letters 6, 330–332 (1999)

11. Gomez-Herrero, G., De Clercq, W., Anwar, H., Kara, O., Egiazarian, K., Van Huffel, S., Van Paesschen, W.: Automatic Removal of Ocular Artifacts in the EEG without an EOG reference channel. In: Signal Processing Symposium, NORSIG, pp. 130–133 (2006)

12. Liu, T., Yao, D.: Removal of the Ocular Artifacts from EEG Data using a Cascaded Spatio-Temporal Processing. Computer Methods and Programs in Biomedicine 83, 95–103 (2006)

13. Zhou, W., Zhou, J., Zhao, H., Ju, L.: Removing Eye Movement and Power Line Artifacts from the EEG based on ICA. In: 27th Annual International Conference on Engineering in Medicine and Biology Society, IEEE-EMBS, pp. 6017–6020 (2005)

14. Zhou, W., Gotman, J.: Automatic Removal of Eye Movement Artifacts from the EEG using ICA and the Dipole Model. Progress in Natural Science 19, 1165–1170 (2009)

15. Flexer, A., Bauer, H., Pripfl, J., Dorffner, G.: Using ICA for removal of Ocular Artifacts in EEG recorded from Blind Subjects. Neural Networks 18, 998–1005 (2005)

16. Klados, M., Papadelis, C., Bamidis, P.: Reg-ica: A New Hybrid Method for EOG Artifact Rejection. In: 9th International Conference on Information Technology and Applications in Biomedicine, ITAB 2009, pp. 1–4 (2009)

17. Li, R., Principe, J.: Blinking Artifact Removal in Cognitive EEG data using ICA. In: 28th Annual International Conference of the Engineering in Medicine and Biology Society, IEEE-EMBS, pp. 5273–5276 (2006)

18. Aspiras, T.H., Asari, V.K.: Analysis of Spatio-temporal Relationship of Multiple Energy Spectra of EEG Data for Emotion Recognition. In: Venugopal, K.R., Patnaik, L.M. (eds.) ICIP 2011. CCIS, vol. 157, pp. 572–581. Springer, Heidelberg (2011)

19. Aspiras, T.H., Asari, V.K.: Log Power Representation of EEG Spectral Bands for the Recognition of Emotional States of Mind. In: 8th International Conference on Information Communications and Signal Processing, ICICS, pp. 1–5 (2011)

20. Obradovic, D., Deco, G.: Blind Source Separation: Are Information Maximization and Redundancy Minimization Different? In: Proceedings of the 1997 IEEE Workshop on Neural Networks for Signal Processing VII, pp. 416–425 (1997)

21. Hyvarinen, A.: Fast ICA for Noisy Data using Gaussian Moments. In: Proceedings of the 1999 IEEE International Symposium on Circuits and Systems, vol. 5, pp. 57–61 (1999)

Effective Multiclassifier for Arecanut Grading

Ajit Danti[1] and Suresha M.[2]

[1] Department of Computer Applications,
Jawaharlal Nehru National College of Engineering, Karnataka, India
ajitdanti@yahoo.com
[2] Department of Computer Science, Kuvempu University, Karnataka, India
srit_suresh@yahoo.com

Abstract. The k-Nearest Neighbour (k-NN) rule is a simple and effective method for multi-way classification that is much used in Computer Vision. However, its performance depends heavily on the distance metric being employed. k-NN classifiers suffer from the problem of high variance in the case of limited sampling. Alternatively, one could use support vector machines but they involve time-consuming optimization and computation of pairwise distances. We propose a combination of these two methods which deals with the multiclass problem, has reasonable computational complexity in classification and gives excellent results in practice. The basic idea is to find support vectors using Support Vector Machine Classifier. k-NN classifier uses only support vectors as a feature space which is given by SVMs in training phase. k is the most important parameter in the arecanut grading system based on k-NN. this method can be applied to large, multiclass data sets.

Keywords: Arecanut, Classification, k Nearest Neighbor Classifier, Support Vector Machines.

1 Introduction

ARECANUT (Areca catechu L.) is one of the important commercial crops of India. It plays a prominent role in the religious, social and cultural functions and economic life of people in India. Its cultivation is concentrated in South Western and North Western regions of India. The economic product is the fruit called "betel nut" and is used mainly for masticatory purposes. Arecanut has innovative in Ayurvedic and Veterinary medicines. The habit of chewing arecanut is typical of the Indian sub-continent and its neighborhood. Arecanut is grown in Bangladesh, China, Malaysia, Indonesia, Vietnam, Philippines and Thailand. India accounts for about 57 percent of world production. The quality, variety and types of arecanut vary from one place to another. Recent studies have shown that arecanut has pharmalogical uses such as hypoglycermic effect, mitotic activity etc. Since, these classification activities are being done manually and is mainly labor dependent and hence automation is necessary. There are several computer based technologies for other crops but there is no computer vision based advanced technology in identifying grade for the arecanut. There is an increasing demand for computer vision based technology to address the above

K.R. Venugopal and L.M. Patnaik (Eds.): ICIP 2012, CCIS 292, pp. 350–359, 2012.
© Springer-Verlag Berlin Heidelberg 2012

issue for arecanut farmers. The SVM, which is based on the theory of structural risk minimization in statistical learning Vladmir Vapnik [1], has outperformed many traditional learning algorithms. It is now generally recognized as a powerful method for various machine learning problems B Scholkf *et al.*[2], Cortes *et al.*[3], J Shave Taylor *et al.*[4], N Christianini *et al.*[5]. As is well known, the SVM first maps the inputs to a high-dimensional feature space and then finds a large margin hyperplane between the two classes. Computationally, this leads to a quadratic programming (QP) problem. Moreover, the SVM relies only on the dot product in the feature space, which can be computed efficiently with the help of kernel trick. An essential thing of the SVM and other kernel methods is the kernel. In principle, the kernel can be chosen by standard model selection methods such as cross validation. However, recent research has focused on developing more efficient kernel optimization algorithms. A Micchelli *et al.*[6], Argyriou *et al.*[7], F. R Bach *et al.*[8], GRG Lankriet *et al.*[9], I Argyriou *et al.*[10], I. W. Tsang *et al.*[11], S. Sonnenburg *et al.*[12], Y. Lin *et al.*[13]. Proposed a new cross-domain kernel learning framework into which many existing kernel methods can be readily incorporated. The framework, referred to as Domain Transfer Multiple Kernel Learning (DTMKL), simultaneously learns a kernel function and a robust classifier by minimizing both the structural risk functional and the distribution mismatch between the labeled and unlabeled samples from the auxiliary and target domains. Under the DTMKL framework, they also propose two novel methods by using SVM and prelearned classifiers, respectively Lixin Duan *et al.*[14]. Large scale nonlinear support vector machines (SVMs) can be approximated by linear ones using a suitable feature map. This work introduces explicit feature maps for the additive class of kernels, such as the intersection, Hellinger's, and χ^2 kernels. In particular, they: 1) provide explicit feature maps for all additive homogeneous kernels along with closed form expression for all common kernels; 2) derive corresponding approximate finite-dimensional feature maps based on a spectral analysis; and 3) quantify the error of the approximation, showing that the error is independent of the data dimension and decays exponentially fast with the approximation order for selected kernels such as χ^2 Vedaldi *et al.*[15]. In this paper, arecanut categorization is done using SVM which is well founded in terms of computational learning theory and very open to theoretical understanding and analysis.

k-Nearest Neighbor is one of the most popular algorithms for text categorization Manning C. D *et al.*[16]. Joachims T *et al.* [17], Li Baoli *et al.* [18]. D S Guru *et al.* [19] proposed an algorithmic model for automatic classification of floweres using k-NN classifier. The proposed algorithmic model is based on textural features such as Gray level co-occurrence matrix and Gabor responses. The idea behind k-Nearest Neighbour algorithm is quite straightforward. To classify a new document, the system finds the k nearest neighbours among the training documents, and uses the categories of the k nearest neighbours to weight the category candidates Manning C. D *et al.* [16]. One of the drawbacks of k-NN algorithm is its efficiency, as it needs to compare a test document with all samples in the training set. In addition, the performance of this algorithm greatly depends on two factors, that is, a suitable similarity function and an appropriate value for the parameter k. In this paper, we focus on the selection of the parameter k. In the traditional k-NN algorithm, the value of k is fixed beforehand. If k is too large, big classes will overwhelm small ones. On the other hand, if k is too small, the advantage of k-NN algorithm, which could make use of many experts, will not be exhibited. In practice, the value of k is usually optimized by many trials on the training and validation sets. Several works done on classification of fruits, flowers and seeds based on color Domingo Mery et al.[21], Meftah et al.[22].

After reviewing the standard feature vector representation of arecanut, we will identify the color properties of arecanut in the section 3.2. The empirical results in section 3 will support our claim. Compared to state-of-the-art methods, SVMs show substantial performance gains. Moreover, SVMs will prove to be very robust, eliminating the need for expensive parameter tuning. We have considered four types of arecanuts for this work, namely Api, Bette, Minne, and Gorublu. For classification problem, the nuts are grouped into only two classes i.e Api, Bette and Minne belongs to one class called Boiling Nuts (BN) and Gorublu belongs to another class called Non Boiling Nuts (NBN). In our approach arecanuts can be classified based on color component. We have conducted a survey about 15 agricultural fields and have got the following observations:

1. All the Gorublu arecanuts will be in reddish yellow color (Belongs to NBN class).
2. All the Bette, Api and Minne are in green color(belongs to the class BN).
3. Nuts which are in transition state(contains 25% of the green color) from Bette to Gorublu also belong to BN class

2   Proposed Methodology

The proposed method has training and classification phases. In the training phase, from a given set of training images the color features are extracted and used to train the system using SVM classifier. In classification phase a given set test arecanut image is segmented and then the color features are extracted for classification. These features are queried to k-NN classifier to label an unknown arecanut. The block diagram of the proposed method is given in Fig. 1.

2.1   Segmentation

In this work, arecant samples are considered for classification problem. The feature space is selected based on color components of the arecanut. The first step in arecanut classification is to segment the arecanut image. Segmentation subdivides an image into its constituent parts or objects. The level to which this subdivision is carried depends on the problem being solved. That is segmentation should stop when the objects of interest in an application have been isolated. In general, autonomous segmentation is one of the most difficult tasks in image processing. The arecanut is segmented from the image using threshold based segmentation algorithm Gonzales et al.[23]. A given image is converted into HSV

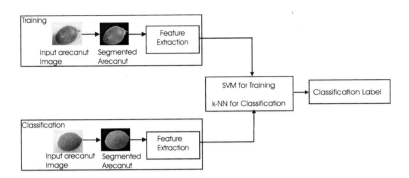

Fig. 1. Block Diagram of the Proposed Method using Multiclassifier

color space and intensity histogram corresponding to each channel is extracted. The histogram intensity values corresponding to two dominant regions belonging to background and arecanut are identified. Based on this intensity values the arecanut is segmented. Fig. 2, shows the results of the arecanut segmentation using threshold based method on a few set of arecanut images. The segmented image is converted into binary image and morphological hole filling algorithm is applied Rafel C. Gonzalez *et al.*[23] in order to fill the possible holes inside the arecanut object. After filling the holes, arecanut object in the image mask will be of same shape and size as in the original image as shown in Fig. 2(c) .Multiply the mask with the original image using equation (1), the arecanut object will be segmented as shown in Fig. 2(d).

$$f_s(x,y) = \sum_{i=1}^{M} \sum_{j=1}^{N} m(i,j) f(x,y) \tag{1}$$

Where *fs, m* and *f* are the segmented image, mask and original images respectively.

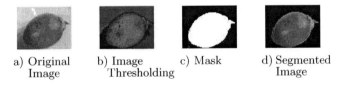

a) Original   b) Image   c) Mask   d) Segmented
   Image   Thresholding   Image

Fig. 2. Sample Experimental Results

Nuts that are turned into yellow color are considered as NBN class. As the nuts mature, green color gets vanished, where as red color gets dominated. The resultant Gorublu nuts color will be turned into reddish yellow. So, average red color component in the Gorublu nuts will be always greater than average green color component. For our problem, Red and Green Color is enough to classify the arecanut.

2.2   Feature Extraction

SVM is used to classify the arecanuts into two classes. Average red color component (μ_R) and green color component (μ_G) is used as feature space for SVM classifier. μ_R and μ_G is determined using the equations (2) & (3).

$$\mu_R = \frac{1}{MXN} \sum_{i=1}^{M} \sum_{j=1}^{N} R(i,j) \tag{2}$$

$$\mu_G = \frac{1}{MXN} \sum_{i=1}^{M} \sum_{j=1}^{N} G(i,j) \tag{3}$$

2.3   Support Vector Machines for Training

We are given l training examples x_i, y_i,i=1 .,l, where each example has 2 inputs ($x_i \epsilon R^2$), and a class label with one of two classes ($y_i \epsilon 1, -1$). Now, all hyperplanes in R^2 are parameterized by a vector (w), and a constant (b), expressed in the equation

$$w.x + b = 0 \tag{4}$$

w is in fact the vector orthogonal to the hyperplane. Given such a hyperplane (w, b) that separates the data, this gives the function

$$f(x) = sign(w.x + b) \tag{5}$$

This correctly classifies the training data. However, a given hyperplane represented by (w, b) is equally expressed by all pairs $\{\lambda w, \lambda b\}$ for $\lambda \epsilon R^+$. So we define the canonical hyperplane to be that which separates the data from the hyperplane by a distance of at least 1. That is, we consider those that satisfy

$$x_i.w + b \geq +1 \quad when \quad y_i = +1 \tag{6}$$

$$x_i.w + b \leq +1 \quad when \quad y_i = -1 \tag{7}$$

or more compactly:

$$(x_i.w + b) \geq 1 \ \forall i \tag{8}$$

All such hyperplanes have a functional distance ≥ 1. For a given hyperplane (w, b), all pairs $\{\lambda w, \lambda b\}$ define the exact same hyperplane, but each has a different functional distance to a given data point to obtain the geometric distance from the hyperplane to a data point. We must normalize by the magnitude of w, this distance is simply:

$$d((w,b), x_i) = \frac{y_i(x_i.w + b)}{||w||} \geq \frac{1}{||w||} \tag{9}$$

Intuitively, we want the hyperplane that maximizes the geometric distance to the closest data points. From the equation we see this is accomplished by minimizing

$\|w\|$ (subjected to the distance constraints). The main method of doing this is with Lagrange multipliers Christopher Jc Burges *et al.*[24], Vladmir Vapnik *el al.*[1]. The problem details are eventually transformed into:

$$Minimize: w(\alpha) = -\sum_{i=1}^{l} \alpha_i + \frac{1}{2}\sum_{j=1}^{l} y_i y_j \alpha_i \alpha_j (x_i.x_j) \qquad (10)$$

$$Subjected\ to: \alpha^T y = 0$$

$0 \leq \alpha \leq C1$ Where α is the vector of l of non-negative Lagrange multipliers to be determined, and C is a constant. We can define the matrix $(H_{ij} = y_i y_j(x_i.x_j))$, and introduce more compact notation:

$$Minimize: w(\alpha) = -\alpha^T + \frac{1}{2}\alpha^T H \alpha \qquad (11)$$

$$Subjected\ to: \alpha^T y = 0 \qquad (12)$$

$$0 \leq \alpha \leq C1 \qquad (13)$$

This minimization problem is what is known as a Quadratic Programming Problem (QP). In addition, from the derivation of these equations, it was seen that the optimal hyperplane can be written as:

$$w = \sum_i \alpha_i y_i x_i \qquad (14)$$

That is, the vector w is just a linear combination of the training examples. Interestingly, it can also be shown that

$$\alpha_i(y_i(w.x_i + b) - 1) = 0 \ (\forall i) \qquad (15)$$

When the functional distance of an example is strictly greater than 1 (when $y_i(w.x_i + b) > 1$), then $\alpha_i = 0$. So only the closest data points contribute to w. these training examples or which $\alpha_i > 0$ are termed support vectors. They are the only ones needed in defining the optimal hyperplane. Assuming we have the optimal α, we must still determine b to fully specify the hyperplane. To do this, take any positive and negative support vector, x^+ and x^-, for which we know

$$(w.x^+ + b) = +1 \qquad (16)$$

$$(w.x^- + b) = -1 \qquad (17)$$

Solving these equations gives us

$$b = -\frac{1}{2}(w.x^+ + w.x^-) \qquad (18)$$

Now, we need for the constraint(eq. 13)

$$\alpha_i \leq (\forall_i) \qquad (19)$$

When $C = \infty$, the optimal hyperplane will be the one that completely separates the data. For finite C, this changes the problem to finding a "soft-margin" classifier, which allows for some of the data to be misclassified. The constant C is a tuneable parameter: higher C corresponds to more importance on classifying all the training data correctly, lower C results in a "more flexible" hyperplane that tries to minimize the margin error for each example. Finite values of C are useful in situations where the data is not easily separable.

2.4   k-NN Classification

What is called supervised learning is the most fundamental task in machine learning. In supervised learning, we have training examples and test examples. A training example is an ordered pair h_x, y_i where x is an instance and y is a label. A test example is an instance x with unknown label. The goal is to predict labels for test examples. k-NN classifiers has two stages; the first is the determination of the nearest neighbors and the second is the determination of the class using those neighbors. Let us assume that we have a training dataset D made up of $(x_i) \in [1, |D|]$ training samples. The examples are described by a set of features F and any numeric features have been normalised to the range [0,1]. Each training example is labelled with a class label $y_j \in Y$. Our objective is to classify an unknown example q. For each $x_i \in D$ we can calculate the distance between q and x_i as follows:

$$d(q, x_i) = \sum_{f \in F} w_f \delta(q_f, x_{if}) \tag{20}$$

There are a large range of possibilities for this distance metric; a basic version for continuous and discrete attributes would be:

$$\delta(q_f, x_{if}) = \begin{cases} 0 & f \text{ discrete and } q_f \doteq x_{if} \\ 1 & \text{discrete and } q_f \neq x_{if} \\ | q_f - x_{if} | & f \text{ continuous} \end{cases} \tag{21}$$

The k nearest neighbors is selected based on this distance metric. Then there are a variety of ways in which the k nearest neighbors can be used to determine the class of q. The most straightforward approach is to assign the majority class among the nearest neighbors to the query. It will often make sense to assign more weight to the nearer neighbors in deciding the class of the query. A fairly general technique to achieve this is distance weighted voting where the neighbors get to vote on the class of the query case with votes weighted by the inverse of their distance to the query.

$$Vote(y_j) = \sum_{c=1}^{k} \frac{1}{d(q, x_c)^n} (y_j, y_c) \tag{22}$$

Thus the vote assigned to class y_j by neighbor x_c is 1 divided by the distance to that neighbor, i.e. $1(y_j, y_c)$ returns 1 if the class labels match and 0 otherwise. The value n would normally be 1 but values greater than 1 can be used to further reduce the influence of more distant neighbors.

3   Results and Discussion

The most common commercial variety of arecanut was considered for this study. The database contains 204 images from 15 different agricultural fields. Images with 3000x4000 pixel resolution were obtained using Canon digital color camera (Power Shot A1100IS). All the Images were taken to approximately fill the camera field of view in natural day light with white background. Images were resized into 150x200 pixel resolution for reasonable computation speed. The proposed method efficiently classifies various arecanuts such as Api, Bette, Minne and Gorublu into two classes BN and NBN as shown in Fig. 3(a). We have used k-fold cross validation-method Pang ning Tan et $al.$[19] for evaluating the performance of the SVM classifier. We have considered the 204 arecanut images for k-fold validation and found 98% success rate, Where k is the 20 in our case i.e., 10 folds of the data.

Table 1. Qualitative analysis of Arecanut Classification

Classifier		Success Rate
Multiple Kernel Classifier		98.06
k	Distance	
3	Euclidean	98.50
	City Block	98.00
5	Euclidean	99.50
	City Block	98.00
7	Euclidean	99.00
	City Block	97.00
9	Euclidean	98.50
	City Block	96.00

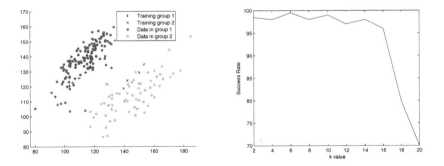

Fig. 3. a) Support Vector based k-NN Classifier b) Plot of Success Rate against Different k Values

The success rate of arecanut against different k values of k-NN is plotted as shown in the Fig. 3(b). The behaviour of the graph indicates that as the k value increases the success rate is remains constant until some optimum value (98%), thereafter success rate reduces as k increase. The k-NN will compare with the highly potential features and reduces number of comparisons with the non potential features. This gives us reduced computational cost and increased performance.

4 Conclusions

In this paper we have used color based classification method. The arecanut is segmented from the image using threshold based segmentation algorithm. In the segmented region, the blue color component is normally suppressed and only red and green components are used to classify the arecanuts. SVM and k-NN classifiers are used in series for training and testing respectively. k-NN suffer from the problem of high variance in the case of limited sampling. Alternatively, one could use support vector machines but they involve time-consuming optimization and computation of pairwise distances. We propose a combination of these two methods which deals with the multiclass problem, which has reasonable computational complexity in testing and gives excellent results in practice. The experimental k-fold cross validation method demonstrated the efficiency of the proposed approach. The proposed method is effective in terms of time complexity because query sample is compared with only support vectors and gives best results for a large training set. This method can be extended to other objects such as classification of fruits, seeds, flowers *etc.* where sorting and quality rating is normally done by experts.

Acknowledgments. Authors would like to thank all the peer reviewers for their valuable comments. The authors also thank Kuvempu University for their support during this work.

References

1. Vapnik, V.: The Nature of Statistical Learning Theory. Springer (1995)
2. Cortes, Vapnik, V.: Support-Vector Networks. Machine Learning, 273–297 (1995)
3. Scholkopf, B., Smola, A.J.: Learning with Kernels. MIT Press, Cambridge (2002)
4. Shawe-Taylor, J., Cristianini, N.: Kernel Methods for Pattern Analysis. Cambridge University Press (2004)
5. Cristianini, N., Shawe-Taylor, J.: An Introduction to Support Vector Machines. Cambridge University Press, Cambridge (2000)
6. Micchelli, A., Pontil, M.: Learning the Kernel Function *via* Regularization. Journal of Machine Learning Research 6, 1099–1125 (2005)
7. Argyriou, Hauser, R., Micchelli, C.A., Pontil, M.: A DC Algorithm for Kernel Selection. In: Proceedings of 23rd International Conference on Machine Learning, Pittsburgh, pp. 41–49 (2006)

8. Bach, F.R., Lanckriet, G.R.G., Jordan, M.I.: Multiple Kernel Learning, Conic Duality and the SMO Algorithm. In: Proceedings of 21st International Conference on Machine Learning, pp. 6–14 (2004)

9. Lanckriet, G.R.G., Cristianini, N., Bartlett, P.L., El Ghaoui, L., Jordan, M.I.: Learning the Kernel Matrix with Semi Definite Programming. Journal on Machine Learning Research 5, 27–72 (2004)

10. Argyriou, A., Micchelli, C.A., Pontil, M.: Learning Convex Combinations of Continuously Parameterized Basic Kernels. In: Auer, P., Meir, R. (eds.) COLT 2005. LNCS (LNAI), vol. 3559, pp. 338–352. Springer, Heidelberg (2005)

11. Tsang, I.W., Kwok, J.T.: Efficient Hyperkernel Learning using Second-Order Cone Programming. IEEE Transaction on Neural Networks 17, 48–58 (2006)

12. Sonnenburg, S., Ratsch, G., Schafer, C., Schalkopf, B.: Journal on Machine Learning Research, PPH 7, 1531–1565 (2006)

13. Lin, Y., Zhang, H.H.: Component Selection and Smoothing in Smoothing Spline Analysis of Variance Models, Technical Report, University of Wisconsin-Madison and North Carolina State University (2003)

14. Duan, L., Tsang, I.W., Xu, D.: Domain Transfer Multiple Kernel Learning. IEEE Transaction on PAMI 34(3), 465–479 (2012)

15. Vedaldi, A., Zisserman, A.: Efficient Additive Kernels via Explicit Feature Maps. IEEE Transaction on PAMI 34(3), 480–492 (2012)

16. Manning, C.D., Schutze, H.: Foundations of Statistical Natural Language Processing. MIT Press (1999)

17. Joachims, T.: Text Categorization with Support Vector Machines: Learning with Many Relevant Features. In: Proceedings of the European Conference on Machine Learning (1998)

18. Li, B., Chen, Y., Yu, S.: A Comparative Study on Automatic Categorization Methods for Chinese Search Engine. In: Proceedings of the Eighth Joint International Computer Conference, pp. 117–120. Zhejiang University Press, Hangzhou (2002)

19. Guru, D.S., Sharath, Y.H., Manjunath, S.: Texture Features and k-NN in Classification of Flower Images. IJCA on Recent Trends in Image Processing and Pattern Recognition (2010)

20. Mery, D., Pedreschi, F.: Segmentation of Colorful Images using a Robust Algorithm. Journal of Food Engineering 66, 353–360 (2005)

21. Alfatni, M.S.M., Shariff, A.R.M., Shafri, H.Z.M., Saaed, O.M.B., Eshanta, O.M.: Oil Palm Fruit Bunch Grading System Using Red, Green and Blue Digital Number. Journal of Applied Sciences 8(8), 1444–1452 (1999)

22. Tan, P.-N., Steinbach, M., Kumar, V.: Introduction to Data Mining. Pearson Education (2009)

23. Gonzalez, R.C., Woods, R.E.: Digital Image Processing. PPH (2008)

24. Burges, C.J.C.: Data Mining and Knowledge Discovery. A Tutorial on Support Vector Machines for Pattern Recognition, 121–167 (1998)

Real Time Human Gender Detection
Based on Facial Features
and Connected Component Analysis

R.S. Vaddi[1], L.N.P. Boggavarapu[1], H.D. Vankayalapati[2], and K.R. Anne[1]

[1] Department of Information Technology,
V R Siddhartha Engineering College, Vijayawada, India
syam.radhe@gmail.com
[2] Department of Computer Science & Engineering,
V R Siddhartha Engineering College, Vijayawada, India

Abstract. Automatic gender detection through facial features has become a critical component in the new domain of computer human observation and Computer Human Interaction (HCI). Automatic gender detection has numerous applications in the area of recommender systems, focused advertising, security and surveillance. Detection of gender by using the facial features is done by many methods such as Gabor wavelets, artificial neural networks and support vector machine. In this work, we have used the facial global feature distance measure as a precursor. The concept of "connected-components" is used to extract the required features. It is implemented in Matlab to predict the gender.

Keywords: Connected-Components, Computer Human Interaction, SVM Classifier.

1 Introduction

In the recent years biometric recognition systems (e.g., face, hand geometry, odor, gait, iris, fingerprints and palm) have taken on a new importance to provide authentication in financial and computer vision applications. Among all the biometric identification methods, researchers put utmost attention on a non intrusive and user friendly way of recognizing face and hence gender of a human being. Gender detection has numerous applications in the fields of surveillance, medical, criminal identification, human identification, smart human computer interface, and passive demographic data collection etc. It is known from literature studies that most of the gender detection techniques are based on face only because the face of a human being contains useful information and used as a clue for recognizing the facial expressions. The present paper illustrates a system which uses image processing methods to automatically detect faces, tracks them across time and finally classifies the particular face as either male or female based on a robust learning technique called kernel functions or Support Vector

K.R. Venugopal and L.M. Patnaik (Eds.): ICIP 2012, CCIS 292, pp. 360–370, 2012.
© Springer-Verlag Berlin Heidelberg 2012

Machine. Further the results of the proposed system and performance are evaluated using receiver operating character curves ROC. This paper is organized as follows: Related work is explained as state or art in Section 1 and Proposed method is described in Section 3 which comprises a series of steps like preprocessing, connected component analysis, facial feature extraction and finally classification using SVM classifier, experimental results are shown in Section 4, these results are analyzed in Section 5. Finally conclusion is given in Section 5.

1.1 Related Work

Moghaddam and Yang [1] developed the first automatic system for both face detection and gender classification. They used maximum-likelihood estimation for face detection and for facial feature detection. For gender classification, they used several different classifiers. The experiments were carried out with a set of FERET images. The most interesting findings in the context of this paper were that the Support Vector Machine (SVM) performed better than the other classifiers and resolution of the face did not affect the classification rate with the SVM. Erno Makinen and Roope Raisamo [2] carried out an experimental evaluation on gender classification. The study includes the comparison of four fundamentally different gender classification methods and four automatic alignment methods together with non-aligned faces and manually aligned faces. They also analyzed how the classification accuracy was affected when face image resizing occurred before or after alignment. Finally, they conducted a sensitivity analysis for the classifiers by varying rotation, scale, and translation of the face images. Shakhnarovich et al. [3] combined the cascaded face detector by Viola and Jones with discrete Adaboost-based gender and ethnicity classification. The advantage of the system is that many preprocessing and calculations can be shared by the face detector and the gender classifier. Hui-Ching Lain and Buo -Liang Lu [4] have proposed a Multi-view gender classification by focusing on shape and texture data for representing facial images. In this, the face area is divided into small regions from which local binary pattern (LBP) histograms are used. Roytatsu Iga et al., [5] proposed an algorithm to classify gender and age using SVM classifier considering the features like geometric arrangement and luminosity of facial images. The graphical matching method is used with GWT method in order to detect the position of the face. For gender classification the following GWT features are considered geometric arrangement of color, hair and mustache and for age classification texture spots, wrinkles and flabs of skin are considered. Baback Moghaddam and Ming-Hsua [6] proposed an appearance based method to identify gender through facial images using SVM nonlinear classifier and compared their results with traditional classifiers and modern techniques such as Radial Basis Function (RBF) networks and large ensemble-RBF classifiers, the differentiation in classification of performance with low-resolution and their corresponding her resolution images is very less. Zehangs Sun et al.,

[7] presented his work on gender classification from frontal faces of images using genetic feature subset selection. Principal Component Analysis (PCA) is also used to represent each image as a feature vector of low-dimensional space. Genetic algorithm selects a subset of features from the low-dimensional representation without taking into an account of certain Eigen values that do not seem to encode important gender detection information. Baluja and Rowley [8] presented an Adaboost system for gender classification with manually aligned faces. They carried out a thorough experimental comparison between the Adaboost and an SVM classifier by varying face image scaling, translation, and rotation. Similar comparative analysis was conducted. Yang et al. [9] reported a detailed analysis of how different normalizations affect gender classification accuracy. They had three different methods for alignment and three gender classifiers: an SVM, an FLD, and a two-layer Real Adaboost classifier. They used Chinese face images in the experiments. The most interesting fact from the viewpoint of this paper was their claim that shape-free alignment may produce better classification results with methods that use local features such as haar-like features, while shape preserving alignment methods may produce better results with global features.

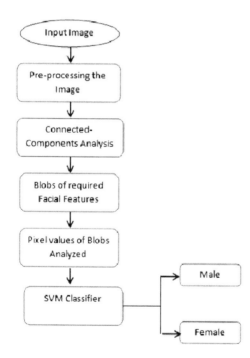

Fig. 1. Flowchart for Gender Detection

1.2   Pre-processing the Image

The pre-processing of a face image will undergo several processes in order to acquire a transformed face image which in turn increases the quality of the face image by holding prominent features of the visual quality. Noise reduction, color conversion and edge detection are some pre-processing techniques. Edge Detection is mainly aimed at the detection and extraction of features in any digital image. The detection is done at the places at which the image brightness changes sharply and formally has discontinuities. The main intension of detecting sharp edges of images is to capture and observe important events which can change entire situation of that particular incident. In an ideal case of an image, the resultant of applying edge detector may lead to the formation of set of connected curves that corresponds to variations in surface orientation. Therefore, implementing edge detection algorithm on any image may significantly reduce the quantity of data to be processed and also removes the undesirable data. Edges are extracted from 2-dimensional image of a 3-dimensional scene can be categorized as either viewpoint dependent or viewpoint independent. A viewpoint dependent edge changes with the viewpoint and reflects the geometry of the scene or image, such as objects occluding one another. A viewpoint independent reflects inherent properties of 3-dimensional objects, which includes surface makings and surface shape. Many edge detection techniques came into existence. A survey was held by Ziou and Tabbone in 1998 to know actually how number of edge detection techniques came into existence. The development of the edge detection algorithm is done based on the following factors: Good detection - the algorithm should point or mark as many as real images that are possible. Minimal response - Edge should mark only once and also in possible way of an image the noise of the image should not create false edge. Good localization - the marked edges must be always nearer to the real in any image. The Sobel edge detector is used in image processing; the resultant of this operator depends on either corresponding gradient vector or the norm of this vector. This mainly depends on the convolving the image with a small, separable and integer valued filter in horizontal and vertical direction of an image. It gives better approximations of the existing derivatives. The kernels can be applied separately to the input image to produce separate measurements of the gradient component in each orientation (call these Gx and Gy) [10].

$$G_x = \begin{pmatrix} -1 & -2 & -1 \\ 0 & 0 & 0 \\ 1 & 2 & 1 \end{pmatrix}; G_y = \begin{pmatrix} -1 & 0 & 1 \\ -2 & 0 & 2 \\ -1 & 0 & 1 \end{pmatrix}; G_x = \begin{pmatrix} -1 & 0 & 1 \\ -1 & 0 & 1 \\ -1 & 0 & 1 \end{pmatrix}; G_y = \begin{pmatrix} 1 & 1 & 1 \\ 0 & 0 & 0 \\ -1 & -1 & -1 \end{pmatrix};$$

Prewitt Edge Detector is similar to the Sobel edge detector but with different coefficients and is also used for detecting vertical and horizontal edges in images.

1.3   Connected Component Analysis

Connected components algorithm finds regions of connected pixels which have the same value. Before applying algorithm let us look in to some Basic notations: A pixel p at a coordinate (x, y) has four direct neighbors, N4(p) and four diagonal neighbors, ND(P). Eight neighbors, N8(p) of pixel p consists of the union of N4(p) and ND(P). To establish connectivity between pixels of 1s in a binary image, three type of connectivity for pixels p and q can be considered. They are i) 4-connectivity - connected if q is in N4(P); ii) 8-connectivity - connected if q is in N8(p); iii) m-connectivity- connected if q is in N4(P), or if q is in ND(P) and N4(p) N4(q) and N4(p) U N4(q)=0 A Connected Component Labeling Algorithm: The labeling algorithm is described below based on 8-connectivity. Step 1: Initial labeling. Scan the image pixel by pixel from left to right and top to bottom. Let p denote the current pixel in the scanning process and 4-nbr denote four neighbor pixels in N, NW, NE and W direction of p. If p is 0, move on to the next scanning position. If p is 1 and all values in 4-nbrs are 0, assign a new label to p. If only one value in 4-nbrs is not 0, assign its values to p. If two or more values in 4-nbrs are not 0, assign one of the labels to p and mark labels in 4-nbrs as equivalent. Step 2:.The equivalence relations are expressed as a binary matrix. For example, if label 1 is equivalent to 2, label 3 is equivalent to 4, label 4 is equivalent to 5, and label 1 is equivalent to 6 then the matrix L is that shown in Figure 2 a). Equivalence relations satisfy reflexivity, symmetry and transitive. To add reflexivity in matrix L, all main diagonals are set to 1. Transitive closure can be obtained by using Floyd-Warshall (F-W) algorithm. After applying reflexivity and the F-W algorithm, the matrix L is that shown in 2 b). After calculating the transitive closure, each label value is recalculated to resolve equivalences. The image is scanned again and each label is replaced by the label assigned to its equivalence class.

	1	2	3	4	5	6			1	2	3	4	5	6
1		1				1		1	1	1				1
2	1							2	1	1				1
3				1				3			1	1	1	
4			1		1			4			1	1	1	
5				1				5			1	1	1	
6	1							6	1	1				1

Fig. 2. a) Matrix before Applying the F-W Algorithm b) Matrix after Applying Reflexivity and the F-W Algorithm

1.4   Blobs of Facial Features

To decide gender of individual mainly 4 types of ratios plays key role [11] these ratios further depends on parameters like Inter-Ocular distance, Eye to Nose, Lips to Nose and Lips to Eyes. (i) Inter-Ocular distance: The distance between the midpoints of right eye-ball to the left eye-ball. (ii) Eye to Nose: The distance between the midpoint of joining of two eyes pixel of the image and nose tip in the image. (iii) Lips to Nose: The distance between nose tips to the midpoint of lips pixel in the image. (iv) Lips to Eyes: The distance between midpoints of the lips pixel to the line joining of two eyes pixel in an image Ratio1 = Lf eye to Rt eye distance/Eye to Nose distance Ratio2 = Lf eye to Rt eye distance/Eye to Lip distance Ratio3 = Eye to Nose distance/Eye to Chin distance Ratio4 = Eye to Nose distance/Eye to Lip distance.

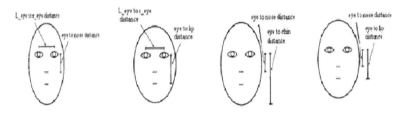

Fig. 3. Facial Features

1.5   Pixel Value of Blob Analysis

Basing on facial features extracted blob analysis can be done blob analysis is the identification and study of blobs (region of connected pixels) The algorithms of this kind fall in to two categories one basing on the foreground (typically pixels with a non-zero value) another is with background (pixels with a zero value). In typical applications that use blob analysis, the blob features usually calculated are area and perimeter, Feret diameter, blob shape, and location. The versatility of blob analysis tools makes them suitable for a wide variety of applications such as pick-and-place, pharmaceutical etc. Blob analysis consists of a series of processing operations and analysis functions that produce information about any 2D shape in an image. Use blob analysis when you are interested in finding blobs whose spatial characteristics satisfy certain criteria. In many applications where computation is time-consuming, you can use blob analysis to eliminate blobs that are of no interest based on their spatial characteristics, and keep only the relevant blobs for further analysis. Blob analysis is a well-known technique to isolate objects and features of an arbitrary kind, analyze their shape or position, and classify them. It combines image binarization and connected component analysis for segmentation.

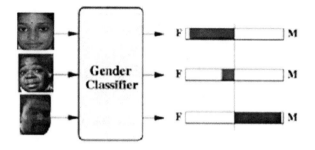

Fig. 4. Gender Classifier

1.6 Support Vector Machine

Support Vector Machines are based on the concept of decision planes that define decision boundaries. A decision plane is one that separates between a set of objects having different class memberships. Support Vector Machines, as in, are based on the concept of decision planes that define decision boundaries. A decision plane is one that separates between a set of objects having different class memberships. A Support Vector Machine (SVM) constructs a hyper plane or asset of hyper planes in a high or infinite dimensional space. Intuitively, a good separation is achieved by the hyper plane that has the largest distance to the nearest training data points of any class. The classification is done based on the particular constraint and the resultant satisfies the constraint after pre-processing of taken image for facial recognition them the classification is done; i.e., if the results are above the constraint then the can be recognized as female or male depending on the constraint we consider as shown in Figure 2.

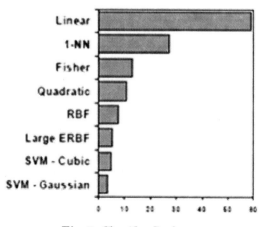

Fig. 5. Classifier Performance

1.7   Experimental Outcomes

Fig. 6. Input Image, Binary Image, Connected Components Image, Blobs Components, Required Parameters

Fig. 7. Input Image, Binary Image, Connected Components Image, Blobs Components, Required Parameters

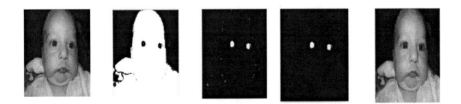

Fig. 8. Input Image, Binary Image, Connected Components Image, Blobs Components, Required Parameters

Fig. 9. Input Image, Binary Image, Connected Components Image, Blobs components, Required Parameters

1.8   Result Analysis

The Receiver Operating Characteristic (ROC) graphs are useful for analyzing the classifier performance. The ROC curve is a plot of the True Positive Fraction (TPF) versus the False Positive Fraction (FPF). It compares the two operating characteristics (TPF, FPF). So ROC is also called as Relative Operating Characteristic curve. These TPF and FPF are calculated by using True Positive (TP), True Negative (TN), False Positive (FP) and False Negative (FN) as shown in

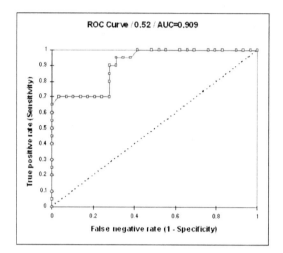

Fig. 10. ROC Curve

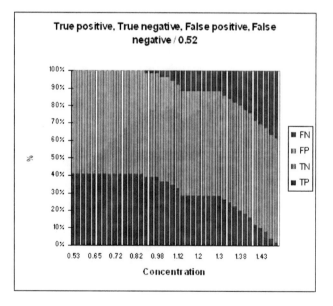

Fig. 11. Graph Showing Areas for FN, FP, TN and TP

Equations (i) and ,(ii). Sensitivity is the true positive fraction, expressed as a percentage. Specificity is the true negative fraction, expressed as a percentage. In Fig. 15 is the example roc curve, Shadow area (ROC space) gives the better classification.

$$TPF=TP/(TP+FN) \qquad (i)$$

$$FPF=FP/(FP+TN) \qquad (ii)$$

1.9 Conclusions

Detecting gender through a machine is a good achievement in a modern era of computer world. A new approach for gender detection is proposed in this paper. This application is really working in many other fields. The face images are preprocessed and edges correctly detected by applying gradient method the features of face are used for matching and finally the gender is classified using svm classifier. The future work should focus on gender detection by considering different races, face angles and illumination variations. The entire work is done using mat lab and results are analyzed with roc curve analysis.

Acknowledgement. This work was supported by TIFAC - CORE (Technology Information Forecasting and Assessment Council Center of Relevance and Excellence) in the area of Telematics, a joint venture of DST (Department of Science and Technology), Govt. of India, V.R. Siddhartha Engineering College, Vijayawada, India.

References

1. Yang, M.-H., Moghaddam, B.: Support Vector Machines for Visual Gender Classification. In: Fifteenth International Conference on Pattern Recognition, pp. 5115–5118 (2000)
2. Makinen, E., Raisamo, R.: Evaluation of Gender Classification Methods with Automatically Detected and Aligned Faces. IEEE Transactions on Pattern Analysis and Machine Intelligence 30(3) (March 2008)
3. Vijaya Kumari, G., Mallikarjuna Rao, G., Babu, G.R., Krishna Chaitanya, N.: Methodological Approach for Machine based Expression and Gender Classification. In: IEEE Internationl Advance Computing Conference, pp. 1369–1374 (March 2009)
4. Lain, H.-C., Lu, B.-L.: Age Estimation using a Min-max Modular Support Vector Machine. In: Twelfth International Conference on Neural Information Processing, pp. 83–99 (2005)
5. Hayashi, H., Fukano, G., Iga, R., Izumi, K., Ohtani, T.: Gender and Age Estimation from Face Images. In: International Conference on the Society of Instrument and Control Engineering, pp. 756–761 (2003)
6. Moghaddam, B.: Mitsubishi Electric Research Laboratories. Gender Classification with Support Vector Machines. In: 4th IEEE International Conference on Face and Gesture Recognition (2000)

7. Boggavarapu, L.N.P., Vaddi, R.S., Vankayalapati, H.D., Anne, K.R.: Edge Detection Using CNN for the Localization of Non-standard License Plate. In: Burduk, R., Kurzyński, M., Woźniak, M., Żolnierek, A. (eds.) Computer Recognition Systems 4. AISC, vol. 95, pp. 685–695. Springer, Heidelberg (2011)
8. Baluja, S., Rowley, H.A.: Boosting Sex Identification Performance. International Journal of Computer Vision 71, 111–119 (2007)
9. Ramesha, K., et al.: Feature Extraction Based Face Recognition, Gender and Age Classification. International Journal on Computer Science of Engineering 2(01), 14–23 (2010)
10. Vaddi, R.S., Vankayalapati, H.D., Boggavarapu, L.N.P., Anne, K.R.: Extraction of Facial Features for the Real-time Human Gender Classification. In: International Conference on Emerging Trends in Electrical and Computer Technology, ICETECT (March 2011)
11. Wu, J., Smith, W.A.P., Hancock, E.R.: Facial Gender Classification Using Shape from Shading and Weighted Principal Geodesic Analysis. In: Campilho, A., Kamel, M.S. (eds.) ICIAR 2008. LNCS, vol. 5112, pp. 925–934. Springer, Heidelberg (2008)

Classification of Categorical Data
Using Hybrid Similarity Measures

Seetha Hari and Srividya V.V.R.

School of Computing Science and Engineering,
VIT University, Vellore-632014, India
hariseetha@gmail.com

Abstract. In conventional classification methods a single similarity measure is applied across all the attributes of a categorical data. But different attributes of a categorical data can have different nature and using a single similarity measure across all the attributes may not always show a better classification performance. So in the present paper classification is performed using different similarity measures for different set of attributes called as hybrid similarity measure. Experimental results using benchmark datasets showed that classification using the hybrid similarity measures showed good classification performance.

Keywords: Categorical Data, Classification, Hybrid Similarity Measure, K-Nearest Neighbor.

1 Introduction

The study of similarity measure plays an important role in the past few decades in the field of data mining, pattern recognition, machine learning, information retrieval and artificial intelligence. Measuring similarity for two data sets is based on several feature variables. Depending on the measurement scale of the feature variable, similarity can be determined. Since measuring similarity for a categorical data is a challenging work there exist only few measures for finding similarity between categorical data. Overlap measure was one of the simplest similarity measure which is defined as $d(x_i, y_i) = 1$ if $x_i = y_i$ else $d(x_i, y_i) = 0$ [1].The number of attributes that match in the two data instances are counted. Stanfill and Waltz [1] used Value Difference Metric (VDM) to measure the distance between two categorical values with respect to class column (supervised learning). It is defined as:

$$d(x_i, y_i) = w(x_i) \sum_{c \in C} (p(c|x_i) - p(c|y_i))^2.$$ (1)

Where C is the set of all classes labels, $p(c|x_i)$ is the conditional probability of class c given x, and

$$w(x_i) = \sqrt{\sum_{c \in C} p(c|x_i)^2}$$

K.R. Venugopal and L.M. Patnaik (Eds.): ICIP 2012, CCIS 292, pp. 371–377, 2012.
© Springer-Verlag Berlin Heidelberg 2012

which attempts to give higher weight to an attribute value that is useful in class discrimination. Cost and Salzberg [2] modified it and proposed Modified Value Distance Metric(MVDM) . Esposito *et al.*,[3,4]modified traditional hamming distance. By using this distance measure various similarity measures e.g., overlap measure, Jaccard(S-coefficient) similarity measure, Sokal-Michener (M-coefficient) similarity measure, Grower-Legendre similarity measure, etc., were suggested to get the similarity or dissimilarity coefficient between two categorical data objects. Goodall proposed another statistical approach, in which less frequent attributes have greater contribution to overall similarity than frequent attribute values [5,6].The Goodall1 measure is the same as Goodall's measure on a per-attribute basis. However, instead of combining the similarities by taking into account dependencies between attributes, the Goodall1 measure takes the average of the per attribute similarities. Boriah *et al.*, [6] proposed Goodall3 and Goodall4 which are the other variants of Goodall's measure. Hirano *et al.*, [7] adopted the hamming distance that counts the number of attributes for which two objects have different attribute values, in order to measure similarity for categorical attributes,

$$d_H\left(x_i, x_j\right) = \frac{1}{p_H} \sum_{k=1}^{p_d} \delta\left(x_i^k, x_j^k\right).$$ (2)

$$\delta\left(x_i^k, x_j^k\right) = \begin{cases} 1 & \text{if } \left(x_i^k = x_j^k\right) \\ 0 & \text{otherwise} \end{cases}$$

If objects have both numerical and categorical attributes, their similarity is calculated as weighted sum of the Mahalanobis distance $d_M\left(x_i, x_j\right)$ of numerical attributes and hamming distance $d_H\left(x_i, x_j\right)$ of nominal attributes as follows:

$$d\left(x_i, x_j\right) = \frac{p_c}{p} d_M\left(x_i, x_j\right) + \frac{p_d}{p} d_H\left(x_i, x_j\right).$$ (3)

2   Similarity Measures Used

Boriah *et al.*,[6] have applied various similarity measures for categorical data for outlier detection. Some of these similarity measures have been used in this paper as shown in Fig.1. The overlap measure simply counts the number of attributes that match in the two instances. The range of per-attribute similarity for overlap measure is [0,1]. This measure fills the diagonal elements only. Eskin measure gives more weight to mismatches that occur on attributes that have many values. This measure fills the off diagonal elements only. The Inverse Occurrence Frequency(IOF) measure assigns lower similarity to mismatches on more frequent values. This measure fills off-diagonal entries only [6]. The Occurrence Frequency(OF) measure gives the opposite weighting of the IOF measure for mismatches, i.e., mismatches on less frequent values are assigned lower similarity and mismatches on more frequent values are assigned higher similarity.

S.No	Measure	Formulas $S_k\,(X_k,Y_k)$	Weight $w_k, k=1\ldots d$
1	Overlap	$\begin{cases} 1 & \text{if } X_k = Y_k \\ 0 & \text{otherwise} \end{cases}$	$\frac{1}{d}$
2	Eskin	$\begin{cases} 1 & \text{if } X_k = Y_k \\ \frac{n_k^2}{n_k^2+2} & \text{otherwise} \end{cases}$	$\frac{1}{d}$
3	IOF	$\begin{cases} 1 & \text{if } X_k = Y_k \\ \frac{1}{1+\log f_k(X_k)\ast\log f_k(Y_k)} & \text{otherwise} \end{cases}$	$\frac{1}{d}$
4	OF	$\begin{cases} 1 & \text{if } X_k = Y_k \\ \frac{1}{1+\log\frac{N}{f_k(X_k)}\ast\log\frac{N}{f_k(Y_k)}} & \text{otherwise} \end{cases}$	$\frac{1}{d}$
5	Goodall3	$\begin{cases} 1 - p_k^2\,(X_k) & \text{if } X_k = Y_k \\ 0 & \text{otherwise} \end{cases}$	$\frac{1}{d}$
6	Goodall4	$\begin{cases} p_k^2\,(X_k) & \text{if } X_k = Y_k \\ 0 & \text{otherwise} \end{cases}$	$\frac{1}{d}$

Fig. 1. Similarity Measures for Categorical Attributes

This measure fills off-diagonal entries only.Goodall3 measure assigns higher similarity if the matching values are infrequent regardless of the frequencies of the other values. This measure fills the diagonal entries only.Goodall4 measure assigns similarity 1-Goodall3 for matches. This measure fills diagonal entries only [6].

Fig. 1 provides the similarity measures that were discussed above with formulas. In this table N is the number of instances, d is the number of attributes, n_k is the number of values taken by each attribute $f_k\,(x)$ is the number of time attributes A_k takes the value x in the data set D. $\widehat{p}_k$ is the sample probability of attribute A_k to take the value x in the data set D. The sample probability is given by

$$\widehat{p}_k = \frac{f_k\,(x)}{N}. \tag{4}$$

$p_k^2\,(x)$ is another probability estimate of attribute A_k to take the value x in a given data set, given by

$$p_k^2\,(x) = \frac{f_k\,(x)\,(f_k\,(x) - 1)}{N\,(N - 1)}. \tag{5}$$

3 Experiments

The experiments are conducted on benchmark datasets collected from UCI ML repository [8] in the following way:

Scheme 1: Classification using single similarity measure across all the attributes.

Scheme 2: Classification using hybrid similarity measure i.e. different similarity measures for different set of attributes.

The properties of the datasets i.e., the the number of attributes,number of patterns and the number of classes in each dataset used in this paper are shown in Table 1 below the dataset name. For each dataset the training set is chosen to be independent of testing set. Two -thirds of the data of each class is used for training and the rest of the data of each class is included in the testing set.

Experimental Results for Scheme 1. The classification using kNN (k Nearest neighborhood) classifier is performed using single similarity measure on Balloons, Hayes Roth, Car Evaluation, Monk, Vote and Nursery datasets. The classification performance obtained on these datasets is shown in Table 1. From

Table 1. CA% vs K Using Single Similarity Measures for Categorical Data

Dataset	Overlap		Eskin		IOF		OF		Goodall3		Goodall4	
	Max	Min	Max	Min	Max	Min	Max	Min	Max	Min	Max	Min
Balloons	86	57	86	57	100	86	86	57	100	86	71	57
(4,20,2)	k=3,5	k=10	k=3,5	k=10	k=10	k=3,5	k=3,5	k=10	k=5,10	k=3	k=3	k=5,10
Monk	83	56	93	56	95	76	90	56	88	56	78	49
(6,160,2)	k=5	k=50	k=5	k=50	k=10	k=50	k=5	k=50	k=3,5,10	k=50	k=10	k=50
Hayes Roth	75	66	77	72	81	68	77	55	85	60	74	58
(6,160,3)	k=3	k=50	k=3	k=30,50	k=50	k=10	k=30	k=10	k=20	k=30	k=20	k=10
Vote	92	88	92	89	90	87	93	88	93	88	93	88
(16,300,2)	k=5	k=50	k=5	k=30,50	k=5	k=30	k=5	k=30,50	k=5	k=20,30	k=3	k=30,50
Car Evaluation	64	60	64	60	64	59	64	60	64	60	67	60
(6,1728,4)	k=3	k=5,10 & 20,30,50	k=3,5	k=10,20& 30,50	k=3	k=5	k=3	k=5,10& 20,30,50	k=3	k=5,10& 20,30,50	k=20	k=5,10,30
Nursery	90	86	94	85	88	84	99	93	97	93	88	85
(8,6000,5)	k=10	k=5	k=3	k=50	k=3	k=50	k=3	k=5,10	k=3	k=5,10,50	k=5	k=3

Table 1 it can be observed that for Balloons data the similarity measures IOF and Goodall3 works excellent with the accuracy of 100% . For Monk dataset IOF has shown superior performance with k=10. For Hayes Roth maximium classification accuracy was obtained using Goodall3 with k=20. In Vote dataset similarity measures of OF, Goodall3 and Goodall4 showed better performance. In Car evaluation dataset Goodall4 performed with 67% accuracy with k=20. The similarity measure OF outperformed other similarity measures in case of Nursery dataset with k=3.

3.1   Experimental Results for Scheme 2

Hybrid 1: In this case we applied a single similarity measure for a set of two different attributes. Thus we combined three different similarity measures for Monk and Car Evaluation dataset. From Table 2, it can be noticed that in Monk data set best performance is given by two combinations. Those combinations are 1.IOF, OF, Overlap and 2.IOF, OF, Goodall3. Poor performance is given by Goodall4, Overlap and Eskin. In Car Evaluation data set best performance is given by four combinations as shown in Table 2. Those combinations are 1.Goodall4, Overlap, IOF 2.Eskin, IOF, Overlap 3.Eskin, IOF, OF and 4.Eskin, IOF, Goodall3.Poor performance was given by OF,Goodall3,IOF combination.

Table 2. CA% vs K Using Hybrid1 Similarity Measures

Dataset	Combinations	k=3	k=5	k=10	k=20	k=30	k=50	Max	Min
	IOF,OF,Overlap	95	93	90	83	90	80	95	80
Monk	IOF,OF,Goodall3	95	93	93	88	88	78	95	78
	Goodall4,Overlap,Eskin	66	59	49	66	59	37	66	37
	Eskin,IOF,Overlap	64	70	70	60	61	61	70	60
Car Evaluation	Eskin,IOF,OF	64	70	70	60	61	61	70	60
	Eskin,IOF,Goodall3	64	70	70	60	61	61	70	60
	Goodall4,Overlap,IOF	64	64	70	60	64	67	70	60
	OF,Goodall3,IOF	64	55	59	60	64	60	64	55

Table 3. CA% vs k using Hybrid2 similarity measures

Dataset	Combinations	k=3	k=5	k=10	k=20	k=30	k=50	Max	Min
	Overlap,Eskin,IOF,Goodall3	100	100	43	-	-	-	100	43
	Eskin,IOF,Goodall3,Overlap	100	100	43	-	-	-	100	43
Baloons	IOF,Goodall3,Overlap,Eskin	71	43	43	-	-	-	71	43
	Goodall3,Overlap,Eskin,OF	71	43	43	-	-	-	71	43
	OF,Goodall4,Overlap,Eskin	100	100	43	-	-	-	100	43
	Overlap,Eskin,IOF,Goodall4	100	100	43	-	-	-	100	43
	Goodall3,Overlap,Eskin,OF	75	75	63	-	-	-	75	63
	IOF,Goodall3,Overlap,Eskin	88	88	63	-	-	-	88	63
	Overlap,Eskin,OF,Goodall4	88	88	63	-	-	-	88	63
Lenses	OF,Goodall4,Overlap,Eskin	75	75	63	-	-	-	75	63
	Goodall4,Overlap,Eskin,OF	75	75	63	-	-	-	75	63
	Overlap,Eskin,IOF,Goodall4	88	88	63	-	-	-	88	63
	IOF,Goodall4,Overlap,Eskin	75	75	63	-	-	-	75	63
	Overlap,Eskin,OF,Goodall4	62	66	70	68	74	68	74	62
Hayes Roth	OF,Goodall4,Overlap,Eskin	62	62	66	68	57	62	68	57
	Goodall4,Overlap,Eskin,OF	85	79	81	79	64	81	85	64
	Goodall4,Overlap,Eskin,IOF	83	74	81	75	70	81	83	70
	Overlap,Eskin,OF,Goodall4	93	93	92	92	92	91	93	91
	Eskin,OF,Goodall4,Overlap	89	89	88	88	85	84	89	84
Vote	OF,Goodall4,Overlap,Eskin	92	93	91	93	90	91	93	90
	Eskin,IOF,Goodall4,Overlap	89	86	86	84	85	84	89	84
	Goodall4,Overlap,Eskin,IOF	85	84	87	88	84	83	88	83
	OF,Goodall3,Overlap,Eskin	90	95	78	99	94	94	99	78
Nursery	Overlap,Eskin,OF,Goodall4	83	97	92	99	87	75	99	75
	OF,Goodall4,Overlap,Eskin	95	98	95	99	96	96	99	95
	Eskin,OF,Goodall4,Overlap	86	88	86	89	84	85	89	84

Hybrid 2: By applying a different similarity measure for each of the attribute we performed classification using kNN on Balloons, Lenses, Hayes Roth, Vote and Nursery datasets and the classification accuracies obtained are shown in Table 3. Table 3 depicts that for Balloons dataset best performance is given by four combinations. Those combinations are 1.Overlap, Eskin, IOF, Goodall3

2.Eskin, IOF, Goodall3, Overlap 3.OF, Goodall4, Overlap, Eskin and 4.Overlap, Eskin, IOF, Goodall4. Poor performance is given by the combinations of 1.Goodall3, Overlap, Eskin, OF and 2.IOF, Goodall3, Overlap, Eskin. In lenses data set best performance is given by three combinations namely, 1.Overlap, Eskin, IOF, Goodall4 2.Overlap, Eskin, OF, Goodall4 and 3.IOF, Goodall3, Overlap, Eskin. Poor performance is given by four combinations. Those combinations are 1.Goodall3, Overlap, Eskin, OF 2.OF, Goodall4, Overlap, Eskin 3.Goodall4, Overlap, Eskin, OF and 4.IOF, Goodall4, Overlap, Eskin. Best performance for Hayes Roth data set is given by 1.Goodall4, Overlap, Eskin, OF and 2.Goodall4, Overlap, Eskin, IOF. Poor performance is given by 1.OF, Goodall4, Overlap, Eskin and 2.Overlap, Eskin, OF, Goodall4. Best performance for Vote is given by 1.Overlap, Eskin, OF, Goodall4 and 2.OF, Goodall4, Overlap, Eskin. Poor performance is given by three combinations i.e.1. Goodall4, Overlap, Eskin, IOF 2.Eskin, IOF, Goodall4, Overlap and 3.Eskin, OF, Goodall4, Overlap. In nursery data set best performance is given by two combinations. Those combinations are 1.OF, Goodall4, Overlap, Eskin 2.OF, Goodall3, Overlap, Eskin. and the combination of Eskin,OF,Goodall4,Overlap showed poor performance for Nursery dataset.

4   Conclusions

In the present paper we performed classification using kNN with single similarity measure across all the attributes and also with hybrid similarity measures. Hybrid similarity measures are useful since each attribute is of different type and nature. So we applied different similarity measures for different set of attributes called as hybrid similarity measures. From the experiments conducted on the bench mark datasets the following conclusions are drawn: (i)No single similarity measure is superior to the other as no single similarity measure consistently showed superior performance in all the datasets. (ii)Although when some of the similarity measures did not show good performance when applied individually across all the attributes ,they showed an improved performance on combining with other similarity measures using hybrid similarity methods.

References

1. Stanfill, C., Waltz, D.: Toward Memory-Based Reasoning. Commun. ACM 9(12), 1213–1228 (1986)
2. Cost, S., Salzberg, S.: A Weighted Nearest Neighbor Algorithm for Learning with Symbolic Features. Machine Learning 10(1), 57–78 (1993)
3. Esposito, F., Malebra, D., Tamma, V., Bock, H.H.: Classical Resemblance Measures. In: Analysis of Symbolic Data, pp. 139–152. Springer (2002)
4. Ahmad, A., Dey, L.: A Method to Compute Distance between Two Categorical Values of Same Attribute in Unsupervised Learning for Categorical Dataset. Pattern Recognition Letters 28(1), 110–118 (2007)
5. Goodall, D.W.: A New Similarity Index Based on Probability. Biometrics 22(4), 882–907 (1966)

6. Boriah, S., Chandola, V., Kumar, V.: Similarity Measures for Categorical Data: A Comparative Evaluation. In: Proceedings of 2008 SIAM Data Mining Conference, pp. 243–254 (2008)
7. Hirano, S., Sun, X., Tsumoto, S.: On Similarity Measures for Cluster Analysis in Clinical Laboratory Examination Databases. In: Compsac, 26th Annual International Computer Software and Applications Conference (2002)
8. Murphy, P.M.: UCI Repository of Machine Learning Databases. Department of Information and Computer Science, University of California, Irvine, CA (1994), http://www.ics.uci.edu/mlearn/MLRepository.html

An Evolutionary Algorithm
for Heart Disease Prediction

M.A. Jabbar[1], B.L. Deekshatulu[2], and Priti Chandra[3]

[1] JNTU Hyderabad, India
jabbar.meerja@gmail.com
[2] IDRBT, RBI Government of India
[3] Advanced System Laboratory, Hyderabad, India

Abstract. This Paper focuses a new approach for applying association rules in the Medical Domain to discover Heart Disease Prediction. The health care industry collects huge amount of health care data which,unfortunately are not mined to discover hidden information for effective decision making.Discovery of hidden patterns and relationships often goes unexploited. Data mining techniques can help remedy this situation.Data mining have found numerous applications in Business and Scientific domains.Association rules,classification,clustering are major areas of interest in data mining. Among these,association rules have been a very active research area.In our work Genetic algorithm is used to predict more accurately the presence of Heart Disease for Andhra Pradesh Population.The main motivation for using Genetic algorithm in the discovery of high level Prediction rules is that they perform a global search and cope better with attribute interaction than the greedy rule induction algorithms often used in Data Mining.

Keywords: Andhra Pradesh, Association Rules, Evolutionary Computation, Heart Disease.

1 Introduction

The Major reason that data mining has attracted great deal of attention in the information industry in the recent years is due to the wide availability of huge amounts of data and imminent need for turning such data into useful information and knowledge. The information gained can be used for applications ranging from business management, production control, and market analysis, to emerging design and science exploration and health data analysis.

Data mining also popularly referred to as Knowledge Discovery in Data bases (KDD), is the automated or convenient extraction of patterns representing knowledge implicitly stored in large data bases, data ware houses, and other massive information repositories[1].

Mining association rules is a field of data mining that has received a lot of attention in recent years. The main Association rule mining algorithm, APRIORI

K.R. Venugopal and L.M. Patnaik (Eds.): ICIP 2012, CCIS 292, pp. 378–389, 2012.
© Springer-Verlag Berlin Heidelberg 2012

not only influenced the association rule mining community, but it affected other data mining fields as well.

Medical diagnosis is regarded as an important yet complicated task that needs to be executed accurately and efficiently.The automation of this system should be extremely advantageous. Medical history of data compromises of a number of tests essential to diagnosis a particular disease. It is possible to acquire knowledge and information concerning a disease from the patient specific stored measurements as far as medical data is concerned. Therefore data mining has developed into a vital domain in health care [2].

Evolutionary algorithm is a subset of Evolutionary computation which is a subfield of Artificial Intelligence. Evolutionary computation is a general form for several computational techniques. Evolutionary computation represents powerful search and optimization paradigm influence by biological mechanism: that of natural selection and genetic. Genetic Algorithms represent the main paradigm of Evolutionary Computation.

In this paper we use genetic algorithm to identify association rules to predict heart Disease. Genetic algorithm is efficient for global search work, especially when the space is too large to use a Deterministic search method. It imitates the mechanics of natural species evolution with genetic principles, such as Selection, Crossover and Mutation. A Brief introduction about association rule mining, genetic algorithms and heart attack data are given in the following sub sections, followed by methodology in section 2. Section 3 deals with results and discussion in section 4 performance evaluation. We will conclude our final remarks in section 5.

1.1   Association Rule Mining

Association Rule mining is one of the fundamental research topics in Data Mining and knowledge discovery that finds interesting association or correlation relationship among a large set of data items and predicts the associative and correlative behaviors for new data . During the development of KDD,Association rule mining has played a fundamental role,which was first proposed by Agrawal et all [3]. Association rule is of the form $X =>$ where X is the antecedent and Y is the consequent.Association rule shows how many times Y has occurred if X has already occurred depending on the support and confidence value. Support is the probability of item or item sets in the given transactional data bases.

$$\text{Support}(X => Y) = P(XUY)$$

Confidence or strength is the ratio of number of transactions that contain XUY to the number of transactions that contain X.

$$\text{Confidence= Support (XUY)/support(X)}$$

Rules that satisfy both minimum support and confidence threshold are said to be strong. The problem of association rule mining can be Decomposed into two sub problems 1) Discovering frequent item sets 2) Generating rules from frequent item sets . Overall performance of mining association rules are determined by

1st step. The main association rule mining algorithm, Apriori also called Level wise algorithm, uses Down ward closure property, it works on the principle of Apriori i.e., subset of any frequent item set is also frequent [4].

Association rules are useful in real word applications and have played a fundamental role in development of data mining. When a data set is very large, association rule mining is challenging, because the no. of rules grows exponentially with the number of items. But this complexity will be tackled with the efficient algorithms which can efficiently prune search space. In order to generate efficient rules we used genetic algorithm to Predict Heart Disease.

1.2   Genetic Algorithms

Genetic algorithms (GA) represent powerful general purpose search method based on Evolutionary ideas of natural selection and genetics. They simulate natural process based on principles of Lamark and Darwin.

The field of Genetic and Evolutionary computation was first explored by Turing, who suggested an early template for the genetic algorithm. Holland performed much of the fundamental work in GEC in 1960 and 1970.His goal of understanding the processes of natural adoption and designing biologically inspired artificial systems led to the formulation of the simple genetic algorithms [5].

Genetic algorithms are typically implemented using computer simulations in which an optimization problem is specified. Members of space of candidate solutions, called individuals are represented as chromosomes. Genetic algorithms works in an iterative manner by generating new populations of strings from old ones .Every string is Encoded in binary, real etc., versions of a candidate solution. An evolution function associates a fitness measures to every string indicating its fitness for the problem.

The evolutionary process of Genetic algorithm is a highly simplified and stylized simulation of the biological version. It starts from a population of individuals randomly generated according to some probability distribution,usually uniform and updates this population in steps called generators. In our method we used the following three operators. The driving force behind genetic algorithm is unique cooperation between three genetic operators.

1) Selection

The application of fitness criteria to choose which individuals will go on to reproduce. Here we used Roulette wheel sampling method procedure. In this method the parents for crossover and mutations are selected based on their fitness.

2) Crossover

It is the exchange of Genetic Material denoting rules, structural components, and features of machine learning, search or optimization problem. Various types of crossover operators are 1)Single point crossover 2)Two point crossover

3)Uniform crossover 4)Half uniform crossover 5) Reduced surrogate crossover 6) Shuffle crossover 7) Segmented crossover[6].For multi parent recombination where more than 2 parents are involved following operators are used. 1) Uniform scanning 2) Occurrence based scanning 3) Fitness based scanning4) Adjacency based scanning[7].

3) Mutation

It is defined as the modification of chromosomes for single individuals. The general process of Genetic algorithm is repeated until a termination condition has been reached.Common terminating conditions are

1. A solution is found that satisfies minimum criteria
2. Fixed no. of generators reached
3. Allocated budget reached (time/money)
4. The highest rankings solutions fitness is reaching or if successive iterations no longer produce better results.
5. Manual inspection.
6. Combination of above [8].

Pseudo Code for Genetic Algorithm
Begin

1. t=0
2. initialize population P(t)
3. compute fitness P(t)
4. t =t+1
5. if termination criterion achieved go to step 10
6. select P(t) from p(t-1)
7. crossover P(t)
8. mutate P(t)
9. go to step 3
10. Output best and stop

End

1.3   Heart Disease

Among the Disease feared the world over are those involving the heart and blood vessels, also called Cardiovascular Disease (CVD). Heart problems are either acquired at birth or later in life. Mortality data from the registrar general of India shows that coronary heart disease (CHD) are a major cause of death in india.studies to determine the precise cause of death in Andhra Pradesh have revealed that CHD cause about 30% death are in rural areas.

Risk Factors for Cardiovascular Disease

Risk factors for heart disease are behaviors or conditions that increase ones chance of having heart problem.CVD can be classified as Controllable and uncontrollable. Controbale risk factors are life style related. They can be altered by changing individual behaviors, while controllable risk factors are not behavior related and are not under the control of individual.

A) Controllable Risk Factors

1)Smoking 2)High blood Pressure 3)Cholesterol 4)Physical inactivity5) Obesity 6)Diabetes 7)Psychological and Social factors like a)High stress b)Suppressing psychological distress c)Hostility, Cynicism d)Depression, Anxiety, and Social isolation e)Low Socio Economic status and low Educational Attainment

B) Un Controllable Risk Factors

1)Heredity 2)Age 3)Gender 4)Ethnicity[9]. The need to contain the epidemics of cardiovascular disease as well as combat its impact and minimize its toll is obvious and urgent.

2 Methodology

In this paper we applied genetic algorithm on medical data and analyzed heart Disease prediction.We have taken a sample of 10 records each consists of 12 Attributes. The genetic algorithm starts as follows.An initial population is created consisting of randomly generated transactions.Each transaction is represented by a string of bits.

Parameters Used in GA Are
Selection: Roulette Wheel Sampling Procedure
Crossover: Two point Crossover
Mutation: 1 Bit mutation
Fitnessfunction: SQRT (TP/TP+FN)*SQRT (TN/TN+FP)
Fitness Threshold: 50%
Range of G-Mean lies between 0 and 1.Confusion matrix is used to define the performance of an association rule.
TP:True Positive=>No.Of attributes satisfying Antecedent and Consequent(11)
FP:False Positive=>No.Of attributes satisfying Antecedent but not Consequent-(10)
FN:False Negative=>No.Of attributes not satisfying Antecedent but satisfying Consequent(01)
TN:True Negative=>No.Of attributes not satisfying Antecedent and also Consequent(00)

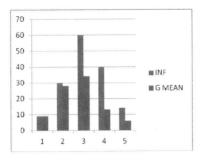

Fig. 1. INF V$_S$ G-Mean Measure

2.1 Data Source

The following features are collected for heart disease prediction in Andhra Pradesh based on the data collected from various corporate hospitals and opinion from expert doctors.

1) Age 2) Sex 3) Hypertension 4) Blood Pressure 5) Hyper Cholestremia 6) Diabetes 7) Resting ECG 8) Smoking 9) Alcohol 10) Family history of CAD 11)Rural/Urban 12) Concept Class
We converted the medical data into binary.Bit 1 represents presence of attribute and 0 represents absence.

Algorithm Description
Begin

1. Read Binary Transactional Data Base D.
2. Calculate fitness of each individual attribute.
3. If fitness of attribute is less than threshold go to step 11.
4. Else Repeat.
5. Select the individual which satisfy fitness threshold And make combinations.
6. Perform crossover to generate new offspring.
7. Perform mutation.
8. Calculate fitness function using G-Mean measure.
9. If calculated fitness threshold is less than minimum threshold go to Step 11.
10. Else goto step 5.
11. Output best and stop.

End

2.2 Explanation of Algorithm

We tested our proposed algorithm on heart disease datasets to study the performance of algorithm. For convenience each attribute will be treated as item. However to illustrate the algorithm,we hereunder provided the solution to a typical example from Table1. Let minimum support=6.

Table 1. Example Medical Data Base

T/A	1	2	3	4	5	6	7	8	9	10	11	12
1	1	1	0	1	0	0	1	1	0	1	1	1
2	1	1	1	1	1	0	1	1	1	1	1	1
3	1	1	1	1	0	0	1	1	1	1	1	1
4	0	1	1	1	1	0	0	1	0	1	1	1
5	0	0	0	1	0	0	1	1	0	1	0	1
6	1	1	0	1	0	0	0	1	0	1	0	1
7	1	0	1	1	1	0	1	1	0	1	1	1
8	1	0	1	0	1	0	0	1	1	0	0	1
9	1	1	1	1	1	0	1	1	0	1	1	1
10	1	1	1	1	0	0	1	1	1	1	1	1

Support of individual items are I1 = 8,I2 = 7,I3 = 7,I4 = 9,I6 = 0,I7 = 7,I8 = 10 I9 = 4,I10 = 9,I11 = 7,I12 = 10.
ItemsI5,I6, I9 having less minimum support. Hence these items are pruned.

Frequent 1 items are I1, I2, I3, I4, I5, I7, I8, I10, I11, I12. To generate Frequent 2 item sets make the combinations of frequent 1 item. Make the combination of (I1,I3) I1 = 1110011111 AND I3 = 0110011111 Perform cross over I1 = 1111001111 I3 = 0110011111 Perform Mutation I1 = 1111011111 AND I3 = 0110001111 TP(11) = 6 TN(00) = 1 FP(10) = 3 and FN(01) = 0

Fitness = SQRT(TP/TP+FN)*SQRT (TN/TN+FP) Fitness = 0.5.

Here Fitness(I1,I3)<Fitness threshold,So(I1,I3)not a frequent item set. Make the combinations of (I1,I4) I1 = 1110011111 AND I4 = 0110001011 Perform cross over I1 = 1110001111 AND I4 = 0110011011 Perform Mutation I1 = 1110011111 AND I4 = 0110001011 TP(11) = 5 TN(00) = 2 FP(10) = 3 and FN(01) = 0. Fitness=0.63.

Here Fitness(I1,I4)>Fitness threshold So(I1,I4)is a 2 frequent item set.

Table 2. G-Mean Values for Weather Data

Rule	TP	FP	FN	TN	Support	Confidence	G-Mean	Strong Rule
1	5	3	2	4	4	100	0.63	y
2	5	0	3	6	4	100	0.79	Y
3	8	1	2	3	4	100	0.77	Y
4	2	3	3	6	3	100	0.51	Y
5	2	2	3	7	3	100	0.55	Y
6	6	2	3	3	3	100	0.62	Y
7	6	2	4	2	3	100	0.54	Y
8	4	1	5	4	3	100	0.47	Y
9	2	3	2	7	2	100	0.59	Y
10	2	2	2	8	2	100	0.63	Y

Frequent 2 item sets are
(I1,I2),(I1,I3),(I1,I7),(I1,I8),(I1,I10),(I1,I12),(I2,I4),(I2,I8),(I2,I10),(I2,I11),
(I2,I12),(I3,I4),(I3,I8),(I3,I10),(I3,I11),(I3,I12),(I4,I7),(I4,I8),(I4,I10),(I4,I11),
(I7,I8),(I7,I11)(I7,I12),(I7,I14),(I8,I0),(I8,I11),(I8,I12),(I10,I11),(I10,I12),
(I11,I12)

Frequent 3 item set generation
To find the 3 item set generation use diagonal crossover and mutation opera-
tions.To find 3 item set (1,2,3)make the combinations of (1,2),(1,3)generate off
springs from (1,2)and (1,3)and perform crossover and mutation.Then find G-
Mean fitness value.

Frequent 3 itemsets are
(1,2,4),(1,2,7),(1,3,7),(1,3,8),(1,3,10),(1,3,12),(1,7,8),(1,7,10),(1,8,10),(1,8,12)
(1,10,12),(1,2,10)

Frequent 4 item sets are
(2,4,8,11),(3,4,7,8),(3,4,10,11),(2,4,10,12),(2,4,7,11),(4,7,8,10),
(7,8,10,10), (7,8,10,12),(7,8,11,12),(8,10,11,12),(2,4,7,8), (3,4,7,11),(3,4,10,12)

Frequent 5 item sets are
(2,4,7,8,11),(3,4,7,8,11),(2,4,7,8,10) (7,8,10,11,12),(4,7,8,10,12),(3,4,10,11,12)

Frequent 6 item sets are
(2,4,7,8,10,11),(3,4,7,8,10,11),(2,4,7,8,10,12),(4,7,8,10,11,12)

Frequent 7 item sets are
(2,4,7,8,10,11,12),(3,4,7,8,10,11,12)

As there is no frequet itemsets generated,and the termination condition achieved,
the algorithm stops. Frequent itemsets are (2,4,7,8,10,11,12),(3,4,7,8,10,11,12).

Table 3. G-Mean Values for Lens Data

Rule	TP	FP	FN	TN	Support	Confidence	G-Mean	Strong Rule
1	13	0	0	11	12	100	1	YES
2	10	3	3	8	6	100	0.74	YES
3	7	4	8	5	6	100	0.5	YES
4	7	6	6	5	6	100	0.49	YES
5	9	2	4	9	6	100	0.74	YES
6	6	4	3	11	5	100	0.66	YES
7	5	5	2	12	5	100	0.7	YES
8	6	5	4	9	5	100	0.62	YES
9	6	7	2	9	5	100	0.64	YES
10	7	3	3	11	5	100	0.7	YES

Table 4. G-Mean Values for Car Data

Rule	TP	FP	FN	TN	G-Mean
PV− >UNACC	39	0	0	1	1
LS− >SL	4	10	9	17	0.43
LS− >P4	6	4	12	18	0.49
PM− >LS	2	7	11	20	0.33
LM− >SM	5	5	11	17	0.4
LB− >P2	7	9	8	16	0.43
MV− >UNACC	39	0	0	1	1
D2− >UNACC	25	0	14	1	0.8

Table 5. G-Mean Values for Students Data

Rule	TP	FP	FN	TN	G-Mean
RIA=>IPR	8	4	4	7	0.64
IPR=>QC	5	5	7	6	0.47
EB=>NFC	4	5	4	10	0.57
VLSI=>QC	2	7	10	4	0.24
NFC=>VLSI	7	7	3	6	0.56
VLSI=>IPR	8	4	5	6	0.6
IPR=>DMW	6	5	8	4	0.43
VLSI=>DMW	7	3	7	7	0.59
VLSI=>BI	8	6	4	5	0.54
BI=>IPR	7	4	9	3	0.42

Table 6. Optimized Rules Generated from Various Data Bases

Sl.no	Data set	Optimized Rules(No)
1	Weather Data	1,2,3,4,5,6,7,9,10
2	Lens Data	1,2,3,5,6,7,8,9,10
3	Car Data	1,7,8
4	Students data	1,3,5,6,8,9

After decoding frequent item sets (2,4,7,8,10,11,12)implies Rule like, (Sex = Male and BP > 120,ECG = 1,smoking = yes and family history of CAD = yes and Rural = Yes and concept class = yes => Heart Disease) and the frequent item sets(3,4,7,8,10,11,12) Implies rule like (Hypertension = yes and BP > 120, ECG = 1, smoking = yes and family history of CAD = yes and Rural = Yes and concept class = yes => Heart Disease).

3   Results and Discussion

In our Research Heart disease patients Data is collected from various corporate hospitals in Andhra Pradesh and analyzed using Genetic algorithm. Some of the rules generated are shown below.

1. Age,alcohol,rural/urban, smoking=> Heart Disease
2. Age,alcohol,rural/urban=> Heart Disease
3. Age,alcohol,smoking=> Heart Disease
4. Age,diabetes=> Heart Disease
5. Age,gender,hypertension,smoking=>Heart Disease
6. Age,gender,smoking=>Heart Disease
7. Age,gender=>Heart Disease
8. Age,hypertension,rural/urban=> Heart Disease
9. Age,hypertension,smoking=>Heart Disease
10. Age,hypertension=>Heart Disease
11. Age,rural/urban,smoking=>Heart Disease
12. Age,smoking=>Heart Disease
13. Age=>Heart Disease
14. Diabetes,gender,smoking=>Heart Disease
15. Diabetes,gender=>Heart Disease

The aetiology of CHD is multifactorial. Apart from the obvious one like increasing age and gender male, the generated rules shows several important factors, which make the occurrence of the disease more probable as below.
1) Hypertension 2) Smoking 3)Diabetes 4)Alcohol

4   Performance Evaluation

In this section we compared the performance of our proposed method with algorithms [11],[12]. We have chosen the dataset from UCI Machine learning repository and from WEKA tool [12] to test the effectiveness of our proposed algorithm. Fig 1 shows comparison of G Mean with INF measure. Our method generates less number of candidates and optimizes the Rules generated. From table 2-5 illustrates calculation of G mean generated for various data sets.

Calculation of G Mean for Weather Data
Best Rules generated are

1. Outlook=overcast==>play=yes
2. Temperature=cool==>humidity=normal
3. Humidity=normal,windy=False==> play=yes
4. Outlook=sunny,play=no==>humidity=high
5. Outlook=sunny,humidity=high==>play=no
6. Outlook=rainy,play=yes==>windy=False
7. Outlook=rainy,windy=False =>play=yes
8. Temperature=cool,play=yes=>Humidity=normal
9. Outlook=sunny,temperature=hot=>,humidity=high
10. Temperature=hot,play=no==>outlook=sunny

Calculation of G Mean on Lens Data

Best Rules generated are

1. Tear-prod-rate=reduced=>contact-lenses=none
2. Spectacle-prescrip=myope tear-prod-rate=reduced==>contact-lenses=none
3. Spectacle-prescrip=hypermetrope,tear-prod-rate=reduced==>contact-lenses=none
4. Astigmatism=no,tear-prod-rate=reduced=>contact-lenses=none
5. Astigmatism=yes,tear-prod-rate=reduced==>contact-lenses= *none*
6. Contact-lenses=soft==>astigmatism= *no*
7. Contact-lenses=soft==>tear-prod-rate=normal
8. Tear-prod-rate=normal,contact-lenses=soft==>astigmatism=no
9. Astigmatism=no,contact-lenses=soft==>tear-prod-rate=normal
10. Contact-lenses=soft==>astigmatism=no,tear-prod-rate=normal

Calculation of G Mean on Car Data

Best rules generated are
1. PV=>UNACC 2. LS=>SL 3. LS=>P4 4. PM=>LS 5. LM=>SM 6. LB=>P2
7. MV=>UNACC 8. D2=>UNACC 9. D4=>UNACC

PV stands for persons more than 4.Ls for legboot small.Lm for Lug boot Medium, Sm stands for safety medium,mv for maintanance very high

Calculation of G Mean for Students Data from Reference[12].

Best rules Generated are
1. RIA=>IPR 2. IPR=>QC 3. EB=>NFC 4. VLSI=>QC 5. NFC=>VLSI
6. VLSI=>IPR 7. IPR=>DMW 8. VLSI=>DMW 9. VLSI=>BI 10.BI=>IPR

A data mining system has the capability to generate thousand of rules or even millions of rules.So all rules are not interesting.Only small fraction of rules potentially generated would actually be interesting to user. Generating only interesting rules is the optimization problem in data mining. In our research we used G-mean Measure to optimize association rules generated.

5   Conclusions

In this paper we proposed a new method for heart disease prediction using genetic algorithm. Our proposed work will mine association rules from heart disease data more efficiently.The association rule mining problem is an NP hard problem because finding all frequent item sets having minimum support results in a search space of 2^m which is exponential in m where m is number of item sets. We have applied genetic algorithm to optimize association rules. We obtain a fitness function for the task of optimizing the number of rules generated by efficiently pruning redundant Rules. In future work we plan to use different fitness functions for genetic algorithm for prediction of Heart Disease.

References

1. Han, J., Kamber: Data Mining Concepts and Techniques, 2nd edn. Morgan and Kaufman (2000)
2. Stilou, S., Bamidic, P.D., Maglareras, N., Papas, C.: Mining Association Rules from Clinical Data Bases An Intelligent Diagnostic Process in Health Care Study of Health Technology, pp. 1399–1403 (2001)
3. Agrawal, R., Imielinski, T., Swami, A.: Mining Association Rules Between Sets of Items in Large Databases ACM SIGMOD. In: International Conference on Management of Data, Washington, D.C. (1993)
4. Agrawal, Srikant, R.: Fast Algorithms for Mining Association Rules. In: Proceedings of the 20th International Conference on Very Large Data Bases, pp. 487–499 (1994)
5. William, H., Hsu: Genetic Algorithms. Kansas State University (2006)
6. Picek, S., Golub, M.: On the Efficiency of Crossover Operators in Genetic Algorithms with Binary Representation. In: Proceedings of the 11th WSEAS International Conference on Neural Networks (2010)
7. Eiben, A.E., Raué, P.-E., Ruttkay, Z.: Genetic Algorithms with Multi-Parent Recombination. In: Davidor, Y., Schwefel, H.-P., Männer, R. (eds.) PPSN 1994. LNCS, vol. 866, pp. 78–87. Springer, Heidelberg (1994)
8. Ghosh, S., et al.: Mining Frequent Item Sets using Genetic Algorithm. IJAIA 1(4) (October 2010)
9. Youmasu, J.S.: Understanding Risk Factors For Heart Disease A Report. Oklahoma State University (2010)
10. Haifeng, S., et al.: The Problem of Classification in Imbalanced Data Sets. IEEE (2010)
11. Anandavalli: Optimized Association Rule Mining using Improved Association Rule Mining. Advance in Information Mining (2009)
12. Manish, Saggar., et al.: Optimizing Association Rule Mining using Improved Genetic Algorithm IEEE (2004)
13. Weka Tool, http://www.cs.waikato.ac.nz/ml/weka

An Efficient Voice Enabled Web Content Retrieval System for Limited Vocabulary

G.R. Bharath Ram[1], R. Jayakumaur[1], R. Narayan[1],
A. Shahina[1], and A. Nayeemulla Khan[2]

[1] Dept. of Information Technology, SSN College of Engineering,
Chennai, India
narayan.libran@gmail.com
[2] School of Computing Sciences and Engineering,
VIT University, Chennai, India

Abstract. Retrieval of relevant information is becoming increasingly difficult owing to the presence of an ocean of information in the World Wide Web. Users in need of quick access to specific information are subjected to a series of web re-directions before finally arriving at the page that contains the required information. In this paper, an optimal voice based web content retrieval system is proposed that makes use of an open source speech recognition engine to deal with voice inputs. The proposed system performs a quicker retrieval of relevant content from Wikipedia and instantly presents the textual information along with the related image to the user. This search is faster than the conventional web content retrieval technique. The current system is built with limited vocabulary but can be extended to support a larger vocabulary. Additionally, the system is also scalable to retrieve content from few other sources of information apart from Wikipedia.

Keywords: Content Retrieval, Regular Expressions, Speech to Text, Sphinx 4, Wikipedia.

1 Introduction

The world wide web is an ocean of information with a large volume of data scattered all over the globe. Obtaining relevant and precise information has become time consuming with the ever growing additions and updates of the web content. For example, a user wishing to learn about the architecture of Hidden Markov Models, types Hidden Markov Model / HMM in the Google search bar and in turn is provided with a list of relevant links. The user then chooses one of them, say the Wikipedia link and clicks on it. The wiki presents all details about HMM, one of them being architecture. The user is now made to run through the page to locate where the architecture is and then read the content under it. This paper aims to overcome this problem by advocating an efficient means for retrieval of content from Wikipedia by eliminating the sequence of re-directions, thereby saving substantial amount of time.

K.R. Venugopal and L.M. Patnaik (Eds.): ICIP 2012, CCIS 292, pp. 390–398, 2012.
© Springer-Verlag Berlin Heidelberg 2012

The organization of the paper is as follows. A review of related works is discussed in Section 2. Section 3 explains the adaptation of Sphinx 4 for the proposed system. The working principle of the content retrieval system has been elaborated in Section 4. Section 5 explains the experimental results and Section 6 summarizes this work with some final remarks.

2 A Review of Existing Web Content Retrieval Systems

Significant research has been carried out with regard to content retrieval from the web. Wikipedia contents were used to automatically generate a dictionary of named entities and their synonyms. This dictionary is used in query expansion to improve the search quality [1]. A web page content retrieval system based on tags had been proposed in [2]. A similar approach is used in the proposed system to fetch web content through parsing, making use of string tokenizers. The results show a notable improvement in the retrieval time. In [3] a template-based Tibetan web text information extraction method which uses regular expression concepts is proposed. However, the system expects a fairly standard web page layout consisting of table tags for better accuracy. Automated extraction of Health Resource URLs from Biomedical Abstracts has been detailed in [4]. Although the paper limited itself to URL extraction from the abstracts alone, it claimed that the method was scalable to obtain content from an entire article. Extraction of news from the web using HTML parsers and regular expressions was proposed in [5].

3 Adaptation of Sphinx 4 for the Proposed System

For the proposed web content retrieval system the open source Sphinx 4 speech recognition system is used [6]. The flexible speech recognizer present in the system is used for the study. The block schematic of the proposed system, to which the Sphinx 4 is adapted, is shown in Fig. 1. The recognizer consists of generalized pluggable front end architecture. The front end comprises of a set of parallel data processors that can obtain the features of any type of speech. The Linguist is a pluggable module that can be dynamically configured according to various spoken languages used. A search graph is constructed using the lexicon, language model and the acoustic model. Here the lexicon is used to map the words of the language model into sequences of acoustic model elements. This permits the use of a lexicon of any size to be incorporated into the speech recognition system. The Decoder block comprises a pluggable *SearchManager* and other supporting code that simplifies the decoding process for an application. The Decoder merely tells the *SearchManager* to recognize a set of feature frames. At each step of the process, the *SearchManager* creates a Result object that contains all the paths that have reached a final non-emitting state. Here also, the *SearchManager* is not limited to any particular implementation. It implements a token passing algorithm to generate a sphinx token, which is an object that is associated with a SearchState and contains the overall acoustic and language scores of the path

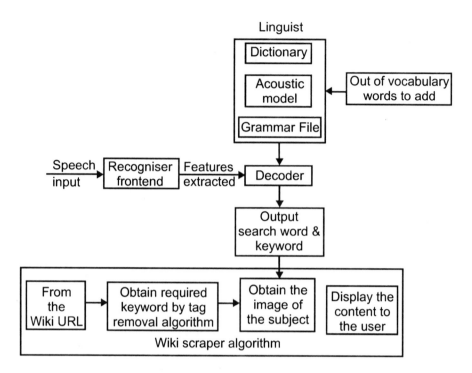

Fig. 1. Block Schematic of the Proposed Voice Based Web Content Retrieval System

at a given point, a reference to the SearchState, a reference to an input feature frame, and other relevant information.

The main objective of adapting the Sphinx 4 speech recognition system is to parameterize the input voice signal into two parts, the search word and the keyword. Sphinx 4 recognizes only the words that are contained in the dictionary file in the linguist module. The dictionary consists of the words to be recognized and the corresponding phoneme transcription of the words. The dictionary can be extended to include more words by incorporating our own words in it. The Sphinx 4 linguist recognizes the words or sentences in a specific format specified in the grammar file. It is highly configurable and can be changed according to the use of the speech recognizer. The decoder uses the features from the front end and the language model from the linguist and produces the recognized speech input. From this output the search word and the keyword are identified and passed to the Wikipedia parser algorithm to display the information and its corresponding image to the user.

4   Voice Enabled Content Retrieval System

The proposed system displays the textual content and the image available in the Wikipedia page, based on the speech input given by the user. The Sphinx

4 speech recognizer is used to convert the input speech into text. The text thus obtained is used to build the Wikipedia URL. Once the wiki URL is obtained, precise information from the page can be extracted by means of suitable parsing. A detailed working of the same is presented below.

4.1   Reaching the Wikipedia Page

Every Wiki page is identified by a distinct URL. It is interesting to note that the initial part of the URL is common to all pages, with the variation occurring only in the last part, which brings the uniqueness to each page. For example the Wiki URLs for speech processing and speech recognition are respectively, *http://en.wikipedia.org/wiki/Speech_processing* and *http://en.wikipedia.org/wiki/Speech_recognition*. Thus, the only difference lies in the last part after wiki/. This part varies according to the search input. To frame the URL, the first letter of the search input is capitalized. Also, if the input consists of two or more words, the URL is formed by replacing the white spaces in between the words by an underscore. Hence, the input speech processing becomes Speech_processing. This homogeneity in the URL makes it easy to access any Wikipedia page once the search input has been pruned suitably.

4.2   Principle of Content Retrieval

It is known that every web page contains a source code which is accessible to the users through the browser. It is also known that the information present on the web page is squeezed within various HTML tags that are a part of the source code. However, the source code is not easy to comprehend due to the presence of a large number of such tags. Upon careful tracking of the right tags, it is possible to pull out the necessary details easily. To do this, the tags along with new line and tab spacing are removed using pattern matching. The pattern matching is done using regular expressions (regex). A regular expression search involves 1) Testing a string for conformance to a pattern, 2) performing a search based on pattern matching, and 3) replacing the text [6]. In pattern matching, the Regex looks for the presence of a pattern string in a source string and returns the latter if present. The same concept is applied here to look out for specific tags in the source code and extract the content embedded within the tags. In the process of extraction, the tags are removed, leaving behind the content alone.

As mentioned above, the source code of any web page is abstruse, cluttered with numerous tags. These include script tags, style tags, primary HTML tags along with a lot of special characters, comments and white spaces such as tabs and new lines. These are essential for the browser to display the information in a proper manner. Consequently, it becomes quite a difficult task to pull the desired information from this clutter. Each of them must be removed in order to get the required information contained within them. It is possible to remove all the tags with the help of pattern matching as shown below. The following snippet shows a sample source code of the definition of the Hidden Markov Model (HMM) as present in Wikipedia.

```
<div id="mw-content-text" lang="en" dir="ltr" class="mw-content-
ltr"><p>A <b>hidden Markov model</b> (<b>HMM</b>) is a <a href=
"/Wiki/Statistical_model"// title="Statistical model">statistical
</a> <a href="/wiki/Markov_model" title="Markov model">Markov model
</a> in which the system being modeled is assumed to be a <a href=
"/wiki/Markov_process" title="Markov process">Markov process</a>
with unobserved (<i>hidden</i>) states. An HMM can be considered as
the simplest <a href="/wiki/Dynamic_Bayesian_network" title=
"Dynamic Bayesian network">dynamic Bayesian network</a>. The mathe
matics behind the HMM was developed by L. E. Baum and coworkers.
```

Upon removing the tags and gathering the HTML content present in-between them, from the above source code, the following information can be extracted. 'A HMM is a statistical Markov model in which the system being modeled is assumed to be a Markov process with unobserved (hidden) states. An HMM can be considered as the simplest dynamic Bayesian network. The mathematics behind the HMM was developed by L. E. Baum and coworkers'. Likewise, information is extracted from the source code for different keywords.

4.3   Extracting Content from a Specific Label in a Wiki Page

The general information about the HMM can be extracted as shown above. However, it cannot extract the required information if, instead, the user wants to know about the architecture of the HMM. To cater to such requirements, Wikipedia classifies every page in it with the help of headings in chronological order. The headings with which the page is classified varies from one page to another. This classification depends on the theme of a page. By analyzing the source code, it is seen that every heading is represented by the tag `<span class="mw-headline" id="Heading">Heading</span>` followed by the content under that heading. Hence, the information under any heading can be extracted if this specified tag can be located in the source page. For example, the architecture heading of the Hidden Markov Model is represented by the tag, `<span class="mw-headline" id="Architecture">Architecture</span>` followed by the architecture of the HMM. Thus, once this particular tag is located, it is possible to extract the information about the architecture of the HMM. In this manner, information regarding any subject and any field can be fetched.

4.4   Image Extraction

The source code of the page is traced for the presence of image tags. When such an instance is found, suitable validation is done to check whether the image corresponds to the particular keyword being searched. The key to find such an image tag is checking for the presence of parts of the keyword in the URL attribute of the image tag. By conducting a pattern matching process (pattern is the search word) the required image tag can be obtained. The obtained image tag contains the URL of the image that resides in the server. Hence the image can be downloaded and displayed to the user. The algorithm of the Image Extraction system is given below.

```
Extract_Image()
Input:Keyword KW
Output :Image I
I is downloaded from the web and displayed to the user
begin
    Identify first instance of image tag
  While(presence of next instance of image tag)
    if(KW  is a part of URLattribute)
      Img_URL=Extracted URLfrom tag;
    else
      continue;
    end
  end
    if(img_URL==NULL)
        Print(Image not available);
    else
        I = Download_Img(Img_URL);
        Display(I);
    end
end

Download_Img()
    Download the Image I into the system.

Display()
    Display the Image I on the screen.
```

5   Experimental Analysis

To evaluate the performance of the proposed system, the working procedure of the web content extraction, as described in Section 4, is implemented using Eclipse software. A screen shot of the obtained output is shown in Fig. 2.

A limited vocabulary consisting of a set of 34 keywords is built and tested against the system to ensure its consistent working. In order to measure the efficiency of the system, an experiment is conducted to calculate the time taken by the proposed system to obtain the textual content and the image from the web. The retrieval time for conventional extraction technique is also computed. Figs. 3 and 4 show the comparative time taken for text extraction and image extraction respectively. It can be interpreted from Fig. 3 that the proposed system takes less than 50 percent of the time taken by the conventional procedure. For example, while the conventional method takes 20 seconds to present content about Albert Einstein from the web, the proposed system does the same in only

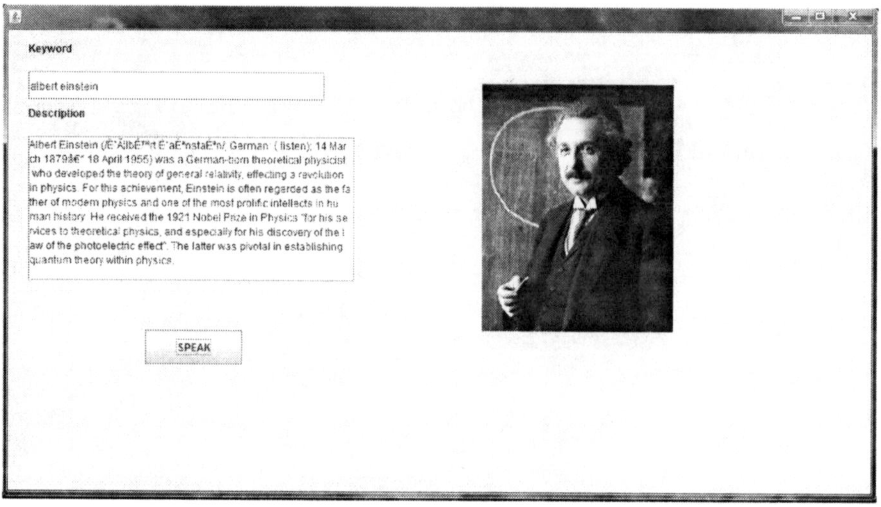

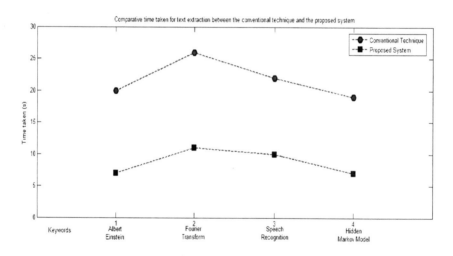

Fig. 2. Screenshot of the Proposed Voice Based Web Content Retrieval System

Fig. 3. Performance of the System for Textual Content Retrieval

7 seconds. Similarly, the system also proves to perform better with respect to image extraction. For example, Fig. 4 indicates that the proposed system takes only 11 seconds to obtain the image of Albert Einstein against the 25 seconds taken by conventional method. Similar results are obtained for various other search keywords.

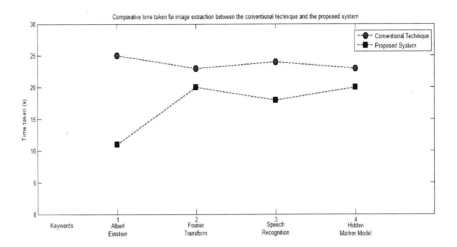

Fig. 4. Performance of the System for Image Content Retrieval

6   Conclusion

In this paper, a voice based textual information and image extraction system is proposed. Optimal content is fetched from the web and presented to the user as expected. Also, a substantial improvement is observed in the time taken by the system to obtain the required information. The efficiency of the system is high enough to deliver content on almost any subject. However, the system cannot retrieve information from web pages whose absolute URI are not available, such as a few ASP.net web pages. The absence of uniformity in the development of the source code of certain wiki pages adds difficulty in locating tags. Although designed for limited vocabulary, there is sufficient scope for extending the system to support a larger vocabulary.

References

1. Bohn, C., Norv, K.: Extracting Named Entities and Synonyms from Wikipedia. In: Proceedings 24th IEEE International Conference Advanced Information Networking and Applications, AINA 2010, pp. 1300–1307. IEEE Computer Society, Washington, DC (2010)
2. Xu, Z., Yan, D.: Proceedings International Conference on Intelligence Science and Information Engineering (ISIE)
3. Chuncheng, X., Yu, W.: A Template-Based Tibetan Web Text Information Extraction Method. In: Proceedings 4th International Conference on Intelligent Networks and Intelligent Systems (ICINIS), pp. 218–221 (2011)
4. Young, J.A., Frenz, C.: Automated Extraction of Health Resource URLs From Biomedical Abstracts. In: Proceedings Island System Applications and Technology Conference (LISAT), pp. 1–3 (2010)

5. Lin Xia, H., Sen Zhang, Y.: Design and Implementation of a Web News Extraction System. In: Proceedings International Conference Fuzzy Systems and Knowledge Discovery (FSKD), vol. 3, pp. 1793–1797 (2011)
6. Walker, W., Lamere, P., Kwok, P., Raj, B., Singh, R., Gouvea, E., Wolf, P., Woelfel, J.: Proceedings Technical Report Sphinx-4: A Flexible Open Source Framework for Speech Recognition (2004)

Face Detection Using a Boosted Cascade of Features Using OpenCV

Chandrappa D.N.[1], Akshay G.[1], and Ravishankar M.[2]

[1] Department of ECE, SJBIT, Bangalore, India
chandrappa.dn@gmail.com
[2] Department of ISE, DSCE, Bangalore, India

Abstract. Face detection in an image is a problem that has gained lots of importance in the last decade. Detecting faces is quite simple for human beings because it comes naturally but it is not so easy to teach a computer to detect faces. We divide the detection problem into three steps. The first step is Integral Image [1] which allows the features used by detector to be computed very quickly. The second step is a learning algorithm, based on AdaBoost, which selects a small number of critical visual features from a larger set and yields extremely efficient classifiers [2]. The third step is combining more complex classifiers in a cascade [3] which allows background regions of the image to be quickly discarded while spending more computation on promising face like regions. We conduct extensive experiments on publicly available databases to verify the efficacy of the proposed algorithm. In real time the detector runs at 15 frames per second without resorting to image difference or skin color detection.

Keywords: Face Detection, AdaBoost, OpenCV, Haar-Like Features.

1 Introduction

Several methods have been proposed for face detection like skin-color, Eigen faces, support vector machines, neural networks [4]. We have constructed a frontal face detection system which has acceptable false positives and negatives. The OpenCV library provides us a greatly interesting demonstration for a face detection. It provides us functions that they used to train classifiers for their face detection system, called Haar-Training. Our system achieves high frame rates working only with the information present in a single image. The integral image can be computed from an image using a few operations per pixel. Once computed, any one of these Harr-like features [5] can be computed at any scale or location in constant time. The second step is constructing a classifier by selecting a small number of important features using AdaBoost [2]. Within any image subwindow the total number of Harr-like features is very large, far larger than the number of pixels. In order to ensure fast classification, the learning process must exclude a large majority of the available features, and focus on a small set of critical features. Feature selection is achieved through a simple modification

K.R. Venugopal and L.M. Patnaik (Eds.): ICIP 2012, CCIS 292, pp. 399–404, 2012.
© Springer-Verlag Berlin Heidelberg 2012

of the AdaBoost procedure: the weak learner is constrained so that each weak classifier returned can depend on only a single feature [6]. As a result each stage of the boosting process, which selects a new weak classifier, can be viewed as a feature selection process. The third step is combining successively more complex classifiers in a cascade structure which dramatically increases the speed of the detector by focusing attention on promising regions of the image.

The rest of the paper is organized as follows, Section 2 describes about proposed method, Section 3 explains about Haar-Like feature for Face detection, section 4 and 5 explains about Learning Classification and Cascade of Classifiers for Face detection, Section 6 demonstrates experimental results. Finally, conclusions are drawn.

2   Proposed Method

The Input Image is given to Face Detection block which performs face detection by using Haar-Like features and compute Integral Image features. For classification, weak classifiers are used initially and later they are boosted using discrete AdaBoost algorithm. In the final step classifiers are cascaded to achieve high accuracy in face detection. This method is implemented using Intel OpenCV library and Microsoft Visual C++.

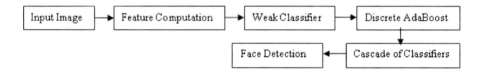

Fig. 1. Block Diagram

3   Haar-Like Features

We use simple Haar-Like features [5] (so called because they are computed similar to coefficients in Haar wavelet transforms) as shown in Figure 2.

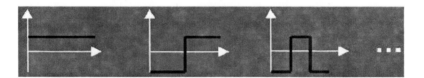

Fig. 2. Basis Functions in Haar Wavelets

Fig. 3. Features used in OpenCV

Pools of features used in OpenCV implementation are shown in figure 3:

Given that the base resolution of the detector is 24x24, the exhaustive set of rectangle features is quite large, over 130,000.

The feature used in a particular classifier is specified by its shape, position within the region of interest and the scale (this scale is not the same as the scale used at the detection stage, though these two scales are multiplied). For example, in the case of the second line second feature, the response is calculated as the difference between the sum of image pixels under the rectangle covering the whole feature (including the two grey stripes and the white stripe in the middle) and the sum of the image pixels under the white stripe multiplied by 3 in order to compensate for the differences in the size of areas. The sums of pixel values over rectangular regions are calculated rapidly using integral images.

The Haar features are computed using the equation:

$$feature_{i,k} = w_{i,k,1} * RectSum_{i,k,grey+white}(I) + w_{i,k,2} * RectSum_{i,white}(I)$$

Weights are compensated:

$$w_{i,k,1} * Area_{i,k,grey+white} + w_{i,k,2} * Area_{i,k,white} = 0$$

Fig. 4. Example Features

In real classifiers, hundreds of features are used, so direct computation of pixel sums over multiple small rectangles would make the detection very slow. But Viola [1] introduced an elegant method to compute the sums very fast. First, integral images (SAT, RSAT) are computed as shown in Figure 5.

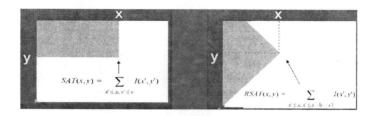

Fig. 5. Calculation of SAT(x,y)and RSAT(x,y)

RecSum(r) = SAT (x - 1, y - 1) + SAT (x + w - 1, y + h - 1) - SAT (x - 1, y + h - 1) - SAT (x + w - 1, y - 1)

RecSum(r) = RSAT (x + w, y + w) + RSAT (x - h, y + h) - RSAT (x, y) - RSAT (x + w - h, y + w + h)

4   Learning Classification

Given a feature set and a training set of positive and negative images, any number of machine learning approaches could be used to learn a classification function. In our system a variant of AdaBoost is used both to select a small set of features and train the classifier [2]. Even though each feature can be computed very efficiently, computing the complete set is expensive. So a very small number of these features can be combined to form an effective classifier.

The weak classifiers are used to select the rectangle feature which best separates the positive and negative examples as shown in Figure 6.

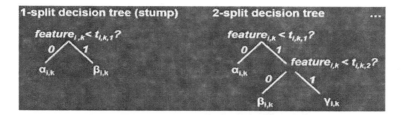

Fig. 6. Weak classifiers

ti,k and the values at leaves are found using L.Brieman CART^{TM} algorithm. To make weak Adaboost classifier stronger we use Discrete Adaboost (Freund, Schapire, 1996) as described below.

1. Given N example

$$(x_1, y_1), \ldots, (x_N, y_N) \text{ with } R^k, y_i \in (-1, 1)$$

2. Start with weights

$$w_i = 1/N, i = 1, \ldots, N.$$

3. Repeat for m = 1,....,M

    (a) Fit the classifier

$f_m(x) \in (-1, 1)$, using weights w_i on the training data $(x_1, y_1), ...(x_N, y_N)$

    (b) Compute

$$err_m = E_w[1_{(y \neq f_m(x))}], cm = log(1 - err_m)/err_m.$$

    (c) Set

$w_i.exp(cm.1_{(y \neq f_m(xi))}), i = 1, ..., N$ and renormalize weights so that $\sum_i w_i = 1$

4. Output the classifier

$$sign[\sum_{m=1}^{M} C_m.f_m(x)]$$

5 Cascade of Classifiers

The overall form of the detection process is that of a degenerate decision tree, a cascade. A positive result from the first classifier triggers the evaluation of a second classifier which has also been adjusted to achieve very high detection rates. A positive result from the second classifier triggers a third classifier, and so on. A negative outcome at any point leads to the immediate rejection of the sub window. Cascade of classifiers (special kind of decision tree) can outperform a single stage classifier because it can use more features at the same average computational complexity.

6 Results and Discussion

In this paper, the OpenCV simulated experiments are performed to verify the effectiveness of the proposed method. These experiments were done on Stanford,

Fig. 7. Examples of Face Detection

MMU and Local test set of image owing to different illumination conditions and cluttered background images with crowded scene. For frontal face detection, we chose haarcascade_frontalface_alt.xml that came with OpenCV in the "data\haarcascades\" folder. Figure 7 shows examples of face detection. The proposed method was tested for standard datasets and results are shown in the Table 1.

Table 1. Statistical Tested Data for Standard Datasets and Results

Database	Number of Faces	Faces Detected	Detection Efficiency
Stanford	142	136	95.77%
MMU	56	51	91.07%
Local	40	36	90%

7   Conclusions

In this paper, face detection using OpenCV is presented, which minimizes computation time while achieving high detection accuracy. However this algorithm will not work well when faces are occluded or pose by an angle or under very bright light conditions. Experiments on a large and complex dataset are difficult and time consuming. We have found that OpenCV is simple and easy to implement approach. Most importantly the algorithm works in real time and it is faster than most of the previous approaches.

References

1. Viola, P., Jones, M.: Rapid Object Detection using a Boosted Cascade of Simple Features. In: CVPR, pp. 511–518. IEEE Computer Society (2001)
2. Freund, Y., Schapire, R.E.: A Decision-Theoretic Generalization of On-Line Learning and an Application to Boosting. In: Vitányi, P.M.B. (ed.) EuroCOLT 1995. LNCS, vol. 904, pp. 23–37. Springer, Heidelberg (1995)
3. Bradski, G., Kaehler, A., Pisarevsky, V.: Intel Corporation Learning-Based Computer Vision with Intels OpenCV, vol. 9 (2005)
4. Tian, Y., Yu, F.-Q.: A Survey on Human Face Detection. Computer Security (2009)
5. Papageorgiou, C., Oren, M., Poggio, T.: A general Framework for Object Detection. In: International Conference on Computer Vision (1998)
6. Lienhart, R., Maydt, J.: An Extended Set of Haar-like Features for Rapid Object Detection. In: IEEE ICIP 2002, vol. 1, pp. 900–903 (2002)
7. Crow, F.: Summed-area Tables for Texture Mapping. Proceedings of SIGGRAPH 18(3), 207–212 (1984)
8. OpenCV library manual by INTEL,
   http://sourceforge.net/projects/opencvlibrary/

Disambiguating Phrasal Verbs
in English to Kannada Machine Translation

Parameswarappa S. and Narayana V.N.

Department of Computer Science and Engineering
Malnad College of Engineering
Hassan, Karnataka, India
param.phd@gmail.com

Abstract. Due to the presence of Phrasal verbs in an English text, the English to Kannada machine translation poses a great challenge. It is because of ambiguous nature of the Phrasal verbs. Each Phrasal verb may have more than one equivalent Kannada translation depending on the context in which it appears. Phrasal verbs are the commonly occurring feature of English and comprise a verb followed by a particle(s). Phrasal verbs have highly context dependent meaning and may be disambiguated only by devising a method involving utilization of semantic information pertaining to the context. The present paper describes the semantic based disambiguation method for ambiguous Phrasal verbs sense disambiguation using hybrid example based approach. It is an essential task for getting the good quality output during English to Kannada Machine Translation. Experiments are conducted and the results obtained are described. The performance of the proposed method is reliable and extendable.

Keywords: Machine Translation, Parallel-aligned Corpora, Phrasal Verbs, Semantic File, Wordnet.

1 Introduction

Phrasal verbs are special kind of Multi Word Expressions (MWE). They occur in numerous languages notably in English. A Phrasal verb, which is a combination of a verb and a particle(s) (adverb or a preposition), creates a meaning different from its constituent verb. It should not be translated by considering its constituent verb alone. Because verb and particle(s) together act in conjunction with each other to produce a specialized context-specific meaning that may not be directly derived from the original meaning of the constituents. But the existing machine translation system handles the translation of a Phrasal verb by translating the constituent verb in it. As an example consider, a sentence 'V.S. Acharya passed away from heart attack'. In a given sentence 'passed away' is a Phrasal verb. The correct meaning of it is died. But the existing translator generates the following wrong output in Kannada.

[V.S. Acharya hrudayaaGaatadinda duura jaarige] 'V.S. Acharya passed far from heart attack'.

K.R. Venugopal and L.M. Patnaik (Eds.): ICIP 2012, CCIS 292, pp. 405–410, 2012.
© Springer-Verlag Berlin Heidelberg 2012

Therefore, the Phrasal verbs have great impact on the accuracy of the English to Kannada machine translation.

As a solution for the above problem, we describe a methodology to translate occurrence of Phrasal verbs in English sentences to their appropriate Kannada equivalent by extracting semantic information about the local context and performing disambiguation based on it. The method uses hybrid example based approach for disambiguation.

2   Related Work

There is not a much work reported on Disambiguating Phrasal verbs. Many earlier MT systems assume that the input text shall be controlled so as to minimize the occurrences of the Phrasal verbs. Some other systems address the problem by including multi word lexical entries in the lexicon. But this strategy has its own limitations. SIMPLE system [1] for Danish language proposes a solution to a disambiguation problem. The system classifies the Phrasal verbs as compositional and non-compositional. In case of compositional Phrasal verbs, the verb and particle retains their core meaning but it is not the case with non-compositional Phrasal verbs. The system introduces the notion of semantic types and semantic units to carry out disambiguation. A methodology and an implementation details for semantic based Phrasal verbs sense disambiguation using hybrid example based approach has been proposed by [2]. They used the module in AnglaBharati English to Hindi MT system. Example-Based technique for disambiguating Phrasal verbs in English to Hindi MT has been proposed by [3]. In this approach, they used generalized examples instead of raw examples containing the Phrasal verbs. They used Wordnet [4] categories for generalization. They integrated the proposed system with MaTra, an existing MT system developed by NCST, Mumbai.

3   Phrasal Verbs

The compositions of a verb followed by a particle(s) are considered as Phrasal verbs [5]. They are very common in English. They can be used in all tenses and has all the same forms as any other verbs. Some of the examples of commonly used Phrasal verbs are put on, put off, get up, check out, bring up, bring down, come to, pickup, call off, call for, take off, pass away, pass out, cut off etc [6].

The Phrasal verbs produce specialized context-specific meanings that may not be derived from the meaning of the constituents. There is almost always an ambiguity during word-to-word translation from source to the target languages. The direct object to the Phrasal verb mostly provides the contextual sense of the sentence. Apart from the direct object, the preposition following it and its indirect object plays an important role in deriving the actual sense of the Phrasal verb and hence of the sentence. Let us consider a Phrasal verb put on. It may be used in any of the following way.

He put on the light (switch on).
[avanu deepa haakida]
The boy put on a cap (wear).
[aa huDuga Toopi darisida]

The correct English to Kannada translation of the Phrasal verb put on for the above sentences are [haaku] and [dharisu] respectively.

Phrasal verbs can be broadly classified into two categories, transitive and intransitive. A transitive phrasal verb can either be followed by an object or it can contain an object between the verb and particle(s). Based on this, they are further classified into separable and inseparable. Separable transitive phrasal verbs are those in which the object is placed between the verb and particle(s). In case of inseparable transitive phrasal verbs, the object is placed after the particle(s). Though some transitive Phrasal verbs can be both separable and inseparable, the Phrasal verb should take only the separable form when the object is a pronoun. An intransitive Phrasal verb should neither be followed by an object nor should it contain an object between the verb and particle(s). Different types of Phrasal verbs are shown in Table 1.

Table 1. Types of Phrasal Verb with an Example

Type	Phrasal verb	Meaning	Example
Separable	Cut off	Interrupt	She cut off the phone while he was speaking. [avanu maatanaaDuttiruvaaga avaLu duuravaaNiyannu stagitagoLisidaLu]
Inseparable	Look into	Investigate	The police are looking into murder. [Aarakshakaru kole tanike naDesuttiddaare]
Intransitive	Pass away	Die	He passed away. [avanu maraNa hondida]

The following issues are to be considered during Phrasal verb translation.

a) To find out the equivalent class of the object in the sentence and to compute the similarity between the classes with some form of knowledge base. The knowledge base may comprise some raw examples or templates (generalized examples) associated with the various sense of the Phrasal verb.

b) To identify the direct and indirect object and the subject associated with the Phrasal verb in a sentence.

c) Finally, in order to identify the sense attributes subject, object and indirect object governed by the preposition in a sentence, the Phrasal verb in a sentence acts as a pivot element. Therefore, correct identification of the Phrasal verb from a sentence is must to disambiguate Phrasal verb.

In summary, in order to disambiguate Phrasal verb, we have to identify the Phrasal verb and its sense attributes and prepare the knowledge base for comparison.

4   Methodology

Fig. 1 shows the pictorial representation of the Phrasal verbs sense disambiguation process. The system takes English sentences containing commonly used Phrasal verbs. It outputs the contextual meaning of the Phrasal verbs in English and Kannada.

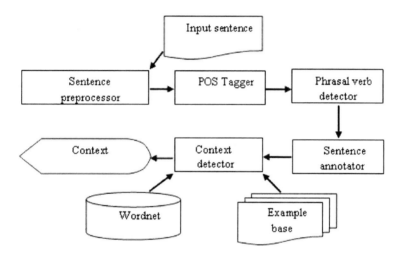

Fig. 1. Phrasal Verbs Sense Disambiguation Process

It contains five components namely Sentence preprocessor, POS (Part-of-speech) tagger, Phrasal verb detector, Sentence annotator, Context detector. In addition, it uses example base and the Wordnet as a lexicon.

The system takes the input sentence containing a Phrasal verb and passes it to the sentence preprocessor to perform the preprocessing task required by the POS tagger. The POS tagger takes the preprocessed sentence and assigns POS tags and chunks it as Phrases. The Phrasal verb detector uses the POS tags and detects the Phrasal verb from the input sentence. The sentence annotator uses POS tags, Phrase chunks and the Phrasal verb to annotate the sentence with subject, object and indirect object governed by the immediate preposition following the Phrasal verb. Finally, the context detector detects the context of the Phrasal verb using the sense attributes, example base and the Wordnet.

5   Evaluation

The proposed method has been tested with 50 randomly selected sentences collected from web corpora. The following example illustrates the disambiguation process.

Sentence: The actor put on some very strange expression during the first scene. Kannada Transliteration: [modala drusyadalliyee aa natanu bahaLa vibhinnavaada abhivyaktiyannu vyaktapaDisidanu]

Table 2 shows the Sentence preprocessing and POS Tagging output.

Table 2. Sentence Preprocessor and POS Tagger Output

Sentence Preprocessor	POS Tagging		
Tokens	POS tags	Tag sets	Meaning
The	DT	B-NP	Determiner, Noun Phrase tag set.
Actor	NN	I-NP	Noun, singular or mass, Noun Phrase tag set.
Put	VBN	B-VP	Verb past participle, Verb Phrase tag set.
On	IN	B-PP	Preposition or subordinating conjunction.
Some	DT	B-NP	Determiner, Noun Phrase tag set.
Very	JJ	I-NP	Adjective, Noun Phrase tag set.
Strange	NN	I-NP	Noun, singular or mass, Noun Phrase tag set.
Expression	NN	I-NP	Noun, singular or mass, Noun Phrase tag set.
During	IN	B-PP	Preposition or subordinating conjunction.
The	DT	B-NP	Determiner, Noun Phrase tag set.
First	JJ	I-NP	Adjective, Noun Phrase tag set.
Scene	NN	I-NP	Noun, singular or mass, Noun Phrase tag set.

The Phrasal verb detector identifies 'put on' as a Phrasal verb.
Table 3 shows the Sentence Annotator output.

Table 3. Sentence Annotator Output

Sense Pattern	Input sentence tokens
Subject	Actor
Phrasal verb	Put on
Object	Expression
Preposition	During
Indirect object	Scene

The output of the Context detector component is 'to assume/[vyaktapaDisu]'.

6 Discussion

During the Phrasal verb disambiguation process, the following observations were made.

a) The accuracy of the system depends on the semantic file. But manually creating such file is difficult, labor intensive and time consuming. Hence it needs automation.

b) The pronoun resolution is needed for Phrasal verb sense disambiguation. As an example, for a sentence 'Earlier they were bit tensed. Now they got over it' [modalu avaru swalpa gaabariyaagiddaru. iiga avaru adarinda horabandiddaare] the system generates wrong output because the 'it' in the second sentence refers to 'tensed', which is referred in the previous sentence. It needs to be resolved to get the correct output.

c) Due to incorrect translation, insufficient context and incorrect sense attributes the proposed method gives correct output for 35 sentences out of 50 test sentences.

7 Conclusion and Future Work

In this paper, we proposed a methodology to disambiguate Phrasal verbs during English to Kannada machine translation. It uses hybrid example based approach to disambiguate the Phrasal verb in an English sentence. Constructed a parallel-aligned (English-Kannada) corpus. Randomly selected 50 sentences from corpora have been used during experimentation. The semantic file required for disambiguation has been created manually. Experiments are conducted and the results obtained are described. The performance of the proposed method with respect to applicability and precision are encouraging.

In future, we are planning to enhance the capability of the proposed method by automating the semantic file creation process, pronoun resolution. The present work allows only one Phrasal verb in a sentence. In future we are planning to extend the present work to handle multiple Phrasal verbs in a sentence.

References

1. Pedersen, B.S., Nimb, S.: Semantic Encoding of Danish Verbs in SIMPLE - Adapting a Verb Framed Model to a Satellite Framed Language. In: 2nd International Conference on Language Resources and Evaluation, LREC 2000, Greece (2000)
2. Jain, A., Sinha, R.M.K.: Machine translation of Phrasal verbs from English to Hindi. Technical Report, IIT Kanpur (2002)
3. Saha, I., Ananthakrishnan, R., Sasikumar, M.: Example-Based Technique for Disambiguating Phrasal Verbs in English to Hindi Translation. Technical Report, CDAC Mumbai (2004)
4. Harold, S.: Example-Based Machine Translation. Review Article, Centre for Computational Linguistics, UMIST (1999)
5. Courtney, R.: Longman Dictionary of Phrasal Verbs. Longman Group UK Limited (1989) ISBN 0-582-55530-2 CSD, ISBN 0-582-05864-3 PPR
6. Common Phrasal Verbs, http://webster.commnet.edu/grammar/phrasals.htm

Extraction of Panic Expression from Human Face Based on Histogram Approach

Mohammed Alamgir Hossain[1], Debabrata Samanta[2], and Goutam Sanyal[2]

[1] Department of MCA,
Calcutta Institute of Technology, West Bengal, India
alamgir_sim@yahoo.com
[2] Department of CSE,
National Institute of Technology, Durgapur,
Mahatma Gandhi Avenue, West Bengal, India - 713209
{debabrata.samanta369,nitgsanyal}@gmail.com

Abstract. Panic expression is one of the most important features of facial recognition in the present era, and it has become a burning issue. It is very difficult to segregate a people whether he or she is in the normal position or barring unexpected circumstances that has occurred abruptly. Over the past 50 years, different researchers have developed human-observer based methods that can be used to classify and correlate facial expressions with human sensation. In this paper we proposed a novel methodology based on histogram classification for extraction of panic moment of a human being. Firstly, we have considered face-mask to collect the maximum information from human face. Then we have set the three coordinate positions for storing the data as a panic-info-mask. Finally, the geometrical value of panic-info-mask represents the data of panic moment.

Keywords: Panic-info-mask, Face detection, K-means clustering.

1 Introduction

Panic face recognition is the programmed assignment of a digital image to a particular person by analyzing the features of panic-info-mask of that image. The method of panic expression recognition consists of three components: face detection, image processing and face state identification and reorganization. Panic state detection uses computer knowledge to detect the location of any faces within an image. Image processing build with scaling and image rendering to prepare the face for identification. Identification of Panic expression of human face based on mathematical techniques on the pixel values or features in the facial area of an image to determine who the face belongs to. The most useful applications contain crowd surveillance, video content indexing, personal identification (ex. driver's license), mug shots matching, entrance security, etc. The face can be correspond to in different ways, e.g., as a whole unit (holistic representation), as a set of features (analytic representation) or as a combination of

K.R. Venugopal and L.M. Patnaik (Eds.): ICIP 2012, CCIS 292, pp. 411–418, 2012.
© Springer-Verlag Berlin Heidelberg 2012

these (hybrid approach). The applied face representation and the kind of input images determine the choice of mechanisms for automatic extraction of facial expression information.

Let us consider a situation where a lot number of people are working and an abnormal situation has occurred all on a sudden. The situation is such that nobody are in the position to dial anybody, can't press alarm, not in the position to move to go out. In this situation if there is a camera placed on the prime positions on the working place then it is very easy to capture images and extract the faces and determine the terror moment of those faces. In this paper we proposed a novel methodology based on histogram classification for extraction of panic moment of a human being. Firstly, we proposed face-mask for collect the maximum information from human face. Then we have set the three coordinate positions for storing the data as a panic-info-mask. Finally, the geometrical value of panic-info-mask represents the data of panic moment.

2   Related Work

During last 10 years, different scientists have a great role to identify the unwanted situation with respect to facial expression. Irene Kotsia and Ioannis Pitas have used the geometrical displacement of certain selected Candide nodes, distinct as the differentiation of the node coordinates between the first and the greatest facial expression intensity frame, is used as an input to a novel multiclass Support Vector Machine (SVM) system of classifiers that are used to recognize either the six basic facial expressions or a set of chosen Facial Action Units (FAUs). Anastasios Koutlas, Dimitrios I. Fotiadis [1] uses Active Shape Models for identification of well-known features of the face and Gabor filters for representation of facial geometry at selected locations of fiducially points. Jun Wang, Lijun Yin, Xiaozhou Wei and Yi Sun [2] proposed 3D facial geometric shapes for reorganization of facial expressions using 3D facial expression range data. Frank Y. Shih, Chao-Fa Chuang [3] look into various feature representation and expression classification schemes to recognize seven different facial expressions, such as happy, neutral, angry, disgust, sad, fear and surprise, in the JAFFE database. Andrew Ryan , Jeffery F. Cohn, Simon Lucey, Jason Saragih, Patrick Lucey, Fernando De la Torre , Adam Rossi [4] used automates the manual practice of FACS for face detection. Mandeep Kaur , Rajeev Vashisht [5] used Principal Component analysis (PCA), PCA with SVD(Singular Value Decomposition) for Facial Expression Recognition.

3   Proposed Methodology

The proposed methodology aims to model a promising facial expression grading system of human being. For the experimentation purpose, three types of human facial expression are considered. The system is divided into the following steps: (1) Face Detection (2) Image Pre-processing (3) Color image segmentation

(4) Panic-Info-Mask based Histogram draw (5) Expression grading by picks value. The proposed system is an efficient module that identifies various facial expression of that human being and also determines the stage in which the face is.

3.1 Face Detection

Face detection and identification of important features is a crucial step for an AFER system. This is the main step of any system that operates automatically and the overall performance of the system mainly based on the truthful identification of the face or certain facial attributes such as eyes, eyebrows, mouth and so on. The most commonly engaged face detection algorithm in automatic facial expression recognition systems is the real-time face detector. The face detector does not work directly with image intensities but there is a set of features extracted related to Haar basis functions.

3.2 Image Pre-processing

Image processing is a arrangement of signal processing for which the input is an image, such as a photograph or video frame; the output of image processing may be either an image or a set of characteristics or parameters related to the image. We performed pre-processing on the face images used to train and test our algorithms as follows:

1. The location of the eye braw is first selected.
2. Images are scaled and cropped to a fixed size (320 x 205) keeping the eyes in all images aligned .
3. The image is histogram stable using the median histogram of all the training images to make it invariant to lighting, skin color etc.
4. Generating threshold adaptively as follows:
5. A fixed oval panic-info-mask is applied to the image to extract face region. This serves to eliminate the fear features in the image which provide no information about facial panic expression.

3.3 Panic Facial Features Extraction

The panic facial feature extraction step aims at mock-uping the panic face using a panic-info-mask. There are two ways to represent the face and consequently facial geometry. Firstly, the face can be processed as a whole often referred to as holistic or analytic approach and secondly it can be represented at the location of specific regions or at the location of fiducial points often referred to as local approach.

3.4   Color Image Segmentation

Image segmentation refers to the sequence of separating the digital image into its ingredient regions or objects so as to change the representation of the image into something that is more consequential and easier to analyze. K-means clustering technique has been used in the present work to carry out segmentation. K-Means Clustering is a method of cluster analysis which aims to partition n observations into k mutually exclusive clusters in which each observation belongs to the cluster with the nearest mean. The objective function is defined as

$$Q = \sum_{j=1}^{k} \sum_{i=1}^{i} |(S^{(j)} - Y_j)^2| ------- (1)$$

Where $S^{(j)} - Y_j)^2$ is a chosen distance measure between a data point $S^{(j)}$ and the cluster centre Y_j is an indicator of the distance of the n data points from their respective cluster centres.

3.5   Panic-Info-Mask Based Histogram Draw

Basically, in image processing facial expressions area of a binary image is the total number of on pixels in the image. The original resized face image is transformed to binary image such that the pixels analogous to the face image are on. Then we plot the histogram for calculate the change the pick value.

3.6   Expression Grading by Picks Value

A histogram based System is developed for expression grading by referring to the expression scoring scale in Table 1. The main grading system depends on:

$$S(p_i, q_j) = \exp(-\varphi[\![p_i - q_j]\!]^2), \varphi > 0 --------- (2)$$

Now we consider the η for extract the fear value from face.

$$\eta(p, q, \phi, \beta) = \frac{1}{2\pi\rho^2} e^{-(\frac{p^2 + q^2}{2\rho})} [e^{i\phi p'} - e^{\phi^2 \rho}] ----(3)$$

$$p' = p \cos \beta + q \sin \beta, q' = -p \sin \beta + q \cos \beta ----(4)$$

3.7   Proposed Work Flow Diagram

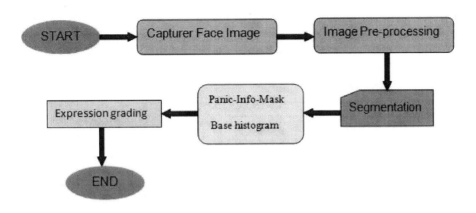

3.8   Result and Discussion

The experiment is implemented on a Compaq nx6120 laptop, running at 1.73 GHz; Ram 2GB, using MatLab. The average time for each image is about 750 milliseconds. Here fig 1, fig 3, fig 5 are representing the original images of facial Expressions of normal, panic, Happiness. Fig 2, fig 4, fig 6 are representing the histogram of those images. Finally, a comparing Bar Chart of facial expressions of normal, panic, Happiness represented by fig 7.

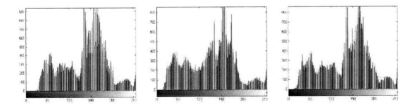

Fig. 1. Facial Expressions of normal, panic, Happiness

Fig. 2. Histogram of Facial Expressions of normal, panic, Happiness

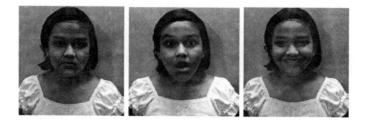

Fig. 3. Facial Expressions of normal, panic, Happiness

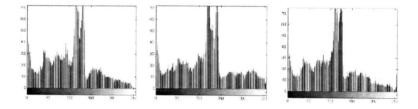

Fig. 4. Histogram of Facial Expressions of normal, panic, Happiness

Fig. 5. Facial Expressions of normal, panic, Happiness

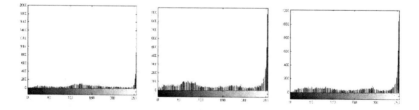

Fig. 6. Histogram of Facial Expressions of normal, panic, Happiness

Table 1. Confusion matrix for Face expression

Expressions	Normal	Fear/Panic	Happiness	Accuracy rate
Normal	47	14	16	87.23%
Fear/Panic	12	43	52	98.75%
Happiness	05	28	13	85.43%

Table 2. Result of detection

Expressions	% of correction	True images (out of 85)
Normal	86.74%	74
Fear/Panic	98.71%	81
Happiness	86.24%	79

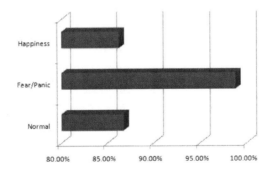

Fig. 7. Recognition Rate of various Facial Expressions

4   Conclusion

In this paper, we proposed a novel histogram based facial expression detection of human being. This histogram classification for extraction of panic moment of a people does not depend on noise removal function. Here face-mask is used to collect the maximum information from human faces. Then we have set the three coordinate positions for storing the data as a panic-info-mask. Finally, the geometrical value of panic-info-mask represents the data of panic moment. The result from the preliminary study indicated that the proposed strategy is effective to assess panic facial expression of human being in more precisely.

References

1. Koutlas, A., Fotiadis, D.I.: Image Processing and Machine Learning Techniques for Facial Expression Recognition, pp. 1–16. IGI Global (January 2009)
2. Wang, J., Yin, L., Wei, X., Sun, Y.: 3D Facial Expression Recognition Based on Primitive Surface Feature Distribution,
   www.cs.binghamton.edu/~lijun/Research/3DFE/Yin_cvpr06.pdf
3. Shih, F.Y., Chuang, C.-F.: International Journal of Pattern Recognition and Artificial Intelligence 22(3), 445–459 (2008)
4. Ryan, A., Cohn, J.F., Lucey, S., Saragih, J., Lucey, P., De la Torre, F., Rossi, A.: Automated Facial Expression Recognition System. IEEE (2009), 978-1-4244-4170-9/09/25.00
5. Kaur, M., Vashisht, R.: Comparative Study of Facial Expression Recognition Techniques. International Journal of Computer Applications (0975 - 8887) 13(1) (January 2011)
6. Zhang, Y., Ji, Q.: Active and dynamic information fusion for facial expression understanding from image sequences. IEEE Trans. Pattern Anal. Mach. Intell. 27(5), 699–714 (2005)
7. Cohen, I., Sebe, N., Garg, S., Chen, L.S., Huanga, T.S.: Facial expression recognition from video sequences: temporal and static modelling. Comput. Vis. Image Understand. 91, 160–187 (2003)
8. Bartlett, M.S., Littlewort, G., Fasel, I., Movellan, J.R.: Real time face detection and facial expression recognition: Development and applications to human computer interaction. In: Proc. Conf. Computer Vision and Pattern Recognition Workshop, Madison, WI, June 16-22, vol. 5, pp. 53–58 (2003)
9. Lyons, M.J., Akamatsu, S., Kamachi, M., Gyoba, J.: Coding facial expressions with G abor wavelets. In: Proc. 3rd IEEE Int. Conf. Automatic Face and Gesture Recognition, pp. 200–205 (1998)
10. Cootes, T., Edwards, G., Taylor, C.: Active appearance models. PAMI 23(6), 681–685 (2001)
11. Bourel, F., Chibelushi, C., Low, A.A.: Robust Facial Expression Recognition Using a State-Based Model of Spatially-Localized Facial Dynamics. In: Proc. Fifth IEEE Int. Conf. Automatic Face and Gesture Recognition, pp. 106–111 (2002)
12. Cootes, T., Kittipanya-ngam, P.: Comparing variations on the active appearance model algorithm. In: BMVC, pp. 837–846 (2002)
13. Chen, Huang, T.S., Cohen, I., Garg, L., Sebe, N.: Facial expression recognition from video sequences: Temporal and static modeling. In: CVIU, vol. 91, pp. 160–187 (2003)
14. Fasel, B., Luettin, J.: Automatic facial expression analysis: A survey. Pattern Recognition 36, 259–275 (2003)

Towards a Novel Statistical Method for Generating Test Sets with a Given Coverage Probability

Cristiane Selem, Eber Assis Schmitz, Fabio Protti,
Antonio Juarez Alencar, and Jorge V. Doria Jr.

The Tércio Pacitti Institute for Computer Reseach
Federal University of Rio de Janeiro, Rio de Janeiro, Brazil
cistianeselem@gmail.com

Abstract. This paper presents a method that uses a small set of execution samples to select a minimal set of execution paths, which has the property of its coverage probability being above a required confidence level, and then generate a natural language specification of the test case set. Experimental results show that it is not only simple to be applied but also generates a reliable test case set. The greatest benefit, however, is the use of a minimal set of test cases, which reduces the computational effort to guarantee that the program reliability is above a required level of confidence.

Keywords: Automatic Efficient Test Case Generator (AETG), Coverage Probability, Statistical Method, Ad-hac, Probabilistic Paths.

1 Introduction

The essence of the "basis path testing", first proposed by McCabe [1] in 1976 is the representation of the source code as a type of graph. The control flow graph is a directed graph where nodes represent computations and edges the transfer of control. From this graph, a set of basis paths are identified and a test case is generated for each one. This provides a minimal set that covers all non-redundant execution scenarios for the module.

The evaluation of decision and loop nodes being dependent on the unknown state of variables at the time of execution implies that each traversed path element of the set can be associated with an execution probability. Since the coverage obtained from the basis test paths set approach is probabilistic, the use of this technique can potentially generate a test paths set which has little chance of being executed in practice.

When the objective is to define a test paths set such that the coverage probability is above a required confidence level, we must take a different approach. The aim now is to find the set of test cases that guarantee the minimum required probability of being executed. If the probability distribution of the execution paths were known, it would be a simple matter of selecting the smallest set that attains to the required level of confidence. Since this distribution is unknown, we

K.R. Venugopal and L.M. Patnaik (Eds.): ICIP 2012, CCIS 292, pp. 419–425, 2012.
© Springer-Verlag Berlin Heidelberg 2012

could use instead, the probability distribution of the paths obtained by running the program a very large number of times, let's say N, which would converge to the real distribution of execution paths. But this solution would require an amount of computational effort equal to the testing the software itself.

This paper presents an efficient method to find the test case set through the selection of a minimal set of paths, that satisfies the coverage probability, by using the combination of execution samples of size n ($n \leq N$) with a generative algorithm, in such a way that this set can be obtained in a very efficient way. The method has been tested on a set of programs and the results show that the set of paths produced is statistically similar to the one obtained by running a very large sample.

The structure of this paper is as follows: Section 2 presents the most important concepts involving white box tests, Chi-Square and K-S tests and graph representation of programs. Section 3 describe in details the method, while Section 4 shows the computational experiments, comparing to other related works. Conclusions are discussed in Section 5.

2   Conceptual Framework

In this section, we present the main concepts to understand how the method works. Expert readers may jump to Section 3.

2.1   Path Based Testing

A program module M can be thought as a function $M : D \to R$, where D is the input domain and R is the output domain. If RM is the specification relation $\{(d_i, r_i)\}$ we say that M is correct if and only if for every $d_i \in D, (d_i, M(d_i)) \in RM$.

A test set is defined as a subset $T \subseteq D$. A test set is said to be ideal if for every $d_i \in D, (d_i, M(d_i)) \notin RM$ implies $d_i \in T$.

We will restrict our efforts to finding a test set based on the coverage of source code. The "basis path testing" is one of the white box test techniques. The program is associated with a control flow graph, that has unique entry and exit nodes. A path is a sequence of connected nodes that traverse the control flow graph from the start node to the end node. Each path corresponds to a test case element. McCabe introduced the concept of independence in a strong connected graph. Each independent path must include at least one edge that has not been crossed when determining the path. The cyclomatic number $V(G)$ of the control flow graph G is equal to its maximum number of linearly independent paths. Its value is given by the formula $V(G) = e - n + p$, where e, n and p are the number of edges, vertices and connected components respectively.

2.2   Probabilistic Paths

The sample space, in probability theory, is used to represent the outcome of a random experiment. In our case, the sample space is the set $\mathcal{P}$ of all paths p_i resulting from the execution of the program under test.

The set $\mathcal{P}$ may be very large. The goal of our method is to obtain a good approximation $\mathcal{P}_A$ which is not compared directly to $\mathcal{P}$, but instead to a representative sample $\mathcal{P}_L$ of $\mathcal{P}$. Here, $\mathcal{P}_L$ denotes a sample (set of paths) obtained by running a program N times. In $\mathcal{P}_L$, each path p_i will appear with a certain frequency f_i. We define the probability of path p_i in $\mathcal{P}_L$ as the relative frequency $f^N(p_i) = f_i/N$. Note that $\mathcal{P}_L$ contains a finite number of paths, say k. We assume an ordering $p_1, \ldots, p_k, p_{k+1}, \ldots, p_i, \ldots$ in $\mathcal{P}$ such that the first k paths are precisely those occurring in $\mathcal{P}_L$, that is, $\mathcal{P}_L = \{p_1, \ldots, p_k\}$ and $\mathcal{P} = \mathcal{P}_L \cup \{p_{k+1}, \ldots, p_i, \ldots\}$. In addition, define $f^N(p_i) = 0$ for $i > k$.

How to choose N in order to obtain a representative sample of $\mathcal{P}$? For large samples, we can use the table of critical values of the Kolmogorov-Smirnov test [2] with desired confidence level α. It is a widely used nonparametric test for the equality of probability distributions, that can be employed to compare a sample (in our case, $\mathcal{P}_L$) with a reference probability distribution (the one associated with $\mathcal{P}$). The Kolmogorov-Smirnov statistic quantifies a distance K_N between the empirical cumulative distribution function of the sample and the cumulative distribution function of the reference. For a distance K_N, it can be shown that the required value for N can be derived from the desired confidence level α. For $alpha = 95\%$ we get $N \geq \frac{1.36}{1-\alpha}$ and, therefore, $N \geq 740$.

Running the module M N times, using samples obtained on D can be very expensive. The goal of our method is to obtain a good approximation to $\mathcal{P}_L$, $\mathcal{P}_A$, using a generative algorithm and a much smaller sample size, n. In other words:

$\mathcal{P}$ = set of all paths p_i resulting from the execution of the program under test
$\mathcal{P}_L$ = sample set of $\mathcal{P}$ after running a program a large number of times (N)
$\mathcal{P}_A$ = approximation sample set of $\mathcal{P}_L$, obtained by our method

The evaluation of the closeness between the distribution frequencies of $\mathcal{P}_A$ and $\mathcal{P}_L$, also known as the problem of probability distribution fitting, is central to the validation of our method. To develop it, we resort to the χ^2 test [2]).

2.3   Control Flow Graph Representation

The module under test M is represented by a control flow graph containing four types of nodes: activity nodes, junction nodes, decision nodes and loop nodes. Each activity node represents a sequence of source code statements executed as a block, and may have several inputs and outputs [3]. A junction node has a syntax role of joining several branches coming from different places (inputs) into only one (output).Decision nodes have one input and several outputs, each one associated with a probability. The loop node has one input and two outputs, one for going to a node outside the loop, and other for going to a new iteration of the loop, It is also associated with probabilities of exiting the loop or going to a new iteration. The programming structures while-do and do-while associated with boolean conditions will be treated as loop nodes, whilst for-do structures with a predefined number of times will be treated as activity nodes.

3   The Method

Step 1 - Generating the control flow graph: The objective of this step is to draw the control flow graph from the source code of program module M. This means replacing if-structures by decision nodes, while-do and do-while structures by loop nodes, for-do structures and actions by activity nodes. Junction nodes are included in the end, when a node with several inputs needs to join them into a single input.

Step 2 - Running the program module n times and obtaining an estimate of the probabilities associated with decision/loop nodes: Probabilities must be assigned to decision and loop nodes. Since we do not have a previous knowledge of the program behavior, these probabilities are estimated from the results of a number n of program runs, using as input a random sample from the program's domain. These values will enable us to calculate the probability of an execution path, by simply multiplying the probabilities associated with decision and loop nodes in the selected path.

Step 3 - Determining the execution path set $\mathcal{P}_A$: After assigning probabilities to decision and loop nodes, we generate execution paths of program M and calculate the probability of each path. This temporary set of paths is denoted by $\mathcal{P}_{A'}$, where each path is identified by a sequence of nodes being traversed.

Then, after generating $\mathcal{P}_{A'}$, we obtain the execution path set $\mathcal{P}_A$, formed by the paths from $\mathcal{P}_{A'}$ whose sum of probabilities is larger than a required confidence level α. Of course, $\mathcal{P}_A \subseteq \mathcal{P}_{A'}$.

Step 4 - Specifying the desired test case set from the execution path set $\mathcal{P}_A$: Each element of the execution path set will be used to generate one element of the test case set. Although a computationally amenable solution could be attempted by the use of an off-the-shelf SAT solver such as [4], we recommend a simple ad-hoc procedure, in which the program developer translates the required node transitions into natural language specifications for the input values.

4   Application

4.1   A Practical Example

We introduce an example of application of this method. The program called c8up transforms lowercase into uppercase letters of a random string in the input.

Step 2. The program is then run $n = 25$ times in order to estimate the decision and loop node probabilities. This number is enough to generate our sample, but can vary according to the set of programs used in the experiment. The results are shown in Table 1.

Step 3. Next, the set of paths $\mathcal{P}_{A'}$ is identified by traversing the control graph. It is formed by seven paths. Then, we estimate the probability of each path.

We sort the estimated probabilities, as shown in Table 2, and include the paths into the set $\mathcal{P}_A$, so that the sum of their associated probabilities reaches

Table 1. Probabilities for Decision and Loop Nodes

	If		While		
	True	False	Loop 0x	Loop 1x	Loop 2x
Prob.	0.28	0.72	0	0.52	0.48
Transition	4-5	4-6	3-8	3-4, 3-8	3-4, 3-4, 3-8

the confidence level α. Thus, if $\alpha = 90\%$, the set $\mathcal{P}_A$ is formed by paths p_3, p_7, p_2, p_5 and p_6, whose sum of associated probabilities is 96.24%.

Table 2. Sorted path set $\mathcal{P}_{A'}$ with their Respective Probabilities

Path	Estimated path probability
p_3:1-2-3-4-6-7-2-3-8	0.72 * 0.52 = 0.3744
p_7:1-2-3-4-6-7-2-3-4-6-7-2-3-8	0.72 * 0.72 * 0.48 = 0.2488
p_2:1-2-3-4-5-6-7-2-3-8	0.28 * 0.52 = 0.1456
p_5:1-2-3-4-6-7-2-3-4-5-6-7-2-3-8	0.72 * 0.28 * 0.48 = 0.0968
p_6:1-2-3-4-5-6-7-2-3-4-6-7-2-3-8	0.28 * 0.72 * 0.48 = 0.0968
p_4:1-2-3-4-5-6-7-2-3-4-5-6-7-2-3-8	0.28 * 0.28 * 0.48 = 0.0376
p_1:1-2-3-8	0

Step 4. Finally, we translate the execution path set into the test case set. Table 3 shows the translation for the program c8up.

Table 3. Translation of Paths in Test Cases

Path	Test Cases
1-2-3-4-6-7-2-3-8	one character out the range a-z
1-2-3-4-6-7-2-3-4-6-7-2-3-8	two characters, both out the range a-z
1-2-3-4-5-6-7-2-3-8	one character in the range a-z
1-2-3-4-6-7-2-3-4-5-6-7-2-3-8	two characters, one out the range a-z and the one inside
1-2-3-4-5-6-7-2-3-4-6-7-2-3-8	two characters, one in the range a-z and one outside

4.2   Validation of the Method

We devised a simple experiment to validate the method. The objective is to confirm that the resulting path set $\mathcal{P}_A$ along with its probability distribution function is sufficiently close to the real path set $\mathcal{P}$, which will be represented by its proxy,the set $\mathcal{P}_L$, obtained by running the program a sufficiently large number N (1000) of times. Denoting by f^* and f the pdf's of $\mathcal{P}_L$ and $\mathcal{P}_A$, respectively, the null hypothesis was formulated as $H_0 : f^* \neq f$.

The method was applied in a set of fourteen programs written in C/C++. For each program, the path set $\mathcal{P}_L$ along with its associated pdf f^* were generated. Each pdf f^* was then compared to f, obtained by our method. The goodness of fit between each f^* and f in the set was verified using the χ^2 test with a confidence level of 95%. The results show that H_0 is rejected thirteen times out of fourteen. The computational effort was also measured, showing an average gain of computational effort of two orders of magnitude.

4.3   Comparison to Other Related Works

The work by Callahan and Schneider [5] analyzes the execution traces created by monitoring statements during white box testing via a model checker. In this work, no probabilistic analysis of decisions and loops is employed. In Whittaker and Poore's work [6], a procedure for modeling software usage with finite states of a Markov Chain is discussed. Our work focus on white box tests. The work by Burr and Young [7] combines table-based testing and code coverage via Bellcore's Automatic Efficient Test Case Generator (AETG) to generate small, efficient sets of test cases. AETG does not use random inputs; instead, the values of the inputs are known, and several possibilities are combined.

5   Conclusions

This paper presents a computationally efficient method to generate a test set that guarantees a probabilistic coverage above a required confidence level. The method consists of obtaining an approximation of the probability distribution of the set of execution paths using a combination of a sampling procedure, which provides a low cost of execution, and a generative algorithm based on the probabilistic analysis of a special form of control flow graph.

The evaluation tests confirmed that not only the method is simple to use, but also provides a good approximation when comparing $\mathcal{P}_A$ (the set of paths which is the outcome of the method) and $\mathcal{P}_L$ (a large sample of the real set $\mathcal{P}$ of execution paths).

The greatest benefit of our method, however, is the use of a minimal set of test cases, which reduces the computational effort to guarantee that the program reliability is above a required level of confidence.

References

1. McCabe, T.J.: A complexity Measure. IEEE Transactions on Software Engineering 2(4), 308–320 (1976)
2. Hoel, P.G.: Introduction to Mathematical Statistics. Wiley, California (1966)
3. Barbosa, V.C., Ferreira, F.M.L., Kling, D.V., Lopes, E., Protti, F., Schmitz, E.A.: Structured Construction and Simulation of Nondeterministic Stochastic Activity Networks. European Journal of Operational Research 198(1), 266–274 (2009)
4. Goldberg, E., Novikov, Y.: Berkmin: A Fast and Robust Satsolver. In: Conference on Design, Automation and Test in Europe, Washington, USA, pp. 142–149 (April 2002)

5. Callahan, J., Schneider, F., Easterbrook, S.: Automated Software Testing using Model-checking. In: Proceedings 1996 SPIN Workshop, Vienna, Austria (August 1996)
6. Whittaker, J.A., Poore, J.H.: Markov Analysis of Software Specifications. ACM Transactions on Software Engineering and Methodology 2(1), 93–106 (1993)
7. Burr, K., Young, W.: Combinatorial Test Techniques: Table-Based Automation, Test Generation and Code Coverage. In: 7th International Conference on Software Testing, Analysis, and Review, San Diego, USA (October 1998)

Compiler Driven Inter Block Parallelism for Multicore Processors

Kiran D.C., Gurunarayanan S., and Misra J.P.

Birla Institute of Technology and Science, Pilani,
Rajasthan, India
{dck,sguru,jpm}@bits-pilani.com

Abstract. The move to multicore processor architecture has been spurred by diminishing returns from micro architectural techniques to extract ILP. It is desirable to exploit task level parallelism by exposing architecture to compiler in multicore processor. A compiler driven global scheduling technique for scheduling disjoint sub blocks belonging to different blocks of CFG on to multiple cores is proposed with a view to balance the execution speedup and power consumption.

Keywords: Data Dependency, Instruction Level Parallelism (ILP), Multicore Processors, Static Single Assignment (SSA).

1 Introduction

The principle behind RISC architecture is to move the architecture boundary down closer to the hardware, exposing key performance features to the compiler. By doing so, it can take advantage of the compiler by off-loading the task like choreographing complex instructions from the hardware to compiler, to get high performance processor. But subsequent generations of microprocessors focused on fully hardware-based approaches for many optimizations, resulting in complex hardware implementations of algorithms such as branch prediction, instruction level parallelism detection, and register renaming/allocation. The analysis at compile time can simplify and eliminate many of the complex algorithms in the hardware. Some architecture like RAW [1] and TRIPS[2] aims to maximally utilize the compiler by fully exposing the hardware and giving control to the software systems. Furthermore, compiler based analysis can be more rigorous and can lead in increase of the effectiveness in optimizations than hardware, because hardware-based approaches work under heavy resource and time constraints. Also todays compilers are capable of analyzing whole program behavior and can infer detailed information about parallelism. Instruction Level Parallelism (ILP) is a technique used in both single core and multicore systems to speed up execution by executing individual machine operations in parallel. ILP indicates which instructions can be executed in parallel and which have to be executed in order. At micro-architectural level there are different techniques like reordering of instructions, out-of-order scheduling, speculative execution, and register renaming, to exploit ILP [3]. Also ILP is introduced in compilers for

K.R. Venugopal and L.M. Patnaik (Eds.): ICIP 2012, CCIS 292, pp. 426–435, 2012.
© Springer-Verlag Berlin Heidelberg 2012

single core architecture and has proved that it can improve the performance [4]. For multicore architectures these techniques can be improved in order to benefit from the extra processing power. The basis of ILP is dependency analysis. The result of this analysis is used by compiler to identify the independent instructions which can be executed in parallel. In most of the techniques split of the code is done on a function basis, making each instruction to execute on a different processor. Here the time spent on communicating the results will be more than the speed-up obtained by running the instruction in parallel. In recent previous work [5], a parallelization scheme involving extracting intra block parallelism within SSA form sequential programs [6]-[8] was shown. An attempt was made to identify parallel constructs in a SSA form program and figuring out a way to represent and to handle them. The disjoint set of instructions was created by looking into true dependency among the instructions in a basic block. The intra block scheduler was used to schedule these disjoint sub-blocks on multiple cores. This technique results in achieving better performance in terms of speedup. Intra block scheduler maps the sub-block on to different cores by taking two factors into consideration, one being the register requirement of each sub-block to avoid spill and other is the power optimization [9]. The entire flow is shown in Figure 2. In the following sections, the steps involved in applying these techniques globally will be discussed. The rest of the paper is organized as follows. Section 2 and 3 gives a brief overview of the architecture and compiler used in the work. Section 4 give details of creating Sub-block Dependency Graph (SDG). Section 5 gives the detail of the inter block scheduling technique. Analysis and discussion of results are given in section 6. Finally, the paper concludes with Section 7.

2   Target Architecture

Fig. 1 shows the architecture targeted by our compiler. This type of architecture fully exposes the low level details of hardware to compiler. They implement minimal set of mechanisms in the hardware and these mechanisms are fully exposed to software, where software includes both runtime system and compiler. Here runtime system manages mechanisms historically managed by hardware, and compiler has responsibility of managing issues like resource allocation, extracting parallel constructs for different cores, configurable logic, and scheduling. These types of architectures can be seen in some network processors and RAW architecture.

The multicore environment has multiple interconnected tiles and on each tile we can have one RISC like processor or core. Each core has instruction memory, data memory, PC, functional units, register files, and source clock. FIFO is used for communication. Here the register files are distributed, eliminating the small register name space problem, thus allows exploiting ILP at greater level.

3   Compiler

This Section briefly describes the compiler which has been used for initial experimentation. For this experiment, Jackcc Compiler [10] has been used. This is

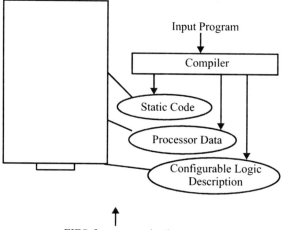

Fig. 1. Compiler Generated Code and their Relation with Architecture (Core/Processor)

an open source compiler developed at university of Virginia. The basic block in CFG of Jackcc is called Arena, and instruction inside the block is called Quad. Instructions are in SSA form. The flow (function calls) of *jackcc* is shown in Fig. 1. The DAG generated by front end of the compiler is converted into quad intermediate representation, and then these quads are used to construct the basic blocks of CFG. The dead code elimination, peephole optimization, common sub-expression elimination, etc, are done by appropriate functions. Register assignments are done by the function color-graph. Assembly level program is generated by quad-2 asm function. The disjoint union operation is performed on the SSA form instruction within a basic block. This is an extra pass of the compiler finds the true-dependency of the instruction and forms disjoint sub-blocksm [8]. These sub-blocks are given as input to intra block scheduler, which maps them on to multiple cores to execute concurrently [9].

4   Inter Block Parallelism

The technique of extracting inter block parallelism is performed by considering all the sub-blocks across the program (CFG). The sub-blocks are disjoint within a basic block of CFG, but the sub-block across the basic blocks need not be disjoint. The non-disjoint sub-blocks should be executed one after the other. Inter block parallelism is a process of finding the non-disjoint sub-blocks across the basic block and define AFTER relation between them.

Definition 1: The sub-block SB_i of block B_p should be scheduled after SB_j of block B_q where $p \neq q$, if one or more instruction in SB_i has true dependency with the instruction in SB_j. Thus SB_i is AFTER related with SB_j and it is denoted as $SB_j \rightarrow SB_i$. In Figure 3, the sub-block SB_1 of block B_2 is AFTER

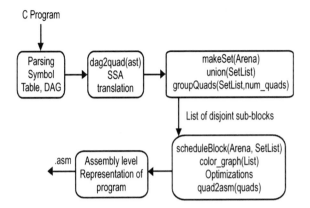

Fig. 2. Work Flow of Jackcc

related on SB_1 of block B_1 and it is denoted as $B_1SB_1 \rightarrow B_2SB_1$ and similarly $B_1SB_2 \rightarrow B_3SB_2$.

There are three steps involved in the process of extracting inter block parallelism.

1. Creating disjoint sub-blocks: The sub-block B_pSB_i is created by analyzing the dependency of instructions locally in a basic block B_p. The instructions showing true dependency are placed in same sub-blocks, thus making disjoint sub-blocks [5]. This process is performed by applying disjoint set functions as shown in Fig. 2.
2. Construction of sub-block dependency graph (SDG): The SDG is graph G (V,E), where vertex viV is sub-block B_pSB_i, and the edge eE, is drawn between vertex SB_iB_p and SB_jB_q where $p \neq q$, and sub-blocks are AFTER related. SDG is represented as dependency matrix as shown in Fig. 3. In dependency matrix all sub-blocks are arranged in first column. If the sub-block B_pSB_i is dependent on sub-block B_qSB_j, then B_qSB_j is added in the dependency list of B_pSB_i, meaning B_pSB_i should be scheduled only after B_qSB_j complete its execution. The sub-block B_pSB_i can be scheduled only if the list is empty otherwise it should wait till the list becomes empty.
3. Global scheduling: Scheduler picks the sub-block BpSBi from the dependency matrix if its dependency list is empty. Once B_pSB_i is scheduled and completes its execution, its entry is removed in all dependency lists. When B_1SB_1 is scheduled and completes its execution, its entry in row 4 is removed. When B_1SB_2 is scheduled and completes its execution, its entry in row 7 is removed. Similarly, when B_2SB_3 is scheduled and completes its execution,, its entry in row 5 and 6 is removed.

4.1   Sub Block of Dependence Graph(SDG)

The data structure of a node of CFG is very much similar to data structure of block with extra pointers to its children and parents in CFG. In CFG, apart from the data elements present in the block, we also have pointers child1, child2 and *parents*[] (list of children and parents the CFG node can have). ϕ[] is the list of ϕ functions. Each element of ϕ[] corresponds to the function of one variable. It has as many columns as number of parents to the node. Each entry stores the version number of the variable from the corresponding branch. *no_rows* indicates the number of ϕ functions. Once the block is split into subblocks, the array *subbl_phi*[] stores the sub-block number to which each function belongs. The dependencies of each sub-block is computed and are stored in structures *dependency_Block* and *dependency_SubBlock* while former stores pointers to blocks to which a sub-block is dependent upon, latter stores the corresponding sub-block number. depcount stores the number of dependencies. *subBlockGraph*[] is an array of nodes of sub-block dependency graph one node corresponding to each sub-block. In SDG node in Sub-block Dependence Graph has list of quads, Sub-block number, size, list of children, list of parents, ϕ functions belonging to the sub-block and a pointer to the node of CFG to which the sub-block belongs.

4.2 Algorithm

Constructing sub-block dependence graph involves two steps. First is computing dependency and next is creating SDG.

```
ComputeDependency
Begin
    for each subBlockSBi in SetList L
    begin
        for each  function belonging to sub-block SBi
        begin
            for each column of  function, j=1 to numparents
            begin
                add [j] to the list use[SBi]
                end for
            end for
        for each quad Q in sub-block SBi
        begin
            add srca and srcb of Q to the list use[SBi]
        end for
        for each variable v in use[SBi]
        begin
            L= find sub-block in which v is defined
            addToDependencyList(SBi,L)
        end for
End
```

1. Dependency is computed block-wise, in the order of CFG. The function *computeDependency*() takes a node of CFG (a block) as input and computes dependency of all subblocks in that block. It goes to every sub-block

and examines all phi functions in the sub-block and identifies the use list of each variable. It then goes to each use and finds in which sub-block and block, it was defined. It then adds this sub-block to the list of dependencies. It repeats the process for each quad in the sub-block, computing use and finding where it was defined. Also, while examining each instruction, whenever there is a definition, it adds the variable to the def list. The function $addToDependencyList()$ will take a sub-block and the sub-block to which it is dependent upon and it will add this sub-block to the list of dependencies, $dependency\_Block$ and $dependency\_SubBlock$.

2. Creating SDG Once the dependencies are computed, the CFG is traversed again and call function $createSDG()$ for each block (each node of CFG). Input to this function is a node A of CFG and SetList corresponding to the node L. Based on dependency computation of the sub-blocks, it creates nodes for each sub-block in A and adds edges to the blocks it is dependent upon its parents. The result of the two steps is illustrated in Fig. 3.

```
createSDG
begin
   for each subBlockSBi in SetList L
   begin
     Create a node of SDG, say v corresponding to SBi
      for j=1 to depcount[SBj]
       begin
         u=SDG node corresponding to dependencyblock [SB_ij] and
         sub-block dependencyblock[SB_ij]
         add the edge u → v
         include v in list of us children
         include u in the list of vs parents
       end for
   end for
End
```

5   Mapping Inter Block Disjoint Sub-blocks on to Multiple Cores

This section explains the proposed dynamic and efficient compiler based scheduling algorithm for multi-core processors. The sub-block dependency graph represented in the form of adjacency matrix is used to capture the execution time of each sub-block and to map them on to multiple cores. The latencies of the sub-blocks are calculated and are arranged in decreasing order of latencies. Then these sub-blocks are scheduled on to different cores.

5.1 Scheduler

In this algorithm the sub-block is picked from top of the list (descending order of latencies) and is scheduled to core with less scheduling time, then one of the child (if any and if ready) of recently scheduled sub-block is also scheduled on the same core, and it continues with next sub-block. Switching of core is done when a leaf sub-block is reached and scheduling time of current core is greater than global maximum scheduling time. The scheduler, keeps track of sub-blocks ready time to execute, and global maximum scheduling time.

```
Ready-time of sub-block
    j = max (finish time of all immediate predecessors).
    Finish time of sub-block i = number of cycles in i + schedule
time of i.
    Scheduler
    Step 1: Find Latency
    Latency of sub-block i = max
    (latencies of all immediate successors) + number of
instructions in sub-block i.
    Step 2: Sort sub-blocks by descending latency.
    Step 3: Schedule
    If Single Core  in order of sorted list.
    If Multi Core:
    i. Repeat steps (ii) to (viii) until list gets empty
    ii. Temp ← complete top (list) (ready sub-block)
    iii. Schedule temp & increment schedule time of this core.
    iv. Update finish-time of temp and ready-time for all
immediate successors.
    v. If any immediate successor of temp is ready
    (check in order of list) & list is non-empty
    temp ← immediate successor
    goto step (iii)
    vi. If schedule time of current core is less than max
schedule time
& list is non-empty
    goto step (ii)
    vii. Max schedule time ← schedule time of current core
    viii. If list is non-empty
    goto step (ii)
end
```

Table 1. Speedup Statistics

System	Test Case 1	Test Case 2	Test Case 3	Test Case 4
Single Core	1	1	1	1
Dual Core(Intra Block)	1.72	1.72	1.65	1.77
Dual Core(Inter Block)	1.93	1.91	1.93	1.89
Quad Core(Intra Block)	2.25	2.69	2.14	1.84
Quad Core(Inter Block)	3.11	3.44	2.93	2.44

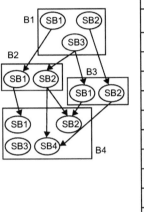

	Sub blocks	Dependency List	
1	B1SB1 ->8		
2	B1SB2 ->6		
3	B1SB3 ->8		
4	B2SB1- ->5	B1SB1	
5	B2SB2 ->6	B1SB3	
6	B3SB1 ->4	B1SB3	
7	B3SB2 ->8	B1SB2	
8	B4SB1 ->5	B2SB1	
9	B4SB2 ->6	B3SB1	B2SB2
10	B4SB3 ->4		
11	B4SB4 ->5	B2SB2	B3SB2

Fig. 3. a. Sub-block Dependency Graph **b.** Dependency Matrix

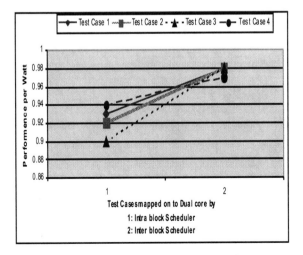

Fig. 4. Performance Watt of each Test Case on Dual Core System

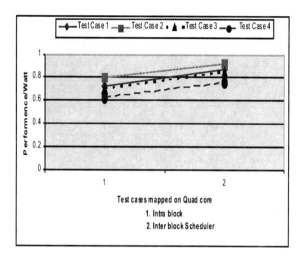

Fig. 5. Performance Watt of each Test Case on Quad Core System

6   Experimental Results

The effectiveness of the proposed technique for detecting and scheduling inter-block disjoint sub-blocks on to multiple cores is assessed in this section. The experiments are done on 3 systems, with one core, 2 cores (Dual core) and 4 cores (Quad core) and the results of 4 different extreme test cases are shown. All the test cases are mapped on to multiple cores using the proposed schedulers and their execution time in terms of cycles are captured. Performance in terms of speed up is calculated using Amdahls law. The result is normalized to the performance metric to that of a basic unit core, which is equivalent to the Base Core Equivalents (BCE) in the Hill-Marty model [11]. Also, the result of proposed technique is compared with the Intra block scheduler. It is observed that the proposed technique attain better performance in terms of speedup with inter-block parallelism than intra-block as shown in Table 1. The speedup for quad-core is more than speedup of dual-core system. To check the energy efficiency of the approach, performance per power model proposed by Woo-Lee model [12] is used. The power consumed to execute the test cases is captured and performance per power of each test case is calculated.

Speedup increases (mostly) with increase in number of cores. It is observed that, more the number of cores used more the power consumed. Since both the factors increase independently it is difficult to predict what will be the change in their ratio. So systems with different number of cores should not be compared with respect to power consumption (Perf/W). Performance per power is compared on same type of system (either dual core or quad core machines) for different schedulers. Here we compare the performance per power using intra block scheduler and the proposed inter block scheduler on dual core and quad core machine independently. The result is shown in Fig. 4 and Fig. 5. It is observed that performance with respect to power consumption (Perf/W) is improved with inter-block scheduling than respective intra-block scheduling.

7   Conclusions

Finding an effective way to exploit the parallelism or concurrency inherent in an application is one of the most daunting challenges in multicore environment. This paper discuss the technique to extract the inter block disjoint sub-bocks and to schedule them on to multiple cores. Here we propose and compare a scheduler to map the disjoint sub-block on to multiple cores. Since power is another important factor in multicore environment, the proposed scheduler will balance power consumption and speedup. The result shows that the inter block scheduler will perform better in terms of speedup by balancing the power consumption.

References

1. Waingold, E., Taylor, M., Srikrishna, D., Sarkar, V., Lee, W., Lee, V., Kim, J., Frank, M., Finch, P., Barua, R., Babb, J., Amarasinghe, S., Agarwal, A.: Baring it all to software: Raw machines. Computers 30(9), 86–93 (1997)
2. Gebhart, M., Maher, B.A.: An Evaluation of the TRIPS Computer System. ACM SIGPLAN Notices ASPLOS, 1–12 (March 2009)
3. Tyson, G., Farrens, M.: Techniques for Extracting Instruction Level Parallelism on MIMD Architectures. In: 26th International Symposium on Microarchitecture, pp. 128–137 (1993)
4. Schlansker, M.C., Dehnert, T.M., Ebcioglu, J., Fang, K., Thompson, J.Z.: Compilers for Instruction-Level Parallelism. IEEE Computer 30(12) (December 1997)
5. Kiran, D.C., Gurunarayanan, S., Misra, J.P.: Taming Compiler to Work with Multicore Processors. In: IEEE Conference on Process Automation, Control and Computing (2011)
6. Cytron, R., Ferrante, J., Rosen, B.K., Wegman, M.N., Zadeck, F.K.: Efficient Computing Static Single Assignment Form and the Control Dependence Graph. ACM Transaction on Programming Languages and Systems 13(4), 451–490 (1991)
7. Briggs, P., Copper, K., Harvey, T., Simpson, T.: Practical Improvements to the Construction and Destruction of Static Single Assignment Form. Software-Practice and Experience 28(8), 859–881 (1998)
8. Aycock, J., Horspool, N.: Simple Generation of Static-Single Assignment Form. In: 8th International Conference, pp. 110–124 (2000)
9. Kiran, D.C., Radheshyam, B., Gurunarayanan, S., Misra, J.P.: Compiler Assisted Dynamic Scheduling for Multicore Processors. In: IEEE Conference on Process Automation, Control and Computing (2011)
10. The Jack Compiler, http://jackcc.sourceforge.net
11. Hill, M.D., Marty, M.R.: Amdahls Law in the Multicore Era. IEEE Computer, 33–38 (2008)
12. Dong, H.W., Hsien, H.S.L.: Extending Amdahls Law for Energy-Efficient Computing in the Many-Core Era. IEEE Computer, 24–31 (2008)

Implementation of Application Specific Network-On-Chip Architectures on Reconfigurable Device Using Topology Generation Algorithm with Genetic Algorithm Based Optimization Technique

Maheswari M.[1] and Seetharaman G.[2]

[1] Department of Electronics and Communication Engineering,
J.J. College of Engineering and Technology,
Trichirappalli-620 009
kousi.rhithi@gmail.com
[2] Oxford Engineering College,
Trichirappalli-620 009

Abstract. In Networks-On-Chip (NOC) architecture, routers are the main sources of power consumption. Hence to reduce the power consumption, the application should be mapped on a custom topology rather than on regular topologies, as custom topology uses fewer routers than regular topologies. This reduces the power consumption. In this paper, we propose a novel topology generation algorithm using genetic algorithm optimization technique to generate a custom topology for Application Specific Networks-On-Chip (ASNOC) architectures. We applied the novel algorithm to benchmark video applications MPEG 4 decoder and PIP. The implementation of the proposed algorithm on Altera cyclone II FPGA device EP2C35F672C6 shows good results in terms of area, power consumption, hop count and number of global links compared to standard topologies like Mesh, Ring, Star and Binary Tree.

Keywords: ASIC, ASNOC, Custom Topology, FPGA, Low Power, NOC.

1 Introduction

Networks-On-Chip (NOC) has emerged as a viable solution for designing energy efficient and high performance architectures for Multi Processor SOC (MPSOC) [1]. In NOC, the design of the topology affects the performance, power consumption and overall area of the on chip interconnection network. In modern ASNOCs, different communication requirement exists between different cores [2]. For these ASNOCs, standard topologies would result in poor performance and large overhead of power consumption and area. The power consumption and area of the topology depends on the number of routers used in the topology and the numbers of hops the data bits take to reach destination [3]. This requires application

K.R. Venugopal and L.M. Patnaik (Eds.): ICIP 2012, CCIS 292, pp. 436–445, 2012.
© Springer-Verlag Berlin Heidelberg 2012

specific topology which requires few routers than standard topologies like Mesh, Ring, Star and Binary Tree to minimize the area and power consumption [4]. The number of routers the data bits take to reach the destination determines the power consumption. The more the number of routers the data bits takes, the higher is the total power consumption. Hence, we must construct application specific topology in such a way that the number of hops or routers the data bits take to reach the destination is reduced [5]. This reduces power consumption and increases the performance, as the message bits take fewer routers to reach the destination.

In this paper, we propose a novel topology generation algorithm using genetic algorithm optimization technique that is capable of generating custom topology for a specific application to reduce the power consumption than that of regular topologies. The rest of the paper is organized as follows: in section 2, we present the overview of the state-of-the-art in the area of application specific topology generation in NOC. In section 3, we present analysis of power consumption in NOC. In section 4, we present the proposed novel algorithm. In section 5, we present the results and discussion and finally the conclusion is given in section 6.

2   Related Work

In recent years, many research works have been carried out in the design of the application specific custom topology. Throughput oriented custom topology is generated by using two algorithms [2] and their topology is compared with standard topologies like Mesh and Fat tree and another custom topology. The authors considered number of hops between two cores for low latency and reduce the inter switch communication traffic volume which is to be minimized for low power. Four various heuristics based algorithms are proposed [5] for generating the optimal tree based topology for multimedia applications. In [6]-[8] mapping of the cores onto NOC standard topology has been proposed. Floor plan information is used to get area estimation for the mapping of the cores onto topology [7]. In [8] a unified approach is used for mapping and routing for only standard topologies.

An application specific topology design has been considered in [9][11]. In [9] and [10] floor plan information is not used for the design of the custom topology. In [11] the authors try to reduce the power consumption on wire using physical planner. In [12], the authors propose an evaluation methodology to compare the performance and characteristics of a variety of standard NOC architectures like SPIN, CLICH, Torus, Folded torus, Octagon, BFT. A prototype implementation of the NOC architecture for multimedia applications in FPGA and ASIC is carried out in [13]. The authors use the SCOTCH partitioning tool and map complex application task graph onto four architecture [14] analysis is performed by OMNET++ simulator. In [15], the authors present a design methodology for the synthesis of application specific NOC architectures and propose a two stage synthesis approach for (i) core to router mapping (ii) custom topology and route generation. They use the port constrained router for their design. They evaluate the performance of multimedia bench mark applications for application specific NOC and compare their results with the existing results. In [16], [17], [18] the authors propose linear programming based custom topology generation from the floor plan of the application. In [19], the authors propose the power aware topology construction method which is used to construct Application Specific low power interconnection topologies based on the traffic characteristics of SOC. In [20], the authors propose a complete NOC Synthesis flow. In [21], the authors propose a partitioning algorithm and apply for the MPEG 4 decoder. The authors analyze and compare the performances of the NOC, like power, hop count and the number of links with the standard topologies and hybrid topologies. In [22], the authors generate custom topology for benchmark video application and they compare their work with the existing algorithm.

The work proposed in [19], [22] for topology generation of ASNOC, use four ports routers. This constrain forces them to use more number of routers. In contrast to these works, the work proposed in this paper, is a three phase novel topology generation algorithm that uses a router with parametrizable number of ports. In our proposed work the number of ports can be parameterized up to seven. The increase in the number of ports in a router from 4 ports to seven ports increases the router crossbar size which in turn increases the power consumption of the single router. Although the power consumed by the single router is increased the overall router power consumption in the topology is reduced. This is because, the number of routers used for the given applications is reduced compared to the work proposed in [19], [22]. To evaluate the effectiveness of the proposed algorithm, we applied the proposed algorithm to two benchmark video applications namely MPEG 4 decoder and PIP. The custom topology generated by the proposed algorithm uses lesser number of routers than standard topologies and the other custom topologies generated by the existing topology generation algorithms. This reduces area, power consumption compared to the previous works.

3   Power Analysis in NOC

Power consumption is the key limitation factor in NOCs, where the power is dissipated in two components: (i) the switches (router) located in the cross points of the network and (ii) the interconnect wires. These interconnect wires consume significant amount of power. A brief power analysis is given for the NOC router and the interconnection links.

3.1   Power Analysis of NOC Router

The design of the network router consists of four parts: (i) input port (ii) arbitration unit (iii) crossbar switch and (iv) output port. The basic router unit is given in the Fig. 1. The input port has buffers to store the data and a header decoder unit to decode the destination address. When the flits arrive at the input port, the flits are stored in the buffer, and the header unit decodes the destination address from the header flit. It sends the request to the output port. When more than one input ports request the same output port, the arbiter in the output port, gives access to one input port at a time in round robin fashion. The input port that receives the access sends the flits through the crossbar switch to the output port. We examined the area and the power consumption of the NOC router for different number of ports, by implementing on Altera cyclone II EP2C35F672C6 device. The results of the area occupancy, power consumption are shown in Fig. 2.

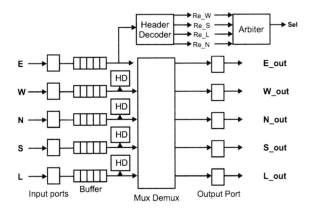

Fig. 1. Router Architecture

3.2   Power Analysis of NOC Links

There are two main sources of power consumption in on chip interconnections. They are: (i) the coupling capacitance between the adjacent wires, and (ii) the capacitance between wire and ground. The power consumed on interconnection wires between two neighbor switches is given as in (1).

$$P_{dyn} = \frac{\alpha \, C \, f \, V_{dd}^2}{2}.$$ (1)

Where, C is the capacitance of the interconnection wires, α is the average switching activity in the wires, f is the signal frequency, V_{dd} is the supply voltage.

4   Proposed Methodology

The idea for generating low power custom topology is to form clusters of the cores. To do this, the cores are clustered based on the communication volume (traffic) between them. The cores that have larger communication volume (traffic) are grouped to the same cluster to form localization. This localization creates shorter communication distance between the cores that have larger communication volume and reduces the average number of hops between sources to destination. We connect one router for one cluster. The number of ports in the router is selected based on the number of cores in the cluster. Hu and Marculescu [10] proposed the average energy consumption of sending one bit of data from tile t_i to t_j is

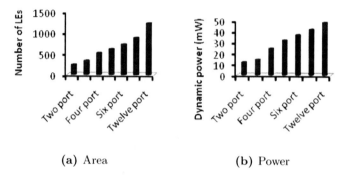

(a) Area   (b) Power

Fig. 2. Comparison of Area, Power of the Router

$$P_{bit}^{t_i.t_j} = n_{hops}E_{sbit} + E_{lbit}(n_{hops} - 1). \tag{2}$$

Where, E_{sbit} is the Energy consumption of a router, E_{lbit} is the Energy consumption of interconnecting wires, n_{hops} is the number of routers the bit passes. To formulate this problem more formally, we propose the following definitions as in [1].

Definition 1. The Communication Task Graph (CTG) is an unidirected Graph, G (V, E), where each vertex $v_i \in V$ represents a core and the directed edge $e_k = (v_i, v_j) \in E$ represents the communication between the cores v_i and v_j. W_{ij} represents the communication volume between two cores v_i and v_j.

Definition 2. The Router Communication Graph (RCG) is a fully connected graph with m vertices, where m is the number of clusters. The edge weights are set to zero.

The bandwidth constrain of the router is Br. We fix the cluster to have number of cores less than or equal to six. In [23], the use of multi local port router increases the router performance and reduces the number of routers used in the topology which in turn reduces the overall power consumption in the topology. Hence, to get better performance of the router and at the same time only small increase in the router size, we select the routers to have number of ports less than or equal to seven. Leaving one port for interconnection, we select the cluster size is less than or equal to 6 cores. Table 1 compares the overall router power consumption for the proposed algorithm with the previous works. In the following sub section, we present the proposed three phase topology generation algorithm.

Table 1. Comparison of the Total Router Power Consumption for MPEG 4 Decoder

	7 Port	6 Port	5 Port	4 Port	3 Port	2 Port	Total Router Power in mW
The Work Proposed in [18]	–	–	–	5	–	–	123.6
The work Proposed in [22]	–	–	–	5	–	–	123.6
The work Proposed in [19]	2	–	–	–	–	3	121.08
Our Proposed Algorithm	2	–	–	5	–	–	84.72

4.1   The Proposed Algorithm

The proposed topology generation algorithm has three phases. They are: (i) Construction of clusters (ii) Optimization of clusters using GA (iii) Topology Generation.

4.2   Genetic Algorithm Based Optimization

In the second phase of the proposed algorithm, optimization of cores is done and RCG is built. The clusters are optimized using Genetic Algorithm (GA) based optimization technique.

(i) **GA Based Optimization:** GA applies crossover and mutation to produce new solutions. A crossover combines two solutions to generate a new solution and mutations modifies an existing solution to generate a new solution. Application of two point crossover in cluster array is shown in Fig. 3.

(ii) **Population Representation:** GA based optimization technique requires a representation of the population for the application of genetic operators [6]. We set the population size is equal to the number of cores n multiplied by the number of clusters m. The total population size is divided equally among the clusters. In each cluster the population is represented as strings of chromosomes in an array and is called as cluster array. We form m cluster arrays. The cluster array is a binary array where a 1 in a location denotes the presence of the core in that cluster and a 0 denotes that the core is not present in that cluster. For example in a cluster array a 1 in 5th location represents the core 5 is present in that cluster and a 0 in 9th location denotes core 9 is not in that cluster.

(iii) **Criteria for Solution Selection:** Since a cluster has number of cores less than or equal to six, the criteria to be satisfied in the cluster array is that the number of 1s in the cluster array is less than or equal to six. We apply two point crossover to produce the solutions. Only the solutions that satisfy the above criteria are considered for the fitness calculation. The fitness functions are given in (3) and (4) in the algorithm. The custom topology generated by the proposed

Table 2. Algorithm: Topology Generation

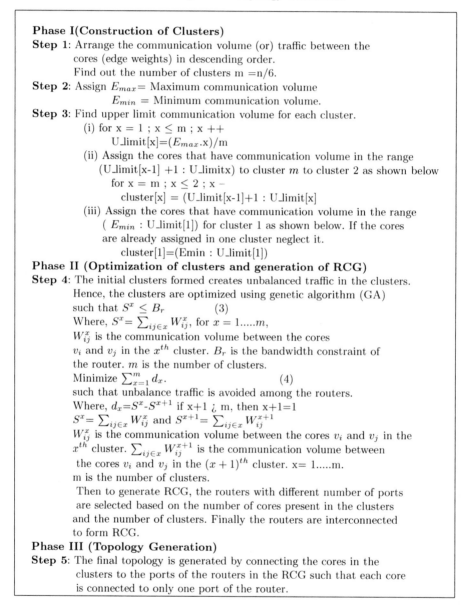

Phase I(Construction of Clusters)

Step 1: Arrange the communication volume (or) traffic between the
cores (edge weights) in descending order.
Find out the number of clusters m =n/6.

Step 2: Assign E_{max}= Maximum communication volume
E_{min} = Minimum communication volume.

Step 3: Find upper limit communication volume for each cluster.
    (i) for x = 1 ; x ≤ m ; x ++
        U_limit[x]=(E_{max}.x)/m
    (ii) Assign the cores that have communication volume in the range
        (U_limit[x-1] +1 : U_limitx) to cluster m to cluster 2 as shown below
        for x = m ; x ≤ 2 ; x -
        cluster[x] = (U_limit[x-1]+1 : U_limit[x]
    (iii) Assign the cores that have communication volume in the range
        (E_{min} : U_limit[1]) for cluster 1 as shown below. If the cores
    are already assigned in one cluster neglect it.
        cluster[1]=(Emin : U_limit[1])

Phase II (Optimization of clusters and generation of RCG)

Step 4: The initial clusters formed creates unbalanced traffic in the clusters.
Hence, the clusters are optimized using genetic algorithm (GA)
such that $S^x \leq B_r$ (3)
Where, $S^x = \sum_{ij \in x} W_{ij}^x$, for $x = 1.....m$,
W_{ij}^x is the communication volume between the cores
v_i and v_j in the xth cluster. B_r is the bandwidth constraint of
the router. m is the number of clusters.
Minimize $\sum_{x=1}^{m} d_x$.   (4)
such that unbalance traffic is avoided among the routers.
Where, $d_x = S^x - S^{x+1}$ if x+1 ¿ m, then x+1=1
$S^x = \sum_{ij \in x} W_{ij}^x$ and $S^{x+1} = \sum_{ij \in x} W_{ij}^{x+1}$
W_{ij}^x is the communication volume between the cores v_i and v_j in the
x^{th} cluster. $\sum_{ij \in x} W_{ij}^{x+1}$ is the communication volume between
the cores v_i and v_j in the $(x + 1)^{th}$ cluster. x= 1.....m.
m is the number of clusters.
Then to generate RCG, the routers with different number of ports
are selected based on the number of cores present in the clusters
and the number of clusters. Finally the routers are interconnected
to form RCG.

Phase III (Topology Generation)

Step 5: The final topology is generated by connecting the cores in the
clusters to the ports of the routers in the RCG such that each core
is connected to only one port of the router.

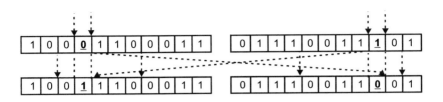

Fig. 3. Cross Over in Cluster Array

algorithm minimizes overall energy consumption because most of the bits travel within the router which takes one hop only. Fig. 4 shows the custom topology generated for MPEG 4 decoder.

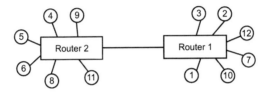

Fig. 4. Custom Topology Generated by the Proposed Algorithm for MPEG 4 Decoder

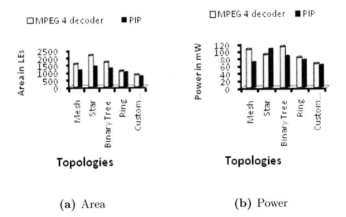

(a) Area   (b) Power

Fig. 5. Comparison of standard topologies on FPGA for Area, Power

5   Experimental Results and Discussion

We have applied the proposed algorithm to two different benchmark video applications MPEG 4 decoder (12 cores) and Picture-in-Picture (8 cores). We implemented the applications using standard topologies and custom topology on

Altera cyclone II FPGA EP2C35F672C6 device by applying a synthetic traffic generator that resembles the applications traffic nature. The area, power consumption, average hop count and number of global links for the standard topologies and the custom topology for the two benchmark applications are shown in Fig. 5. The custom topology generated by proposed topology generation algorithm results in 1.31× improvement in area, 1.26× improvement in power consumption and 2.6× improvement in hop count for MPEG 4 decoder. For PIP application, the proposed algorithm results in 1.4× improvement in area, 1.13× improvement in power consumption and 4.5× improvement in hop count.

6   Conclusions

In this paper, we presented a novel custom topology generation algorithm using genetic algorithm based optimization technique to generate the custom topology for ASNOCs. We evaluate the performance of the proposed algorithm for two benchmark applications MPEG 4 decoder and PIP. We compare the custom topology generated by the proposed algorithm with the standard topologies like mesh, star, binary tree, ring. We implement the topologies on cylone II FPGA EP2C35F672C6 device. From the experimental results we find that the proposed algorithm generates custom topology which consumes less power and occupies lesser area compared to the standard topologies.

References

1. Murali, S., et al.: Designing Application Specific Network on Chips with Floorplan Information. In: Proceedings of ICCAD 2006, pp. 355–362 (November 2006)
2. Dumitriu, V., Gui, N.K.: Throughput Oriented NoC Topology Generation and Analysis for High Performance SoCs. IEEE Transactions on Very Large Scale Integration, 1433–1446 (2009)
3. Guoming, L., Lin, X.: Floor Plan Aware Application Specific Network on Chip Topology Synthesis using Genetic Algorithm Technique. The Journal of Super Computing (2011) (online first)
4. Srinivasan, K., Karam, S., Chatha: A Technique for Low Energy Mapping and Routing in Network on Chip Architectures. In: Proceedings of ISLPED 2005, pp. 387–392 (2005)
5. Deepak, M., Pasalapudi, A., Yalamanchili, K.: Low Energy Tree Based Network on Chip Architectures using Homogeneous Routers for Bandwidth and Latency Constrained Multimedia Applications
6. Hu, J., Marculescu, R.: Exploiting the Routing Flexibility for Energy/performance Aware Mapping of Regular NOC Architectures (2003)
7. Murali, S., De Micheli, G.: SUNMAP: A tool for Automatic Topology Selection and Generation for NOCs. In: Proceedings of DAC (2004)
8. Hansson, A., et al.: A unified Approach to Constrained Mapping and Routing on Network on Chip Architectures. In: Proceedings of ASPDAC, pp. 75–80 (2005)
9. Pinto, A., et al.: Efficient Synthesis of Network on Chip. In: ICCD 2003, pp. 146–150 (2003)

10. Ho, W.H., Pinkson, T.M.: A Methodology for Designing Efficient on Chip Interconnects on Well Behaved Communication Patterns. In: HPCA 2003, pp. 377–388 (2003)

11. Ahonen, T., et al.: Topology Optimization for Application Specific Network On Chip. In: Proceedings of SLIP 2004 (2004)

12. Pande, P.P., et al.: Performance Evaluation and Design Trade Offs for Network-On-Chip Interconnect Architectures. IEEE Transactions On Computer, 1025–1040 (2005)

13. Umit, Y., Ogras, et al.: Challenges and Promising Results in NOC Prototyping using FPGAs. IEEE Microelectronics, 86–95 (2007)

14. Luciano, B., et al.: NoC Topologies Exploration Based on Mapping and Simulation Models. In: Proc. of Euromicro Conference on DSD (2007)

15. Karam, S.C., Srinivasan, K., Konjevod, G.: Automated Technique for Synthesis of Application Specific Network on Chip Architectures. IEEE Transactions On Computer Design of Inte. Circuits and Systems, 1425–1438 (2008)

16. Srinivasan, K., Chatha, K.S., Konjevod, G.: Linear programming based Techniques for Synthesis of Network on Chip Architectures. IEEE Transactions on Very Large Scale Integrated System 14(4), 407–420 (2004)

17. Leary, G., Srinivasan, K., Metha, K., Chatha, K.S.: Design of Network-on-Chip Architectures with a Genetic Algorithm based Techniques. IEEE Transactions on Very Large Scale Integrated System 17(5), 674–687 (2009)

18. Srinivasan, K., Chatha, K., Konjevod, G.: An Automated Technique for the Topology and Router Generation of Application Specific on Chip Interconnection Networks. In: Proceedinds of IEEE/ACM Int. Conf. on Computer Aided Design, pp. 231–237 (2005)

19. Chang, K.C., Chen, T.F.: Low Power Algorithm for Automatic Topology Generation for Application Specific Networks on Chips. IET Comput. Digital Techniques 2(3), 239–249 (2008)

20. David, A., et al.: Network on Chip Design and Synthesis Outlook. Integration the VLSI Journal 41, 340–359 (2008)

21. Haythem, E., et al.: Power Optimization for Application Specific Networks-on-Chips: A Topology Based Approach. Elsevier -Microprocessor and Microsystems 33, 343–355 (2009)

22. Yilmaz, A., Suleyman, T., Hasan, K.: TopGen: A New Algorithm for Automatic Topology Generation for Network on Chip Architectures to Reduce Power Consumption. IEEE (2009)

23. Sethuraman, B.: Novel Methodologies for Efficient Network-on-Chip implementation on Reconfigurable Device, Ph.D thesis (November 2007)

Painting an Area by Swarm
of Mobile Robots with Limited Visibility

Deepanwita Das[1] and Srabani Mukhopadhyaya[2]

[1] Department of Information Technology,
National Institute of Technology, Durgapur, West Bengal, India
[2] Birla Institute of Technology, Mesra, Kolkata Extension Centre,
Kolkata, West Bengal, India
deepanwita.das@it.nitdgp.ac.in

Abstract. This paper presents a distributed algorithm for painting a priori known obstacle free rectangular region by swarm of mobile robots with limited visibility capability. We have assumed that initially the visibility graph is connected. Our approach is to divide the region into some non overlapping strips, and to let each robot to paint one of these strips assigned to it. Width of the strips may vary for different robots. In the proposed algorithm, the robots follow the basic *Wait-Observe-Compute-Move* model together with the *Asynchronous* timing model.

Keywords: Coverage, Distributed Algorithm, Limited Visibility, Painting, Robot Swarm.

1 Introduction

Applications of scanning or covering a free space by a swarm of robots, such as painting a rectangular area [1], search and rescue of victims, space exploration, terrain mapping etc. can be achieved by using the concept of distributed coverage. Previous research works on multi robot area coverage [1], [2], [3], [4], [5] consider that each robot in the swarm can sense or see the entire space together with the position of all the robots. But in reality, robots can view only upto certain distance.

In this paper, we have studied the problem of painting a known obstacle-free rectangular area, by a swarm of mobile robots with limited visibility. We have assumed that a swarm of N robots are placed within the region, with a restriction that multiple robots will not be located on the same vertical line. We also assume that robot can view upto a fixed distance d. For painting the region, the whole area is divided into a number of parallel vertical strips, may not be all of equal width. Each strip is assigned to be painted by one robot. A robot calculates the boundary of its assigned strip, based on the position of the nearest neighbour and/or the boundary (either left or right) of the region. When each of the robots completely paints its assigned strip, the whole area will be painted.

The algorithm proposed in this paper, is strongly based on the concept of visibility graph, in which the nodes represent robots and the edges represent the

K.R. Venugopal and L.M. Patnaik (Eds.): ICIP 2012, CCIS 292, pp. 446–455, 2012.
© Springer-Verlag Berlin Heidelberg 2012

connection between the nodes which are at distance less than or equals to d. It is assumed that the visibility graph is connected in the initial situation. The proposed algorithm is based on the basic *wait-observe-compute-move* model [1]. The robots are assumed to follow the *full-compass* and *asynchronous* timing model and all of them remains active throughout the process.

Large amount of research work has been done to solve Multi Robot coverage problem where mostly team based approach [3], [4] and completely distributed approach [1], [2], [5] have been considered. In the team based approach, multiple robots move in a team and when the team finds any obstacle the team and the current cell is divided into two sub-teams and sub-cells. The sub-teams rejoin on complete coverage of the sub-cells. In distributed approaches, the whole area is divided into a number of disjoint sub-areas and each robot has at least one individual sub-area to cover, so that when each of them completes their assigned job the whole area will be covered. Both the approaches consider that the robots are having unlimited visibility.

Some algorithms for the robots with limited visibility have been reported in the area of swarm spreading [6], convergence [7] and gathering [8] problems. Cohen et. al.,[6] presents a local spreading algorithm for the robots with limited visibility to achieve equally spaced configuration. Another study related to limited visibility of robots is presented by Ando et. al.[7]. In this paper, an algorithm is proposed to converge different robots towards a single point. All the robots are having limited visibility and mutual visibility graph is used. The main idea is to make the robots get closer while maintaining the mutually visible robots to remain within the visible distance of each other. Flochinni et. al.[8] presents an algorithm that allows anonymous, oblivious robots with limited visibility to gather at a single point within a finite amount of time. All the robots are having same orientation. It has also used the concept of maintaining mutual visibility graph throughout the process.

The problem of area coverage with robots with limited visibility has been studied very less. In this paper, we propose a completely distributed algorithm to solve the problem.

2 Problem Definition, Assumptions and Models

Our problem is to paint a priori known obstacle free rectangular area by a swarm of N robots. It is assumed that no two robots can occupy the same position or positions on the same vertical line. The robots are initially distributed within the region, such that the visibility graph is connected initially. It is assumed that, both the left and right boundary of the rectangular area must be viewed by at least one robot. The robots, considered here are assumed to have the following characteristics.

2.1 Characteristics of the Robot

1. Identical and Homogeneous - All robots are identical and have the same computational ability. The robots are assumed to be point robots. The visibility range of the robots is limited.

2. Autonomous - There is neither any central authority nor any external control over the robots. Thus the robots work in completely distributed manner, asynchronously and independently of other robots. They do not even communicate among themselves.

3. Mobile - All robots are allowed to move on a plane.

4. Computational Model - Here we follow the basic *Observe-Compute-Move* [1] model. A *computational cycle* is defined to be a sequence of "observe", "compute" and "move" steps. Each of the robots executes same instructions in all the computational cycles. Once a robot completes one computational cycle, it starts executing the next one. The actions taken by a robot in *compute* and *move* steps, entirely depend on the observations made in *observe* step. In some situations, an observation might lead a robot not to change its position in *move* step. In such cases the robot seems to be idle, though it is actually executing all the three steps.

5. Limited Visibility - Robots have limited visibility. Each robot can view only those robots which are located within a distance d from it. So, the area of visibility for each robot can be measured by a circle with radius d and the robot is located at the center of the circle. This circle is known as the *circle of visibility* and d is known as the *visibility radius*.

6. Non-Oblivious - Robots will have some amount of memory and can retain the information gathered in the previous computational cycle. We have assumed that the robots observe and store certain parameters. The parameters with their initial values are shown in Fig.1. These values may change during the execution of the algorithm.

Parameters	Descriptions	Initial Value
UB	Upper boundary of the assisgned strip	Infinite
LoB	Lower boundary of the assisgned strip	Infinite
LB	Left boundary of the assigned strip	d
RB	Right boundary of the assigned strip	d
State	The direction of robot's movement	Upward
(X_d, Y_d)	Co-ordinate of the next destination	(0,0)
PhaseICompleted	Completion of first phase	False

Fig. 1. Parameters to be Considered by the Robots Together with their Initial Values

2.2 Visibility Graph

Based on the relative positions of the robots in the region, we define a visibility graph $G = (V, E)$. The vertices in the graph correspond to the robots in the swarm. Moreover, two additional nodes are also taken in the graph which represent the left and the right boundary of the region to be painted. Thus $|V| = N+2$. Two nodes in the graph are connected by an edge iff the corresponding robots are mutually visible. Two robots R and S are defined as mutually visible iff the distance between them is less than or equals to d. That means, when two robots are located within each others *circle of visibility* then they are known as mutually visible robots. If the left or right boundary is visible to any robot, then the corresponding nodes are also connected. Fig.2(b) shows the visibility graph corresponding to the distribution of robots shown in Fig.2(a), where LB and RB are the left and right boundary walls respectively. We assume that for initial distribution of the robots, the visibility graph is connected. However, during execution of the algorithm, the visibility graph may not necessarily remain connected.

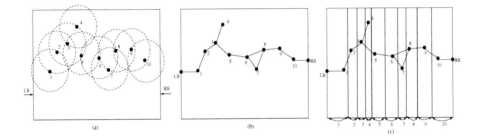

Fig. 2. (a)Distribution of Robots, (b) Visibility Graph Corresponding to (a), (c) Final Partition of the Region

2.3 Models

The models considered here are as follows:

Asynchronous Model: The robots operate on independent computational cycles of variable lengths. They do not share any common clock and are active in every cycle.

Full-Compass: Directions and orientations of both axes are common to all the robots. Each robot has its local co-ordinate system. All the robots would assume that they occupy the position $(0, 0)$ with respect to their local co-ordinate system.

In the proposed work, we have assumed that there will not be more than one robot on a same vertical line. The *"painting"* operation considered here is assumed to be an *atomic* operation. Once a robot starts painting the assigned strip, it completes its job without any further interruption.

3   Coverage Algorithm

The first part of this section describes the proposed algorithm. The correctness of the Algorithm is proved in the second part.

3.1   Algorithm

The basic idea of the algorithm is to divide the whole rectangular region into a number of disjoint parallel vertical strips. Each robot will be assigned the responsibility of painting one strip. Based on the information gathered in the observe step, a robot calculates its own strip boundaries. The robots retain the information regarding strip boundaries and these parameters are updated during the execution of the algorithm. Let us first discuss some terminologies that will be used later.

   (a) Nearest right (left) neighbour: For a robot R, the nearest right (left) neighbour is the robot R' such that (i) R' is on the right (left) of R, (ii) $hdist[R, R']$ is minimum among all robots which are on the right (left) of R. It is not necessary that initially R' is visible to R.

   (b) Nearest visible right (left) neighbour: At a particular instant of time, among all the visible robots which are on the right (left) of R, the one whose $hdist$ from R is minimum, will be called as the nearest visible right neighbour at that instant of time.

In the first phase of the algorithm, a robot calculates the boundaries of the strip which is to be painted by itself and in the second phase the robot actually paints the strip. A strip is defined as a rectangular part of the whole area of painting. The upper and the lower boundaries of each of the strip is same as that of the whole region. Only the right and left boundaries of the strips are to be calculated by the robots. A robot would finally fix its right (left) boundary at a distance $x/2$ from itself where x is the horizontal distance of the robot from its nearest right (left) neighbour. Since nearest neighbours (right/left) may not be visible initially, robots initially set the left and right boundaries at a distance of d from itself. To finalize the positions of the boundaries, in every computational cycle throughout the first phase of the algorithm, a robot computes the distances of the nearest visible neighbours left and right. Based on that distances, it estimates the position of the (right and left) boundaries. It then compares the estimated one with the stored one, whichever is nearer, it accepts that as the tentative position of the boundaries and store it.

   From the initial position, each of the robots moves in the upward direction first until it reaches the upper boundary of the region. It then moves in the vertically downward direction to reach the lower boundary of the region. While traversing this route, the robot finalize its strip boundaries, left, right, bottom and top. For the initial distribution of the robots shown in Figure 2(a), the nearest right neighbour of robot 4 is robot 5. However, robots 4 and 5 are not visible to each other initially. Later, during execution of the first phase of the algorithm, when they become visible to each other, the common boundary in between them would be finalized by themselves. Figure 2(c) shows the final position of the strip boundaries for the initial distribution shown in Figure 2(a). After reaching the lower boundary of the strip to be painted, i.e., the lower boundary of the region, the robot starts painting from the bottom left-most corner of the strip.

Algorithm *Paint*
Phase I

Observe:
Step 1: Robot R checks the status of the *PhaseICompleted* flag. If it is *True*, R will not execute the next steps. It will directly go to Phase-II, where it will start the painting operation. If *PhaseICompleted* = *False*, then R executes the following steps.

Step 2: According to the local co-ordinate system, the robot R first observes the position of the neighbours within its area of visibility. Suppose, the robot R have $n - 1$ number of visible neighbours. Let their co-ordinates be (a_1, b_1), (a_2, b_2), $\cdots$, (a_{n-1}, b_{n-1}), and its own co-ordinate is $(0, 0)$. Robot R would also observe whether the boundaries are visible or not. If left and/or right boundaries are visible, it would observe its perpendicular distance from those boundaries. If upper or lower boundary is visible it will set $UB = Seen$ or $LoB = Seen$ respectively.

Compute:
Step 1: If R observes the left and/or right boundary of the rectangular region and if k_1 and k_2 be its distances from those boundaries, then it will generate the co-ordinates of the points on the boundaries as $(-k_1, 0)$ and $(k_2, 0)$ (in case the boundary is on the left side or right side respectively). R inserts these points into the list of visible neighbours.

Step 2: Robot R orders the list of visible neighbours according to the increasing values of x-coordinate. It then chooses two coordinates, having largest negative x co-ordinate and least positive x co-ordinate. Let R' and R'' be these two points respectively. Hence, R' and R'' are the nearest visible left and right neighbours of R respectively. These points may represent the boundary also. From now on, we assume that the co-ordinate of R' and R'' be (x_L, y_L) and (x_R, y_R).

Step 3: After determining the nearest left and right coordinates, robot R calculates the boundary of the strip to be painted by it. We consider the following possible cases.

Case 1: The co-ordinates R' and/or R'' represent robots.
    If R' represents a robot, then set $LB = \max(\frac{x_L}{2}, LB)$.
If R'' represents a robot, then set $RB = \min(\frac{x_R}{2}, RB)$. Fig. 3 shows the positions of the computed strip boundaries where both R' and R'' are robots.

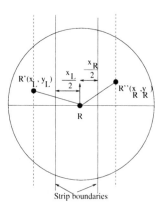

Fig. 3. Calculation of Strip Boundaries with Neighbour Robots in both Sides

Case 2: The co-ordinates R' and/or R'', represent boundaries of the rectangular region.
If R' represents the boundary, then set $LB = \max(x_L, LB)$.
If R'' represents the boundary, then set $RB = \min(x_R, RB)$.

Case 3: Robot R does not find any neighbour or boundary of the region on its right and/or left side.
In this case, R would not change the value of RB and/or LB.

<u>Step 4:</u> If $UB = Seen$, then robot R sets $state = Downward$.

<u>Step 5:</u> If $LoB = Seen$, then
(5.1): R computes the vertical distance of the lower boundary from its current position. Let it be y, where $y \leq 0$.
(5.2): If $UB = Seen$ and $y = 0$ then R sets $state = Painting$.

<u>Step 6:</u> Depending on the values of UB, LoB and $state$, robot R will compute its next destination (X_d, Y_d) as per the rules shown in Figure 4.

UB	LoB	state	Destination (X_d, Y_d)	
Not Seen	Not Seen	Upward	$X_d = 0$	$Y_d = d/2$
Seen	Not Seen	Downward	$X_d = 0$	$Y_d = -d/2$
Not Seen	Seen	Upward	$X_d = 0$	$Y_d = d/2$
Seen	Seen	Downward	If the lower boundary of the region is at a distance y from R, $X_d = 0$ $Y_d = \min(d/2, y)$	
Seen	Seen	Painting	$X_d = LB$	$Y_d = 0$

Fig. 4. Destination Coordinate (X_d, Y_d) based on UB, LoB and $state$ Values

Move:
In this step the robot moves to the destination point (X_d, Y_d) as calculated in the *compute* step. After reaching the destination, if *state* = *Painting*, the robot sets *PhaseICompleted* = *True*. This signifies that, Phase I is completed and the robot will start painting the assigned area.

Phase II
In this phase the robot executes the painting operation. Within a finite amount of time, robot R completes the job successfully, without any interruption as the *painting* is an *atomic* operation.

3.2   Correctness Proof

Lemma I: In the horizontal projection of the initial distribution of robots, the distance between any two consecutive robots is atmost d.

Proof: On the horizontal projection of the initial distribution of the robots, let R_1 and R_2 be two consecutive robots, R_2 be on the right of R_1. There may arise two possible situations, (I) the distance between R_1 and R_2 on the horizontal line $(hdist[R_1, R_2])$ is less than or equal to d, (II) the distance between R_1 and R_2 on the horizontal line $(hdist[R_1, R_2])$ is greater than d. First case supports the result. We now proceed to prove that the second case is not possible.

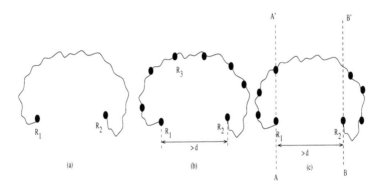

Fig. 5.

Let us assume that, $hdist[R_1, R_2] > d$. Therefore, initially the Euclidean distance between R_1 and R_2 $(dist[R_1, R_2])$ is also greater than d. Hence, in the visibility graph, there does not exist any direct edge between R_1 and R_2. As we know that the visibility graph G is connected initially, therefore in G, R_1 and R_2 must be connected to each other through a path passing through some other node(s) in G. Figure 5 illustrates the situation.

We claim that, there must exists at least one node R_3 whose initial position was on the right of R_1 and left of R_2, as shown in Figure. 5(b). If that is not the case, then all the intermediate nodes on the path must be either on or left of the vertical line $\overline{AA'}$ (passing through R_1) or on or right of the vertical line $\overline{BB'}$ (passing through R_2), as shown in Figure.5(c). Since the distance between $\overline{AA'}$ and $\overline{BB'}$ is greater than d, this contradicts the existence of such a path in the visibility graph. Hence R_3 lies on right of R_1 and left of R_2. Thus, on the horizontal projection, R_3 appears between R_1 and R_2. This is a contradiction to the fact that R_1 and R_2 are two consecutive robots on the horizontal projection. Hence, in the horizontal projection of the initial distribution of robots, the distance between two consecutive robots can be atmost d but not more than that.

Lemma II: By execution of the proposed algorithm, the robots partition the whole region into a number of non-overlapping strips.

Proof: In the initial distribution of the robots, a robot may not observe its nearest neighbours. In those cases, robots determine its strip boundaries on the basis of the positions of its visible nearest neighbours. Thus the initial formation may results in overlapping strips. During to and fro movement of a robot in phase I, first towards upper boundary and then towards lower boundary, robots, being able to observe the position of their nearest neighbours at least once (by lemma I), can uniquely and unanimously determine the strip boundaries (left and right). Hence the strips defined by the robots are non-overlapping. Moreover, as we have assumed that the boundaries of the region are visible to at least one robot initially, all the strips defined by the robots cover the whole region.

Lemma III: There will be no repeated coverage during the painting operation.

Proof: From lemma II, we see that at the end of phase I of the algorithm, the whole region is divided into some non-overlapping strips. Since each robot is responsible for painting only one such strip, there will not be any repeated coverage in the proposed algorithm.

Lemma IV: The movement of the robots are collision free.

Proof: During the calculation of the strip boundaries, a robot moves only in vertically upward or downward direction along the same line passing through its initial position. As per the assumption that no two robots are located on the same vertical line, during vertical movement there is no chance for collision. After reaching the lower boundary of the region the robots move along horizontal direction within its own strip boundary. Since the strips are non-overlapping, during horizontal movement also there will be no collision.

Lemma V: The overall painting process will be completed within finite amount of time.

Proof: By lemmas II, III and IV, we can say that determination of corresponding strip boundaries can be completed within finite amount of time. Moreover, according to our assumption, *painting* is an atomic operation and hence painting of the strips by the corresponding robots will also be completed within finite amount of time. Hence, a swarm of mobile robots can paint the given region using the proposed algorithm in finite amount of time.

4 Conclusions

In this paper, an algorithm is presented to paint a known rectangular region by a swarm of N robots with limited visibility capabilities. This algorithm is based on *Full-compass* and *Asynchronous* model. The algorithm guarantees complete coverage within a finite time. As future work, we would like to extend the algorithm for painting a convex or concave region with obstacles inside the region.

References

1. Das, D., Mukhopadhyaya, S.: An Algorithm for Painting an Area by Swarm of Mobile Robots. In: International Conference on Control, Automation and Robotics, Singapore, pp. C1–C6 (2011)
2. Kong, C., Peng, N.A., Rekletis, I.: Distributed Coverage with Multi-Robot System. In: IEEE International Conference on Robotics and Automation, pp. 2423–2429 (June 2006)
3. Rekletis, I., Lee-Shue, V., New, A.P., Choset, H.: Limited Communication, Multi-Robot Team Based Coverage. In: IEEE International Conference on Robotics and Automation, pp. 3462–3468 (April 2004)
4. Latimer, D., Srinivasa, S., Lee-Shue, V., Sonne, S., Choset, H., Hurst, A.: Toward Sensor Based Coverage with Robot Teams. In: IEEE International Conference on Robotics and Automation, vol. 1, pp. 961–967 (August 2002)
5. Rekletis, I., New, A.P., Rankin, E.S., Choset, H.: Efficient Boustrophedon Multi-Robot Coverage: An Algorithmic Approach. Proceedings Annals of Mathematics and Artificial Intelligence 52(2-4), 109–142 (2008)
6. Cohen, R., Peleg, D.: Local Spreading Algorithms for Autonomous Robot Systems (November 16, 2007)
7. Ando, H., Oasa, Y., Suzuki, I., Yamashita, I.: Distributed Memoryless Point Convergence Algorithm for Mobile Robots with Limited Visibility. In: IEEE International Conference on Robotics and Automation, vol. 15(5), pp. 818–828 (October 1999)
8. Flocchini, P., Prencipe, G., Santoro, N., Widmayer, P.: Gathering of Asynchronous Oblivious Robots with Limited Visibility. In: Ferreira, A., Reichel, H. (eds.) STACS 2001. LNCS, vol. 2010, pp. 247–258. Springer, Heidelberg (2001)

Design of RISC Based MIPS Architecture with VLSI Approach

Munmun Ghosal and A.Y. Deshmukh

Department of Electronics Engineering,
G.H. Raisoni College of Engineering, Digdoh Hills,
Nagpur, India
munmun_ghosal@yahoo.co.in

Abstract. This paper describes the design and analysis of the functional units of RISC based MIPS architecture. The functional units includes the Instruction fetch unit, instruction decode unit, execution unit, data memory and control unit. The functions of these modules are implemented by pipeline without any interlocks and are simulated successfully on Modelsim 6.3f and Xilinx 9.2i. It also attempts to achieve high performance with the use of a simplified instruction set.

Keywords: Interlocking, Memory, MIPS, Pipelining, RISC.

1   Introduction

MIPS stands for microprocessor without interlocked pipeline stages. It is a reduced instruction set computer (RISC) instruction set architecture (ISA) [1] and is now a performance leader within the embedded industry. MIPS is a load/store architecture in which all operations are performed on operands held in the processor registers.

RISC CPU has advantages such as faster speed, simplified structure & easier implementation. The decision to include a microprocessor in a design is that it transforms the design effort from a logic design into a software design. In this paper the design of various functional units of RISC based MIPS processor using VHDL has been presented. The goal of this work was to evaluate the performance of various units of the MIPS processor.

2   Salient Features of MIPS Architecture

2.1   Instructions Set Architecture

The MIPS Architecture defines thirty-two[6]. 32-bit general purpose registers (GPRs). All instructions of MIPS microprocessor are 32 bit and are available in three formats: R-type, I-type and J-type [4].MIPS instructions are three address operations taking two sources and one destination.

K.R. Venugopal and L.M. Patnaik (Eds.): ICIP 2012, CCIS 292, pp. 456–466, 2012.
© Springer-Verlag Berlin Heidelberg 2012

31	26 25	21 20	16 15	11 10	6 5	0
Opcode (6 bits)	Rs (5 bits)	Rt (5 bits)	Rd (5 bits)	Sa (5 bits)	Function (6 bits)	

Fig. 1. (a) MIPS (R-Type) CPU Instruction Format

31	26 25	21 20	16 15	0
Opcode (6 bits)	Rs (5 bits)	Rt (5 bits)	Address immediate (16 bits)	

Fig. 2. (b)MIPS Immediate (I-Type) CPU Instruction Format

Fig. 1(a) explains the format of R-Type CPU instruction format which is meant for performing arithmetic operations. It allows a range of register to register operations.

Fig. 1(b) explains the I-type instructions format that allows a 16 bit immediate to replace one of the operands and is also used for memory accesses and for conditional branches.

Fig. 1(c) explains the J-type format with a 26 bit immediate field. The only instruction to use this format is a jump which places the value in the bottom 26 bits of the program counter.

1. **Register**

   A MIPS microprocessor has 32 addressable registers. The registers are preceded by $ in assembly language instruction. Two formats for addressing are used i.e, using register numbers ($0 through $31) or using equivalent names ($t1, $sp).Special registers Lo and Hi used to store result of multiplication and division. The stack of MIPS grows from high memory to low memory [3].

2. **Memory**

   Memory access instructions are included in the I-type format. The source register (RS) is added to the immediate to create an effective address which is used to reference the memory. The second register (RT) is either used as the destination in a memory load or as a source in a memory store. The memory is byte addressed but is 32 bit wide so all word loads and stores have to be word aligned. Half word accesses have to be aligned to half word boundaries. To help with unaligned loads and stores there are two more memory access instructions. Load Word Left (LWL) and Load Word Right (LWR) in combination allow word loads from unaligned addresses.

31	26 25	21 20	16 15	0
Opcode (6 bits)		Instr_index (26 bits)		

Fig. 3. (c)MIPS Jump (J-Type) CPU Instruction Format

3. Pipeline Interlocking

In the MIPS microprocessor this means that some instructions have an implicit delay before their effect takes place [1].The general philosophy is to construct the hardware as simply as possible and, if a result is not ready for use in the next instruction then not to stop the whole processor but use the software to insert instructions into the space. The two main delays in the MIPS microprocessor are branch shadows and memory load delays.

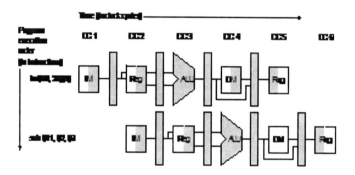

Fig. 4. Five Stage Pipelining

4. Condition

There are no condition flags but instead all branches are conditional on the values of the registers in the main register bank. Each conditional branch instruction specifies two registers (RS and RT) to be fetched and tested. A branch is conditional on the results of two tests. The first is compare the two registers together to test whether they are equal (RS=RT). The other test is simply to look at the sign value (bit 31) of the first register (RS<0). By choosing the second register to be R0 (RT=0) it becomes possible to test RS for less than greater or equal to zero or any combination of the three. For an unconditional branch the Branch if Greater or Equal to Zero instruction (BGEZ) is used with R0 as an operand. This condition will always be true.

3   MIPS Functional Units

3.1   Instruction Fetch Unit

The function of the instruction fetch unit is to obtain an instruction from the instruction memory using the current value of the PC and increment the PC value for the next instruction. The block diagram for the Instruction fetch unit is shown in Fig. 3.

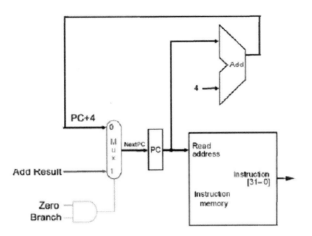

Fig. 5. Instruction Fetch unit

3.2   Instruction Decode Unit

The main function of the instruction decode unit is to use the 32-bit instruction provided from the previous instruction fetch unit to index the register file and obtain the register data values. The block diagram for the Instruction decode unit is shown in Fig. 4(a).

3.3   The Control Unit

The control unit examines the instruction opcode bits [31 − 26] and decodes the instruction to generate nine control signals to be used in the additional modules. The block diagram for the Control unit is shown in Fig. 4(b).

3.4   Execution Unit

The execution unit contains the arithmetic logic unit (ALU) .The branch address is calculated by adding the PC+4 to the sign extended immediate field shifted left 2 bits by a separate adder. The logic elements include a MUX, an adder, the ALU and the ALU control. The block diagram for the Execution unit is shown in Fig. 5.

3.5   Data Memory Unit

It is only accessed by the load and store instructions. The load instruction asserts the MemRead signal and uses the ALU Result value as an address to index the data memory. The read output data is then subsequently written into the register file. A store instruction asserts the MemWrite signal and writes the data value previously read from a register into the computed memory address.

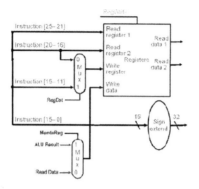

Fig. 6. (a) MIPS Instruction Decode Unit

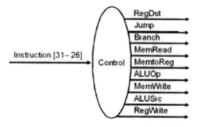

Fig. 7. (b) MIPS Control Unit

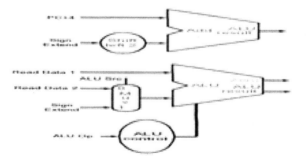

Fig. 8. MIPS Execution Unit

4   Synthesis and Simulation Results

4.1   Instruction Fetch Unit

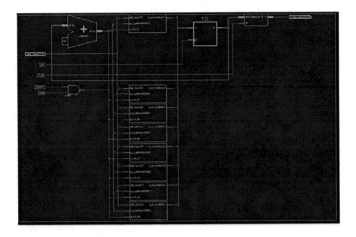

Fig. 9. RTL Schematic of MIPS Instruction fetch Unit Obtained by Synthesis Using Xilinx 9.2i

Fig. 10. Block diagram of MIPS Instruction Fetch Unit Obtained by Synthesis Using Xilinx 9.1

Fig. 6 explains the RTL Schematic of MIPS Instruction fetch Unit which gives a detailed structure of the unit consisting of adder, AND gate, Program counter and Instruction memory. The Instruction memory consists of a series of latches which holds the instruction. Fig. 7 explains the block diagram of Instruction fetch unit showing the input and output ports. The inputs to the unit are the instruction from the instruction memory given as add_result, zero and branch. The unit is also fed by the global clock and enable inputs. The output of the unit is a 32 bit instruction format which is obtained only when the enable input is high. Fig. 8 explains the status of the memory obtained after the simulation of the Instruction Fetch Unit in which the instruction is written into the Instruction Memory. Fig. 9 explains the simulation results of the Instruction fetch Unit. The waveforms show the various possible combinations of inputs and its corresponding outputs.

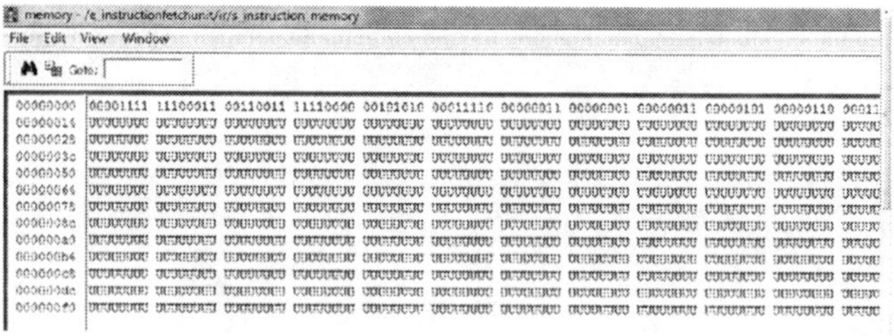

Fig. 11. Memory Assigned for the Analysis of Instruction Fetch Unit in Modelsim 6.3f

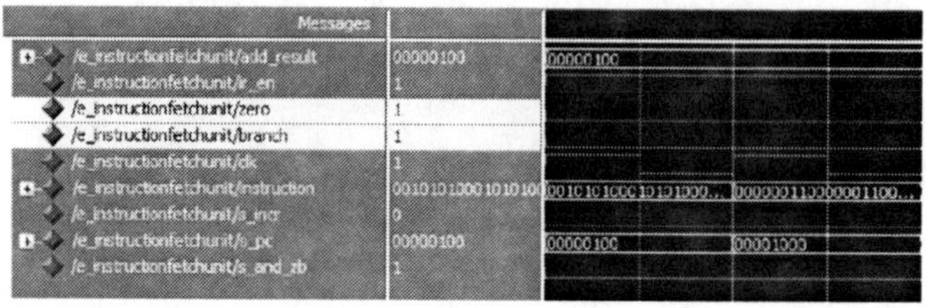

Fig. 12. Waveforms of MIPS Instruction fetch Unit Obtained by Simulation Using Modelsim 6.3f

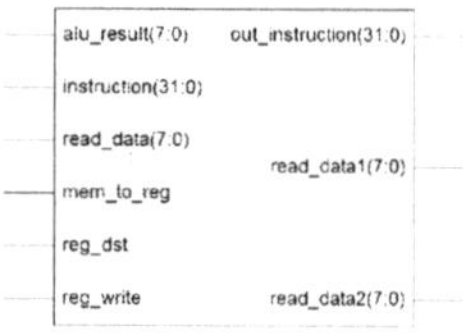

Fig. 13. (a) Block Diagram of MIPS Instruction Decode Unit Obtained by Synthesis Using Xilinx 9.1

Fig. 14. (b) RTL Schematic of MIPS Instruction Decode Unit obtained by Synthesis using Xilinx 9.2i

Fig. 10(a) explains the block diagram of Instruction decode unit showing the input and output ports. The inputs to the unit are the outputs from the instruction fetch unit. It decodes the instruction obtained from the previous instruction fetch unit.

Fig. 10(b) explains the RTL Schematic of MIPS Instruction Decode Unit which gives a detailed structure of the unit consisting of registers, MUX and sign extend unit.

Fig. 15. Memory assigned for the Analysis of Instruction Decode Unit in Modelsim 6.3f

Fig. 11 explains the contents of the memory obtained after the simulation of the Instruction Decode Unit.

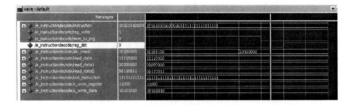

Fig. 16. Waveforms of MIPS Instruction Decode Unit Obtained by Simulation using Modelsim 6.3f

Fig. 12 explains the simulation results of the Instruction decode Unit. The waveforms show the various possible combinations of inputs and its corresponding outputs whereby depending on the state of MemtoRegsignal, the ALUresult or the readData is written into the registers. The RegDat signal determines if instruction bits [20-16] or [15-11] is provided to the write registers.

Fig. 13(a) explains the block diagram of control unit showing the input as a 32 bit instruction and outputs as various control signals which are used to execute a given instruction and hence the given program.

Fig. 13(b) explains the RTL Schematic of MIPS Control Unit which gives a detailed structure responsible for the generation on control signals.

Fig. 14 explains the simulation results of the Control Unit which shows various possible values of the given Instruction and the corresponding values of the control signals which are alu_op, alu_src, branch, jump, mem_read, mem_to_reg, mem_write, reg_dst and reg_write .

Fig. 15(a) explains the block diagram of Execution unit. The inputs to the unit are the data from decode unit and the ALU operation which is to be performed.

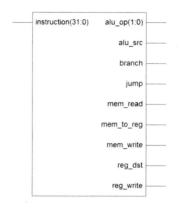

Fig. 17. (a) Block diagram of MIPS Control Unit obtained by Synthesis using Xilinx 9.1

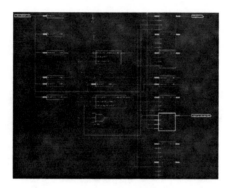

Fig. 18. (b) RTL Schematic of MIPS Control Unit obtained by Synthesis using Xilinx 9.2i

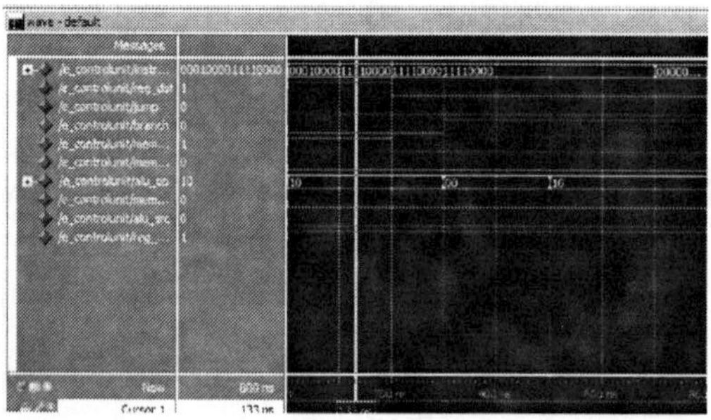

Fig. 19. Waveforms of MIPS Control Unit Obtained by Simulation using Modelsim 6.3f

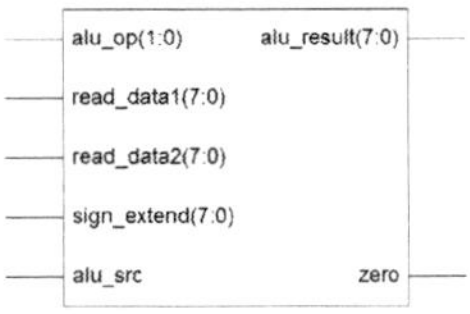

Fig. 20. (a) Block Diagram of MIPS Execution Unit obtained by Synthesis using Xilinx 9.1

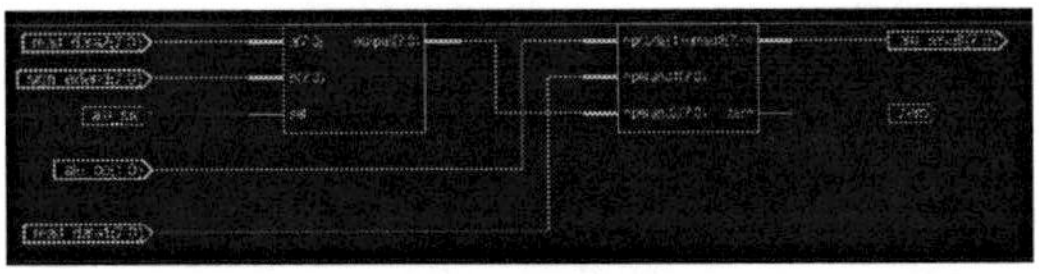

Fig. 21. (b)RTL Schematic of MIPS Execution Unit obtained by Synthesis using Xilinx 9.2i

The outputs consist of the result obtained on the desired operation and a zero signal which indicates if the result is zero or not.

Fig. 15(b) explains the RTL Schematic of MIPS Execution Unit which gives a detailed structure consisting of Arithmetic and logical Unit together with multiplexers, shift registers and sign extend unit. Fig. 16 explains the simulation result of the Execution Unit whereby the output alu_result is obtained with various possible combinations of inputs i.e. read_data1 and read_data2 and the opcode which specifies the operation to be performed.

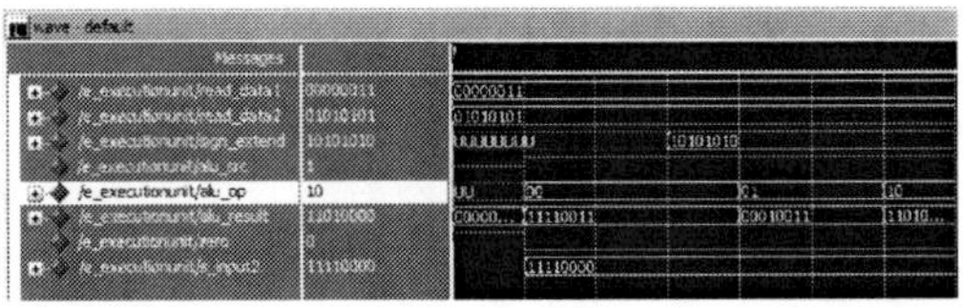

Fig. 22. Waveforms of MIPS Execution Unit obtained by Simulation using Modelsim 6.3f

5   Conclusions

A complete realistic, parameterized, synthesizable, modular, single clock and multiple clock multicore architecture of RISC based MIPS is studied. MIPS is a fully pipelined architecture having an efficient instruction scheduling. The functionality of the instruction fetch unit, Instruction decode unit, Control unit and the execution unit has been synthesized and verified using Modelsim 6.3f and Xilinx 9.2i.

References

1. Charles, B.: A MIPS R3000 microprocessor on an FPGA (February 13, 2002)
2. MIPS Technologies, Inc. MIPS32 Architecture For Programmers, vol. 2. The MIPS32 Instruction Set (June 9, 2003)
3. MIPS Technologies, Inc. MIPS32 Architecture For Programmers Volume I:Introduction to the MIPS32 Architecture (June 25, 2008)
4. Gautham, P., Parthasarathy, R.: Karthi Balasubramanian.: Low-Power Pipelined MIPS Processor Design, ISIC (2009)
5. Zulkifli, Y., Soetharyo, A.: Reduced Stall MIPS Architecture using Pre-Fetching Accelerator. In: International Conference on Electrical Engineering and Informatic, Selangor, Malaysia (August 2009)
6. Yi, K., WuHan, Ding, Y.-H.: 32-bit RISC CPU Based on MIPS Instruction Fetch Module Design. In: International Joint Conference on Artificial Intelligence (2009)
7. Tyson, Romas, A.L., Rd. Siti Intan, P., Adiono, T.: A Pipelined Double-Issue MIPS Based Processor Architecture. In: International Symposium on Intelligent Signal Processing and Communication Systems, ISPACS (2009)
8. Reaz, M.B.I., Shabiul Islam, M., Sulaiman, M.S.: A Single Clock Cycle MIPS RISC Processor Design using VHDL. In: Proceedings of ICSE 2002, Penang, Malaysia (2002)
9. Bashteen, A., Lui, I., Mullan, J.: A Superpipeline Approach to the MIPS Architecture, MIPS Computer Systems

A Fair and Efficient Gang Scheduling Algorithm for Multicore Processors

Viswanathan Manickam and Alex Aravind

Department of Computer Science
University of Northern British Columbia
Prince George, BC, Canada - V2N 4Z9
{manickam,csalex}@unbc.ca

Abstract. The trend in multicore processors indicates that all future processors will be multicore, and hence the future cloud systems are expected to have nodes and clusters based on multicore processors. On the application front, to utilize these multicore processors, most future applications are expected to be parallel programs. Gang scheduling is a popular strategy of scheduling parallel programs on multiprocessor systems. 'Adaptive First-Come-First-Served' and 'Largest-Gang-First-Served' are most popular gang scheduling algorithms, but they are susceptible to starvation and hence high variance in response time. To address starvation, process migration mechanisms have been proposed in the literature. Migrating a process to a new processor is generally expensive, and also it does not eliminate starvation. This paper presents a starvation free gang scheduling algorithm for multicore processors without using process migration. The algorithm is simple, fair, and efficient.

Keywords: Scheduling, Gang Scheduling, Adaptive First-Come-First-served, Largest Gang First, Multicore Systems, Cloud Computing, Fairness, Starvation, predictability.

1 Introduction

Multicore systems and cloud computing are two popular recent hot research topics in Computer Science. It is expected that all future computer systems will be based on multicore processors, and cloud computing is emerging as the dominant approach to provide computing services. Therefore, future cloud systems will be typically built using multicore processors.

As limited by the law of physics, the microprocessor design hit the clock cycle wall, and the chip makers had to come up with the way to exploit the benefit of Moore's law. The new way is to use the extra transistors to add multiple processors (referred to as cores). Thus, multicore processor systems have emerged as the mainstream computing platforms. Intel, AMD, Fujitsu, IBM, and Sun Microsystems are shipping their desktops and workstations with multicore processors. This hardware trend seems to continue and we will have hundreds and even thousands of cores in a single machine in the near future.

K.R. Venugopal and L.M. Patnaik (Eds.): ICIP 2012, CCIS 292, pp. 467–476, 2012.
© Springer-Verlag Berlin Heidelberg 2012

This shift in technological trend is expected to revolutionize the way we will design and use software on these systems.

Cloud computing is designed to provide services such as computation, software applications, data access, data management and storage resources to its customers through internet transparently. As cloud computing is fundamentally a service oriented system, its primary goal must be providing quality service to its customers. Although the term quality of service is often used and directly related with response time, it is not well interpreted in the context of computing and communication systems. As indicated in [1], perceived quality of customers need not be directly related with minimal response time. The study indicates that users are often unaware of the quality differences until it crosses certain threshold. Therefore, quality of service need not always be related to the widely used metrics such as minimal response time or minimal average response time.

A similar observation is made in the operating system context. We quote from [2]: "it is more important to minimize *variance* in the response time than to minimize the average response time. A system with reasonable and *predictable* response time may be considered more desirable than a system that is faster on the average but highly variable. However, little work has been done on CPU scheduling algorithms to minimize the variance." Thus, we believe that a predictable response time is more appropriate measure for the quality of service in the cloud computing context than other measures such as average response time and resource utilization.

As cloud computing offers computing as a service, customer satisfaction about the services they receive is extremely important. Customer satisfaction is mainly related to cost, fairness, and quality of service. In that, fairness in service and quality of service are often related to system performance. Particularly, these metrics are primarily influenced by the execution of applications in the cloud. That in turn heavily depends on the processor scheduling in the cloud. That is, to offer services effectively to customers, the service requests must be properly mapped with the available computing resources in the cloud. This is simply a scheduling problem, and it generally involves sequencing and assigning a set of processes (customers) on one or more processors (servers) such that the intended criterion is met while maintaining maximum possible utilization of system resources. Therefore, processor scheduling is a fundamental problem in cloud computing as it is involved in almost all services that the cloud can offer.

Among the applications of cloud computing, parallel applications are dominant, as they require huge computational resources. Some of these applications typically involve execution of parallel threads with frequent synchronization (referred to as fine-grained synchronization) among themselves. During their executions, threads communicate for synchronization and data exchange. Often, a thread cannot proceed further without sufficient progress from other threads. Such threads either do busy waiting or block themselves by suspending from execution until other threads progressed enough.

A long busy wait on a processor wastes its execution time. On the other hand, suspending and resuming processes often are also not good, when only a small wait is needed. Blocking results in context switches, which are costly. For several applications inducing small waits, research shows that, busy wait is better than blocking. Based on these observations, Ousterhout introduced a simple scheduling idea called co-scheduling (later referred to as gang scheduling) to efficiently use busy waiting for fine-grained synchronization[3–5]. The idea behind gang scheduling is simple that threads of a same process are scheduled together as a 'gang' on distinct processors so that they can progress in parallel and synchronize with minimal busy waiting involved.

1.1   Gang Scheduling

Gang scheduling has been extensively analysed and several studies have concluded that gang scheduling is one of the best approaches for parallel applications [6–14]. Gang scheduling is a generic approach which can be loosely defined as a scheduling policy which maps a set of threads of a gang simultaneously on a set of processors using one-to-one mapping for execution. It does not specify which gang to be scheduled, when more than one gangs are waiting.

There are several approaches to schedule gangs to processors on different time slots. There are two popular algorithms: First Fit (or First-Come-First-Served (FCFS)) and Best Fit (or Largest-Gang-First-Served (LGFS))[12]. When enough processors are free, FCFS chooses the process in the head of the queue to schedule and LGFS chooses the largest process in the queue to schedule. FCFS assures high fairness, but need not guarantee the best processor utilization. Consider that a larger gang G is in the head of the queue, and several other smaller gangs are waiting behind G. Assume that there are not enough processors to schedule G, but several other processes from the queue can be scheduled. Now, in FCFS, these processors will be idle until enough processors become free and G is scheduled. Such situations will not only make the processor utilization low, but also have potential to increase the average waiting time. To avoid such situations, a modification called adaptive FCFS (AFCFS) was introduced in the literature. When a gang in the head of the queue cannot be scheduled, AFCFS schedules other gangs behind in the queue.

1.2   Motivation and Contributions

The trend in multicore processors indicates that all future processors will be multicore, and hence the future cloud systems are expected to have their nodes and clusters based on multicore processors. So the processor scheduling in the future systems will most likely be all multicore processor scheduling. Therefore, multicore scheduling is fundamental to future cloud computing performance. Also, due to multicore revolution, a considerable portion of large applications will be parallel programs. As described above, gang scheduling is a dominant strategy to schedule parallel programs. Therefore, gang scheduling in multicore processors is an important problem with practical appeal.

Between AFCFS and LGFS algorithms, AFCFS is simple that it does not involve sorting of gangs and therefore has less scheduling overhead than LGFS.

In terms of performance, they are very similar under moderate loads, AFCFS performs better in light loads and LGFS performs better in heavy loads[12]. In terms of fairness, both does not assure freedom from starvation. In practical terms, there is no guarantee of a bound on number of bypasses by new gangs on a waiting gang by both algorithms.

To avoid starvation or long wait time, these algorithms adopt a process migration policy. Process migration may not be even possible between two heterogeneous multicore systems, and generally expensive even between two homogeneous systems. Also, although it alleviates, process migration does not eliminate starvation.

These observations bring us a question: Can we design a gang scheduling algorithm with the following characteristics?

1. Freedom from starvation.
2. Predictable and acceptable response.
3. Better processor utilization.
4. Simple.

Fairness and predictable performance are important particularly in cloud environment where customer satisfaction hugely depends on fairness and predictable response time. In practice, the customers who receive a little faster service (at the expense of others' long wait) may not be overly satisfied. But, the customers who experience unpredictably long delay, on the other hand, will readily notice the unfairness and unpredictable response and that could potentially drive the cloud business in a negative direction. Therefore, in addition to fast response and high processor utilization, minimal variance in response is extremely important for better cloud services.

1.3   Contributions

This work presents a gang scheduling algorithm that satisfies the characteristics listed in the motivation section under light loads. From the quality of service point of view, we have demonstrated the importance of standard deviation in response time than the average response time. With respect to fairness, we introduce a new metric called bypass count, demonstrated its use in assuring fairness by setting a bound on the number of bypasses possible over a waiting gang. The performance and the fairness of the proposed algorithm in comparison with the current best algorithm are demonstrated through a simulation study.

Fairness and predictability are particularly important that the expectation of users under light load is normally high, and failure provide such guarantee even under light load could expose the system very badly.

2   Fair and Efficient Gang Scheduling Algorithm

The gang scheduling algorithm proposed in this paper is a minor modification of AFCFS, and that retains the simplicity of AFCFS almost intact. AFCFS algorithm proposed for multicore clusters in [12], each multicore has a run queue and all gangs stay in the run queue until it gets a chance to execute. The scheduler always chooses the next fit gang from the run queue so that overall response time will be reduced. Such a behaviour could degrade the overall core utilization, which in turn could increase the variation in response time, we have observed in the experiments.

The proposed algorithm uses an additional variable for each gang which stores the information about how many gangs bypassed it for execution when it stayed in the run queue. We call that variable *'bypass count'*. When the gang's bypass count reaches the threshold value T, it gets the highest priority to schedule next. This pushes other gangs to force wait until the highest priority gang gets scheduled. The proposed algorithm is given in Table 1.

A new gang joins RQ, and its bypass count is set to zero. Whenever a gang is scheduled, the bypass count of gangs precedes the scheduled gang in RQ will be incremented by 1. At any time, gang in RQ with bypass count greater or equal to the threshold value has the highest priority over other gangs. This guarantees that the gangs will be served in a predictable time period. When there is no gang with bypass count greater or equal to the threshold value, it acts as AFCFS algorithm.

Table 1. New Gang Scheduling Algorithm

<u>Data Structures:</u>RQ:Queue of gangs; T:Threshold value;$i.bpc$:bypass count of gang i
1. **while** $(RQ \neq$ empty $)$ **do**
2.   **for** $i = 1$ to size of RQ **do**
3.   **if** $RQ[i].bpc \geq T$ **then** wait until $RQ[i]$ fits in free cores
4.   **if** $RQ[i]$ fits in free cores **then**
5.   **for** $k = 1$ to $i - 1$ **do** $RQ[k].bpc + +$ **end for**
6.   schedule $RQ[i]$
7.   **end if**
8.   **end for**
9. **end while**

When not enough cores are available to schedule the highest priority gang, the system has to wait for some of the currently executing gangs to leave, and this delay is unavoidable to assure fairness and predictable response. The simulation result shows that such a wait rarely happens.

Note: The proposed algorithm becomes AFCFS if the threshold is set to ∞. When the threshold is 0, it emulates FCFS algorithm. So, choosing a proper threshold is the key of the proposed algorithm.

3   Simulation Experiment

As mentioned earlier, the proposed algorithm tries to achieve predictable and fast response for gangs (users) and better utilization for the system. To study these measures, we use average response time, standard deviation in response time, and average core utilization. The definitions of these metrics are given next.

3.1 Performance Metrics

Average Response Time: The response time is the time taken from the arrival of the gang until it completes it's execution. Consider a_j is the arrival time of gang j and e_j is the execution completion time of gang j, then the average response time ART for n gang is defined as:

$$ART = \frac{1}{n} \times \sum_{j=1}^{n} (e_j - a_j)$$

Standard Deviation in Response Time: Standard deviation in response time tells the accuracy of the prediction of response time based on its mean. Consider, μ is the mean response time for n gangs and R_j is the response time for j gang, then the variance in response time $SDRT$ can be calculated as:

$$SDRT = \sqrt{\sum_{j=1}^{n} (R_j - \mu)^2}$$

Average Core Utilization: Core utilization is the percentage amount of time the core spent executing the gangs. Let's say, there are m number of cores and ex_i is the total time spent by core i for executing the gangs, then the average core utilization ACU is:

$$ACU = \frac{1}{m} \times \sum_{j=1}^{m} ex_i \times 100$$

3.2 Simulation Setup

For our simulation experiments, we used the parameters given in Table 2. To keep the results generic, the execution is shown in terms of simulation clock ticks. Through simulation study, we observed average response time, standard deviation in response time, average core utilization, and bypass count for the gangs. The observations are presented next.

- *Observation on Average Response Time:* Fig. 1 shows that the average response time of the proposed algorithm is better than that of AFCFS. This is because, whenever the bypass count reaches the threshold, it guarantees to schedule next which reduces the response time of long waiting gangs. Choosing a proper threshold value is crucial. Choosing a small number will unnecessarily make other gangs to wait more often, which will in turn

Table 2. Simulation Parameters

Parameter	Value(s)
Number of Cores	200
Time	1 minute
Tasks per Gang	Uniformly distributed over [2..200]
Mean Arrival Rate	4, 5, 7.5
Arrival Rate Distribution	Poisson
Mean Service Rate	2
Service Rate Distribution	Exponential
Threshold	700

increase the average response time. For our experiments, we have chosen 700[1] bypass count as the threshold value. From the graph, it is clear that the average response time performs better than AFCFS consistently.

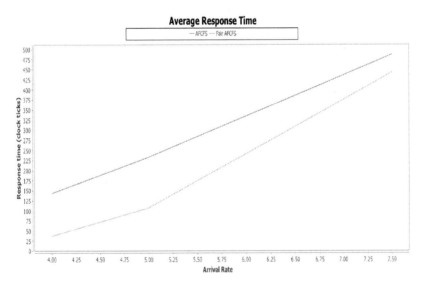

Fig. 1. Average Response time

- *Observation on Average Core Utilization:* The average core utilization of the proposed algorithm outperforms AFCFS algorithm. This is because, AFCFS favors only small gangs but the proposed algorithm favours all sized gangs after reaching the threshold.

- *Observation on Standard Deviation of Response Time:* To measure the predictability, we computed the average response time to see how soon a gang will execute in the cloud. Fig. 3 shows that the proposed algorithm is better

---

[1] The threshold value is derived from the set of experiments.

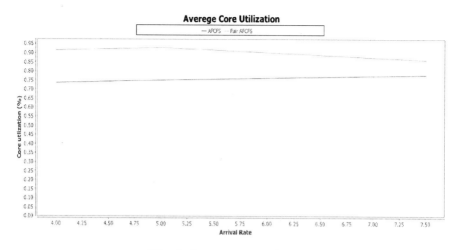

Fig. 2. Average core utilization

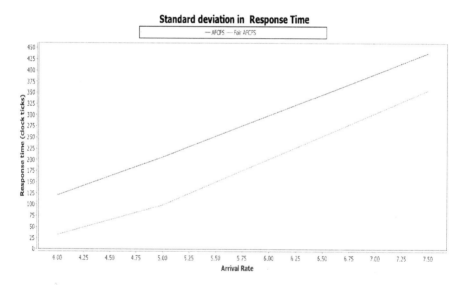

Fig. 3. Standard deviation of Response time

than AFCFS. Since, the proposed algorithm avoids longer wait times, the predictability in response time will be lower than AFCFS. By controlling the bypass threshold value, better predictability may be assured.

– *Observation on Bypass Count Graph:* The bypass count tells how many gangs overtake a waiting gang which is a fairness matter. Fig. 4 shows the bypass counts of gangs. The proposed algorithm shows the fairness among gangs, once it reaches the threshold shown by green color line, it starts giving the priority for long waited gangs. The longer wait time is completely avoided in the proposed algorithm, which makes our algorithm interesting.

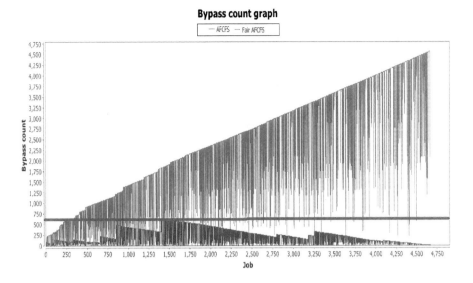

Fig. 4. Bypass counts of gangs

From these observations, we conclude that, the proposed algorithm outperforms AFCFS in all three metrics, and of course solves the starvation problem completely.

4 Conclusions

In this paper, we proposed a fair and efficient gang scheduling algorithm for multicore processors. The algorithm is simple, fair, and gives predictable performance. Such a predictable performance is attractive from the service point of view. Since this algorithm solves the problem locally without using process migration, it is scalable and attractive for cloud computing involving a large number of multicore processors.

As indicated earlier, fairness and predictability under light load are particularly important, as it could be easily considered by the users as the test case for the quality of service of the system.

References

1. Ghinea, G., Chen, S.Y.: Perceived Quality of Multimedia Educational Content: A cognitive style approach. Multimedia Systems 11(3), 271–279 (2006)
2. Silberschatz, A., Galvin, P.B., Gagne, G.: Operating System Concepts. John Wiley & Sons, Inc. (2010)
3. Ousterhout, J.K.: Scheduling Techniques for Concurrent Systems. In: Proceedings of the IEEE Distributed Computing Systems, pp. 22–30 (1982)

4. Chai, L., Gao, Q., Panda, D.K.: Understanding the Impact of Multi-Core Architecture in Cluster Computing: A Case Study with Intel Dual-Core System. In: Seventh IEEE International Symposium on Cluster Computing and the Grid, CCGrid 2007, pp. 471–478 (2007)
5. Frechette, S., Avresky, D.R.: Method for Task Migration in Grid Environments. In: Fourth IEEE International Symposium on Network Computing and Applications, pp. 49–58 (2005)
6. Batat, A., Feitelson, D.G.: Gang Scheduling with Memory Considerations. In: 14th International Parallel and Distributed Processing Symposium, pp. 109–114 (2000)
7. Hyoudou, K., Kozakai, Y., Nakayama, Y.: An Implementation of a Concurrent Gang Scheduler for a PC-based Cluster System. Systems and Computers in Japan 38(3), 39–48 (2007)
8. Karatza, H.D.: Scheduling Gangs in a Distributed System. International Journal of Simulation: Systems, Science and Technology 7(1), 15–22 (2006)
9. Moschakis, I.A., Karatza, H.D.: Evaluation of Gang Scheduling Performance and Cost in a Cloud Computing System. Journal of Supercomputing 59, 975–992 (2012)
10. Papazachos, Z.C., Karatza, H.D.: The Impact of Task Service Time Variability on Gang Scheduling Performance in a Two-Cluster System. Simulation Modelling Practice and Theory 17(7), 1276–1289 (2009)
11. Papazachos, Z.C., Karatza, H.D.: Gang scheduling in a Two-Cluster System Implementing Migrations and Periodic Feedback. Simulation: Transactions of the Society for Modeling and Simulation International 87(12), 1021–1031 (2010)
12. Papazachos, Z.C., Karatza, H.D.: Gang scheduling in Multi-Core Clusters Implementing Migrations. Future Generation Computer Systems 27, 1153–1165 (2011)
13. Wiseman, Y., Feitelson, D.G.: Paired Gang Scheduling. IEEE Transactions on Parallel and Distributed Systems 14(6), 581–592 (2003)
14. Zhang, Y., Franke, H., Moreira, J.E., Sivasubramaniam, A.: An Integrated Approach to Parallel Scheduling using Gang-Scheduling, Backfilling and Migration. IEEE Transactions on Parallel and Distributed Systems 14(3), 236–247 (2003)

Identifying the Most Efficient Implementation Sequence of IT Projects Broken Down into MMFs and AEs

Antonio Juarez Alencar[1], Ivan Maia Vital Jr.[1],
Eber Assis Schmitz[1], Alexandre Luis Correa[2], and Jorge V. Doria Jr.[1]

[1] The Tércio Pacitti Institute for Computer Research
Federal University of Rio de Janeiro (UFRJ)
[2] Department of Applied Informatics
State of Rio de Janeiro Federal University (UNIRIO)
juarezalencar@br.inter.net

Abstract. This papers presents a method that allows for the identification of the most efficient implementation sequence of IT projects broken down into minimum marketable feature units (MMFs) and architectural elements (AEs).

Keywords: Efficiency, Incremental Funding Method, IT Investment Analysis, Minimum Marketable Features, Software Engineering.

1 Introduction

The economic downturn that has been affecting the prosperity and wealth of nations worldwide has created a need for immediate reductions in business budgets, while increasing the demand for timely access to quality decision-enabling information [1].

Consistent with this view, a large variety of IT Investment Analysis concepts, methods, techniques and tools have been put forward in recent years [2]. Regretfully, many of these proposals have chosen to ignore that it is frequently the case that IT projects may be decomposed into smaller valuable units with high internal cohesion and low coupling [3]. As a consequence, they completely miss the fact that the order in which these units are implemented may considerably change the value of IT projects [4].

Among those who acknowledge the decomposition aspect of IT projects, some take into consideration a single performance indicator such as return on investment (ROI) or net present value (NPV), while others suggest the use of a multi-criteria framework as a means of making their methods better suited to cope with a wider range of circumstances [5].

However, so far very little has been said about how to improve the Efficiency of investments made in IT projects that have been decomposed into smaller units from a multi-criteria perspective. This paper presents a method that goes towards filling this gap. The remainder of this paper is organized as follows.

K.R. Venugopal and L.M. Patnaik (Eds.): ICIP 2012, CCIS 292, pp. 477–486, 2012.
© Springer-Verlag Berlin Heidelberg 2012

Section 2 presents a review of the principal concepts and results used in this paper. Section 3 introduces the method proposed by the authors together with an example of the use of the method. Section 4 presents the conclusions of this paper.

2 Conceptual Framework

2.1 The Incremental Funding Method

The Incremental Funding Method (IFM), credited to Denne and Cleland-Huang [6], is a financially oriented approach to software development that advocates the break down of an IT project to be developed into smaller self-contained units that create value for business and can be deployed in shorter periods of time. According to Denne and Cleland-Huang [6] such units are called *Minimum Marketable Features* (MMFs).

Although an MMF is a self-contained unit, it is often the case that it can only be developed after other project parts have been completed. These project parts may either be other MMFs or the architectural infrastructure, i.e., the set of basic features and services that offers no direct value to customers, but that is required by the MMFs.

It is important to note that the architectural infrastructure itself can usually be decomposed into self-contained deliverable units. These units, called *architectural elements* (AEs), enable the architecture to be delivered according to demand, further reducing the initial investment needed to run an IT project.

Furthermore, the total value brought to a business by an IT project consisting of several interdependent MMFs and AEs, each one with its own cash-flow stream and precedence restrictions, is highly dependent on the order in which these units are developed. Consider the diagram presented in Figure 1, which describes the dependency relations that hold true among the units (U) of an IT project that has been divided into MMFs and AEs.

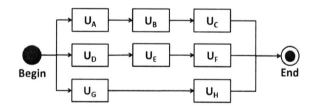

Fig. 1. A Precedence Diagram

In the diagram $U_{X \in \{A,B,\cdots,H\}}$ are either MMFs or AEs. *Begin* and *End* are dummy software units signalling respectively the beginning and end of the project. They take no time to be developed, require no capital investment and yield no returns.

In addition, an arrow going from one software unit to another, e.g. $U_A \to U_B$, indicates that the development of the former (U_A) must precede the development of the latter (U_B). In these circumstances, U_A is called a predecessor of U_B. It should be noted that predecessor is a transitive relation. Therefore, as $U_A \to U_B$ and $U_B \to U_C$, then necessarily $U_A \to U_C$.

Table 1 shows the undiscounted cash-flow elements of each software unit in the diagram introduced in Figure 1. See Schniederjans [7] for an introduction to the basic concepts of IT project financial appraisal.

Table 1. An IT project Unit's Cash-flow Elements

Unit	Cash-flow Elements (US$ 1K) Period															
	1	2	3	4	5	6	7	8	9	10	11	12	13	14	15	16
U_A	-200	98	89	81	72	63	54	45	36	27	18	9	5	4	3	2
U_B	-250	0	0	0	0	0	0	0	0	0	0	0	0	0	0	0
U_C	-250	63	90	117	144	171	198	200	225	225	225	225	225	225	225	225
U_D	-200	0	0	0	0	0	0	0	0	0	0	0	0	0	0	0
U_E	-350	35	35	70	90	108	126	144	162	180	180	180	180	180	180	180
U_F	-120	90	90	90	135	135	135	135	135	135	135	135	135	135	135	135
U_G	-350	60	80	100	60	70	70	70	80	120	150	250	450	100	100	100
U_H	-100	50	50	50	25	5	5	5	100	20	20	20	20	20	20	20

For example, according to the information presented in Table 1, U_A requires an initial investment of US$ 200,000, or US$ 200K for short. Once its development is completed at the end of the first period, it provides a series of positive returns until the sixteenth period when the unit as a whole becomes obsolete and has to be replaced by a new and more suitable tool. A similar path is followed by units U_C, U_E, U_F, U_G and U_H. Therefore, all of these units are indeed MMFs.

A different path is followed by units U_B and U_D. Once they are completed, they provide no financial returns on their own in respect of the investment required for their development. Hence, these units are architectural elements.

The number of periods comprising the beginning of an IT project and the point in time when the project's final product is replaced by a more suitable alternative is often referred to as the project's *window of opportunity*.

Because it is improper to perform mathematical operations on monetary values without taking into account a discount rate, in order to compare the financial value of different MMFs and the investment required by AEs, one has to resort to their discounted cash-flow [7]. The sum of all cash-flow elements of a unit is the unit's net present value (NPV). For instance, according to the information presented in Table 1, if U_C is developed in the first period, it yields an NPV of

$$\text{US\$2,398K} = \frac{-250K}{(1+0.5\%)^1} + \frac{63K}{(1+0.5\%)^2} + \cdots + \frac{225K}{(1+0.5\%)^{16}},$$

considering a discount rate of 0.5% per period. On the other hand, if U_C is developed in the second period, it yields an NPV of US$ 2,179K, in the third, US$ 1,962K and so on.

In order to make understanding easier, all the monetary figures presented in this paper are rounded to the nearest integer value. Also, when its use is required the cash-flow discount rate is kept at 0.5% per period.

Clearly, not every MMF can be developed in the very first period. The precedence diagram presented in Figure 1 indicates that only U_A, U_D and U_G can be developed in that period. If at any given time, only one unit can be in its development phase, U_C, for example, cannot be developed until the third period at best.

Furthermore, each particular sequence of project units yields its own NPV. For instance, the sequence $U_D \to U_E \to U_F \to U_G \to U_A \to U_B \to U_C \to U_H$ yields US\$ 5,154K, which is the highest NPV among all possible development sequences.

It is important to note that the NPV of a project unit development sequence is the sum of the NPV of each of its components, considering the period in which they are expected to be built. Therefore,

$$\text{NPV}(SU_D \to SU_E \to SU_F \to SU_G \to SU_A \to SU_B \to SU_C \to SU_H) =$$
$$\text{NPV}_1(SU_D) + \text{NPV}_2(SU_E) + \text{NPV}_3(SU_F) + \cdots \text{NPV}_8(SU_H) =$$
$$(-199 + 1,405 + 1,420 + \cdots + 176) \times \text{US\$ 1K}, =$$
$$\text{US\$ 5,154K},$$

where $\text{NPV}_t(U_X)$ is the NPV of unit U_X, considering that its development starts in period t.

Note that the financial data presented throughout this paper was obtained considering that: (a) the first non-dummy unit must be developed in period one, (b) at any given period only one unit can be in its development stage, (c) once the development of a project unit starts it cannot be stopped or paused, (d) there is no delay between the completion of a project unit and the beginning of the development of the next, and (e) all project units have to be developed eventually.

2.2 Data Envelopment Analysis

Data Envelopment Analysis (DEA), due to Charnes et al. [8], is a non-parametric linear programming method used to estimate the relative Efficiency of production units of the same kind. Such units take in a set of inputs in order to yield a set of outputs. For example,

- *Branches of a chain of furniture stores* - which take in capital investment to be set up, products to be sold and employees to attend potential buyers, yielding financial returns and satisfied customers;
- *Agencies of the same government* - which take in taxpayers' money, yielding public services; and
- *Different implementation sequences of the units comprising the same IT project* - which take in capital to be built, yielding financial returns and increased productivity.

In DEA jargon such production units are called *decision making units* (DMUs).

To estimate the relative Efficiency of DMUs, DEA takes into account a relevant set of measurements that are collected about the decision making units one wants to analyze, being the most efficient those that have the highest ratio between the products and services yielded and the resources used to make them. In formal terms, *DMU Efficiency* is defined as $\frac{DMU_{Output}}{DMU_{Input}}$, where DMU_{Input} and DMU_{Output} are linear combinations of the measurements describing the resources consumed and the products and services yielded by the DMU respectively.

The most efficient units are then connected by a hyperplane in the n-dimensional space defined by the set of relevant measurements. This hyperplane defines an efficient frontier, against which the other DMUs are analyzed.

The problem of figuring the relative Efficiency of n decision making units with multiple inputs and outputs has been generalized by Charnes, Cooper and Rhodes [8] with the following optimization model, which is often referred to as the CCR model for obvious reasons:

$$\max_{u,v} \theta = \frac{u_1 y_{1o} + u_2 y_{2o} + \cdots + u_s y_{so}}{v_1 x_{1o} + v_2 x_{2o} + \cdots + v_m x_{mo}} \tag{1}$$

subjected to

$$\frac{u_1 y_{1j} + u_2 y_{2j} + \cdots + u_s y_{sj}}{v_1 x_{1j} + v_2 x_{2j} + \cdots + v_m x_{mj}} \leq 1, \text{ for } j = 1, \cdots, n,$$

$$v_1, v_2, \cdots, v_m \geq 0, \text{ and}$$

$$u_1, u_2, \cdots, u_s \geq 0,$$

where $1 \leq o \leq n$, $x_{1o}, \cdots, x_{mo}$ and $y_{1o}, \cdots, y_{so}$ are respectively the measurements of the inputs and outputs of a given DMU_o, and $u_1, \cdots, u_s$ and $v_1, \cdots, v_m$ are the weights whose value one is interested in determining.

Because only very simple DEA problems can be solved by analytical means, one has frequently to resort to a computer tool to evaluate the relative efficiently of IT projects' implementation sequences. A comprehensive list of DEA solvers can be found in [9].

Before one may use a DEA solver for CCR calculation, it is important to bear in mind that some additional restrictions are often imposed on the optimization-model input and output variables, so that the software tool can be used in a variety of circumstances. While it is expected that the smaller the value of an input variable, the better; the converse holds true for output variables, i.e., the higher the value of those variables the better [10].

If one's data does not comply with these additional restrictions, then some linear transformations may be applied to the model variables. For example, the self-funding point (SFP) and break-even point (BEP) do not comply with these restrictions, as the higher the value of these performance indicators are, the worse it is. However, $\frac{1}{SFP}$ and $\frac{1}{BEP}$ do comply with the additional restrictions. Therefore, the latter should replace the former when using a general purpose DEA solver.

Table 2 presents the relative Efficiency (Effcy) of the IT project's implementation sequences introduced in Figure 1, obtained with the assistance of the CCR model. In these circumstances, the capital investment (CI) was taken as the input of each possible implementation sequence and the return on investment (ROI), internal rate of return (IRR), $\frac{1}{SFP}$ and $\frac{1}{BEP}$ as the outputs. To make understanding easier the SFP and BEP are presented in Table 2 in their original form.

Table 2. The Relative Efficiency of Implementation Sequences

#	Period								CI	ROI	IRR	SFP	BEP	Effcy
	1	2	3	4	5	6	7	8	($ 1K)	(%)	(%)			(%)
1	U_D	U_E	U_F	U_G	U_A	U_B	U_C	U_H	851	606	23,8	5	9	65,9
2	U_G	U_D	U_E	U_F	U_A	U_B	U_C	U_H	768	670	23,7	6	9	73,1
3	U_D	U_E	U_G	U_F	U_A	U_B	U_C	U_H	881	581	22.9	5	9	63,7
⋮	⋮	⋮	⋮	⋮	⋮	⋮	⋮	⋮	⋮	⋮	⋮	⋮	⋮	
1,120	U_D	U_A	U_B	U_E	U_F	U_G	U_C	U_H	880	379	18.4	8	10	57,4

Considering that the NPV is the ratio between the CI and ROI, its presence in the CCR model adds no new information to the optimization model, nevertheless, increasing the computational effort required to yield a solution. Therefore, for obtaining the relative Efficiency of each sequence the NPV remains unused either as an input or output in the CCR model.

The relative Efficiency presented in Table 2 was obtained with the support of the *Efficiency Measurement System* (EMS), an MS-Windows DEA solver developed at the Technical University Dortmund, Germany [11].

2.3   The Analytic Hierarchy Process

When the number of possible implementation sequences is considerable, it is not uncommon that two or more sequences turn out to be equally efficient. In these circumstances, management may find themselves in a situation in which they have to choose one implementation sequence among several different but equally efficient sequences, so that the underlying IT project can actually be developed.

For example, consider the data presented in Table 3, which is in fact a subset of the data presented in Table 2. Note that only the most efficient sequences are displayed in Table 3.

Altogether there are five possible implementation sequences that are equally efficient from the financial point of view, nonetheless, only one implementation sequence shall be used to implement the IT project under analysis. In these circumstances, management may benefit from using Saaty's Analytic Hierarchy Process (AHP) [12] in order to make the choice wisely.

According to Saaty, the decisions in which one has to consider several performance indicators, such as CI, ROI, IRR, etc., are often more easily accomplished when these indicators are compared to each other in pairs. Therefore, for a given set of performance indicators $\{PI_1, PI_2, \cdots, PI_n\}$, Saaty's pairwise comparison leads to the construction of a valuation $n \times n$ matrix V as shown in Table 4.

Table 3. The Most Efficient Development Sequences

#	Period								CI	NPV	ROI	IRR	SFP	BEP	Effcy
	1	2	3	4	5	6	7	8	($ 1K)	($ 1K)	(%)	(%)			(%)
298	U_A	U_G	U_H	U_E	U_E	U_F	U_B	U_C	573	4,353	760	24.9	6	10	100.0
331	U_D	U_E	U_F	U_H	U_A	U_B	U_C	U_G	630	4,328	687	23.7	4	9	100.0
370	U_D	U_E	U_G	U_F	U_A	U_B	U_C	U_H	568	4,277	753	25.2	8	10	100.0
432	U_D	U_E	U_F	U_H	U_A	U_B	U_G	U_C	630	4,229	671	23.2	4	9	100.0
642	U_A	U_D	U_E	U_F	U_H	U_B	U_C	U_G	561	4,026	718	24.5	5	9	100.0

Table 4. Saaty's Squared Valuation Matrix

$$
\begin{array}{c}
\quad PI_1 \; PI_2 \; PI_3 \; PI_4 \; \cdots \; PI_n \\
\quad \downarrow \;\; \downarrow \;\; \downarrow \;\; \downarrow \;\;\;\;\; \downarrow \\
\begin{array}{c}
PI_1 \rightarrow \\
PI_2 \rightarrow \\
PI_3 \rightarrow \\
PI_4 \rightarrow \\
\vdots \\
PI_n \rightarrow
\end{array}
\left[
\begin{array}{cccccc}
1 & \frac{1}{v_{2,1}} & \frac{1}{v_{3,1}} & \frac{1}{v_{4,1}} & \cdots & \frac{1}{v_{n,1}} \\
v_{2,1} & 1 & \frac{1}{v_{3,2}} & \frac{1}{v_{4,2}} & \cdots & \frac{1}{v_{n,2}} \\
v_{3,1} & v_{3,2} & 1 & \frac{1}{v_{4,3}} & \cdots & \frac{1}{v_{n,3}} \\
v_{4,1} & v_{4,2} & v_{4,3} & 1 & \cdots & \frac{1}{v_{n,4}} \\
\vdots & \vdots & \vdots & \vdots & \vdots & \vdots \\
v_{n,1} & v_{n,2} & v_{n,3} & v_{n,4} & \cdots & 1
\end{array}
\right]
\end{array}
$$

Each element in V is the result of a direct comparison between two performance indicators, using the scale described in Table 5. Therefore, if experience and judgement strongly favour PI_2 over PI_1 in reaching one's objective, then $v_{2,1} = 5$ and, as a consequence, the opposite also holds true, implying that $v_{2,1} = \frac{1}{5}$. On the other hand, if it is PI_1 that is strongly favored over PI_2 in reaching one's objective, then $v_{2,1} = \frac{1}{5}$ and, as a consequence, $v_{2,1} = 5$.

All of this paves the way for the construction of a matrix in which all the main-diagonal entries are 1s, because when compared to themselves every performance indicator contributes equally to reaching a predefined objective. Also, every $v_{i,j}$ in the off-diagonal lower and upper triangular parts of V is either drawn out of the scale presented in Table 5 or is the inverse of $v_{j,i}$.

According to Saaty [12] the relative importance of each performance indicator under consideration is given by the components of the principal eigenvector E of V. For example, consider the financial performance indicators presented in Table 3. In a financially stable environment in which the IRR is considerably higher than the discount rate, the implementation sequences that provide higher ROIs are often preferable to those that offer smaller figures.

Moreover, if obtaining capital investment is a question of concern, smaller CIs may be preferable over higher ROIs and reduced SFPs and BEPs. Finally, in many circumstances, having the implementation project self-funded earlier, may be preferable to returning capital to the project's investors. Table 6 reflects these ideas.

As a result, $(0.53, 0.23, 0.04, 0.12, 0.08)^T$ is the eigenvector of the valuation matrix presented in Table 6, being its elements the weights to be used evaluate

Table 5. The Fundamental Scale of Pairwise Comparison

Intensity of Importance	Definition	Explanation
1	Equal importance	The two performance indicators contribute equally to the objective one has in mind
3	Moderate importance	Experience and judgement slightly favour one performance indicator over another
5	Strong importance	Experience and judgement strongly favour one performance indicator over another
7	Very strong	A performance indicator is favoured very strongly over another
9	Extreme importance	The evidence favouring one performance indicator over another is of the highest possible order of affirmation
2, 4, 6, 8	Intermediate values	When compromise is needed

Table 6. Saaty's Valuation Matrix for Financial Performance Indicators

$$
\begin{array}{c}
\begin{array}{cccccc}
\text{CI} & \text{ROI} & \text{IRR} & \text{SFP} & \text{BEP} & \quad \text{E} \\
\downarrow & \downarrow & \downarrow & \downarrow & \downarrow & \quad \downarrow
\end{array}\\
\begin{array}{c}
\text{CI} \rightarrow \\
\text{ROI} \rightarrow \\
\text{IRR} \rightarrow \\
\text{SFP} \rightarrow \\
\text{BEP} \rightarrow
\end{array}
\begin{bmatrix}
1 & 5 & 7 & 7 & 7 \\
\frac{1}{5} & 1 & 5 & 5 & 5 \\
\frac{1}{7} & \frac{1}{5} & 1 & \frac{1}{5} & \frac{1}{5} \\
\frac{1}{7} & \frac{1}{5} & 5 & 1 & 3 \\
\frac{1}{7} & \frac{1}{5} & 5 & \frac{1}{3} & 1
\end{bmatrix}
\begin{bmatrix}
0.53 \\
0.23 \\
0.04 \\
0.12 \\
0.08
\end{bmatrix}
\end{array}
$$

the most efficient implementation sequences. Hence, the CI is $\frac{0.53}{0.23} = 2.2$ times more relevant than the ROI and $\frac{0.53}{0.12} = 4.4$ times more important than the SFP. Table 7 presents the combined performances of the most efficient implementation sequences.

Table 7. The Combined Performances of the Most Efficient Implementation Sequences

#	0.53×CI	0.23×ROI	0.04×IRR	$0.04 \times \frac{1}{\text{SFP}}$	$0.04 \times \frac{1}{\text{BEP}}$	Σ
298	0.53×-573	0.23×760%	0.04×24,9%	$0.12 \times \frac{1}{6}$	$0.08 \times \frac{1}{10}$	-299,04
331	0.53×-630	0.23×687%	0.04×23,7%	$0.12 \times \frac{1}{4}$	$0.08 \times \frac{1}{9}$	-329,13
370	0.53×-568	0.23×753%	0.04×25,2%	$0.12 \times \frac{1}{8}$	$0.08 \times \frac{1}{10}$	-296,44
432	0.53×-630	0.23×671%	0.04×23,2%	$0.12 \times \frac{1}{4}$	$0.08 \times \frac{1}{9}$	-329,17
642	0.53×-561	0.23×718%	0.04×24,5%	$0.12 \times \frac{1}{5}$	$0.08 \times \frac{1}{9}$	-292,84
					Max	-292,84

According to the information presented in Table 7, 642 is the sequence with the best performance, followed by sequences 370, 298, 331 and 432. One may rightfully wonder why the CI bears a negative sign in Table 7. Also, why the inverse of the SFP and BEP are used to calculate the combined performance of sequences. This has been done so that for all financial performance indicators the higher they are the better, thus allowing Σ to be a coherent indicator of sequence Efficiency.

3   The Method

Organizations that are interested in increasing the Efficiency of the investments being made in IT projects may benefit from taking the steps described in Table 8.

Table 8. A Method to Increase the Efficiency of an Investment made in IT

Step	Action
1	Select an IT project that has been broken down into MMFs and AEs
2	Determine the project's window of opportunity
3	Elicit the project units' dependency relations
4	Figure the cash-flow elements of each project unit
5	Identify an appropriate cash-flow discount rate
6	For each project unit, calculate its NPV according to the period in which its development may start
7	Generate all possible implementation sequences
8	Compute the financial performance indicators of each possible implementation sequence
9	Select a solver to help with the DEA calculations
10	Submit the implementation sequences together with the relevant financial performance indicators to the selected DEA solver for CCR optimization
11	Use the DEA results to identify the most efficient sequences
12	If several implementation sequences turn out to be equally efficient, use Saaty's AHP to select the one that is going to be used in the implementation of the IT project under consideration

4   Conclusions

In production engineering being efficient indicates that production units are using their resources to yield products and services in the most efficient way possible, thus allowing for reduced production cost and better selling prices for consumers and clients. In this paper, IT project units are taken as production units, the dependency relations that hold true among them are acknowledged, the order in which these units can be developed is considered, the financial performance of each possible development sequencing is evaluated and the most efficient implementation sequences are identified.

However, it is important to bear in mind that Efficiency is highly dependent on the measurements collected about the production units. In this paper the capital investment, return on investment, internal rate of return, self-funding point and break even point have been used to exemplify the use of the method being put forward. These particular performance indicators have been selected because they are widely used in many different circumstances in a large variety of industries. Nevertheless, other quantitative financial performance indicator such as liquidity ratios and risk indicators can be easily added to the suggested method, further increasing the number of circumstances in which it can be used successfully.

As information technology has, with time, permeated all business functions, making financially efficient IT investment has become a matter of concern for decision makers. Therefore, the ideas presented in this paper contribute not only to increasing the perceived business value of IT, but also to enhancing the overall financial performance of businesses in which investments in IT are being made.

References

1. Luftman, J., Zadeh, H.: Key Information Technology and Management Issues 2010-11: an International Study. Journal of Information Technology 26(3), 193–204 (2011)
2. Rosacker, K.M., Olson, D.L.: An Empirical Assessment of IT Project Selection and Evaluation Methods in State Government. Project Management Journal 39(1), 49–58 (2008)
3. Gomez, A., Rueda, G., Alarcón, P.P.: A Systematic and Lightweight Method to Identify Dependencies between User Stories. In: Sillitti, A., Martin, A., Wang, X., Whitworth, E. (eds.) XP 2010. LNBIP, vol. 48, pp. 190–195. Springer, Heidelberg (2010)
4. Alencar, A.J., do Nascimento, R.A., Schmitz, E.A., Correa, A.L., Dias, A.F.S.: Unleashing the Potential Impact of Nonessential Self-Contained Software Units and Flexible Precedence Relations Upon the Value of Software. Journal of Software 6(12), 2500–2507 (2011)
5. Danesh, A.S.: A Survey of Release Planning Approaches in Incremental Software Development. In: Das, V.V., Thankachan, N. (eds.) CIIT 2011. CCIS, vol. 250, pp. 687–692. Springer, Heidelberg (2011)
6. Denne, M., Cleland-Huang, J.: Financially Informed Requirements Prioritization. In: Roman, G.C., Griswold, W., Nuseibeh, B. (eds.) Proceedings of ICSE, May 15-21, pp. 710–711. IEEE, Chicago (2005)
7. Schniederjans, M.J., Hamaker, J.L., Schniederjans, A.M.: Information Technology Investment: Decision-making Methodology, 2nd edn. WSPC (March 2010)
8. Charnes, A., Cooper, W.W., Rhodes, E.: Measuring the Efficiency of Decision Making Units. EJOR 2(6), 429–444 (1978)
9. Cooper, W.W., Seiford, L.M., Zhu, J.: Handbook on Data Envelopment Analysis. Kluwer Academic (March 2004)
10. Cooper, W.W., Seiford, L.M., Tone, K.: Introduction to Data Envelopment Analysis and Its Uses. Springer (2005)
11. Scheel, H.: EMS: Efficiency Measurement System - a Data Envelopment Analysis (DEA) Software. Information available in the Internet (2011) (Site last visited on February 5, 2000)
12. Saaty, T.L.: Decision Making with the Analytic Hierarchy Process. International Journal of Services Sciences 1(1), 83–98 (2008)

IBGA: An Incentives Based Grant Allocation Algorithm for Academic Institutions

Ash Mohammad Abbas

Department of Computer Engineering, Aligarh Muslim University
Aligarh - 202002, India
am.abbas.ce@amu.ac.in

Abstract. Devising a scheme for allocation of grant to academic institutions is a challenging task. In this paper, we propose an incentive based scheme for allocating the grant to academic institutions. Our schemes has a provision of base grant that is allocated to each faculty member/research student irrespective of his/her performance. The grant is further augmented based on the quality of research papers published and the amount of augmentation is computed based on the impact factors of journals where the research papers of the faculty member/research student are published.

Keywords: IBGA, Grant Allocation.

1 Introduction

Research is an integral part of academic activities for faculty members of an academic institution or an institute of higher education such as a university. Without adequate research one cannot imagine the existence of a department, an institute, or a university. To carry out research, each faculty member requires appropriate funding from government, semi-government, or private agencies. Allocating grants to a university and its departments that the university contains is a challenging task. The challenge comes from the fact that the resources (in terms of grant) are limited and the funding agency or the government wishes to allocate it in the best possible manner.

Since the resources are finite, therefore, those should be allocated in a manner that leads to excellence. Metrics for evaluating quality of research are described in [1] and their relationships are presented in [2]. It is mentioned in [3] that there are two factors for an excellent research: the quantum of research funding and an appropriate mechanism to allocate limited funding to the most promising and high quality research. In [3], it is felt that there is a need for a sound mechanism to allocate grants in such a way so as to achieve excellence.

Trends and practices in assessment of education research are described in [4]. An empirical exploration of changing allocation models for public research funding which is based on project funding data is presented in [5]. Impact of metrics based allocation of research grant together with its merits and demerits

K.R. Venugopal and L.M. Patnaik (Eds.): ICIP 2012, CCIS 292, pp. 487–492, 2012.
© Springer-Verlag Berlin Heidelberg 2012

is discussed in [6]. On the other hand, there are opponents of impact based allocation of research grant. In [7], the views of employees about meritocracy in equitable organizations are discussed. In [8], it has been discussed that the mechanisms of assessing research performance are complicated and burdensome. The reason is that there is no unique definition of impact and it may depend on the context, therefore, its assessment is far from straight forward.

A major issue is that the research grant should be allocated in such a manner so that it provides equal opportunities to all researchers as well as it motivates the researchers to be more productive and creative. In this paper, we try to answer the following research question: Can there be an allocation scheme such that it motivates the employees to be *more creative and productive* and simultaneously it tries to adhere as far as possible the *equal opportunity principle*. We propose a scheme which is based on incentives provided to the academic employees in addition to a bare minimum (however, sufficient for their individual growth) research grant called the base grant

In this paper, we propose a scheme to allocate the grants to each faculty member of a department. Our scheme is based on incentives to be provided to a faculty member based on his/her performance in research. The merits of our scheme are (i) a faculty member who performs better is allocated relatively larger grant, and (ii) the one who was not able to perform in the last session still has chances to perform better by allocating him a bare minimum grant called the *base grant*.

The rest of this paper is organized as follows. In Section 2, we describe the proposed scheme. Section 3 contains results and discussion. The last section is for conclusion.

2   Incentive Based Scheme

We assume that a monthly assistantship or fellowship is provided to each research student and similarly, a monthly salary is provided to each faculty member by the government. These salaries and/or fellowships are provided irrespective of the country of origin of either a faculty member or a research student. We assume that such a salary provided to a faculty member or stipend/fellowship provided to a research student is enough to support himself/herself together with his/her family to live a modest life. All grants are over and above his/her salary/stipend/fellowship etc.

2.1   Grants for Faculty Members

Let there be a base grant, γ_b, for each faculty member irrespective of his/her performance in research activities. This is the grant at the disposal of a faculty member, which he/she can recommend or can utilize himself/herself in attending the conferences/symposia/workshops or procuring equipment for his/her research and academic activities.

Let there be k articles published by an author. Let ith article be published in a journal with an impact factor $\mathcal{F}_i$, and let there be a_i number of authors in paper i. It has been argued in [1] that the credit of a published paper should be divided among all authors of the paper. Therefore, if we assume that the impact factor of a journal represents the credit of an author, then the impact factor of the journal divided by the number of authors should represent the credit of each author under an equal weight assignment scheme.

Let Δ be an increment in the grant if an author publishes an article, independently, in a journal with an impact factor equal to 1. Augmentation in the grant for the next academic session on the basis of the quality of research papers published is as follows.

$$\gamma_r = \begin{cases} \sum_{i=1}^{k_f} \frac{\mathcal{F}_i}{a_i} \Delta_f & \text{if } \gamma_r < \gamma_{\max} \\ \gamma_{\max} & \text{if } \gamma_r \geq \gamma_{\max} \end{cases}. \tag{1}$$

where, $\gamma_{\max}$, is the ceiling on the amount of annual augmentation in the research grant due to publications in journals.

Incorporating the augmentation, the grant of the faculty member is given by the following expression.

$$\gamma_f = \gamma_b + \gamma_r. \tag{2}$$

Let S be the annual salary provided to a faculty member. Then, the amount of expenditure incurred due to a faculty member is,

$$E_f = S + \gamma. \tag{3}$$

2.2   Grants for Research Students

Let the base grant of a research student be ξ_b, which can be utilized in attending conferences/workshops/seminars or for procuring equipments related to his/her own research. If a research student publishes ith paper in a journal with an impact factor $\mathcal{F}_i$, his annual research grant can be augmented by

$$\xi_r = \begin{cases} \sum_{i=1}^{k_s} \frac{\mathcal{F}_i}{a_i} \Delta_s & \text{if } \xi_r < \xi_{\max} \\ \xi_{\max} & \text{if } \xi_r \geq \xi_{\max} \end{cases}. \tag{4}$$

where a_i is the number of authors of ith paper. The amount of grant provided to a research student after this augmentation is,

$$\xi = \xi_b + \xi_r. \tag{5}$$

Let the annual stipend/assistantship/fellowship provided to a research student be X. Then, the amount of expenditure incurred due to a research student is,

$$E_s = X + \xi. \tag{6}$$

Algorithm 1. Incentives Based Grant Allocation Scheme (IBGA).

1: *Input:* γ_b, $\gamma_{\max}$, k, a_i, $\mathcal{F}_i$, Δ_f
2: {C}ompute the augmentation in research grant
3: $\gamma_r = 0$
4: **for** $i = 1$ to k **do**
5:     $\gamma_r = \gamma_r + \frac{\mathcal{F}_i}{a_i} \Delta_f$
6: **end for**
7: **if** $\gamma_r \geq \gamma_{\max}$ **then**
8:     $\gamma_r = \gamma_{\max}$
9: **end if**
10: {C}ompute the grant of the faculty member
11: $\gamma_f = \gamma_b + \gamma_r$

2.3   Balancing Meritocracy and Equitability

Let us first consider the grant allocation for faculty members. The research grant provided to a non-performer is γ_b and that to a performer is $\gamma_b + \gamma_r$. The excess research grant provided to a performing researcher is γ_r. We define a parameter that we call *meritocratic factor*, μ, as follows.

$$\mu = \frac{\gamma_r}{\gamma_b + \gamma_r}. \tag{7}$$

In other words, the *meritocratic factor* is a ratio of the augmentation in research grant due to journal publications and the sum of the base grant and augmentation in research grant. Now consider special cases of (7). If $\gamma_r = 0$, then $\mu = 0$. It corresponds to a purely equitable allocation of the research grant. If $\gamma_b = 0$, then $\mu = 1$. It corresponds to a purely meritocratic allocation of grants. For $\gamma_r = \gamma_b$, then $\mu = 0.5$. In this case, there is an equal weightage to equitable and meritocratic allocations of research grant. If $\gamma_r > \gamma_b$, it means that more weightage is given to meritocratic allocation as compared to equitable allocation and vice-versa. Similarly, one may define a meritocratic factor in case of the grant allocation to research students.

On the other hand, using (7), we have,

$$1 - \mu = \frac{\gamma_b}{\gamma_b + \gamma_r}. \tag{8}$$

We may call $1 - \mu$ as equitability (or equality) ratio. Further, from (7), we have,

$$\frac{\mu}{1 - \mu} = \frac{\gamma_r}{\gamma_b}. \tag{9}$$

In other words, the ratio of meritocratic factor and equitability factor is the ratio between the grant allocated on the basis of merit and that allocated equitably.

3   Results and Discussion

Let the increment in the grant of a faculty member for an article published in a journal with an impact factor equal to 1.0 be \$5000. For research students, let

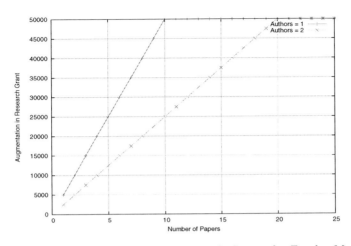

Fig. 1. The Augmentation in the Annual Research Grant of a Faculty Member as a Function of the Number of Papers Published in Journals

this increment be $4000. Let the annual ceiling of augmentation due to research publications of a faculty member be $50000 and that of a research student be $20000.

Fig. 1 shows the augmentation in the annual research grant as a function of the number of papers published in journals for faculty members. We observe that as the number of papers published is increased, the augmentation in the research grant increases linearly up to the ceiling in the augmentation and then remains constant. If the number of authors are increased, the increase in the augmentation due to research papers becomes smaller as compared to single authored papers.

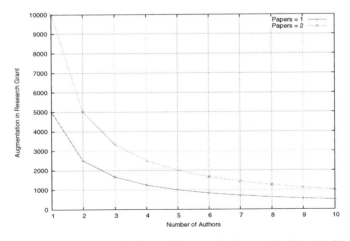

Fig. 2. The Augmentation in the Annual Research Grant of a Faculty Member as a Function of the Number of Authors of the Papers Published in Journals

Fig. 2 shows the augmentation in the annual research grant as a function of the number of authors of the papers published in journals for faculty members. We observe that as the number of authors are increased, the augmentation in research grant decreases. This is in accordance with (1), which says that the augmentation in research is inversely proportional to the number of authors in papers.

4   Conclusions

In this paper, we proposed an incentive based scheme for allocating the grant to academic institutions. Our scheme is based on incentives to be provided to a faculty member based on his/her performance in research. The merits of our scheme are (i) a faculty member who performs better is allocated relatively larger grant, and (ii) the one who was not able to perform in the last session still has chances to perform better by allocating him a bare minimum grant called the *base grant*. In this way, our scheme tries to fill the gap between the allocation of the grant based on the performance of a researcher and the allocation where performance is not an issue.

References

1. Abbas, A.M.: Weighted Indices for Evaluating Quality of Research with Multiple Authors. Scientometrics 88(2), 107–131 (2011)
2. Abbas, A.M.: Bounds and Inequalities Relating h-Index, g-Index, e-Index, and Generalized Impact Factor: An Improvement over Existing Models. PloS One 7(4), e33699 (2012)
3. Allocation of Research Funding and Undergraduate Student Places by the University Grant Committee, LEGCO Panel on Education, LC Paper No. CB(2) 2291/10-11(07) (2011),
   http://www.ugc.edu.hk/eng/doc/hgc/publication/prog/lc-paper.pdf
4. Oancea, A.: From Procrusters to Proteus: Trends and Practices in the Assessment of Education Research. International Journal of Research and Method in Education 30(3), 243–269 (2007)
5. Poti, B., Reale, E.: Changing Allocation Models for Public Research Funding: An Empirical Exploration Based on Project Funding Data. Science and Public Policy 34(6), 417–430 (2007)
6. Sastry, T., Bekhradnia, B.: Using Metrics to Allocate Research Fund,
   http://www.hepi.ac.uk/files/Usingmetricstoallocateresearchfunds.pdf
7. Deem, R.: Managing a Meritocracy or Equitable Organization? Senior Managers and Employee's Views About Equal Opportunities Policies in UK Universities. Journal of Education Policies, Taylor and Francis 22(6), 615–636 (2007)
8. Martin, B.R.: The Research Excellence Framework and the Impact Agenda: Are We Creating a Frankenstein Monster? Research Evaluation 20(3), 247–254 (2011)

On the Merits and Pitfalls of the Incremental Funding Method and Its Software Project Scheduling Algorithms

Antonio Juarez Alencar[1], Jorge V. Doria Jr.[1],
Eber Assis Schmitz[1], Alexandre Luis Correa[2], and Ivan Maia Vital Jr.[1]

[1] The Tércio Pacitti Institute for Computer Reseach
Federal University of Rio de Janeiro (UFRJ)
[2] Department of Applied Informatics
State of Rio de Janeiro Federal University (UNIRIO)
juarezalencar@br.inter.net

Abstract. This paper analyses the merits of the IFM and its software project scheduling algorithms; challenges the claim of efficacy and efficiency of those algorithms made by their authors; indicates alternative solutions to the IFM's pitfalls; and points towards research directions that could further improve the method.

Keywords: Incremental Funding Method, Minimum Marketable Feature Software Units, Value-Based Software Engineering, Weighted Look-Ahead Algorithm.

1 Introduction

Despite the vital contribution that computer technology has been making to many lines of businesses over the years, funding software development projects today has become a central issue for both managers and practitioners. Claiming for better financial returns, shorter payback time, less risk exposure, faster time to market and improved ability to adapt to new market conditions have become common place concerns among those who make their investment capital available for software building.

Consistent with this view, Denne and Cleland-Huang [1] have introduced the Incremental Funding Method, an approach to bring financial discipline to software development. This paper analyses the IFM and each of its accompanying scheduling algorithms, unveiling their merits and pitfalls so that developers may acquire a better understanding of what they may gain and lose when using each one of them.

The remainder of this paper is organized as follows. Section 2 presents a review of the principal concepts and methods used in the coming sections. Section 3 introduces the scheduling algorithms conceived by Denne and Cleland-Huang [1]. Section 4 discusses the merits and pitfall of the IFM and its scheduling algorithms, while also recommending alternative solutions to the IFM's pitfalls. Section 5 points towards future research directions. Section 6 presents the conclusions of this paper.

K.R. Venugopal and L.M. Patnaik (Eds.): ICIP 2012, CCIS 292, pp. 493–502, 2012.
© Springer-Verlag Berlin Heidelberg 2012

2   The Incremental Funding Method

The Incremental Funding Method (IFM) advocates the partitioning of the software to be developed into smaller self-contained units that create value to business and can be deployed in a shorter period of time. According to Denne and Cleland-Huang [1] such units are called *Minimum Marketable Features* or *MMFs*.

Although an MMF is a self-contained unit, it is often the case that it can only be developed after other project parts have been completed. These project parts may be either other MMFs or the architectural infrastructure, i.e., the set of basic features that offers no direct value to customers, but that is required by the MMFs. It also important to keep in mind that the architectural infrastructure itself can usually be decomposed into self-contained deliverable units. These units are called *architectural elements*, or AEs for short.

Moreover, the total value brought to a business by a software consisting of several interdependent MMFs and AEs, each one with its own cash flow stream and precedence restrictions, is highly dependent on the order in which these units are developed. For instance, Figure 1 presents the precedence diagram of a software that has been divided into MMFs and AEs.

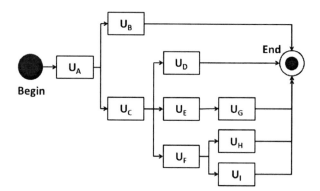

Fig. 1. A precedence diagram

In the diagram *Begin* and *End* are dummy units that take no time to be developed, require no capital investment and yield no returns. Also, an arrow going from one software unit to another, e.g. $U_A \rightarrow U_C$, indicates that the development of the former (U_A) must precede the development of the latter (U_C). In these circumstances, U_A is called a predecessor of U_C.

Table 1 shows all possible development sequences for the units introduced in Figure 1, considering that: (a) the first non-dummy unit must be developed in period one, (b) at any given period only one unit can be in its development stage,(c) once the development of a software unit starts it cannot be stopped or paused, (d) there is no delay between the completion of a software unit and the beginning of the development of the next, and (e) all software units have to be developed eventually,

Table 1. Scheduling options

Sched.	Period								
Option	1	2	3	4	5	6	7	8	9
1	U_A	U_B	U_C	U_D	U_F	U_E	U_G	U_I	U_H
2	U_A	U_B	U_C	U_D	U_F	U_E	U_G	U_H	U_I
3	U_A	U_B	U_C	U_D	U_E	U_G	U_F	U_I	U_H
$\vdots$	$\vdots$	$\vdots$	$\vdots$	$\vdots$	$\vdots$	$\vdots$	$\vdots$	$\vdots$	$\vdots$
960	U_A	U_C	U_E	U_F	U_H	U_I	U_G	U_D	U_B

Table 2 shows the undiscounted cash-flow elements of each software unit in the diagram introduced in Figure 1. For example, according to the information presented in Table 2, U_D requires an initial investment of US$ 35 thousand. Once its development is completed at the end of the first period, it provides a series of positive returns until the sixteenth period, when the software as a whole becomes obsolete and is replaced by a new and more advanced tool. A similar path is followed by units U_B, U_F, U_G, U_H and U_I. Therefore, all these units are indeed MMFs.

A different path is followed by units U_A, U_C and U_E. Once they are completed they provide no financial returns on their own in respect to the investment required for their development. Hence, these units are architectural elements.

Table 2. Software unit cash-flow elements

Unit	Cash-Flow Elements (US$ 1,000)															
	Period															
	1	2	3	4	5	6	7	8	9	10	11	12	13	14	15	16
U_A	-35	0	0	0	0	0	0	0	0	0	0	0	0	0	0	0
U_B	-20	-20	100	90	50	70	95	90	95	65	40	115	80	80	80	75
U_C	-10	0	0	0	0	0	0	0	0	0	0	0	0	0	0	0
U_D	-35	15	15	20	10	10	20	30	20	35	15	40	25	40	50	40
U_E	-45	0	0	0	0	0	0	0	0	0	0	0	0	0	0	0
U_F	-40	10	10	10	15	20	10	40	25	15	25	10	15	20	20	20
U_G	-20	-10	5	5	20	20	25	35	60	55	55	95	95	95	90	95
U_H	-20	-10	-5	20	20	20	20	20	20	20	20	20	20	20	20	20
U_I	-10	5	5	5	5	10	10	10	10	10	10	10	5	5	5	5

Because it is improper to perform mathematical operations on monetary values without taking into account a discount rate, in order to compare the financial value of different MMFs and the investment required by AEs one has to resort to their discounted cash flow [2]. Throughout this paper a discount rate of 0.5% per period is used wherever it is appropriate.

For instance, if U_D is developed in the first period, it yields an NPV of US\$ 330 thousand i.e., $\frac{-35}{(1+\frac{1}{2}\%)^1} + \frac{15}{(1+\frac{1}{2}\%)^2} + \frac{15}{(1+\frac{1}{2}\%)^3} + \cdots + \frac{40}{(1+\frac{1}{2}\%)^{16}}$. On the other hand, if U_3 is developed in the second period, it yields an NPV of US\$ 292 thousand, in the third period US\$ 245 thousand and so on.

Obviously, not every MMF can be developed in the first period. The precedence diagram presented in Figure 1 indicates that only U_A can be developed in that period. Because in this example at any given time only one unit can be in its development phase, U_D cannot be developed until the third period at best.

Furthermore, each particular sequence of software units yields its own NPV. For instance, the sequence $U_A \rightarrow U_B \rightarrow U_C \rightarrow U_D \rightarrow U_F \rightarrow U_E \rightarrow U_G \rightarrow U_I \rightarrow U_H$ yields US\$ 1,365 thousand, which is the highest NPV among all the possible development sequences.

It is important to note that the NPV of a software-unit development sequence is the sum of the NPV of each of its components, considering the period in which they are expected to be built. Therefore,

$$NPV(U_A \rightarrow U_B \rightarrow U_C \rightarrow U_D \rightarrow U_F \rightarrow U_E \rightarrow U_G \rightarrow U_I \rightarrow U_H) =$$
$$NPV_1(U_A) + NPV_2(U_B) + NPV(U_C, 4) + \cdots NPV_{14}(U_H) =$$
$$(-35 + 960 + -10 + \cdots + -33) \times US\$\, 1,000 =$$
$$US\$\, 1,365 \text{ thousand,}$$

where $NPV_t(U_X)$ is the NPV of unit $U_{X \in \{A,B,\cdots,I\}}$ considering that its development starts in period t.

3   The IFM's Scheduling Algorithms

Because the number of possible implementation sequences grows exponentially with the number of software units, it is often the case that the sequence that maximizes the financial return of a software project cannot be found in polynomial time [1]. Therefore, for software development projects that have been divided into MMFs and AEs, the IFM provides managers and developers with three distinct approximation algorithms to find the implementation sequence that maximizes a project's NPV, i.e., the greedy, the simple look-ahead and the weighted look-ahead approaches.

3.1   The Greedy Approach

The greedy approach is based upon a shortsighted heuristics, which selects the next software unit to be built among those whose predecessors have already been fully developed. According to the greedy approach, the unit to be developed next is always the one with the highest NPV, considering the development period the software project is currently in. For instance, consider the example introduced in Section 2. Initially, the greedy approach selects unit U_A for development, because it is the only unit that can be developed in period 1.

In period 2, units U_B and U_C are both candidates for development, as all their respective predecessors have already been built. However, at this point in the development cycle U_B yields an NPV of US\$ 1,024 thousand, whereas U_C yields US\$ -10 thousand. Therefore, U_B, which takes two periods to be built, yields a higher NPV and is the unit selected for development. The process continues until the last undeveloped unit is selected for development.

For the example introduced in the previous section $U_A \rightarrow U_B \rightarrow U_C \rightarrow U_D \rightarrow U_F \rightarrow U_H \rightarrow U_I \rightarrow U_E \rightarrow U_G$ is the implementation sequence selected by the greedy approach, which yields an NPV of US\$ 1,311 thousand.

3.2   The Simple Look-Ahead Approach

The simple look-ahead approach is a farseeing heuristics, which analyses the paths connecting the units that have already been built to the undeveloped software units. Denne and Cleland-Huang [1] call these paths *strands*.

According to the simple look-ahead approach the next unit to be developed is always the one heading the strand that yields the highest NPV, considering the development period the software project is currently in.

Consider the example introduced in Section 2. As the dummy unit *Begin* requires no time to be built, at the very beginning of period 1 its development will have already been completed. Therefore, the initial set of strands analysed by the simple look-ahead approach contains the strands $U_A {}^\frown U_B$ and $U_A {}^\frown U_C {}^\frown U_D$, which are the paths connecting the already developed unit *Begin* to the undeveloped units U_B and U_D respectively.

At this point in time the set of strands also contains $U_A {}^\frown U_C$ and U_A which are the paths leading to the undeveloped units U_C and U_A, and so on and so forth. Table 3 shows all possible initial strands for the example introduced in the previous section.

The NPV of a strand is the sum of the NPV of each of its components, considering the period in which they are expected to be developed. Hence,

$$NPV(U_A {}^\frown U_C {}^\frown U_D) = NPV_1(U_A) + NPV_2(U_C) + NPV_3(U_D) = -15 - 10 + 245 = 200$$

Table 3 also shows the NPVs of all possible initial strands.

Based upon the information presented in Table 3, $U_A {}^\frown U_B$ is the strand with the highest NPV. Therefore, the software project starts with the development of unit U_A.

In the beginning of the second period unit U_A will have already been built, so the set of strands requires some updating accordingly. Table 4 presents the strands that are identified by the simple look-ahead approach at the beginning of that period.

Because U_B is the strand that yields the highest NPV, U_B is selected for development. The process continues until the last undeveloped unit is selected for development. For the example introduced in the previous section the simple look-ahead approach selects the following strand for development $U_A \rightarrow U_B \rightarrow U_C \rightarrow U_F \rightarrow U_D \rightarrow U_H \rightarrow U_I \rightarrow U_E \rightarrow U_G$, which yields an NPV of US\$ 1,283 thousand.

Table 3. All possible initial strands

Strand	NPV (US$ 1,000)
U_A	-35
$U_A \frown U_B$	925
$U_A \frown U_C \frown U_D$	200
$U_A \frown U_C$	-45
$U_A \frown U_C \frown U_E \frown U_G$	322
$U_A \frown U_C \frown U_E$	-89
$U_A \frown U_C \frown U_F \frown U_H$	284
$U_A \frown U_C \frown U_F$	129
$U_A \frown U_C \frown U_F \frown U_I$	209

Table 4. Strands for the second period

Strand	NPV (US$1,000)
U_B	960
$U_C \frown U_D$	235
U_C	-10
$U_C \frown U_E \frown U_G$	357
$U_C \frown U_E$	-54
$U_C \frown U_F \frown U_H$	319
$U_C \frown U_F$	164
$U_C \frown U_F \frown U_I$	244

3.3 The Weighted Look-Ahead Approach

If one negatively weights the number of periods required for the development of each strand, the chances of the simple look-ahead approach selecting the actual strand that maximizes the financial return of a software project increases considerably [1].

This weighting favours the development of strands that are delivered over a shorter period of time, despite the fact that they may provide the same NPV as others. Therefore, the weighted look-ahead approach facilitates even further the earlier appropriation of the financial benefits yielded by a software project.

According to Denne and Cleland-Huang [1] the most effective weighting factor depends on a number of project characteristics such as the shape of the precedence diagram and the window of opportunity, i.e., the length of time from the beginning of a software project and the time when the project's final product becomes obsolete and has to be replaced by a more attractive solution.

Denne and Cleland-Huang (*op. cit.*) suggest the use of the following formula to negatively weight the NPV of a given strand S:

$$\text{WNPV(S)} = \text{NPV(S)} \times (1 - (\text{WF} \times (p - 1))), \tag{1}$$

where WF is a pre-selected weighting factor and p is the number of periods necessary to built all software units in S.

For example, consider a strand $U_X \frown U_Y \frown U_Z$ that takes three periods to be developed and yields an NPV of $50 thousand if its development starts in period 1. Also, allow for a weighting factor of 10%. In these circumstances

$$\text{WNPV}(U_X \frown U_Y \frown U_Z) = \$50,000 \times (1 - (10\% \times (3 - 1))) = \$40,000$$

Now, consider a strand $U_V \frown U_W$, which yields the same NPV, if its development starts in period 1 but takes only two periods to be developed. Hence, this strand yields a weighted NPV of

$$\text{WNPV}(U_V \frown U_W) = \$50,000 \times (1 - (10\% \times (2 - 1))) = \$45,000$$

indicating that it is a more attractive choice for development.

It is important to keep in mind that both the simple and weighted look-ahead approaches share same strategy for strand identification. For the example introduced in Section 2 with a weighting factor of 10%, the weighted look-ahead approach selects for development the strand $U_A \rightarrow U_B \rightarrow U_C \rightarrow U_D \rightarrow U_F \rightarrow U_H \rightarrow U_I \rightarrow U_E \rightarrow U_G$, which yields an NPV of US\$ 1,311 thousand.

4   The Merits and Pitfalls of the IFM Algorithms

4.1   The Merits

The IFM has the merit of providing a very practical way of making software development an important element in the conception and implementation of competitive business strategies. By exploiting the possibility of dividing a software to be built into modules that have value to business, the IFM favors the early appropriation of the benefits yielded by a variety of software projects.

Moreover, the IFM not only suggests that those modules should contain the minimum amount of features that have value to corporate clients, end customers or both, but it also provides consistent guidelines on how to identify the most valuable modules once the software architecture has been decided upon [3].

In addition, the IFM clearly indicates that the total value brought to a business by a software consisting of several interdependent Minimum Marketable Feature Software Units and architectural elements, each one with its own cash-flow stream and precedence restrictions, is highly dependent on the development order of these units. Hence, further facilitating the early appropriation of benefits. Finally, the IFM's scheduling approaches are easy to understand and implement.

4.2   The Pitfalls

The well-known Heisenberg's *Uncertainty Principle* implies that the future cannot be accurately predicted [4]. However, a closer look at the IFM reveals that it requires a precise knowledge of the future value of the development cost and financial benefits from both MMFs and AEs. Regretfully, the longer the estimated project window of opportunity is, the less consistent the results provided by the IFM tend to be.

Furthermore, the IFM, as presented in [5] and [6], does not contemplate the possibility that it may actually be more profitable not to build all units comprising a software project. In the very competitive world in which software is developed these days, it is not uncommon that market conditions change quite substantially overnight. A new market scenario may very well make the future development of certain AEs and MMFs a financially unwise undertaking [7].

Finally, because all the scheduling approaches proposed by Denne and Cleland-Huang are indeed approximation algorithms, one would most certainly benefit from a mathematical foundation that could be used to estimate how far from the ideal solution the results presented by those algorithms are. Unfortunately, at present, such a mathematical foundation is not available for the IFM's scheduling algorithms. Therefore, in general, the IFM's users can never be sure whether the ideal solution is just around the corner or lightyears away.

4.3   Overcoming the Pitfalls and Extending the IFM

As the pitfalls of the Incremental Funding Method have become evident, several valuable suggestions have been made to extend the capabilities of the IFM, while preserving the basis upon which it is built.

For instance, Alencar et al. [8] claim that the use of a branch & bound approach, as a substitute for the IFM's scheduling algorithms, can increase considerably the size of the projects that can be successfully dealt with by the method in a variety of circumstances.

Schmitz et al.[9] indicate how the introduction of uncertain cash-flow elements can make the IFM's assumptions about the value of software units more realistic. Thus, allowing for the identification of scheduling sequences of software units that are more likely to bring value to business.

Barbosa et al.[10] show that it is possible to conceive an effective decision making environment based upon the IFM, uncertain cash-flow estimates and classification trees[1]. Such an environment allows for the creation of sets of disjoint rules that indicate the best course of action in each possible business scenario. Hence, transforming the IFM into an attractive planning tool to be used in the customarily uncertain context in which software is developed today. See [11] for a thorough introduction to classification trees.

Fernandes et al. [12] combine Information Economics (IE), an IT multicriteria investment model due to Parker and Benson [13], and the IFM to allow for the identification of a scheduling development order that maximizes not one, but several critical variables. In Fernandes et al.[14]'s multicriteria IFM variables are connected using Saaty's Analytical Hierarchical Process (AHP).

Alencar et al.[15] argue that the introduction of non-essential minimum marketable feature units (NMMFs), non-essential architectural elements (NAEs) and flexible dependency relations in a project, may considerably increase its financial value to business.

Adric [16] extends the notion of effect mapping, a project visualization model due to Balic [17], to encompass the ideas of minimum marketable features and the early appropriation of financial value stemming from the IFM. As a result, Adric creates a compound model that is suitable to the management of software projects based on the agile development paradigm.

5   Future Research Directions

In spite of the improvements that have been put forward in recent years, there are still areas in which the IFM is unable to deliver consistent results. For example,

---

[1] Classification trees are also known as decision trees in certain information technology circles.

when the software to be developed is connected to the creation or improvement of governmental services, such as as housing, health care and public safety, it is highly unlikely that the NPV is the only performance indicator that should be used to determine the best implementation order of software units.

By not making provision for the inclusion of performance indicator that are important to tax payers, government officials and members of congress in the Incremental Funding Method, Denne and Cleland-Huang [1] managed to make the IFM less attractive to one of the biggest spenders in information technology in the market, i.e., the government.

According to Peter Drucker (1909-2005), the well known philosopher and economist, the purpose of strategy is to not to eliminate risk, but to allow managers to take the right risks [18]. However, so far, the ideas laying the conceptual basis of the IFM, i.e., maximizing the NPV of an of interconnected set of software units, cast the method adrift from any strategic goal, but making money as fast as possible. Because it is not always the case that making money fast constitutes a sound business strategy, it is possible, and sometimes very likely, that by using the IFM as it is structured today, one may be doing efficiently what should not be done in the first place [19].

Although both Denne and Cleland-Huang [1] advocate for the use of the NPV as the one and only financial measure that one should take into consideration when maximizing the business value of a software project. By avoiding combining the most common financial measures Denne and Cleland-Huang (*op. cit.*) restrict the number of projects in which the IFM can provide a consistent result.

For instance, one may not have the necessary capital investment to run a project the way the IFM indicates. Also, one may not have the necessary resources to wait until the break even point. In both circumstances it is advisable to be aware of those limitations before committing capital investment and other resources to a project.

6   Conclusions

Since it was first presented to the software engineering community back in 2003, the Incremental Funding Method has found many enthusiasts among academics and practitioners alike.

Easy to understand and apply, the IFM has already been used in a variety of software projects, especially in conjunction with the ideas introduced by the agile software development paradigm. Hence, a large number of articles, comments and case reports have emerged in the Internet[2]. However, it is not always the the case that the IFM, as described in [5] and [6], presents consistent results.

This article analyses the merits of the IFM, together with its pitfalls, with the intent of not only making the enthusiasts aware of them, but also promoting further research towards increasing the number of situations in which the IFM (and its extensions) can successfully be used.

---

[2] A search in the Google Scholar supports this claim.

References

1. Denne, M., Cleland-Huang, J.: Financially Informed Requirements Prioritization. In: Proceedings of the 27th International Conference on Software Engineering (ICSE), St. Louis, Missouri, USA, pp. 710–711. ACM (2005)
2. Groppelli, A.A., Nikbakht, E.: Finance, 5th edn. Barron (2006)
3. Chang, C.K., Hua, S., Cleland-Huang, J., Kuntzmann-Conbelles, A.: Function-Class Decomposition. IEEE Computer 34(12), 87–93 (2001)
4. Heisenberg, W.: Über Den Anschaulichen Inhalt Der Quantentheoretischen Kinematik Und Mechanik. Zeitschrift für Physik 43(3-4), 172–198 (1927) (in English: "On the Perceptual Content of Quantum Theoretical Kinematics and Mechanics")
5. Denne, M., Cleland-Huang, J.: Software by Numbers: Low-Risk, High-Return Development, 1st edn. Prentice Hall (October 2003)
6. Denne, M., Cleland-Huang, J.: The Incremental Funding Method: Data-Driven Software Development. IEEE Software 21(3), 39–47 (2004)
7. Dolci, P.C., Macada, A.C.G., Becker, J.L.: IT Investment Management using the Real Options and Portfolio Management Approaches. In: AMCIS, Lima, Peru, August 12-15. ESAN University (2010) AIS Electronic Library Paper 370
8. Alencar, A.J., de Abreu, E.P., Schmitz, E.A.: Maximizing the Business Value of Software Projects: a Branch & Bound Approach. In: 10th ICEIS, Barcelona, Spain, June 12-16, vol. 1, pp. 200–206. Institute for Systems and Technologies of Information, Control (INSTICC) (2008)
9. Schmitz, E.A., Alencar, A.J., de Azevedo, C.M.: Defining the Implementation Order of Software Projects in Uncertain Environments. In: 10th ICEIS, Barcelona, Spain, June 12-16, vol. 1, pp. 100–105. Institute for Systems and Technologies of Information, Control (INSTICC) (2008)
10. Barbosa, B.P., Schmitz, E.A., Alencar, A.J.: Generating Software-Project Investment Policies in an Uncertain Environment. In: IEEE SIEDS, Charlottesville, Virgina, USA, April 25, vol. 1, pp. 30–35. University of Virginia, IEEE Press (2008)
11. Rokach, L., Maimon, O.: Data Mining with Decision Trees: Theory and Applications. World Scientific Publishing Company (April 2008)
12. Fernandes, M.C., Alencar, A.J., Schmitz, E.A., Alves, C.H., Ferreira, A.L.: A Multicriteria Approach to the XP Release Plan that Maximizes Business Performance in Uncertain Environments. In: IEEE SIEDS, Charlottesville, Virgina, USA, April 25, vol. 1, pp. 30–35. University of Virginia, IEEE Press (2008)
13. Benson, R.J., Bugnitz, T., Walton, B.: From Business Strategy to IT Action: Right Decisions for a Better Bottom Line. Wiley (2004)
14. Saaty, T.L.: Decision Making with the Analytic Hierarchy Process. International Journal of Services Sciences 1(1), 83–98 (2008)
15. Alencar, A.J., do Nascimento, R.A., Schmitz, E.A., Correa, A.L., Dias, A.F.S.: Unleashing the Potential Impact of nonessential Self-Contained Software Units and Flexible Precedence Relations upon the Value of Software. Journal of Software 6(12), 2500–2507 (2011)
16. Adzic, G.: Agile Product Management Using Effect Maps. Agile Record 6, 6–12 (2011)
17. Balic, M., Ottersten, I.: Effect Managing IT. Copenhagen Business School (2007)
18. Drucker, P.F.: The Essential Drucker. Harper (July 2008)
19. Porter, M.E.: The Five Competitive Forces that Shape Strategy. Harvard Business Review 86(1), 78–93 (2008)

Statistical Interpretation
for Mining Hybrid Regional Web Documents

Kolla Bhanu Prakash[1], M.A. Dorai Rangaswamy[2], and Arun Raja Raman[3]

[1] Sathyabama University, Chennai, India
[2] AVIT, Chennai, India
[3] IIT Madras, Chennai 600 036, India
bhanu_prakash231@rediff.com

Abstract. Media mining has taken a major shift from conventional data mining due to the ever increasing complexity of web documents. Another new dimension gets added when the web documents are of Indian origin since variety of languages and dialects get into the development of web pages. These web documents wherein words in different languages are used with or without translation can be termed as hybrid documents. A typical *yahoo news page* in different languages is an example of this. The complexity of extracting information or content and eventually knowledge gets more involved when words from other languages are used as yjet are without translation like 'computer' or 'mobile' being used freely in regional languages. Even though the reader/ surfer can follow the content easily, no translation has been done. Such documents are the focus of this study and a statistical approach for describing the features of the words in different languages is used as the basis for correlation to assess the content of such web documents. As a benchmark study six words related to education are taken in four different languages, English, Tamizh, Telugu and Hindi and different ways of normalizing within and outside the group are taken as the base vectors and using correlation study, any new data or group of data is checked for assessing the probability of getting the content. The words being in different scripts are converted to a three layer pixel map groups so that translational and text related issues do not affect the mining procedure. Further as textual data is well-structured irrespective of language, this approach of getting attributes and using them as bases is more general and does have the ability to include texts from any language.

Keywords: HTML, Media Mining, Multi-Lingual, Web Communication, Web Documents.

1 Introduction

Web communication is becoming increasingly a powerful medium in variety of disciplines and with the spread of mobile and ad-hoc networks, it is an essential component in many areas of application. But with English as the main language used in the development in many of these conceptual and innovative applications,

K.R. Venugopal and L.M. Patnaik (Eds.): ICIP 2012, CCIS 292, pp. 503–512, 2012.
© Springer-Verlag Berlin Heidelberg 2012

its adoption in regional and multi-lingual level needs more and more extensive work. One of the main problems here is in assessing the content of a web document and NOT the translated version of it which may take more time when one looks at this from on-line perspective. So if a content mining approach based on the file format of the web document is developed so that the user or the node can react immediately for getting an in-depth view of a particular aspect in the document [1]–[5]. It is the focus of the present study to look into aspects dealing with web documents either in English or in a regional language like Hindi, Tamizh, Telugu are prepared in different modes.

2   Features of Regional Web Documents

Web documents are prepared in different ways with HTML occupying a standard form for developing web pages. But if one looks at the documents generated by a browser for presenting various aspects, the content might differ. Fig. 1 shows a web page in English, Hindi, Tamizh and Telugu on a particular day. It may be seen that contents are completely different. Here the top one is in English with content completely different from the one in regional language Tamizh, shown next. Whereas for Hindi web page on that day shows a different content.

Even confining to one language like English, web pages in different regions show different content, depending on which is current in that region. This divergence is shown in Fig. 2.The web page in USA on top is completely different from the one for the world or for Asia as shown in Fig. 2 So, content extraction is more needed than literal translation of the document. Many times the format of the web page is such that video, audio and text are in built in such a way that content is very apparent from the audio and video so that the user or node can decide immediately which is his need for further browsing [6]–[8]. With this in view, it is proposed to develop a method based on pixel maps alone which any computer can 'understand' and use to extract content. In this study pixel map attributes for texts and characters of different languages are discussed to form the basis for classification and training.

3   Need for Media Mining from Data Mining Approaches

It may be seen from the above display of web documents, that surfer from different parts of India should be able to assess the content of each of the above web pages in a short period of time so that his interest in surfing further on a topic can continue [9]–[12]. While the English web document gives details of Air India, the Hindi one below gives more details about finance. This could be seen from the images in the document and the text in the documents contains details about those topics. So the surfer of English documents may not know the content of the Hindi document and vice versa. So extracting the content of the documents which have text , images, figures has to cater for an approach above that of text documents where the data is structured and organized. But a new dimension of complexity in the above three documents is the mix up of words with or without translation. An example is shown below from http://tamil.yahoo.com/national/ dated 4th March 2012: The corresponding news item in English is also shown

போலீஸ்செக்போஸ்ட்மீதுலாரிமோதல்   and in English
Lorry collision with police checkpost

and one can see words 'police' ,'checkpost','lorry' are used as they are in Tamil as and these make it difficult to use conventional data mining approaches. The

போலீஸ்,செக்போஸ்ட்,. லாரி

focus of current study is such documents and the development of a methodology to handle without translation and applicable to any hybrid document.

Fig. 1. Web Pages on the Same Day in Different Languages

One of the basic steps in mining is in processing the data as it may be in different forms like pictures, texts or media or in different formats either in full form or compressed form. So the pixel map of any data can be seen as a matrix of columns and rows with each element giving the color scheme for the pixel. Typically the matrix could be [Nx, Ny, Ip] where Nx indicates the rows Ny the columns and Ip the value of each element. The matrix is rectangular with rows being less than columns mostly in the case of texts and letters and the values

Fig. 2. Web Pages on the Same Day in Different Regions

Ip may be either 0 or 1 for black and white and 0 to 255 for colour depending on the resolution. So the characteristic and attribute of any pixel map can be deduced from these three values and most of image processing and data mining depend on this basic matrix. In this study this is used to assess the content. Fig.3 shows typical letters and words with sizes of pixel maps and irrespective of which language, the image or pixel map is what the computer stores as data and interpretation through different software allows one to display or use as input. This is the basic data taken up for processing.

4   Content Features in Multi-lingual Documents

Letters and words in different languages have their own unique and distinctive features; but with English dominating the web in the last two decades, a tendency to use words mutually in English and regional languages has become popular [13]–[16]. For example the word 'computer' is used as it is in many languages and communication. So, content extraction calls for similar and dissimilar features in letters and words for better assessment of pixel map attributes. Examples shown in Fig. 4 are for letter 'a' having the same content.

Normally text in any languages consists of words formed in a certain structured way and each of these words consists of characters native to the language in which the text is prepared. So it is preferable to look at extraction of features in characters and here one can see how it is quite complicated between English and any regional language like Tamil or Telugu or Hindi.

Fig. 5 gives a comparison of features of "education". This gives us a clear idea of feature extraction. Since regional language letters have characters surrounding

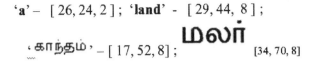

'a' – [26, 24, 2] ; 'land' - [29, 44, 8] ;

'காந்தம்' – [17, 52, 8] ; மலர் [34, 70, 8]

Fig. 3. Pixel Maps of Letters and Words

a   अ   அ   ഒ

Fig. 4. Pixel-Maps of Characters in Four Languages of Same Content

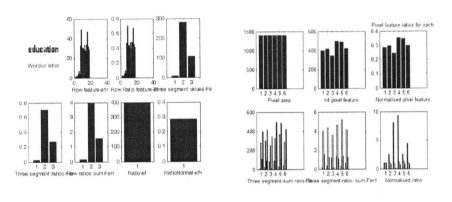

Fig. 5. Feature Extraction for 'Education'

Fig. 6. Pixel Feature Comparison

the main body, the pixel map is divided into three segments like 25% top, 50% middle and 25% bottom. Letters 'g' and 'y' in English have bottom 25% for example.

Since parent language is taken as English one can normalise features and this is given in Fig. 6. One can see clearly the variation in features in three segments and this can be used for classification and training.

Fig. 7 given below shows the variations of ratio plot for the six words considered taking into consideration "education" as the parent word.

5   Statistical Interpretation

With the complexities mentioned above in the attributes of pixel maps, it is preferable that statistical pattern recognition approach can give ideas on the

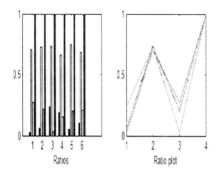

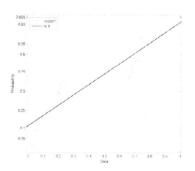

Fig. 7. Ratio Plot Interpretation

Fig. 8. Probability variation for the basic six words-vector1

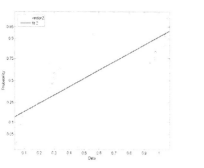

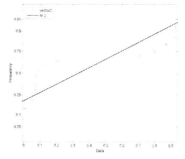

Fig. 9. Probability Variation for Vector2

Fig. 10. Probability Variation for Vector3

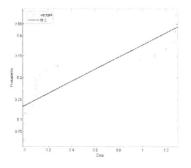

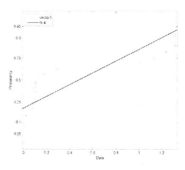

Fig. 11. Probability Variation for Vector4

Fig. 12. Probability Variation for Vector5

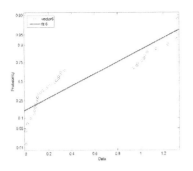

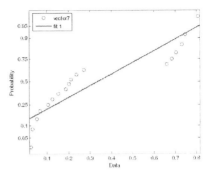

Fig. 13. Probability Variation for Vector 2 and 5

Fig. 14. Probability Variation for Vector 7

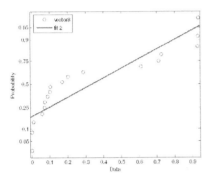

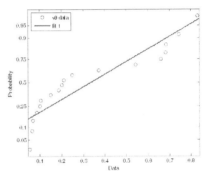

Fig. 15. Probability Variation for Vector8

Fig. 16. Probability Variation for Three Words not Related to Education

content and as is normal when more data are added the probabilistic predictions may be closer to reality. This approach is taken here. Six words in English and Hindi are taken which relate to education as

   [book, class, college, school, student, teacher] in English
   In Hindi

किताब ग्रगे मश्रविद्यान्व शिधालय छात्र शिक्षक

In this study results are given for two sets English and Hindi.

   Probability variation for the basic six words in English are given and this is termed as Vector1,below: the figure gives us explanation of the content in two different ways. The circles between the range 0 to 0.3 indicate that these have a less probability of related to the content considered. The circles between the range 0.6 to 0.8 indicate that these have a high probability of related to the content considered.

Since it is known that all the basic six words are related to 'education', it is preferable that their pixelmap attributes are normalized with those of 'education' given earlier. Vector2 is considered as the second case of study which is normalized with respect to "education" as the parent word. Its corresponding probability variation is shown in Fig. 9 given below.

Vector3 is considered as the third case of study which consists of all the six words written in Hindi, as shown earlier.. Its corresponding probability variation is shown in Fig. 10 given below using the name vector3.

Vector4 is considered as the fourth case of study which consists of all the six words in translated form written in Hindi and normalized with respect to "education" in Hindi as the parent word. Its corresponding probability variation is shown in Fig. 11 given below.

Vector5 is considered as the fifth case of study which consists of all the six words in translated form written in Hindi and normalized with respect to "education" in English as the parent word. Its corresponding probability variation is shown in Fig. 12 given below.

As a special case to find better probability we have considered both vectors 2 and 5 and plotted the graph as shown in Fig. 13 given below.

Vector7 is considered as the next case of study which consists of one word among six words not belonging to education, for eg., here we used "light" in English. Its corresponding probability variation is given below.

Vector8 is considered as the next case of study which consists of one word among six words not belonging to education, for eg., here we used "light" in hindi. Its corresponding probability variation is given below.

As a final study we considered word "tatkal" in hindi, its transliteration in English and its translation "immediate" in English which are not related to content of education, along with three words that are related to education, its probability variation is as shown in Fig. 16. The figure clearly shows different variations as most of the circles lie in the lower probability region indicating that some of the words considered are not related to education. This clearly supports our theory of content prediction.

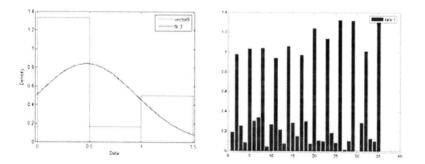

Fig. 17. Distribution variation for vector 6 data

Normal distribution gives us a better general idea regarding the content variation, which is shown in Fig. 17, density as a function of the data considered for 36values of vector6. The figure gives us an idea regarding the mean and standard deviation variation. The figure on the right side shows the bar chart for the 36 values considered which shows the variation in features of pixel maps.

Table 1. Mean and Standard Deviation Variation

Vector	Mean	Standard Deviation
1	0.3333	0.2772
2	0.4738	0.394
3	0.3333	0.3905
4	0.4593	0.5382
5	0.47382	0.5551
6	0.47382	0.4744
7	0.3333	0.292
8	0.3333	0.3592

The mean and standard deviations were computed for all the vectors that are considered above and are given in the table above in Fig. 1.

6   Conclusions

Extraction of content in multi-lingual web documents is essential for education and other activities on the net so that the user can surf on interested areas immediately. A method based on feature extraction for words in multi-lingual documents is developed and the complexities and numerical aspects are discussed for typical examples in [17,18,19,20]. The examples are from letters to words bringing out the need to include character variations in developing the mining approach. The work will be expanded in future in observing how the features vary as the content varies when different languages are taken into consideration.

References

1. Rafael, C.G., Richard, E.W., Steven, L.E.: Digital Image Processing using Matlab (2002)
2. Renu, D.: Feature Extraction and Classification for Bilingual Script (Gurumukhi and Roman) (April 2007)
3. Bing, Z., Stephen, V.: Adaptive Parallel Sentences Mining from Web Bilingual News Collection (2002)
4. Chen, S.C., Rubin, S.H., Shyu, M.L., Zhang, C.: A Dynamic User Concept Pattern Learning Framework for Content-Based Image Retrieval. IEEE Transactions on Systems, Man, and Cybernetics, Part C 36(6), 772–783 (2006)
5. Li, Z.N., Drew, M.S.: Fundamentals of Multimedia. Prentice Hall, NJ (2004)

6. Pan, L., Zhang, C.N.: A Criterion-Based Role-Based Multilayer Access Control Model for Multimedia Applications. In: Eighth IEEE Int. Symposium on Multimedia, San Diego, CA, USA, pp. 145–152 (2006)
7. Lu, G.: Multimedia Database Management Systems. Artech House Publishers, Boston (1999)
8. Li, Y., Kuo, C.C.J., Wan, X.: Introduction to Content-Based Image Retrieval-Overview of Key Techniques. In: Castelli, V., Bergman, L.D. (eds.) Image Databases: Search and Retrieval of Digital Imagery, pp. 261–284. John Wiley, New York (2002)
9. Iqbal, Q., Aggarwal, J.K.: CIRES: A System for Content-Based Retrieval in Digital Image Libraries. In: Int. Conf. Control, Automation, Robotics and Vision (ICARCV), Singapore, pp. 205–210 (2002)
10. Kuchinsky, A., Pering, C., Creech, M., Freeze, D., Serra, B., Gwizdka, J.: Fotofile: A Consumer Multimedia Organization and Retrieval System. In: ACM CHI Conference, New York, NY, USA, pp. 496–503 (1999)
11. Gupta, A., Jain, R.: Visual Information Retrieval. Communications of the ACM 40(5), 71–79 (1997)
12. Pentland, A., Picard, R.W., Sclaroff, A.: Photobook: Content Based Manipulation of Image Databases. Int. J. Computer Vision 18(3), 233–254 (1996)
13. Prakash, K.B., Dorai Ranga Swamy, M.A., Raja Raman, A.: Mining Approach for Documents Containing Multilingual Indian Texts (NCRTAC 2009). Bharath University, Chennai (2009)
14. Prakash, K.B., Dorai Ranga Swamy, M.A., Raja Raman, A.: A Two-Input Neuron Model for Documents Containing Multingual Indian Texts (EPPCSIT 2009). Guru Nanak Dev Engineering College, Ludhiana (2009)
15. Prakash, K.B., Dorai Ranga Swamy, M.A., Raja Raman, A.: Feature Extraction for Content Mining in Multi-Lingual Documents (NCICN 2010). Sathyabama University, Chennai (2010)
16. Prakash, K.B., Dorai Ranga Swamy, M.A., Raja Raman, A.: A Neuron Model for Documents Containing Multilingual Indian Texts (ICCCT 2010), Allahabad (2010)
17. Prakash, K.B., Dorai Ranga Swamy, M.A., Raja Raman, A.: Text Studies Towards Multi-Lingual Content Mining for Web Communication (TISC 2010), Sathyabama University, Chennai (2010)
18. Prakash, K.B., Dorai Ranga Swamy, M.A., Raja Raman, A.: Content Extraction for Multi-lingual Web Documents. CIT Journal of Research 1(3), 93–101 (2010)
19. Prakash, K.B., Dorai Ranga Swamy, M.A., Raja Raman, A.: Performance of Content Based Mining Approach for Multi-Lingual Textual Data. International Journal of Modern Engineering Research (IJMER) 1(1), 146–150
20. Prakash, K.B., Dorai Ranga Swamy, M.A., Raja Raman, A.: Content Extraction with Web Pages having Hand-Written Texts. In: NCEVENT 2011, Sathyabama University, Chennai (2011)

Ontology Based Text Processing for Context, Similarity and Key Word Extraction

Raja S.[1], Jaya Chandra M.A.N.[2], Valli Kumari V.[2], and Raju K.V.S.V.N.[2]

[1] Naval Science & Technological Laboratory (NSTL),
Visakhapatnam, Andhra Pradesh, India, 530 027
sunkararaja@gmail.com
[2] Dept. of Computer Science & Systems Engineering, Andhra University,
Visakhapatnam, Andhra Pradesh, India, 530 003

Abstract. Semantic similarity plays a vital role in Q & A systems, Text Mining, Language modeling, Information Retrieval, Natural Language Processing (NLP), text-related research and applications. Measuring Semantic similarity between sentences is closely related to Semantic similarity between words. Key word extraction is useful to understand the important information contained in a document or in a short text. This paper proposes two strategies for: (i) finding the similarity and context between two sentences. (ii) Extending this approach for a paragraph of sentences using the WordNet lexical database.

Keywords: Common Root Word (CRW), Hierarchical Ontology (HO), Similarity Measure Value (SMV), Word-pair similarity.

1 Introduction

Ontologies like WordNet [1] are the structural frameworks for organizing information as a form of knowledge representation in Semantic Web. Information is mostly available in sentences on the web and it is necessary in applications like IR, LP and Q & A systems to find the Semantic similarity. This paper proposes an approach for finding the Semantic similarity between the sentences based on context. For this Word-pair similarity was measured in the range [0-1] and a Common Root Word (CRW) was then found for these two given words, using WordNet. The work is mainly divided into two strategies, namely (i) SenCon: An approach for finding the similarity between the sentences based on their context (ii) KeyWordEx: An approach for extracting the key words from the given set of sentences or a paragraph. The results of the proposed work help in judging the context of the domain.

2 Related Work

In the Elemental Level Matching Techniques, Semantic similarity was measured by the involvement of the Web Search Engines which dealt with Linguistic analysis- comprising Page Counts and Lexico-Syntactic Patterns [2]. For

K.R. Venugopal and L.M. Patnaik (Eds.): ICIP 2012, CCIS 292, pp. 513–518, 2012.
© Springer-Verlag Berlin Heidelberg 2012

measuring Semantic similarity between words, ontology with is-a hierarchy is considered by the researchers. Semantic similarity between concepts using Hierarchical Ontologies (HO) was broadly classified into two categories: *Edge based* and *Node based* approaches. Leacock proposed an edge based approach metric, which scales the shortest path by twice the maximum depth of the HO [3]. The Node based approach was proposed by Resnik [4] to overcome the drawbacks of the edge-counting approach, and defined the similarity between two concepts as the information content of the Lowest Common Ancestors (LCA) [4]. A novel similarity measure for Hierarchical Ontologies called OSS approach, has been proposed for similarity measure[5]. Semantic similarity measure using WordNet is proposed in [6]. Semantic similarity measures have evolved in the recent decade from the word-similarity to that of sentence similarity. The current research in this area includes, the evaluation of sentence similarity measures where we can judge whether two sentences are semantically equivalent or not[7].

3   Proposed Work

Semantic similarity is a special case of textual similarity. Semantic similarity uses the actual meaning of words to decide similarity and is a special case of the concept of Semantic Relatedness. Relatedness between words can be determined by the use of hyponymy and meronymy. This similarity measure can be extended to find the Semantic similarity between the sentences. The overall architecture consists of the following modules:

(i) Tokenization: As text is an unstructured source of information, to make it a suitable input to system, it is usually transformed into a structured format. This involves preprocessing of the input text.

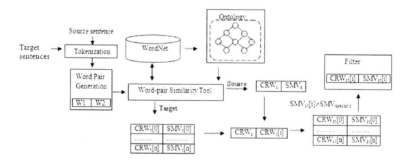

Fig. 1. Architecture of SenCon

(ii) Word-pair Similarity Tool: It is a word similarity metric using WordNet and other resources. The words are represented in is-a taxonomy using WordNet. It is an advanced tool, which gives the Similarity Measure Value (SMV) between the pair of words in the scale of [0-1] and Least Common Ancestor (LCA) of both words in is-a taxonomy, given as Common Root Word (CRW).

(iii) Filter: In this step, the actual processing of the word-pairs is done. The SC set consisting of SMV-CRW pair is tabulated and only those values that cross a threshold are selected for further processing. The threshold is set as the mean value of all the SMVs obtained.

Table 1. Algorithm: SenCon

Input : Source Sentence(SS), Target Sentences TS = $\{TS_1, TS_2, ..., TS_n\}$
Output : SenCon, SimVal
Assumptions : ST = $\{\phi\}$; //Set of source sentence tokens
TT = $\{\phi\}$; //Set of target sentence tokens
TW = $\{\phi\}$; //Set of CRWs of target sentences
TV = $\{\phi\}$; //Set of SMVs for target sentences, SimVal = 0;
Method :
ST = ST ∪ Ttokens(SS); // preprocess source sentence to extract 2 tokens
CRW = WordpairSim(ST_1,ST_2);// returns the Common Root Word
SMV = WordpairSimVal(ST_1,ST_2);// returns the Similarity Measure Value
for each TS_i in TS
begin
TT = TT ∪ Ttokens(TS);// preprocess source sentence to extract 2 tokens
TW = TW ∪ WordpairSim(TT_1,TT_2);
TV = TV ∪ WordpairSimVal(TT_1,TT_2);
end for
for each TW_i in TW
Word = WordpairSim(CRW,TW_i);
Value = WordpairSimVal(CRW,TW_i);
if(SimVal ≤ Value) **then**
SimVal = Value; // returns the Similarity Measure Value
SenCon = Word; // returns the Common Root Word
end if
end for

3.1   SenCon

In this strategy, we attempt to find the Semantic similarity between sentences and thereby, selecting the sentences which are closer to (or) semantically related to the given source sentence. This will result in less Recall & high Precision, in retrieving the sentences from the web. The strategy is explained as follows: Consider the following three sentences: (a) Leech is a segmented-worm,

(b) Worm is a type of virus, (c) Spider is an insect. Consider sentence (a), as a source sentence, we parse this sentence using the techniques of NLP, and extract the tokens as Leech and segmented-worm. Now these tokens form a word-pair which are fed as an input to the word-pair similarity tool, which outputs an SMV for this word-pair along with CRW. Let this Similarity measure of sentence (a) be smv_a and the Common Root word be crw_a. Now, we consider only the crw_a, for further processing. Similarly, we consider the target sentences (b) and (c), and extract their tokens in the above manner and consider their respective word-pairs. The word-pairs of sentences (b) and (c) are fed as input to the tool, which outputs similarity measure value along with Common Root Word each time as (smv_b, crw_b) and (smv_c, crw_c) respectively. The tokens of the target sentences are now replaced with their respective CRWs. The source crw_a is compared with the target CRWs crw_b and crw_c, each time with the tool. The word-pairs (crw_a, crw_b) and (crw_a, crw_c) are compared using the tool and in each case we obtain the SMV along with CRW as (smv_{ab}, crw_{ab}) and (smv_{ac}, crw_{ac}). The sentence pair (ab or ac) with a higher SMV value is considered to be more similar relatively when compared to the other pair and the CRW corresponding to that pair gives most probable context of the two sentences.

3.2 KeyWordEx

The first strategy, SenCon is further extended from two sentences to a paragraph which is taken from a text document, usually a set of sentences. Generally this text is in unstructured format which makes it difficult for the machine to retrieve the key words under which the text is giving narration.

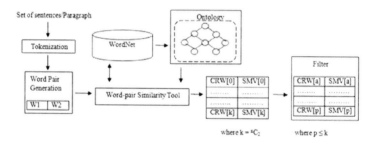

Fig. 2. Architecture of KeyWordEx

In this strategy, we attempt to retrieve the relevant key words, from text document, which helps in information retrieval from the system.The algorithm of KeyWordEx is given in Table 2.

4 Experimental Results

4.1 SenCon

Sentence1: Program is a set of instructions. CRW1(program, instructions): Computer program).
Sentence2: Applet is a simple program. CRW2(applet, program): Computer program
Sentence3: Program is a course of study. CRW3(program, study): Document
SMV(CRW1,CRW2): 1.0 & SMV(CRW1,CRW3): 0.0

Table 2. Algorithm: KeyWordEx

```
Input : S = {S₁, S₂, S₃, ..., Sₙ} // set of sentences
Output : K = {K₁, K₂, K₃, ..., Kₙ} // set of Keywords
Assumptions : T = {φ}, KW = {φ}, KV = {φ}, Avg = 0;
Method :
for each Sᵢ in S
T = T ∪ Tokens(Sᵢ) //preprocess the sentences to extract the tokens
end for
for each Tᵢ in T
begin
for each Tⱼ₌ᵢ₊₁ in T
begin
KeyWord = WordpairSim(Tᵢ, Tⱼ);// returns the CRW
Value = WordpairSimVal(Tᵢ, Tⱼ);// returns the SMV
KW = KW ∪ KeyWord; KV = KV ∪ Value; Avg = Avg + Value;
end for
end for
Avg = Avg/KV;//Avg is set as threshold
for each KWᵢ in KW
begin
if (KVᵢ < Avg) then
KW = KW - KWᵢ;// Keywords that cross the threshold are selected
end for
end
```

Fig. 3. Ontology

Hence sentence 1 and 2 are similar when compared to sentence 1 and 3, it is further inferred that the Context of sentence 1 and 2 is Computer program. This is represented in Fig.3

4.2 KeyWordEx

Sample text for Key word extraction:

> Tree is a woody-plant. It has branches supported on a single main stem called as Trunk. Woody-plants that have multiple stems are called as Shrubs. Shrubs are usually small in size.

Word-pair	CRW	SMV
Tree, woody-plant	Woody-plant	0.300
Tree, branch	Null	0
Tree, stem	Null	0
Tree, Trunk	Tree	0.300
Tree, shrub	Woody-plant	0.090
Woody-plant, branch	Plant	0.001
Woody-plant, stem	Plant	0.027
Woody-plant, Trunk	Woody-plant	0.090

Word-pair	CRW	SMV
Woody-plant, shrub	Woody-plant	0.300
Branch, stem	Stem	0.300
Branch, Trunk	Stem	0.090
Branch, shrub	Plant	0.001
Stem, Trunk	Stem	0.300
Stem, shrub	Plant	0.001
Trunk, shrub	Woody-plant	0.027

Fig. 4. KeyWordEx

Token set of the above sentences: Tree, woody-plant, branch, stem, Trunk, Shrub
Average SMV = 0.1218, CRWs above Average SMV are considered.
  1. Woody-plant, 2.Tree, 3.Stem are identified as the key words.

5   Conclusions

This paper gives the context of the sentences and extracting the key words in a paragraph. The experimental results have been verified with human intuition values and correlation was obtained. However, the limitations of the word-pair similarity tool have direct impact on identifying the context and the keywords. Further research in word-pair similarity tool will contribute towards the correct identification of the context of sentence and retrieving the keywords from sentences.

References

1. Miller, G.A., Beckwith, R., Fellbaum, C., Gross, D., Miller, K.: Introduction to WordNet: An On-line Lexical Database. Technical Report, CSL, Princeton University (1993), http://wordnetweb.princeton.edu/perl/webwn
2. Danushka, B., Yutaka, M., Mitsuru, I.: Measuring Semantic Similarity between Words using Web Search Engines. In: Proceedings of WWW, Banff, Alberta, Canada, pp. 757–766 (2007)
3. Chodorow, M., Leacock, C.: Combining Local Context and WordNet Similarity for Word Sense Identification. Fellbaum, 265–283 (1997)
4. Resnik, P.: Using Information Content to Evaluate Semantic Similarity. In: Proceedings of IJCA 2005, pp. 448–453 (1995)
5. Schickel-Zuber, V., Faltings, B.: OSS: A Semantic Similarity Function based on HO. In: Proceedings of IJCAI 2007, pp. 551–556 (2007)
6. Zhongcheng, Z., Jinzhou, Y., Liying, F., Pu, W.: Measuring Similairty Based on Word Net. In: Proceedings of WISA, pp. 89–92 (2009)
7. Achananuparp, P., Hu, X., Shen, X.: The Evaluation of Sentence Similarity Measures. In: Song, I.-Y., Eder, J., Nguyen, T.M. (eds.) DaWaK 2008. LNCS, vol. 5182, pp. 305–316. Springer, Heidelberg (2008)

Reduction of Variation in Mooney Viscosity of Polybutadiene Rubber

Sriram M.V.V.N.[1], Kanti Amin[2], and G. Padmavathi[3]

[1] Department of Mechanical and Mining Machinery Engineering,
Indian School of Mines, Dhanbad, India
[2] Polybutadiene Rubber Plant
[3] RTG, Reliance Industries Limited, Vadodara -391345, India
garimella.padmavathi@ril.com

Abstract. Poly Butadiene Rubber (PBR) is used in rubber processing industries. Mooney viscosity is an important quality parameter of PBR. The design range of Mooney viscosity of the product from last reactor outlet is in the range of 37-47. The existing variation of Mooney viscosity is between 37 and 43 for 92% of the product. Further reduction in the variation in Mooney viscosity improves product quality and results in greater customer satisfaction. Data mining techniques have been used to analyze the Mooney viscosity and process variable data to obtain range of values of process variables that gives Mooney in the desired range of 37-43. Data partitioning and interval plots are used to obtain the range of process variables that will keep the Mooney viscosity in the desired range.

Keywords: Data Partionin, Mooney Viscosity, Polybutadiene Rubber.

1   Introduction

Achieving a uniform product quality is more difficult in polymerization processes than in short chain reactions as the product quality properties are very sensitive to process conditions. Any upsets in feed and catalyst conditions, mixing and temperature, can change the critical product properties such as viscosity, molecular weight and degree of branching. Most of the advanced process control methods are limited to temperature and pressure control. The lack of on line sensors for the product quality properties is due to the complex nonlinear dynamics of the polymerization processes. Control of the product quality requires an accurate model that can predict desired properties as a function of operating variables. The mechanistic modeling of polymerization processes is very complex, time consuming and difficult.

The conventional approach based on linear models like multiple linear regression and principle component analysis are not suitable for highly nonlinear polymerization processes [1]. Data mining is the analysis of large data sets with the goal of finding unsuspected relationships. Large data sets include large number of records noted on large number of variables. Data mining techniques can

K.R. Venugopal and L.M. Patnaik (Eds.): ICIP 2012, CCIS 292, pp. 519–528, 2012.
© Springer-Verlag Berlin Heidelberg 2012

lead to local models and global models. Local models are limited to restricted range of variable values. Models associated with data mining techniques include regression analysis, clustering and neural networks. Neural net works are data based models and given sufficient data the neural networks are capable of modeling nonlinear processes to a desired degree of accuracy [2-4]. The neural network models have been applied in process modeling and control [5-7]. Model is useful for inferential estimation and control of the quality. But if the objective is reduction of variation in quality parameter, then range of process variables that will result the quality parameter in the desired range is required so that action can be taken in case of deviation in controllable variables.

1.1   Process

PBR is produced by solution polymerization of 1-3 butadiene in four continuous stirred tank reactors in series. Fig. 1 shows the block diagram of the process.

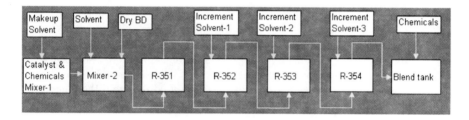

Fig. 1. Block Diagram of the Process

The monomer, the solvent, the catalyst, the cocatalyst and the chain modifier (BRF) are mixed thoroughly before entering the first reactor. The reactor feed temperature is lowered before entering the reactor to prevent premature polymerization in the reactor in let. The reactors are provided with jackets for temperature control and an agitator of a double helical ribbon type for mixing of high viscosity polymer solution. The reaction temperature is approximately 60 70° C and about 88% of monomer is converted into polymer at the outlet of last reactor. In the first reactor, a large amount of polymerization heat is generated and the heat is removed by a combination of the sensible heat required to heat up reactor feed (monomer and solvent) and of the heat required to vaporize the refrigerant in the jacket.

In the second to fourth reactors a comparatively smaller amount of the polymerization heat is generated and the heat is removed by a combination of the sensible heat required to heat up the incremental solvent to be used in the 2nd-4th reactors. The reactants enter from bottom of reactors and come out from the top. After the polymer is formed, the conversion and the physical properties such as Mooney and solution viscosity are analyzed and they are controlled so that they fall within each process control standards. The Mooney viscosity is controlled by chain modifier level and traces of moisture in solvent. The polymer solution produced is mixed with a chain modifier and an antioxidant and held in blend tank and the final control of physical properties in the polymerization step is performed by blending operation. Mooney viscosity is an important quality property of PBR. Mooney viscosity indirectly represents molecular weight and it is a critical property. It has significant effect on end use properties of the polymer. It is a difficult to measure property and its analysis is labor intensive and time consuming. Mooney viscosity is measured once in two hours off line in the plant laboratory.

The results are available after measurement delay which results in infrequent feedback and makes automatic process control impossible. This can be overcome by development of a model that can infer the quality of the product properties from easily available process variables or at least development of range of controllable process variables that will allow keep the target variable in the desired range. Changes in some of the process variables indicate the change in product quality. Hence this work has been undertaken with an objective to analyze the process input-output data using data mining techniques with an objective to extract a range of operating conditions that will help engineers to maintain Mooney within the desired range.

2 Data Mining

Often no obvious relationships exist between the dependent variable Y (response variable of interest) and the independent variables Xs (other process variables in the data set). The starting data tends to be messy in the respect that all rows and records may be incomplete for all variables, and there may be many missing data values. Extensive pre-processing of large data sets may be a required prior to application of data mining. Extensive study of the process is carried out to identify the all possible independent variables (Xs). Gathered information on the impact of variation in each variable on Mooney value in terms of high, medium and low. Also identified whether the variable is with in control. Based on the process experience short listed fourteen important variables for further processing from the 36 important process variables. The process variables considered include flow rates of 1. monomer (BD), 2. solvent, 3. cocatalyst (TAL), 4. BRF, 5. catalyst (NIC), 6.wet solvent, and 7-9. temperatures of reactors 1,2, & 4 (R1T, R2T, R4T)), 10. Ageing temperature, 11. Feed temperature, 12. solvent to monomer ration (S/M) 13. TAL/NIC 14. BRF/TAL.

2.1 Data Partitioning

Around 2906 data sets are collected bihourly over a period of one year for one dependent variable and fourteen process variables. The data distribution analysis shows non normal distribution as is evident from p value < 0.05 (Fig. 2). Run chart is generally used for analyzing non normal distribution data.

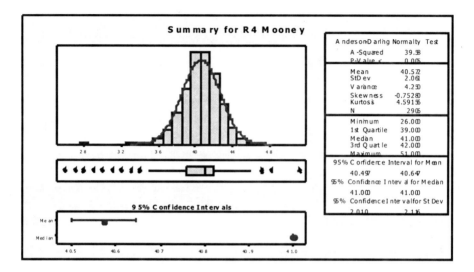

Fig. 2. Data Distribution Analysis

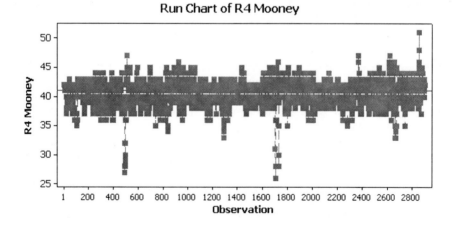

Fig. 3. Run Chart of Mooney Viscosity

The run chart (Fig. 3) indicates that the process is mostly stable except at few places which may be during startup or shutdown.Hence the data were divided in to three groups A. Data with Mooney value less than lower specification limit, B. Data with Mooney value in the desired range and C. Data with Mooney value more than the higher specification limit for further processing. The interval plots and one way ANOVA analysis indicates that the group A data is significantly different from the other 2 groups. Overlapping was observed between the B & C group data as can be seen from Fig. 4. & 5 for the controllable process variables. Hence the A group data was removed from the data set assuming that it is due to some disturbance and it is not a regular process. Since the objective is reduction of variation, the data was subjected to partitioning in JMP software [8].

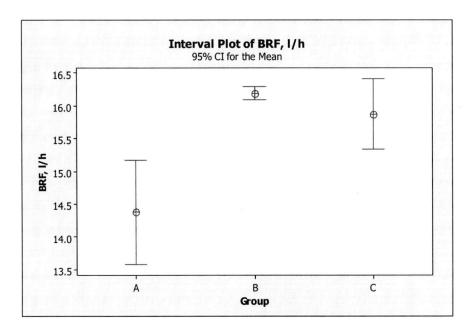

Fig. 4. Interval Plot for BRF

The data partitioning gives the best possible range of operating conditions that will allow us to maintain the Mooney in the desired range of 37-43 with minimum standard deviation. The Partition platform recursively partitions data creating a tree of partitions. It is good for exploring relationships among variables without knowledge of a prior model, it handles large data sets easily, and the results are interpretable. JMP software is used for data partitioning. Partition is done according to cutting values. The splits are done so as to maximize the difference of the two groups as measured by sum of squares due to the differences between means. Fig. 6 shows the partition plot generated. Mooney is Y variable

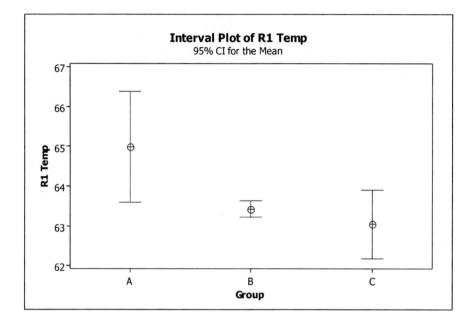

Fig. 5. Interval Plot for Temperature

and all the other process variables as X variables. Criteria used for the split is best split and maximize significance which takes groups with small within-sample variances.

Column Contributions brings up a report showing how each independent variable X contributed to the fit, including how many times it was split and the total sum of squares attributed to that variable. The first major contributing parameter is found to be feed temperature which should be greater than or equal to -23. There are only five data points in the split that feed temperature is < -23 as can be seen in tree split (Fig. 6) which can be considered as outliers. The complete tree split is not shown in Fig. 7 for the sake of brevity. Only three splits are shown. The column contribution (Fig. 8) information indicates that feed temperature, BRF/TAL, TAL/NIC, monomer load, first reactor temperature are the contributing to the variation of Mooney. The following are the range of process variables required to be maintained to obtain Mooney viscosity in the range of 37.22-44.03 (mean = 40.63; std. = 1.708) which is closer to our desired range of 37-43. 1. *Feedtemperature* ≥ -23. 2. BRF/TAL < 1.9. 3. TAL/NIC < 7.8 4. R1 temperature < 61.4 5.$TAL \geq 68l/h$. It is possible to specify an X variable to be used as the splitting variable for any split instead of using the variable identified by JMP soft ware as being the next best predictor of Y. This is useful in situations when the best X variable has no meaning or has no practical value. The data partitioning gives range of process conditions that lead to get Mooney in the desired range based on the data.

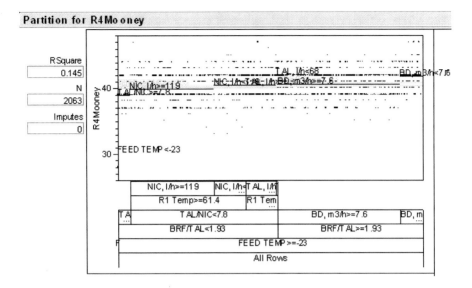

Fig. 6. Partition Plot for Mooney Viscosity

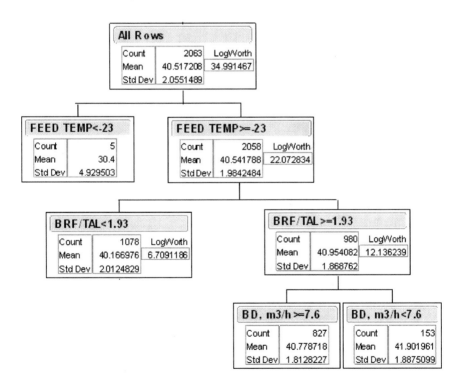

Fig. 7. Tree Split

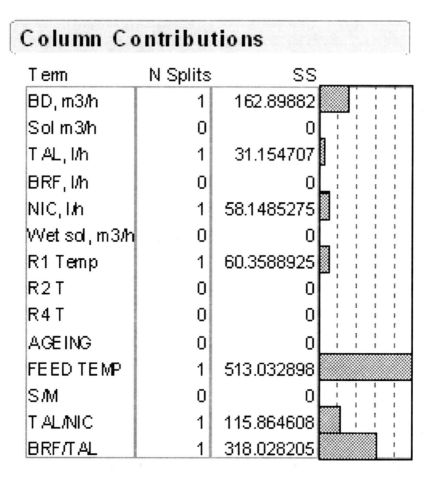

Fig. 8. Column Contribution

2.2   Interval Plots

As the data partitioning results show that monomer flow rate is important variable, it is required to predict the range of control variables as a function of monomer load. Hence the data has been sorted out in ascending order with respect to monomer load and divided in to 8 sets covering the entire range of monomer operation load. Interval plots are drawn in Minitab software. Interval plots are used to compare means of different groups. These plots plot mean of each variable corresponding to each monomer load group. The summary of the results are presented in Table 1. The confidence interval of each process variable value presented in the Table 1 is 95%. The results presented in the Table 1 will help to select the value of controllable process variable that would results in average Mooney of around 40. From the interval plots of Mooney viscosity, BRF,

R1T and Wet solvent flow against monomer load it is observed that wet solvent and BRF are important controlling variables. The results presented in the Table have been sent to plant for implementation.

Table 1. Interval Plot Results

	A	B	C	D	E	F	G	H
BD	4-5.6	5.7-6	6.1-6.9	7-7.4	7.5-7.9	8-8.5	8.6-8.9	9-9.3
Mooney	40.87	40.58	40.81	41.05	40.5	40.43	40.19	40.4
Solvent	15.1	14.65	17.08	18.21	19.65	21.22	22.39	22.83
BRF	12.31	12.41	13.96	13.95	16.63	16.51	16.77	16.75
TAL	54.09	53.18	65.27	67.27	71.2	77.72	85.15	88.145
NIC	83.7	81.58	101.882	102.265	109.85	119.81	128.389	132.44
Wet Solvent	231.21	188.5	240.58	290.735	376.61	346.07	401.195	452.81
R1 T	65.34	61.8	61.51	63.13	63.27	62.78	63.73	64.53
R2 T	79.35	79.9	79.8	80.19	81.43	83.52	83	81.68
R4 T	72.38	75.01	75.53	75.76	77.7	78.69	79.21	79.38
Ageing T	18.45	18.6	18.59	18.54	18.49	18.52	18.52	18.53
Feed T	-5.04	-5.41	-5.68	-8.51	-6.25	-7.1	-9.24	-10.23
TAL/NIC	7.34	7.47	7.556	7.6	7.42	7.39	7.49	7.54
BRF/TAL	2.198	2.228	2.019	1.96	2.22	2.02	1.88	1.796

3   Conclusions

Real time data of Mooney viscosity of PBR has been analyzed systematically to derive range of process variables that allows to maintain the desired response variable in the range of interest. Data partitioning and interval plots are used to get the desired result. The critical variables that will have major impact on Mooney obtained from the data analysis are as expected and inline with the actual process. Minitab and JMP software were used to analyze the data [8][9]. The results give direction to reduce the variation in Mooney viscosity which results in greater customer satisfaction. The approach presented in the paper can be used for analysis other processes also.

References

1. Pradeep, B.D., Srinivas, S.V.: Predict Difficult -To-Measure Properties with Neural Analyzers. Control Engineering (1997)
2. Hornik, K.M., Stinchomobe, White, H.: Multi Layer Feed Forward Networks are Universal Approximators. Neural Networks 2, 359–366 (1989)
3. Funahashi, K.: On The Approximate Realization of Continuous Mapping by Neural Network. Neural Netwrok 2, 183–192 (1989)
4. Cybenko, G.: Approximation by Superposition of a Sigmoid Function. Mathematics of Control, Signals and Systems 2, 303–314 (1989)
5. Saint Donal, J., Bhat, N., McAvoy, T.J.: Neural Net Based Model Predictive Control. International Journal of Control 54(6), 1453–1468 (1991)

M.V.V.N. Sriram, K. Amin, and G. Padmavathi

6. Hernandez, E., Arkun, Y.: Study of the Control Relevant Properties of Backpropagation Neural Network Models of Nonlinear Dynamical Systems. Computers and Chemical Engineering 6(4), 227–240 (1992)
7. Chen, F.C., Khalil, H.K.: Adaptive Control of Non-Linear Systems Using Neural Networks. International Journal of Control 55(6), 1299–1317 (1992)
8. JMP Software 5.1.1 (2004)
9. Minitab software 15.1 (2006)

Assesement of Freeware Data Mining Tools over Some Wide-Range Characteristics

B. Madasamy[1] and J. Jebamalar Tamilselvi[2]

[1] Anna University of Technology, Chennai
bmadasamy@gmail.com
[2] Dept. of Computer Applications
Jaya Engineering College, Anna University, Chennai

Abstract. Data mining is the process of analyzing data from different aspects and summarizing it into novel information. Open source data mining software is one of a number of analytical tools for analyzing data. Open source software provided for the user gives freedom to change and improve the software. As the number of available tools is more, the choice of the most suitable tool becomes increasingly difficult to select.

This work has conducted a comparative study between a number of some of the liberated available data mining and knowledge discovery tools and software packages. The performance of the tools for the mining task is affected based on various things such as the users, data structures, data mining tasks and methods, visualization and interaction patterns, import and export options for data, platforms and license policies. Here a comparative study on various open source data mining tools and software packages are done. The various tools compared are as follows RAPID MINER (YALE), WEKA, ORANGE, KNIME, TANGRA, KEEL, WAFFLES, and MEGA. This paper attempts to support the decision-making process by discussing the historical development and presenting a range of existing state-of-the-art data mining and related tools. Finally, the paper briefly discusses the comparison of high-end data mining tools including capabilities, ease of use, and practical tips with an uncertain real world situation.

Keywords: Correlation, Data Mining, Discovery, Knowledge, Orange, Weka.

1 Introduction

Data mining is the process which automated extraction of predictive information discovers the interesting knowledge from large amounts of data stored in databases, data warehouses or other information repositories. Open source data mining software represents a new drift in data mining research, education and industrial applications. As the number of available tools continues to grow, the choice of one special tool becomes increasingly difficult for each potential user. This decision making process can be supported by criteria for the categorization of data mining tools[1]-[10].

K.R. Venugopal and L.M. Patnaik (Eds.): ICIP 2012, CCIS 292, pp. 529–535, 2012.
© Springer-Verlag Berlin Heidelberg 2012

In this paper we conducted a comparative study between a number of some of the liberated available data mining and knowledge discovery tools and software packages. In Section 2 describes about open-source Data Mining System. In Section 3 describes different table carry out comparative survey between the tools using different parameters. In Section, 4 5 & 6 describes a summary of the work, conclusion and future enhancements.

2   Open-Source Data Mining

RAPID MINER (YALE), (Yet Another Learning Environment), is an environment for machine learning, data mining, text mining, predictive analytic, and business analysis. It is the world-wide leading open-source data mining solution and is widely used by researchers. The Rapid Miner is written in the Java programming.

WEKA, The prominent example is Waikato Environment for Knowledge Analysis (WEKA). WEKA started in 1994 as a C++ library. In 1999, it was completely rebuilt as a JAVA package. It is a widely used toolkit for machine learning.

KNIME (Konstanz Information Miner) is a user-friendly and comprehensive open-source data integration, processing, analysis and exploration platform. KNIME is a modular data exploration platform that enables the user to visually create data flows.

TANAGRA, offers several data mining methods like data analysis, statistical learning and machine learning. The intention of the Tanagra project is to give easy-to-use data mining software, adding own data mining methods and free access to source code.

ORANGE, is a library of C++ core objects and routines that includes a large variety of standard machine learning and data mining algorithms, plus routines for data input and manipulation.

KEEL, (Knowledge Extraction based on Evolutionary Learning) is a open source Java software tool which empowers the user to assess the behavior of evolutionary learning and Soft Computing based techniques for different kinds of DM problems.

MEGA, (Molecular Evolutionary Genetic Analysis) is engineered to be an 'extensible framework' that facilitates expansion with any bioinformatics software tool used for molecular evolutionary genetic analysis, graphical and visual representations.

WAFFLES, is a collection of tools that seek to provide a wide diversity of useful operations in machine learning and related fields without imposing unnecessary process or interface restrictions on the user.

3   Comparative Survey

Data Mining Software list, Many advanced tools for data mining are available either as open-source or commercial software. In this Table 1, eight different types of Open source tools are presented.

Table 1. Some of the Open-Source Data Mining Tool List

Tool Name	Company Name	URL
KNIME	KNIME Tech	www.knime.org
KEEL	University of Granada	www.keel.es
MEGA	MEGA Soft Solutions	www.megasoftware.net
ORANGE	University of Ljubljana, Slovenia	http://orange.biolab.si
RAPID MINER(YALE)	rapid-i.com	www.rapidminer.com
TANGRA	University Lumiere Lyon 2 (France	http://eric.univ-lyon2. fr/~ricco/tanagra
WAFFLES	Brigham Young University	www.waffles.sourceforge.net
WEKA	University of Waikato	http://www.cs.waikato.ac.nz

Table 2. Open Source Data Mining Tool Vs Platforms

Tool Name	PC Stand alone (98/2000)	Stand alone	Unix Client/ Server	Mac	Activity	License	Language
KNIME	Y	Y	Y	Y	High	GPL	Java
KEEL	Y	Y	Y	Y	High	GPL	Java
MEGA	Y	Y	N	Y	Medium	GPL	SQL, jQuery,
ORANGE	Y	Y	Y	Y	High	GPL	C++/Python
RAPID MINER	Y	Y	Y	Y	High	GPL	Java
TANGRA	Y	N	N	N	Medium	GPL	C++
WAFFLES	Y	Y	N	Y	High	GPL	CLI, C++
WEKA	Y	Y	Y	Y	High	GPL	Java

Platforms, We consider some general system features, including Activity, License, Programming Language and Operating Systems. The results are listed in Table 2. The activity is measured by the frequency of updates and time of latest update. The common open sources licenses include the GPL, LGPL, BSD, NPL, and MPL.

Data Input forms, In real world applications data comes from different sources in different formats. The ability to access different data formats is important in selecting an open source system is described in Table 3.

Functionality Aspect (Algorithm), To be able to solve different data mining problems, the functionality of an open source data mining system is an important feature. Table 4 lists the summary of algorithmic functionality of the 8 systems where DT(Decision Tree), L/S(Linear/Statistical), RF(Random Forest),NN(Nearest Neighbour), RI(Rule Induction), E(Evaluation), B(Boosting), KM(K Means), AR(Association Rules).

Visualization, Good data and model is visualization. The data mining visualization capabilities such as Histograms, Pie charts, Scatter/ Line Plots, classification Tree, Correlation plots are compared in Table 5.

Table 3. Open-Source Data Mining Tools Vs Input Data Format

Tool Name	Statistical-analysis packages (SAS SPSS)	Spread sheets (Excel Lotus)	Rational Databases (Informix Oracle)	Data Translation Tool
KNIME	No	Yes	Yes	Xsl or Translated into ARFF
KEEL	No	Yes	Yes	Xsl or Translated into ARFF
MEGA	No	No	No	Export Xsl to CSV
ORANGE	No	No	No	MY SQL Data format
RAPID MINER	Yes	Yes	Yes	Translated to .csv format
TANGRA	No	Yes	No	Xsl or Translated into ARFF
WAFFLES	No	Yes	No	XSL or .csv
WEKA	No	Yes	Yes	Translated to ARFF format

Table 4. List of Algorithms in Open-Source Data Mining Tool

Tool	DT	L/S	RF	NN	RBF	Bayes	RI	N N/W	SVM	E	B	KM	A
KNIME	Y	Y	Y	Y	Y	Y	Y	Y	Y	Y	Y	Y	Y
KEEL	Y	Y	Y	Y	Y	Y	Y	Y	Y	Y	Y	Y	Y
MEGA	Y	Y	N	N	N	Y	Y	Y	Y	Y	N	Y	Y
ORANGE	Y	N	Y	Y	N	Y	Y	Y	Y	Y	N	Y	Y
RAPID MINER	Y	Y	Y	Y	Y	Y	Y	Y	Y	Y	Y	Y	Y
TANGRA	Y	N	N	Y	N	Y	Y	Y	Y	Y	N	Y	Y
WAFFLES	Y	N	N	Y	N	Y	N	Y	Y	Y	N	Y	Y
WEKA	Y	Y	Y	Y	Y	Y	Y	Y	Y	Y	Y	Y	Y

Table 5. Visualization Chart in Open-Source Data Mining Tool

Tool Name	Histograms	Pie Chart	Scatter/Line Plots	Classification Tree	Correlation Plots
KNIME	Yes	Yes	Yes	Yes	No
KEEL	Yes	Yes	Yes	Yes	No
MEGA	No	No	No	Yes	No
ORANGE	Yes	Yes	Yes	Yes	No
RAPID MINER(YALE)	Yes	Yes	Yes	Yes	Yes
TANGRA	No	No	Yes	Yes	Yes
WAFFLES	Yes	No	Yes	Yes	No
WEKA	Yes	Yes	No	Yes	No

Applied Fields, The following applications are all FOSS, in most cases the result of many years of wide user involvement and continuing improvement listed in Table 6.

Usability Aspect, describes how easy an open source data mining system can be used in solving real world problems in different data and system environments are listed in Table 7. Here, we consider human interaction, interoperability and extensibility.

Table 6. Open-Source Data Mining Applied in Various Applications

Tool Name	Marketing	Direct Mail	Financial Service	Manu-facturing	Health Care	Military
KNIME	Y	Y	Y	Y	Y	Y
KEEL	Y	Y	Y	Y	Y	Y
ORANGE	Y	Y	Y	Y	Y	Y
MEGA	N	N	N	Y	N	N
RAPID MINER	Y	Y	Y	Y	Y	Y
TANGRA	N	N	Y	Y	N	N
WAFFLES	N	N	N	Y	N	N
WEKA	Y	Y	Y	Y	Y	Y

Table 7. Usability of Various Open-Source Data Mining Tool

Tool Name	Human Interaction	Interoperability	Extensibility
KNIME	Manual	PMML	Excellent
KEEL	Manual	Self	Excellent
MEGA	Manual	PMML	Simple
ORANGE	Manual	Self	Excellent
RAPID MINER(YALE)	Manual	Self	Excellent
TANGRA	Manual	Self	Simple
WAFFLES	Manual	PMML	Simple
WEKA	Manual	Self	Excellent

Table 8. Weaknesses and Strengths of Various Open-Source Data Mining Tool

Tool Name	Advantages	Disadvantages
KNIME	Scalability, cluster execution	Plug in needed
KEEL	Evolutionary Computation	Hacking
MEGA	Sequence Analysis	Visualization
ORANGE	Component based Framework	Communication
RAPID MINER(YALE)	Powerful hardware, scheduling, web based access, shared repository, industry standard application	Hacking, user training
TANGRA	compatibility	Data base connectivity is difficult
WAFFLES	Handle different kind of data format. Fast Algorithms.	Limited Graphical Interface
WEKA	Can be working on any platform	Low speed

Advantages & Disadvantages are concluded in Table 8. That there is no tool is better than the other if used for a mining task, since the mining task itself is affected by the type of parameter and the way the analyzer was implemented within the toolkit.

4   Summary

This study is to support the decision-making process by discussing the historical development and related tools can be used to study knowledge and data mining software. Analysis criteria are based on user groups, data structures, data mining tasks and methods, import and export options, license models, Platforms, Algorithms, Visualization, Applied fields, software's general characteristics, data source accessibility and data mining functionality.

This work has conducted a comparative study between a number of some of the free accessible data mining and knowledge discovery tools and software packages. This research has conducted a comparison between 8 data mining toolkits such as RAPID MINER (YALE), WEKA, ORANGE, KNIME, TANGRA, KEEL, WAFFLES and MEGA for analysis purposes, different above mentioned parameters used to judge the toolkits tested using different algorithms.

5   Conclusions

The performance of the tools for the mining task is affected by the kind of above mentioned parameters were implemented within the toolkits. For the applicability issue, the RAPIDMINER (YALE) toolkit has achieved the premier applicability followed by WEKA, KNIME, KEEL, ORANGE, MEGA, TANGRA, WAFFLES, respectively. Finally; RAPIDMINER (YALE) toolkit has achieved the highest improvement in evaluation performance. It has applicable in many research areas, problem domain and suitable for major Data Mining Algorithms. This technique is fit for all types of project development.

Our most significant result is that there is no particular data mining technique that is more powerful or suitable for all type of projects. In order to choose a better data mining algorithm, domain expert must consider the various factors like problem domain, type of data sets, nature of project, and uncertainty of parameters. Multiple classifiers were combined by majority determination of experts to get more precise result.

6   Future Work

To check the efficiency and accuracy of the tools will be finding by various problem domains such as classification, clustering, and preprocessing algorithm using different type of data sets. Another important task is to compare using data streams, extremely large datasets, graph mining, text mining. In the near future, methods for high-dimensional problems such as image retrieval and video mining will also be comparing and embed into powerful tools.

References

1. Han, J., Kamber, M., Jian, P.: Data Mining Concepts and Techniques. Morgan Kaufmann Publishers, San Francisco (2011)
2. Hen, L.E., Lee, S.P.: Performance Analysis of Data Mining Tools Cumulating With a Proposed Data Mining Middleware. Journal of Computer Science (2008)
3. King, M.A., Elder, J.F.: Evaluation of Fourteen Desktop Data Mining Tools. In: Proceedings of the 1998 IEEE International Conference on Systems (1998)
4. Witten, I.H., Frank, E.: Data Mining: Practical Machine Learning Tools and Techniques with Java Implementations, 2nd edn. Morgan Kaufmann, San Francisco (2005)
5. Wang, J., Hu, X., Hollister, K., Zhu, D.: A Comparison and Scenario Analysis of Leading Data Mining Software. International Journal of Knowledge Management 4, 17–34 (2008)
6. Wang, J., Chen, Q., Yao, J.: Data Mining Software. In: Tomei, L. (ed.) Encyclopedia of Information Technology Curriculum Integration, pp. 173–178. Information Science Publishing, Hershey (2008)
7. Data Mining Group (PMML) (January 2003), http://www.dmg.org
8. Blaz, Z., Janez, D.: Open-Source Tools for Data Mining. Clin Lab. Med. 28, 37–54 (2008)
9. Christian, T., Christian, T.: A Survey of Open Source Tools for Business Intelligence. International Journal of Data Warehousing and Mining 5(3) (2009)
10. Xiaojun, C., Graham, W., Xiaofei, X.: A Survey of Open Source Data Mining Systems (2009)

Dimensionality Reduction for Efficient Classification of DNA Repair Genes

Vidya A.[1], Manohar V.[1], Shwetha V.P.[1], Venugopal K.R.[1], and Patnaik L.M.[2]

[1] Department of Computer Science and Engineering
University Visvesvaraya College of Engineering
Bangalore University, Bangalore, India
vidyaananth16@gmail.com
[2] Indian Institute of Science, Bangalore, India

Abstract. DNA damage is an imperative process which plays a crucial role in ageing demanding the need for classification of DNA repair genes into ageing and non-ageing. In our paper, we employ a data mining approach for classifying DNA repair genes using their various characteristic features. The classification models built were difficult to analyze and interpret due to the curse of dimensionality present in the gene dataset. This difficulty is overcome by adopting Dimensionality Reduction which is a well-known pre-processing technique. The Feature subset selection technique along with various search methods is used to reduce the dataset without affecting the integrity of the original dataset. The reduction in the dataset enabled the use of Multilayer perceptron in the efficient analysis of the dataset. The classifiers showed better performance on the reduced dataset when compared to the original dataset.

Keywords: Ageing Genes, Classifiers, Data Mining, Dimensionality Reduction, DNA Repair Genes, Feature subset.

1 Introduction

Living organisms are a complex universe of activities and functionalities. Among all these important biological activities, ageing plays a vital role. Ageing is a pleiotropic, progressive degenerative process that involves a number of molecular events at various levels. Ageing manifests itself both physically and biologically. It is discovered that the longevity mutant gene daf-2 [1] is responsible for extended lifespan in C.elegans. It is found that the molecular mechanisms of complex diseases like Progeriod Syndrome and Alzheimer are similar to the mechanisms of ageing process. Thus, the study of ageing and its functionalities paves an easier way for decoding these complex diseases [2]. DNA damage is a deterministic process affecting ageing and thus its study is of great importance to understand different DNA repair pathways and their role in ageing. In our work we analyze the important features of DNA repair genes to understand their unique characteristics which differentiate them from non-ageing repair genes. DNA, in spite of having a stable structure is constantly damaged by change

K.R. Venugopal and L.M. Patnaik (Eds.): ICIP 2012, CCIS 292, pp. 536–545, 2012.
© Springer-Verlag Berlin Heidelberg 2012

in temperature, pH and deamination of cytosine to uracil bases causing major changes in evolution [3].

Research in the field of ageing over the past few years has resulted in the accumulation of large amounts of data. Extracting the pertinent data sets from this vast ocean of data is a challenging task. Data mining techniques make it easier for extracting essential patterns which help in the study of ageing and understanding its importance. The patterns thus extracted are analyzed and categorized into their respective classes by using classification methods [4].

To design a model which efficiently and accurately classifies the data objects, a number of classification techniques can be used, by which analysis can be performed more easily when compared to the trial and error methods of in-vitro techniques. These techniques are very advantageous in terms of their accuracy, cost of computation, scalability, robustness, simplicity and interpretability which makes the process of classification a less complicated one. Although these algorithms give accurate results, efficiency is an issue of concern in biological data-mining due to their vast and complex datasets. Dimensionality reduction is an important data reduction technique that is used to simplify the dataset.

Motivation: Among all the factors of DNA which play a vital role in ageing, DNA repair mechanism is found to be at the top of the list. DNA repair genes have been studied extensively to understand their properties which help in classifying them as ageing and non-ageing genes [3]. Despite continuous efforts that have been put into analyzing the characteristics of these genes to classify them efficiently, studies have not been able to produce accurate results due to the presence of noise, inconsistencies and vast size of the biological datasets. For better accuracy the adoption of a classifier like Multilayer perceptron which is insensitive to these discrepancies would be ideal. Biological datasets are characterized by huge dimensions and complex attribute correlations which can easily be handled using Dimensionality reduction techniques. These techniques not only reduce the complexity of datasets but also maintain the integrity of the original, unsimplified dataset.

Contribution: To achieve accurate classification of DNA repair genes into ageing and non ageing, the biggest obstacle encountered was the complexity of the dataset. In order to overcome this difficulty, we propose the idea of adopting Dimensionality reduction techniques which reduce the datasets complexity drastically and make it easier for understanding and interpreting the data, still maintaining the integrity of the original dataset.

Organization: The remainder of this paper is organized as follows: Section 2 presents the overview of Literature Survey. Section 3 describes the background. Section 4 describes the proposed method and Section 5 depicts the design and implementation of the proposed method. Section 6 presents the results and a comparative assessment of the different classifiers. Concluding remarks are presented in section 7.

2   Related Work

A lot of research has been carried out in the field of data mining for classification and data reduction.

Yan-Hui Li *et al.*, [2] have used statistical methods to analyze the topological features of genes in order to classify them into ageing and non-ageing and have also analyzed the importance of PPIs, which define the characteristic features of human genes. The study can be further used for the analysis of disease genes.

Alex A Freitas *et al.*, [3] have analyzed Human DNA repair genes using their biological features and then classified using machine learning techniques. The analysis showcases the use of protein interaction partners to improve accuracy in various data mining methods. The study can also be applied to other ageing related pathways.

Mark Hall and Eibe Frank [5] have investigated a semi-nave Bayseian ranking method that compares the results of the combined model to the either component techniques. The combined approach builds a powerful model which increases the AUC when compared to the stand-alone models. The ranking model along with attribute selection methods can be used to achieve better accuracy.

Asha Gowda Karegowda *et al.*, [6] have employed Gain Ratio and Correlation based feature selection (CFS) to handle the curse of dimensionality. Subsets selected by CFS resulted in better accuracy than those selected by information gain. The attribute selection techniques can be used to classify very large biological datasets.

M. Vasantha and Dr.V.Subbiah Bharathy [7] have explored the attribute selection methods along with search methods and have used the reduced dataset for comparing the accuracies of various classification algorithms. Dimensionality reduction techniques have shown an increase in the accuracy of the models without losing the integrity of the original dataset. An integrated or a hybrid variety of the attribute selection methods can be used to classify different datasets.

3   Background

The challenge of increasing the longevity of living organisms and decoding the molecular mechanisms of deadly diseases has been a fascination among researchers since decades. This quest has led to many revelations that have unveiled hidden knowledge about the ageing process. Studies have shown that DNA plays a very important role in ageing. Yan-Hui Li et al., [2] have analyzed the molecular mechanisms of ageing genes showing their characteristic features such as higher interaction degree, high neighbour ratio, being the centre of the PPI network and high correlated expressions [8]. Alex A Freitas et al.,[3] have successfully classified human DNA Repair genes into ageing and non-ageing showing the importance of ageing in DNA repair genes. Research is focussed on classifying genes into ageing and non-ageing due to the abundance of genes, where the human genome itself ranges over ten thousand. However the ratio of ageing genes in the human genome is very less. Hence, there is a need for classifying ageing genes accurately in order to understand the complex processes occurring in living organisms.

4   The Proposed Method

4.1   Problem Statement

To classify human DNA repair genes into ageing and non-ageing and to develop a model that can accurately label a novel gene.

Assumptions: Datasets retrieved from different sources are assumed to be precise and accurate.

5   Design and Implementation

DNA repair gene play a key role in ageing. A model has been proposed to efficiently classify DNA repair genes. The proposed model is as depicted in Fig.1. The model contains several modules like: Data Collection module, Data Cleaning and Data Reduction as preprocessing module, Classification module and result evaluation module.

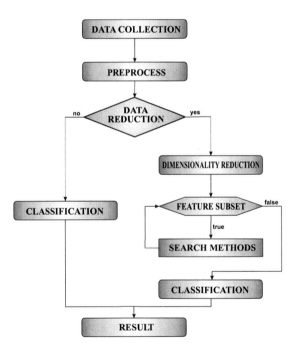

Fig. 1. Model for Efficient Classification of DNA Repair Genes

5.1   Data Collection

The datasets used in this work comprises of five subsets: no PPI related attributes (D1), only number of interaction partners as PPI related attribute(D2), 10 BPI(D3), 20 BPI(D4) and 30 BPI(D5). The dataset used in this work is retrieved from the senescence website [9].

5.2   Data Preprocessing

Data preprocessing generally involves data cleaning, data integration, data transformation and data reduction. In our work, data preprocessing mainly concentrates on data cleaning and data reduction, as the dataset created is complex and contains missing values which when neglected can drastically affect the results. In order to treat missing values one of the well-known methodologies, KNN (K-nearest neighbour) algorithm is employed [10].

Data Reduction: Data mining on very large amounts of data is time consuming, making analysis an uphill task. Data reduction techniques are thus used to obtain a reduced representation of the dataset without losing the integrity of the original dataset. In our work we employ feature subset selection which is a dimensionality reduction technique that compresses the dataset by removing the redundant and irrelevant attributes. Methods used for feature subset selection are classified into embedded, wrapper and filter methods. In our work, we use the Correlation-based Feature Subset selection method which is a filter approach [11].

The CFS method estimates the importance of a subset of attributes by considering the individual predictive ability of each feature along with the degree of redundancy between them. Correlation coefficient is then used to determine the correlation between the subsets of attributes and the target class label, along with the inter-correlations between the features. The feature subsets that are highly correlated with the class but having low inter-correlation are preferred. We then combine the CFS method with search strategies like best-first search, linear forward search and rank search. We finally consider the attributes that are common to the aforementioned search techniques to obtain better accuracy and number of correct classifications.

5.3   Classification Models

We are using the classification models like the J48 Decision Tree, Naive Bayes and Multilayer perceptron, supported by a data mining tool WEKA [12][13]. (i) J48 Decision Trees: The decision tree uses a top-down approach to classify the data tuples wherein every internal node represents a test on any attribute. The branches of the tree represent the outcome of the test on the predictor attribute and the leaf nodes represent the class label which classifies the genes into two classes, namely, ageing and non-ageing.

(ii) Naive Bayesian Classifier: Bayesian classifers are statistical and are based on Baye's theorem. Bayesian classifiers can predict the class membership probability, that a given sample belongs to a particular class. Bayesian classifiers are scalable and they can predict the class membership probability very fast. Accuracy of the Bayesian classifiers are very high, when applied to a large databases. In comparison with other classifiers Bayseian classifiers have minimum error rate.

(iii) Multilayer Perceptron: Multilayer Perceptron is a neural network learning algorithm which uses backpropagation to classify data instances. It is one of the most robust and versatile algorithms available for classification. It is characterized by the presence of one input layer, one or more hidden layers and an output layer in its completely connected network where each layer is made up of units. The attributes of the training tuples are fed as inputs to the units forming the input layer. These inputs are propagated forward through the feed-forward network till the output layer. These inputs are made to undergo mathematical transformation using weights and biases at each unit of all the layers. The backpropagation algorithm builds the classification model by performing non-linear regression. The Fig. 2 depicts the network model that is used while classifying the WRN gene.

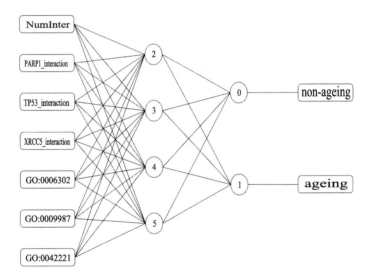

Fig. 2. Multilayer Perceptron Model

5.4   Accuracy Measures

The performance of a classification model is estimated in terms of its predictive accuracy. The accuracy of a classifier is determined by different evaluator measures. The evaluator measures used in our work include CCI, F-score and ROC, which are determined using 10-fold cross validation.

6   Results and Discussions

The dataset collected varied in the number of attributes and instances making analysis a difficult task. Among the various classification methods available in WEKA, J48, Naive Bayesian and Multilayer perceptron are used in the classification of genes. J48 and Naive Bayesian classifiers could interpret this complex dataset without much difficulty giving acceptable accuracies. However Multilayer perceptron developed are complicated models having large time and space complexities. These models were very difficult to analyze and interpret and thus could not be used for classifying the data instances. This drawback demanded the need for dimensionality reduction methods which could reduce the size of the dataset without losing the integrity of the original dataset.

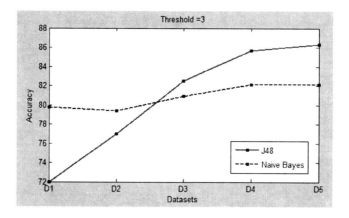

Fig. 3. Comparison of different Classifiers v/s Datasets for Thershold 3 before Dimensionality Reduction

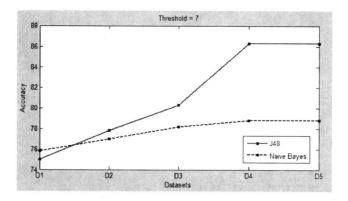

Fig. 4. Comparison of different Classifiers v/s Datasets for Thershold 7 before Dimensionality Reduction

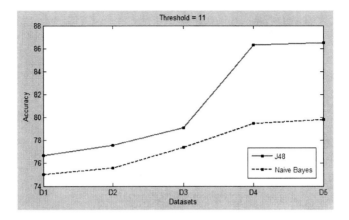

Fig. 5. Comparison of different Classifiers v/s Datasets for Thershold 11 before Dimensionality Reduction

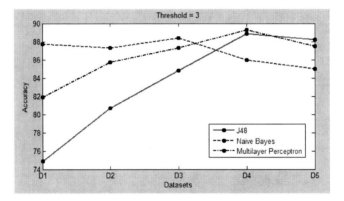

Fig. 6. Comparison of different Classifiers v/s Datasets for Thershold 3 after Dimensionality Reduction

The accuracy versus dataset line for J48 is linear with a positive slope. The lines show a drastic increase in the slope at dataset D3 due to the presence of distinguishing attributes like BPI interactions in datasets D3, D4 and D5. This is in accordance with the fact that the decision trees classify based on the splitting criterion attributes. The graphs for Naive Bayes show a linear line with negligible slope. The lines show a gradual decrease in the average accuracy from threshold 3 to threshold 11 as shown in Fig. 3, Fig. 4 and Fig. 5, due to the decrease in the number of attributes in the datasets for the corresponding thresholds. This is in accordance with the fact that the Naive Bayesian classifies based on probability distribution of classes.

The results obtained for J48 and Naive Bayesian classifier after Dimensionality Reduction(DR) as shown in Fig. 6, Fig. 7 and Fig. 8, are similar to those obtained before DR. However the difference lies in the presence of a considerable

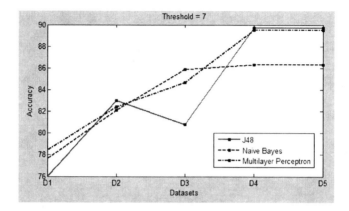

Fig. 7. Comparison of different Classifiers v/s Datasets for Thershold 7 after Dimensionality Reduction

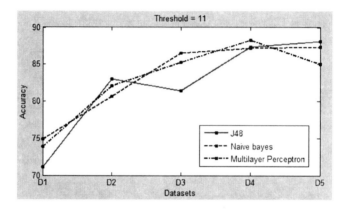

Fig. 8. Comparison of different Classifiers v/s Datasets for Thershold 11 after Dimensionality Reduction

amount of increase in the accuracy values. This clearly highlights the significance of Dimensionality Reduction techniques employed on the dataset. The results for Multilayer perceptron could be obtained only after the reduction of the dataset. The graphs show a relatively smooth line for Multilayer perceptron when compared to that of J48 and Naive Bayesian classfier owing to the fact that it can efficiently handle dubious dataset.

7   Conclusions

Classification on reduced dataset proves to be more efficient and interpretable making data analysis an easier task. Reduced datasets are model-friendly thus helping in the development of simpler and efficient classification models. Dimensionality Reduction technique can be used to analyze humungous biological dataset with ease. This greatly contributes to the study of many complex diseases related to ageing.

References

1. Kenyon, C., Chang, J., Gensch, E., Rudner, A., Tabtiang, R.: A C.elegans Mutant that Lives Twice as long as Wild Type. Nature 366, 461–464 (1993)
2. Li, Y.-H., Zhang, G.-G., Guo, Z.: Computational Prediction of Aging Genes in Human. In: Biomedical Engineering and Computer Science (ICBECS) (2010)
3. Freitas, A.A., Vasieva, O., de Magalhaes, J.P.: A Data Mining Approach for Classifying DNA Repair Genes into Ageing-Related or Non-Ageing-Related. BMC Genomics 12(27) (2011)
4. Han, J., Kamber, M.: Data Mining Concepts and Techniques, 2nd edn. Morgan Kauffmann (2006)
5. Hall, M., Frank, E.: Combining Naive Bayes and Decision Tables. In: Twenty First International FLAIRS, pp. 318–319 (2008)
6. Asha Gowda, K., Jayaram, M.A., Manjunath, A.S.: Feature Subset Selection using Cascaded GA and CFS: A Filter Approach in Supervised Learning. International Journal of Computer Applications 23(2), 0975–8887 (2011)
7. Vasantha, M., Subbiah Bharathy, V.: Evaluation of Attribute Selection Methods with Tree Based Supervised Classification-A Case study with Mammogram Images. International Journal of Computer Applications 8(12), 975–8887 (2010)
8. Przulj, N., Wigle, A.D., Jurisica, I.: Functional Topology in a Network of Protein Interactions. Bioinformatics 20(3), 340–348 (2004)
9. http://genomics.senescence.info/genes/DNA_repair.html
10. Acuna, E., Rodriguez, C.: The Treatment of Missing Values and its Effect in the Classifier Accuracy. In: Classification, Clustering and Data Mining Application, pp. 639–648 (2004)
11. Tan, P.-N., Steinbach, M., Kumar, V.: Introduction to Data Mining, 3rd edn. Pearson Education (2009)
12. Witten, H.I., Eibe, F.: Data Mining: Practical Machine Learning Tools and Techniques, 2nd edn. Morgan Kauffmann, San Francisco (2005)
13. The Weka Data Mining Software: an update, http://www.cs.waikato.ac.nz/ml/weka/

Comparison of Supervised Learning and Reinforcement Learning in Intrusion Domain

Nandita Sengupta[1] and Jaya Sil[2]

[1] University College of Bahrain,
P.O. Box 55040, Manama, Bahrain
ngupta@ucb.edu.bh
[2] Bengal Engineering and Science University Shibpur,
P.O.B. Garden, Howrah, WB, India 711103

Abstract. In modern world use of network is increasing exponentially. Network security needs attention of computer science researchers. Intrusion Detection System is software / hardware which detects intruder in the network or host system. Classification plays an important role in Intrusion Detection System. Detection of anomaly or normal traffic is main working philosophy for such type of system. For detection of online traffic, learning of the system is required. In our paper, performance of Supervised Learning and Reinforcement Learning is compared in Intrusion Domain. NSL-KDD data is considered for our work. In that dataset for each object 41 conditional attributes and one decision class attribute are mentioned. Out of 41 attributes, 7 attributes are discrete and 34 attributes are continuous. Using feature ranking method, number of discrete attributes are reduced and these reduced number of attributes are used for classification in Supervised Learning. Some Supervised Learning like CS-MC4, Decision List, ID3, Naive Bayes, C4.5, Rnd Tree are applied on this data set and compared this classification result with classification accuracy derived from Reinforcement Learning combined with Rough Set Theory classifier.

Keywords: Classification, Intrusion Detection System, Reinforcement Learning, Supervised Learning.

1 Introduction

Online classification of network traffic data is very important to develop intrusion detection system (IDS) that automatically monitors the flow of network packets. Existing works on intrusion detection have been carried out to classify the network traffic as anomaly or normal. A majority of current IDS follow signature based approach [1] in which, similar to virus scanners, events are detected that match specific predefined patterns known as "signatures". The limitation of these signature-based IDS is their failure to identify novel attacks and even minor variation of patterns are not detected accurately. In addition, sometimes IDS generate false alarm for alerting network administrator due to failure of handling imprecise data which has high possibility to appear in network traffic

K.R. Venugopal and L.M. Patnaik (Eds.): ICIP 2012, CCIS 292, pp. 546–551, 2012.
© Springer-Verlag Berlin Heidelberg 2012

data. Therefore, accuracy, computation time and system learning are the key issues to be addressed properly for classifying such data.

Classification is an important task in data mining research that facilitates analysis of huge amount of data. Learning plays an important role in classification for any dataset. A lot of research work on supervised learning, unsupervised learning has been carried out for intrusion detection system. Reinforcement Learning for intrusion detection system is an active research area where researchers can contribute to improve the performance of IDS. Feature reduction helps in optimization of classification with respect to time and efficiency. In the paper, network traffic data [2] of NSL-KDD has been considered for generating training and testing patterns. Feature ranking technology is used for feature reduction. In our work, 7 discrete attributes are considered and applying feature ranking technology, number of discrete attributes is reduced to 5. Using these 5 discrete attributes, supervised learning algorithm is applied for classification. Reinforcement learning is used for RST [3] classifier in NSL-KDD data. Finally, classification accuracy has been expressed in terms of confusion matrix[4] for all these supervised learning methods. Classification accuracy for supervised learning and reinforcement learning is compared for IDS dataset.

Supervised learning [5]-[8] like CS-MC4, Decision List, ID3, Naive Bayes, C4.5, Rnd Tree are applied on this data set and compared this classification result with reinforcement learning. Using Tanagra software, feature reduction is done by Feature ranking method and classification accuracy is found out for supervised learning. Reinforcement Learning (RL) is used for facilitating RST [9]-[11] classifier and it is observed that RL yields better result than Supervised Learning in intrusion domain.

Section 2 explains requirement of feature reduction, Section 3 describes supervised learning, Section 4 mentions reinforcement learning, Section 5 depicts experimental results and Section 6 concludes the paper and mentions future work.

2   Feature Reduction

Almost every real world system deals with huge dimension in the information system table which makes the system complicated. Operational complexity, timing complexity increases for such type of real world system. To achieve efficient performance from classifier, dimension reduction becomes essential. Different machine learning techniques are used for dimension reduction of information system to retrieve concise, useful, precise, general, understandable information. In RST, reducts are found out by different techniques. The attributes which primarily help in determination of classification is known as reduct. In the work, feature ranking method is applied for feature reduction for Supervised Learning. In feature ranking technology, relevance of each attribute is calculated and accordingly, features are selected for classification. Reinforcement Learning is applied for discretization of continuous attributes and then RST is used as classifier. In paper, NSL-KDD data set, 7 discrete attributes, protocol_type, service, flag, land, logged_in, is_host_login, is_guest_login are considered and applying feature ranking method, 7 attributes have been reduced to 5 attributes. Supervised Learning algorithm is applied for classification with these 5 attributes. Applying Reinforcement Learning, discretization is done and then reduct is calculated for RST.

3   Supervised Learning

In Supervised Learning, along with input sequence x1,x2,x3,.....,xn, output sequence for that input sequence is also known y1,y2,y3,.....,yn. The objective of such type of learning is that machine generates the correct output for a given input. Label of classification is known for Supervised Learning. Supervised Learning like CS-MC4, Decision List, ID3, Naive Bayes, C4.5, Rnd Tree are applied on this data set. Some of the Supervised Learning algorithms (like CS-MC4,Naive Bayes) are explained here. CS-MC4 [6] is cost sensitive supervised decision tree algorithm. It uses a generalization of LaPlace estimate, smoothed probability estimation. It minimizes the expected loss using misclassification cost matrix for the detection of best prediction within leaves. It is also known as statistical classifier. A naive Bayes classifier is a simple probabilistic classifier based on applying Bayes' theorem. Naive Bayes classifiers can be trained very efficiently in a Supervised Learning setting. In spite of their naive design and apparently oversimplified assumptions, naive Bayes classifiers have worked quite well in many complex real-world situations. An advantage of the naive Bayes classifier is that it only requires a small amount of training data to estimate the parameters (means and variances of the variables) necessary for classification.

4   Reinforcement Learning

In Reinforcement Learning (RL), machine receives input sequence and depending on its action on a particular state machine receives positive reward or negative reward (punishment) for the environment. Thus the machine learns the path from environment for achieving its goal through which reward can be maximized. There are plenty of scope of research work on Reinforcement Learning.

5   Experimental Results

NSL-KDD data set is considered for our experiment. Total 11850 objects have been considered for the whole information system. Each object has 42 attributes. 34 are continuous conditional attributes, 7 are discrete conditional attributes and 1 is discrete decision attribute. 42 attributes are shown in Table 1. Using feature ranking technology, number of discrete attributes are reduced from 7 to 5. Those 5 attributes are mentioned in Table 2. Supervised Learning like CS-MC4, Decision List, ID3, Naive Bayes, C4.5, Rnd Tree are applied on this data set and classification accuracy are mentioned in Table 3, Table 4, Table 5, Table 6, Table 7 and Table 8 respectively. Whereas, we applied Reinforcement Learning for discretization of continuous attributes and we applied on all 41 attributes, reducts are formed with only 12 attributes and we got efficiency which is much higher than any of the Supervised Learning algorithms mentioned here. Comparison of classification accuracy is mentioned in Table 9.

Table 1. Attributes of Network Traffic

Sl. No.	Attributes	Sl. No.	Attributes
1	Duration	22	is_guest_login
2	protocol_type	23	count
3	service	24	srv_count
4	flag	25	serror_rate
5	source_bytes	26	srv_serror_rate
6	destination_bytes	27	rerror_rate
7	land	28	srv_rerror_rate
8	wrong_fragment	29	same_srv_rate
9	urgent	30	diff_srv_rate
10	hot	31	srv_diff_host
11	failed_logins	32	dst_host_count
12	logged_in	33	dst_host_srv_count
13	num_compromised	34	dst_host_same_srv_rate
14	root_shell	35	dst_host_diff_srv_rate
15	su_attempted	36	dst_host_same_srv_rate
16	num_root	37	dst_host_srv_diff_host_rate
17	num_file_creations	38	dst_host_serror_rate
18	num_shells	39	dst_host_srv_serror_rate
19	num_access_files	40	dst_host_rerror_rate
20	num_outbound_cmds	41	dst_host_srv_rerror_rate
21	is_host_login	42	class

Table 2. Attributes after Feature Reduction for Supervised Learning Algorithm

Sl No	Name of the Attribute)
1	protocol_type
2	service
3	flag
4	logged_in
5	is_guest_login

Table 3. Confusion Matrix using CS-MC4 Supervised Learning

	Anomaly	Normal	Sum
Anomaly	8859	839	9698
Normal	753	1399	2152
Sum	9612	2238	11850

Table 4. Confusion Matrix using Decision List Supervised Learning

	Anomaly	Normal	Sum
Anomaly	8961	737	9698
Normal	713	1439	2152
Sum	9674	2176	11850

Table 5. Confusion Matrix using ID3 Supervised Learning

	Anomaly	Normal	Sum
Anomaly	8975	723	9698
Normal	726	1426	2152
Sum	9701	2149 11850	

Table 6. Confusion Matrix using Naive Bayes Supervised Learning

	Anomaly	Normal	Sum
Anomaly	8858	840	9698
Normal	750	1402	2152
Sum	9608	2242	11850

Table 7. Confusion Matrix using C4.5 Supervised Learning

	Anomaly	Normal	Sum
Anomaly	8980	718	9698
Normal	736	1416	2152
Sum	9716	2134	11850

Table 8. Confusion Matrix using Rnd Tree Supervised Learning

	Anomaly	Normal	Sum
Anomaly	8964	734	9698
Normal	700	1452	2152
Sum	9664	2186	11850

Table 9. Comparison of Classification Performance

Classifiers	Accuracy(%)
CS-MC4	86.57
Decision List	87.76
ID3	87.76
Naive Bayes	86.58
C4.5	87.73
Rnd Tree	87.9
Reinforcement Learning	96.0

6   Conclusion and Future Work

It is clear from Table 9 that Reinforcement Learning, along with rough set, produces higher classification accuracy with respect to some Supervised Learning classification algorithm in Intrusion Domain. In future, this work can be extended with multiagent Reinforcement Learning. Multiagent reinforcement can yield more efficient classification accuracy which can consider other environmental aspects in Intrusion Domain.

References

1. Neelakantan, S., Rao, S.: A Threat-Aware Signature Based Intrusion-Detection Approach for Obtaining Network-Specific Useful Alarms. In: Proceedings of the Third International Conference on Internet Monitoring and Protection (2008)
2. NSL-KDD Data Set for Network-Based Intrusion Detection Systems, http://iscx.ca/NSL-KDD/
3. Beaubouef, T., Petry, F.E.: Uncertainty Modeling for Database Design using Intuitionistic and Rough Set Theory. Journal of Intelligent & Fuzzy Systems: Applications in Engineering and Technology 20(3) (August 2009)
4. Sengupta, N., Sil, J.: Decision Making System for Network Traffic. In: Proceedings of International Conference and Exhibition on Knowledge Business, Industry and Education (KBIE), Bahrain (2011)
5. Kumar, Y., Upendra, J.: Intrusion Detection using Supervised Learning with Feature Set Reduction. Proceedings of International Journal of Computer Applications 33(6) (2011)
6. Nancy, P., Ramani, G.R.: A Comparison on Performance of Data Mining Algorithms in Classification of Social Network Data. International Journal of Computer Applications 32(8) (October 2011)
7. Hu, W., Hu, W., Maybank, S.: AdaBoost-Based Algorithm for Network Intrusion Detection. IEEE Transactions On Systems, Man, and Cybernetics 38, 2 (2008)
8. Chen, C., Gong, Y., Tian, Y.: IEEE International Conference on Systems, Man, and Cybernetics, SMC (2008)
9. Sengupta, N., Sil, J.: An Integrated Approach to Information Retrieval using RST, FS and SOM. In: Proc. ICIS, Bahrain (2008)
10. Dembczynski, K., Pindur, R., Susmaga, R.: Generation of Exhaustive Set of Rules within Dominance-based Rough Set Approach. In: Proceedings of International Workshop on Rough Sets in Knowledge Discovery and Soft Computing (March 2003)
11. Li, L., Zhao, K.: A New Intrusion Detection System Based on Rough Set Theory and Fuzzy Support Vector Machine. In: Proceedings of IEEE 3rd International Workshop on Intelligent Systems and Applications (2011)

An Improved Set-Valued Data Anonymization Algorithm and Generation of FP-Tree

Tripathy B.K.[1], Manusha G.V.[2], and Mohisin G.S.[2]

[1] School of Computing Science and Engineering,
VIT University, Vellore, TN, India
tripathybk@vit.ac.in
[2] School of Information Technology and Engineering,
VIT University, Vellore, TN, India
manushagv@gmail.com, gshahidmohisin2008@vit.ac.in

Abstract. Data anonymization techniques enable publication of detailed information, while providing the privacy of sensitive information in the data against a variety of attacks. Anonymized data describes a set of possible worlds that include the original data. Generalization and suppression have been the most commonly used techniques for achieving anonymization. Some algorithms to protect privacy in the publication of set-valued data were developed by Terrovitis et. al.,[1]. The concept of k-anonymity was introduced by Samarati and Sweeny [2], so that every tuple has at least (k-1) tuples identical with it. This concept was modified in [1] in order to introduce km -anonymity, to limit the effects of the data dimensionality. This approach depends upon generalisation instead of suppression.To handle this problem two heuristic algorithms; namely the DA- algorithm and the AA-algorithm were developed by them.These alogorithms provide near optimal solutions in many cases.In this paper,we improve DA such that undesirable duplicates are not generated and using a FP-growth we display the anonymized data.We illustrate through suitable examples,the efficiency of our proposed algorithm.

Keywords: Count-tree, Direct anonymization, FP-growth, k-anonymization, k^m-anonymization.

1 Introduction

In [3] supermarket transactions were considered as the motivating example to describe the requirement of anonymization of set valued data. Suppose an adversary finds some of the items purchased by a customer. If the supermarket database is published later, even after removing the personal identities, there is a chance that the database contains only one transaction containing the items seen by him. Then the adversary can easily identify the other items purchased by the particular customer and get useful information out of it. Identifying the transaction details in this way is known as re-identification. Inorder to preserve the data from being re- identified data can be k-anonymized. According to Sweeney[1] the data is k-anonymized if the information for each person contained in the release cannot be distinguished from at least k -1 individuals whose

K.R. Venugopal and L.M. Patnaik (Eds.): ICIP 2012, CCIS 292, pp. 552–560, 2012.
© Springer-Verlag Berlin Heidelberg 2012

information also appears in the release. So, we need to transform the original database D to the anonymized database D'. Even after the data is k-anonymized the data cannot be completely protected from being re-identification.

However, in this approach the set of attributes in a database are divided into two broad categories. These are the sensitive attributes and the non-sensitive attributes. So, making use of this concept a k^m -anonymization model was developed in [3] and algorithms were developed to deal with such type of set-valued data. A subset of items in a transaction play the role of quasi-identifier.By which the data can be re-identified by linking techniques. So, the Generalization technique is used for transactional database or "market basket" data analysis. Three algorithms were introduced in [1] to achieve k^m-anonymization. However, the problem in these algorithms is the generation or redundant transactions while generating the additional tuples to achieve anonymization. In this paper we improve upon the two algorithms (DA and AA algorithms) in [1] by adding several steps so that the number of transactions generated is the exact number required.

2   Literature Survey

As mentioned in the introduction, one of the earliest attempts to anonymisation of databases is the introduc- tion of the notion of k-anonymity by Samarati [4] and Sweeny [2]. A table is k-anonymised if each record is indistinguishable from at least k-1 other records with respect to a set of quasi-identifier (QI) attributes. The QIs are than generalised and the records with identical QI values thus form an anonymised group. The process of transforming a database table D into a table D' after anonymisation is called recoding. These are in [5] with a bound of O(k.logk), in [6] with a bound of O(k), and with a bound of O(logk) in [7]. In [8] an algorithm called Incognito is proposed, which uses dynamic programming approach to find an optimal solution.

The problem here is the concept of full-domain recoding, which requires that all values in a dimension must be mapped to the same level of hierarchy. Inspired by Incognito, Terrovitis et. al., [1] proposed three algorithms, the optimal anonymisation (OA) algorithm and two heuristic algorithms called the direct anonymisation (DA) algorithm and the apriori anonymisation (AA) algorithm. Here, the full-domain recoding is not assumed. Also, in k- anonymity the set of QI attributes are known beforehand. However, in case of [1], since any set of m items (which corresponds to the attributes) can be used by the adversary, no QI set can be predetermined. Frequent Pattern(FP)-growth algorithm [9],is one of the association algorithms,to mine frequent data items from large databases without the generation of candidate sets.

Repeated database scans are avoided by implementing this algorithm by which both time and resources can be saved.The required statictics from large database are gath- ered into a smaller data structure(FP-tree),which is generated with just two database scans.This FP-tree is used to generate frequent patterns in transactions.These patterns are used ad profiles to check against future transactions.Transactions that do not match these patterns are identified as malicious transactions.FP-growth adopts a divide-and -conquer approach to decompose both the mining tasks and the database.FP-tree uses a pattern fragment growth method to avoid the costly process of candidate generation and testing used by apriori.

3   Concepts and Existing Algorithms

In this section we introduce some concepts to be used in the paper and also introduce the existing algorithms proposed in [1] along with explanations.

3.1   Generalization

The data generalization concept explored from data mining as a way to hide detailed(more specific) informa- tion, rather than discover trends and patterns. In k^m-anonymization model there is no fixed,well defined set of quasi-identifier for the sensitive data.A subset of items in a transaction can act as quasi-identifier for the sensitive ones or vice versa. To solve the k^m -anonymization problem for a transactional database, generalization is in use.If original database D does not satisfy the k^m -anonymity then it is transformed to D' by replacing items with their generalized ones.Here in supermarket database while entering the item is provided with its respective generalization. Generalization replaces intial attribute with generalized attribute.

For example consider T=orange,goodday,mango,timepass,in thisorange,mango can be generalized to fruits and goodday,timepass can be generalized to biscuits and total transaction to fruits, biscuits . Example 3.1.1 : In the table below we present a set of items along with their generalisations, which form the components of any transaction in a super market.

Table 1. Database of Items and their Generalizations

ITEMID	Items	Generalization	ITEMID	Items	Generalization
1	Apple	Fruit	6	Aswini	Oil
2	Orange	Fruit	7	VVD	Oil
3	Pineapple	Fruit	8	Margo	Soap
4	Clinicplus	Shampoo	9	Lux	Soap
5	Dove	Shampoo	10	Chik	Shampoo

3.2   Count Tree

To find whether generalization applied provides k ^{m} -anonymity,it is to count efi- ciently the support of all combina- tions of m-items that appear in the database. To avoid scanning the database each and every time generalization has to be checked. To acheive these two goals a datastructure was constructed which keep track of not only all combinations of m items from the generalized database but

Table 2. Transactions in the Database

Transaction ID	Transaction Items	Transaction ID	Transaction Items
1	Apple, Aswini, ClincPlus	8	Aswini, ClinicPlus, Orange
2	Dove, ClincPlus, Aswini	9	Aswini, ClinicPlus, Orange
3	Apple, Aswini, ClincPlus, Orange, Pineapple	10	ClincPlus, Orange, Margo
4	ClinicPlus, Apple, Dove, Pineapple	11	ClincPlus, Dove
5	Aswini, ClincPlus, Orange	12	Aswini
6	Apple, Orange, Pineapple	13	PineApple, Chik,Lux
7	Apple, Aswini, ClincPlus,Dove, Margo, Orange, PineApple, VVD	14	Apple, Dove, Margo
		15	ClinicPlus, Aswini

also it must know how each generalized value effects the database.The support value of each combination of all items in the transactions is calculated.Inorder to keep track of the support of all the transactions a count tree-data structure was constructed.

To count the support of all these combinations and to store them the count-tree is used, based on the count tree algorithm. The tree assumes an order of items and their generalizations, based on their frequencies(supports)in D.To compute this order, a database scan is required.The support of each itemset with upto m items can be computed by following a corresponding path in the tree and using the support value of the corresponding node [1].Count-tree follows the apriori principle which states that the support of an item set is always less than or equal to the support of its subsets.

Here in the database the items which are present and not present in the transaction are represented 1 's and 0 's respectively.Based on this the frequent item sets are generated. A frequent item set is an item set whose number of occurrences is above a threshold. For each combination of items in the transaction the support value is calculated and is displayed. The items which are having the support value less than the minimum support value then those items are neglected.

Based on the count tree two anonymization techniques can be performed i.e.,Direct Anonymization (DA) and Apriori -based anonymization (AA).

Support: The support or utility or prevalence for an association rule X=>Y is the percentage of transactions in the database that contains both X and Y.

$$\text{Support } (X \rightarrow Y) = \frac{\text{No. of tuples containing both X and Y}}{\text{Total no. of tuples}} = P(X \bigcap Y)$$

3.3 Direct Anonymization

Direct anonymization is to scan the count tree once and then use the generalized combinations to find a solution that optimizes problem of re-identification. Optimal Anonymization method is based on pre-computation of complete count tree for sets consisting of up to m item sets [1].Direct anonymization scans

Table 3. Algorithm Creation of the Tree for k^m-Anonymity

Populate Tree (D, tree, m)
1:**For all** t in D do for each transaction
2: expand t with the supported generalized items
3: **For all** combination of cm items in the expanded t do
4: **If¬∃** i,j ∈ c such that i generalizes j **then**
5: insert c in *tree*
6: increase the support counter of the final node

Table 4. Output of the Above Algorithm

Item	No. of occurences	Support	Item	No. of occurences	Support
Apple	1	0.5	VVD	1	0.142857142
PineApple	1	0.357142857	Orange	1	0.5
Dove	1	0.214285714	Aswini	1	0.571428571
Margo	1	0.142857142	ClincPlus	1	0.714285714
Lux	1	0.071428571	Chik	1	0.071428571

the tree to detect m-sized paths that have support less than k.For each such paths,it generates all possible generalization. In this direct anonymization, the database is scanned and a count tree is constructed. Once the count tree has been created; direct anonymization initializes the output generalization C_{out} as bottommost cut of the lattice (i.e. no generalization).Then performs preorder traversal of count tree. Based on the initial support count neglect the item sets whose support count is less than the initial. For every node encountered, if the item corresponding to that node has already been generalized in C_{out}, direct anonymization backtracks as all complete m-sized paths passing from there correspond to itemsets that will not appear in the generalized database based on C_{out} (and therefore their supports need not be checked).The algorithm corresponding to this process comprise of the first 11 steps of the Improved direct anonymization algorithm(Table 5 below).Due to shortage of space we do not reproduce it here.

3.4 FP-Growth Algorithm

Algorithm: We refer to the FP-growth(Han and Kamber [9]), which mines frequent itemsets using an FP-tree by pattern fragment growth.

4 The Proposed Algorithms

As mentioned earlier we improve the algorithm DA and FP-growth in order to reduce the generation of redundant transactions which makes the further analysis of the output eficient and simpler. First we present the improved DA algorithm below. We have added new steps from 12 to 25 in the existing algorithm.

4.1 Improved Direct Anonymization

Table 5. Algorithm Improved Direct Anonymization

Algorithm DA (D, I, k, m)	13. Initialize count=0
1: Scan D and create count-tree	14. Scan each transaction in C_{out}
2: Initialize C_{out}	15. Seperate each item in a transaction and
3:**For** each node v in preorder count-tree	and store it in p
tranversal do	16. Increment count.
4: **If** the item of v has been generalized	17.**For** j: =1 to count do
in C_{out} then	18. **For** all g belongs C_{out} do
5: backtrack	19. Compare each item of p with that of C_{out}
6: **If** v is a leaf node and v.count < k then	20. **If** all items of i equal to c_{out}
7: J: = item set corresponding to v	21. Increment r
8: find generalization of items in J that	22. **If** k_a equal to r then backtrack to i
make J k-anonymous	23. **Else if** r is greater than k_a then get the
9: merge generalization rules with C_{out}	index position of the similar transactions
10: backtrack to longest prefix of path J,	24. make them NULL until k_a equal to r
wherein no item has been generalized in	25. **Else** update the transactions in
C_{out}. 11.Return C_{out}	database, where k_a-anonymization value
12:**For** i:=1 to C_{out} d	

Table 6. Improved FP-Growth Algorithm

1:**Retrieve** C_{out} from database
2:**Procedure** FP growth(Tree,C_{out})
3:**If** Tree contains a single path P then
4:**For** each combination(denoted as β)of the nodes in the path P
5:Generate pattern $\beta \bigcup C_{out}$ with support_count=minimum support count of nodes in β;
6:**Else for** each a_i in the header of Tree
7:Generate pattern $\beta= a_i \bigcup C_{out}$ with support_count=a_i.support_count;
8:Construct β's conditional pattern base and then β's conditional FP_{tree} $Tree_\beta$
9:**If** Tree $\beta \neq \phi$ **then**
10:Call FP-growth($Tree_\beta,\beta$);
Where a_i=item in the transaction.

4.2 Improved FP-Growth Algorithm

Here we present the modified and improved FP-growth algorithm.

5 Comparison of the Algorithms

Here we representing the anonymized data using FP Tree.We are reducing the number of the duplicate trans- actions that are generated by the previous algorithm ie DA.

Table 7. Output of the Direct Anonymization Algorithm

Transaction ID	Generalized transactions	Transaction ID	Generalized transactions
1	fruit, shampoo, oil	14	oil, shampoo
2	oil, shampoo	15	fruit, shampoo, oil
3	fruit, shampoo,oil	16	fruit, soap, shampoo, oil
4	fruit, shampoo	17	fruit, shampoo, oil
5	fruit, shampoo,oil,	18	fruit, soap, shampoo
6	Fruit	19	fruit
7	fruit, shampoo,oil	20	oil
8	fruit, soap, shampoo, oil	21	shampoo, oil
9	shampoo, oil	22	fruit, shampoo
10	fruit, soap, shampoo	23	oil, shampoo
11	Oil	24	fruit, soap, shampoo
12	fruit, soap, shampoo,	25	oil, shampoo
13	fruit, soap, shampoo	26	fruit, soap, shampoo

Table 8. Output of the Direct Anonymization Algorithm

Transaction ID	Generalized Transactions	Transaction ID	Generalized Transactions
1	fruit, shampoo, oil	8	oil, shampoo
2	oil, shampoo	9	oil
3	fruit, shampoo	10	oil
4	fruit	11	fruit, shampoo, oil
5	fruit, soap, shampoo, oil	12	fruit, soap, shampoo, oil
6	fruit, soap, shampoo	13	fruit
7	fruit,soap,shampoo	14	fruit,shampoo

5.1   Experimental Analysis

We consider here a Supermarket database where there is a provision to add an item,add an transaction as well as to view the transactions.Here a database is created with limited number of transactions let us consider 10 transactions.

Database and Transaction in Database. We consider the Database and set of transaction in the Table 1 and Table 2 for our discussion in this section.

Output Using Eariler Algorithms. We implemented the following algorithms in NETBEANS IDE using JAVA SWINGS with backend technology as SQL SERVER. Outputs of both the algorithms are similar.

Output Based on New Approach. In this new approach, the number of duplicate transactions is decreased because the algorithm checks for all the conditions inorder to achieve k^m-anonymity completely. As said earlier the outputs are same for both algorithms.

Output of the Improved FP-Growth Algorithm. Let us consider a supermarket database of six transactions and perform the FP-Growth.This procedure will be applicable to even large database also.

Table 9. Transaction in the database

Transaction ID	Transactions Items	Generalized Transactions
1	Apple, Aswini, ClincPlus	fruit, shampoo, oil
2	Dove, ClincPlus, Aswini	oil, shampoo
3	Apple, Aswini, ClincPlus, Orange, Pineapple	fruit, shampoo, oil
4	ClinicPlus, Apple, Dove, Pineapple	fruit, shampoo
5	Aswini, ClincPlus, Orange	fruit, shampoo, oil
6	Apple, Orange, Pineapple	Fruit

Output of FP-TREE

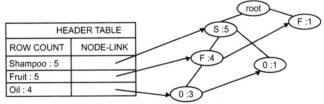

Fig. 1. Output of FP-Tree

6   Conclusions

In this paper we have improved the k^m-anonymity algorithms developed in [1] for anonymization of set-valued data. The algorithms in [3] generate many redundant transactions and it is very inconvenient for further analysis. The improved algorithms generate the exact number of tuples required for the generalisation.The anonymized data is used to construct the FP-tree which reduces the number of comparisions and provides an easy way to find the count of the generalized items in the transactions. This reduces the size of the output table considerably and makes it simpler for further analysis. We provided an example to illustrate the efficiency of the new algorithms over the existing algorithms. Also, theoretically we have computed the extent of improvement in the results.

References

1. Terrovitis, M., Mamoulis, N., Kalnis, P.: Privacy Preserving Anonymization of Set-Valued Data. In: PVLDB 2008, Auckland, New Zeland, pp. 115–125 (2008)
2. Sweeney, L.: K-Anonymity: A Model for Protecting Privacy. International Journal of Uncertainty, Fuzziness and Knowledge-based Systems 10(5), 557–570 (2002)
3. Li, N., Li, T., Venktasubramanian: t-closeness Privacy Beyond k-Anonymity and l-Diversity. In: Proceedings of ICDE, pp. 106–115 (2007)
4. Samarati, P.: Protecting Respondents Identities in Microdata Release. IEEE TKDE 13(6), 1010–1027 (2001)
5. Meyerson, A., Williams, R.: On the Complexity of Optimal k-Anonymity. In: Proceedings of ACM PODS, pp. 223–228 (2004)
6. Aggarwal, G., Feder, G., Kenthapadi, R., Motwani, R., Panigrahy, D., Thomas, Zhu, A.: Approximation Algorithms for k-Anonymity. Journal of Privacy Technology (2005)
7. Atzori, M., Bonchi, F., Giannotti, F., Pedreschi, D.: Anonymity Preserving Pattern Discovery. VLDB Journal (2008) (accepted for publication)
8. LeFevre, K., DeWitt, D.J., Ramakrishnan, R.: Incognito: Efficient Full-domain k-anonymity. In: Proceedings of ACM SIGMOD, pp. 49–60 (2005)
9. Han, J., Kamber, M., Pei, J.: Data mining: Concepts and Techniques Text Book

Cryptanalysis of Simplified-Data Encryption Standard Using Tabu Search Method

Rajashekarappa[1] and Soyjaudah K.M.S.[2]

[1] Department of Computer Science and Engineering,
JSS Academy of Technical Education Mauritius, Avenue Droopnath Ramphul,
Bonne Terre, Vacoas, Mauritius
rajashekarmb@gmail.com
[2] Dept. of Electrical and Electronic Engineering,
University of Mauritius, Reduit, Mauritius

Abstract. Cryptanalysis with Tabu Search method has attracted much interest in recent years. This paper presents an approach for the cryptanalysis of Simple Data Encryption Standard (S-DES) using Tabu Search method. In this paper, cipher text only attack is adopted and variety of optimum keys are generated based on the cost function values. S-DES keys can be found faster using the proposed approach. Tabu Search applications has been discussed in this paper. A Tabu Search algorithm has been implemented using a dynamically changing tabu tenure, a frequency based long term memory structure and an aspiration criterion. The experimental results indicate that, Tabu Search is a promising method and can be adopted to handle other complex block ciphers like DES.

Keywords: Cipher Text, Cipher Text Attack, Cryptanalysis, Plain Text, Simplified-Data Encryption Standard (S-DES), Tabu Search.

1 Introduction

Cryptography is the study of methods of sending messages in disguised form so that only intended recipients can remove the disguise and read the message. The process of converting a plaintext to cipher text is called enciphering and the reverse process is called deciphering. Cryptanalysis is the study of methods for obtaining the meaning of encrypted information, without access to the secret information which is normally required to do so. Cryptanalysis is one of the challenging research areas in the discipline of security. Typically, this involves finding the key that is used for disguising the message. An attack on Cipher text may be of various types. One type of attack namely Cipher text only attack is considered in this paper. In cipher text only attack, the encryption algorithm used and the cipher text to be decoded are known to cryptanalyst. This is the most difficult attack among the classes of attacks encountered in cryptanalysis. This paper considers cryptanalysis of S-DES ciphers. Though S-DES is a much simplified version of DES, Cryptanalysis of S-DES will give a better insight into the attack

K.R. Venugopal and L.M. Patnaik (Eds.): ICIP 2012, CCIS 292, pp. 561–568, 2012.
© Springer-Verlag Berlin Heidelberg 2012

of DES and other block ciphers [1]. In the brute force attack, the attacker tries every possible key on the piece of cipher text until an intelligible translation of the cipher text into plaintext is obtained. Cryptographic algorithms are designed to make the brute force attack almost infeasible. Generally, the key space considered by any secret key based algorithm is large enough so that it is not possible for an attacker to try every possible key. But, Tabu Search efficiently solves this problem without searching the entire key space. The objective of the study is to determine the efficiency and accuracy of Tabu Search algorithm for the cryptanalysis of SDES and compare the relative performance of Brute Force attack with tabu search. Hence, the focus of this work is breaking the S-DES key by conducting a directed random search of a key space using Tabu Search. Since Tabu Search are considered as one of the most efficient search techniques, this paper considers Tabu Search as a tool to solve the key breaking problem. Cryptanalytic attack on SDES belongs to the class of NP-hard problem. Due to the constrained nature of the problem, this paper is looking for a new solution that improves the robustness against cryptanalytic attack with high effectiveness.

The rest of the paper is or organized as follows: Section 2 discusses the earlier studies and works done in this area. Section 3 presents a brief overview of S-DES and Section 4 gives the overview of Tabu Search. Experimental results are discussed in Section 5. Finally, Conclusion and Future work are presented in section 6.

2   Related Work

The Tabu search is a widely used modern local search technique. Using cost function values as well as historical information (i.e., it uses memory of some form) enables the search to escape from local optima and to explore the search space in a productive fashion. Tabu search generally adopts a best improvement local search but moderates this policy using historical information [2].

For example, the actual cost associated with a solution could be made tabu. The search would be prevented from visiting solutions with the same cost function value for the tabu tenure. The tabu status of a move can be relaxed if taking that move would give rise to a particularly good solution, most typically a solution better than any reached so far (this is generally referred to as the aspiration criterion). Other aspects of history can also be taken into account, such as long-term frequencies of particular move types. The notion of influence is also used to guide the search; a move that causes greater change (measured in some fashion) is deemed to be more influential. Thus, influence criteria can be created and applied to diversify the search. An excellent discussion of tabu search is provided in the chapter on tabu search by Glover in Colin R. Reeves [2].

3   S-DES Algorithm

This section briefly gives the overview of S-DES Algorithm. The SDES encryption algorithm takes an 8-bit block of plaintext and a 10-bit key as input and produces an 8-bit block of ciphertext as output. The decryption algorithm takes an 8-bit block of ciphertext and the same 10-bit key used for encryption as input and produces the original 8-bit block of plaintext as output. The encryption algorithm uses five basic functions: 1. An initial permutation (IP). 2. A complex function called fK which involves both permutation and substitution operations and depends on a key input. 3. A simple permutation function (SW) that switches the two halves of the data. 4. The function fK a TS in and 5. A permutation function that is the inverse of the initial permutation (IP-1).The function fK takes as input the data passing through the encryption algorithm and an 8-bit key [4].

A. Key Generation

For key generation, a 10-bit key is considered from which two 8-bit sub keys are generated. In this case, the Key is first subjected to a permutation P10= [3 5 2 7 4 10 1 9 8 6], then a shift operation is performed. The numbers in the array represent the value of that bit in the original 10-bit key. The output of the shift operation then passes through a permutation function that produces an 8-bit output P8 =[6 3 7 4 8 5 10 9] for the first sub key (K1). The output of the shift operation also feeds into another shift operation and another instance of P8 to produce the second sub key K2. In all bit strings, the leftmost position corresponds to the first bit.

B. Encryption Algorithm

The encryption process involves the sequential application of five functions:

1. Initial and Final Permutation (IP): The input to the algorithm is an 8-bit block of plain text, which is first permuted using the IP function IP = [2 6 3 1 4 8 5 7]. This retains all 8-bits of the plain text but mixes them up. At the end of the algorithm, the inverse permutation is applied; the inverse permutation is done by applying, $IP^{-1} = [4 1 3 5 7 2 8 6]$ Where, $IP^{-1}(IP(X)) = X$.

2. Function fK: The function fk, which is the complex component of S-DES, consists of a combination of permutation and substitution functions. The functions are given as follows:
fK (L, R) = (L XOR f(R, key), R)where, L, R be the left 4-bits and right 4-bits of the input, XOR is the exclusive-OR operation and key is a sub-key. Computation of f(R, key) is done as follows.

1. Apply expansion/permutation E/P= [4 1 2 3 2 3 4 1] to input 4-bits.
2. Add the 8-bit key (XOR)
3. Pass the left 4-bits through S-Box S0 and the right4-bits through S-Box S1
4. Apply permutation P4 = [2 4 3 1]

The S-boxes operate as follows: The first and fourth input bits are treated as 2-bit numbers that specify a row of the S-box and the second and third input bits specify a column of the S box. The entry in that row and column in base 2 is the 2-bit output.

Table 1. S- Boxes

S0	S1
1032	0123
3210	2013
0213	3010
3132	2103

3. The Switch Function (SW): Since the function fK allows only the leftmost 4-bits of the input, the switch function (SW) interchanges the left and right 4-bits so that the second instance of fK operates on different 4-bits. In this second instance, the E/P, S0, S1 and P4 functions are the same as above but the key input is K2 [6].

4   Tabu Search

Any application of tabu search includes as a subroutine a local search procedure that seems appropriate for the problem being addressed. A local search procedure operates just like a local improvement procedure except that it may not require that each new trial solution must be better than the preceding trial solution. The process begins by using this procedure as a local improvement procedure in the usual way (i.e., only accepting an improved solution at each iteration) to find a local optimum [3]. A key strategy of tabu search is that it then continues the search by allowing non-improving moves to the best solutions in the neighborhood of the local optimum [8]. Once a point is reached where better solutions can be found in the neighborhood of the current trial solution, the local improvement procedure is re-applied to find a new local optimum.

This use of memory to guide the search by using tabu lists to record some of the recent history of the search is a distinctive feature of tabu search. This feature has roots in the field of artificial intelligence [7].

4.1   Outline of a Basic Tabu Search Algorithm

Initialization: Start with a feasible initial trial solution.

Iteration: Use an appropriate local search procedure to define the feasible moves into the local neighborhood of the current trial solution. Eliminate from consideration any move on the current tabu list unless that move would result in a better solution than the best trial solution found so far. Determine which of the remaining moves provides the best solution. Adopt this solution as the next trial solution, regardless of whether it is better or worse than the current trial solution. Update the tabu list to forbid cycling back to what had been the current trial solution. If the tabu list already had been full, delete the oldest member of the tabu list to provide more flexibility for future moves.

Cost Function: The ability of directing the random search process of the tabu search by selecting the fittest chromosomes among the population is the main characteristic of the algorithm. So the fitness function is the main factor of the algorithm. The choice of fitness measure depends entirely on the language characteristics must be known. The tabu search technique used to find the candidate key is to compare n-gram statistics of the decrypted message with those of the language (which are assumed known). Equation 1 is a general formula used to determine the suitability of a proposed key(k), here, K is known as language Statistics i.e., for English, [A,.......,Z],D is the decrypted message statistics, and u/b/t are the unigram, bigram and trigram statistics. The values of α, β and γ allow assigning of different weights to each of the three n-gram types where $\alpha + \beta + \gamma = 1$.

$$C_k \approx \alpha. \sum_{i \in A} |K_i^u - D_i^u| + \beta. \sum_{i,j \in A} |K_{i,j}^b - D_{i,j}^b| + \gamma. \sum_{i,j,k \in A} |K_{i,j,k}^t - D_{i,j,k}^t| \quad (1)$$

When trigram statistics are used, the complexity of equation (1) is O (P3) where P is the alphabet size. So it is an expensive task to calculate the trigram statistics. Hence we will use an assessment function based on bigram statistics only. Equation 1 is used as fitness function for tabu search attack. The known language statistics are available in the literature [2]. The size of the tabulist influences the performance of the algorithm. Two randomly chosen key elements are swapped to generate candidate solutions. In each iteration, the best new key formed replaces the worst existing one in the tabu list [9]. The algorithm is presented as below.

1. Input: Intercepted ciphertext, the key size P, and the language statistics.
2. Initialise parameters: The size of the tabu list STABU, the size of the list of possibilities considered in each iteration SPOSS, and the maximum number of iterations MAX.
3. Initialise the tabu list with random and distinct keys and calculate the cost for each key in the tabu list.
4. For I =1...., MAX do:
   (a) Find the best key with the lowest cost in the current tabulist, K_{BEST}.
   (b) For j=1...., SPOSS do:
      i. apply the perturbation mechanism to produce a new key K_{NEW}.
      ii. Check if K_{NEW} is already in the list of possibilities generated for this iteration or the tabu list. If so, return to step 4(b) i.
      iii. Add K_{NEW} to the list of possibilities for this iteration.
   (c) From the list of possibilities for this iteration, find the key with the lowest cost, P_{BEST}.
   (d) From the tabu list, find the key with the highest cost, T_{WORST}.
   (e) While the cost of P_{BEST} is less than the cost of T_{WORST}:
      i. Replace T_{WORST} with P_{BEST}.

  ii. Find the new P_{BEST}.

  iii. Find the new T_{WORST}

5. Output the best solution from the tabu list, K_{BEST} (the one with the least cost)

5   Experimental Setup and Results

A number of experiments is carried out to outline the effectiveness of Tabu Search. The Tabu Search algorithm is coded in MATLAB 7, and tested on more than 60 benchmark data sets adapted from literature [10]. Among the unigrams, bigrams and trigrams, Unigram is more useful and the benefit of trigram over digram is small.

For S-DES, the key size required is 10bits. The plain text and cipher text size are 8 bits. Initially, start with a feasible initial trial solution size of 40 is taken with a chromosome size of 10 bits i.e., 40 sets of 10 bit keys are taken randomly and the known cipher text is decrypted using the initial keys. The results are promising, yielding solutions between 60 and 112 seconds on a standard Intel Pentium Desktop computer with a 1.5GHz processor and 1GB of RAM. Four independent runs are executed for each of the 60 problems.

The parameters for TS areas follow in Table 2.

Table 2. Illustrates the Tabu Search Input Data

Initialization	40
Chromosome Size	10 bits
No. of Iteration	10
Mating Scheme	Best-Worst Mating

The total number of generations taken is 10. The key was recovered on an average of 5 generations. The size of the search space used by TS is only 40 where as in Brute-force attack, it is 65. Thus, in case of cryptanalysis using TS there is reduction in search space by a factor of 4 approximately. In the worst case the number of generations is increased to 15.

Table 3. Result Tabu Search and Brute-force attack

Time Taken for Tabu Search attack to attack S-DES	Time Taken for Brute-force attack to attack S-DES
4 Seconds	9 Seconds

The Table 3 depicts the time taken for Brute-force attack to attack S-DES is approximately 9 Seconds if 1 decryption /second was performed. But using TS the time taken is reduced to 4 Seconds. This is actually, a factor of half the time required to attack by Brute Force attack. In this section a number of experiments are carried out which outlines the effectiveness of both the algorithm described above. The purpose of these experiments is to compare the performance of Brute-force algorithm approach with tabu search approach for the cryptanalysis of simplified SDES algorithm. The experiments were implemented in MATLAB 7 on a Pentium IV(1.83 Ghtz). Experimental results obtained from these algorithms were generated with 100 runs per data point e.g. ten different messages were created for both the algorithms and each algorithm was run 10 times per message. The best result for each message was averaged to produce data point. This table 4 shows the average number of key elements (out of 10) correctly recovered versus the amount of cipher text and the computation time to recover the keys from the search space. The table shows results for amounts of cipher text ranging from 100 to 1000 character.

Glover [2] used TS to attack S-DES; the time taken is around 6 min. But in our approach, the time required is reduced and it is less than a minute to break the cipher SDES. This confirms that this method of Cryptanalysis of S-DES using TS can be extended to attack DES which uses 64 bit key size. The time taken for attacking the DES using Brute-Force technique is approximately 10 Hours if 56 bit key is considered and the encryption is done at 1 microsecond per encryption. Using TS the time taken can be reduced by at least by a factor of half, the time taken by Brute Force attack [5].

Table 4. The number of bits recovered from the key

Amount of Cipher Text	Tabu Search	
	Time(minutes)	Number of bits matched in the key
100	7.9	5
200	8.7	6
300	8.5	7
400	8.6	7
500	10.3	7
600	8.7	8
700	8.5	7
800	9.2	8
900	8.4	7
1000	8.8	9

6   Conclusions and Future Work

In this paper, Tabu Search for the cryptanalysis of Simplified Data Encryption Standard is presented. The time complexity of the proposed approach has been reduced drastically when compared to the Brute-Force attack. Though SDES is a simple encryption algorithm, this is a promising method and can be adopted to handle other complex block ciphers like DES and AES. The cost function values used here can be applied for other block ciphers also. The future works are extending this approach for attacking DES and AES ciphers.

References

1. Poonam, G.: Crypatanalysis of SDES via Evolutionary Computation Techniques. International Journal of Computer Science and Information Security 1(1) (May 2009)
2. Glover, F.: Tabu Search-Part I. ORSA Journal on Computing 2(1), 4–32 (1990)
3. Frederick, S., Gerald, J.L.: Introduction to Operations Research Concepts and Cases, 8th edn. McGraw-Hill (2009)
4. William, S.: Cryptography and Network Security Principles and Practices, 4th edn. McGraw-Hill (2003)
5. Behrouz, A.F.: Cryptography and Network Security, 1st edn. McGraw-Hill (2006)
6. James, K., Russell, E.: Particle Swarm Optimisation. In: Proceedings of the IEEE International Conference on Neural Networks, pp. 1942–1948 (1995)
7. Laguna, M., Barnes, W., Glover, F.: Intelligent Scheduling with Tabu Search: An Application to Jobs with Linear Delay Penalties and Sequence Dependent Setup Costs and Times. Journal of Applied Intelligence 3, 159–172 (1993)
8. Chanas, S., Kobylanski, P.: A New Heuristic Algorithm Solving the Linear Ordering Problem. Computational Optimization and Applications 6, 191–205 (1996)
9. Derisi, A., Donateo, D., Paolo, C., Ficarella, A.: A Combined Optimization Method for Common Rail Diesel Engines. In: Proceedings of 2002 Spring Technical Conference of the ASME Internal Combustion Engine Division, Rockford Illinois (2002)
10. Sommerville, L.: Software Engineering, 6th edn. Pearson Education, Asia (2006)

QoS Improvement Using NLMPC
for Congestion Control and Co-operative
Information Processing

M.V. Parulekar, V. Ramesh, Viraj Padte, Prerak Dalal, and Prajeet Nair

Research and Innovation Center,
Dwarkadas J. Sanghvi College of Engineering,
Plot No. U-15, J.V.P.D Scheme, Mumbai, India
mvparulekar@gmail.com

Abstract. Congestion control in packet switching networks for improved Quality of Service (QoS) is extensively needed in Inter-Vehicular and Vehicle to Infrastructure Communication due to deployment of the Dynamic Short Range Protocol for communication. We will be investigating the Non-linear Model Predictive Dynamic Matrix Control for modeling the stochastic nature of changing vehicular traffic dynamics (mobile nodes). In this Letter we also propose a modification in the leaky bucket algorithm for variable traffic flow rate and a reverse mapping of location input to GPS co-ordinate conversion to IP address conversion and then provide auto-routing for vehicles from source to destination. Distributed and centralized information processing and data logging for performance analysis computing will be deployed using LabVIEW for peer-to-peer communication, collision avoidance and QoS improvement by reducing congestion.

Keywords: Congestion Control, Dynamic Matrix Control, Dynamic Short range Communication, GPS routing, LabVIEW.

1 Introduction

Dynamic Matrix Control is a sub-class of Model Predictive Controllers [1, 2] where the primary advantage to any stochastic process input change or disturbance is the explicit handling of constraints. We will be using the Dynamic Matrix Control [2] to provide us with a constantly updated model for changing traffic scenarios. The stochastic nature of traffic based on Dynamic Short Range Communication Protocol (DSRC) [3, 4] provides a controller constraint where we can never predict how many cars will be forming a peer set. Hence we need to change the matrix parameters governing the speed, direction and position of a mobile node to update our model continuously at run time. Here we will be building our model based on optimization where our objective will be to continuously minimize the difference between our set point and the output actually obtained i.e. by employing Least Minimum Mean Square Error estimation. We will minimize the error between the predicted value and the output value using

K.R. Venugopal and L.M. Patnaik (Eds.): ICIP 2012, CCIS 292, pp. 569–577, 2012.
© Springer-Verlag Berlin Heidelberg 2012

which we will be manipulating our set-point of the mobile node continuously at run time. Here the calculated values will be valid for a prediction horizon say P time intervals however only the first time instant value will be actually used and a new model will be created from that value providing a continuous updating of our model and minimizing error as shown

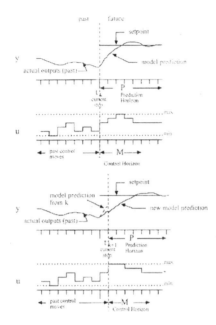

Fig. 1. Model Predictive Control - Basic concept of Prediction and Contol horizon

When this behavior is applied to packets or mobile nodes that are moving from say Node *A* to Node *B* based on optimization principles using either OSPF or EIGRP algorithms. They can deployed along with variable source quenching such that congestion is at its minimum, since the source even if bursts will be quenched without affecting flow rates from any other source. Also since the application is being created for smart traffic routing [4] it needs to be adaptive thus introducing our system to non-linearity. We hence propose for fig. 2 shown below an adaptive Non-Linear Model Predictive Dynamic Matrix Control to modify packet/traffic behavior characteristics. This will then be deployed on mobile nodes for smart traffic routing and minimizing congestion such that peer-to-peer communication will be possible and collision avoidance systems [5–8] can be deployed.

2   Dynamic Matrix Control for Collision Avoidance

Here we address issues related to control and co-ordination of peer set of cars where they will be making and breaking formations thus manipulating our

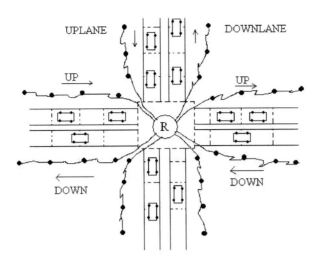

Fig. 2. Scenario of Centralised and Distributed Computing for Random Traffic Scenario

matrix controller input disturbances .Here the cars are required to follow a trajectory for transitioning from source to destination avoiding obstacles and negotiating with peers to set itself to the optimum set-point [3, 4]. Here we focus on the main problems of 1) speed, direction and position adjustment 2) Peer-to-Peer communication for information relay 3) Formation control for collision avoidance. The feedback is responsible for maintaining a safe distance from the peer cars failing which the failsafe manoeuvre [7] is executed and string stability [9, 10] of the entire system is maintained. We design a generalized system where each car is performing distributed computing to have say Np (prediction for N time slots) future outputs that match some optimum set-point by finding best values of Nc (controller action for N time slots) to manipulate our control variables. This is same as fitting Np data points with an equation with Nc coefficients.

Generalizing our model to consist of Nc parameters for Nc variables our performance index becomes

$$J = \sum_{i=1}^{Np} \left((yi - \tilde{yi})^2 \right) + \lambda^2 \sum_{k=1}^{Nc} (mk)^2 \ . \tag{1}$$

Using a partial derivative of J and generalizing these equations in matrix form we have :

$$\left[X^T X + \lambda^2 I \right] M = X^T Y \ . \tag{2}$$

The DMC algorithm finds the best values for the manipulated variables, Δm by minimizing a performance index J.

$$J = \sum_{i=1}^{Np}(yi - yi)^2 + \lambda^2 \sum_{k=1}^{Nc}(\Delta mi)^2 \tag{3}$$

$$= \sum_{i=1}^{N}\left\{ y^{set} - yoL, i - \sum_{k=1}^{Nc} wik(\Delta mk)^{new} \right\}^2 + \lambda^2 \sum_{k=1}^{Nc}(\Delta mi)^n \tag{4}$$

By Least Squares formulation we can write:

$$(\Delta m^{new}) = [A^T A + \lambda^2 I]^{-1} A^T Y \tag{5}$$

DMC Algorithm:

Calculate Np values of yoL, i from the past manipulated and present variables.
Calculate the Nc values of the future changes in the manipulated variables.
Implement the first change Δ m1.
Measure the controlled variable y^m at the next instant.
Repeat.

3   Reverse Mapping of Location to IP Using Domain Name Server and GPS

We are employing the same concept of Domain Name Server (DNS) for retrieving the IP address by just providing the input of source and destination location to the user. Here a GPS co-ordinate based IP address discovery [11] for high speed vehicular users is tested where the vehicles move from home location with an assigned IP address and reconfigure their IP address using DHCP [12] as a Foreign Agent (FA) or Care-of-Address (COA) after moving away from home location. Since these vehicles will be provided with an IPv6 number plate a stateless IP address auto-configuration will be deployed based on subnet prefix advertised by router and link local prefix using which a media redirect to the vehicle will be sent from the router as shown in fig.3 below.

Geocast [11] explains how IP address can be augmented with geographic address space using GPS coordinates [13]. Geographical Routing of messages can be obtained by using a GPS Multicast or extended DNS. Using this methodology vehicular and base station positions can be a-priori obtained for adaptive and ad-hoc routing to inform vehicles about their new prospective location and the optimum least cost path.

3.1   Navigational Control Using GPS, IP and LabVIEW

The figures(4-5) below shows the mapping of location say Source: Mumbai, Destination: Bangalore into IP address and then changes Source IP using stateless auto-configuration to adapt to new Care-off address (COA) and then routing using hops at various routers that exist between source and destination.

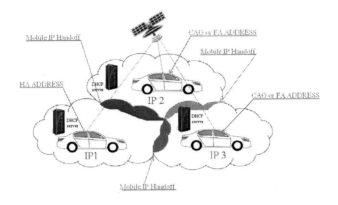

Fig. 3. DHCP in different Cells after Mobile IP Handoff

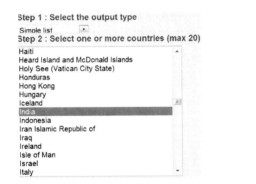

Fig. 4. Select Country of Vehicle Location

Fig. 5. IP Address Block Assigned to India

4   Modelling of Stochastic Traffic Flow Based on Variable Leaky Bucket Algorithm

The Leaky Bucket Algorithm is used in packet switched networks to check if the data transmissions conform to defined limits on bandwidth and burstiness (a measure of unevenness or variations in traffic flow). The leaky bucket algorithm is also used in leaky bucket counters, to detect when the average or peak rate of the source has been violated. The modified leaky bucket algorithm will accept unregulated and random flow of packets (vehicles in our case) and give a regulated and stable output flow. The algorithm is adaptive and hence when the bucket is 70 percent full, it will inform the sender and the flow will be reduced by quenching the source. This process will be repeated until a stable flow is obtained which will not overflow the bucket. The figure 8 below shows the

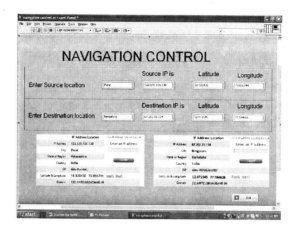

Fig. 6. Navigational Control using IP Addressing GPS and LabVIEW

description for a sequence of events for modeling the traffic flow and its graphical implementation using java applet.

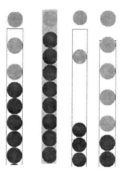

Fig. 7. Modified Leaky Bucket in Java Applet as per given Condition

The description for the sequence of events is as given below:
Normal Steady State - Unregulated related Traffic flow
Buffer 50 percent full - Traffic Policing Initiated.
Buffer 75 percent full -Variable Leaky Bucket initialized.
Buffer 90 percent - Traffic is regulated.
Traffic restored to normal state after congestion is overcome.

On 75 percent full, a warning is dispatched to violating source to reduce traffic flow and Variable Leaky Bucket initialized.Then when the buffer is 90 percent full,the traffic is regulated by quenching source, providing new route and adapting to a new flow rate.

This provides us with modelling the traffic packets or vehicular users to adhere to pre-agreed flow parameters however it would be constraint if a vehicular breakdown has led to the congestion in which case the traffic conditions would not be updated such that they are given a priority scheduling. This requires again a a-priori information of events taken place to be multicasted to all users on that route.

5   Data Logging Using Hardware Implementation

Experimental results for data logging were based on a test vehicle-Hyundai Santro for data logging and monitoring the temperature of engine, temperature of the cabin, speed of the car and date of occurrence of event to the accuracy of millisecond real time clock and its x-y axis tilt using a accelerometer is also being recorded by LabVIEW [14] for further analysis. Fig 10 shows all the actual logged data values in run time test and Fig.11 shows graphical analysis of speed v/s time and X-Y axis tilt for accelerometer.

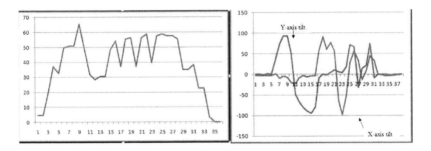

Fig. 8. Speed vs Time and Graph 2- X-Y axis Tilt Measurement using Accelerometer Output

6   Vehicle Position Tracking Using Arduino and LabVIEW

The block diagram of the vehicle tracking system for the car developed using LabVIEW, Arduino Board, magnetic is shown below:

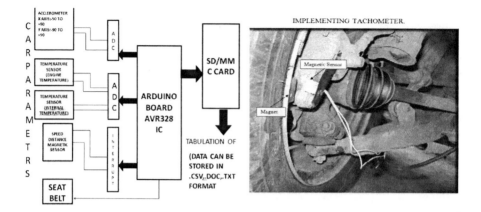

Fig. 9. Block Diagram for Vehicle Tracking and Hardware Interface using Magnetic Sensor

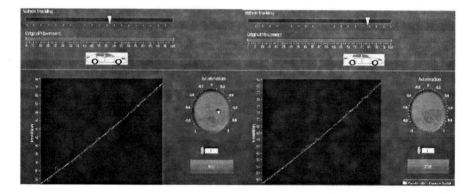

Fig. 10. Vehicle Tracking Using LabVIEW

7   Conclusions

We have formulated the Dynamic Matrix Control Algorithm for MPC analysis using which stochastic flows of traffic can been modelled. The modified leaky bucket algorithm has been implemented for bursty traffic. We have provided a reverse mapping of location to IP to GPS using DNS and LabVIEW. Navigational Control using LabVIEW and modified leaky bucket algorithm has been implemented. Auto-routing using OSPF algorithm has been implemented on Matlab for route optimization. Data logging with hardware implementation has been completed using which distributed control for collision avoidance will be executed.

8 Further Work

Currently work is underway on indoor mapping using image processing where camera positioning would be used to relay co-ordinates to vehicles. Also since all data is sent wirelessly security and integrity of wireless data is a major cause of concern as frames are viable to be corrupted and also ability to discard opposite lane information is being carried out. High gain omni-directional microstrip antenna array is currently being designed along with the onboard Single board computer for interface with navigation maps. Swarm logic control will be our next step where genetic algorithms designed by nature to create a semblance in swarms will be deployed such that the control will be robust as well as cohesive with the importance of human life in a scenario where we would let the car take decisions but at the same time make it responsible to be failure proof.

References

1. Wayne Bequette, B.: Non-Linear Predictive Control using Multi-rate Sampling. The Canadian Journal of Chemical Engineering 69(1), 136–143 (1991)
2. http://www.ni.com/labview/
3. Huang, Q., Miller, R., McNeille, P., Dimeo, D., Roman, G.-C.: Development of a Peer-to-Peer Collision Warning System. Ford Technical Journal 5(2) (March 2002)
4. Rappaport, T.S., et al.: Position Location using Wireless Communication on Highways of Future. IEEE Communications Magazine, 33–41 (October 1996)
5. Wayne Bequette, B.: Process Control: Modeling, Simulation and Design. Prentice Hall (2003) ISBN: 0-13-353640-8
6. Xu, Q., Sengupta, R., Jiang, D.: Design and Analysis of Highway Safety Communication Protocol in 5.9Ghz DSRC. Proceedings IEEE VTC 57(4), 2451–2455 (2003)
7. Biswas, S., Raymond, T., Francois, D.: Vehicle-to-Vehicle Wireless Communication Protocol for Enhancing highway Traffic Safety. Proceedings IEEE Communication Magazine 44(1), 74–82 (2006)
8. Desai, J.P., Ostrowski, J.P., Kumar, V.: Modeling and Control of Formations of Nonholonomic Mobile Robots. IEEE Transactions on Robotics and Automation 17(6), 905–908 (2001) ISSN- 1042-296X
9. Fierro, R., Das, A.K., Kumar, V., Ostrowski, J.P.: Hybrid Control of Formation of Robots. In: IEEE International Conference on Robotics and Automation, Proceedings 2001 ICRA (2001)
10. Swaroop, D., Hedrick, J.K.: String Stability of Interconnected Systems. IEEE Transactions Automatic Control 41, 349–357 (1996)
11. National Highway Traffic Safety Administration, "Automotive Collision Avoidance Systems (ACAS)
12. Yanakiev, D., Kanellakopoulos, I.: A Simplified Framework for String Stability in AHS. Preprints of the 13th IFAC World Congress, vol. Q, pp. 177–182 (1996)
13. GPS based Addressing and Routing-RFC (2009)
14. McAuley, A. et al.: Dynamic Rapid Configuration Protocol, IETF Draft RFC 2131 updated by 4361

Modeling Access Permissions in Role Based Access Control Using Formal Concept Analysis

Ch. Aswani Kumar

School of Information Technology and Engineering
VIT University, Vellore 632014, India
cherukuri@acm.org

Abstract. One of the most popular access control model is Role Based Access Control (RBAC). The main aim of this paper is to model the access permissions of various roles in RBAC using mathematical lattice approach, Formal Concept Analysis (FCA).

Keywords: Access control models, FCA, RBAC.

1 Introduction

Access control is an important security concern in information, computer and network security. Role Based Access Control (RBAC) is a form of mandatory access policy that supports function based access control [1]. The main components of RBAC are Users, Roles, Permissions, Data items and Sessions. RBAC controls all access to the resources, through the roles assigned to the users where each role assign a collection of permissions. The main advantage of RBAC is that it supports data abstraction, seperation of duties and least previlege [2]-[3]. The roles in RBAC form a hierarchy based on the permission inheritance. The relation between the components of RBAC can be represented in the form of an access control matrix. Recently lattice theory has become popular under the framework of Formal Concept Analysis (FCA). The main feature of FCA is the discovery of formal concepts, derive the hierarchical partial order among the discovered concepts and visualize them as concept lattice [4]. Lattices have been proved and widely used for implementing access control policies by interpreting the access control matrix as a formal context. Recently there are growing interests to use FCA for modeling and implementing RBAC [5]. In this paper we model the access permissions in RBAC using FCA. We show them as a lattice structure and derive the dependencies among them.

2 Background

Research on RBAC is recently intensified due to its potential in reducing the complexity and costs of access control administration. Sandhu et al., [1] have provided a detailed discussion on RBAC. Kuhn et al., [6] have demonstrated how RBAC can be implemented using traditional multilevel security systems.

K.R. Venugopal and L.M. Patnaik (Eds.): ICIP 2012, CCIS 292, pp. 578–583, 2012.
© Springer-Verlag Berlin Heidelberg 2012

Ma et al., [7] have designed a role hierarchy with constraints in RBAC. FCA support knowledge representation and discovery. From the data represented as formal context, FCA finds set of formal concepts, where each concept contains a set of objects and set of attributes which relate each other. All these concepts are partially ordered and forms a complete lattice. A very good illustration of the FCA and its applications, can be found in [8]-[14] and references therein.

Priss [15] has reviewed FCA research for security and demonstrated the use of FCA for analyzing Unix system data. Obiedkov et al., [16] have performed attribute exploration from FCA to build a lattice structure based access control model. Dau and Knechtel [2] have formalized a RBAC control matrix as a triadic security context and derived different dyadic contexts to conduct attribute exploration. Further they have applied Description Logic to formalize RBAC. Recently Sobieski and Zielinski [5] have modeled the role hierarchy for RBAC from the access control matrix using FCA.

3   Modeling Access Permissions Using FCA

An RBAC matrix contains set of roles (R), set of documents (D) and set of access permissions (P). This three dimensional matrix can be formalized as a triadic formal context $K_{R,D,P} = (R, D, P, I)$ [17]. By interpreting RBAC matrix as formal context in which the formal attributes are set of elements of access permissions and cross product of user roles and data items as formal objects, we can apply FCA process. We can derive the dyadic contexts from the triadic security contexts either by slicing or by the cross product of two sets among R,D,P [2].

With slicing we can derive dyadic contexts from two sets by fixing a value from the third set, i.e. for a particular $p \in P$, we can derive a dyadic context $K_{R,D}^p = (R, D, I^p)$. However slicing will narrow down the analysis only to any two sets. Applying cross product on any two of the above three sets, we can derive six dyadic contexts such as $K_{R \times D,P}$, $K_{P \times D,R}$, $K_{R \times P,D}$ etc. Our objective is to model the access permissions. Hence we apply the cross product on the sets: Roles and Data items. So we create dyadic context $K_{R \times D,P}$ having the access permissions as attributes and the cross product of roles and data items as objects.

4   Illustration

We consider a rural healthcare unit operations [18]. Different data items including Family Folders (FF) etc, different roles (R) that include Office Assistant etc are listed in Table 1. The access permissions (P) are Create, Input, Modify, Verify, Delete. Table 1 lists access permissions on data items for each of the roles. These details form a triadic context $K_{R,D,P} = (R, D, P, I)$. We show a sample triadic context in Table 2, containing three roles (OA, HV and MCU), three data items D_1, D_2 and D_3 and three access permissions (Input, Modify and Delete). From this context, we can understand that the role OA has Input permission on the data items D_1 and D_2. To apply FCA on the context, we transform the triadic context into dyadic context $K_{R \times D, P}$. Table 3 shows the dyadic context having the access permissions as attributes and the cross product of roles and data items as objects. Generally a single role can not possess all the access permissions on all the data items. However from Table 1 we can understand that the Basic Health Unit In-charge can have all the access permissions on all the data items during emergency. In order to incorporate this constraint, we have added an extra attribute emergency in the formal context.

Table 1. Roles and their Permissions on Different Data Items

No.	Role	Functions
1	Office Assistant	Input data into Family folders
2	Health Visitor	Input Modify mother nutrition chart, Vaccination information for children
3	MCU In-Charge	Create & Delete family folders in addition to functions of Office Assistant and Health Visitor
4	Nurse	InputModify In-Patient Record
5	OT In-Charge	Input Modify OT Record
6	Doctor	Create Modify Delete In-Patient & OT record,Input Prescription and all the functions of Nurse and OT-In Charge
7	Accountant	Input all the health unit transactions and create ledger reports
8	Accounting Manager	Modify ledger reports in addition to all the accountant functions
9	Internal Auditor	Verify all the transactions and Ledger reports
10	Basic health unit In-Charge	Perform all the above operations in emergency

The concept lattice structure, containing 10 concept nodes is shown in Figure 1. Each node of the lattice structure indicates a concept. The bottom node of the structure indicates a specialization while the top node indicates a generalization. From the roles and the access permissions listed in the Table 3, we can understand that during emergency, a BHU Incharge will have all the access permissions on all the data items. This specialization is represented in the form of bottom node shown in the lattice. Since there is no attribute (access permission) common to all the objects, the generalized node at the top of the lattice is blank.

The partial ordering hierarchy among the roles produces a permission inheritance up or down the ordering. In the Figure 1, roles at a node inherit the permissions from the roles above it, provided there is a path between the both. For e.g. the node just above left side of the bottom node indicate that a Doctor can delete OTR and IPR records. Based on the permission inheritance disccused above, we can infer from the lattice that the Doctor can create, input and modify these two records. The partial order hierarchy on the roles reduces the allocation of access permissions to the roles. We can verify that Accounting Manager is having the permissions to create, input and modify. Only the Internal Auditor has permission to verify. Table 4 lists DG basis of implications. From the first

Table 2. A sample Triadic Context

| | OA | | | HV | | | MCU | | |
	D_1	D_2	D_3	D_1	D_2	D_3	D_1	D_2	D_3
Input	X	X		X			X		
Modify	X		X		X	X	X	X	X
Delete	X		X		X	X	X		

implication we can understand that a role that has the permissions to Create, Input and Modify is also having the permission to Delete. All the other implications can be understood analogously. The three dimensional RBAC matrix can be interpreted as context and transformed appropriately to apply FCA. An important issue is to handle the large size RBAC formal contexts. Investigations in this direction can be found in FCA literature [4][14][19]. The lattice and the attribute implications model the access permissions and their dependencies.

Table 3. Dyadic Security Context

	Create	Input	Modify	Verify	Delete	Emergency
(OA, FF)		X				
(HV, MNC)		X	X			
(HV, VI)		X	X			
(MCI,FF)	X	X	X		X	
(NUR,IPR)		X	X			
(OTI,OTR)		X	X			
(DOC,IPR)	X	X	X		X	
(DOC,OTR)	X	X	X		X	
(DOC,PRE)	X	X				
(ACC,HUT)		X				
(ACC,LR)	X					
(ACM,LR)	X		X			
(ACM,HUT)	X	X				
(IA,HUT)				X		
(IA,LR)				X		
(BHU,FF)	X	X	X	X	X	X
(BHU,MNC)	X	X	X	X	X	X
(BHU,VI)	X	X	X	X	X	X
(BHU,IPR)	X	X	X	X	X	X
(BHU,OTR)	X	X	X	X	X	X
(BHU,PRE)	X	X	X	X	X	X
(BHU,HUT)	X	X	X	X	X	X
(BHU,LR)	X	X	X	X	X	X

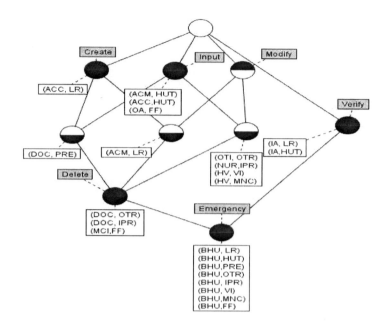

Fig. 1. Modeling Access Permissions As Concept Lattice

Table 4. Implications Representing Dependencies Between Access Permissions

No.	Implications
1	Create, Input, Modify→ Delete
2	Delete → Create, Input, Modify
3	Emergency →Create, Input, Modify, Verify, Delete
4	Create, Verify →Input, Modify,Delete,Emergency
5	Input, Verify →Create, Modify, Delete, Emergency
6	Modify, Verify →Create, Input, Delete, Emergency

5   Conclusions

In this paper our aim is to model the access permissions in RBAC using FCA. We have transformed the three dimensional RBAC matrix to a dyadic security context where the access permissions are the attributes and the cross product of roles, data items are the objects. The resultant lattice and the implications model the access permissions.

Acknowledgments. Author acknowledges the support from NBHM, DAE, Govt. of India under the grant 2/48(11)2010-R&D 11/10806.

References

1. Sandhu, R., Coyne, E.J., Feinstein, H., Youman, C.: Role Based Access Control Models. IEEE Computer 29(2), 38–47 (1996)
2. Dau, F., Knechtel, M.: Access Policy Design Supported by FCA Methods. In: Rudolph, S., Dau, F., Kuznetsov, S.O. (eds.) ICCS 2009. LNCS, vol. 5662, pp. 141–154. Springer, Heidelberg (2009)
3. Bertino, E.: RBAC Models-Concept and Trends. Computers & Security 22(6), 511–514 (2003)
4. Aswani Kumar, C.: Knowledge Discovery in Data using Formal Concept Analysis and Random Projections. International Journal of Applied Mathematics and Computer Science 21(4), 745–756 (2011)
5. Sobieski, S., Zielinski, B.: Modelling Role Hierarchy Structure using The Formal Concept Analysis. Annals UMCS Informatica 2, 143–159 (2010)
6. Kuhn, D.R., Coyne, E.J., Weil, T.R.: Adding Attributes to Role Based Access Control. IEEE Computer 43(6), 79–81 (2010)
7. Ma, X., Li, R., Lu, Z., Wang, W.: Mining Constraints in Role Based Access Control. Mathematical and Computer Modeling 55, 87–96 (2012)
8. Ganter, B., Wille, R.: Formal Concept Analysis: Mathematical foundations. Springer (1999)
9. Stumme, G.: Formal Concept Analysis. In: Handbook of Ontologies, pp. 177–199. Springer (2009)
10. Aswani Kumar, C., Srinivas, S.: Mining Associations in Health Care Data using Formal Concept Analysis and Singular Value Decomposition. Journal of Biological Systems 18(4), 787–807 (2010)
11. Aswani Kumar, C., Srinivas, S.: Concept Lattice Reduction using Fuzzy k Means Clustering. Expert Systems with Applications 37(3), 2696–2704 (2010)
12. Aswani Kumar, C.: Mining Association Rules Using Non-Negative Matrix Factorization and Formal Concept Analysis. In: Venugopal, K.R., Patnaik, L.M. (eds.) ICIP 2011. CCIS, vol. 157, pp. 31–39. Springer, Heidelberg (2011)
13. Priss, U.: Formal Concept Analysis in Information Science. Annual Review of Information Science and Technology 40(1), 521–543 (2007); Snasel, V., Polovincak, M., Dahwa, H.M., Horak, Z.: On Concept Lattices and Implication Bases from Reduced Contexts. In: Proc. of ICCS Supplement, pp. 83-90 (2008)
14. Aswani Kumar, C.: Fuzzy Clustering Based Formal Concept Analysis for Association Rules Mining. Applied Artificial Intelligence 26(3), 274–301 (2012)
15. Priss, U.: Unix Systems Monitoring with FCA. In: Andrews, S., Polovina, S., Hill, R., Akhgar, B. (eds.) ICCS 2011. LNCS (LNAI), vol. 6828, pp. 243–256. Springer, Heidelberg (2011)
16. Obiedkov, S., Derrick, G.K., Eloff, J.H.P.: Building Access Control Models with Attribute Exploration. Computers & Security 28(1-2), 2–7 (2009)
17. Belohlavek, R., Osicka, P.: Triadic Concept Analysis of Data with Fuzzy Attributes. In: Proceedings of IEEE International Conference on Granular Computing, pp. 661–665 (2010)
18. Memon, Q.A.: Implementing Role Based Access in Healthcare Ad Hoc Network. Journal of Networks 4(3), 192–199 (2009)
19. Singh, P.K., Aswani Kumar, C.: A Method for Reduction of Fuzzy Relation in Fuzzy Formal Context. In: Balasubramaniam, P., Uthayakumar, R. (eds.) ICMMSC 2012. CCIS, vol. 283, pp. 343–350. Springer, Heidelberg (2012)

A Hybrid Fractal-Wavelet Digital Watermarking Technique with Localized Embedding Strength

M. Jayamohan and K. Revathy

Department of Computer Science
University of Kerala, Kariavattom, Trivandrum 695 581, India
jmohanm@gmail.com

Abstract. We propose a hybrid image watermarking technique making use of the advantages of fractal theory and wavelet transforms. Generally, the strength of watermarking is set to be a fixed value for the entire image. In our work the strength of watermarking in cover image is customized according to the complexity of image portions. The image is separated into complex and smooth regions based on fractal dimension. Fractal dimension measured with differential box counting (DBC) method is used to estimate the complexity of image portions. A higher value of embedding strength is used for complex regions, whereas a smaller embedding strength for smooth regions which are more sensitive to human vision system. Results show that the method produces imperceptible watermarks with higher detector response.

Keywords: Digital Watermarking, Fractal, Wavelet.

1 Introduction

Image watermarking is the technique of hiding data within an image, in order to ensure copyright protection, source authentication, or for sending a secret message. The strength of a watermarking technique is evaluated by its invisibility, robustness and recoverability. Though there are visible watermarks like those used in printed materials or television displays, digital image watermarks are designed to be completely imperceptible. The watermark must be scattered throughout the image in such a way that they cannot be identified and manipulated. Except for some very early watermarking schemes, all robust watermarking algorithms operate in a transform domain that offers access to the frequency components of the host image. In the embedding stage, the host image is first transformed to a domain that facilitates data embedding. A selected subset of the transform coefficients are modified with the prepared signature data. The inverse transform is applied on the modified coefficients to get the watermarked image. The choice of the host features and the definition of the embedding rule have implications on watermark robustness and imperceptibility.

K.R. Venugopal and L.M. Patnaik (Eds.): ICIP 2012, CCIS 292, pp. 584–591, 2012.
© Springer-Verlag Berlin Heidelberg 2012

2   Fractal Encoding

The fractal image encoding theory is developed based on the concept of Iterated Function Systems (IFS) [1]. Barnsley used IFS for image encoding [2]. The current investigations in fractal encoding are rooted in Jacquin's Partitioned Iterated Function Systems (PIFS) [3], finding self-similarity among portions within the image. The image is first partitioned into fixed sized non-overlapping blocks called range blocks. A set of larger blocks called domain blocks are taken from the same image in order to check for similarity. A best-matching domain is found out for each range block. The matching is based on various features like mean square error [4]-[5]. Contractive affine transformations in both spatial and luminance aspects are derived to transform the domain blocks to their corresponding range blocks. Affine transformation coefficients that maps each domain block to its matching range block along with the spatial information required for each partition constitute the compressed image information.

2.1   Fractal Watermarking

Many researchers have attempted to use fractal encoding concepts to image watermarking. Puate and Jordan proposed to insert a digital signature, which is a short-length (32 bit) binary data, into an image using fractal theory [6]. The method is robust against low-pass filtering, and to a good extent to JPEG compression. It is infeasible to find out the presence of watermark bits. Using the entire domain blocks in the image instead of local search region might increase the robustness of the signature as well as the retrieving reliability. Bas et al., [7] used artificial similarities to embed watermark bits. Kamal [8] gives a detailed study of the fractal watermarking, using the same basic approach of Puate [6] in his methods.

An advantage of the fractal techniques over other methods is that it is infeasible to identify watermark bits in the cover image in fractal techniques. Though the methods are resistant to image processing attacks like compression and filtering, they are vulnerable to geometric attacks like cropping, as well as the variations in brightness and contrast.

2.2   Fractal Dimension

Fractal dimension has been used as an efficient indicator of shape information and texture complexity of an image. There are various techniques for measuring fractal dimension of images. The most popular and straight forward method is box counting. According to the box counting theorem [2], the image is assumed to be covered with closed square boxes of size $1/2^n$. Let $N(A)$ denote the number of boxes of side length $1/2^n$, which intersects the attractor. Then A has the fractal dimension **D**, if

$$D = lim_{n \to \infty} \frac{log(N(A))}{log 2^n} \tag{1}$$

The value of **FD** will be stable over a pure fractal image. But natural images are not having pure fractal nature. Hence if we estimate fractal dimensions of local areas of the image, it will be different from the FD of the entire image, and the results may vary depending on the local texture variations.

Sarkar and Choudhari [9] use an improved approach to determine the fractal dimension of images, known as differential box-counting (DBC), taking into account the graylevel values of pixels in each box. The image is viewed as a terrain surface of graylevel plot. Let an $m \times m$ image be covered with boxes of size $b \times b$. Let $r = m/b$ be the ratio of partitioning. (If box size is half of the image, $r = \frac{1}{2}$). Let L be the maximum graylevel and l be the minimum graylevel value of pixels in a box (i, j). Then the number of boxes is counted as

$$N_r = \Sigma n_r(i, j) \tag{2}$$

where $n_r(i,j) = L - l + 1$. Conci & Campos have improvised the method with minor modifications in DBC [10]. When the method is used, we get the fractal dimension of graylevel images generally in [2.0, 3.0].These works [9]-[10] show that fractal dimension can be used to identify texture variations in images.

3   Wavelet Transforms in Watermarking

The excellent spatio-frequency localization properties of the discrete wavelet transform makes it well suited to identify areas in the cover image where a watermark can be imperceptibly embedded. The most of the energy of the image is concentrated in the low-frequency approximation of the carrier image after wavelet decomposition. It is the smooth part of the image and the human eye is more sensitive to it. Hence embedding watermark into the approximation coefficients may result in perceptible distortions in the cover image. So, in order to meet transparency and robustness requirements, the watermark is normally embedded in the second or third level of wavelet coefficients which has medium frequency characteristics.

Dugad et al., [11] have investigated the possibilities of watermarking in wavelet transform coefficients. The idea is to select coefficients in DWT domain above a threshold. The amount of watermark added is adapted to the image, so that less amount of watermark is added to smooth images and more to more complex images. A three level DWT with a Daubechies 8-tap filter of the cover image is taken. Watermark is added to all coefficients in the sub-bands except low-pass, which are above a given threshold. The method is more resistant than DCT based methods to image processing attacks including cropping. The major advantage of using DWT is the implicit visual masking due to the time-frequency localization property of wavelets. Setting a threshold for selecting coefficients remains a matter of concern. Podilchuk and Zeng [12] use the just noticeable difference (JNC) to determine an image dependant perceptible mask for watermarking. The method has been applied in both DWT and DCT domains. The method does not take into account the perceptual significant regions, thus the watermark can be erased from the insignificant coefficients. So the method is vulnerable against filtering attacks. Xia et al., [13] proposed an algorithm for watermarking in second level decomposition coefficients using Haar wavelets. The coefficients in detail subbands are used for watermark embedding. This increases the invisibility of watermark, since detail subbands corresponds to edges and textures which are less sensitive to human visual system. Detection is made using the intercorrelation between original watermark and the difference of the two images. Kundur and Hatzinakos [14]-[15] use quantization for embedding the watermark bits. A reference watermark is used to estimate whether the watermark bits have been embedded.

Barni et al., [16] use the texture and luminance content of all the image subbands to mask a watermark. The image is decomposed into 4 levels using Daubechies-6 mother wavelet. The watermark strength is varied across various layers of the image. Highest level of strength is used for image contours, a medium strength for textures a lower strength for regions with high regularity which is more sensitive to human visual system. The texture activity around a pixel is composed of the product of the local mean square value of DWT coefficients in all detail subbands and the local variance of the forth level approximation image. Both are calculated in a small 2×2 neighbourhood of each pixel. Detection is made using correlation between the marked DWT coefficients and the watermarking sequence to be tested for presence. Barni's method is robust against image processing attacks like filtering, compression, cropping etc. The disadvantage is that it is easy to erase the watermark since it is embedded in the last resolution level only.

4   Hybrid Methods

Ni and Ruan [17] have made a significant step forward in using fractal theory effectively in digital watermarking in wavelet domain. Featured regions are extracted from the image using fractal dimension based estimates. The watermark is scaled to match the region of interest in the image. The ROI is determined by the user and is mapped to the wavelet decomposition subbands. Shahraeini and Yaghoobi [18], tried to search similarities using fractal mappings, among the coefficients obtained after applying DWT on the cover image.

5   Embedding Strength

Watermarking in transform domains use a parameter α defined as the embedding strength for embedding the watermark bits into the cover image. A general basic expression for watermarking is [11][16][19]

$$V_i' = V_i + \alpha \mid V_i \mid x_i \tag{3}$$

where V_i is the DWT coefficient (or DCT) of original image and V_i' is that of the watermarked image. x_i is the watermark value at the position of V_i. The transparency of watermark depends on the value of the coefficient α chosen. If

α is high the watermark turns to be perceptible as it increases the contribution of watermark in the new embedded image. But, higher the value of α, the watermark will be more robust to image processing attacks including compression and filtering. Increasing the embedding strength α causes the PSNR of the watermarked image to decrease. That is when α is increased the watermarking results in perceptible distortions [20]. Generally, for a PSNR of 30dB or more, the original image and the watermarked one are considered indistinguishable. Since high values of α gives more robust data hiding, but with visible distortion in the cover image, the choice of α is a matter of concern. Using different strength values (α) for image separations like image contours, edges, redundant portions etc. have been investigated [16].

6   Proposed Method

We propose to decide the value of embedding strength α, based on the complexity of image portions. Different values of α will be used for different regions over the cover image. Fractal dimension can be used as an estimate of the complexity of image. Selection of α will be based on the local fractal dimension of the image portions.

The basic box counting algorithm [2] cannot be used to measure the complexity of grayscale or color images, since the value of FD estimated depends on the threshold chosen to convert the given image to binary. The Differential Box Counting method [10] has proven to be a better estimate as it uses the distribution of intensity levels over the image surface to count the number of boxes. Improvements have been suggested over the DBC to make it a better measure for texture and complexity [21]-[22].

In order to embed a watermark first the image is be divided into blocks, square sized for computational convenience. The size of the block can be in proportion to the image size. The local fractal dimension (LFD) of each block shall be computed using DBC. The image blocks are separated into two pools based on the LFD values. Complex regions over the image will be having higher values for LFD and blocks with smaller LFD represent smooth portions. Two different levels of α can be used for embedding watermark into image portions in these two pools. Since the complex portions are less sensitive to HVS than smooth portions, one can use a higher value of α for complex regions and the watermark can be embedded lighter in smooth portions.

The three level wavelet decomposition of the image blocks are computed using Db2 mother wavelets. Third level coefficients have medium frequency characteristics and hence gives optimum performance for robustness and transparency requirements. The computational complexity for db2 is less compared to other wavelet filters in db series, since the convolution process consumes less time as the number of filter coefficients decrease. The watermark image is also transformed using DWT. The watermark is to be embedded into all coefficients of detailed subbands.

7   Experimental Results

Watermark detection uses a symmetric process. Pearson's correlation coefficient is measured to detect the watermark. The performance has been compared with that proposed by [16] and [18].The peak signal-to-noise ratio is used as a measure of imperceptibility. Table 1. shows the PSNR values obtained against 10 images watermarked with the selected methods and the new one. The watermarked image was given to different attacks including cropping, rotation, noising (Gaussian noise), filtering and JPEG Compression and histogram equalization. The original and extracted watermarks have been compared using Pearson's correlation coefficient. The results are shown in Table 2. Sample images showing the results are given in figure 1.

Table 1. Impercebility of Watermarks (PSNR values)

Images	Barni	Shahraeini	Proposed
Sachu	39.7863	40.8945	42.4607
Road	38.6653	40.2268	40.9654
Boy& Girl	40.2011	41.3256	42.6536
X-mas	39.3259	39.5934	40.0757
Astronomic	35.9864	37.9564	38.6565
Lena	39.5133	39.6509	40.3365
Flowers	38.5424	39.7751	40.5506
Passport	39.9218	41.2033	41.6934
Document	37.4655	39.4869	40.5982
Medical	39.7606	40.7578	41.0275

Table 2. Correlation Coefficient Values

Image	JPEG	Cropping	Hist. Eq.	Noising
Sachu	0.9571	0.9782	0.9818	0.9345
Road	0.9648	0.9846	0.9658	0.9355
Boy& Girl	0.9385	0.9875	0.9706	0.9378
X-mas	0.9558	0.9864	0.9647	0.9485
Astronomic	0.9654	0.9795	0.9675	0.9494
Lena	0.9432	0.9809	0.9733	0.9396
Flowers	0.9595	0.9788	0.9768	0.9402
Passport	0.9686	0.9886	0.9785	0.9433
Document	0.9537	0.9763	0.9855	0.9381
Medical	0.9627	0.9799	0.9804	0.9383

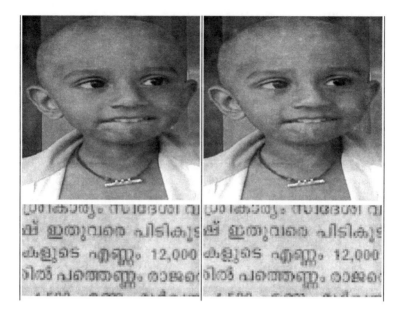

Fig. 1. (a) Original Image (top left) (b)Watermarked Image (top right) (c) Watermark (bottom left) (d) Extracted Watermark (bottom right)

8 Conclusions

The work shows that texture classification based on fractal dimension improves the imperceptibility and robustness of wavelet-domain watermarking techniques. Fractal dimension, if properly measured, can effectively be used to classify image portions based on texture complexity. The results show that use of localized strength values for watermark embedding improves quality of watermarked images. This allows to have varied watermarking strengths over a single image. The method can be improved using multiple levels of strength values for various clusters of image blocks with different texture levels. Using the proposed method after classifying the image based on overall image features is also under study.

References

1. Hutchinson, J.E.: Fractals and Self Similarity. Indiana Univ. Math. J. 30(5), 713–747 (1981)
2. Barnsley, M.F.: Fractals Everywhere. Academic Press, New York (1993)
3. Jacquin, A.E.: Image Coding Based on a Fractal Theory of Iterated Contractive Image Transformations. IEEE Trans. on Image Processing 2, 18–30 (1992)
4. Welstead, S.T.: Fractal and Wavelet Image Compression Techniques. SPIE Press (1999)
5. Welstead, S.: Self-organizing Neural Network Domain Classification for Fractal Image Coding. In: Proceedings IASTED, Banff, Canada, pp. 248–251. IASTED Press (1997)

6. Puate, J., Jordan, F.: Using Fractal Compression Scheme to Embed A Digital Signature into an Image. In: Proceedings of SPIE Photonics East 1996 Symposium, Boston, Massachusetts (1996)
7. Bas, P., Chassery, J.M.: Using Fractal Code to Watermark Images. In: Proceedings International Conference Image Processing (ICIP), Chicago, vol. 1 (1998)
8. Gulati, K.: Information Hiding Using Fractal Encoding, MTech Thesis, IIT, Bombay, India (2003)
9. Sarkar, N., Choudhuri, B.B.: An Efficient Differential Box Counting Approach to Compute Fractal Dimension of Image. IEEE Transactions. on Syst. Man and Cybernetics 24, 115–120 (1994)
10. Conci, A., Campos, C.F.J.: An Efficient Box-Counting Fractal Dimension Approach for Experimental Image Variation Characterization. In: Proceedings of IWISP 1996 3rd International Workshop in Signal and Image Processing, pp. 665–668. Elsevier Science, UK (1996)
11. Dugad, R., Ratakonda, K., Ahuja, N.: A New Wavelet-Based Scheme for Watermarking Images. In: Proceedings of the IEEE International Conference on Image Processing, ICIP 1998, Chicago (1998)
12. Podilchuk, C., Zeng, W.: Image Adaptive Watermarking using Visual Models. IEEE Journal on Selected Areas in Communications 16(4), 525–539 (1998)
13. Xia, X., Boncelet, C.G., Arce, G.R.: Wavelet Transform Based Watermark for Digital Images. Optics Express 3(12), 497–505 (1998)
14. Kundur, D., Hatzinakos, D.: Digital Watermarking using Multiresolution Wavelet Decomposition. In: Proceedings IEEE Int. Conf. on Accoustics, Speech and Signal Processing, Washington, vol. 5, pp. 2969–2972 (1998)
15. Kundur, D., Hatzinakos, D.: Diversity and Attack Characterization for Improced Robust Watermarking. IEEE Trans. on Signal Processing 49(10), 2383–2396 (2001)
16. Barni, M., Bartolini, F., Piva, A.: Improved Wavelet-based Watermarking through Pixel-Wise Masking. IEEE Transaction Image Processing 10(5), 783–791 (2001)
17. Ni, R., Rual, Q.: Region of Interest Watermarking Based on Fractal dimension. In: Proceedings ICPR 2006, Pattern Recognition. IEEE (2006)
18. Sharaeini, S., Yaghoobi, M.: A Robust Digital Image Watermarking Approach against JPEG Compression Attack based on Hybrid Fractal-Wavelet. In: Proceedings of International Conference on Computer Communications and Management, vol. 5. IACSIT Press, Singapore (2011)
19. Cox., I.J., Miller, M.L.: A Review of Watermarking and the Importance of Perceptual Modeling. In: Proceedings of Electronic Imaging (1997)
20. Nafornita, C.: Contributions to Digital Watermarking of Still Images in the Wavelet Transform. PhD Thesis, Technical University of Cluj-Napoca, Romania (2008)
21. Jin, X.C., Ong, S.H., Jayasooriah: A Practical Method for Estimating Fractal Dimension. Pattern Regnition Letters 16, 457–464 (1995)
22. Liu, S.: An Improved Differential Box-Counting Approach to Compute Fractal Dimension of Gray-Level Image. In: International Symposium on Information Science and Engineering (ISISE 2008), pp. 303–306 (2008)

Digital Signatures Using Multivariate Polynomial Systems with Relatively Simpler Central Maps

Sivasankar M. and Padmanabhan T.R.

Department of Mathematics, Amrita Vishwa Vidyapeetham, Coimbatore, India
m_sivasankar@cb.amrita.edu

Abstract. Multivariate polynomials, especially quadratic polynomials, are very much used in cryptography for secure communications and digital signatures. In this paper, polynomial systems with relatively simpler central maps are presented. It is observed that, by using such simple central maps, the amount of computational work of the Signer, is considerably reduced.

Keywords: Affine Transformations, Digital Signatures, Eigen Values, Multivariate Polynomial Cryptography, Ring Representation.

1   Introduction

Multivariate Polynomial Cryptography ($\mathcal{MPC}$), uses polynomial systems in many variables, for secure asymmetric communications. Announcing a randomly looking, tough public key is the prime aim of the designer of the public key cryptosystem. Secure public keys with relatively simpler base structures are very much in demand in any public key cryptosystem [1],[2]. In $\mathcal{MPC}$ also if we can construct a strong public key, starting from a simple base key, we can save considerable amount of computational work while using the system. We present a way of designing such strong public keys for $\mathcal{MPC}$.

The remaining sections of this paper are organized as such. Section 2: Multivariate Polynomial Cryptography and Digital Signatures, Section 3: Eigen values and diagonalization of matrices, Section 4: Ring representation of elements for solving Polynomial Systems, Section 5: Grobner Basis technique for solving Polynomial Systems, Section 6: Affine transformations and hiding the central map, Section 7: Conclusion.

2   Multivariate Polynomial Cryptography and Digital Signatures

2.1   Introduction to $\mathcal{MPC}$

Let F be a finite field. In Multivariate Cryptography, a set of m polynomials, say, $C(X) = \{c_i(x_1, x_2, .., x_n)\}, i = 1, 2, ...m$, in n variables $x_1, x_2, ..., x_n$, called the central map, is selected. *i.e,*

K.R. Venugopal and L.M. Patnaik (Eds.): ICIP 2012, CCIS 292, pp. 592–598, 2012.
© Springer-Verlag Berlin Heidelberg 2012

$$C(X) = \{c_1(x_1, x_2, .., x_n), c_2(x_1, x_2, .., x_n), \, ... \, , c_m(x_1, x_2, .., x_n)\}.$$

is the central map.

These polynomials actually define a mapping from F^n to F^m, by transforming $(x_1, x_2, .., x_n)$ to $(c_1, c_2, .., c_n)$. To complete the construction of the public key two invertible trapdoor transformations $S : F^n \longrightarrow F^n$ and $T : F^m \longrightarrow F^m$ are selected and will be used to hide the central map C.

These transformations S and T are affine transformations and are of the format,

$$S(x_1, x_2, .., x_n) = A_{n \times n} \, X_{n \times 1} + C$$

$$T(x_1, x_2, .., x_m) = B_{m \times m} \, X_{m \times 1} + D$$

here A and B are $n \times n$ and $m \times m$ invertible matrices ;also $C \in F^n$ and $D \in F^m$.

Now the public key is obtained by composition of these transformations with the central map to produce the public key

$$P(X) = (T \circ C \circ S)(X) = T(C(S(X))).$$

Note that the public key $P(X)$ is again a set of m polynomials in n variables $x_1, x_2, .., x_n$. We can symbolize them as

$$P(X) = \{p_1(x_1, x_2, .., x_n), p_2(x_1, x_2, .., x_n), \, ... \, , p_m(x_1, x_2, .., x_n)\}.$$

Only the set of polynomials $P(X)$ is announced publicly, and the transformations C, S and T are kept secretly [3].

2.2 Encryption and Decryption Using $\mathcal{MPC}$

Encryption is performed by inputting the message, say $X = (x_1, x_2, .., x_n) \in F^n$, into the public key set of m polynomials to yield, say , $Y = P(X) = (y_1, y_2, .., y_m) \in F^m$. The received Y is decrypted back to X, through inverting T, C and S. i.e.

$$X = S^{-1}(C^{-1}(T^{-1}(Y))) \, .$$

The need of invertible transformations can be obviously understood by the decryption process. Clearly affine transformations are easily inverted,as they are defined through invertible matrices.

The difficulty involved in inverting the central map C, depends on the structure of C. Infact it can be easily seen that inverting the central map automatically leads to solving a polynomial system of m equations in n variables.Mostly quadratic multivariate polynomials are used for C [4]. A lot of techniques like Grobner Bases [5], Homotopy Continuation methods and Numerical Methods are available to solve polynomial systems.

2.3   Digital Signatures Using $\mathcal{MPC}$

It is interesting to note that, in any public key cryptosystem, the person having the secret key, can securely sign any document send by him [6]. Hence, apart from used for encryption purpose, public key cryptosystems can be used for producing digital signatures also.

For the hash value $h = H(m)$ of a (possibly encrypted)message m, the designer of the cryptosystem, who possesses the secret keys C, S and T and hence C^{-1}, S^{-1} and T^{-1}, signs by evaluating $S^{-1}(C^{-1}(T^{-1}(h)))$ to get the signature DS. Actually the designer solves the system $P(X) = h$, to get the solution DS. Note that, only the designer can generate this DS, as he only can solve the system.

When h and DS are received by any third party, it can be verified by the third party, using the designer's public key; i.e. by checking whether $P(DS) = h$. When DS is put into P(X) naturally h will be produced, as DS is the solution of $P(X) = h$.

More applications of multivariate schemes can be found in [3].

Keeping in mind that, cryptography is difficult, even with the simple case of quadratic central maps, difficulties arising out of non linear transformations has to be explored. Polynomial systems of degree $n > 2$ will naturally consume more computation time for solving the encryption/decryption/signature verification and will also pose an additional threat of unavailability of inverse transformations. A balance should be achieved amongst the degree of the polynomials used,the computational time required for encryption/decryption and security [7].

3   Eigen Values and Diagonalization of Matrices

Definition 1. *Given a matrix* $A = \begin{pmatrix} a_{11} & a_{12} & \dots & a_{1n} \\ a_{21} & a_{22} & \dots & a_{2n} \\ \dots & \dots & \dots & \dots \\ a_{n1} & a_{n2} & \dots & a_{nn} \end{pmatrix}$ *the eigen values of* A *are the values* λ *such that* $AX = \lambda X$. *The* $n \times 1$ *vector* X *is called an eigen vector of* A *corresponding to the eigen value* λ.

All the n eigen values of A are obtained by solving the characteristic equation $|A - \lambda I| = 0$ of A. The eigen vector corresponding to the eigen value λ can be obtained by solving the homogeneous system $(A - \lambda I)X = 0$.

We state few fundamental theorems of matrix algebra without proof.

Theorem 1. *Let* λ_1, λ_2, $\cdots$, λ_n *be distinct eigen values of an* $n \times n$ *matrix. Then, the corresponding eigen vectors* $X_1, X_2, \cdots, X_n$ *form a linearly independent set.*

Theorem 2. *An* $n \times n$ *matrix* $\hat{A}$ *is called similar to another* $n \times n$ *matrix* A *if*

$$\hat{A} = M^{-1}AM,$$

for some nonsingular matrix M. The transformation effected is called a similarity transformation.

Further similar matrices have same eigen values and the eigen vectors $\hat{X}_i$ of $\hat{A}$ and X_i of A, are related by $\hat{X}_i = P^{-1}X_i$.

Theorem 3. *If an $n \times n$ matrix A has n linearly independent eigen vectors, $X_1, X_2, \cdots, X_n$, then the matrix M, whose column vectors are the eigen vectors of A, diagonalizes A.*

i.e. if $M = [X_1|X_2|...|X_n]$ then

$$M^{-1}AM = D,$$

a diagonal matrix, with eigen values of A occupying the diagonal.

4   Ring Representation of Elements for Solving Polynomial Systems

4.1   Solving One Variable Polynomials Using Eigen Values

Definition 2. *Given a polynomial $h(x) = c_0 + c_1 x + c_2 x^2 + ... + c_n x^n$, the companion matrix of $h(x)$ is given by*

$$\mathcal{C} = \begin{pmatrix} 0 & 1 & 0 & \cdots & 0 \\ 0 & 0 & 1 & \cdots & 0 \\ \cdots & \cdots & \cdots & \cdots & \cdots \\ 0 & 0 & 0 & \cdots & 1 \\ -c_0 & -c_1 & -c_2 & \cdots & -c_{n-1} \end{pmatrix}.$$

The importance of the companion matrix is that, the eigen values of $\mathcal{C}$ are the roots of $h(x)$. So in one way the companion matrix helps us to solve for the roots of $h(x)$.

It is interesting to note that the eigen vectors of the companion matrix are easily obtained from the Vandermonde matrix,

$$V(\lambda_1, \lambda_2, \cdots, \lambda_n) = \begin{pmatrix} 1 & 1 & \cdots & 1 \\ \lambda_1 & \lambda_2 & \cdots & \lambda_n \\ \cdots & \cdots & \cdots & \cdots \\ \lambda_1^{n-1} & \lambda_2^{n-1} & \cdots & \lambda_n^{n-1} \end{pmatrix}.$$

4.2   Solving Multivariate Polynomial Systems Using Ring Representations

Similar to how companion matrices convert the problem of solving one variable polynomials into an eigenvalue/eigenvector problem, ring representations convert the problem of solving multivariate polynomial systems in to eigen value problem [8].

Consider the system of multivariate polynomials

$$c_1(x_1, x_2, .., x_n) = 0$$
$$c_2(x_1, x_2, .., x_n) = 0$$
$$................$$
$$c_m(x_1, x_2, .., x_n) = 0$$

The ring representations $\mathcal{X}_1, \mathcal{X}_2, ..., \mathcal{X}_n$ of the elements $x_1, x_2, .., x_n$ has to satisfy,

$$c_1(\mathcal{X}_1, \mathcal{X}_2, ..., \mathcal{X}_n) = 0$$
$$c_2(\mathcal{X}_1, \mathcal{X}_2, ..., \mathcal{X}_n) = 0$$
$$................$$
$$c_m(\mathcal{X}_1, \mathcal{X}_2, ..., \mathcal{X}_n) = 0$$

Also if $\mathcal{X}_1, \mathcal{X}_2, ..., \mathcal{X}_n$ have the same basis of eigen vectors, they can be simultaneously diagonalizable.

Hence, the eigen values of the matrix of the ring representation of x_i will give the possible values of x_i and the system stands solved.

Ring representation of elements can be obtained using the algorithm in [9].

5   Grobner Basis Technique for Solving Polynomial Systems

Grobner basis technique is a powerful tool to solve multivariate polynomial systems. For a detailed introduction to Grobner bases [10] can be referred, but a few basic definitions are recalled here.

Definition 3. *Let* $p_1, p_2, \cdots, p_n \in K[X]$ *be polynomials. The ideal generated by these polynomials in* $K[X]$ *is the subset of* $K[X]$ *which consists of all the possible linear combinations of the type* $a_1 p_1 + a_2 p_2 + \cdots + a_n p_n$, *where* $a_i \in K[X]$. *This ideal is denoted by* $I = \langle p_1, p_2, \cdots, p_n \rangle$.

Definition 4. *A monomial ordering* $\prec$ *on* $K[X]$ *is a total ordering relation on the set of monomials if* $x^\alpha \prec x^\beta$ *then* $x^{\alpha+\gamma} \prec x^{\beta+\gamma}$ *and* $\prec$ *is a well-ordering.*

Definition 5. *Given a monomial ordering* $\prec$, *for a polynomial* $h(X) = \Sigma_\alpha c_\alpha x^\alpha$, *its leading term is defined by* $LT(h) = c_\alpha x^\alpha$ *where,* c_α *is referred to as the leading coefficient.* x^α *called the leading monomial, is the largest monomial appearing in* h *in the ordering* $\prec$. *Then, we can also define a division algorithm, which generalizes the division algorithm in the case of one variable as "Every polynomial* $h \in K[X]$ *can be written as* $h = a_1 p_1 + a_2 p_2 + \cdots + a_n p_n + r$, *where* r *is the remainder".*

The remainder r in this decomposition is not unique in general with a lucky exception, when the set of generators satisfy the following definition [5].

Definition 6. *The polynomials $\{g_1, g_2, \cdots, g_r\}$ is a Grobner basis of the ideal $I =< p_1, p_2, \cdots, p_n >$ if and only if the remainder r is uniquely determined for all $h \in K[X]$.*

Grobner basis of a set of polynomials is obtained by a systematic procedure, similar to Gauss elimination method for linear systems. After efficiently eliminating all but one variable, we get a one variable polynomial which can be solved and the solution can be used to find the values of the other variables.

There exists an algorithm, developed by Buchberger for converting a given generating set to a Grobner basis. Algorithms F_4, F_5 are some improved versions of Buchberger algorithm.

6   Affine Transformations and Hiding the Central Map

The trapdoor affine transformations S and T, play a vital role in hiding the central map. In general an affine transformation can be described by various parameters which account for translation, rotation, scaling and shear [11]. Hence affine transformations can be efficiently used to make a simple central map into a randomly looking set of polynomials. This can be achieved by selecting a set of m biquadratic forms and exaggerating the number of cross terms through an affine transformation.

For the understanding of quadratic forms we give a definition:

Definition 7. *A quadratic form Q, in n variables is a function of the form $X^T A X = Q$, where $X = (x_1, x_2, \cdots, x_n)^T$. In an expanded manner we can write it as*

$$Q = x_1{}^2 + x_2{}^2 + \cdots + x_n{}^2 + x_1 x_2 + x_1 x_3 + \cdots + x_1 x_n + x_2 x_3 + \cdots + x_n x_{n-1}$$

The noteworthy point about quadratic forms is the matrix A of the quadratic form is symmetric and provides an easy way of diagonalizing the system [11].

With these ideas we are now ready to present a simpler central map.

Step 1. Select a set of m simultaneously diagonalizable quadratic forms in n variables $u_1, u_2, \cdots, u_n$ as the central map
Step 2. Letting $u_1 = x_1{}^2;\ u_2 = x_2{}^2;\ \cdots\ u_n = x_n{}^2$, make the quadratic central map into a biquadratic one. Let this be the new central map $C(x)$
Step 3. Select two invertible affine transformations S and T carefully
Step 4. Perform the composition $T \circ C \circ S$ to get the public key set of m polynomials. Keep C,S and T secretly.

The main advantage of the quadratic forms constituting the central map is, quadratic forms are easily solvable, either by ring representations or by Grobner bases. So while digitally signing a hashed message $h = H(m)$, we easily get the signature and as a biquadratic central map is announced publicly, it will be very difficult to forge the signature.

7   Conclusions

In this paper we have presented a new way of hiding a simpler quadratic central map. The public key deceives the user as it looks like a random set of polynomials. Keeping in mind the effect of Quantum computers in cryptanalysis, introducing invertible non-quadratic central maps and hiding then using affine transformations will be in demand in near future.

References

1. Wolf, C., Preneel, B.: Superfluous Keys in Multivariate Quadratic Asymmetric Systems. Cryptology ePrint Archive, Report 2004/361 (2004)
2. Albrecht, P., Enrico, T., Stanislav, B., Christopher, W.: Small Public Keys and Fast Verification for Multivariate Quadratic Public Key Systems. In: Proceedings of the Workshop on Cryptographic Hardware and Embedded Systems, CESS (2011)
3. Wolf, C.: Introduction to Multivariate Quadratic Public Key Systems and Their Applications. In: Proceedings of Yet Another Conference on Cryptography, YACC 2006, France (2006)
4. Wolf, C., Preneel, B.: Taxonomy of Public Key Schemes based on the Problem of Multivariate Quadratic equations. Cryptology ePrint Archive, Report 2005/077 (2005)
5. Buchberger: An algorithmic Method in Polynomial Ideal Theory. In: Multidimensional Systems Theory, pp. 184–232. D, Reidel Publishing Company (1985)
6. Alfred, J., Van Menezes Paul, C., Oorschot, S., Vanstone, A.: Handbook of Applied Cryptography. CRC Press LCC (1996)
7. Sivasankar M.: Multivariate Non-quadratic Public Key Schemes. In: Proceedings of the International Conference on Algebra and Its Applications, ICOAA 2011 (2011)
8. Williams, M.P.: Solving Polynomial Equations Using Linear Algebra. Johns Hopkins APL Technical Digest 28(4) (2010)
9. Emiris, I.Z.: On the Complexity of Sparse Elimination. J.Complexity 12, 134–166 (1996)
10. Cox, D.A., Little, J., O'Shea, D.: Ideals: Varieties and Algorithms: An Introduction to Computational Algebraic Geometry and Commutative Algebra II. Springer (1996)
11. Anton, H., Rorres, C.: Elementary Linear Algebra, IXth edn. John Wiley & Sons (2005)

Analysis and Comparison of Fully Layered Image Encryption Techniques and Partial Image Encryption Techniques

Parameshachari B.D.[1] and K.M.S. Soyjaudah[2]

[1] Dept. of Electronics and Communication Engineering,
JSS Academy of Technical Education, Mauritius, Avenue Droopanath Ramphul,
Bonne Terre, Vacoas, Mauritius
parameshbkit@gmail.com
[2] Dept. of Electrical and Electronic Engineering, University of Mauritius, Reduit,
Mauritius

Abstract. In traditional image and video content protection schemes, called fully layered, the whole content is first compressed. Then, the compressed bitstream is entirely encrypted using a standard cipher (DES, AES, IDEA, etc.). The specific characteristics of this kind of data (high-transmission rate with limited bandwidth) make standard encryption algorithms inadequate. Another limitation of fully layered systems consists of altering the whole bitstream syntax which may disable some codec functionalities. Partial encryption is a new trend in image and video content protection. It consists of encrypting only a subset of the data. The aim of partial image encryption using SCAN mapping method is to reduce the amount of data to encrypt while preserving a sufficient level of security than the fully layered image encryption using SCAN method. In this paper, we analyzed Image encryption techniques and Partial image encryption techniques and present the comparative results.

Keywords: Image Encryption, Mapping, Partial Image Encryption, Security, SCAN.

1 Introduction

Today with the rapid growth in the number of telecommunications and computer networks as well as with the growing increase in the amount of multimedia transmission, securing video content is becoming more important than ever before. A traditional approach [1][2] for content access control is to first encode data with a standard compressor and then to perform full encryption of the compressed bitstream with a standard cipher. In this scheme called fully layered and the compression and encryption processes are totally disjoint.

Another limitation of fully layered scheme consists of altering the original bitstream syntax. Therefore, many functionalities of the encoding scheme may be disabled (e.g., scalability). Some recent works explored a new way of securing the content, named, partial encryption or selective encryption, soft encryption,

K.R. Venugopal and L.M. Patnaik (Eds.): ICIP 2012, CCIS 292, pp. 599–604, 2012.
© Springer-Verlag Berlin Heidelberg 2012

perceptual encryption, by applying encryption to a subset of a bitstream. The main goal of partial encryption is to reduce the amount of data to encrypt while achieving a required level of security. An additional feature of selective encryption is to preserve some functionalities of the original bitstream (e.g., scalability).

The rest of this paper is organized as follows: Section 2 explains the related work. The results are described in Section 3. This paper is concluded by providing the summary of the present work in Section 4.

2 Related Work

2.1 Image Encryption Techniques

A Technique for Image Encryption Using Digital Signatures : Aloka et al., [3] have proposed a new technique to encrypt an image for secure image transmission. The digital signature of the original image is added to the encoded version of the original image. Image encoding is done by using an appropriate error control code, such as a Bose-Chaudhuri Hochquenghem (BCH) code. At the receiver end, after the decryption of the image, the digital signature can be used to verify the authenticity of the image.

Lossless Image Compression and Encryption Using SCAN : Maniccam et al., [4] have presented a new methodology which performs both lossless compression and encryption of binary and gray-scale images. The compression and encryption schemes are based on SCAN patterns generated by the SCAN methodology. The SCAN is a formal language-based two-dimensional spatial-accessing methodology which can efficiently specify and generate a wide range of scanning paths or space filling curves.

A New Encryption Algorithm for Image Cryptosystems : Chin-Chen et al., [5] use one of the popular image compression techniques, vector quantization to design an efficient cryptosystem for images. The scheme is based on vector quantization (VQ), cryptography, and other number theorems. In VQ, the images are first decomposed into vectors and then sequentially encoded vector by vector. Then traditional cryptosystems from commercial applications can be used.

2.2 Partial Image Encryption Techniques

In this subsection, a few newly proposed techniques for partial image encryption, which will improve the complexity of algorithm as well as make the key stronger has been introduced.

Partial Encryption Algorithms : Cheng et al., [6] proposed partial encryption methods that are suitable for images compressed with two specific classes of compression algorithms: (a) quadtree compression algorithms, and (b) wavelet compression algorithms based on zero trees.

Selective Encryption Methods for Raster and JPEG Images : Droogenbroeck et al., [7] proposed the selective encryption methods for uncompressed (raster) images and compressed (JPEG) images. According to Droogenbroeck et al., at least 4-5 least significant bitplanes should be encrypted to achieve the satisfactory visual degradation of the image.

Selective Bitplane Encryption Algorithm : Podesser et al., [8] proposed a selective encryption algorithm for the uncompressed (raster) images, that is quite opposite from the first method by Droogenbroeck et al., [7]. In the raster image that consists of 8 bitplanes, Schmidt and Uhl's algorithm encrypts only the most significant bitplanes. The proposed underlying cryptosystem for this method was AES. However, without loss of generality, any fast conventional cryptosystem may be chosen instead.

On Partial Encryption of RDF-Graphs : In 2005, Mark et al., [9], proposed a method to partially encrypt RDF-graphs. It differs from other approaches in that the result is a single self-describing RDF compliant graph containing both encrypted data and plain text data. The method allows for fine grained encryption of subjects, objects, predicates and sub graphs of RDF graphs.

Selective Image Encryption Using JBIG : In 2005, Roman et al., [10],proposed selective encryption of JBIG encoded visual data exploiting the interdependencies among resolution layers in the JBIG hierarchical progressive coding mode. Contrasting to earlier ideas when selectively encrypting a subset of bitplanes, they able to show attack resistance even in case of restricting the amount of encryption to 1% - 2% of the data only. The extremely low amount of data required to be protected in their technique also allows the use of public-key cryptography thereby simplifying key management issues.

A Partial Image Encryption Method with Pseudo Random Sequences : In 2006, Y.V. Subba Rao et al.,[11], proposed partial encryption of image using pseudo random sequences with simple hardware. According to [11] partial encryption method achieves the same security with the improvement in processing speed. The performance of the method mainly depends on the differentiation of correlated and uncorrelated information in the image. Here we have treated the MSB planes as correlated information.

   Region-Based Selective Encryption for Medical Imaging : In 2007, Yang et al., [12], proposed two novel region-based selective encryption schemes for medical imaging. The first scheme is to randomly invert the first two MSBs of ROI coefficients in wavelet transform domain. It can be efficiently implemented and only incurs little compression efficiency overhead, also it can be extended to other motion formats. The second scheme, selective encryption of the compressed ROI data, provides a high level security and has no file size changes.

   Selective Encryption of Multimedia Images : In 2008, Nidhi et al., [13], proposes a selective encryption technique in wavelet domain for conditional access

Table 1. Processing Time for Fully Layered Encryption and Partial Image Encryption for Different Image Sizes

Image Size	Fully Layered Encryption Using SCAN Method(second)	Partial Image Encryption SCAN Mapping Method(second)
457X700	1.230	1.065
500X446	0.847	0.652
400x568	0.706	0.521
434x823	1.333	1.101

Table 2. Memory usage for Fully Layered Encryption and Partial Image Encryption for Different Images

Image	Fully Layered Encryption Using SCAN Method(bytes)	Partial Image Encryption SCAN Mapping Method(bytes)
Radiological image(gray scale)	1112004	0900112
Radiological image(color)	1224125	1004105
Lena(gray scale)	2406239	2009106
Lena(color)	2709752	2100219
Coffeemaker (grayscale)	4709605	4201517
Coffeemaker (color)	5206807	4711302

Table 3. Results of Fully Layered Encryption using SCAN Method and Partial Image Encryption SCAN Mapping Method for Gray Scale Images

Image	Amount	Image Correlation	Reconstructed Image Correlation
Radiological image	Full	0.0067	0.999918
	25%	0.0575	0.999952
	8.5%	0.2367	0.999976
	2.5%	0.1978	0.999987
Lena	Full	0.0023	0.999998
	25%	0.0304	0.999926
	8.5%	0.0745	0.999915
	2.5%	0.1987	0.999968
Coffeemaker	Full	0.0085	0.999971
	25%	0.0786	0.999941
	8.5%	0.3456	0.999986
	2.5%	0.5483	0.999974

systems. The encryption is applied only to a subset of multimedia data stream rather than the multimedia data in its entirety to save the computational time and computational resources. According to [13], encryption technique controls

Table 4. Results of Fully Layered Encryption using SCAN method and Partial Image Encryption SCAN mapping method for Color Images

Image	Amount	Image Correlation	Reconstructed Image Correlation
Radiological image	Full	0.0095	0.999911
	25%	0.0589	0.999919
	8.5%	0.2014	0.999925
	2.5%	0.1245	0.999963
Lena	Full	0.0012	0.999921
	25%	0.0201	0.999902
	8.5%	0.0541	0.999901
	2.5%	0.1252	0.999923
Coffeemaker	Full	0.0076	0.999989
	25%	0.0532	0.999962
	8.5%	0.3135	0.999976
	2.5%	0.5012	0.999912

the transparency and security in an efficient manner by selecting the coefficients for encryption based on predefined criteria.

3   Results and Discussion

In this paper image processing software package MATLAB 7.0 is used as the engine for the image processing experiments for fully layered image encryption and partial image encryption techniques. An RGB image is stored in MATLAB as an M-by-N-by-3 data array that defines red, green and blue color components for each individuals pixel. The color of each pixel is determined by the combination of the red, green and blue intensities stored in each color plane at the pixels location. Images that were used during full layered encryption as well as used during partial image encryption these experiments shows that the partial image encryption method as given best results than fully layered image encryption. As the comparative results of partial image encryption using SCAN mapping method given best results than the fully layered image encryption using SCAN method [14] as shown in tables.

4   Conclusions

As combined and effective methods has been proposed in this paper for fully layered image encryption using SCAN method and partial image encryption using SCAN mapping method. Many of the proposed schemes only achieve moderate to low level of security which may find applications in which quality degradation preferred over absolute security. Partial image encryption using SCAN mapping method provided higher security, flexibility, multiplicity, spatial selectively and format compliance than fully layered image encryption.

References

1. Zhang, S., Karim, M.A.: Color Image Encryption Using Double Random Phase Encoding. Microwave And Optical Technology Letters 21(5), 318–322 (1999)
2. Hou, Y.-C.: Visual Cryptography for Color Images. Pattern Recognition 36, 1619–1629 (2003)
3. Sinha, A., Singh, K.: A Technique for Image Encryption using Digital Signature. Optics Communications, 1–6 (2003) (article in press)
4. Maniccam, S.S., Bourbakis, N.G.: Lossless Image Compression and Encryption using SCAN. Pattern Recognition 34, 1229–1245 (2001)
5. Chang, C.-C., Hwang, M.-S., Chen, T.-S.: A New Encryption Algorithm for Image Cryptosystems. The Journal of Systems and Software 58, 83–91 (2001)
6. Cheng, H., Li, X.: Partial Encryption of Compressed Images and Video. IEEE Transactions on Signal Processing 8(8), 2439–2451 (2000)
7. Van Droogenbroeck, M., Benedett, R.: Techniques for a Selective Encryption of Uncompressed and Compressed Images. In: Proceedings of Advanced Concepts for Intelligent Vision Systems (ACIVS) 2002, Belgium (2002)
8. Podesser, M., Schmidt, H.P., Uhl, A.: Selective Bitplane Encryption for Secure Transmission of Image Data in Mobile Environments. In: Proceedings of 5th Nordic Signal Processing Symposium, Norway (2002)
9. Giereth, M.: On Partial Encryption of RDF-Graphs. In: Gil, Y., Motta, E., Benjamins, V.R., Musen, M.A. (eds.) ISWC 2005. LNCS, vol. 3729, pp. 308–322. Springer, Heidelberg (2005)
10. Pfarrhofer, R., Uhl, A.: Selective Image Encryption Using JBIG. In: Dittmann, J., Katzenbeisser, S., Uhl, A. (eds.) CMS 2005. LNCS, vol. 3677, pp. 98–107. Springer, Heidelberg (2005)
11. Subba Rao, Y.V., Mitra, A., Mahadeva Prasanna, S.R.: A Partial Image Encryption Method with Pseudo Random Sequences. In: Bagchi, A., Atluri, V. (eds.) ICISS 2006. LNCS, vol. 4332, pp. 315–325. Springer, Heidelberg (2006)
12. Ou, Y., Sur, C., Rhee, K.-H.: Region-Based Selective Encryption for Medical Imaging. In: Preparata, F.P., Fang, Q. (eds.) FAW 2007. LNCS, vol. 4613, pp. 62–73. Springer, Heidelberg (2007)
13. Kulkarni, N.S., Balasuramanian: Selective Encryption of Multimedia Images. In: XXXII National Systems Conference, NSC 2008 (2008)
14. Parameshachari, B.D., Chaitanyakumar, M.V.: Image Security Using SCAN Based Encryption Method. In: 42nd IETE Mid-term Symposium on Telecom Paradigms - Indian Scenario, pp. 115–118 (2011)

Performance Analysis of TEA Block Cipher for Low Power Applications

Ruhan Bevi A. and Malarvizhi S.

Department of Electronics and Communication Engineering,
SRM University, India
ruhanmady@yahoo.co.in

Abstract. The FPGA based embedded system plays a vital role in the implementation of many cryptographic applications especially in the field of wireless communication. The security constraint applications increasingly demand the encryption process for sensitive data transfer from one end to the other end. The software implementation of security algorithms are easy to implement but it lags in its execution speed and performance. Therefore, hardware implementations are considered to be a good alternate, since they provide additive performance along with the low power and less memory consumption. The Tiny Encryption Algorithm (TEA) is one of the fastest and efficient cryptographic algorithms well suited for many real time data communications with moderate security. This paper analyzes the hardware implementation of TEA in FPGA with different approaches that consumes lesser resources with increased execution speed. This work emphasizes the efficient implementation of TEA algorithm for various applications where the hardware resources are limited and power constraints are stringent.

Keywords: TEA, RFID, Encryption, Feistal Block Cipher, Round Function.

1 Introduction

The need for secured data transfer is more essential in the rapid development of communication systems. This is achieved by using cryptographic algorithms which can be classified into symmetric or asymmetric algorithms. Symmetric algorithms are divided into stream ciphers and block ciphers. Stream ciphers encrypt a single bit of plain text at a time, whereas block ciphers take a number of bits (say 64 bits) and encrypt them as a single unit. The cryptographic algorithms are claiming importance, as the threats for secure data communication [1],[2] keeps increasing. The TEA is a symmetric cipher which uses secret key, where the same key is used for both encryption and decryption. It is prominent for its simplicity of implementation with reduced power and memory consumptions. This paper uses the hardware description language VHDL to describe the performance and efficiency of TEA with different approaches. The primary objective is to focus on the evaluation fast hardware implementation with less

K.R. Venugopal and L.M. Patnaik (Eds.): ICIP 2012, CCIS 292, pp. 605–610, 2012.
© Springer-Verlag Berlin Heidelberg 2012

memory and to minimize the chip area with its expected performance. The paper comprises of various Sections, the Section 2 explores the related works, Section 3 deals with the implementation of TEA with various approaches, Section 4 depicts the performance and comparative analysis of these approaches with results and conclusions drawn in Section 5.

2 Related Works

A secured XTEA system to build a high performance core for secure application is developed in [3] which does not discuss any architectural implementations. An efficient verilog description for XTEA is discussed in [4],[5],[6] but it does not report the power consumed and energy parameters. A low cost secure RFID based on TEA encryption is proposed in [7], [8] with their architectural implementations using HDL. The genetic based description is employed for the round function implementation in [6] but the work does not discuss the utilization of slices and other parameters such as the target device, memory, LUTs, flipflops and delay introduced in FPGA. The TEA algorithm for wireless sensor network application was discussed in [9], where the implementation was done in microcontroller. In [10], the software analysis of different block ciphers using microcontrollers is presented. The performance these block ciphers are compared with that of the AES implementation and it has been proved that TEA/XTEA consumes less memory than all the others. The proposed work focuses the implementation of TEA with reduced slice counts to offer the relatively better performance and to adopt with the time and area constraint applications such as RFID and wireless data communication.

3 Implementation of TEA with Different Approaches

TEA operates on 64 (block size) data bits and 128-bit key with 32 cycles. In this block cipher, 64-bit data block is separated into two halves and 128-bit key is divided into four subkeys. The round function is applied to one half of the data M0, using the subkeys and the output is (exclusive-or-ed) with the other half M1. Each cycle follows the same model and the two halves are then fed back as an input for the next round function. The constant $delta = \delta = \sqrt{5}1 * 2^3 1 = 9E3779B9h$ is derivative of the golden number ratio to distinguish the sub keys. The TEA algorithm is implemented using various design approach and the performance of each method is analysed. The number of clocks required to perform a complete encryption of a 64-bit data block is 32 cycles and a single round fuction is executed one per clock cycle. The different approaches are discussed in this section and all the methods are implemented in xilinx vertex II pro device and analysed for various performance parameters.

3.1 Method I : Sequential Approach

The proposed architecture for TEA encryption with single round function is shown in the Fig. 1. In the TEA encryption process, the 64 bits block cipher is divided into two halves say M0, M1 and the key is divided into four subkeys say K0, K1, K2 and K3 of size 32 bits each. These data and subkeys are then applied to the round function which performs 32 iterations.

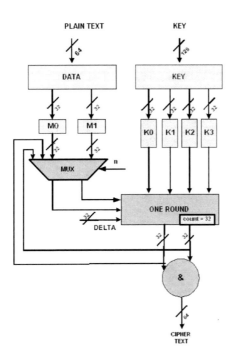

Fig. 1. TEA Architecture

TEA is an iteration cipher, whose ith round has the inputs M0(i-1) and M1(i-1), which is derived from the previous round and the subkey K(i) derived from the 128 bit key K. It uses big endian approach for every round function. The each iteration executes a single round function using one half of the data and subkeys.

The multiplexer is used to select the block cipher either from input or from the feedback to proceed with the further iterations. At the end of the 32nd iteration, it outputs the complete cipher text. The single TEA round function in Fig. 2 performs the simple mixed orthogonal algebraic functions such as right/left shifts, integer addition and xor operations.

3.2   Method II : Structural Approach

This method uses structural modelling to instantiate (port map) the single TEA round. The architecture of this method is shown in the Fig. 3 with their required inputs and outputs. The single round function is designed and executed as a separate module. The component that is created for a single round function is

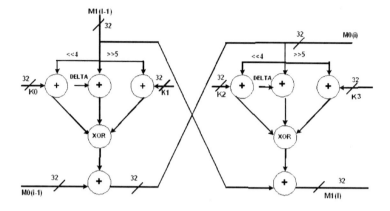

Fig. 2. Single TEA Round Function for Encryption

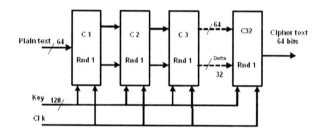

Fig. 3. Architecture of Structural Approach

instantiated to perform 32 TEA round functions. These instances of components are represented as Ci (where, i =1 through 32) each performing a single round function. The top module accepts the plain text, key and clock as the inputs, whereas, each single round uses delta count in addition to the above inputs. The key and clock is common for all the intances as shown in the Fig. 3. The intermediate cipher text and delta count which is the output of each round is applied as a input for the next instance and the output from the last intance is taken as a complete cipher text of TEA encryption process.

3.3   Method III : Subprogram Approach

The method III uses a subprogram technique of coding to implement the TEA algorithm. The single round function is coded as a subprogram and the counter is enabled to count the execution of the subprogram for 32 times. Each time when the sub program is executed the output is intermediate and stored in a temporary register. Upon the completion of the 32nd round function, the output is taken as the complete cipher text.

4   Performance Analysis and Results

The different methods of TEA are implemented and analyzed using xilinx vertex II pro device. The analysis deals with the parameters such as slice counts, memory consumption, delay, etc. that are occupied by each method. The Table 1 shows the implementation results for the resources utilised using all the methods. It is clearly seen that method I uses less memory, slices, LUTs, power compared to the other types.

Table 1. Resource Utilisation for the Three Methods

Parameters	Method1	Method2	Method3
No. off Slices	233	6510	3964
No. of FFs	139	3005	0
Delay (ns)	7.68	8.78	167.66
Logic Delay(ns)	4.563	5.57	100.76
Routing Delay (ns)	2.669	3.21	66.89
Throughput (Mbps)	266.65	264.32	122.1
Memory(KB)	226.956	286.4	347.5
Total Power(mw)	145.27	449.77	279.2
Energy (Gbits/J)	1.83	0.58	0.43

Table 2. Comparison with other works

Parameter	This work	Ref1	Ref2	Ref3
Slices	233	266	294	4608
Delay	4.5(ns)	13.8(ns)	10.9(ns)	6.4(ns)
Throughput	266(Mbps)	19(Mbps)	85(Mbps)	73.3(Mbps)

The throughput is measured as the number of cipher text bits delivered per second and energy is evaluated as the number of bits delivered at the output at the cost of one joule of energy. The results proposed in method I is compared with other existing works for the parameters lile slices used,delay and throughput and shown in Table 2. The comparison shows that the proposed work offers a high throughput for the lesser slices and delay. This indicates that the proposed method I for TEA architectue is highly performing and can be used for applications on stringent constraint of resourses.

5   Conclusion

The presented performance analysis of different approaches concludes that the Method I (sequential approach) is proved to be an efficient implementation of

TEA encryption algorithm. This paper justifies that this method occupies less chip area and power and relatively faster than the other approaches which satisfactorily proves the objective. As a result, the proposed architecture is well suitable for any real-time area and time constraint applications with the expected efficiency and performance.

References

1. Vladimirova, T., Banu, R., Sweeting, M.: On-Board Security Services in Small Satellites. In: MAPLD Proceedings (2005)
2. Ravi, S., Raghunathan, A., Kocher, P., Hattangady, S.: Security in Embedded Systems.: Design Challenges. ACM Transaction Embedded Computation System 3, 461–491 (2004)
3. Kaps, J.P., Chai: TEA Cryptographic Hardware Implementations of XTEA. In: 9th International Conference on Cryptology INDOCRYPT, pp. 363–375. ACM Press, India (2008)
4. Issam, D., Samer, H., Hassan, D.: Efficient Tiny Hardware Cipher under Verilog. In: High Performance Computing and Simulation Conference (2008)
5. Steven, M.A., Michael, D.K.: Hardware Implementation of XTEA. In: Proceedings of the Security and Cryptography Conference, China (2009)
6. Julio, C.H.: Finding Efficient Distinguishers for Cryptographic Mappings, with an Application to the Block Cipher TEA. International Journal of Computer Intelligence 20(3), 517–523 (2004)
7. Israsena, P.: Design and Implementation of Low Power Hardware Encryption for Low Cost Secure RFID using TEA. In: 5th International Conference on Information, Communications and Signal Processing (2006)
8. Israsena, P.: On XTEA-based Encryption/Authentication Core for Wireless Pervasive Communication. In: International Symposium on Communications and Information Technologies, ISCIT (2006)
9. Devesh, J., Dhiren, P., Kankar, D.: Configurable Link Layer Security Architecture for Wireless Sensor Networks. Journal of Information Assurance and Security 4, 582–603 (2009)
10. Thomas, E., Sandeep, K., Christof, P., Axel, P.L.U.: A Survey of Lightweight Cryptography Implementations. IEEE Design and Test of Computers, Special Issue on Secure ICs for Secure Embedded Computing 24, 522–533 (2004)

Robustness Test Analysis of Histogram Based Audio Watermarking

Manisha D. Mali[1] and Khot S.R.[2]

[1] Bharat Ratna Indira Gandhi College of Engg., Solapur
manishamali2008@gmail.com
[2] SD.Y. Patil College of Engg. and Technology, Kolhapur, Maharashtra

Abstract. Audio watermarking is the process that imperceptibly watermarks the audio file with a specific watermark for the purpose of content authentication, data monitoring and tracking, and copyright protection. In histogram based algorithm watermark in text form is embedded by dividing histogram into different groups. Three bins are used to embed one bit. By modifying number of samples in bins bits are embedded. In the paper performance of histogram based audio watermarking technique is tested by applying different attacks such as low pass filtering , cropping, jittering, amplification etc.

Keywords: Audio Watermarking, BER Cropping, Histogram, Jittering, SNR, Synchronization, TSM.

1 Introduction

Rapid evolution of digital technology has improved the ease of access to digital information. Digitizing of multimedia data has enabled reliable, faster, efficient storage, transfer and processing of digital data. It also leads to the consequence of illegal production and redistribution of digital media. Duplication and modification of such digital data has become very easy and undetectable. The risk of copyright violation of multimedia data has increased .Due to the enormous growth of computer networks that provides fast and error free transmission of any unauthorized duplicate and possibly manipulated copy of multimedia information. One way to protect multimedia data against illegal recording and distribution is to embed a secondary signal or pattern into the image, video or audio data that is not perceivable. Data is mixed so well with the original digital data that it is inseparable and remains unaffected against any kind of multimedia signal processing. This embedded secondary information is digital watermark which is, in general, a visible or invisible identification code. It contains some information about the intended recipient, the lawful owner or author of the original data, its copyright etc. in the form of textual data or image, audio. In order to be effective for copyright protection, digital watermark must be robust, recoverable from a document, provide the original information embedded reliably, be non-intrusive and also removable by authorized users. This framework is then used to evaluate Histogram based audio watermarking.

K.R. Venugopal and L.M. Patnaik (Eds.): ICIP 2012, CCIS 292, pp. 611–620, 2012.
© Springer-Verlag Berlin Heidelberg 2012

In this paper, a multi-bit watermark aiming to solve the TSM manipulations is discussed. The watermark insertion and recovery are described by the histogram specification. The robustness of the audio mean and the relative relation in the number of samples among different bins is used in the design. The mean invariance property is used to select the amplitude range to embed bits so that the watermark can resist amplitude scaling attack and avoid exhaustive search.[1] The basic idea of the embedding strategy is to extract the histogram from a selected amplitude range. Divide the bins into many groups, each group including three consecutive bins. For each group, one bit is embedded by reassigning the number of samples in the three bins. The watermarked audio is obtained by modifying the original audio according to the watermarking rule[2].Histogram based algorithm[2] is applied for 20s file and watermark in 60 digit sequence. In this paper results with different length watermark are shown.

2   Performance Parameters

The parameters used to check the performance are bit error rate (BER), signal to noise ratio (SNR) are discussed below.

2.1   Bit Error Rate

Bit error rate can be defined as the percentage of bits corrupted in the transmission of digital information due to the effects of noise, interference and distortion. For example, the bits to be transmitted are 11001100 and the received bits are 10000100. Comparing the number of bits transmitted and received, two bits are affected by transmission. Hence, the BER in this example is 2/8*100 = 25%
BER = Number of error bits/Number of total bits (1)

2.2   Signal to Noise Ratio

Signal to noise ratio is a parameter used to know the amount by which the signal is corrupted by the noise. It is defined as the ratio of the signal power to the noise power. Alternatively, it represents the ratio of desired signal (say a music file) to the background noise level. Signal to noise ratio can also be calculated by equation below. x (i) is the un-watermarked audio signal and is the watermarked audio signal [3].

2.3   Experiment Result of Histogram Based Approach

The Histogram based algorithm [2] is applied to an audio signal in wav format Danube.wav (20s). The parameter =2.4 is selected to extract the histogram. The watermark is binary conversion of text information with the embedding threshold T=1.5. Robustness of algorithm is verified according to BER. In Figure 3 watermark bits verses beta is plotted. Beta represents relationship between different bins a, b, c. From the Watermarked bin samples a, b, c, beta is calculated as $2b/(a+c)$. If beta is greater than or equal to one, watermark bit is one otherwise zero [1].

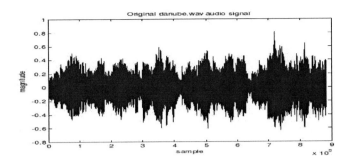

Fig. 1. Original Audio Signal

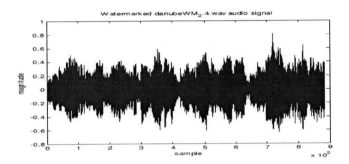

Fig. 2. Watermarked Wav File

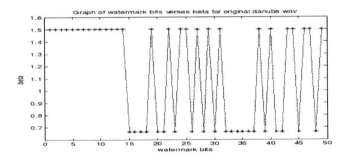

Fig. 3. Watermark Bits Vs Beta

2.4   Results with Different Length Watermark

The output of the experiment is obtained by using different length watermark signals. Watermark in text is converted into binary sequence, BER is observed to check recovery of watermark.

Table 1. Performance evaluation of Danube.wav audio signal with different length watermark signal

WM Character	WM Bits	SNR	BER	Mean before watermark	Mean after watermark
8	56	43.80	0	4001.3	4001.3
9	63	44.68	0	4001.3	4001.4
10	70	45.59	0	4001.3	4001.4
12	84	17.72	0	4001.3	4001.5
14	98	48.57	0	4001.3	4001.4
15	105	18.26	0	4001.3	4001.5

3 Robustness Test

In robustness test, typical signal manipulations for audio watermarking are adopted to attack the watermarked signal, such as adding noise, resampling, low pass filtering, jittering, random sample cropping, zeros inserting [1]. All experimental results are tabulated in Table, where BER represents bit error rate for every detection. The following signal processing attacks are performed to assess the robustness. The audio editing and attacking tools adopted in the experiment are MATLAB 7.1, Audacity, Cool Edit Pro v 2.1, and Gold Wave 5.18. The Histogram based algorithm is applied to an audio signal in wav format Danube.wav (20s). The parameter =2.4 is selected to extract the histogram, watermark is seven character text information with the embedding threshold T=1.5. The different attacks are applied to the watermarked file.

- Amplification
- Resampling
- Filtering
- Random cropping
- Even cropping
- Addition of noise

3.1 Amplification

Amplification is applied to the watermarked audio signal with different factors 110% , 150%, 200%. Change Volume modifies the selection so that it sounds louder. The volume is given in decibels with a 0dB reference level. Positive values above 0dB increase the volume. Negative values below 0dB decrease the volume. A value of 0dB leaves the volume unchanged. The amplitude scale simply maps the states to a linear range of -1.0 to +1.0, with zero being silence. The waveform levels or states can be interpreted in a number of different ways. Reading the states in their binary form is impractical, so the states are mapped to different scales that are more human-readable. These include a simple amplitude scale, a percentage scale, and a decibel scale. The absolute value of the amplitude scale converted to a percentage by multiplying by one hundred and adding a percent sign.

Table 2. Performance Evaluation of Danube.wav Audio Signal with Different amplification Factor

Amplification Factor %	BER
110	0
150	0
200	0

3.2 Resampling

Sampling rate, Fs, is an important parameter for digital signal. In this work, all the audio files are sampled at 44.1 k Hz and quantized in 16 bits, with CD quality. So the sampling frequency of the watermarked signal is also equal to 44.1 kHz. To examine the property of resisting resampling, the watermarked signal originally sampled at 44.1 kHz, is resampled at 32 kHz, 48kHz, 96kHz.

Table 3. Performance Evaluation of Danube.wav Audio Signal with resampling

Resampling %	BER
32kHz	0
48kHz	0
96kHz	0

3.3 Low-Pass Filtering

With watermarks embedded in the frequency domain, low-pass filtering could effectively eliminate the embedded watermarks. Definitely, low-pass filtering attracts more attention than high-pass filtering, because the low frequency components of audio signals are much more perceptually significant. Although music has a wide dynamic range in frequency from 20 Hz to about 20 kHz, low frequency period contains most influential information. For example, human speech typically falls into the frequency range comprised between 100 Hz and 8 kHz. A tenth-order Butterworth filter with cut-off frequency 8kHz, 9kHz, 10kHz is used for evaluation.

Table 4. Performance Evaluation of Danube.wav sudio Signal with Low-pass Filters

Low pass filter with different cut off	BER
8k	0
9k	0.3061
10k	0.3061

3.4 Random Cropping

Random samples cropping belong to geometric distortions, producing disastrous synchronization problem. Random samples cropping refers to deleting some samples at some randomly selected locations, at the beginning, somewhere in the middle, or in the end. Perception of cropping depends not only the amount of samples removed, but also the amplitude of that clipping. Roughly speaking, one cropping less than 10 samples would not give rise to obvious discontinuity under the normal volume. For robustness test, a large number of samples, 500 and 1000, at a certain position will be cropping. In cropping, watermarked file is applied cropping of 10s segment in front side, back side, middle, five segments of 2s randomly.

Table 5. Performance Evaluation of Danube.wav audio Signal with Cropping Watermarked File of Different Length

Cropping length	Direction	BER
10s	Front side	0
10s	Back side	0
10s	Middle	0
10s	Randomly each 2s	0
12s	Front side	0
15s	Front side	0.0408

3.5 Jittering

Jittering is an evenly performed case of random samples cropping, which means randomly cropping A samples out of every B samples. As a continuous case of random samples cropping, jittering will lead to loss of synchronization. For evaluating jittering 1 sample is cropped in every 10, 100, 500 samples, from the watermarked audio signal.

Table 6. Performance Evaluation of Danube.wav Audio Signal with Jittering Watermarked File

Jittering	BER
1/10	0.3265
1/30	0
1/50	0
1/100	0
1/400	0
1/500	0
1/1000	0

3.6   Addition of Noise

Signal is often polluted by the noise during the transmission. To evaluate for robustness against noise addition, white Gaussian noise and normal distributed noise are applied separately to the watermarked signal. Cool Edit Pro v 2.1, and Gold Wave 5.18. generate random noise in a variety of colors. Color is used to describe the spectral composition of noise. Each color has its own characteristics.

Table 7. Performance Evaluation of Danube.wav Audio Signal with Different Noise Addition

Type of Noise	BER
White noise	0.3061
Pink noise	0.3061
Brown noise	0.3061

Table 8. The Performance of Histogram based Algorithm with Amplification (110%), Low-pass Filtering (8 KHz), Resampling (32 KHz), and Cropping in Forward Direction-10s Segment for Different Watermark Length

No of WM Character	No of WM Bits	Attacks			
		Amp BER	LPF BER	Resamp BER	Cropp BER
7	49	0	0	0	0
8	56	0	0	0	0
9	63	0	0.015	0	0
10	70	0	0.02	0.157	0
12	84	0.3452	0.071	0	0
14	98	0	0.11	0.47	0
16	112	0.04	0.24	0.0089	0

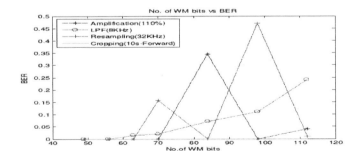

Fig. 4. Number of Watermark Bits Vs BER(Table 8)

Table 9. The Performance of Histogram based Algorithm with Amplification (150%), Low-pass Filtering (9 KHz), Resampling (48 KHz), and Cropping in Forward Direction-10s Segment for Different Watermark Length

No of WM Character	No of WM Bits	Attacks			
		Amp BER	LPF BER	Resamp BER	Cropp BER
7	49	0	0.34	0	0
8	56	0	0.30	0	0
9	63	0	0.3	0	0
10	70	0	0.3	0	0
12	84	0.32	0.33	0	0
14	98	0	0.36	0.47	0
16	112	0.28	0.34	0.0089	0.0089

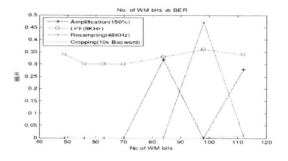

Fig. 5. Number of watermark bits Vs BER(Table 9)

Table 10. The Performance of Histogram based Algorithm with Amplification (200%), Low-pass Filtering (10 KHz), Resampling (96 KHz), and Cropping in Forward Direction-15s Segment for Different Watermark Length

No of WM Character	No of WM Bits	Attacks			
		Amp BER	LPF BER	Resamp BER	Cropp BER
7	49	0	0.28	0	0
8	56	0	0.28	0	0
9	63	0	0.34	0.44	0
10	70	0	0.3	0	0
12	84	0	0.35	0	0
14	98	0	0.37	0.47	0
16	112	0.27	0.36	0.0089	0.0089

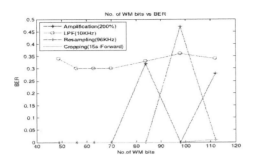

Fig. 6. Number of Watermark Bits Vs BER(Table 10)

Table 11. The Performance of Histogram based Algorithm with Different WM Bits and SNR

No of WM Character	No of WM Bits	SNR
7	49	42.59
8	56	43.75
9	63	44.68
10	70	45.54
12	84	17.72
14	98	48.52
16	112	14.63

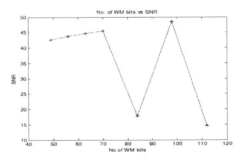

Fig. 7. Number of Watermark Bits Vs SNR

4 Conclusions

In this paper, performance of histogram based watermarking algorithm is evaluated based on bit error rate, robustness to signal processing operations. By applying amplification, resampling BER is zero and the watermark is recovered correctly. For low pass filtering with different cut-off frequencies, 9 kHz, 10 kHz the BER is occurred as 0.3061. Cropping in different direction and of different length is applied. The BER is observed zero up to the cropping of 14s segment. In jittering, the BER observed is 0.3265 at 1/10 and in other cases zero. For noise addition White, pink and brown noise BER is observed as 0.30, 0.32, and 0.30 respectively. With this it is realized that the Histogram based algorithm is more robust to TSM modification including scaling, cropping and jittering. Histogram based watermarking scheme can be considered time scale invariant. Greater than 14 character watermark is less resilient to TSM attacks.

References

1. Xiang, S., Huang, J., Yang, R.: Time-scale Invariant Audio Watermarking Based on the Statistical Features in Time domain. In: 8th International Workshop on Information Hiding, vol. 66(3), pp. 337–355 (2006)
2. Shijun, X., Jiwu, H.: Histogram-Based Audio Watermarking Against Time Scale Modification and Cropping Attacks. IEEE Transactions on Multimedia 9(7), 232–241 (2007)
3. Zhang, X.: Segmenting Histogram-based Robust Audio Watermarking Approach. Journal of Software 3(9), 69–76 (2008)
4. Arnold, M., Schmucker, M., Wolthusen, S.D.: Techniques and Applications of Digital Watermarking and Content Protection. IEEE 93(12), 2083–2126 (2005)
5. Todorov, T.: Spread Spectrum Watermarking Technique for Information System Securing. International Journal Information Theories & Applications 11, 405–408 (2004)
6. Polikar, R.: Home page - Dr. Robi Polikar (January 2001), http://users.rowan.edu/~polikar/WAVELETS/WTtutorial.html (accessed July 21, 2010)
7. Bender, W., Gruhl, D., Morimoto, N.: Techniques for Data Hiding. IBM Systems Journal 35(3), 313–336 (1996)
8. Bassia, P., Pitas, I., Nikolaidis, N.: Robust Audio Watermarking in the Time Domain. IEEE Transaction Multimedia 3, 232–241 (2001)
9. Hong, D.G., Park, S.H., Shin, J.: A Public Key Audio Watermarking using Patchwork Algorithm. In: IEEE International Conference on Multimedia and Expo., New York, vol. 2, pp. 1013–1016 (2000)
10. Charmchamras, B., Kaengin, S., Airphaiboon, S., Sangworasil, M.: Audio Watermarking Technique using Binary Image in Wavelet Domain. Signal Process 66(3), 337–355 (1998)
11. Delforouzi, A., Pooyan, M.: Adaptive Digital Audio Steganography Based on Integer Wavelet Transform. IEEE Transaction Signal Process 54, 570–584 (2006)
12. Wei, F.S., Mun, H.S., Mei, N.L.: Audio Watermarking Using Time-Frequency Compression Expansion. IEEE Transaction Image Process 6, 1673–1687 (1997)

A Secured-Concurrent-Available Architecture for Improving Performance of Web Servers

N. Harini and T.R. Padmanabhan

Department of Computer Science and Engineering,
Amrita Vishwa Vidyapeetham, Coimbatore, India
n_harini@cb.amrita.edu

Abstract. As Internet services become more popular and pervasive, a serious problem that arises is managing the performance of services under intense overload. Models and mechanisms proposed by researchers till date either stop answering requests or give answers based on incomplete/stale data, specifically when Web servers become saturated. The paper provides two contributions to the study of improving the performance of Web servers in terms of support for massive concurrency. Firstly it outlines the factors necessary to build scalable Web servers and the research contributions made to these. Secondly it illustrates how these factors can be combined and applied to obtain architecture for highly concurrent Internet services. The proposed scheme addresses the issues of overload and staleness effectively and ensures that more number of legitimate requests is answered with complete data. It is shown to improve Web QoS for commercial Web servers through control mechanisms that offer adaptive load shedding,improved availability, and secure transactions using a multi layered filtering scheme. Our experimental results show that the proposed architectural framework provides a simpler programming model that achieves superior performance.

Keywords: Availability, Distributed Denial of Service, Massive concurrency, Multi Layered Filtering, Overloaded Web Server.

1 Introduction

Web-based applications have experienced astonishing growth in recent years and all indications are that such applications will continue to grow in number and importance. The performance of Web servers plays a major role in satisfying the needs of a large growing population of Web users. Improving the performance of the Web has been the subject of much recent research,addressing various aspects of the problem such as better Web caching, HTTP protocol enhancements, server OS implementations *etc.*. The facts: Yahoo! receives over 1.2 billion page views daily [1], and AOL's Web caches service over 10 billion hits a day [2]-[3] and "Slashdot Effect" shows that it is very common for a Web server to experience more than 100-fold increase in demand when a site becomes popular [4]. Today increasing numbers of events are being watched live on the Internet. Such

K.R. Venugopal and L.M. Patnaik (Eds.): ICIP 2012, CCIS 292, pp. 621–631, 2012.
© Springer-Verlag Berlin Heidelberg 2012

events include Olympic Games, Worldcup Cricket, daily stock trading, *etc.*. The client population for these Websites is characterized by large peaks in access rates during such events. Also, there are strong geographic variations in access rates based on the popularity of local sports teams, stocks or other interests. The dynamic nature of these events requires live data to be made available to clients. Perhaps one of the most compelling problems of the modern Internet is the lack of a comprehensive and unifying approach to dealing with service concurrency, security, and availability. Although many such individual mechanisms exist, no general set of policies or standards exist where these mechanisms can be combined to achieve an overall robust state for the Internet service. In short, no "secured concurrent available" architecture exists. Moreover, the available models aim to improve the uptime of the server only in terms of the number of connections accepted. The suggested framework focuses on improving the quality of service by providing complete data rather than simple uptime. We propose and evaluate practical mechanisms that use multi layered filtering (MLF) approach which does not require over-provisioning of resources and provides better QoS to bring more reward for having serviced in terms of minimized user frustration and request rejection rates at times of emergency. Our goal is to provide practical end-to-end framework that improves service availability. The rest of the paper is organized as follows: Section 2 presents literature review, Section 3 describes the MLF architecture in detail. Finally Section 4 offers conclusions.

2   Background Study

Internet design principles do not provide any form of control for a server to state the amount of load it wants to receive and from whom. A Web server has defined load limits, it can handle only a limited number of concurrent client connections (usually between 2 and 80,000, by default between 500 and 1,000) per IP address (and TCP port) and it can serve only a certain maximum number of requests per second depending on, its own settings, HTTP request type, whether content is static or dynamic, whether content is cached, and hardware and software limitations of the OS of the computer on which the Web server runs *etc.* A flash crowd is a large spike or surge in traffic to a particular Web site. Major news Web sites experience this during major world events. The degraded Internet performance experienced during a Victorias Secret Web cast (February 5, 1999) was due to flash crowds. Flash crowds often cause very poor performance at the server side and result in a significant number of unsatisfied clients. To manage the multi fold increase in number of clients the available solutions are over-provisioning of resources or use of an appropriate concurrency model to support more connections. Though the second approach seems to be feasible in terms of implementation, at times of peak load Web servers obviously will have to make a choice between stopping to answer the requests and giving answers based on stale data (available with it). Moreover, Internet was initially designed for openness and scalability without any security concern; malicious users exploit this weakness to achieve their purpose. In recent years, the number of network-based threats has significantly increased. For example, the Internet blockages and slowdowns in Myanmar on October 25, 2010 that caused "big problems" for tourism businesses in Yangon, was due to DDoS attacks on local servers. Widely known Web sites, such as Yahoo, CNN, eBay, and Amazon.com are well-equipped in security; however DDoS attacks can degrade their performance substantially [9].

2.1 Distributed Denial of Service (DDOS)

In the Distributed Denial of Service (DDoS) attacks, network machines (called bots) are manipulated by the attacker to produce an excessive surge of traffic toward a target server. The surge of malicious traffic effectively blends in with legitimate or normal traffic, making it difficult to weed them out causing starvation for the unaware clients. The annual infrastructure security report compiled by ArborNetworks [5] shows that DDoS and Bots top the chart as the primary security concerns at 46% and 31% respectively. Flash crowds that access Internet services may also include denial-of-service attacks that can knock a service out of commission. Evolution in intruder tools is a long- standing trend and it will continue; DDoS attacks by their very nature are difficult to defend against and will continue to be an attractive and effective form of attack. Automation of attack tool deployment - despite the plethora of research on this topic still remains as one of the largest concerns of many Internet services. DDoS attacks have had a major impact on the performance of sites such as Buy.com, Yahoo!, and whitehouse.gov [3]; this clearly shows that Internet hosts whose economic and social impact have grown to considerable proportions are vulnerable to this.

2.2 Support for Concurrency in Web Servers

The most common approach to dealing with heavy loads is to over-provision resources. However, over- provisioning is infeasible when the ratio of peak to average load is very high; it is not practical to purchase 100 or 1000 times the number of machines needed to support the average load case. The two most common programming models for concurrency support are thread-based (or process-based) concurrency, which is generally used for ease of programming, and event-driven concurrency, which is used for scalability and performance. SEDA [6] draws together these two approaches and proposes a hybrid model that exhibits features of both. Though the SEDA architecture and its variations using admission control policies manage the multifold increase in load with peaceful degradation of service, they do not address the issue of data availability.

2.3 Replication of Resources

It is generally difficult to share data while providing high availability, good performance, and strong consistency. Replication techniques are primarily employed to improve the availability and the performance of distributed applications and Web services deployed over wide area networks. However, in order to maintain a consistent view across all replicas in the system, additional workload may be imposed on the system on both client reads and writes. As the result, the replication systems usually gain better availability and performance at the cost of reducing the overall system capacity. Researchers have investigated the scalability, communication overhead, and availability of various replication protocols under different workloads. Lei Gao *et al.*[8], in their research work show that by taking object specific workload characteristics DQ protocol shows much better performance in terms of data availability and reduced communication overhead.

2.4   Summary of Findings

Internet services experience huge variations in service load, with bursts coinciding with the times that the service has the most value. As mentioned earlier there are two types of events that overload Websites to a point where their services are degraded or disrupted entirely flash events and distributed denial of service attacks (DDoS). While the intent and the triggering mechanisms for DDoS attacks and flash crowds are quite different, from the network's perspective both events are quite similar. The persistent congestion in the network is due to an undifferentiated overall increase in traffic. Although commercial solutions promise full protection from DDoS, their demand on IP address space is too high to be affordable for small organizations.

The major strategies used for constructing high performance servers can be broadly categorized as event-driven concurrency and thread-based concurrency [10]. The debate over which approach is better has waged for a long time and still appears an open issue. Given a service instance that can sustain a certain level of performance, it must be replicated to sustain a many-fold increase in load. Efficient replication of data on a wide scale is difficult because it implies significant replica update traffic or high latencies for write access. Moreover, synchronous updation of all replicated copies is a static approach that does not offer much flexibility and more difficult to exercise when the data is upgraded more frequently or when new data is added suddenly. Unfortunately, in traditional operating system designs, common models of concurrency and replication protocols are not integrated to provide graceful management of such peak loads.

2.5   Problem Statement

To provide a practical (secured-concurrent-available)end-to-end framework based on admission control policies - a strategy that achieves robust performance on a wide range of Internet services subject to huge variation in load, while preserving ease of implementation and improves the service availability at varied load levels by using adaptive protocols and filtering capabilities and evaluate the same.

3   Proposed Architecture

As the Internet services are extremely popular, there is an increasing demand for Internet servers to meet customer's expectations in terms of the QoS delivered in order to increase client's satisfaction and in turn achieve more profits. A new architecture called "multi layer filtering" is proposed here; this architecture aims to minimize resource utilization (amount of wasted server work) by removing a malicious request at the very beginning of its transaction. This helps in shaping the traffic (reduces the load on the Web server), and improves the throughput. It provides improved QoS by providing fresh data in addition to increased uptime of the server. The scheme allows access to Web servers through specialized access-nodes. This provisioning achieves two purposes firstly it helps to drop malicious attacks well ahead of the Web server and secondly it masquerades the actual Web servers serving the client. All client requests are directed to a public server (does not store anything) that implements a light weight protocol to select one of the suitable access nodes. MLF framework does request-processing in two stages.

3.1   Stage 1

The scheme offers resistance to peak loads by filtering malicious requests at an initial stage thus avoiding bottlenecks. Filtering at the first level is done using Completely Automated Public Turing test to tell Computers and Humans apart. These tests are easily solvable by human users but hard to break for bots [7]. Therefore, this can offer effective protection against bots that attempt to flood a server with requests and thus help in preventing DDoS attacks originating from bots. The next level of filtration is done at the public server / Router by the Detection module that detects the DDoS attack far ahead of servers'location using a Fuzzy C Means algorithm that does network anomaly detection. The Figures 1 and 2 show the operation of Stage1. Fuzzy C-means (FCM) clustering

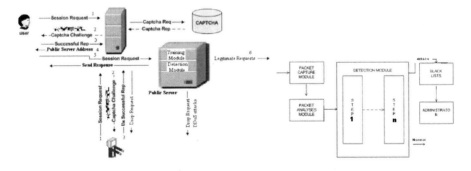

Fig. 1. Architecture of Stage 1   **Fig. 2.** Steps in Detection

algorithm can be defined as a mechanism to discover certain features in a set of data and classify each element of data into a number of clusters with different degree of memberships. The operation of the algorithm is as follows: X is matrix of size nXN and U is the membership matrix expressed as:

$$X = \begin{bmatrix} x_{11} & x_{12} & \cdots & x_{1N} \\ x_{21} & x_{22} & \cdots & x_{2N} \\ \vdots & \vdots & \ddots & \vdots \\ x_{n1} & x_{n2} & \cdots & x_{nN} \end{bmatrix} \qquad U = \begin{bmatrix} \mu_{11} & \mu_{12} & \cdots & \mu_{1N} \\ \mu_{21} & \mu_{22} & \cdots & \mu_{2N} \\ \vdots & \vdots & \ddots & \vdots \\ \mu_{n1} & \mu_{n2} & \cdots & \mu_{nN} \end{bmatrix}$$

Each $X_j \in R^p, j = 1, 2 \ldots n$ is a given set of feature data representing a number of features $p(16\ chosen)$for the packet $x_i, i = 1 \ldots N$. FCM operates on the matrix X and minimizes the FCM objective function using $f(x : U, V) = \sum_{i=1}^{c} \sum_{j=1}^{n} (\mu)^n D_{ij}{}^2$ in order to partition matrix X into C (normal and attack) clusters. The value m controls the degree of fuzziness for the membership of the cluster ($chosen\ as\ 1.2\ here\ as\ is\ done\ widely$). Each value of matrix U indicates the degree of membership between vector X_j and cluster C_i satisfying the criteria $\mu_{ij} \in [0,1], \forall_i = 1 \ldots C, \forall_j = 1, \ldots n \sum_{i=1}^{c} \mu_{ij} = 1, \forall_j = 1, \ldots n$ During the clustering process, the elements of U are updated using $\mu_{ij} = \dfrac{1}{\sum_{k=1}^{c} \left(\frac{\|x_j - v_i\|}{\|x_j - v_k\|} \right)^{\frac{2}{m-1}}}$

where $1 \leq i \leq C, 1 \leq j \leq n$. The clusters' centers $V = v_1, \ldots v_c$ are calculated using $v_i = \dfrac{\sum_{j=1}^{n} (\mu_{ij})^m x^j}{\sum_{j=1}^{n} (\mu_{ij})^m}$, $\forall_i = 1, \ldots . C$. The Distance D_{ij}^2 is the Euclidean distance between x_j to the centre v_i of the cluster i which is defined by $D_{ij}^2 = \|x_j - v_i\|^2$. The process is repeated until the maximum number of iterations is reached or the objective function improvement between two consecutive iterations is less than the minimum amount of improvement ($< 1e\text{-}4$ in our case). At the end of processing in stage 1 legitimate request are forwarded for further processing. The above filters helped us to drop nasty requests that are not legitimate at a very early stage thereby improving the server throughput.

3.2   Stage 2

Legitimate requests successfully crossing stage 1 are directed to access nodes introduced earlier. The MLF model categorizes resources into two types namely, resources that may not be replicated due to security concerns ($e.g.$ building structure reports, intelligence, etc) and those that may be replicated (News articles, Game scores etc). This differentiation is essential as the availability is closely affected by the number of replications. For resources of the first category the access node verifies the authenticity of the request and then directs it to the corresponding front-end-server. For the other category it sets priority levels and other parameters in the TCP header of the request before it is forwarded. At this stage the architecture can use any replication protocol to ensure completeness of the data made available. Our implementation uses DQ protocol for ensuring better data availability and minimized communication overhead. The front end server's act as edge server clients or just clients to the DQ storage system (guarantees availability of complete data). Figure 3 shows the interaction of various components in Stage 2. The architecture details for the case of replicated resources follow.

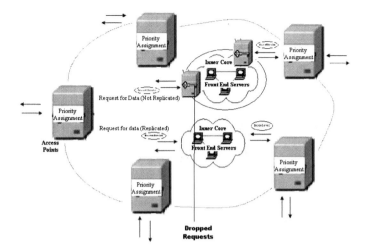

Fig. 3. Architecture of Stage 2

3.3   Operation of the Inner Core

The inner core consists of front end Web servers which are responsible for processing of the client request. To maintain concurrency over multiple copies of database Quorum systems are used. The front end server performs the following: accepts a client request, sets admission control parameters and directs request to Read/Write quorum. The event pipeline used by front end servers to fulfill its task helps in conditioning the load. The architecture of the inner core is shown in Figure 4.

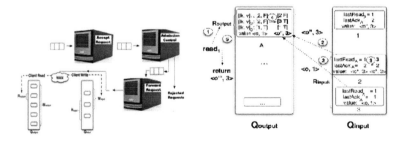

Fig. 4. Architecture of Inner Core   **Fig. 5.** Operation of Protocol

Admission Control. The admission control is based on the policies defined by the administrator on input parameters (Max clients, Queue length, Arrival rate *etc.* set by him initially). An additional set of parameters based on the information generated from user behavior can improve the architecture in terms of cost-effectiveness and this could particularly benefit e-commerce application and deployed in Websites like Buy.com.

Read and Write Operations. The DQ protocol uses two separate quorum systems (see Figure 5) , an input quorum system Q_{input} for write and an output quorum system Q_{output} for read and optimizes both write and read's availability and performance. Upon receiving a read request from a client, the server contacts a read quorum R_{output} of the output quorum system Q_{output}. R_{output} server can return a read immediately if it holds a valid copy of the object('*read hit*'). A *read miss* occurs when A does not have the latest data. Otherwise, it must renew the object by communicating with a read quorum R_{input} of the input quorum system ('*read miss*'). Upon receiving a write request from a client, the server contacts every server in a write quorum W_{input} of the input quorum system Q_{input}. Writing is done in two phases. First, a server i that receives the client's write request retrieves the highest logical clock from every server in R_{input} via QRPC(Quorum Remote Procedure Call); then, the server advances the logical clock and assigns it along with its unique id as the write version number. Second, the server sends the write request with the version number to a W_{input} quorum via QRPC. The write completes after i receives acknowledgments from every server in a W_{input} quorum. Figure 5 illustrates *read miss* scenario with three Q_{input} servers (1, 2, 3) and multiple Q_{output} servers (A, B,C,...). With input quorum configured as majority quorum, initially all Q_{input} servers replicate the object (value-o; version Num-i) and all Q_{output} servers cache the object from each Q_{input} server (last known - lk, valid-v and state (T/F)). Suppose A selects servers 2 and 3 as the R_{input} quorum for its object renewal, Servers 2 and 3 send the data to A and after A applies these two replies it will have the latest version of the data (state-T). Because the W_{input} quorum of write1 intersects the R_{input} quorum of read1, A is able to read the newest data (completed version). For a detailed understanding of the protocol [8] may be referred.

3.4   Evaluation of the Architecture

Dataset Specification. A realistic performance analysis of the architecture demands a dataset comprising of requests from all types discussed earlier. The data set included intrusion samples from the widely used DARPA datasets, requests from bots, and requests that would fail at the last stage due to unavailability of complete data. The information used for experimenting is as follows: Protocol, Flag, No. of error fragments, Connections having "SYN" errors, No. of compromised conditions, % of connections to the same services, % of connections to the different services, No.of connections from same source host to the same destination host, No.of connections from same source service to the same destination service, No. of connections from same destination host to the same source host, No. of connections from same destination service to same source host , Destination IP address, Destination port, Source bytes, Destination bytes, The dataset includes Requests from bots - 12%, DDoS Attacks - 33% ,Legitimate - 50%, Incomplete - 5%

Testing - Stage 1. CAPTCHA test filtered about 10% of the requests that were generated from bots and with 16 attributes 81.2 % of the DDoS attacks were detected by our detection module that used FCM algorithm. The throughput achieved in stage 1 and the resource utilization are shown in The Figures 6 and 7 respectively. The graph in The Figure 6 clearly shows that the performance of the MLF architecture is decidedly better than thread based schemes - specifically with 400 clients the average response time with MLF scheme is only 70ms whereas it is 80ms with threaded scheme. The figure 7 the resource utilization. The service rate attains the peak value of 10 requests/second with 10 threads and sustains at that level up to 20 threads and tapers rather slowly with MLF scheme; in contrast the thread based model attains a peak value of service rate of 8 requests per second that too only with 15 threads; further it tapers much more rapidly. It is interesting to note that this conspicuous improvement in resource utilization is due to drop of malicious requests early enough.

Table 1. Graphs showing Performance Achieved in stage 1 and stage 2

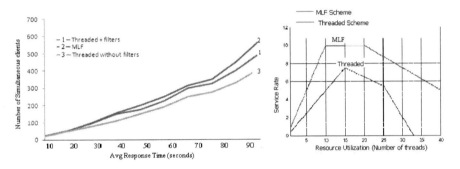

Fig. 6. Throughput Achieved   **Fig.7.** Resource Utilization

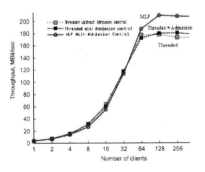

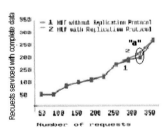

Fig. 8. Throughput Achieved   **Fig.9.** Performance of the Web Server

Testing - Stage 2. The packet structures used to establish the connection are shown below:

Event	Field 1	Field 2	Field 3	Field 4	Field 5
Client Request for session	Client IP	Destination IP	Time	nil	nil
Return Public Server IP	Sender ID	Public Server IP	Session key	Pkt. seq. range	Time Status Flags
Request Forwarding	Pkt. seq.	Session key	IDs flag	Time	IP packet from application

The legitimate requests that passed stage 1 were accepted and granted admission based on admission control strategy used by the front end Web server which included the factors max clients, arrival rate, queue length, and priority. The pipelined front end servers in our implementation allowed new requests to be queued as long as the queue size was below a threshold value T. The graphs in Figures 8 and 9 show the throughput achieved in stage 2 and the performance of the Web server measured in terms of complete data delivered respectively. The throughput achieved with MLF architecture can be seen to be clearly higher than that with the threaded model; the gain is because of the event pipeline that does parallel processing. The improvement in the quality of service can be seen at point "a" where the residual 5% of the incomplete requests were also serviced with fresh data with the proposed scheme.

4   Conclusions

The primary goal has been to develop a framework that simplifies the development of highly concurrent Internet services and builds real world applications that can take advantage of this functionality. Our overall observation was that there was not much of a performance improvement till the load on the Web server was about serving 300 clients. When the number of clients was increased to 500 the MLF scheme showed a better throughput than the traditional thread based model. There is a clear case for examining reduction in the dimensionality of the dataset used with algorithm 1 to achieve the same level of performance. Similarly exercising better admission control strategies taking into consideration business metrics can benefit E-Commerce applications. These require detailed investigation. Next, our plan is to critically analyze the contribution of each filter to the performance of our architecture by varying the algorithms used at different levels and investigate the impact on the architecture as users move from one edge server to another. It would be also interesting to tune Web server parameters in real time by using a neural network model supported by a feedback control strategy.

Acknowledgments. We are grateful to our institution for their constant support. We sincerely thank Dr. Vidya Balasubramaniam for her suggestions, useful remarks, and productive discussion which helped to improve the content and presentation of this paper.

References

1. Yahoo! Inc. Yahoo! reports Second Quarter, Financial results (2001), http://docs.yahoo.com/docs/pr/release794.html
2. America Online Press Data points, http://corp.aol.com/press/pressdatapoints.html
3. Lemos, R.: Web Worm Targets White House (July 2001), http://news.com.com/2100-1001-270272.html
4. Wald, L.A., Schwarz, S.: The 1999 Southern California Seismic Network Bulletin. Seismo logical Research Letters 71(4) (July/August 2000)
5. MacPherson, D., Labovitz, C.: Worldwide Infrastructure Security Report, vol. 2 (September 2006)
6. Welsh, M., David, E.C., Eric, A.B.: SEDA: Architecture for Well Conditioned, Scalable Internet Services. In: Proceedings of the Symposium on Operating System Principles (2001)
7. Morein, W., Stavrou, A., Cook, D., Keromytis, A., Misra, V., Rubenstein, D.: Using Graphic Turing Tests to Counter Automated DDoS Attacks Against Web servers. In: Proceedings of ACM CCS 2003, Washington DC (October 2003)
8. Lei, G., Mike, D., Jiandan, Z., Lorenzo, A., Arun, I.: Dual-Quorum: A Highly Available and Consistent Replication System for Edge Services. IEEE Transactions on Dependable and Secure Computing 2 (Apri-June 2010)
9. Zhang, F., Abe, S.: A Heuristic DDoS Flooding Attack Detection Mechanism Analyses Based on the Relationship between Input and Output Traffic. Computer Communications and Networks, 798–802 (August 2007)
10. Bacon, J.: Concurrency Systems. Addison Wesley, Reading (1997)

Text Steganography through Quantum Approach

Indradip Banerjee, Souvik Bhattacharyya, and Gautam Sanyal

Department of Computer Science and Engineering
University Institute of Technology
The University of Burdwan
Burdwan, West Bengal, India
ibanerjee2001@yahoo.com

Abstract. Steganography maintain the security of the secret data through a communication channel, which causing attempts to break and reveal the original messages. In this paper, a text steganography technique has been proposed with the help of Bengali language. Text steganography including quantum approach based on the use of two specific characters and two special characters like invited comas (opening and closing) in Bengali language and mapping technique of quantum gate truth table have been used.

Keywords: Cover Text, Quantum Steganography, Security, Stego Text, Text Steganography.

1 Introduction

Information hiding is the ability to prevent or hidden certain aspects from being accessible to others excluding authentic user. It has many sub disciplines. One of the most important sub disciplines is steganography [1], [2] as shown in Fig. 1. Steganography diverges from cryptography in the sense that where cryptography focuses on keeping the contents of a message secret by encryption technique, steganography focuses on keeping the presence of a message secret.

A hidden channel could be defined as a communications channel that transfers some kind of information using a method originally not intended to transfer this kind of information. Observers are unaware that a covert message is being communicated. Only the sender and recipient of the message notice it. Steganography works have been carried out on different media like images, video clips, text, music and sound [3],[4].

The most difficult kind of steganography is text steganography or linguistic steganography because due to the lack of redundant information in a text compared to an image or audio. The text steganography is a method of using written natural language to conceal a secret message.

1.1 Quantum Steganography

Comparatively very little research work has been done in quantum steganography also. The idea of hiding secret messages as the error syndromes of a quantum

K.R. Venugopal and L.M. Patnaik (Eds.): ICIP 2012, CCIS 292, pp. 632–643, 2012.
© Springer-Verlag Berlin Heidelberg 2012

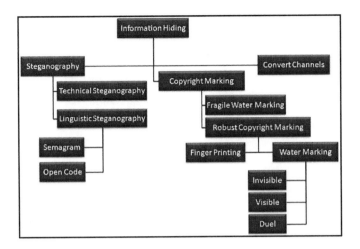

Fig. 1. A Classification of Information Hiding techniques

error-correcting code (QECC) was introduced by Julio Gea-Banacloche in [5]. In his work Alice and Bob use the three-bit repetition code to transmit messages to each other using a shared secret key. All the noise in the channel that Eve perceives is because of these deliberate errors that Alice applies. In his model he assumes that Alice and Bob share a binary-symmetric channel. This work does not address the issue of whether the errors would resemble a plausible channel, nor does it consider the case where the channel contains intrinsic noise. Natori gives a simple treatment of quantum steganography which is a modification of super-dense coding [6]. Martin introduced a notion of quantum steganographic communication based on a variation of Bennett and Brassard's quantum-key distribution (QKD), hiding a steganographic channel in the QKD protocol [7]. Curty e.al. proposed three different quantum steganographic protocols [8].

1.2   Quantum Gate[9]

Quantum circuit model of computation in quantum computing[10]-[12], a quantum gate or quantum logic gate is a basic quantum circuit which operates on a small number of qubits. They are the building blocks of quantum circuits, like classical logic gates are basically for conventional digital circuits. Quantum logic gates are reversible like other classical logic gates. However, classical computing can be performed by the help of only reversible gates. Quantum gates are represented as matrices. A gate which acts on k qubits is represented by a 2^k x 2^k unitary matrix. The number of qubits in the input and output of the gate is equal.

1.3   Reversible Classical Logic

The first concept of the reversibility of computation were raised in the 1970s. There were two issues which are logical reversibility and physical reversibility,

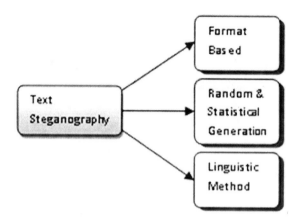

Fig. 2. Type of Steganography

both were intimately connected. Logical reversibility reconstruct the input from the output of a computation or gate function. The NAND gate is explicitly irreversible, it has two inputs and one output, while the NOT gate is reversible (its own inverse). In case of Physical reversibility the NAND gate has only one output, one of it's inputs has effectively been erased in the process, whose information has been irretrievably lost. The change in entropy that we would associate with the lost of one bit of information is ln 2, which, thermodynamically, corresponds to an energy increase of kT ln 2, where k is Boltzmans constant and T is the temperature. The heat dissipated during a process is usually taken to be a sign of physical irreversibility, that the microscopic physical state of the system cannot be restored exactly as it was before the process took place.

NOT	<0>	<1>
<0>	0	1
<1>	1	0

Fig. 3. NOT Gate Truth Table

Reversible logic gates are symmetric with respect to the number of inputs and outputs. The reversible NOT gate, whose truth table is given in Fig. 3. It can also write this in the form of a matrix, or as a graphic. The matrix form lists the lines in the truth table in the form $\langle 0 \rangle$, $\langle 1 \rangle$. The matrix field with 1's and 0's such that each horizontal or vertical line has exactly one 1, which is to be interpreted as a one-to-one mapping of the input to the output. A two-bit gate closely related to the NOT gate is the two-bit Controlled-NOT (or C-NOT) gate.

C-NOT	<00>	<01>	<10>	<11>
<00>	1	0	0	0
<01>	0	1	0	0
<10>	0	0	0	1
<11>	0	0	1	0

Fig. 4. Quantum Truth Table

Controlled-NOT gate shows in Fig. 4, performs a NOT on the second bit if the first bit is $\langle 1 \rangle$, but otherwise has no effect. The C-NOT is sometimes also called XOR, since it performs an exclusive OR operation on the two input bits and writes the output to the second bit.

1.4 Text Steganography

The Text is one of the ancient media used in steganography. Letters, books and telegrams hide secret messages within their texts in earlier time i.e. before the electronic age comes. Text steganography refers to the hiding of information within text i.e. character-based messages. There are three basic categories of text steganography 2 maintained here: *format-based methods, random and statistical generation and linguistic methods* [13].

Format-Based Methods. This methods [13] use the physical formatting of text as a space in which to hide information. Format-based methods usually modify existing text for hiding the steganographic text. Insertion of spaces or non-displayed characters, careful errors tinny throughout the text and resizing of fonts are some of the many format-based methods used in text steganography.

Random and Statistical Generation Method. This [13] avoid comparison with a known plaintext, steganographers often resort to generating their own cover texts. Character sequences method hide the information within character sequences.

Linguistic Methods. The affluence of electronic documented information available in the world as well as the exertion of serious linguistic analysis makes this an interesting medium for steganographic information hiding [13]. Fig. 5 shows the mechanism of text steganography. Firstly, a secret message will be covered up in a cover-text by applying an embedding algorithm to produce a stego-text. The stego-text will then be transmitted by a communication channel to a receiver.

In this paper, an approach of quantum text steganography using Bengali character mapping method has been proposed based on the use of some special character. The explanation of text steganography remains wide in order to differentiate it from the more specific "Format-based methods of steganography".

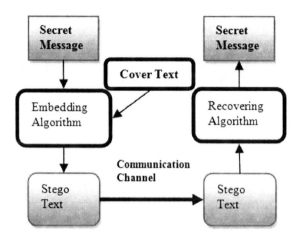

Fig. 5. Steganography Mechanism

Here the quantum truth table also mapped to increase the security level and complexity. In this method the length of the stego and the cover are same so prediction of existence of message is difficult in view of that characteristics, so this one is the unique method which has been developed in this steganography approach.

The proposed scheme has been enthused by the author's previous work [14]-[22] on various approaches of steganography methods. The quantum truth table approach has been incorporated from previous work [22].

This paper is organized into the following sections. Section 2 describes the proposed model. Algorithms of various processes like embedding, extracting and GUI are discussed in Section 3. Analyses of the results are in Section 4. The last section descries the concluded part of the work.

2 Proposed Model

This paper exactly deals with Text steganography using Indian regional language, specifically the Bengali text as the medium where to hide information. Text steganography can involve anything from changing the ASCII character from the specific position of an existing text. The input messages can be in any digital form and are often treated as a bit stream. Then select the proper Bengali Text as cover and change it to it's equivalent binary code. Then a matrix formed with the help of message length and map the C-NOT truth table (shown in Fig. 7) from left most corner in a sequence (vertically or horizontally), after that start embedding one by one if the mapped value showing not '1' value. After that secret message has been embed to the cover text by replacing the next ASCII of "ক" and "র" by ASCII 34 i.e. ['] and 39 i.e. ['] in Bengali language based on the mapping information given in Fig. 6 to generate the stego text.

By the help of replacing technique the stego length are being same as cover. At the receiver side with the help of same mapping algorithm and other different reverse operation has been carried out to get back the original information.

ASCII	Character	ASCII	Character		
69	ক	34	'	0	0
69	ক	39	'	0	1
77	ম	34	'	1	0
77	ম	39	'	1	1

Fig. 6. Mapping Technique

C-NOT	<00>	<01>	<10>	<11>
<00>	1	0	0	0
<01>	0	1	0	0
<10>	0	0	0	1
<11>	0	0	1	0

1	89	52	46	1	82	45	65	62	66
63	1	50	120	125	1	68	55	86	57
52	46	75	1	45	120	125	1	68	52
50	120	1	92	68	125	1	75	64	50
52	125	52	75	64	52	46	75	82	45
50	45	50	125	63	50	120	125	92	68
75	82	45	45	52	120	125	92	68	52
125	92	68	68	50	125	52	75	64	50

Fig. 7. Quantum Truth Table Mapping

Solution Methodology. The proposed system involves two windows i.e. SENDER SIDE and RECEIVER SIDE. The user will be someone who is aware with the process of information hiding and will have adequate knowledge of steganography systems. The user have a duty to select a plain text message from a file, another Bengali text to be used as the carrier (cover text) and then use the proposed embedding method which will hide the message in the selected cover text and will procedure the stego text. The user at the receiver side should be able to extract the message from the stego text with the help of different reverse process in chronological manner to un-hide the message from the stego text. The GUI of the proposed solution has been shown in Fig. 8.

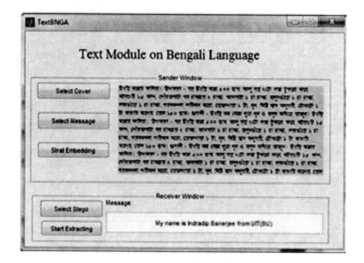

Fig. 8. GUI Representation

3   Algorithms

In this section, algorithms for different processes used both in the sender side and receiver sides are described which are furnished below:

3.1   Algorithm for Message Embedding

1. Select the message and Bengali cover. Check whether the selected text is capable of embedding. If not possible repeat this step otherwise continue.
2. Map the quantum C-NOT gate to the matrix MATMSG (N x N) vertically or horizontally and Put the message value by replacing '0' in the matrix MATMSG.
3. Check the message sequence and pick first two bit sequence (MSG). Start from the first character of the cover text (TX).
4. Start checking and embedding.
   - If MSG='11' and character "ঝ" from the TX then change from ASCII (77,245) to (77,39)
   - Else If MSG='10' and character "ঝ" from the TX then change from ASCII (77,245) to (77,34)
   - Else If MSG='01' and character "ক" from the TX then change from ASCII (77,245) to (77,39)
   - Else If MSG='00' and character "ক" from the TX then change from ASCII (77,245) to (77,34)
5. Repeat the above step for the remaining bit sequence of the message (two bit at a time) and prepare the stego text.

3.2   Algorithm for Message Extracting

1. Select the stego text put in MATMSG (N x N) matrix and map the quantum C-NOT gate to the matrix vertically or horizontally.
2. Extract the message value from the '0' th position of C-NOT. Pick values one by one from MATMSG and create MSG.
3. Select the stego text TX.
   - If "ৰ" and next ASCII is 39, MSG='11'.
   - Else If "ৰ" and next ASCII is 34, MSG='10'.
   - Else If "ক" and next ASCII is 39, MSG='01'.
   - Else If "ক" and next ASCII is 34, MSG='00'.

3.3   Algorithm for GUI

In this section the two algorithmic approach is described one for the function of the Sender Side and another for the Receiver Side.

Sender Side

1. Select the Cover Text from the set of Text files.
2. Check whether the selected text is capable to do the embedding or not. If not possible then error.
3. Select the message in text form.
4. Embed the message in the cover text to form the stego text.
5. End.

Receiver Side

1. Receive the text with embedded message along with positions.
2. Extract the message from the Stego Text.
3. End.

4   Results Analysis

There are mainly three phases that should be reserved into account when discussing the results of the proposed method of text steganography with the help of Bengali Language. The authors simulated the proposed system and the results are shown in the Fig. 9, 10 and 11. It generates the stego text with minimum degradation which is not very revealing to people about the existence of any hidden data, maintaining its security to the eavesdroppers. This method hides two bit per word in the Bengali cover text which reflects the high embedding capacity of the system. The embedding capacity of the proposed method depends upon the embedding character of cover and Quantum Table. This method hides two bit per word in the cover text which reflects the high embedding capacity of the system. Although the embedding capacity of the proposed method is depends upon the Bengali characters.

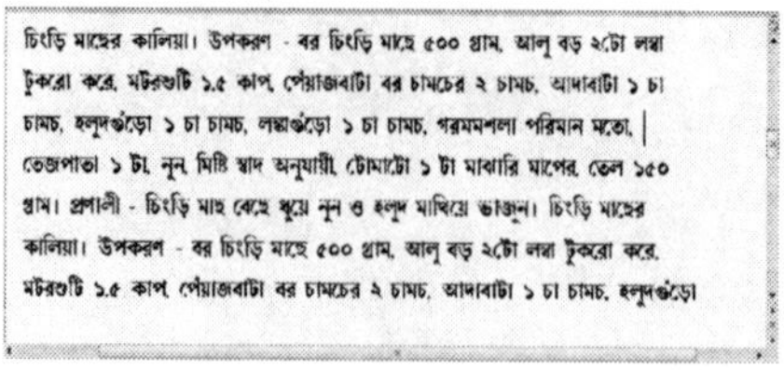

Fig. 9. Cover Text 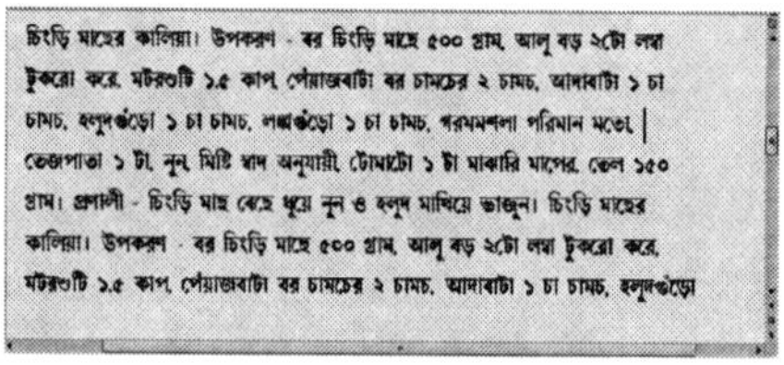   **Fig. 10.** Stego Text

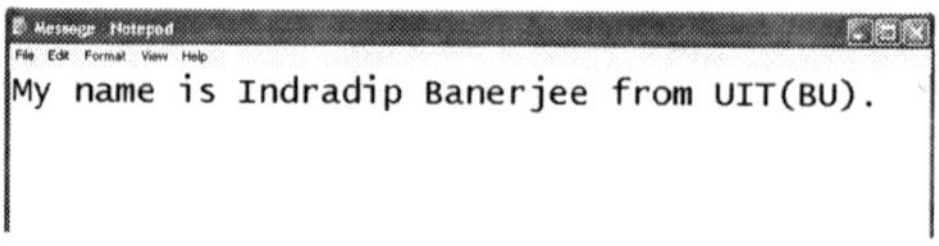

Fig. 11. Secret Message

4.1 Similarity Measure

For comparing the similarity between cover text and the stego text, the Correlation method for measuring similarity between two strings has been computed. The most familiar measure of dependence between two quantities is the Pearson product-moment correlation coefficient [23], or "Pearson's correlation". It is obtained by dividing the covariance of the two variables by the product of their standard deviations. The Pearson correlation is +1 in the case of a perfect positive (increasing) linear relationship (correlation), -1 in the case of a perfect decreasing (negative) linear relationship (anticorrelation)[24] and some value between -1 and 1 in all other cases, indicating the degree of linear dependence between the variables. As it approaches zero there is less of a relationship (closer to uncorrelated). The closer the coefficient is to either -1 or 1, the stronger the correlation between the variables. If the variables are independent, Pearson's correlation coefficient is 0, but the converse is not true because the correlation coefficient detects only linear dependencies between two variables If we have a series of n measurements of X and Y written as x_i and y_i where $i = 1, 2, ..., n$, then the sample correlation coefficient can be used in Pearson correlation r between X and Y. The sample correlation coefficient is written

$$r_{xy} = \frac{\sum_{i=1}^{n}(x_i - \bar{x})(y_i - \bar{y})}{(n-1)s_x s_y} \tag{1}$$

where $\bar{x}$ and $\bar{y}$ are the sample means of X and Y, s_x and s_y are the sample standard deviations of X and Y. The number of matching (but different sequence order) characters divided by two defines the number of transpositions. The Correlation score of comparing cover text and stego text is shown in Fig. 12 and the chart in Fig. 13 represent the Correlation of different stego of various length of message. The Fig. 14 shows that the Input and Output message are remain same.

MESSAGE LENGTH (in Character)	CORRELATION VALUE
0	1.000000000000000
10	0.999990260304237
50	0.999951327098684
100	0.999902718146403
150	0.999854173130309
200	0.999805692033057
250	0.999757274844497
300	0.999708921545378
350	0.999660632121283
400	0.999612406558322

Fig. 12. Correlation Values of Cover and Stego Text in Different Length of Message in Character

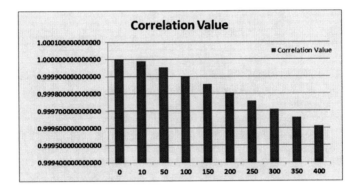

Fig. 13. Representation Correlation Values

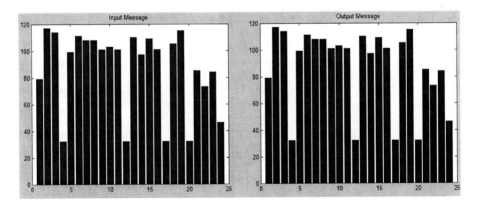

Fig. 14. Input and Output Message Graphical Representation

5   Conclusions

In this paper the authors presented an approach of text steganography method using Bengali language by the help of quantum truth table mapping technique. This property generates the stego text with minimum degradation. In this method the length of stego and cover remain same and this property enables the method to avoid the steganalysis also. The result shows that the performance of the technique is satisfactorily. This work can be extended by using other Indian regional language.

References

1. Al-Mualla, M., Al-Ahmad, H.: Information Hiding: Steganography and Watermarking, http://www.emirates.org/ieee/information_hiding.pdf
2. Ross, J.A., Petitcolas, F.A.P.: On the Limits of Steganography. IEEE Journal on Selected Areas in Communications (J-SAC), Special Issue on Copyright and Privacy Protection 16(4), 474–481 (1998)
3. Bailey, K., Curran, K.: An Evaluation of Image Based Steganography Methods (1999)
4. Mrkel, T., Eloff, J.H.P., Olivier, M.S.: An Overview of Image Steganography. In: Proceedings of the Fifth Annual Information Security South Africa Conference, South Africa (2005)
5. Gea-Banacloche, J.: Journal of Mathematical Physics (2002)
6. Natori, S.: Quantum Computation and Information. In: Topics in Applied Physics, vol. 102, pp. 235–240. Springer, Heidelberg (2006)
7. Martin, K.: Lecture Notes in Computer Science (2008)
8. Curty, M., Santos, D.J.: 2nd Journal Bielefeld Workshop on Quantum Information and Complexity (2000)
9. Muthukrishnan, A.: Classical and Quantum Logic Gates: An Introduction to Quantum Computing. In: Quantum Information Seminar, Rochester Center for Quantum Information (RCQI) (1991)
10. Feynman, R.P.: Quantum Mechanical Computers. Found. Phys. 16, 507 (1986)
11. Deutsch, D.: Quantum Theory, the Church-Turing Principle and the Universal Quantum Computer. Proceedings of Roy. Soc. Lond. A 400, 97–117 (1985)
12. Deutsch, D.: Quantum computational networks. Proceedings of Roy. Soc. Lond. A 425, 73–90 (1989)
13. Bennett, K.: Linguistic Steganography: Survey, Analysis, and Robustness Concerns for Hiding Information in Text, Purdue University, CERIAS Technical Report (2004)
14. Bhattacharyya, S., Banerjee, I., Sanyal, G.: Design and Implementation of a Secure Text Based Steganography Model. In: Proceedings of 9th Annual Conference on Security and Management (SAM) under The 2010 World Congress in Computer Science, Computer Engineering and Applied Computing (WorldComp 2010), LasVegas, USA (July 2010)
15. Bhattacharyya, S., Banerjee, I., Sanyal, G.: Implementation of a Novel Text Based Steganography Model. In: National Conference on Computing and Systems (NACCS), Dept. of Computer Science, The University of Burdwan, Burdwan (2010)

16. Bhattacharyya, S., Banerjee, I., Sanyal, G.: A Novel Approach of Secure Text Based Steganography Model using Word Mapping Method (WMM). Proceedings of International Journal of Computer and Information Engineering 4(2) (2010); World Academy of Science, Engineering and Technology (WASET), 4(2), 96–103 (2010)
17. Bhattacharyya, S., Mazumdar, A.P., Banerjee, I., Sanyal, G.: Text Steganography using Formatting Character Spacing. Proceedings of IJICS 13(2) (December 2010)
18. Bhattacharyya, S., Banerjee, I., Sanyal, G.: Data Hiding Through Multi Level Steganography and SSCE. Journal of Global Research in Computer Science 2(2) (2011)
19. Bhattacharyya, S., Banerjee, I., Sanyal, G.: The Text Steganography using Article Mapping Technique (AMT) and SSCE. Journal of Global Research in Computer Science 2(4) (April 2011)
20. Bhattacharyya, S., Banerjee, I., Sanyal, G.: A Survey of Steganography and Steganalysis Technique in Image, Text, Audio and Video as Cover Carrier. Journal of Global Research in Computer Science 2(4) (April 2011)
21. Bhattacharyya, S., Banerjee, I., Sanyal, G.: Novel Text Steganography through Special Code Generation. In: Proceedings of International Conference on Systemics,Cybernetics and Informatics (ICSCI 2011), Hyderabad, India (2011)
22. Bhattacharyya, S., Banerjee, I., Sanyal, G.: An Approach of Quantum Steganography through Special SSCE Code. Proceedings of International Journal of Computer and Information Engineering - World Academy of Science, Engineering and Technology (WASET) 175, 939–946 (2011)
23. Correlation and Dependence, http://en.wikipedia.org/wiki/Correlation_and_dependence
24. Dowdy, S., Wearden, S.: Statistics for Research. Wiley (1983) ISBN 0471086029

A Novel Approach
of Video Steganography Using PMM

Souvik Bhattacharyya and Gautam Sanyal

University Institute of Technology, Burdwan, India
souvik.bha@gmail.com

Abstract. Steganography is an emerging area, used for secured data transmission trough any public media. Different researcher's developed newer steganographic techniques. This paper proposes a novel video steganography technique for data hiding. In this approach data hiding operations are executed entirely in the discrete integer wavelet domain. This method also uses our developed Pixel Mapping Method (PMM) in order to enlarge the capacity of the hidden secret information and provide an imperceptible stego-frame/stego-video for human vision. Experimental results demonstrate that the proposed algorithm has high imperceptibility and capacity and produces satisfactory results in terms of security of the hidden data.

Keywords: Steganography, Cover Image, Cover Video, Stego Image, Stego Video, PMM (Pixel Mapping Method), Integer Wavelet Transform.

1 Introduction

Steganography is a technique to hide a text in a manner that is both invisible and undetectable. The majority of today's steganographic system uses multimedia objects like image, audio, video etc as cover media [1]. Coding secret messages in digital images is by far the most widely used of all methods in today's digital world [2,3]. Text steganography [4,5] and [6]can be a very challenging task due to lack of redundant data. Encoding secret messages in audio is the most challenging techniques to use when dealing with Steganography [7]due to the dynamic range of the human auditory system (HAS). Steganography in video [8,9] is similar to that of Steganography in image, except that information is hidden in each frame of the video.

This paper has been organized as following sections:- Section 2 discusses about some of the related works done based on image steganography and video steganography. Section 3 deals with proposed method on video steganography. Section 5 describes different algorithms for different functions used at both at sender side and receiver side. Experimental results and analysis are shown in Section 6 and Section 7 respectively. Finaly Section 8 draws the conclusion.

K.R. Venugopal and L.M. Patnaik (Eds.): ICIP 2012, CCIS 292, pp. 644–653, 2012.
© Springer-Verlag Berlin Heidelberg 2012

2   Review of Related Works on Image and Video Steganography

In this section various image and video based steganography method has been presented.

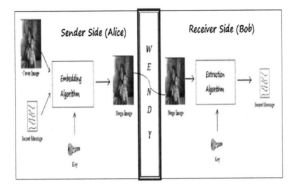

Fig. 1. Generic Form of Image Steganography

A message is embedded in a cover image through an embedding algorithm at the sender side, with the help of a secret key. The resulting stego image is transmitted over a channel to the receiver side where it is processed by the extraction algorithm using the same key. During transmission the stego image can be monitored by unauthenticated viewers who will only notice the transmission of an image without discovering the existence of the hidden message.

2.1   Existing Data Hiding Methods in Image

Various techniques of data hiding have been proposed in literature. One of the common techniques is based on manipulating the least-significant-bit (LSB) [9,10] and [11] planes by directly replacing the LSBs of the cover-image with the message bits. LSB methods typically achieve high capacity but vulnerable to slight image manipulation such as cropping and compression. The pixel-value differencing (PVD) method proposed by Wu and Tsai [12] can successfully provide both high embedding capacity and outstanding imperceptibility for the stego-image. In 2004, Potdar et al.[13] proposes GLM (Gray level modification) technique which is used to map data by modifying the gray level of the image pixels. Ahmad et al. [14] presents a novel steganographic method for hiding information within the spatial domain of the gray scale. The proposed approach works by dividing the cover into blocks of equal sizes and then embeds the message in the edge of the block depending on the number of ones in left four bits of the pixel.

2.2   Bhattachayya and Sanyal's Transformation

Bhattachayya and Sanyal proposed a new image transformation technique in [15,16] known as Pixel Mapping Method (PMM), a method for hiding data within the spatial domain of any gray scale image. Embedding pixels are selected based on some mathematical function which depends on the pixel intensity value of the seed pixel and its 8 neighbors are selected in counter clockwise direction. Data embedding are done by mapping each two or four bits of the secret message in each of the neighbor pixel based on some features of that pixel. Figure 2 shows the mapping information for embedding two bits and four bits respectively.

PAIR OF MSG BIT	PIXEL INTENSITY VALUE	NO OF ONES (BIN)
01	EVEN	ODD
10	ODD	EVEN
00	EVEN	EVEN
11	ODD	ODD

TWO BIT MAPPING METHOD

MSG BIT SEQ	2nd SET RESET BIT	3rd SET RESET BIT	PIXEL INTENSITY VALUE	NO OF ONES(BIN)
0000	EVEN	EVEN	EVEN	EVEN
0001	EVEN	EVEN	EVEN	ODD
0010	EVEN	EVEN	ODD	EVEN
0011	EVEN	EVEN	ODD	ODD
0100	EVEN	ODD	EVEN	EVEN
0101	EVEN	ODD	EVEN	ODD
0110	EVEN	ODD	ODD	EVEN
0111	EVEN	ODD	ODD	ODD
1000	ODD	EVEN	EVEN	EVEN
1001	ODD	EVEN	EVEN	ODD
1010	ODD	EVEN	ODD	EVEN
1011	ODD	EVEN	ODD	ODD
1100	ODD	ODD	EVEN	EVEN
1101	ODD	ODD	EVEN	ODD
1110	ODD	ODD	ODD	EVEN
1111	ODD	ODD	ODD	ODD

FOUR BIT MAPPING METHOD

Fig. 2. PMM Mapping Technique for Embedding of two and four Bits

Extraction process starts again by selecting the same pixels required during embedding. At the receiver side other different reverse operations has been carried out to get back the original information.

2.3   Existing Data Hiding Methods in Video

The most common method is Least Significant Bit method (LSB) which hide secret data into the least significant bits of the host video [17] and [18]. Another well-known method which has been still researching is called Spread Spectrum [18] and [19]. This method satisfies the robustness criterion also. Wang et al.[20] presented a technique for high capacity data hiding using the Discrete Cosine Transform (DCT) transformation. Its main objective is to maximize the payload while keeping robustness and simplicity. There exits some other methods like multi-dimensional lattice structure [21] or enable high quantity of hidden data and high quantity of host data by varying the number of quantization levels for data embedding [20]. Lane proposed a vector embedding method [22] that uses a robust algorithm with video codec standard (MPEG-I and MPEG-II).

3   Proposed Method on Video Steganography

In this paper a new approach of Video Steganography in un-compressed domain has been proposed which uses the PMM technique for data embedding in the video frames. GUI of the proposed system has been shown in Figure 3. The major challenges involved in design and implementation of video steganography are:

1. Video Format Selection: Different video formats have different way of packing data into itself. So it's quite a challenging task to design a general algorithm which work's for all/most of the video formats.
2. Lack of References: Very less of work has been done in this field, so the approach towards the goal to obtain a Multimedia Steganographic system is a very challenging task.
3. Disintegrating and integrating the Image Sequence and Audio: Obtain the Stego Video with no/unrecognizable distortion and at the same time maintaining the properties of the stego video with respect to the original cover video file.

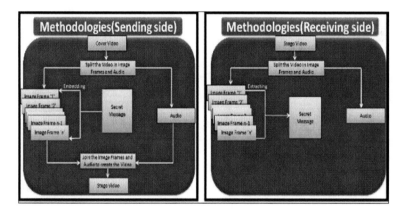

Fig. 3. GUI of the Proposed System

4   Algorithms

In this section algorithms for various sub processes has been discussed.

4.1   Data Hiding in Image Using PMM

1. Select a cover image and a secret message.
2. Select the Embedding Seed Pixels and its 8 neighbors.
3. Check whether the selected seed pixel or its neighbor lies at the image boundary.
4. Map each two bit of the secret message in each of the neighbor pixels as shown in Fig 2 to form the stego image.

4.2   Data Extraction through PMM

1. Extraction process starts again by selecting the same pixels required during embedding. At the receiver side other different reverse operation has been carried out to get back the original information.

4.3   Wavelet DPCS (Division-PMM-Combination-Sending) Algorithm

1. Input: Height and width of a particular frame and the Message to be embedded.
2. Divide the msg into 4 parts viz msg1, msg2, msg3, msg4.
3. Let 'els' be an array of elementary lifting steps and lshaarInt is Integer to Integer wavelet transform in Haar lifting scheme.
4. lsnewInt is New Lifting Scheme obtained by appending the elementary lifting step els to the lifting scheme lshaarInt.
5. Apply 2D lifting wavelet decomposition w.r.t the existing wavelet and store it in parts viz. CA, CH, CV and CD.
6. Call the Pixel Mapping Method for mapping data in the four above mentioned parts.
7. Return the 2D lifted and reconstructed wavelet.

4.4   Wavelet DPCR (Division-PMM-Combination-Receiving) Algorithm

1. Input height and width of a particular frame and the length of the message.
2. Divide the length of the message by 4 and store it in 'l'.
3. Let 'els' be an array of elementary lifting steps and lshaarInt is Integer to Integer wavelet transform in haar lifting scheme.
4. lsnewInt is New Lifting Scheme obtained by appending the elementary lifting step 'els' to the lifting scheme' lshaarInt'.
5. Apply 2D lifting wavelet decomposition w.r.t the existing wavelet and store it in parts viz. A, H, V, D.
6. Call the Pixel Mapping Method Receiving to extract the data in the four above mentioned parts.
7. Return the 2D lifted and reconstructed wavelet.

4.5   Data Hiding in Video Using PMM

The idea as discussed earlier is to hide a message in a cover video i.e. in the image sequence extracted from the cover video and send the stego video to the receiver end, where in the receiver end the message is extracted.

Sender Side

1. Select a cover video and a secret message.
2. Divide the Video in Two parts: Visual Image Sequence and the Audio.
3. Embed the secret message in the Visual Image Sequence using Wavelet DPCS.
4. Recombine Visual Image Sequence and the Audio part to generate the Stego Video.

Receiver Side

1. Select a Stego Video and divide the Video in Two parts: Visual Image Sequence and the Audio.
2. Extract the secret message from Visual Image Sequence using Wavelet DPCR.

5   Experimental Results

Experimental results of the proposed method has been discussed based on two benchmarks namely the embedding capacity of cover carrier and the imperceptibility of the stego image. A comparative study of the proposed method with the existing methods are also shown based on embedding capacity, mean square error (MSE) and peak signal-to noise ratio (PSNR). Normalized cross correlation coefficient has been used for computing the similarity measure between the cover image and stego image. The security of the hidden data has been tested using the relative entropy distance through K-L Divergence.A comparative study of embedding capacity has been depicted in Figure 4.

IMAGE	IMAGE SIZE	PVD	GLM	AHMAD ET ALL.	PMM
LENA	128x128	++	2048	2493	2393
	256x256	++	8192	10007	10012
	512x512	50960	32768	40017	45340
PEPPER	128x128	++	2048	2443	2860
	256x256	++	8192	9767	11694
	512x512	50685	32768	39034	46592

Fig. 4. Comparison of Embedding Capacity

5.1   Mean Squared Error (MSE) and Peak Signal to Noise Ratio (PSNR)

The PSNR is used to evaluate the quality of the stego-image.Assume a cover image $C(i,j)$ of size NxN and a stego image $S(i,j)$ is produced by embedding / mapping the message bit stream.

Mean squared error (MSE) is calculated as follows:

$$MSE = \frac{1}{[N \times N]}\sum_{i=1}^{N}\sum_{j=1}^{N}[C(ij) - S(ij)]^2$$

The PSNR is computed using the following formulae:

$$PSNR = 10\log_{10} 255^2 / \ MSE \ db.$$

IMAGE	IMAGE SIZE	PVD	GLM	AHMAD ET ALL	PMM
LENA	128x128	36.20	30.5	44.30	49.0296
	256x256	35.00	33.20	46.80	50.3489
	512x512	41.79	35.50	55.00	54.1515
PEPPER	128x128	38.70	38.00	43.50	47.9463
	256x256	35.00	37.20	47.50	48.3668
	512x512	40.97	34.00	52.50	54.1521

Fig. 5. Comparison of PSNR for Lena Image

5.2   Similarity Measure

For comparing the similarity between cover image (C) and the stego image (S), the normalized cross correlation coefficient (r) has been computed.

$$r = \frac{\sum_{(C(i,j)-m_1)(S(i,j)-m_2)}}{\sqrt{(\sum_{C(i,j)-m_1})^2}\sqrt{(\sum_{S(i,j)-m_2})^2}}$$

Here m_1 is the mean pixel value of C and m_2 is the mean pixel value of S.

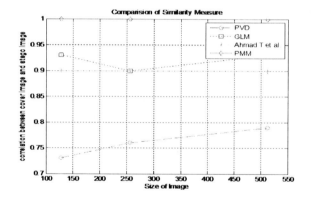

Fig. 6. Comparison of Similarity Measure for Lena Image

5.3   Steganography Security Using KullbackLeibler Divergence

Cachin's definition of steganographic security [23] is based on the assumption that the selection of covers from C can be described by a random variable c on C with probability distribution function (pdf) P. A steganographic scheme, S, is a mapping $C \times M \times K \rightarrow C$ that assigns a new (stego) object, $s\epsilon C$, to each triple (c,M,K), where $M\epsilon M$ is a secret message selected from the set of communicable messages, M, and $K\epsilon K$ is the steganographic secret key. Assuming the covers are selected with pdf P and embedded with a message and secret key both randomly (uniformly) chosen from their corresponding sets, the set of all stego images is again a random variable s on C with pdf Q. The measure of statistical detectability is the Kullback Leibler divergence is given by

$$D_{\mathrm{KL}}(P\|Q) = \sum_{c\epsilon C} P(c) \log \frac{P(c)}{Q(c)}.$$

when $D_{\mathrm{KL}}(P\|Q) < \epsilon$,the stego system is called ϵ secure.

The steganographic security of the hidden data in various video frames has been shown in Figure 9.

5.4 Case Study of Video Steganography Technique in Terms of MSE and PSNR

Case Study 1: Video name : Traffic.avi. Embedding Message : "I am an Indian and I feel proud to be an Indian". The data is inserted in the frame number 1, 3, 6, 10 and 11.

Case Study 2: Video name : Ronaldo.avi. Embedding Message : "University Institute of Technology". The data is inserted in the frame number 1, 3, 6, 10 and 11.

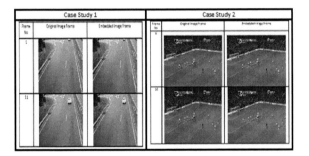

Fig. 7. Video Frame Before and After Data Embedding

6 Analysis of the Results

Experimental results shows that the embedding capacity of the PMM method is better in most cases compared to other existing methods except the PVD. Similarity measures proves that the proposed method is best among these four methods ensuring that cover image and the stego image is almost identical.Also as the message bits are not directly embedded at the pixels of the cover image, steganalysis may be avoided. PSNR value of the proposed method is moderate comparing other methods. This method can produce a good quality stego video with high embedding capacity and moderate PSNR. This method is highly secure as the relative entropy distance is very low between the cover frame and stego frame.

Case Study1			Case Study2		
Frame No.	PSNR	MSE	Frame No.	PSNR	MSE
1	61.6923	0.0440	1	31.2860	48.3595
3	61.4383	0.0467	3	31.2099	49.2139
6	61.4190	0.0469	6	31.2318	48.9665
10	34.2765	24.2902	10	31.3008	48.1945
11	34.3523	23.8698	11	31.2535	48.7224

Fig. 8. PSNR and MSE Values for Two Cases

Video	Frame No		Data Embedding Capacity in character						Video	Frame No		Data Embedding Capacity in character					
			100	500	1000	2500	5000	10000				100	500	1000	2500	5000	10000
Traffic.avi	1	Security of hidden data	0.0001	0.0004	0.0010	0.0022	0.0033	0.008	Ronaldo.avi	1	Security of hidden data	0.0001	0.0003	0.0010	0.0019	0.0032	0.0075
	3	Security of hidden data	0.0001	0.0003	0.0011	0.002	0.036	0.0077		3	Security of hidden data	0.0001	0.0004	0.0011	0.0022	0.0035	0.0013
	6	Security of hidden data	0.0001	0.0004	0.0010	0.0021	0.004	0.0078		6	Security of hidden data	0.0001	0.0003	0.0010	0.0021	0.0038	0.0080
	10	Security of hidden data	0.0001	0.0004	0.0012	0.002	0.0041	0.0082		10	Security of hidden data	0.0001	0.0003	0.0015	0.0027	0.0040	0.0081
	11	Security of hidden data	0.0001	0.0003	0.0013	0.0025	0.0039	0.0080		11	Security of hidden data	0.0001	0.0004	0.0011	0.0022	0.0036	0.0080

Fig. 9. Security Value of Hidden Data in Various Video Frame

7   Conclusion

A new Un-Compressed Video Steganographic Scheme was proposed in this paper, operating directly in discrete wavelet domain. For data hiding pixel mapping method (PMM) algorithm has been used which provides high embedding capacity and imperceptible stego-image for human vision of the hidden secret information. The performance of the steganographic algorithm is studied and experimental results conclude that this scheme can be applied on un-compressed videos with no noticeable degradation in visual quality.

References

1. Mrkel, T.: JHP Eloff and MS Olivier: An Overview of Image Steganography. In: Proceedings of the Fifth Annual Information Security South Africa Conference (2005)
2. Marvel, L.M., Boncelet Jr., C.G., Retter, C.T.: Spread Spectrum Image Steganography. IEEE Trans. on Image Processing 8(8), 1075–1083 (1999)
3. Chandramouli, R., Memon, N.: Analysis of LSB Based Image Steganography Techniques. In: Proceedings of IEEE ICIP (2001)
4. Brassil, J.T., Low, S., Maxemchuk, N.F., Gorman, L.O.: Electronic Marking and Identification Techniques to Discourage Document Copying. IEEE Journal on Selected Areas in Communications 13(8), 1495–1504 (1995)

5. Por, L.Y., Delina, B.: Information Hiding: A New Approach in Text Steganography. In: Proceedings of 7th WSEAS International Conference on Applied Computer & Applied Computational Science, pp. 689–695 (April 2008)
6. Alattar, A.M., Alattar, O.M.: Watermarking Electronic Text Documents Containing Justified Paragraphs and Irregular Line Spacing. In: Proceedings of SPIE - Security, Steganography and Watermarking of Multimedia Contents-VI, vol. 5306, pp. 685–695 (June 2004)
7. Gopalan, K.: Audio Steganography using Bit Modification. In: Proceedings of the IEEE International Conference on Acoustics, Speech and Signal Processing (ICASSP 2003), vol. 2, pp. 421–424 (April 2003)
8. Doerr, G., Dugelay, J.L.: Security Pitfalls of Frameby-Frame Approaches to Video Watermarkin. IEEE Transactions on Signal Processing: Supplement on Secure Media 52(10), 2955–2964 (2004)
9. Chang, C.C., Hsiao, J.Y., Chan, C.S.: Finding Optimal Least-Significant-Bit Substitution in Image Hiding by Dynamic Programming Strategy. Pattern Recognition 36, 1583–1595 (2003)
10. Chan, C.K., Cheng, L.M.: Hiding Data in Images by Simple LSB Substitution. Pattern Recognition 37(3), 469–474 (2004)
11. Wang, R.Z., Lin, C.F., Lin, J.C.: Image Hiding by Optimal LSB Substitution and Genetic Algorithm. Pattern Recognition 34, 671–683 (2001)
12. Wu, D.C., Tsai, W.H.: A Steganographic Method for Images by Pixel-Value Differencing. Pattern Recognition Letters 24, 1613–1626 (2003)
13. Potdar, V., Chang, E.: Gray Level Modification Steganography for Secret Communication. In: Proceedings of IEEE International Conference on Industria lInformatics, Berlin, Germany, pp. 355–368 (2004)
14. Al-Taani, A.T., AL-Issa, A.M.: A Novel Steganographic Method for Gray-Level Images. International Journal of Computer: Information and Systems Science and Engineering 3(1) (2009)
15. Bhattacharyya, S., Sanyal, G.: Hiding Data in Images using Pixel Mapping Method (PMM). In: Proceedings of 9th Annual Conference on Security and Management (SAM) under The 2010 World Congress in Computer Science,Computer Engineering and Applied Computing (WorldComp 2010), LasVegas, USA, July 12-15 (2010)
16. Bhattacharyya, S., Kumar, L., Sanyal, G.: A Novel Approach of Data Hiding using Pixel Mapping Method (PMM). International Journal of Computer Science and Information Security (IJCSIS) 8(4) (2010)
17. Lu, C.S.: Multimedia Security: Steganography and Digital Watermarking Techniques for Protection of Intellectual Property. Artech House, Inc. (2003)
18. Provos, N., Honeyman, P.: Hide and Seek: An Introduction to Steganography. IEEE Security & Privacy Magazine (2003)
19. Cox, I.J., Kilian, J., Leighton, T., Shamoon, T.: Secure Spread Spectrum Watermarking for Multimedia. In: Proceedings of IEEE Image Processing (1997)
20. Wang, Y., Izquierdo, E.: High-Capacity Data Hiding in MPEG-2 Compressed Video. In: Proceedings of 9th International Workshop on System: Signals and Image Processing, UK, (2002)
21. Chae, J.J., Mukherjee, D., Manjunath, B.S.: A Robust Data Hiding Technique using Multidimensional Lattices. In: Proceedings of the IEEE Forum on Research and Technology Advances in Digital Libraries, Santa Barbara, USA (1998)
22. Lane, D.E.: Video-in-Video Data Hiding (2007)
23. Cachin, C.: An Information-Theoretic Model for Steganography. In: Aucsmith, D. (ed.) IH 1998. LNCS, vol. 1525, pp. 306–318. Springer, Heidelberg (1998)

Author Index